Recreation and Leisure
in Modern Society

This book was originally published by Appleton-Century-Crofts as a volume in its SERIES IN HEALTH, PHYSICAL EDUCATION, PHYSICAL THERAPY, AND RECREATION

CHARLES A. BUCHER, EDITOR

RICHARD KRAUS

Herbert H. Lehman College of the City University of New York

Recreation and Leisure in Modern Society

GOODYEAR PUBLISHING COMPANY, INC.,
Pacific Palisades, California

Plate 2. Kalapalo Indian wrestlers, Stan Wyman, *Life* Magazine © Time, Inc.
Plate 4. Jousting scene, Frank Scherschel, *Life* Magazine © Time, Inc.
Plate 9. Rugby playfield, copyright Associated Newspapers Limited, London.
Plate 15. Japanese recreation, Larry Burrows, *Life* Magazine © Time, Inc.

To Michael and Vera Kraus

Contents

Preface   xi

PART ONE   THE RECREATION MOVEMENT TODAY

Chapter 1. An Overview of Recreation and Leisure in the
United States   3
    The Role of Government in Recreation   3
    The Role of Voluntary Agencies in Recreation   4
    The Role of Private Organizations   5
    The Role of Commercial Recreation Agencies   6
    Social Factors Supporting Recreation Movement   6
    Challenges to the Recreation Movement   13

Chapter 2. Role of Federal and State Governments   25
    Functions of Federal Government in Recreation   25
    Involvement in Outdoor Recreation Programs   27
    Programs under Health, Education, and Welfare   34
    Functions Related to Housing and Urban Development   36
    Federal Antipoverty Programs   37
    Recreation and the Armed Forces   41
    Functions of the States in Recreation   46

Chapter 3. The Role of County and Local Governments   55
    County Programs of Recreation and Parks   55
    Municipal Recreation and Park Programs   59
    Administrative Structure of Public Recreation Departments   61
    Program Services of Municipal Recreation Agencies   64
    Profiles of Municipal Departments   65
    Trends in Local Recreation and Parks Sponsorship   73

Chapter 4. Recreation in Other Settings: Voluntary, Private,
and Commercial   75
    Voluntary Agencies in the Leisure Field   76
    Youth Serving Organizations   78
    Religious Social Agencies   82
    Settlement Houses and Community Centers   87

Organizations Serving the Disadvantaged   88
Special-Interest Organizations   90
Organizations Serving the Ill and Disabled   94
Private Agencies Providing Recreation Programs   95
Commercial Recreation Programs   96
Industrial Recreation Sponsorship   97

Chapter 5. Professionalism in Recreation and Parks   103
Numbers of Recreation Professionals   104
Characteristics of a Profession   105
Professional Preparation in Recreation and Parks   109
The National Recreation and Park Association   113
Other Professional Associations   115
The Recruitment of Recreation and Park Professionals   116
Certification of Recreation and Park Professionals   119
Civil Service Procedures in Recreation and Parks   121
Clarifying the Role of the Professional   122

PART TWO   THE HISTORY OF RECREATION AND LEISURE

Chapter 6. The Early History of Recreation and Leisure   129
The Play of Primitive Man   129
Recreation and Leisure in Pre-Christian Civilizations   132
The Dark and Middle Ages   142
The Renaissance and Reformation   148
The Development of Parks and Recreation Areas   154

Chapter 7. Recreation and Leisure in Colonial America   160
Puritan Attitudes toward Play   161
Parks and Conservation in the Colonial Era   164

Chapter 8. The Nineteenth Century in Europe and America   168
Influence of the Industrial Revolution: Urbanization and the
    Reduction of Leisure   169
The Protestant Work Ethic   170
Growth of Popular Participation in Recreation   172
Expansion of Sports   173
The Adult Education Movement   179
National and State Parks   179
Urban Parks   180
Establishment of Voluntary Organizations   182
The Playground Movement   183

Chapter 9. The Recreation and Parks Movement During the
Twentieth Century   186
The Growth of Public Recreation and Parks Agencies   186
The Development of the Recreation Movement   188
The Rationale for Organized Recreation Programs   190
Commercial Amusements   194
Settlement Houses and Community Centers   197
Growth of Voluntary Organizations   198

Role of the Schools   199
World War I   201
Public Recreation During the 1920's   202
Depression of the 1930's   203
World War II   206
Trends During the 1950's and 1960's   208

Chapter 10. Recreation on the International Scene   211
Great Britain   212
Soviet Union   217
Germany   222
Recreation in Other European Countries   225
Recreation in Eastern Nations   227
International Recreation Association   231
Recreation and the Peace Corps   232

PART THREE   CONCEPTS OF RECREATION
               AND LEISURE

Chapter 11. Early Theories of Play and Recreation   237
Early Theories of Play   238
The Philosophy of Organized Recreation Service   245
Other Contributions to Play and Recreation Theory   249

Chapter 12. Recreation, Play, and Leisure: A Conceptual
Analysis   253
Four Views of Leisure   254
Concepts of Recreation   260
The Meaning of Play   263
Recent Theories of Play and Recreation: Mitchell and Mason,
    Huizinga, Caillois, Keesing   266

Chapter 13. Psychological Aspects of Play   274
Play in Personality Development   275
Play in the Learning Process   279
Play in Psychoanalytical Theory   286

Chapter 14. The Sociology of Leisure   290
Studies of Leisure Participation   291
Social Class as a Determinant of Leisure   295
Recreation and Race   300
Changing Work Attitudes in American Society   303

Chapter 15. The Economics of Leisure: Its Amounts and Uses   307
Availability of Leisure Today   308
Patterns of Leisure Availability   313
Total Spending on Leisure and Recreation   316
Patterns of Leisure Activity in the United States   319
Sports Participation and Spectator Sports   320
Travel as Leisure Activity   324
Cultural Activities   327
The Growth of Television   328
Technological Influences on Leisure   330

PART FOUR   GOALS AND PROBLEMS IN ORGANIZED
RECREATION SERVICE

Chapter 16. Recreation and Human Values   335
    Physical Growth and Development   335
    Emotional Aspects of Recreational Participation   338
    Social Values of Recreation   340
    Intellectual Growth Through Recreation   344
    Recreation and the Needs of Major Age Groups: Children, Youth,
        Adults, Aging   346

Chapter 17. Recreation and Social Functions   357
    Improving Quality of Community Life   357
    Improving Quality of Urban Environment   360
    Economic Functions of Recreation   361
    Recreation as a Health-Related Service   364
    Recreation Services and the Aging   372
    Recreation and Juvenile Delinquency   376
    Recreation's Function with the Disadvantaged   387
    Recreation as an Outlet for Violence   391
    Recreation and the Need for Ritual   395

Chapter 18. Problems and Issues in Organized Recreation Service   398
    Social Role of Community Recreation Service   398
    Changing Framework of Leisure Values   401
    Preserving and Improving the Physical Environment   407
    Financial Support for Parks and Recreation   412
    Fees and Charges as Sources of Revenue   415
    Changing Role of Voluntary Agencies   419
    Role of Schools in Recreation and Leisure   420
    Professional Development in Recreation and Parks   424
    National Awareness of Recreation and Leisure   428

Chapter 19. Urban Planning for Recreation and Parks   429
    Problems of the Cities   430
    Urban Planning Approaches   432
    Park and Recreation Space Standards   436
    Guides for Recreation and Park Planning   438

Chapter 20. The Challenge of the Future   454
    Population Growth   455
    Effects of Technology and Automation   456
    Predicted Growth of Leisure   463
    Defining the Needs of the Future   465

    Suggested Topics for Examination Questions,
        Student Papers, or Panel Reports   475
    Bibliography   479
    Picture Credits   483
    Index   485

Preface

This book is intended to serve as a text in college and university courses dealing with the history and theory of recreation and leisure. Scholars in a number of disciplines have written extensively on these subjects. Historians have detailed the history of sport and the performing arts or have portrayed the pastimes of certain eras. Sociologists have examined leisure activities as a function of social class or occupation. Psychologists have seen play as part of the developmental process, and economists have seen it as an aspect of national spending.

Few of these scholars have, however, addressed themselves directly to recreation as a form of community service; instead, each has been narrowly concerned with his own discipline and has had a limited vision of the total field. Generally, recreation educators or practitioners who have authored textbooks in this field have written knowledgeably of the total range of organized recreation programs in the United States or of administrative structures and processes in this field. But few have integrated current information drawn from the social and behavioral sciences into their discussions.

This book therefore provides an analysis of the total field of recreation and leisure which includes a thorough description of its current scope, organizational practices, and problems and a detailed discussion of relevant findings and information drawn from the scholarly fields of history, sociology, psychology, philosophy, and economics. It provides a basic understanding of recreation and leisure as increasingly important aspects of our culture.

Why is such an understanding necessary? It is obvious that recreation has grown steadily as a form of public and voluntary agency service in the United States during the past several years, particularly with respect to outdoor recreation facilities and programs. Leaders and administrators in recreation and park agencies have become skilled in the planning and development of facilities, personnel policy, and financial management. Yet, in a field intended to meet significant human needs, it is essential that the practitioner become capable of doing more than a "nuts-and-bolts" job.

He *must* have a thorough and sophisticated understanding of the role of recreation and leisure in human life and of the changing functions of recreation in modern society.

This book is divided into four major sections. Part One, The Recreation Movement Today, provides a detailed account of organized recreation service on the American scene today and of its sponsors in government, voluntary, private, and commercial agencies. It examines the goals and functions of major programs and the nature of professional development in this field in terms of current practices, problems, and issues.

Part Two, The History of Recreation and Leisure, traces the past development of the field, concluding with an examination of its recent history in the United States and in a number of other nations throughout the world. It views recreation in relation to such major social events as wars, depressions, and migrations and also with respect to social customs, class structure, and religious influence.

Part Three, Concepts of Recreation and Leisure, provides an overview of recent and contemporary writing in the social and behavioral sciences with respect to recreation, play, and leisure. It critically examines fundamental concepts in these fields and offers succinct interpretations of a number of important recent studies in the sociology of leisure, the theory of play and recreation, and trends in participation.

Part Four, Goals and Problems in Organized Recreation Service, describes at length the specific values and functions of recreation, both as a form of individual human experience and as an important aspect of community life. It examines its role in contributing to economic and social well-being and as part of the spectrum of social services that attack such problems as juvenile delinquency, mental illness and retardation, and the needs of special populations. It deals with such concerns as environmental pollution, antipoverty programs, and race relations, particularly in our rapidly expanding metropolitan regions. After discussing new approaches to urban planning, it concludes by examining predictions for the future in terms of technological and demographic change and attempts to define the major constructive approaches that those in the field of recreation may follow.

Throughout, this text takes the position that those who have portrayed recreation as a form of service primarily designed to meet the needs and interests of middle-class Americans (economically comfortable, fairly well-educated, mobile, and recreationally literate) in what is generally seen as a suburban or small-town setting have presented an idealistic and limited view of our society. Today it must be recognized that the United States has become predominantly an urban society and that it is marked by major differences in terms of social class, racial affiliation, economic status, and attitudes of morality. Particularly in the cities, the pressure upon the tax dollar is tremendous. Within this context, the notion of recreation as an experience which, by definition, is not designed to meet important social needs or achieve "extrinsic" outcomes can no longer be applicable. Every area of service that is provided by government and voluntary agencies today *must* be purposeful and *must* achieve significant outcomes.

Thus, in this book, recreation is viewed as an important element within the total spectrum of community services. In some cases, it plays a secondary role; in others, as in those efforts which are concerned with improving the environment or with meeting the needs of those with physical, social, or mental disability, it is seen as playing a primary role. This concept of recreation departs from traditional views; however, it is compelled by the reality of the present era.

The author acknowledges certain inevitable limitations in the text. First, in reporting the literature related to recreation, play, and leisure in the social and behavioral sciences, he has necessarily chosen only those reports or selections which seemed to be most relevant. Similarly, his discussion of recreation policies and practices in other nations has been highly selective. Only a few specific community programs in the United States have been described in detail. Much of the information about the use of recreation in antipoverty programs and other specialized agencies has been drawn from his experience or direct observation; it therefore relates heavily to practices found in the eastern part of the United States. Based on reports in the literature and presentations made at professional conferences, however, they appear to be representative of programs in the nation as a whole.

The author wishes to express his appreciation to a number of administrators of public and voluntary agencies and professional organizations who responded cheerfully to his requests for information about their programs. These agencies and organizations include the Bureau of Indian Affairs, Bureau of Reclamation, Fish and Wildlife Service, and National Park Service, all in the Department of Interior; the United States Forest Service, in the Department of Agriculture; the Departments of the Army, the Navy, and the Air Force, and the Veterans' Administration; voluntary organizations such as the Girl Scouts of the United States of America, the Boy Scouts of America, the Boys' Clubs of America, and the Young Men's Christian Association; and the National Industrial Association, the Athletic Institute, the National Recreation and Park Association, and the National Conference on State Parks. He received information from many directors of state recreation and park departments, regional or metropolitan park districts, and community recreation departments, only a few of which can be named here: Mountain View, California; Kansas City, Missouri; Omaha, Nebraska; Greensboro, North Carolina; Portland, Oregon; Long Beach, California; and Philadelphia, Pennsylvania. He also received assistance from administrators of the Central Council of Physical Recreation and the National Association of Youth Clubs in Great Britain and from Canadian educational and youth service authorities.

Considerable use was made of the professional writing of such recreation educators as Elliott M. Avedon, David Gray, John Nesbitt, H. Douglas Sessoms, and Louis Twardzik, both through direct quotation and a review of their ideas. Among his former students, the author acknowledges the assistance of Mark Stempa, Walter Schatz, and Shalom Hermon. It is his hope that this text will prove of real value to professors and students in courses and seminars, both undergraduate and graduate, dealing with the history, philosophy, current trends, and issues in organized recreation service.

R.K.

ONE

The Recreation Movement Today

1

An Overview of Recreation
and Leisure in the United States

Man has always had, since the earliest recorded civilizations, some degree of unobligated time. History describes countless forms of recreative pursuits which have been used to fill leisure hours—particularly by the wealthy and influential social classes of each era. But it has only been within the past century, particularly among the highly industrialized Western nations, that both leisure and economic growth have made it possible for recreation to be widely available to all social classes.

Within the United States, there has been a vast expansion of recreational programs, services, and facilities under four different types of sponsorship. These categories of sponsors which provide pleasurable leisure opportunities to the American people may be regarded as the institutional basis of the twentieth-century recreation movement. They are found on four levels: government, voluntary agency, private, and commercial.

The Role of Government in Recreation

On every level of government—Federal, state, county, township, municipal, and school-district—the provision of recreation programs, services, and facilities, has become an important responsibility.

Federal Functions. Today, over fifty Federal agencies, including major departments such as Agriculture, Commerce, Interior, and Health, Education and Welfare, and a number of independent agencies, commissions, and councils within the Office of the President, hold functions with respect to recreation. These relate chiefly to outdoor recreation; in addi-

3

tion, however, Federal funds and personnel are used to provide or assist direct recreation services in hospitals, armed forces, disadvantaged neighborhoods in American cities, and a variety of other settings. The Federal government today supports the professional training of recreation personnel, sponsors special research relating to recreation and park development, promotes program development for children and for disabled and aging persons, and assists this field in many other ways.

State Functions. On the state level, over 230 different state agencies throughout the nation play an essential role with respect to recreation and park development. This role stresses the provision of outdoor recreation opportunities but also includes special services for youth, aging persons, disadvantaged urban areas, and similar functions. All fifty states in the nation today have legislative codes which empower local government to acquire land, develop recreation and park facilities, tax for recreation purposes, and provide direct program services. Many states sponsor professional education in this field, in public colleges and universities. As a brief indication of the growth of state-sponsored outdoor recreation, the total attendance at state park and recreation areas climbed from 232 million in 1955 to 263 million in 1960 and 391 million in 1967. Similarly, total expenditures related to parks and recreation reported by states were $87 million in 1955, $152 million in 1960, and $295 million in 1967.

Local Government Functions. The provision of recreation and park facilities and programs by America's counties, cities, towns, villages, and school districts has grown steadily since the early decades of the twentieth century. As an example, the number of local and county agencies reporting public recreation and park programs was 2,277 in 1950 and 3,142 in 1966. Total professional leadership, including both full-time and part-time or seasonal workers, was 58,029 in 1950 and 119,515 in 1966. Acreage in municipal and county-owned parks and recreation departments rose from 644,000 in 1950 to 1,490,000 in 1966. Total local government expenditures for recreation rose from $269 million at mid-century to $905 million in 1966, not including the cost of many recreation services provided in our cities and towns by public museums, libraries, colleges and universities, housing authorities, and other agencies. Today it is undoubtedly well over a billion dollars a year.

The Role of Voluntary Agencies in Recreation

A major force in the modern recreation movement is the work of so-called voluntary agencies, both locally and on the national scene. Such agencies are nongovernmental and nonprofit; they usually rely either completely or primarily on private contributions for financial support. They offer an important segment of recreational opportunity to the American public, although they often are organized for purposes that are not primarily recreational. They include the following types: nonsectarian youth-serving organizations, religious social agencies, settlement houses and community centers, special interest organizations, agencies serving special populations, and professional organizations serving the park and recreation field.

Many industrial concerns throughout the nation offer extensive social and recreation programs for their employees and their families. Community service clubs, such as the Elks, Kiwanis, or American Legion, also sponsor recreation programs, particularly for youth. In a number of cities, police-affiliated groups like the Police Athletic League offer comprehensive recreation programs. Anti-poverty organizations in cities and towns frequently provide diversified recreational activities. While such groups are heavily dependent on federal or municipal funding, they are nonprofit in nature, and are usually operated by private citizens—rather than government officials.

Thus, a major sphere of recreational opportunity is provided by voluntary community organizations. While they may serve special clienteles (in terms of age, religion, disability, or other factors), they tend to be open to the public at large. Because of their special concerns and program emphasis, they are often able to satisfy major needs for recreation service which government agencies cannot.

The Role of Private Organizations

Many private organizations, in the form of clubs or societies, have as their primary purpose the provision of social and recreational opportunities for their members. These include yacht clubs, golf clubs, hunting and fishing clubs, tennis clubs, and sometimes organizations concerned with other cultural or hobby pursuits, such as garden clubs. Typically, such organizations have been socially exclusive; membership committees or fee structures have served to screen out those who did not "belong." Thus, they have provided their members both with privacy and with the opportunity to enjoy a variety of pastimes not generally available to the public at large. Often such clubs have developed and operated extensive grounds and buildings.

In recent years, owing to the rapid growth of suburbia, there has been an expansion of membership clubs providing recreation services, on a somewhat less exclusive basis. In many suburban communities, large numbers of new residents have banded together to build their own recreation facilities. The most common type of development has been the cooperatively owned and operated swimming pool; in many cases these have been extended into widespread and varied recreation complexes, with sports, social, and dining facilities as well.

The Role of Commercial Recreation Agencies

While government, voluntary organizations, and private membership groups provide substantial recreational opportunities in the United States today, the bulk of recreational opportunity—as well as the highest proportion of leisure spending—is offered by commercial sponsors.

Such popular recreation facilities as bowling alleys, billiard parlors, motion-picture houses or drive-in movies, golf driving ranges, ski centers, night clubs and bars, theaters—to name only a few—are usually commercially operated. Thus, recreation has become a widely marketed product in our society. Even when it is not the primary product, it may be an attractive accessory that makes the primary product more attractive to the buyer. Many apartment buildings today (even those in the heart of cities) are built with swimming pools, lounges, tennis courts, playgrounds, and other recreational facilities which add to their appeal for the prospective tenant. Similarly, many private home developments are designed to have elaborate recreational facilities, both in the home package itself and also in the development community.

America's financial stake in recreation as an industry is tremendous. Certain forms of activity, such as boating and water sports, are multi-billion-dollar industries in themselves, supporting hundreds of thousands of workers. Typically, one form of recreational involvement tends to be linked with, and to support, others. A host of products are constantly being marketed for reasons that are clearly recreational: radios and television, phonographs and records, toys and games, sports equipment, hobby equipment, and art equipment. Many other products may be viewed as partly utilitarian and partly recreational: books and magazines, leisure clothing, do-it-yourself home-repair or craft equipment, gardening supplies, and outdoor cooking equipment.

Thus, recreation pervades almost every area of American life and involves a tremendous output of energy, interest, and expenditure both on the part of participants and those who sponsor recreation programs. What are the factors that led to this growth of the recreation movement and to the establishment of government, voluntary, private, and commercial recreation services? The following passage summarizes them briefly; they are analyzed in fuller detail in later chapters.

SOCIAL FACTORS SUPPORTING RECREATION MOVEMENT

1. *Growth of Leisure.* In modern, industrialized society, leisure has grown markedly for the great mass of people. Thanks to advanced mechanical processes in factories, agriculture, and service fields, the productive capacity of workers has been dramatically multiplied. In effect, the work

week has been cut in half since the early days of the Industrial Revolution. More and more holidays and longer vacations are now being made available to the American worker. With improved government social benefits and company pension plans, the average employee is today assured twelve years of full-time leisure, following his retirement. Taken all together, these factors mean that Americans have been given a dramatic gift of free time to spend throughout their lifetimes in ways of their own choosing. One major research study has estimated that most adults today have between 25 and 50 hours of unobligated time per week and that young and old persons have between 50 and 70 hours per week.[1] The average employed adult has far more hours of leisure per year than he has hours of paid work.

2. *Increasing Affluence.* Particularly in the years since World War II, the United States has witnessed a steady growth of national income, buying power, and total productivity. Over the nine-year period of the "Soaring Sixties," as some financial analysts called the years from 1960 to 1969, personal income climbed from $383 billion to $686 billion, and the Gross National Product (total output of goods and services) rose almost 80 percent, from $484 billion to $861 billion. In this period, the number of Americans at work climbed from 64.6 million to 76.6 million.

Despite an inflationary trend in the country, the real buying power of the American public has expanded steadily; an enormous amount of money is available to be spent, beyond taxes and expenditures related to food, clothing, shelter, medical care, and education. A high proportion of this discretionary income is spent on leisure pursuits and involvements. A leading firm of stock market analysts estimates the total amount of leisure spending in the United States today as $150 billion.[2] A major financial publication calculates combined annual spending on education and leisure (which it sees as closely related) at $200 billion.[3]

As a consequence, recreational participation has received a tremendous impetus. With the exception of certain disadvantaged groups, Americans are now able to indulge their leisure wishes to a point never before possible. And, just as growing national affluence makes leisure spending possible— so a continued expansion of the leisure market is essential to a healthy national economy.

3. *Higher Level of Education.* Sociologists have noted that those with more advanced levels of educational background tend to engage more widely and intensely in varied forms of recreation. The Outdoor Recreation Resources Review Commission found, for example, that those with a college education engaged in a greater number of outdoor recreation ac-

[1] *The Challenge of Leisure: A Southern California Case Study* (Claremont: Southern California Research Council, Pomona College, 1967), p. 17.

[2] *Leisure: Investment Opportunities in a $150-Billion Market* (New York: Securities Research Division, Merrill Lynch, Pierce, Fenner and Smith, 1968), p. 4.

[3] "Leisure and Education," *Forbes*, January 1, 1969, p. 170.

tivities, on far more occasions per year, than those who held only a high school diploma.

One of the effects of higher education is that it exposes one to a variety of ideas and experiences which inevitably broaden leisure interests and promote habits of varied participation. Thus, the student who has studied music, art, and literature, who has been part of the cultural life of a university with its opportunities for drama, dance, and social activity, may be expected to be far more active in his own community's cultural life than an individual with a narrower background. As an increasingly high proportion of American youth go on to college today (the number was recently estimated to be about 6.5 million, about 55 percent of those in the college-age bracket) it is likely that the national interest in varied leisure pursuits will also continue to grow.

4. *Urbanization and Suburbanization.* One of the key factors in the early development of the recreation movement was the growth of America's factory cities. Millions of European immigrants settled in urban areas during the nineteenth and early twentieth century, as well as great numbers who left the rural areas of the nation to find work when their farms became mechanized. As people huddled together in crowded slums—without the natural play space of the outdoors and with the traditional forms of folk recreation no longer available—it became obvious that leisure posed an important problem.

Many social critics and reformers concluded that commercialized forms of recreation contributed to serious social problems in urban slums. So it was that the recreation movement in the United States got under way. It took the form of "tot-lots" and playgrounds for children, playfields for youth and adults, networks of small and large parks throughout our cities, and the establishment of settlement houses, community centers, and "character-building" organizations for children and youth. Thus, urbanization created a need for organized recreation service which was met by both public and voluntary agencies.

Today, the most striking aspect of growth in metropolitan regions is suburbanization. Great numbers of people have moved out of the cities of the United States into large new suburban settlements on their periphery. In these new settings, public recreation and park departments have expanded rapidly. Today, they provide varied recreation services and facilities. Today the larger cities tend to be heavily populated by socioeconomic extremes—the very well-to-do and the poor, particularly the black or Spanish-speaking poor. This situation has posed an entirely new kind of challenge to recreation administrators, one that will be analyzed in detail elsewhere in this text.

5. *Expanding Population.* In November, 1967, the Bureau of the Census reported that the population of the United States had passed the 200-million mark. It had taken the first 150 years of our nation's existence

to reach the first 100 million and only 35 years to reach the second hundred million. It is estimated that unless present trends are radically reversed, we will reach the 300 million mark by 1985.

The implications of this for recreation are clear. Great new numbers of people, as well as sharply expanded communities, will need to be served with leisure activities. This will be particularly true of young people, whose proportion in the population has steadily increased, and also of older persons who, with improved retirement benefits and longer life spans, will provide a growing market for extended programs to fill leisure hours.

Closely linked to this is the fact that urban and suburban construction has proceeded at such a rapid pace that approximately a million acres of open space per year have been taken over for building in recent years. At the same time, industrial concerns, lumbering companies, mining, and similar enterprises have slashed through America's forests, made deserts out of its grassy plains, laid waste great regions of formerly green hillsides, poisoned its waterways, and killed its wildlife. All of this has highlighted the need for more effective programs of land and water conservation, to preserve and recover our natural heritage for the future population of the United States to use.

The conservation movement has at many points been closely allied to the outdoor recreation movement. Both have received major assistance from government efforts to save and improve land and water resources. Typically, many projects which have conservation, flood control, or rural electrification as their primary objectives also have resulted in the creation of vast new outdoor recreation facilities to serve America's vacation-minded public.

6. *Mobility of the Population.* Closely linked to the growth of the recreation movement in the United States has been the mobility of the American people. Far more than the people of any other nation, we have been a land of travelers. The very settlers who landed on our shores during the period of early colonization were mobile, footloose people, compared with those they left behind. Throughout the period of westward expansion, Americans were on the go—on foot, on horseback, in ox carts, and in wagon trains.

When the automobile was invented and became widely popular throughout the United States, this new form of personal transportation gave a major impetus to recreational participation. People surged like lemmings to seek amusement. They drove at night to theaters, movie houses, dance halls, bowling alleys, and night clubs. They thronged in their Model T's and Model A's to the great new stadiums that were built during the 1920's to see professional baseball, college football, and championship boxing matches.

Travel in itself became a popular new form of entertainment. People were able to drive to state and Federal parks for camping and to see the great national monuments. The nearby county or regional park became a place to visit for swimming, picnicking, and similar pursuits. Thus, in many ways, recreation has evolved based on the readiness of Americans to travel. Many industrial recreation departments, as well as other clubs and organizations, today schedule charter flights for vacation travel abroad for their members. Even flying has become a major recreational pursuit for many who are able to afford it.

Thus, the increasing mobility of our population typifies the American pattern of leisure participation. This is a two-sided coin, however. One of the most serious problems with respect to providing recreation and park services in disadvantaged urban neighborhoods today is that poor people are *not* mobile. They are often confined tightly within their own ghettos. Thus, providing transportation becomes an important part of the work of the planner who is concerned with urban recreation and park opportunity.

7. *Advances in Modern Technology.* Closely allied to mobility as a social factor in the growth of recreation has been the effect of modern technology. Not only has technology created more leisure, by shortening the work week and providing more vacation time and longer retirement, it has also simplified household tasks through labor-saving devices such as dishwashers, automatic waxers, and power mowers.

Technology has also contributed greatly by providing entirely new forms of play that are dependent on devices created by modern science. Within the mass media, such popular forms of entertainment as movies, radio, and television are obvious examples. Many other pursuits—such as power boating, skin and scuba diving, a variety of home crafts, popular music-making (the typical teen-age rock-and-roll band is a triumph of modern electronics), or automobile hobbies—are based on technological development.

Without question, entirely new forms of play will come into existence as scientists and engineers, having met the material and survival needs of mankind with increasing success, devote themselves to making man's total existence richer and more enjoyable.

8. *The Cultural Explosion.* A vital aspect of the recreation movement throughout the United States has been the so-called "cultural explosion." During the 1950's and 1960's, there was a remarkable surge of interest in the graphic and plastic arts, in theater-going, literature, music and dance, and museum attendance throughout the United States. The growth of interest in music provides a single example. In 1966, a survey conducted by the American Symphony Orchestra League indicated that since 1950 there had been an 85 percent increase in the number of persons playing musical instruments in the United States. In terms of the number of orchestras, bands, dance bands, opera productions and school-age instrumentalists, the growth rate was nearly five times that of the nation's population during the period from 1950 to 1964.[4]

[4] "Concert Music U.S.A., 1966," *Music Journal*, February, 1966, p. 94.

Similar figures reporting the growth of amateur participation and audience participation in the other arts suggest that the United States, after a long period of comparative disinterest in the arts, has finally become fully involved in this vital aspect of life. It should be noted, however, that the term "cultural explosion" refers to an essentially *amateur* and therefore recreational approach to the arts. This growth of interest has been marked by several factors, including the building of cultural centers throughout the country, the sponsorship of expanded arts programs by many colleges and universities, and the increased involvement of community recreation departments in sponsorship of creative arts activities. Taken all together, they suggest that the area of cultural activity will be an increasingly significant aspect of the recreation movement in the United States in the decades to come.

9. *The Expansion of Social Welfare.* A striking aspect of governmental policy in the industrialized nations of the world over the past several decades has been the expansion of social welfare programs for those groups of the population suffering from disability or deprivation of any kind. Within the recreation movement, this is most strikingly illustrated by the growth of concern about retarded children and youth which began in the early 1960's under the administration of President Kennedy. The Kennedy Foundation itself, along with the Federal and state governments and a number of professional organizations in physical education and recreation, joined forces to promote improved recreation services for the retarded. They initiated research, supported demonstration projects and pilot programs, and assisted the professional preparation of personnel in this field.

Similarly, during the middle 1960's, concern began to grow about aging persons in the United States. The recommendations of the White House Conference on Aging in 1960 had included strong statements about the need for expanded and improved leisure programs for older persons. With the establishment of the Federal Administration on Aging by the Older Americans Act of 1965, a major impetus was given to the field of recreation for aging persons. Assistance was given to the preparation of recreation personnel who would direct multiservice centers serving aging persons throughout the nation. In a number of other areas, programs concerned with the total rehabilitation of the physically disabled, the mentally ill, and the socially disadvantaged have given new emphasis to recreation.

10. *Professional Development in Recreation and Parks.* A significant aspect of the growth of the recreation and park movement in the 1960's was its improved and strengthened professional identification. Recreation has for years been a fragmented field of public service. Typically, it was housed administratively in a variety of different types of structures: park departments, recreation departments, park and recreation departments, school boards, departments of highways and public properties, and welfare. Practitioners belonged to a variety of professional organizations, each

with a different concern—one with the interests of professional recreation workers, another with lay groups in community life, another with parks management, another with conservation, another with therapeutic recreation service.

An important trend in American life over the past several decades has, however, been toward consolidating professional areas of service and strengthening them through improved programs of professional preparation, certification, and accreditation. The recreation and park field has responded to this trend in a number of constructive ways. Many municipal and county governments have combined their operations relating to leisure services under single merged park and recreation departments—thus lending this area of service increased efficiency and visibility. At the same time, several major national organizations joined together in 1965, to establish the National Recreation and Park Association. Accompanying these changes, there has been a rapid growth of college and university programs preparing professionals in this field throughout the United States. With the exception of a substantial number of two-year community colleges, which have recently established degree programs intended to prepare recreation "technicians," the emphasis in higher education today is on the preparation of supervisors and administrators for a high level of professional service.

These three trends—the merger of municipal and county agencies in this field, the merger of professional organizations, and the healthy expansion of higher education—all contribute to an improved public understanding and acceptance of recreation.

11. *Public Attitudes Regarding Recreation.* Early in our nation's history, Americans had a stern and repressive view of recreation and leisure. The Puritan heritage in colonial New England strongly forbade many forms of play and recreation. While much of the opposition to recreation and leisure had been overcome by the time of the American Revolution, we continued during the period of industrial expansion to regard work as the primary aspect of life, as a matter of popular morality and even religious teaching. Only as educators began to become aware of the values of recreational experience in the upbringing of children and youth and as psychologists began to document its contribution to emotional stability and intellectual growth did we accord it more respect.

With the growth of leisure and affluence for large sectors of our society, there has come a new acceptance and respect for recreation as a form of public responsibility. This has been supported by American voters in the most practical and meaningful way possible—through positive action on steadily increasing budgets for the expansion of municipal, county, and state programs of parks and recreation. Each year, more and more funds are approved for land acquisition, facilities construction, the hiring of personnel, and overall operational support of recreation and park departments. This support is based on a growing recognition on the part of the American public that organized recreation accomplishes more than simply using up idle hours; instead it meets important social and personal needs in our society.

CHALLENGES TO THE RECREATION MOVEMENT

The social factors which have just been presented account for the rapid growth of the recreation movement in the United States during the past several decades. They describe a period of uninterrupted growth of facilities and expansion of services. It would be a mistake, however, to assume that the prospect is such a simple one for the United States. Clearly, there are a number of major challenges which face us all in the period of years that lie ahead and that will be of particular concern to government officials and recreation and park professionals.

1. *The Challenge of Increased Leisure.* One might view the prospect of vastly increased amounts of discretionary time with great enthusiasm. After all, it will mean that for the first time in history the average man will no longer be compelled to work long hours of each day but will be able to choose his involvements—to carry on pursuits that bring pleasure, creative fulfillment, relaxation, growth, and knowledge. Although some occupational groups or social classes have comparatively less free time than others, there is little doubt that we are steadily moving toward an era in which we will possess an overwhelming bulk of leisure time for the mass of the population.

As manufacturing and agricultural productivity per man-hour increases, and particularly with the widespread application of automation in industry, some social scientists have estimated that within two or three decades we shall approach a point where 2 percent of the nation's workers will be able to produce all the goods and services needed for the entire population.[5] Unless artificial restraints are applied on technological advances or union or governmental pressures exerted to keep people at work, there will be few jobs for the least capable and most poorly educated in our society. Those with marginal skills will probably have intermittent periods of employment. Labor economists assure us that the manual jobs, which used to occupy such workers, are rapidly disappearing.

How will people live if there is no work for them to do? The welfare process, which removes pride and incentive, has been responsible, in the eyes of many observers, for perpetuating the poverty cycle for large numbers of disadvantaged families. A number of economists and social scientists have proposed alternative solutions to the problem of economic maintenance of the unemployed or underemployed, and it appears probable that

---

[5] Richard Bellman, quoted in Edward T. Chase, "Four Days Shalt Thou Labor," *New York Times Magazine*, September 20, 1964, p. 28.

some form of guaranteed annual income will be adopted as a national solution to the problem.

But, even if the economic difficulties stemming from inadequate amounts of work can be solved—what of the problems related to human satisfactions and sense of self-worth? When people no longer have work to fill substantial portions of their time and to provide them with a sense of involvement and contributing to society, it will be necessary for them to find other kinds of commitments or outlets. How will our nation face this challenge of ever-increasing leisure? Will we use it in empty, negative, ultimately demoralizing ways? Or will we discover ways to use leisure so that it makes life more fulfilling and rewarding and contributes constructively to the physical, cultural, and intellectual well-being of the nation?

This sense of meaning and purpose in one's leisure life is something which has not yet been widely accepted by the American public. In the past, we tended to view recreation narrowly, as a means of helping the worker recuperate from his toil and gain energy for new labor. More recently, some social critics believe that our "fun morality"—a headlong pursuit of pleasure and a continuous search for novelty, excitement, and entertainment, as opposed to the use of free time for rest, for contemplation, for knowing oneself, for learning and enrichment—is actually a reflection of work attitudes. They suggest that play is only satisfactory when people *work* at it, when they commit themselves fully to it, when it governs their lives, when it imposes obligations on them. This total commitment to play implies that, for many, recreation has simply become a counterpart or substitute for work.

Today, the nature of work has changed considerably; it is marked by a high degree of job specialization, complex bureaucratic structures and personnel systems jointly created by the union and the industry's personnel experts. All of these have made the worker's role as a *person* so minimal and his task so lacking in decision-making or meaningful involvement that sociologists report that the *meaning* of work and the work situation has radically declined for most employees. In essence, the worker now sells his time for money rather than the other satisfactions that once came from the job.

There is the growing likelihood that for the great mass of employed persons the deepest satisfactions of life and the most meaningful kinds of involvement (apart from family relationships) will come to be found in one's away-from-work experiences—i.e., within one's leisure. Some of these experiences may involve formal education, community service, or religious participation. The bulk of them, however, are likely to be found in areas which are widely perceived as recreational: travel, hobbies, group associations, sports, cultural activities, entertainment, and the like. What can be done to help people recognize the need for these experiences to become meaningful rather than trivial and superficial?

2. *The Challenge of Education for Leisure.* Far from being a problem of strictly contemporary concern, the need to educate for leisure has been recognized in a number of earlier societies. Even in ancient Athens, as a later chapter will show, the proper use of leisure was very much the concern of such philosophers as Plato and Aristotle; education for the young Athenian citizen was heavily based on developing the arts of leisure for lifetime use. Similarly, in the courts of the Renaissance, education of the youth of the nobility dealt extensively with the social and cultural skills expected of adult members of the court.

In the United States, with the publication in 1918 of the "Cardinal Principles of Secondary Education,"[6] there was a formal recognition for the first time of the need to prepare people for the constructive and creative use of leisure. The alternative—that without such education there was the danger that great masses of free time would be used in negative, harmful, and socially pathological ways—was clearly foreseen. Through the decades that have followed, this goal of education has been reaffirmed by a number of major statements of educational policy. However, few school or college educators have actually attempted to come to grips with it as a realistic concern or to deal meaningfully with it in curricular programs.

If education is to be concerned with the real lives of students, it should prepare people to use their time wisely and constructively. This means that, in addition to the total process of general education, with in-depth exposure to the arts, literature, science, social studies, and other areas relevant to the creative use of leisure, there should be a direct concern with exploring the role of leisure in one's life. Schools should offer learning experiences in a wide variety of skills and interests useful in enriching lifelong recreational pursuits.

This can no longer be viewed as a task lying solely within the province of the formal educational structure—the schools and colleges of the nation. Increasingly, other types of agencies are beginning to provide a setting for education for leisure. Education is found throughout the life span today and is provided within business and industrial programs, in the armed forces, in rehabilitative settings, and in many other community settings. The task of teaching knowledge, skills, and attitudes related to the constructive and creative use of leisure must no longer be seen as a narrow concern of the schools but of all agencies concerned with meeting human needs.

3. *The Challenge of Meeting Special Needs.* It was indicated earlier that one of the social factors contributing to the growth of the recreation movement in the United States has been the rising level of social expectations for all groups in our population, including those with social, emo-

---

[6] "Cardinal Principles of Secondary Education," *Report of the Commission on the Reorganization of Secondary Education of the National Education Association* (Washington, D.C.: Dept. of the Interior, Bureau of Education Bulletin No. 35, 1918).

tional, or physical disability. Tremendous numbers of Americans are limited in the way in which they are able to use their leisure. Paradoxically, these tend to be the individuals who have the greatest amounts of free time.

What are the special groups which suffer from recreational disability in our society? Most obviously, they include the physically handicapped—the blind, those with hearing loss, those who have suffered a disabling trauma because of an accident, stroke, or operation, the child or adult with cerebral palsy, the person confined to the wheelchair. Often they are barred from participation either because of their own lack of skill or desire to become involved or because of the design of the facility or because administrative policy does not *allow* them to enter the program. For such persons, free time tends to be spent in repetitious, uninteresting, often passive ways.

Physical limitations are not the only ones that restrict recreational participation for special groups in our society. The mentally retarded tend to lack opportunities for recreational participation in the majority of American communities. While a number of outstanding pilot programs have involved the retarded, by far the greatest bulk of them still are unserved in structured recreation programs. Similarly, there is great relevance for recreation in the lives of the mentally ill. It is used in many psychiatric hospitals as part of the treatment process; increasingly it has become recognized that it is necessary to provide opportunities for discharged mental patients to become involved in constructive social programs on their return to community life. While many such individuals are able to make use of existing programs and services provided for the community at large, others require a protected environment with specially skilled leadership. Thus far, the social club or halfway-house movement, which is the major source of such recreational opportunities in America's cities and towns, has barely gotten under way. As we move away from the practice of assigning the mentally ill to institutions shut off like prisons from community life, it will be increasingly necessary to develop community programs in which the mentally ill are able to participate freely.

Other special groups in our population require special attention in terms of recreational opportunity. At one end of the age scale, there is the growing adolescent population—rebellious, searching for "kicks," and engaging in antisocial, defiant acts which challenge and perplex adult society. At the other end of the scale, the increasing number of aging persons, many of whom are physically or economically dependent, lack resources for the constructive and enjoyable use of leisure. It has recently been recognized that among America's poor, particularly black and Spanish-speaking minority groups, the lack of adequate opportunity for recreation has been one of the important factors which has led ghetto residents to strike out angrily in urban rioting over the past several summers. It will take—and this is one of the most significant challenges facing the recreation profession today—a full determination to play a more meaningful social role, if all these groups with special needs are to be properly served.

4. *The Challenge of Conservation.* It has already been suggested that one of the factors supporting the growth of the recreation movement in the United States has been the effort to reclaim its forests, mountains, waterways, and air—all of which have been thoughtlessly despoiled and polluted. A number of significant open-space programs have been initiated, and the Federal government, through the Bureau of Outdoor Recreation and the Land and Water Conservation Fund Act, has begun to help the states initiate massive programs of land acquisition for outdoor recreation purposes.

But this battle is only beginning. It involves a realistic determination of national priorities—particularly in those cases where industrial development and job opportunity for the residents of a region come directly in conflict with the need to protect and set aside natural resources which might otherwise be lost forever. Even when land has successfully been set aside for national, state, or regional park purposes, there is the further issue of whether it should be developed for intensive recreation use or left in its natural state. Experience in national parks has shown that recreation, when permitted to flood an area with overwhelming crowds of picnickers, campers, and fishermen, can result in the creation of "forest slums"— destroying vegetation and wildlife, littering, and poisoning the natural environment. The effort to bring additional highways into major national parks has been strongly resisted by many conservationists who believe that such intrusions destroy the quality of the wilderness by their physical presence and by the additional swarms of vehicles and families they bring. To solve such problems, the report of the Outdoor Recreation Resources Review Commission outlined a system of six classifications in 1962, suggesting the levels of use to which park and recreation areas might be put. Depending on their location, degree of wildness, specific recreational opportunities and similar factors, such areas might be classified as "high-density recreation areas," "general outdoor recreation areas," "natural environment areas," "unique natural areas," "primitive areas," and "historic and cultural sites."[7]

We have begun to acquire and set aside land for outdoor recreation at a rate comparable to the pace at which it is being ground up by bulldozers for residential and business construction. However, the process of developing and enforcing a program that will keep human needs (both economic and recreational) and the need to protect the natural environment in balance is one of the most difficult challenges facing recreation and park professionals and government planners today.

[7] "Outdoor Recreation for America," *Report to the President and Congress by the Outdoor Recreation Resources Review Commission* (Washington, D.C.: U.S. Government Printing Office, 1962), pp. 95-117.

5. *The Challenge of Planning.*   Implicit in the preceding sections has been the crucial need today for more effective concepts and models for planning park and recreation resources and programs. In the past, urban land-use planning consisted of defining the major uses to which land should be put, based on existing resources and needs and projected population and economic trends, and then assigning areas of the city for development or renewal. Recreation and parks have been seen as part of the network of public service facilities and have been assigned to neighborhoods, much as public schools are, with smaller and simpler facilities to serve local neighborhoods and larger and more complex facilities serving larger communities. Typically, planning approaches have been based on a system of standards which prescribe the minimum number of recreation facilities or the amount of needed acreage, according to population totals and density. Such standards have been widely accepted by leading planners and professional organizations.

Today it is recognized by many planning authorities that this traditional approach to planning needs radical rethinking. The old concept of providing facilities and services based strictly on neighborhood needs—with the implied assumption that all neighborhoods have similar needs and are to be served equally—has worked neither in practice nor in theory. Today, because of rapid shifts of population, changing patterns of living, and new kinds of urban problems, there is a need for more innovative and sophisticated city planning.

Our complex governmental structures today, with overlapping school districts, municipalities, and park districts in many metropolitan areas, call for entirely new methods of determining needs and planning land acquisition and facilities construction. There is serious question as to whether we can effectively meet our needs through separate action by municipal governments or whether we must not involve, at every level of decision making and action, the suburban towns that cluster like satellite communities around larger cities. In many antipollution and land-and-water reclamation projects, we are beginning to see regional action with cooperation by numbers of cities and states; in some cases two or more states are joining together with the Federal government to initiate plans. Ultimately, the only viable planning approach may be one in which smaller communities become part of large metropolitan park and recreation districts. The rapid growth of county-sponsored or regional park and recreation departments and commissions in recent years is a good example of this trend.

Modern concepts of planning suggest that recreation and park planning must also be closely linked to other relevant aspects of urban life and governmental responsibility. As an example, transportation has become an increasingly important factor in urban planning for parks and recreation. While mobility was certainly a positive factor in the growth of the recreation movement, it represents for many today (particularly for disadvantaged minority groups in our large cities) a major problem in terms of getting access to attractive recreation facilities. Thus, any attempt to develop meaningful park and recreation programs must realistically consider the possibility of providing subsidized transportation.

Similarly, many city planners are coming to see recreation as part of a total economic system which involves such elements as supply and demand, cost accounting of units of participation, and the establishment of a fees-and-charges approach in which major components of the public park and recreation offering are expected to pay for themselves through revenues derived from public use. When recreation is considered as part of a total marketing system (including voluntary, private, and commercial leisure opportunities), it becomes possible for planners to make intelligent decisions as to what kinds of facilities or services the city *should* provide and how it should finance these—through taxes, direct fees and charges, or the use of concessionaires. In many other ways, recreation and park planning must become a fuller part of total urban planning.

6. *The Challenge of Economic Support.* It has already been pointed out that there has been a major and dramatic expansion of America's resources and programs. While this growth has been impressive, it should be recognized that the entire sum spent by all government in combination with the amount spent by voluntary agencies probably amounts to no more than four or five billion dollars a year—in contrast to about thirty times that amount spent in the purchase of commercial recreational opportunities.

This means that as a nation we are entirely willing to spend vast sums of money privately on commercially purchased pleasure pursuits—including an estimated $50 billion on gambling and comparably high amounts on alcohol and similar leisure pursuits. In contrast, we lend grudging and limited support to programs provided by public and voluntary agencies which serve the public at large through constructive and creative leisure programs. When recreation is viewed as a form of public service, it must compete with many other areas of governmental operation—education, law enforcement, welfare, highways, housing, health, and sanitation. In a period of growing inflation and increased demand on government in every sphere, these agencies need ever-increasing amounts of tax money. While most people must rely completely, or almost completely, on public authorities to meet their needs with respect to education, law enforcement, sanitation, and highways, middle- and upper-class families are generally capable of meeting most of their leisure needs through private expenditure. Therefore, there is a tendency for them to resist major expansion of recreation and park programs on the local level today—unless they perceive it as meeting their needs directly.

We have, as a consequence, seen a considerable recent emphasis on local development in those areas of recreation service which meet middle-

and upper-class needs and interests and which depend on self-supporting or self-amortizing fee structures. The poor, who need public programs and opportunities the most, tend to be served the least. Clawson and Knetsch point out:

In a great many American cities, park and playground acreage is more unevenly distributed than is personal income. The lowest income areas of the city have an even smaller share of recreation area than they have of personal income, while the higher income sections have relatively generous parks and recreation areas. The poorest people, who most need easily accessible parks and playgrounds, often have them least. This situation is made still worse by the racial pattern of urban living. The low-income central city areas so deficient in recreation space are likely to be Negro; the suburban and outer city ring areas, generously supplied with recreation, are likely to be white. One of the great myths of the outdoor recreation field is that free public parks are a boon to "poor" people; actually it is the poor who frequently lack them.[8]

When fees and charges are attached to facilities or programs, they tend to exclude those at the lower end of the socioeconomic scale. Thus, major aspects of what once was regarded as a public service, freely available to all, are now being restricted to a specially privileged population.

To what extent is recreation to be regarded as a fundamental community service that *must* be provided—at least on a minimal basis—to all community residents? There is no question that vast sums of discretionary spending go into private amusement and entertainment. Whether government is justified in saying that a fuller portion of the wage-earner's dollar must go into the support of programs that meet total needs, rather than into the satisfaction of private wants and interests, is a question that must still be resolved.

In *The Affluent Society*, Galbraith made the point that we as a nation have been willing to spend huge sums *privately* to purchase expensive goods and services. However, he suggests that we are unwilling to spend a sufficiently high proportion of our income to support essential public services. He writes that:

an aspect of increasing private production is the appearance of an extraordinary number of things which lay claim to the interest of the young. Motion pictures, television, automobiles, and the vast opportunities which go with the automobile, together with such less enchanting merchandise as narcotics, comic books, and pornographia, are all included in an advancing gross national product.[9]

Galbraith suggests that in a well-organized community, with a strong school system, recreational opportunities, and effective police force, these

---

[8] Marion Clawson and Jack L. Knetsch, *Economics of Outdoor Recreation* (Baltimore: Johns Hopkins Press, published for Resources for the Future, Inc., 1960), p. 151.
[9] John Kenneth Galbraith, *The Affluent Society* (Boston: Houghton Mifflin, 1958), pp. 256-57.

diversionary forces operating on modern youth may do no great damage. The social, athletic, dramatic, and other activities of the school and community serve to hold his attention and meet his needs for leisure involvement. However, in a community where public services have failed to keep abreast of private consumption, things are quite different: "Here, in an atmosphere of private opulence and public squalor, the private goods have full sway."[10] Galbraith suggests that many of our most serious social problems, particularly those concerned with youth, stem from our unwillingness to divert our financial resources as a nation from private spending to public spending. Clearly, as we face the issue of attempting to bridge the gap between the haves and the have-nots in our society, this issue of developing fuller economic support will be primary.

7. *The Challenge of Professional Development.* As recreation and park programs continue to expand throughout the United States, it will be essential for recreation and park leadership, supervision, and administration to be strengthened as areas of professional service.

It has been pointed out that the image of recreation and park professionals is still unclear in the public mind. Their functions range widely from those concerned primarily with facilities and natural resources to those concerned with people; from a concentration on problems of direct leadership and program service to administrative concerns with personnel, finance, construction, maintenance, and public relations; from the needs of the population at large in the community to the needs of special groups in institutional settings.

Closely linked to this problem is the fact that recreation has until recently drawn its practitioners from a variety of other fields. Many early recreation workers were drawn from the field of physical education, for reasons that will be described in Chapter 5. The majority of park directors in past years had training related to landscape architecture, forestry, or conservation.

A primary challenge to the profession will be to define the broad area of professional preparation as an umbrella-like field, which will provide a core of theoretical knowledge germane to all areas of leisure service. It will be this common core that will strengthen universal professional preparation in this field and that will hold its diverse branches together, particularly when it is more clearly defined and its instruction enforced and upgraded, through a process of national accreditation of recreation and park curriculums.

Obviously, there are other important challenges related to strengthening recreation and parks as professional career service. These include the need to improve personnel practices in this field, to clarify and strengthen the public image of recreation service, to recruit qualified candidates for the field at an early age, to screen all professionals through state or regional

[10] *Ibid.*, p. 257.

certification or registration, and to clarify the relationship of recreation to other fields of related public service.

Particularly in the great cities of the nation and in their surrounding metropolitan areas, it will be increasingly important to encourage greater numbers of disadvantaged minority-group individuals to enter this field. Career-entrance programs for black or Spanish-speaking youth at the subprofessional level, linked to opportunities for community college training, or four-year college programs for those with academic potential, will have to be widely established.

8. *The Challenge of the Cities.* Without question, the most serious problems America faces today are rooted in its giant cities. Our great urban complexes in one sense are the pride of our nation; they are the seat of huge skyscrapers, industrial centers, communications, culture, colleges, and universities. At the same time, many of them are increasingly rotten at the core, wracked by problems of congested transportation, growing crime, slums inhabited by families caught deep in the cycle of poverty, and many other pathologies of body and spirit. The urban riots that took place during the 1960's were only one symbol of the discontent and frustration endemic in America's cities. Equally significant was the flight of millions of white middle-class families to the suburbs and the consequent socioeconomic and racial polarization of our metropolitan regions.

But it is clear that America's cities are not going to be abandoned. While their problems are great, so is the determination to solve them. Through programs of vocational training and remedial education, business and government cooperation in the development of new job opportunity programs, slum clearance, and the development of "model cities" with a substantial degree of local participation in planning and decision-making, government at all levels is working to solve the problems of the cities.

But the problems are not only related to the economy, to housing, and to education. They also involve the human spirit and the total quality of living that is available to urban residents. Planners are coming to recognize more and more that the city must be transformed into a pleasant and happy environment in which to live. This implies change for both the physical and the social setting. In terms of the physical, it is essential that more open spaces, air, light, greenery, expanded vistas, decorative buildings, art, sculpture, and places for play on all levels be provided. In terms of the social environment, the city must become a place where the leisure of all classes can be filled with pleasure and challenge—through exciting events and "happenings," through interesting places to stroll and explore, and through the opportunity to become creatively involved with others in a host of exciting and stimulating enterprises.

It has long been recognized that leisure opportunity is not inherently good or bad. It provides the potential for pathological use or for creative and constructive involvement. In the remaking of America's cities, it is clear that these alternative choices must be clearly recognized and that every effort must be made to employ leisure in the most beneficial and constructive ways.

9. *The Challenge of Change.* We are living in a world of fantastically rapid social and technological change. Inventions have transformed the means of production and the character of daily living, of travel, and of business. The race to the moon that Americans won during the late 1960's, the computer-based economy, the tremendous proliferation of knowledge— all these affect our lives radically.

But beyond these physical and economic changes have been other even more striking changes of a spiritual or moral nature. Many of the old rules and values which have been long accepted in society no longer hold. What was first described as the "beat" and then the "hippie" movement represents far more than a comparatively small segment of American youth's "tuning out" by seeking sexual freedom and a hedonistic way of life. Today a very substantial number of young people, not only in the United States but throughout the world, are challenging old values and seeking to establish a new, franker, and freer kind of society. The emphasis on sexual freedom is matched by the widely expanded use of consciousness-expanding or mood-changing drugs. Both forms of release are found not only in rebellious school or college students but also among many middle-class adults who are apparently in other ways highly responsible and law-abiding citizens.

Other factors seem to have played a part. The American family structure is far less stable and secure today than in the past, and parental authority has been sharply undermined. The major religious denominations have lost much of their influence in a moral sense; there is a widespread attempt on the part of younger clergy and many communicants to challenge and change traditional religious practices. Certainly, this breakdown of the traditional roles of the church and the family with respect to human behavior both reflects and adds to the current turbulence in society.

A final factor is the wave of student rebellion that has swept schools and colleges. While this has been a worldwide movement, it has nowhere been as widespread as in the United States. Here it received its initial impetus from the Civil Rights movement during the late 1950's and early 1960's and then shifted into an attack upon the Vietnam war and the role played by universities within the military-industrial establishment. Finally it turned into a broad rejection of adult authority and societal values and a demand for control of schools and colleges in hundreds of disruptive riots throughout the country.

What does all this have to do with recreation and leisure? It would be foolish to suggest that students take drugs, become involved in sex, or engage in campus rebellion only because they are bored. Clearly those who are the leaders in politically oriented campus rebellions hope to overthrow or at least to radically alter both the school or college and the over-all society. Many of those who are involved in sex do so out of a meaningful search for human relationships, just as others who take drugs do so not merely for "kicks" but because they believe that it will enrich them as people.

But there are great masses of others who are frankly seeking sensation, excitement, personal release, and other outlets that might lead to self-discovery, to human contacts, and to a sense of meaningful interpersonal involvement. It is within this sphere that recreation has a major role to play —by providing flexible, responsive, and imaginative ways to meet human needs. Without question, as we move ahead through the final decades of the century, there will be many such challenges—not only from the young but from the aging, from minority groups, from the wealthy, and from the urban and the rural dweller.

It will be necessary for those who provide leisure services to help people deal with vast portions of free time, far beyond that existing in any previous day. They will have the task of providing services and opportunities that are so exciting and attractive that they can counter the strong attractions of antisocial forms of amusement as well as the equally strong tendency to withdraw from active involvement in a spectator-oriented age. The new recreation will have to make the fullest use of modern technology and embody the most relevant concepts of modern psychology. America's cities will need innovative planning in which recreation and parks are closely linked to transportation, housing, education, the economy, and law enforcement.

It is impossible to predict the total challenge of the future. We know only that the rate of change is so tremendous that the society of tomorrow will be vastly different from that of today. Man's possibilities for transforming his environment, his economy, and, indeed, himself are endless—and organized recreation service must respond to these possibilities and challenges fully.

2

Role of Federal and State Governments

This chapter is concerned with the role of the Federal and state governments in the United States with respect to recreation and park facilities, programs, and services. In general, the functions of the Federal government in providing recreation have developed without a systematic plan. No single agency or authority has been responsible for determining appropriate goals. Instead, government functions in recreation have developed either to meet human needs that fell logically into the area of concern of a specific agency or because major programs developed secondary outcomes that related to the provision of recreational opportunities.

As an illustration, the initial purpose of the Tennessee Valley Authority in the Appalachian Mountain region of the United States was to provide badly needed flood and erosion controls, and inexpensive sources of electric power for rural regions. It soon became apparent that the great T.V.A. lakes and reservoirs had the potential for providing enjoyable recreational opportunities for millions of campers and boating enthusiasts. Leisure activities rapidly became a major industry within the Appalachian region and contributed substantially to the economies of the communities and states involved. In many other similar government programs having to do with land, water, and wildlife maintenance or development, recreation use has become an increasingly important concern.

FUNCTIONS OF FEDERAL GOVERNMENT IN RECREATION

1. *Direct Management of Outdoor Recreation Resources.* The Federal government, through the work of such agencies as the National Park

Service, the Forest Service, or the Bureau of Land Management, owns and operates a vast network of parks, forests, lakes and reservoirs, seashores, and other facilities which are extensively used by the public for outdoor recreation. In these, the government may develop access and specific areas for varied use, manage wildlife resources, provide campgrounds or lodges, and carry on other varied functions.

2. *Conservation and Resource Reclamation.* Closely related to the preceding function, the government reclaims natural resources which have been destroyed, damaged, or threatened and promotes programs related to conservation, wildlife propagation, and antipollution controls throughout the nation.

3. *Assistance to Open-Space Programs.* Chiefly through the work of the Bureau of Outdoor Recreation, with funding authorized by the 1965 Land and Water Fund Conservation Act, the Federal government has provided hundreds of millions of dollars in matching grants to states and localities to promote open-space development. In addition, through programs of direct aid to municipalities administered by agencies concerned with housing and urban development, the Federal government has subsidized the development of many parks, playgrounds, and other urban open spaces.

4. *Direct Programs of Recreation Participation.* The government operates a number of direct programs of recreation service in Veteran's Administration Hospitals and other Federal institutions and in the armed forces on bases and armed-forces installations throughout the world. In these settings, recreation is seen as an important form of rehabilitative service or as directly linked to health and morale services.

5. *Advisory, Consultative, and Financial Assistance Programs.* The government provides varied forms of assistance to states, localities, and community agencies to help them in meeting the needs of special population groups. For many years, it has provided extension programs operated by the Department of Agriculture to meet the recreational needs of rural youth and families. More recently, it has supported extensive programs serving the economically and socially disadvantaged populations in major cities. Certain programs relating to physical fitness and mental health have also received Federal assistance.

6. *Aid to Professional Education.* During the 1960's the Federal government—particularly agencies within the Department of Health, Education and Welfare—has provided training grants for professional education in recreation in colleges and universities throughout the United States. These have been specially directed at meeting the needs of the physically or emotionally disabled, including the mentally retarded, the mentally ill, and aging persons. A number of major grants have also been provided to support research and demonstration projects involving recreation.

7. *Promotion of Recreation as an Economic Function.* The Federal

government has been active in promoting tourism, providing aid to rural residents in developing recreation enterprises, and assisting Indian tribes in establishing recreational and tourist facilities on their reservations. Such agencies as the Bureau of the Census and the Coast Guard also provide needed information for travel, boating, and similar pastimes.

The growth of involvement of Federal agencies in recreation is evidenced by the *Recreation and Park Yearbook*, which indicated in 1961 that there were 13 agencies that played a role in this field; by 1966, the number had grown to 72 Federal agencies, including 9 cabinet-level departments (with 49 separate agencies or programs), 11 independent agencies or commissions, and 3 Presidential Committees.[1]

Examples of Federal Involvement in Recreation and Parks

The work of a number of the major Federal agencies in this area is described in the following section.

The National Park Service. The National Park Service has the responsibility for protecting and maintaining all national parks and monuments, battlefield parks and sites, national memorials, national military parks, the National Capital Parks, and certain national cemeteries so that they may yield the maximum benefit and service to the American people. The concept of providing outdoor recreation resources has become so strongly accepted within the National Park Service that it now provides tent, cabin, and hotel accommodations, bridle and hiking trails, marinas and boat docks, museums, and picnic facilities for public use. In many parks, it offers an interpretive nature program with conducted walks, tours, museums and other displays, lectures, and campfire programs. The Park Service does not allow hunting or commercial fishing, cutting of timber, or exploitation of other natural resources; its emphasis is strongly conservationist.

Most of the property administered by the National Park Service in its early years was west of the Mississippi, but, particularly in recent decades, a number of major seashore parks and other areas have been set aside in other areas of the country. In 1956, a ten-year plan, "Mission 66," was set in motion to safeguard the parks and to provide facilities for an anticipated 88 million visitors by 1966. So great has been the wave of interest in outdoor recreation and vacation travel that this goal has long since been surpassed. In 1955 there were 50 million visitors and by 1965 over 121 million visitors. The total in 1968 was 150.8 million. The National Park Service today administers over 214 areas, including 231 million acres of parkland, and had a total budget in 1967 of $147.6 million.

There are 33 specially designated National Parks. In 1967, the Senate

[1] *Recreation and Park Yearbook, 1966* (Washington, D.C.: National Recreation and Park Association, 1967), pp. 1-23.

Interior Committee approved a new Federal outdoor playground, stretching from the Canadian border, with a total of 1.2 million acres to be preserved, of which 503,500 acres would be in a new North Cascades National Park in the State of Washington. Following much legislative and public negotiation, a 58,000-acre Redwoods National Park has been established in northern California, and plans are under way to establish a new Potomac Valley Park in Maryland, Virginia and West Virginia and a new 1.7-million-acre National Park in the Adirondack Mountain area of New York State.

In addition, the National Park Service has been active in developing such East Coast sites as the Fire Island National Seashore on Long Island, Acadia National Park in Maine, Assateague National Seashore on the Maryland coast, and Cape Hatteras National Seashore in North Carolina.

The National Forest Service. The second great Federal agency with a major responsibility for administering extensive preserves of wild land for public recreation use is the National Forest Service, within the Department of Agriculture. This differs from the National Park Service in several respects. First, it does not control great scenic monuments and historical or geological treasures but rather huge areas of forests and grasslands. Unlike the National Park Service, which is dedicated to a single-use concept of preservation and public enjoyment of natural areas, the Forest Service accepts the multiple-use concept of Federally owned land under its control. Such functions as mining, grazing, lumbering, and hunting may all be permitted in national forests. Actually, its responsibilities include the following: national forest management, forestry research, and cooperative state and Federal programs for forest protection and development.

A total of 154 national forests, 19 national grasslands, and various small land utilization projects located in 41 states comprise the 186-million-acre system. There are great differences among the various sites; the most pristine and untouched areas are found within the National Wilderness Preservation System, totaling over 15 million acres, established by the Wilderness Act of 1964. A network of National Recreation Areas, with greater emphasis on development of recreation facilities, winter sports areas, and camping sites, is also being established.

Over all, recreation has become the fastest growing use of the national forests. Over the past decade, it has increased about 8 percent per year, climbing from a reported 45.7 million visitor-days in 1955 to 92.5 million in 1960 and 156.5 million in 1968. So broad is the scope of this agency that about one acre out of twelve in the United States is administered by the Forest Services, and it has been estimated that with full use of all its facilities it is able to accommodate about 800,000 persons at one time.

Today public recreation areas are found in all national forests. In addition, many resorts and hotels have been allowed to operate within national forests under special-use permits. Use of the forests extends from primitive exploration of wilderness areas by horse, by canoe, or on foot, to tent and trailer camping, and staying at comfortable hotels and lodges.

U.S. Army Corps of Engineers. The Corps of Engineers of the U.S. Department of the Army, organized in 1775, is responsible for the improvement and maintenance of rivers and other waterways to facilitate navigation and flood control. It constructs reservoirs, protects and improves beaches and harbors, and administers over 8 million acres of Federally owned land, including 28,000 miles of improved inland and intercoastal waterways; it also operates about 350 reservoirs in 44 states covering approximately 8 million acres. All these facilities are used by the public for camping, hunting, fishing, and boating. Visitor-days at Army Corps of Engineer recreation sites in 1965 totaled 128.6 million, compared with 109 million in 1960 and 63 million in 1955. Based on the Water Project Recreation Act of 1965, recreation and fish and wildlife development are regarded as equal in priority to other uses for which Federal water resource projects may be initiated.

The Corps of Engineers makes many sites available to state and local governments to develop for recreation use. Over all, these levels of government have spent more than ten times as much as the Federal government in developing parks and water recreation facilities on Corps of Engineer lands. In many cases the Corps leases shorelines along its reservoirs to commercial concessionaires or makes them available for private citizens and organizations to build camps and summer homes.

The Bureau of Land Management. Established in 1946, the Bureau of Land Management has jurisdiction over Federally owned public lands which have not been incorporated into specific national forests, parks, or other recreation areas. This includes a total of about one-fifth of the land area of the United States, amounting to about 470 million acres, chiefly in Alaska and the western states. The management of this property is guided by the Classification and Multiple Use Act of 1964, which allows recreation use, along with grazing, wildlife management, forestry, and mineral development, as an important function of public lands. Thus, there are increasing numbers of camping and picnic sites, trailer areas, swimming beaches, and boat-launching ramps on Bureau of Land Management properties; estimated visitor days at these sites in 1968 totaled 24 million.

The Bureau of Indian Affairs. The Bureau of Indian Affairs exists primarily to give service to American Indian tribes in such areas as health, education, economic development, and land management. First established in 1824 in the War Department, the Bureau was transferred to civilian control with the creation of the Department of the Interior. Today, Indian-owned properties aggregate about 58 million acres, including over 5,500 lakes. On their reservations, the various tribes develop and manage recreation facilities, such as campgrounds, museums, restaurants, hunting and fishing areas (including the provision of guides and "packaged" hunt parties), lodges, and ski resorts. The Bureau of Indian Affairs gives technical assistance to tribesmen in operating these facilities and programs, which in 1965 attracted approximately 6.5 million visitors and in 1968, 10.1 million. The cultural heritage of the American Indian is of special interest to many visitors, so the Bureau, along with the Indian Arts and Crafts Board, promotes the development of native arts and crafts and costumed ceremonials.

The Bureau of Reclamation. This agency, housed within the Department of the Interior, has a primary responsibility for water resource development, chiefly in seventeen western states. Although its function has been largely to promote irrigation and electric power, recreation was accepted as one of the important purposes of the Bureau since 1936. The policy of the Bureau of Reclamation is to transfer reservoir areas wherever possible to other Federal agencies; frequently these become classified as National Recreation Areas and are assigned to the National Park Service for operation. They differ from National Parks in that greater stress is placed on active recreation use—such as boating, camping, hiking, hunting, and fishing—rather than sightseeing. By the late 1960's, reclamation project areas totaled over 216, involving over 4.5 million acres of land and 1.5 million surface acres of water. Attendance at Bureau of Reclamation sites climbed from 6 million in 1950 to 24.3 million in 1960 and an estimated 49.5 million in 1968.

The Tennessee Valley Authority. The Tennessee Valley Authority was created by Congress in 1933 with the original purpose of developing the Tennessee River for flood control, navigation, and electric power. Its reservoirs have become increasingly valuable as outdoor recreation resources in Kentucky, North Carolina, Tennessee, and other southern and border states. The Tennessee Valley Authority itself does not develop or operate recreation facilities but makes land available to other public agencies or private groups to develop parks, group camps, marinas, and other recreational areas. By 1965, over 178,000 acres had been transferred to Federal, state, or local authorities for recreation use.

The value of recreation facilities and equipment that have been placed on the shores of T.V.A. reservoirs and lakes was estimated in 1969 at $255 million, a twentyfold increase over 1947, the first year when such statistics were available. T.V.A. water properties today include over 600,000 surface acres of water and over 10,000 miles of shoreline—almost all accessible for recreation use. Visitor-days have tripled since 1950 and in 1968 were calculated at 44.3 million.

The Fish and Wildlife Service. Housed in the Department of the Interior, the Fish and Wildlife Service has a direct responsibility for the protection of fish and wildlife on Federal properties throughout the United States. It administers laws designed to increase and protect birds, mammals, reptiles, and amphibians, carries out research studies, conducts wildlife conservation education, enforces Federal game laws, and cooperates with state fish and game agencies in the control of destructive or injurious birds, animals, and fish.

The Fish and Wildlife Service consists of two separate bureaus: the Bureau of Commercial Fisheries and the Bureau of Sports Fisheries and Wildlife. The latter bureau is most directly concerned with meeting recreational interests of Americans, particularly those related to hunting and fishing. In 1962 Congress declared recreation to be an appropriate "secondary purpose" of the National Wildlife Refuge system, and in 1966 it passed the Endangered Species Preservation Act; both of these steps have given strong support to the wildlife conservation program of the Bureau of Sports Fisheries and Wildlife. Today the Bureau operates a 321-unit chain of nature preserves totaling 28.6 million acres. Such refuges are strong tourist attractions: in 1955 they had 6.9 million visitors; this figure rose to an estimated 17 million visits in 1968.

In view of the fact that at least 78 kinds of animals are regarded as being on the verge of extinction in the United States—as a consequence of rapid urbanization, air and water pollution, large-scale farming, careless shooting, and the free use of pesticides—the work of the Fish and Wildlife Service has become of ever-greater importance.

The Bureau of Outdoor Recreation. A major step was taken toward the unification and promotion of all Federal programs related to open space, the protection of natural resources, and outdoor recreation development with the establishment of the Bureau of Outdoor Recreation in the Department of the Interior in 1962. This action was taken by President Kennedy, based on the report of the Outdoor Recreation Resources Review Commission, which stressed the need for fuller attention to major priorities in the area of natural resources and outdoor recreation. It recommended that the Bureau of Outdoor Recreation be founded to provide leadership, coordinate programs and services, and stimulate the states and local government throughout the country to promote open-space and outdoor recreation resource development.

The Bureau of Outdoor Recreation is responsible for carrying out an inventory of the nation's outdoor recreation needs and resources, formulating an outdoor recreation plan for the nation, classifying recreation resources, providing technical assistance and promoting research and education in this field, and encouraging interstate and regional cooperation in the acquisition and development of outdoor recreation resources. Recently, the Bureau of Outdoor Recreation has made a special effort to stimulate state and local efforts to meet the needs of urban populations. It has been able to do this chiefly through the Land and Water Conservation Fund Act.

Land and Water Conservation Fund Program. This fund was created to provide urgently needed public outdoor recreation areas and facilities.

It was enacted into law by Congress in 1965 to provide a substantial fund over a 25-year period, to assist states and local governments in their outdoor recreation and open-space programs. Its funding was originally intended to be derived from (1) admission and user fees at Federal recreation areas, (2) net proceeds from the sale of surplus Federal property, and (3) the Federal tax on motorboat fuels. Of this total amount (projected at the outset to be about $160 million per year), 40 percent was to be made available to Federal agencies for purchase of recreation areas and 60 percent to states as grants-in-aid, on a 50 percent matching basis, for planning, acquisition, or development projects. Each state was required to prepare a comprehensive outdoor recreation plan, including a full analysis of its cities and their needs, in order to be eligible for funding assistance. The emphasis in this program was to be placed on acquisition rather than development and on sites for direct recreation use rather than historic sites or museums.

By the end of the 1967 fiscal year, Congress had appropriated a total of $251 million for open space and outdoor recreation; of this, $160 million was for assistance to states and $86 million for the acquisition of recreation lands and waters by the National Park Service, the Forest Service, and the Bureau of Sports Fisheries and Wildlife. The Bureau of Outdoor Recreation has channeled substantial assistance into cities, chiefly for land acquisition but also including in some cases such recreation facilities as swimming pools and bathhouses, skating rinks, and sports complexes. Two new supplemental sources were provided in 1968: direct appropriations by Congress and revenues from Outer Continental Shelf leases for oil drilling. It was anticipated that these sources would guarantee an annual Fund income of $200 million.

Thus far, the role of the Bureau of Outdoor Recreation in coordination and providing leadership has been limited, and there is widespread belief that fuller authority needs to be given to a single government agency to provide direction for the total Federal effort in recreation and parks.

Other Federal Programs Related to Outdoor Recreation

A number of other Federal agencies have responsibilities related to outdoor recreation, particularly with respect to its economic function. The Agricultural Stabilization and Conservation Service has assisted many farmers in developing ponds and reservoirs on private land and stocking them with fish; of 700,000 such water sites throughout the country, almost half are open to public use today, many on a fee basis. The Farmers Home Administration gives credit and management assistance to rural organizations and farmers in developing recreation facilities, farms and cabins for vacationers, camping areas, nature trails, fishing sites, hunting preserves, marinas, and similar facilities. The Soil Conservation Service has assisted over 34,000 rural landowners in establishing one or more income-producing recreation areas during the period of the middle 1960's.

The Department of Agriculture provides assistance to rural residents in developing their own recreation programs and establishing recreation enterprises for income purposes. Its Federal Extension Service aids community recreation planning in rural areas and advises states on outdoor recreation development. It works through extension agents at land-grant agricultural colleges in many states to promote wildlife propagation, resource development, and rural recreation activities through the 4-H Clubs, which have well over two million young members today.

A number of agencies in the Department of Commerce have also given assistance to recreation ventures. The Bureau of the Census furnishes population statistics and projections needed for recreation planning and surveys, including trends in outdoor recreation demand and uses. The Business and Defense Services Administration provides useful material, in the form of publications, guides, and special studies for businessmen involved in the operation of resorts, restaurants, ski centers, golf courses, sports arenas, riding academies, and other recreation facilities or in the manufacture of recreation equipment. The Economic Development Administration does economic research related to the effects of recreation development on business opportunity in local communities and provides grants and loans for public works and the development of facilities, including matching funds for park and recreation projects. The Coast and Geodetic Survey Nautical Charting program provides charts and related information about tides, currents, weather, and marine facilities for safe navigation by boating enthusiasts. The Weather Bureau has 300 stations manned by full-time personnel throughout the United States which broadcast weather information helpful to participants and operators of such outdoor recreation activities as boating, skiing, camping, hunting, and fishing. Finally, in the area of economic development, the U.S. Travel Service promotes the nation's tourist attractions and facilities and encourages a steady growth of vacationers throughout the tourist regions of the country.

The Office of the President has been active in calling for the establishment of commissions, advisory bodies, and conferences relating to open space and beautification. Recently, it has promoted major efforts to combat water and air pollution, expanded the National Wilderness Preservation system, established a Clean Rivers Demonstration Program and a national system of hiking trails, and mounted numerous other Federal efforts to protect and improve the natural environment. Its focus has been strongly on encouraging citizen and local participation in these efforts. It has sponsored a number of conferences on natural beauty and conservation and established a Council on Recreation and Natural Beauty, charged with reviewing Federal plans and programs concerned with recreation and natural beauty and encouraging effective coordination among Federal programs in this area.

Other Federal Programs Related to Recreation

Another substantial sphere of Federal activity has related to urban populations and meeting the needs of special groups. Such programs have been found chiefly in three categories: programs in the Department of Health, Education and Welfare, the Department of Housing and Urban Development, and the antipoverty program coordinated by the Office of Economic Opportunity during the 1960's.

Programs under Health, Education and Welfare

The U.S. Office of Education has had, since its establishment in 1867, a concern with recreation in its relationship to education for children and youth. In recent years it has helped to promote workshops and conferences on school-community recreation and professional preparation for recreation leaders.

A number of recent acts of Congress have promoted the work of educational agencies in community-oriented programs, adult education, and informal social education; several of these have had implications for the support of recreation as a school-connected service. For example, Title I of the Higher Education Act of 1965 provided grants to states to enable colleges and universities to strengthen programs aimed at the solution of community problems, including recreation and land-planning programs. The Elementary and Secondary Education Act of 1965 provided grants for supplemental educational centers and services, in-service training programs, and institutions. These have included assistance to camping, cultural activities, physical education and recreation programs, and special programs to serve the physically and mentally handicapped. The Supplemental Education Centers and Services, under Title III of this act, authorizes projects related to outdoor education and recreation, such as nature centers, teacher training, museums, and field trips. The Office of Education has also supported several projects concerned with the adaptation of facilities and the development of recreation programs for chronically ill or disabled children and youth. Through its Bureau for Handicapped Children and Youth, the Office of Education has funded training programs in recreation in over a dozen colleges throughout the United States.

The Administration on Aging. Authorized by the Older Americans Act of 1965, this Federal agency replaced the Office of Aging. It serves as the central Federal office concerned with problems of older persons in society. It promotes comprehensive programs for aging persons, providing grants for training of professional personnel (including graduate study in recreation) and demonstration projects intended to prepare leaders and professional staffs to work with older people. It acts as a clearinghouse for information on new or expanded programs and services for the aging and supports research projects in this field. During its first three years of operation, the Administration on Aging assisted a variety of local projects to improve the lives of older persons, with emphasis on community planning, program coordination, training of special personnel, and information and referral services. By the beginning of 1969, almost a thousand such projects had received assistance from the Administration on Aging. In January, 1969, it was reported that the largest number of such programs (34 percent) were for recreation and leisure time activities, including 250 senior centers. Over three times as many older persons (288,545) participated in recreation and other leisure-time activities under Title III of the Act than in any other special service provided in these programs.

The Children's Bureau. This agency, created in 1912, is specifically concerned with the welfare of children and youth, especially in migrant worker families and among the physically and mentally disabled, the institutionalized, and the socially deviant. It publishes guides and handbooks related to recreation and works through states and a variety of national organizations to promote improved services for young people. One of the Children's Bureau's most important functions is the sponsorship of major White House Conferences on Children and Youth that are called each ten years by the President. In the past, leisure problems of youth have been an important area of concern of these conferences, with many important recommendations being made with respect to recreation needs and services.

The Public Health Service. Through the Bureau of State Services, the Public Health Service provides technical assistance for the improvement of environmental, sanitation, and accident-prevention aspects of recreation facilities and programs. It is concerned with the usability of lands and waters for recreation. Working chiefly through the states, it assists in planning standards and inspection programs for bathing sanitation, food handling, disposal of refuse and sewage, and similar problems in parks and camps. The Public Health Service has also awarded grants to the National Recreation and Park Association for the training of professionals and subprofessionals working with the ill and disabled, particularly the mentally retarded, in community settings. The National Institute of Mental Health, a branch of the Public Health Service, assists research into the cause, prevention, and treatment of mental illness, including recreation-related projects. In addition to sponsoring a number of direct programs which have recreation services, such as the leprosarium at Carville, Louisiana, or St. Elizabeth's Hospital in Washington, D.C., the Public Health Service, through its Environmental Control Program, is particularly active in combatting air and water pollution.

Rehabilitation Services Administration. This major agency in the

Department of Health, Education and Welfare administers the Federal law authorizing vocational rehabilitation programs designed to help the physically and mentally disabled gain employment and lead fuller lives. It assists state rehabilitation programs and is responsible for a number of special projects in the area of research, demonstration, and training. During the 1960's, a number of college programs training therapeutic recreation specialists were given curriculum development and scholarship grants by the Vocational Services Administration (which in 1967 became part of the Rehabilitation Services Administration). These grants represent an important step of recognition and support for recreation by the Federal government.

Bureau of Family Services. Housed within the Welfare Administration, this agency is concerned with the need to strengthen family living; generally it assists community social and recreational programs as supportive of healthy physical and emotional environments for families. Specifically, it gives assistance to low-income families, as authorized under Social Security legislation. It provides grants-in-aid programs for the needy and to the blind, aged, and disabled and encourages states to make recreation services available to public assistance recipients.

Recreation Functions Related to Housing and Urban Development

The Federal government has had an extensive record of promoting slum clearance and assisting housing programs in America's cities. Its policy has been to encourage the provision of recreation areas and facilities to meet the needs of the residents of housing projects. As early as World War II, the Public Housing Administration of the Housing and Home Finance Agency helped provide recreation facilities in low-rent housing developments. In subsequent Federal Acts, in 1949 and 1954, the Urban Renewal Administration provided assistance to park and outdoor recreation development linked to urban housing programs.

The Housing Act of 1961 provided grants to state and local government for the acquisition of open-space lands in urban areas for park, recreation, conservation, scenic, or historic purposes. These grants included up to 30 percent of the cost of the property. Administered by the Urban Renewal Administration within the Housing and Home Finance Agency, this Act represented the first major effort by the Federal government to promote open-space development in urban areas. By 1966, over 750 grants had been approved, totaling $98.9 million of Federal funds and considerably larger state and local government expenditures. This resulted in the acquisition of 197,800 acres of land to meet existing and projected park and recreation needs of urban residents. The projects that were assisted ranged from tiny parks tucked into crowded city neighborhoods to such extensive developments as San Diego's Mission Bay Park, a project involving the transformation of over 4,600 acres of tidelands, marsh, and water into an impressive multi-use recreation site.

The Department of Housing and Urban Development was established in 1965, with responsibility for a broad range of Federally assisted programs, including urban renewal and planning, public housing, mass transit, community facilities, and open space. The act authorizing H.U.D. provided $7.5 billion for a period of four years and liberalized the authority for open-space grants by providing for 50 percent of costs of land acquisition, development, beautification, and improvement. Section 705 of the Housing and Urban Development Act, known as the "small parks program," authorized grants for the demolition of slums to create urban open spaces, and the Urban Beautification and Improvement Program supported numerous projects aimed specifically at beautification.

Increasingly, the Federal government has provided support for parks and recreation in urban areas. The 1966 Demonstration Cities and Metropolitan Development Act provides up to 80 percent of the cost of projects improving the physical environment of cities—preserving historic structures and acquiring and developing parks, playgrounds, community centers, and related facilities. Similarly, the Neighborhood Facilities Program gives assistance to local government in financing neighborhood or youth centers, health stations, and other public buildings for health, recreation, or similar services. Throughout these programs, the coordination of Federal, state, and local agencies is stressed.

The Model Cities Program, initiated in 1967, has provided extensive planning grants for cities to support urban renewal efforts. By 1968, sixty-five communities had received planning grants totaling $11 million, to assist them in developing projects that would then permit them to share in the large sum of $300 million for further Model Cities development. Parks and recreation have been regarded as an integral element in these planning projects.

Federal Antipoverty Programs

The so-called Federal "war on poverty" which was initiated during the early 1960's under the Johnson Administration gave considerable support to the provision of recreation services for economically disadvantaged urban populations. Its major impetus came from the Economic Opportunity Act of 1964, which created the Office of Economic Opportunity to coordinate all anti-poverty programs on the Federal government level. Among the major programs sponsored by OEO with relevance for recreation were the Job Corps, VISTA, the Neighborhood Youth Corps, and an aggregate of special projects known as Community Action Programs.

Job Corps. Operated until 1969 by the Office of Economic Opportunity, this was a program established to provide training in vocational and basic academic subjects for out-of-work, out-of-school, young men and women between the ages of sixteen and twenty-one. It was established as a voluntary residential program, operating in two types of settings: Urban Centers for Men and Urban Centers for Women (usually located in or close to cities and operated by large industries, educational institutions, or social service agencies, with an emphasis on developing business or industrial skills) and on public lands under the direction of the National Park Service or Forest Service and with a special emphasis on conservation. At its peak, in 1967, the Job Corps served approximately 57,000 young men and women in 116 centers throughout the United States, drawn from all sections of the country and both rural and urban depressed areas. Within this setting, recreation was seen as contributing to six broad categories, including (1) physical development, (2) morale-building, (3) intergroup relations on base, (4) community relations (with people in surrounding communities), (5) personal growth, and (6) employability. Job Corps administrators took the position that more than academic and vocational skills were required to insure that its graduates would be capable of getting and holding jobs. It would also require adequate self-concepts, acceptance of community values, and the ability to use one's leisure in constructive and socially acceptable ways—and it was felt that the extensive Job Corps recreation program (which encompassed a wide range of social, athletic, and cultural programs) would contribute significantly to these needs.

In addition to recreation within the Job Corps program, many of the Corps' projects, particularly in Conservation Centers, were concerned with recreational facility development and maintenance in communities surrounding their centers or on Federally owned properties.

VISTA (Volunteers in Service to America). This was a much smaller part of the antipoverty program, viewed by many as a domestic Peace Corps. It involved assignment of several thousand workers—chiefly young college graduates—to work in poverty areas, including urban slums, impoverished rural communities, and Indian reservations. The roles of VISTA volunteers have varied considerably, but in many cases they have included the development of constructive recreation programs for youth and adults. This area of service has been linked to developing community organizations, improving home life, establishing social service programs to meet the needs of youth, neighborhood or community beautification and sanitation, and economic improvement through the establishment of recreation enterprises.

Neighborhood Youth Corps. The Neighborhood Youth Corps was established under Title 1-B of the Economic Opportunity Act, as a work-training program for unemployed young people—chiefly in urban slums but also in suburban or rural pockets of poverty. Subcontractors (those employing youth on Neighborhood Youth Corps projects, with government funding of their salaries) were either governmental or voluntary nonprofit agencies, with some restrictions being placed on sectarian agencies. During 1967, over 1,000 projects were supported for over 300,000 young workers at a cost to the Federal government of $235 million. A high proportion of these projects involved work for park and recreation departments, school recreation programs, hospitals, welfare centers, and settlement houses, often with direct responsibility for assisting in recreation leadership.

Community Action Programs. A major component of the war on poverty was the Community Action Program. This consisted of a considerable number of separate projects carried on in local communities, sponsored by a variety of governmental, voluntary, or "indigenous" groups —referring to newly developed bodies of poor people themselves—organized on a neighborhood or community basis.

The Economic Opportunity Act of 1964 was intended to combat poverty in the United States by strengthening, expanding, and innovating services in the fields of "education and training, provision of jobs, youth opportunities, family units, better living conditions, and better housing." It was considered that recreation services and facilities contributed to these goals, and so the staff manual of the Office of Economic Opportunity indicated that applications based on projects to provide recreation services in disadvantaged communities would be considered. As an example of actual Community Action Programs during the first summer, 1965, the grant to New York City provided $2.7 million to support programs sponsored by thirty-three different public, voluntary, and neighborhood organizations.

In this, as in hundreds of other Community Action Programs around the nation, the major service provided was recreation. The following statement of the role of recreation within the "poverty program" was developed:

Recreation and leisure-time activities are no longer regarded as luxury items in a person's budget or his life. They are recognized as essential to individual and community well-being, to be planned for and made available to everyone irrespective of their ability to pay. That recreation needs are far greater for those families living under crowded conditions in substandard housing and with scant financial resources is generally accepted. The increasing provision of public recreation service and facilities on all levels of government illustrates this recognition. It is therefore natural—indeed, essential—that recreation planning should have a role in the Anti-Poverty programs which the City of New York is providing for its disadvantaged. . . .

1. Recreation activities provide concrete services for all ages in a nonthreatening, non-stigmatized "threshold" experience which can involve almost everyone as a participant or spectator. Through this satisfying entry experience, the way can be paved for the acceptance of other aspects of the Poverty Program which dig more deeply towards the roots of the problem, such as counselling, skill training, education, and job-finding.

2. It is possible to offer recreation-type responsibilities to existing neighborhood instrumentalities (both formal organizations and informal associa-

tions) whereas it is more difficult to involve neighbors in providing counselling, case finding, job training and job finding roles. These latter functions require specialized skills and longer training.

3. Recreation in family groups is a welding experience. Doing things together which are enjoyable places a different aspect on all intrafamilial relations. Opportunities can also be provided for temporarily separating children from parents, providing much-needed relief and growth for all concerned.

4. A recreation program can provide a training ground for neighborhood youth and adults in assumption of responsibility and in the leisure-time and human relations fields specifically—two of the most promising future areas for service.

5. Recreation planning offers an opportunity for neighborhoods to feel a part of the War on Poverty since they can easily be involved around these problems and programs.

6. A good recreation program has been proven to be a positive social control mechanism. Major social organizations, including law enforcement agencies, have traditionally sponsored recreation activities as a safety valve mechanism, channelling energies in a positive direction.[2]

In the years that followed, recreation services continued to be a major part of Federal summer grants to communities for two reasons: (1) the communities themselves *wanted* improved recreation services and were able to organize themselves to provide such services, with Federal funding, and (2) with growing racial friction in the large cities and frequent summer outbursts, particularly by youth, recreation was increasingly viewed as a useful safety valve for ghetto neighborhoods.

During 1967, over 1,300 C.A.P. grants were awarded to the cities, totaling $222 million. Chiefly summertime grants, these were intended to

bring jobs, skills, and employment opportunities to . . . more young Americans . . . provide recreation opportunities . . . keep their schools, libraries, and playgrounds open, build swimming pools, provide special remedial education courses for children, light their basketball courts and baseball diamonds in the evening.[3]

As a further example of Federal policy in this area, the director of the Community Action Programs clarified OEC guidelines and criteria for funding, in May, 1967:

Summer youth programs are intended to provide jobs, additional steps in preparation for work, educational upgrading, recreation, cultural enrichment, improved physical well-being, leadership training, and constructive community impact. Ideally, any summer program should offer each participant active experiences in a number of areas. It is anticipated that the impact of summer pro-

[2] "Summer in New York—1965," *Report of Community Council of Greater New York to Office of Economic Opportunity*, October, 1965, pp. 1-2.
[3] New York *Times*, May 21, 1967, p. 41.

grams on the participants will be to increase their self-respect, self-direction, practical skills, community awareness and interests, as well as their capacity to work and play with others.[4]

As the Nixon Administration entered office in 1969, it appeared that the scope of the Job Corps and other antipoverty operations would be sharply reduced and that opportunities for employment in inner cities would be made to supersede all other programs.

Recreation and the Armed Forces

Another major function of the Federal government with respect to recreation has been its role in providing facilities and programs for the armed forces, both in the continental United States and abroad. For the past several decades, it has been the official policy of the Department of Defense to provide a well-rounded "morale, welfare, and recreational program" for the physical, social, and mental well-being of its personnel. The rationale justifying this area of service is that recreation services are as necessary for young men in the armed forces as for civilians—and often more so. Taken away from their home communities and families and friends, exposed to the strain and tension of battle or alternative periods of training or comparative boredom, they must be provided with interesting and constructive leisure outlets within each branch of the armed forces.

The provision of recreation for the military is not a modern concept. Even the most ancient military campaigns were marked by athletic contests, games, and other amusements provided to improve morale and counter disciplinary problems among the troops. In the armed forces of the United States, it became apparent during World War I that many types of service were needed that had formerly not been provided as part of the normal military operation. Special Services Divisions were established to provide social and recreational programs to help sustain favorable morale, curb homesickness and boredom, minimize fatigue, and reduce AWOL (absent without leave) and VD (venereal disease) rates. At the time of World War II, these special service programs were widely expanded, receiving considerable assistance from such civilian-supported agencies as the United Service Organization and the American Red Cross.

The United Service Organization (consisting of six organizations, the Jewish Welfare Board, the Salvation Army, the National Catholic Community Service, the National Travelers Aid Association, the Young Men's Christian Association, and the Young Women's Christian Association) provided recreational, social, and spiritual opportunities for men of the armed forces when on leave from their bases, or off duty. Within the conti-

[4] Theodore M. Berry, *Memorandum by Director of Community Action Programs to Selected Community Agencies*, May 8, 1967, p. 2.

nental United States, the U.S.O. has established many centers and clubs in cities where members of the armed forces gather, making considerable use of mobile units for reaching scattered locations. The U.S.O. Camp Shows, Inc., has through the years brought professional theatrical performers to entertain troops overseas and in Veterans Administration hospitals. During World War II, the American National Red Cross provided recreation facilities and services in leave areas overseas; it operated about 750 clubs and 250 mobile units employing over 5,500 workers in all theaters. Today its primary function is to provide ongoing recreation services in military hospitals.

Each branch of the service has its own pattern of recreation sponsorship and administration. The most diversified and strongly supported programs are within the Army and the Air Force.

Recreation in the Department of the Army. Within the Army, a division within the Adjutant General's office has the function of "morale support"; its purpose is officially described as "provide for the wholesome utilization of off-duty hours, and eventually return these young men and women to their homes better equipped to accept their full share of responsibility as useful, well-adjusted, constructive and patriotic citizens."[5] A substantial number of military personnel, both officers and enlisted men, are assigned to Special Services for recreation work; in addition, many civilians, hired according to Civil Service regulations, hold posts such as base recreation directors, librarians, service-club directors, and specialists in various recreation activities. In 1969, the total number of such full-time personnel was 13,123; part-time workers numbered 219,048.

The Department of the Army recreation program has five major branches of activity: sports, entertainment, crafts, service clubs, and libraries. It relies heavily on the use of Service-Club/Community Centers; such facilities offer a wide variety of activities attracting all age levels and special-interest groups.

Military recreation has become increasingly professionalized, and its practitioners are regarded as integral parts of the total recreation movement. Today, the Department of the Army operates a far-flung network of facilities throughout the world, including:

Service-club/community centers	282
Theaters and entertainment workshops	385
Showmobiles	30
Crafts facilities	788
Swimming pools	269
Gymnasiums	327

Recreation in the Department of the Air Force. This too is a highly developed operation. It operates under a Division of Special Services which

---

[5] *Policy Statement on Recreation* (Washington, D.C.: Office of the Adjutant General, Department of the Army, April 24, 1969).

includes (1) sports of all types (self-directed, competitive, instructional, and spectator events), (2) motion pictures, (3) service clubs and entertainment, (4) crafts and hobbies, (5) youth activities, (6) special interest groups (flying, automotive, motorcycle, power-boat, hiking, skydiving, and rod-and-gun clubs), (7) rest centers and recreation areas, (8) open messes (described as "facilities, equipment and services for recreation and morale," and (9) libraries.

The Air Force does not make a sharp distinction between community and military recreation but sees their purposes and concepts to be virtually identical:

The Special Services program fulfills the recreation needs and interests of Air Force personnel and their families by providing maximum opportunities for them to participate in leisure-time activities that help to stimulate, develop, and maintain their mental, physical and social well-being. Recreation is a fundamental part of the American way of life; and Air Force military personnel and their families need and deserve self-rewarding, creative recreation programs and opportunities equal in variety and quality to the best offered in the most progressive civilian communities. Proper recreation activities improve the individual's mental state, character growth, and job performance. Moreover, military personnel and their families who participate in recreation activities are more likely to have favorable attitudes toward an Air Force career.[6]

The trend over the past two decades in both the Army and the Air Force to make full use of military personnel with a primary concern for recreation, along with well-qualified civilian administrators and leaders, is less evident within the Navy and the Marine Corps.

Recreation in the Department of the Navy. This function is carried out by the Recreation and Physical Fitness Branch of the Bureau of Naval Personnel in the Department of the Navy. There is no standard structure or recommended organization of Special Services throughout the Navy and funds are derived largely from Navy Exchange sales. Commanding officers are charged with the responsibility of providing adequate recreation programs for their personnel; these programs are conducted and administered under the direction of the Special Services Officer and his staff. Most naval installations ashore have gymnasiums, golf courses, swimming pools, hobby shops, athletic fields, tennis courts, and movie theaters. Many in larger ports involve extensive program facilities and services. For example, the enlisted men's club at Yokosuka, Japan, offers a tremendous range of activities in a huge, colorful installation; it takes in almost $2 million a year in fees (although many of its programs and services are free) and has served as many as 25,000 persons a day.

Because of a less professional philosophy of recreation service and the fluctuation of personnel who are assigned to afloat units, the Navy's pro-

[6] "Air Force Special Programs," *Air Force Regulation No. 215-1* (Washington, D.C.: Department of the Air Force, July, 1966), p. 1.

gram of Special Services is less developed than that of the Army or Air Force. Recreation on shipboard is difficult to standardize because of limited space. The Fleet Motion Picture Service provides free movies to ships at sea at a cost of about $5 million per year. Most larger ships also have spaces available for physical fitness programs, hobby shops, cards and table games, and similar activities. In general, however, the Navy's operation in this field is considerably less well developed than that of the Army or Air Force.

Recreation in the Marine Corps. The Marine Corps assigns recreation as a responsibility to its Personnel Department and places strong emphasis on physical fitness within this program. Its strongest programs tend to be found in war zones, provided as a rest-and-recuperation service for fighting personnel. For example, in the Vietnam zone, the U.S. government has spent several million dollars in the northernmost military zone for marine recreation facilities:

Near Da Nang where the headquarters of the fifty-thousand man Third Marine Amphibious Force directs the fighting of two marine divisions and . . . a reinforced wing of jets and helicopters, plans are on the drawing board to build a massive recreation complex which will include an Olympic Swimming pool, a miniature golf course, a twenty-lane bowling alley, amphitheater, archery range, tennis courts, and a thousand-seat indoor theater.

At China Beach, the marines' community beach on the South China Sea, U.S. Navy Seabees are erecting a beer garden and seashore cafe . . . nearby, Vietnamese workers are hewing out an outdoor movie theater in a patch of shady pine trees not far from the rolling blue surf . . . when the China Beach center is completed, it will be able to handle ten thousand people daily.[7]

Marine recreation in Vietnam is also assisted by other services. The American Red Cross provides field centers, books, games, and hostesses for social programs in the field, and the Army and Navy motion picture services circulate over 200 films or television programs through the two divisions and air wing each week. As with the other branches of the armed forces in Vietnam, marines are given a five-day rest and recreation trip to any of nine Oriental cities (see page 405) once a year; the cost of travel is free, and men are encouraged to detach themselves from the military while on leave. The U.S.O. also offers armed forces personnel in Vietnam a number of well-equipped centers, with libraries, lounges, snack bars, taprooms, and game-rooms.

Other Aspects of Armed Forces Recreation

On a number of major bases overseas, where many family units live in self-contained communities, it is necessary for armed forces recreation

---

[7] Donald V. Joyce, "Recreation with the Marines in Viet Nam," *Parks and Recreation*, October, 1966, p. 842.

programs to provide youth services. Typically, on Okinawa, where there are thousands of children of military personnel in residence, there is an extensive program of services for young people between the ages of seven and nineteen, including sports, Teen Clubs, community relations programs involving Okinawan youth, evening social programs, continuous programs in judo, ballet, bowling, and driver training, drum-and-drill teams, and an extensive Youth Employment program which hires young people as clerks, assistant instructors, maintenance groundskeepers, bus and beach tour assistants, and concession operators. The Teen Club program operates evening programs, such as pool, bingo, bowling, and music sessions, weekend beach parties, boating, dancing, and sports leagues, and over twenty-five special activities ranging from arts and crafts, to dog-obedience training, Japanese doll making, ballet, photography, and scuba diving. Young people on such bases are probably more fully served with social and recreational opportunities than their counterparts in typical communities within the United States itself.

A final important aspect of military recreation consists of programs provided within armed-forces and veterans' hospitals. Within a network of Veterans' Administration hospitals throughout the country, recreation services are provided (1) to improve and maintain patient morale, (2) to act as a specified tool within the total rehabilitation process, and (3) to facilitate the patient's adjustment to the hospital and to aid in his return to community life.[8] It is carried on by the Physical Medicine and Rehabilitation Service of the Department of Medicine and Surgery of the Veterans' Administration in approximately 170 hospitals serving about half a million patients each year. Trained personnel in this field are classified by the Veterans' Administration as recreation therapists, comparable to corrective, educational, manual arts, and music therapists. Of these various types, the largest single group of specialists (635) was assigned to recreational therapy in Veterans' Administration hospitals in 1967.

Overview of Federal Recreation Programs

The preceding section has described a number of ways in which various Federal agencies have provided recreation facilities or direct services. Clearly, this aspect of Federal functioning is growing steadily; however, there are three broad areas of concern:

1. The strongest Federal emphasis has been directed to the development of outdoor recreation resources and facilities. Clearly, there needs to be a much greater effort to support and improve people-oriented services—particularly in the great metropolitan areas where the bulk of our population lives. Although it does not seem likely that the Federal government

[8] C. C. Bream, Jr., "Rehabilitative Recreation in Veterans' Administration Hospitals," *Recreation*, May, 1964, pp. 224-25.

will assume direct operating responsibility for local programs, it could, through training, research, subsidies, or matching grants, help to upgrade the level of program administration and leadership in many areas where facilities have been provided but where there is a dearth of competent personnel.

2. Although the Bureau of Outdoor Recreation has been assigned the task of coordinating outdoor recreation, it lacks sufficient authority to bring about joint planning and coordination among all government agencies in this field—much less those concerned with other aspects of recreation. A Federal agency, preferably on the cabinet level, with jurisdiction over all recreation programs and governmental operations (including those related to health, education, and welfare, housing and urban development, antipoverty programs, and the armed forces) would provide greatly needed national leadership and direction in this field.

3. Several agencies, particularly in the Department of Health, Education and Welfare, have taken major steps to recognize and promote recreation as a field of professional service. There is, however, a strong need for the Federal government to recognize the growing importance of leisure as an area of national concern. For decades, it has been urged that the Federal government take the leadership in defining recreation and leisure policy and in supporting more fully professional development in this field. Such a program might well become the function of a single unified Federal recreation department.

FUNCTIONS OF THE STATES IN RECREATION

The role of state governments within the broad field of recreation and parks has generally rested upon the section of the Tenth Amendment to the Constitution, which states, "The powers not delegated to the United States by the Constitution, nor prohibited by it to the States, are reserved to the States respectively, or to the people." This amendment, commonly referred to as the "states' rights amendment," is regarded as the source of state powers in such areas as public education, welfare, and health services. Under this mandate, each state has seen fit to provide recreation facilities and services to meet the needs of its citizens, within the following eight functions:

1. *Enabling Legislation.* The enactment of laws which authorize local authorities, such as county or municipal governments, or school districts, to operate recreation and park facilities and programs.

2. *Outdoor Recreation Resources and Programs.* The development of a network of state parks and other physical resources, to meet the need for outdoor recreation of the state's population or of visiting vacationers.

3. *Promotion of Conservation and Open Space.* State governments

today have assumed the responsibility for promoting conservation programs and educational efforts and stimulating and supporting open-space and beautification efforts by counties and municipalities within their borders. States serve as intermediaries between Federal and local governments, for guiding planning efforts and channeling Federal grants-in-aid.

4. *Assistance to Local Governments.* State governments assist municipalities and other local governments in the conduct of park and recreation programs by giving technical guidance or consultation, providing subsidies for special programs for youth and aging persons or sharing the cost of development. Today, they may actually move into urban areas to develop resources and provide bussing or other needed services.

5. *Recreation Sponsorship in Other Settings.* All states operate institutions serving special populations, such as aging persons, the mentally ill or retarded, and inmates of penal or corrective centers. Within many of these, state governments operate varied recreation programs.

6. *Promotion of Professional Advancement.* State governments in the majority of states today provide higher education in recreation and park administration through state colleges or universities. They also are involved in the recruitment, selection and training of recreation personnel, through Civil Service and other personnel codes or systems, and through conferences, consultation and research services, and through the publication of manuals and training guides.

7. *Development and Enforcement of Standards.* Both with respect to personnel, as indicated earlier, and in such areas as health and safety or facilities development, states may pass restrictive legislation or may develop standards to be followed by public or voluntary agencies.

8. *Promotion of Recreation as an Economic Asset.* State governments today promote all aspects of leisure activity that contribute to the economic development of their cities and countryside, particularly through the promotion of tourism and outdoor recreation opportunities.

Today, most states have at least one agency whose primary function is recreation, and at least sixteen states have recreation councils or interagency committees which serve to coordinate the recreation functions of various departments. In a number of states, such as Vermont, California, and North Carolina, recreation commissions were established during the 1930's or 1940's to carry on this task. The most common pattern, however, is to have the primary task of outdoor recreation development (including land acquisition and resource management) in the hands of a Department of Parks, Conservation and Recreation, or similar agency, while other functions related to recreation are carried on by departments concerned with a specific area of service, such as youth, education, or aging. As many as 233 different state agencies were reported as having made major expenditures related to parks and recreation, in the *1966 Recreation and Park Yearbook.*

The following section describes the recreation function of state governments in greater detail.

1. *Enabling Legislation.* The power to establish public recreation and parks programs is generally granted to municipal governments by constitutional, statutory, or charter provisions granted by the state legislature. Although local governing bodies have general powers in this area, through the principle of "police powers" or the "general welfare" clause in the Federal Constitution, specific legal powers are needed for them to acquire, develop, and maintain recreation facilities, purchase supplies and equipment, and employ personnel. These powers may be granted through constitutional provisions—that is, permanent state statutes approved by the public and alterable only by them—or, more commonly, by state statutes (laws passed by state legislatures which may be repealed or superseded by subsequent legislation). Most recreation enabling acts are in the latter form.

The first state recreation enabling act was passed by New Jersey in 1915. Other states rapidly followed suit. By 1947, thirty-four states had such laws, and by 1965, at least forty-one states had detailed recreation enabling laws, with others having less well developed permissive legislation. In almost all states today, county, municipal, and school authorities are authorized to operate recreation facilities and provide programs. Enabling legislation may range from rather simple statements which briefly authorize the performance of the recreation function to fully detailed statements of the power, structure, and procedures which apply to local managing authorities in this field, including such elements as the method of acquiring and developing properties, financing recreation and park programs, and establishing public authorities, boards, and commissions.

2. *Outdoor Recreation Resources and Programs.* Each state government today operates a network of parks and other outdoor recreation resources. Such areas provide for varied pursuits, including camping, hiking, picnicking, water sports, and many others. Particularly over the last fifteen years, such programs have expanded dramatically (Table 2-1).

TABLE 2-1   *Growth of State Park and Recreation Programs*

	1955	1960	1967
Total attendance in recreation and parks	232 million	263 million	391 million
Total expenditure (capital and operating budgets)	$87 million	$152 million	$295 million

SOURCE: *Recreation and Park Yearbook, 1966* (Washington, D.C.: National Recreation Association, 1967), pp. 24–40; see also: *Recreation and Park Yearbook, 1961,* pp. 11–15, and *1967 State Park Statistics* (Washington, D.C.: National Conference on State Parks, June, 1968).

Among the leading states in a recent year, in terms of the total number of outdoor recreation visitor-days were: New York, 42 million; California, 35 million; Ohio, 26 million; and Illinois, 20 million. The most popular activities engaged in by those visiting state parks are picnicking, small-game hunting, driving and sightseeing, and fishing.

States have been spending increasing funds on land acquisition and related functions. For example, between 1960 and 1966, the voters of eleven states authorized $656.9 million in bond issues for outdoor recreation, frequently linked with conservation or antipollution projects. Such major programs include the following recent actions: Alabama voters approved a $43-million bond issue in 1967, for state parkland acquisition and development. California voters approved a $150-million bond issue in 1964, for conservation and outdoor recreation purposes. Michigan voters in 1968 approved a $435-million bond program for clean water and recreation. One hundred million dollars of this was designated specifically for outdoor recreation; the remaining $335 million to combat water pollution will create improved water recreation opportunities. New York voters approved a $200-million bond issue in 1966 for park and recreation development having already voted for $100 million a few years earlier. The largest single appropriation thus far was in Pennsylvania, where the state legislature has approved a $500-million Land and Water Conservation and Reclamation Fund Bill for the large-scale development of state and local parks and recreation areas, pollution control, and other conservation programs.

3. *Promote Conservation and Open Space.* The function of providing outdoor recreation resources, as indicated, is closely linked to the promotion of conservation and open-space programs. Typically, New Jersey has introduced a major new program relating conservation and recreation functions, by establishing the "Skylands of New Jersey," an interregional public land preserve in the north-central portion of the state. Its plan is to promote a new concept of environmental conservation, by establishing a huge green belt to enhance the natural environment and protect natural resources from urban sprawl. The first major step in the "Skylands" program was achieved

through New Jersey's pioneering Green Acres program in the establishment of a public preserve in the heart of the Skylands area of north-central New Jersey . . . encompassing a vast 100,000 acres—150 square miles—of New Jersey's prime public forests and woodlands . . . including fresh water lakes, unobstructed miles of mountain trails and vistas, protected wilderness and natural areas . . . irreplaceable national historic markers.[9]

The New Jersey "Skyland" program involves a variety of public, quasi-public, and private recreation lands and watershed or reservoir areas.

[9] Robert A. Roe, "Skylands of New Jersey," *Parks and Recreation*, September, 1967, pp. 17, 61.

Under proper land management and with needed safeguards, recreation pursuits such as hunting, fishing, sailing, camping, and hiking will be made possible without harmfully affecting the water supply. This multi-use concept of water supply facilities has already been implemented at some state-owned reservoirs in New Jersey and is seen as making an important contribution to the economic health of the region.

Beyond the immediate task of acquiring open spaces or preventing pollution, states have other conservation functions. They manage wildlife resources, establish policies or laws governing hunting and fishing, plant trees and bird cover, and carry on intensive conservation education programs with children and youth, hunters, fishermen, and boating enthusiasts. Many state fish and game departments administer wildlife areas, such as reserves, sanctuaries, game farms, and fish hatcheries, and provide technical assistance to local conservation organizations or government agencies, often bringing several communities together for joint action.

4. *Assist Local Government.* In a variety of ways, state park, recreation, or conservation agencies provide assistance to local authorities. Apart from leadership training, they often provide consultants and experts, do research studies, call special conferences, and promote the development of effective recreation agencies on the local level. Recently, because of the increasing concern about urban problems and the requirement of the Bureau of Outdoor Recreation that all statewide plans include projections of the needs of cities, states have begun to assist cities more directly. Heretofore, most state park and recreation facilities have been in their most wooded or mountainous regions—usually at a considerable distance from metropolitan areas and therefore inaccessible to most city dwellers, particularly poor and minority-group members. A number of states have, however, begun to acquire and develop park land close to or actually within the boundaries of their most crowded cities, in order to provide needed services to urban populations.

One example is the state of California, which has been expanding its total recreation and park acreage rapidly. Recognizing the special problems of metropolitan Los Angeles, the state park and recreation department recently established Malibu Lagoon State Beach as an intensive-use area close to metropolitan Los Angeles. It also recently acquired 310 acres for a new park in the Santa Monica Mountains, within the City of Los Angeles, and doubled the size of Mount Tamalpais State Park with the purchase of 2,150 acres in the San Francisco Bay region.

The most dramatic example, however, has been in New York State, where the legislature created a new State Park Commission in 1967, for the City of New York. The new Commission has been given the power to recommend new park sites and acquire property within the city, although it will not have jurisdiction over existing city parks. At the inception of the plan, Governor Rockefeller stated:

Now for the first time the state will be able to develop and operate parks in New York City. In the past the state's efforts have been outside the city, up-state, so that many New Yorkers who do not own automobiles have found it difficult to take advantage of state park facilities. The creation of the new state park district means that the state can now develop parks in our most populous urban center.[10]

The new State Park Commission intends to develop a number of major parks within the city, including such facilities as pools and beaches, ice-skating rinks, and marinas, all readily accessible to major public transit systems. Its first important project will be a park being planned on the east shore of the Harlem River, in the borough of the Bronx. Here the plan is to integrate a new park and recreation complex (including sports, nature, a large stadium, cultural activities, an outdoor center, and a small stadium) with a large new housing project—all to be developed on a run-down waterfront site, where rundown and abandoned shipping piers and factories will be razed.

5. *Recreation Sponsorship in Other Settings.* Another important recreation function of state governments is to provide direct program serv-ices within institutions or agencies which it sponsors, such as mental hos-pitals, homes or schools for mental retardates, and penal or correctional institutions. Recreation is widely accepted as an area of service which con-tributes to the rehabilitation of patients and which helps to maintain favorable institutional morale by reducing friction and boredom and sub-stituting constructive interests and attitudes for antisocial ones while help-ing to prepare individuals for return to society.

Limited statistics are available as to the scope of state recreation oper-ations through departments of mental health, aging, mental hygiene, social services, and welfare, although the *Supply/Demand Manpower Study* published by the National Recreation and Park Association in 1968 estimated that there were 3,320 full-time recreation personnel (or part-time equivalent) in state hospitals and 2,352 full-time personnel in state residential centers for the mentally retarded. It is apparent that this is a growing area of state involvement in recreation.

6. *Promote Professional Advancement.* While states promote effec-tive leadership and administrative practices in recreation and parks by developing standards related to personnel and providing conferences, work-shops, and research in recreation, their major function lies in the profes-sional preparation of recreation practitioners in state colleges and univer-sities. Many leading departments of health, physical education, and recreation have been found in state teachers' colleges, which assume a major responsibility for training individuals for socially oriented and public

[10] Nelson A. Rockefeller, quoted in New York *Times*, December 3, 1967, p. 71; see also Wilbur A. Wright, "State Parks Within a City," *Parks and Recreation*, March, 1968, pp. 31-32.

service fields—as compared with private liberal arts colleges, which tend to reject the goal of vocational education for undergraduates. In addition, a number of state agricultural colleges have developed park and recreation curriculums concerned with park management, resource planning, and conservation. Of 183 colleges and universities reported to have recreation and park curriculums in 1967, a substantial majority are state-sponsored.

7. *Develop and Enforce Standards.* In addition to preparing leaders to enter the field, states also have the function of screening personnel by establishing standards, regulations, and other criteria for personnel. Through Civil Service Commissions, employment procedures are established, and a number of states have developed certification and personnel registration programs in recreation and parks.

Many states also promote professional development in this field by developing standards related to health practices in camping and other recreational settings, enforcing safety codes, promoting facilities standards, insuring that the physically handicapped may use recreation resources, regulating or prohibiting certain types of commercial amusements, and inspecting camps, swimming pools, resorts, and similar operations of voluntary or private agencies.

8. *Promote Recreation as Economic Asset.* A final important function of state governments is to promote all aspects of leisure involvement that support economic development. In a number of states, tourism and vacation spending represent a leading form of industry. Those states which, by virtue of climate, are suited to retirement and year-round recreation or vacation travel (such as Florida, Arizona, or California) promote all sorts of events, facilities, and colorful regional recreational opportunities that will draw tourists. Other states with scenic views, forests, lakes, ocean front, or winter sports areas describe themselves as "vacation lands" and actively promote such tourist attractions.

Tourism represents a multifaceted economic asset. When tourists visit a particular site or event, they spend substantial sums while traveling, for food, purchase, or leisure items, for resort expenses, and in other ways. Economically, this money is turned over several times on various levels of the local economy and provides substantial employment. As an example, when a water recreation area is developed, all sorts of local businesses may profit from the flow of vacationists, such as gas stations, motels and hotels, marinas, sports equipment suppliers, boating manufacturers, salesmen, and camp equipment suppliers. When a ski region is developed in New England, it provides a host of employment opportunities through several months of the winter to accompany summer vacation employment. Most states sponsor and encourage festivals, tournaments, displays, and other programs to attract tourists. Such events then provide the basis for more extended vacations or even for considerable spending within a short period. When about 70,000 sports fans traveled to Miami to attend the 1969

Super-Bowl football championship game, their total spending was estimated at $50 million.

The trend among states appears to be to move ahead vigorously in all of the areas described here, with the extension and protection of open space and the provision of outdoor recreation as the key element. Recognizing the inadequate provision for recreational opportunity and the overlapping and competitive nature of many suburban agencies in large metropolitan areas, it would appear that states should play an increasing role in promoting larger park and recreation districts, coordinating the efforts of smaller communities and carrying on more effective planning.

It is becoming increasingly clear that we can no longer afford to think in terms of strictly separate Federal, state, county, or local operations with respect to recreation resource development or land and water conservation. Just as water flows throughout a state (and therefore no single municipality can clean up a polluted stream), in the broad field of urban planning, recreation resource development, and conservation, problems *must* be approached on a regional basis.

An example of such regional planning has been the development of the Delaware River Basin. This is a major watershed and outdoor recreation resource development program, which has involved the states of New York, New Jersey, and Pennsylvania in a joint effort since the 1950's. The use of the headwaters of the Delaware River has been a cause of concern for city administrators in all three states since the 1920's. In 1931, New York City was permitted to divert water from the Delaware River, and by the mid-1950's the river was supplying all or an important part of the water needs of a service area with a population of 23 million people. But who had priority on it, and how could it best be developed to meet a multiplicity of needs? Dressler writes:

Two of the major problems of "megalopolis" are its need for vast quantities of free water and its equally great need for water sites that can be used for recreation purposes; two of its major characteristics are its continuing reach into the lightly populated, water-rich hinterlands for the needed supplies of water and the periodic migration of its population to the same areas for water-based recreation activities.[11]

In 1955, Congress directed the Army Corps of Engineers to do a comprehensive survey of the water problems and needs of the Delaware River Basin and develop a plan to solve these needs with the assistance of the National Park Service. Projections were that outdoor recreation demand in the area served by the Delaware River would increase by more than six and a half times over the next several decades, and it was recommended that a multipurpose system of fifty-eight dams and reservoirs

[11] Frank W. Dressler, "Outdoor Recreation and the Delaware River Basin," *Recreation*, June, 1962, pp. 299-301.

should be developed to meet water-use needs and provide recreation opportunities for about 38 million visitors annually. Of these, the 37-mile-long Tocks Island Reservoir and Dam was to become the first National Recreation Area in the United States. Situated within 100 miles of 30 million residents, its hundred miles of shoreline provide the potential for situating ten major recreation areas that by the early 1970's are expected to offer an estimated 7 million visitors a year a choice of camping, fishing, hunting, swimming, and hiking. This project represents a good example of joint planning between the Federal government and the states to solve joint watershed and recreation problems.

This chapter has described the role of the Federal and state governments with respect to recreation and parks in the United States. The following chapter describes recreation services on a local level, sponsored by county, municipal, and school agencies.

3

The Role of County
and Local Governments

The major responsibility for providing recreation services and facilities to the mass of the population belongs to local government in the United States on two levels of operation: (1) the county, township, or park-district level and (2) the local political subdivision, consisting of the city, town, village, or school district.

COUNTY PROGRAMS OF RECREATION AND PARKS

In 1963, the National Association of Counties presented a series of guides to assist county governments in promoting more effective recreation and park facilities and programs. Based in part on the recommendations made by the Outdoor Recreation Resources Review Commission in the previous year, the guide stated:

The special role of the county is to acquire, develop, and maintain parks and to administer public recreation programs that will serve the needs of communities broader than the local neighborhood or municipality, but less than state-wide or national in scope. In addition, the county should plan and coordinate local neighborhood and community facilities with the cooperation of the cities, townships, and other intra-county units, and should itself cooperate in state and federal planning and coordinative activities. Where there is no existing unit of local government except the county to provide needed local neighborhood or municipal facilities and programs, the county should provide such facilities and programs, utilizing county service districts, local assessments, and other methods by which those benefited will pay the cost.[1]

[1] "Policy for County Parks and Recreation," *Recreation*, June, 1964, pp. 271-72.

The county park and recreation department today represents an intermediate stage between the state and local governments. County governments today are expected to provide large-scale or regional facilities and resources to meet outdoor recreation needs which cannot be readily met by other units of local government. With a larger population and covering wider geographical areas, county governments are more capable of providing such facilities.

County governments often provide services meeting specialized needs (such as programs for aging or disabled persons or youth services) which cannot be adequately met by municipalities. They may also develop extensive programs in the fine and performing arts to serve all county residents. Counties today provide a variety of supplemental services which assist local governments, such as (1) consultation services, training workshops, planning specialists, (2) major program events, such as large-scale tournaments, drama festivals, or art exhibitions, which motivate local groups and participants, and (3) direction to antipoverty organizations, helping them make contact with appropriate state or Federal agencies. Counties may also provide direct program services in some areas where the local town or village has not provided leadership.

Current Status of County Programs

County governments in the United States have been growing steadily in importance and scope since World War II. During the early part of the century, such general functions as the administration of justice, assessment and collection of property taxes, recording of legal papers, maintenance of county roads, charitable and correctional institutions, and county sheriff's offices, tended to be the major areas of county responsibility. In many respects the county was regarded as losing its powers and influence as a branch of government.

Since World War II, however, the county system of government has been revitalized. First, it has become a base for numerous Federal grants-in-aid programs in such areas as agriculture, health, and welfare and has assumed responsibility for coordination of local programs, funneling of applications, and financial aid. The rapid expansion of suburban communities surrounding the major cities of the country has given many county governments new influence and power. Finally, an expanded and revitalized professional organization, the National Association of Counties, has done much to promote this level of governmental operation. As a consequence, since World War II, county airports, hospitals and health service, utility systems, highways systems and law enforcement agencies, and park and recreation operations have all expanded significantly.

Today, of the 3,080 counties in the nation, ranging widely in size and population, 358 operate park and recreation systems, with a total of

4,149 separate park areas including 691,042 acres. The recent rate of growth in county departments may be seen in Table 3-1.

TABLE 3-1   *County Recreation and Park Operations*

	1960	1966
Number of county park and recreation agencies	290	358
Number of park and recreation areas	2,610	4,149
Total number of employed professionals	7,990	11,912
Total acreage	430,707	691,042
Total expenditure	$95.5 million	$195.7 million

SOURCE: *Recreation and Park Yearbook, 1966* (Washington, D.C.: National Recreation and Park Association, 1967), p. 59, and *Recreation and Park Yearbook, 1961*, pp. 28–31.

The county's role in recreation and parks is growing at a faster rate than that of municipalities, particularly in terms of land acquisition. In part, this is because there is such a pressing need for large open spaces near urban centers. While local municipalities tend to lack adequate space for park expansion, counties, because of their larger geographical area and broader tax base, are able to finance major land acquisitions and the development of specialized facilities. The greatly increased interest in outdoor recreation following World War II and the increased mobility of the public have also stimulated county activity in providing day-use outdoor recreation sites at comparatively short distances from masses of the population.

Current Examples of County Expansion

The King County, Washington, Park and Recreation Department is an excellent example of how such departments have expanded to meet growing urban and suburban needs during the 1950's and 1960's. This extensive system, which includes the City of Seattle, was established in 1949. At that time, it included 20 parks on 236 acres. By 1968, it had expanded to 55 parks with a total of 2,365 acres with plans to expand to a total of 190 parks on 5,965 acres by 1974. Attendance climbed from 644,000 in 1949 to 3,200,000 in 1967. Like a number of major county and municipal recreation departments, King County has a cooperative arrangement with twelve large school districts, under which the schools install major sports areas and outdoor recreation facilities and the county maintains them. In addition to operating varied facilities, the King County Park and Recreation Department provides specialized programs, including extensive cultural activities, and services to specialized population groups.

Its plans for expansion, approved in 1968 by the voters, encompass a $118-million park-bond issue. Scheduled to be constructed are four large regional parks, each of several hundred acres, eleven major new urban parks, thirteen community parks totaling 320 acres, nine major new swimming pools to be constructed in county parks, and three new boat-launching areas. Substantial sums are to be expended on improvements to large existing parks and the development of new neighborhood and local parks with $10 million to be used for new special structures, including a large new county park and athletic center.

While this is an outstanding example, other county departments throughout the county have shown similar patterns of growth.

Nassau County, adjacent to New York City on Long Island, was a comparative late-comer in park development; it was only in 1945 that the first Nassau County park, Salisbury Park, was established. For a number of years, this huge facility, including three golf courses, many ballfields, and other types of recreation areas, was the only real county park. But, like other suburban areas, Nassau's population grew rapidly: in 1940, it was 406,748; in 1950 it was 672,765; and by 1960, over 1.3 million. The number of single-family homes in the county multiplied over five times during this period. In the early 1960's, progress was accelerated in the development of new park sites, boat-launching ramps, historical restorations, and natural history museums. A major new harbor area was developed, along with several ice skating rinks and other specialized facilities and programs. Within the five years prior to 1966, park holdings of the Nassau County park and recreation system were doubled, and funds set aside for park development during the six years following 1966 totaled $73 million.

Such vigorous programs of land acquisition as those described for King County and Nassau County, are essential to obtain and protect land while it is still available and before prices have skyrocketed to even higher levels. Land acquisition programs should be carried on as part of regional master-planning, with assistance from state and Federal funding programs. In a number of cases, counties have enacted laws requiring home developers to set aside community recreation areas. One such example is Anne Arundel County, Maryland, which since 1957 has required all developers to set aside park areas amounting to 5 percent of the land to be developed. In a number of cases, the developer, seeing the value of such improvements, has also taken on responsibility for fully developing park and recreation areas for use by those who purchase his homes. Some county governments are establishing permanently protected green belts to halt the tide of construction. Strengthened zoning policies and more flexible building codes to permit cluster zoning of homes with larger and more concentrated open spaces are also helpful.

The migration of middle-class whites out of our cities into suburban communities has resulted in the population of the central cities becoming increasingly black and Spanish-speaking. What should be a pattern of co-operation and joint planning between the city and its surrounding counties, both to meet immediate needs and to promote effective long-term planning, tends not to be the case. Indeed, many suburban counties have enacted regulations that prevent the residents of adjacent cities from using their facilities—even when such policies are not justified on a financial basis or because of overcrowding. This problem, plus the burgeoning number of municipalities and townships that overlap each other and cause either gaps or in some cases overlapping in service, poses a serious problem for the county form of government. In a number of cases, the solution has simply been for cities to expand, bringing immediately surrounding suburban communities into their incorporated structures. In others, the county, including the city *and* its outlying areas, provides certain major services, while the city proper provides others.

To fully understand this picture, we move now to an examination of the role of local government in providing recreation and park programs and services.

MUNICIPAL RECREATION AND PARK PROGRAMS

Municipal government is the term generally used to describe the local political unit of government, such as the village, town, or city, that has responsibility for providing the bulk of direct community service, such as street maintenance, police and fire protection, and education. In the area of recreation and parks, most people are dependent on municipal governments for day-by-day recreation opportunities (apart from those provided by commercial, private or voluntary agencies).

Butler suggests the following reasons for the marked growth of municipal recreation and park programs: (1) municipal government offers many individuals their primary or only opportunity for wholesome recreational involvement, particularly among poorer people in large cities; (2) only through government can adequate lands be acquired for playgrounds, parks, and other outdoor recreation areas; (3) municipal recreation is "democratic and inclusive"; it serves all ages, races, and creeds and places the burden of support upon the entire community; (4) municipal recreation is comparatively inexpensive, when compared with private expenditure for recreation; yet, by spreading the cost of development over many families, it can provide major facilities needed; (5) the local government gives permanency to recreation, assuring both continuity and the ability to respond to the changing needs of the population; (6) the job is too large for a private agency, whereas the city, with its powers of land acquisition and taxation, can provide inexpensive citywide nonprofit services to meet total community needs; (7) recreation plays an important role in the local economy, helping to stabilize property values and reduce social pathology, thus making communities more attractive for industries seeking new location and families seeking new homes; and (8) the people demand it and are willing to be taxed for it, as evidenced by steady growth of programs, passage of referendums and bond issues, and overall support of recreation.[2]

The overall growth of local recreation and park programs is illustrated in Table 3-2, including both municipal and county agencies.

TABLE 3-2 *Growth of Local Recreation and Park Agencies*

	1946	1950	1960	1965
Total number of park and recreation agencies reported	1,743	2,277	2,968	3,142
Personnel:				
Total full- and part-time paid leadership	41,159	58,029	99,696	119,515
Full-time year-round	5,147	6,784	9,216	19,208
Volunteer	. . .	104,589	277,072	494,407
Total acreage in parks and recreation areas	. . .	644,000	1,015,461	1,496,378
Playgrounds under leadership	. . .	14,747	20,107	24,298
Buildings of all types	. . .	9,617	16,970	22,527
Total expenditures (in millions)	$51.7	$269	$567	$905

SOURCE: *Recreation and Park Yearbook, 1966* (Washington, D.C.: National Recreation and Park Association, 1967), pp. 41, 44–58, and *Recreation and Park Yearbook, 1961*, pp. 27–46; see also *Recreation Yearbook, 1946*, n.p.

Another yardstick of growth is the total amount of municipal and county capital expenditure for parks and recreation. During the period of 1956 to 1960, it totaled $566.5 million. For the comparable period of 1961 to 1965, it totaled $1.05 billion; and it seems clear that the totals for 1966 to 1970 will far surpass these earlier periods, although figures are not yet available. These statistics reflect the operations of only those municipal and county agencies which have a primary concern for recreation and parks. They do not include the involvement of many housing, welfare, or other social agencies, nor do they include substantial Federal expenditures on antipoverty programs in the cities, which have amounted to hundreds of millions of dollars assigned to recreation during the 1960's.

Functions of Municipal Recreation and Park Agencies

The responsibilities of municipal recreation and park departments fall under several headings:

1. *Direct Provision of Recreation Service.* They acquire, develop,

[2] George D. Butler, *Introduction to Community Recreation* (New York: McGraw-Hill, 1967), pp. 66-70.

and maintain facilities (land and water areas and structures) needed for recreational participation and provide skilled leadership to meet the needs of various age groups and individuals within the community.

2. *Coordination of Other Programs.* They provide in-service training and advisory services for other groups in the municipality involved in leisure programs and help them coordinate their services to avoid duplication and overlap.

3. *Cooperate with Other Governmental Agencies.* They work closely with other branches of government (housing, police, education, highways) and with Federal, state, and county authorities to develop innovative programs, long-range planning, and effective programs of land acquisition.

Obviously, the first area of responsibility is the most important one. Municipal agencies must (1) provide a total network of facilities, such as parks, playgrounds, swimming pools, sports areas, and indoor centers, to meet the needs of all citizens for recreation places in which to enjoy their leisure; (2) provide leadership and organized program services to serve all persons (children and youth particularly, but also adults and aging persons) with leisure opportunities; (3) recognize and meet the specialized needs of disadvantaged populations, such as physically or mentally disabled individuals, or dependent aging persons; and (4) generally promote recreation as an important area of public service, taking the leadership for promoting leisure needs, problems, and programs among civic-minded people in the community.

Obviously, the role of the municipal recreation and park agency in any given community will depend on such factors as its financial capability, the availability of other voluntary, private, or commercial opportunities, the public attitude toward government involvement in social programs, and other community traditions, which may be influenced by regional practices or political structures. It would be convenient if one could assume that governmental operation in this area were like an accordion—able to expand or contract readily. If there were strong voluntary, private, and commercial services that met leisure needs of all residents, then municipal public recreation and park services would tend to be minimal and would focus on the provision of major or specialized facilities. On the other hand, if opportunities offered by other agencies were inadequate, then the public department would expand rapidly to meet obvious needs. As a rule, however, those communities which have the poorest voluntary and private social agencies also tend to have minimal facilities and services.

THE ADMINISTRATIVE STRUCTURE OF PUBLIC RECREATION DEPARTMENTS

During the early years of development of public recreation services in American communities, several different types of administrative structures were found. Such factors as the nature of state enabling laws, the ability to obtain necessary funding, the availability of areas and facilities, freedom from political controls, and the development of a positive public image, were all factors considered by communities that chose one pattern or another. In general, the favored pattern through the period preceding the 1950's was to establish recreation as an independent department.

Gradually, following World War II, park administrators became increasingly concerned with recreation functions, and recreation departments moved steadily in the direction of providing outdoor play facilities, such as golf courses, tennis courts, sports fields, swimming pools, and skating rinks. By the late 1950's the two fields became involved on a large-scale merger: (1) many existing separate park and recreation agencies joined forces in single departments; (2) the majority of the new ones which came into being during this period were joint park and recreation departments; and (3) the national organization in this field merged into a single umbrella organization, the National Recreation and Park Association. This development is illustrated in Table 3-3.

TABLE 3-3   Types of Recreation and Park Agencies Reported in 1966

Combined park and recreation	1,304
Separate recreation	818
Separate park	428
School Department	142
Other public agencies (combined grouping)	425
Private*	25
Municipal agencies	2,784
County agencies	358
Total number of agencies	3,142

SOURCE: *Recreation and Park Yearbook, 1966* (Washington, D.C.: National Recreation and Park Association, 1967), p. 45.

* Since these are reported in a listing of local public agencies, the assumption is that they are voluntary agencies which receive public support and have quasi-official responsibility for meeting community recreation needs.

In many of the largest cities throughout the United States, it is common for more than one major public agency to have recreation and park functions. In Los Angeles, the Park and Recreation Department, and the Youth Services Section of the Board of Education, share major responsibilities. In Chicago, the City Park District and the Board of Education, through its Division of Recreation and Playgrounds and its Division of Social Centers, share these functions. In Philadelphia, the Department of

Recreation, the Fairmount Park Commission, and the Division of Health and Physical Education of the Board of Education all cooperate closely. Hjelte comments:

> No single agency can be expected to administer all of the public parks and recreation facilities in the metropolitan city. Inevitably there will be a park or recreation department of the municipal government, usually one with consolidated park and recreation functions. Such an agency will of necessity be limited by city charter or by legal interpretation to the operation of properties of which the city has title. Additionally, the school district or districts will permit school buildings and grounds to be used for recreational purposes with much, if not all, of this program directly under school administration and financed from school funds or conducted on permit by community-serving agencies.
>
> The provision of neighborhood playgrounds cannot be complete according to any reasonable standard in any large metropolitan city unless the school grounds complement the municipal park and recreation centers. Parks and recreation centers will always be fewer than schools within a city.[3]

When several such agencies exist side by side within large metropolitan areas, it is essential that they cooperate closely with each other in terms of planning and organization of services and programs. This should include (1) joint use of facilities, (2) exchange and joint training of personnel, (3) efforts to determine community needs and plan for total recreation development, (4) promotion and public relations efforts, and (5) joint projects and research.

In addition to agencies that have the provision of recreation facilities and services as a primary function, many large cities also have other departments that offer it as a secondary responsibility. They include such areas of service as:

Police Department.   In many larger cities, the police operate youth service bureaus or precinct councils which have direct programs of recreational activity such as recreation centers, play streets, and sports leagues for youth. They may also assign detached workers to contact and work with unaffiliated youth.

Welfare Department.   Such departments are generally concerned with the needs of disadvantaged and dependent children, families, and aging persons. They may operate day-care centers for children of working mothers, after-school recreation-and-study centers for children of school age, multiservice family centers, or programs for aging persons. In such settings, recreation represents an important program area.

Youth Board.   Youth Boards, Commissions, or other service agencies

[3] George Hjelte, quoted in John L. Hutchinson, ed., *Leisure and the Schools* (Washington, D.C.: Yearbook of the American Association for Health, Physical Education and Recreation, 1961), pp. 182-83.

tend to be generally concerned with reducing the school dropout rate, providing educational and vocational assistance, counseling "problem" youth, and working constructively with antisocial gangs and individuals. While they are often specifically concerned with such problems as delinquency and drug addiction, one of their common functions is to provide teen-age recreation and social programs.

Department of Hospitals. Many public hospitals provide therapeutic recreation services as part of the rehabilitation process, particularly in settings which deal with psychiatric patients, or through out-patient clinics, after-care centers, and "halfway houses."

Housing Departments. Particularly in larger cities, many public housing agencies have a direct concern with recreation services. This may consist chiefly of providing playgrounds or indoor centers; the range of service may also include tenants' clubs, libraries, craft shops, centers for aging persons, and youth programs. In many cases, these programs are operated by outside agencies that come in under special contracts to provide recreation. In others they are carried on by the housing authority itself.

Thus, we see that the total picture of municipal recreation is a complex one. In addition to public departments with functions in this field, there are many voluntary agencies, some of which have substantial public funding. In *most* American cities today, however, the primary responsibility for providing and coordinating a total recreation program within a framework of social purpose is assigned to one major agency, for which this is the primary function. What are the program services offered by such departments?

Program Services of Municipal Recreation Agencies

These tend to fall into several major categories of activity, grouped under the following headings: (1) games and sports, (2) outdoor activities, (3) water sports, (4) winter sports, (5) crafts, (6) fine arts, (7) performing arts, (8) special services, and (9) miscellaneous. To illustrate some of the most common activities, the *1966 Recreation and Park Yearbook* offers a detailed listing of varied activities, with the percentage of local public agencies which provide them. Among the most popular activities among youth and adults are the following: *games and sports*: archery, baseball, basketball, touch football, golf, horseshoes, softball, table tennis, tennis, track and field, and volleyball; *outdoor activities*: day and overnight camping, picnicking, and trips and tours; *water sports*: boating, fishing, and swimming; *winter sports*: coasting, ice-skating, and skiing; *crafts*: clay modeling, ceramics, leathercrafts, metalcrafts, papercrafts, and weaving; *fine arts*: drawing and painting; *performing arts*: ballet, band concerts, choral activities, creative dramatics, folk and square dancing, social dancing, orchestral concerts, and storytelling; and *special services*, programs for the ill and handicapped, ranging from preschool children to senior citizens. In addition, public recreation and park departments offer an extremely broad range of opportunities for self-directed activities, including the use of playgrounds, picnic areas, camping sites, lakes for fishing, park areas, bicycling and riding trails, and similar facilities. They also sponsor large-scale special programs, such as holiday celebrations, festival programs, art and hobby shows, and sports tournaments.

In addition to those programs which they sponsor directly, public recreation and park departments also provide assistance to many other community agencies. In some cases, they may provide help in organizing, publicizing, and scheduling activities. In other cases, they may cooperate with other organizations by providing facilities for them to use and coordinating their activities with other community recreation events. Frequently, sports programs for children and youth, such as Little League or Biddy Basketball, are affiliated with and nominally sponsored by public recreation departments but are actually run by associations of interested parents who provide the overall management of the activity, coaching, financing, and similar responsibilities. Similarly, many cultural programs, such as Civic Opera or Little Theater associations, are affiliated with public recreation departments. They are, however, basically independent organizations and provide the bulk of their own financing and organizational control.

In order to provide a more meaningful picture of the variety and scope of municipal park and recreation departments, a series of brief profiles of municipal departments follows. They are based upon departmental reports and brochures published, in most cases, in 1968. These profiles serve to illustrate varied types of administrative structures and budgetary approaches, the range of program emphasis and departmental functions, and other aspects relating to facilities development and personnel.

PROFILES OF MUNICIPAL DEPARTMENTS

The cities described here range in population from less than 100,000 to over one million. Some are described very briefly, others in much fuller detail.

Mountain View, California (Population 53,800)

Many western communities, particularly those in California, are especially vigorous in their development of recreation and park facilities and services. Mountain View represents such a community, with an annual budget for recreation and parks of approximately $770,000. The recreation staff includes seven full-time professionals and five clerical workers, and there is a total park staff of 29. The Parks and Recreation Department has been expanding both facilities and programs at a dramatic rate. In 1967, it received final approval from the state, county, and Federal governments for a cooperative plan to develop a 500-acre shoreline park promising to become one of the finest regional parks in California, with a wide variety of recreational and cultural facilities.

Overall facilities include extensive use of public schools (gymnasiums, art rooms, auditoriums, pools, athletic fields, and tennis courts), and the department's own recreation centers and amphitheaters. Program activities fit under six major headings, including sports and games, hobbies and crafts, performing arts, social activities, outdoor recreation, playground, and Playground Olympics.

In each area, there is an exceptional amount of activity. Within a single sport such as softball, there are four regular men's and boys' leagues, plus girls' and women's leagues, exhibitions, industrial tournaments, and "slow-pitch" competition. Swimming activities include instructional, competitive, life-saving, water show, and synchronized swimming. Social activities include charm courses for women and girls, fashion shows, game rooms for adults and teen-agers, movie showings, teen-age evening programs, ladies' "slim-trim" classes, a special club for widows and widowers, and varied senior citizen activities. Attendance has climbed rapidly, as illustrated by annual reports of recreation participation:

Year	Attendance Total
1954–55	135,715
1958–59	609,850
1962–63	846,763
1966–67	966,446

The Mountain View recreation and parks staff offers a consulting service to community organizations regarding their recreation programs, makes facilities available on a rental or free reservation basis, lends athletic kits and provides game leadership for picnics; and has a speakers' bureau and similar services for other civic groups.

Kansas City, Missouri (Population 617,000)

Kansas City represents an excellent example of a well-established midwestern city Parks and Recreation Department, with an extensive program of activities and a strong network of varied indoor and outdoor facilities. The Department operates under a Board of Park and Recreation Commissioners, consisting of three members appointed by the Mayor to serve during the term for which he is elected.

Park and recreation facilities in Kansas City include the following: eight major recreation centers spaced throughout the city; the Kansas City

Zoo, two municipal golf courses, a giant swimming-pool complex accommodating 3,000 swimmers, a Starlight Theater with nightly light opera performances during the summer, and varied other sports, picnic, and nature areas. Much of the city's leisure is spent in Swope Park, a 1,766-acre facility which was given to Kansas City by a public-spirited citizen in 1896 and has been fully developed since.

While the program includes the normal range of activity, it gives particularly strong emphasis to three areas: art and crafts, summer programming for inner-city youth, and services for disabled persons and other special groups.

Arts and Crafts. These include such varied activities as dressmaking, upholstery, ceramics, leathercrafts, decoupage, sculpture, puppetry, stained glass arts, lapidary, silver-smithing, and other crafts and hobbies.

Summer Programs. These include extensive Summer Olympics sports competition, summer dances and popular music entertainment, a teen-age summer-stock theater, and an "action wagon" which provides entertainment involving music, movies, and sports personalities in disadvantaged neighborhoods six nights a week, busing programs to five large municipal day camps, and similar activities. The Kansas City Park and Recreation Department operates a large resident camp on 350 woodland acres in Swope Park, serving 144 racially mixed boys and girls at a time for ten-day sessions with a program heavily oriented toward nature activities.

Services for Disabled Persons. The Department also operates special camping sessions for handicapped children in the following categories: diabetic, cardiac, cerebral palsy, retardation, and epilepsy. Each of these sessions runs for seven to ten days and is carried on in cooperation with voluntary organizations in Kansas City that serve disabled children. During the regular year, special programs for the handicapped are carried on in nine community centers throughout the city, including a wide range of activities similar to those enjoyed by "normal" youngsters.

Older citizens in Kansas City are also served by a special program, with a summer camping program designed for them especially, and the Golden Age Clubs operated in thirteen different locations throughout the city. These clubs, which are operated by the department both in its own centers and in churches, provide many special events, trips, service projects, publications, and other activities for aging persons.

The Kansas City Park and Recreation Department's budget in a recent year was approximately $6.4 million, including capital and maintenance expenditures. However, substantial sums amounting to almost $2 million are returned to the department each year from licences, permit fees, and charges for current services. Similar administrative practices are found in many municipal park and recreation departments which institute fees and charges that either make certain activities or facilities self-sustaining or significantly reduce the cost of operation.

Omaha, Nebraska (Population 301,598)

Omaha has a well-established Department of Parks, Recreation, and Public Property which operates a major auditorium and stadium complex, extensive boating facilities, and other unusual physical facilities. In the late 1960's, it underwent a major program of physical expansion, acquiring several large new parks. It operates one of the first large municipally owned and operated indoor-tennis centers in the country. A $2.65-million bond issue was passed to finance a major three-year expansion program, including a 50-meter swimming pool, an artificial ice-skating rink, a garden center, lighted softball complex, and improvements in about 100 areas throughout the city.

As in other cities cited, much of this operation is conducted on a fees-and-charges basis, with substantial income derived from marinas, day-camp charges, golf courses, instructional sports programs, and auditorium and stadium receipts. Over all, departmental expenditures in 1967 were $2,013,628, while total receipts were $589,502. Within this picture of dramatic expansion, Omaha has suffered from racial disturbances by inner-city Negro residents who protested—among other grievances—about the lack of adequate recreation and park facilities. With the assistance of Federal funds, Omaha has opened a number of "Postage Stamp Parks" in poverty areas of the city and expanded other special recreation services. They have been particularly effective in terms of expanding city-school recreation programs and adding Senior Citizens activities, under a Federal grant to operate recreation centers in new senior-citizens' apartments. A new citywide Senior Citizens center was constructed in 1969, under a cooperative arrangement with the Public Housing Authority, to be operated by the Recreation Division of the overall Department.

Omaha demonstrates how a city can operate large-scale recreation and park facilities which meet important needs of the community (as an illustration, the municipal auditorium is almost completely booked during the course of the year with entertainment, conventions, sports events, and fairs that attract 1.25 million spectators and contribute to the city's economy). It also recognizes, however, that there is increasing need to provide special services for disadvantaged populations in its inner-city areas. This problem of meeting the needs of varied socioeconomic levels and developing varied policies and programs on each level is becoming an increasingly important challenge in municipal recreation today.

Greensboro, North Carolina (Population 150,000)

Operating under the council-manager form of government through a charter enacted by the North Carolina General Assembly, Greensboro's

Parks and Recreation Commission consists of members appointed by the council and the mayor. It is supported—unlike many cities in which recreation monies are drawn from general tax funds—by a special recreation tax which supplements other allocations and yields a total of $1.27 per $100 of assessed valuation. Greensboro has supported recreation and park development strongly; public funds are supplemented annually by contributions and program co-sponsorship involving various industries and businesses, civic clubs, foundations, and other interested groups. During the decade from 1956 to 1966, Greensboro's annual expenditures for parks and recreation rose from $241,400 to $677,000; by 1969-'70, it was over $1 million. In 1967 there were 52 permanent and 125 temporary or seasonal employees in the Parks and Recreation Department. Some 39,000 persons registered for over 500 different programs during the course of the year, and participation reached an all-time high of 1.5 million participation units.

In Greensboro, program activities are provided under several major headings, including a Youth Division, Athletics, Community Centers and Playgrounds, and Ill and Handicapped.

The Youth Division operates some 35 different programs for teenagers, including weekly television and radio shows, talent shows, youth week, and a variety of projects and services such as youth recreation councils, youth employment services, and school beautification programs.

The Ill and Handicapped Division provides 18 different programs for the mentally retarded, cerebral palsied, blind, orthopedically handicapped, emotionally disturbed, and other disabled individuals. Special programs are provided for nursing homes, and a six-week summer day camp serves a substantial number of disabled children with music, nature activities, games, sports, and crafts.

Recreation and park staff members also assist many local organizations and groups by providing leadership for conferences, workshops, and training institutes. They lend equipment to such groups, set up show wagons, move bleachers, and provide the use of facilities and leadership for recreational events of other organizations and for public functions.

Portland, Oregon (Population 377,800)

In the city of Portland, Oregon, recreation is operated as a division within the larger Bureau of Parks and Public Recreation. The Recreation Division directly sponsors many programs and also relies heavily on affiliated civic organizations to sustain and carry on many recreation activities. In Portland these include many cultural and artistic organizations such as the Civic Contemporary Dance Theater, a Junior Museum, a Community Music Center, Portland Parks Art Center, Portland Actors Company, Little Loom House (weaving), Ballet Workshop, Teen-Age Theater

Workshop, Portland Opera Association, and other performing groups and recreational dance and music activities.

Since 1940, the Recreation Division has had a close working relationship with the Portland public school system, involving a comprehensive exchange of school and park facilities. When, in May, 1967, the failure of a school bond issue compelled the school board to restrict use of school facilities and establish a fee system for their use, the question of having one city department paying another arose. It was found that the school administration used 32,000 hours per week of Park Bureau facilities for classes, playground activities, and competitive sports, while the Bureau of Parks and Public Recreation used 26,000 hours of school facilities, predominantly gymnasiums and auditoriums. Recognizing the mutual benefit of this arrangement, the park and recreation department and the schools continue to exchange facilities by means of a permit system, with fees being charged only for special uses at certain times.

Over the past several years, Portland, like other large cities, has experienced severe financial pressures. Recreation administrators have responded by obtaining increased funds from nontax sources such as fees, charges, and gifts. In 1969, the total budget for parks and recreation was $5.5 million, with several hundred thousand dollars being returned to the department from fees and charges.

Long Beach, California (Population 385,000)

Long Beach is described here in detail primarily because of its administrative structure. Founded in 1929, under what has been known as the Long Beach Coordinated Recreation Plan, the Long Beach Recreation Commission has the following working arrangement: (1) the City Charter provisions which created it defined "public recreation" very broadly in terms of ages served, activities and settings; (2) the program is supervised by a Recreation Commission of nine members, including the City Manager, Superintendent of Schools, a member of the City Council, and a member of the Board of Education; (3) the Director of Health and Physical Education of the city school system is director of the total playground and public recreation department; (4) under him is an Associate Director with a major responsibility for recreation who is responsible also to the City Manager; (5) the City Manager is responsible for all hiring; and (6) funding is based on a special recreation tax of at least 5 cents per $100 assessed value of all property in the city. The overall budget in 1968–69 was $2.4 million, with the municipality contributing about three-quarters and the school district about one-quarter of this amount. A substantial portion of the money spent was returned to the Commission in the form of fees and charges, as in other cities described.

The Long Beach Recreation program is an extremely diversified one, under the following major headings: adult programs, aquatics, crafts, dance, drama, outdoor education, playgrounds, special events, sports, and youth clubs. Their variety may be illustrated by the specific activities offered under only two of these headings:

Aquatics. This includes instruction (recreational, competitive, and synchronized swimming), water safety, diving, building model boats, youth and adult sailing, life saving, water polo, boating, water skiing and canoeing. Long Beach operates a huge Marine Stadium which plays host to many aquatic shows and other special water events. In 1968 it also completed the new Belmont Plaza Olympic Pool, which was used as the site for Olympic tryouts and for aquatic programs thereafter for the community. This huge building (five stories high, 240 feet long, and 150 feet wide) has a million-gallon eight-lane pool, fitted with an underwater television and sound system, with seating facilities for 2,700 spectators and the most modern electronic scoring and timing equipment, plus other facilities for community aquatic activities.

Outdoor Education. This program, carried on in close cooperation with the school system, involves such activities as conservation and nature study, nature crafts, safety, astronomy, animal study, exploration of natural sites, and programs concerned with healthful living. The outdoor education program makes intensive use of a new Nature Center building in El Dorado Park, an 860-acre regional park with extensive facilities for outdoor education.

The Long Beach Recreation Commission also places major emphasis on developing special programs for each age group. Teen-agers are served through four large youth clubs with a total membership of close to 5,000. Since 1944, the Long Beach Recreation Commission has provided facilities, equipment, and trained personnel for this youth club program. Senior citizens are served by programs in several recreation centers, involving cards, chess, checkers, shuffleboard, lawn bowling, horseshoes, and similar activities, as well as Golden Tours, a travel club for older persons in the community. In addition, Long Beach is one of the few municipal programs which operates a "singles" club, open to unmarried persons who are twenty-five years of age or older. It operates a "University by the Sea," involving public forums and discussions, and has numerous other creative and experimental programs in all forms of recreation.

Over all, the Long Beach Recreation Commission is an excellent example of school-community cooperation. Unlike many other school-related programs, it serves all age groups fully and, rather than rely solely on school facilities, has constructed many other park, aquatic, and sports centers around the city for fully diversified leisure opportunities.

Philadelphia, Pennsylvania (Population 2,002,512)

Philadelphia serves as an excellent example of a large city faced by problems of urban blight, poverty, and racial conflicts which has moved ahead aggressively to provide intensified and imaginative new programs. It also demonstrates how the services of several major municipal governmental agencies can be coordinated to meet human and social needs most economically and efficiently.

In Philadelphia, recreation functions are filled by three tax-supported agencies, the Department of Recreation, the Board of Public Education, and the Fairmount Park Commission. When the Philadelphia City Charter was inaugurated in 1951, it made provision for a Recreation Coordination Board to further full cooperation among these agencies. This board coordinates recreation programs administered by different bodies of the city government and also consults with and assists many voluntary organizations concerned with recreation.

Throughout Philadelphia, the Recreation Department works closely with the schools. Schools use Recreation Department sites to conduct programs, seven municipal swimming pools are used for physical education classes, and extensive school use is made of tennis courts, recreation centers, and other recreation-owned facilities for baseball, softball, soccer, and track and field. Similarly, the Recreation Department works closely with the schools, providing leadership for athletic and social activities at schools in neighborhoods that lack other recreation facilities. At a large number of school recreation centers, the Board of Education furnishes utilities and janitorial services, while the Recreation Department provides leadership for joint programs. Both agencies also work closely with the Fairmount Park Commission, using its various facilities throughout the city and participating in joint planning of capital construction projects. Similarly, the Recreation Department provides recreation leadership at a number of different housing projects throughout the city.

The Recreation Department recognizes that while it is its responsibility to provide basic facilities and programs (there are over 425 different playgrounds, parks, and centers throughout the city), in many cases private agencies, voluntary organizations and community groups and clubs can meet specialized community needs. Thus, it works closely with such groups as the Philadelphia Society for Crippled Children and Adults, the Cerebral Palsy Association, the Retarded Children's Association, the Pennsylvania Association for the Blind, and the Health and Welfare Council. It coordinates services with the Crime Prevention Association, the Youth Services Board, and the Police Athletic League in an effort to reduce juvenile crime in disadvantaged sections of the city. In order to insure the fullest use of all programs, the Recreation Coordination Board has prepared an extensive directory of all recreational activities and agencies in the Philadelphia metropolitan area to help educators and recreation and social workers in replying to inquiries from the general public and in making referrals more efficiently.

The Philadelphia Recreation Department has a substantial group of leaders working with "Youth-in-Conflict" groups, attempting to reduce problems such as antisocial gangs, teen-age drinking and narcotics use, and vandalism. These youth workers have close contact with such agencies as the Juvenile Aid Division, the Gang Control branch of the Narcotics Squad of the Police Department, and the Youth Conservation Services Division of the Welfare Department. Sixteen leaders have major portions of their time assigned to working on detached duty in problem neighborhoods. They not only cooperate with the agencies mentioned earlier but also receive training through special courses offered by the State Department of Welfare. In a recent year, forty-four staff members of the recreation department received training given by state experts in such areas as law, social work, sociology, psychology, and youth services. In addition, close contact is maintained with local communities through advisory councils dispersed throughout the city.

The Philadelphia Recreation Department has been heavily involved in the city's antipoverty program. For example, a "new careers" program funded by the U.S. Labor Department, titled "Project Human Renewal," has given training in recreation leadership, including on-the-job involvement, to over 1,000 persons in twelve poverty areas, many of them teen-agers.

Many other special services have been developed to serve disadvantaged areas, particularly in ghetto neighborhoods. These have included summer job programs, expanded play-street programs, family camping programs, officiating clinics, neighborhood teen canteens, college-based "motivation" programs, educational field trips for youth, summer science projects and art classes in junior and senior high schools, Afro-American dance groups, dramatic groups, "Gospelramas" (rock-and-roll spirituals), bookmobiles and touring branch libraries, coffee houses and creative writing programs—all under the Recreation Department's direction.

In terms of physical facilities, the Philadelphia Recreation Department has expanded steadily. During 1967, new or improved facilities were put into operation on the average of one every two weeks, including new modern community playgrounds and centers, pedestrian malls, sports centers, covered sitting pavilions, spray pools, and new swimming sites and ballfields. A six-year capital program for the period from 1968 to 1973 totaled $20.9 million, including both open space programs and development of physical facilities for recreation.

TRENDS IN LOCAL RECREATION AND PARKS SPONSORSHIP

This chapter has outlined some of the major characteristics and trends in county and municipal recreation departments today. It has shown the range of services provided, and such developments as growing services to age groups other than children and youth, rapid expansion of physical facilities, increased reliance on fees and charges, and linkage with other community agencies and social programs. Typically, within larger cities, there has been a growth of services for special populations, including the physically and mentally handicapped or the socially disadvantaged.

The overall expansion of municipal recreation is demonstrated by statistics of expenditures over the past decade, gathered by the National League of Cities (Table 3-4). These figures show, however, that while a number of cities have shown an uninterrupted rise in park and recreation expenditure, others have either slackened off or have declined as a result of severe financial pressures stemming from today's urban crisis.

TABLE 3-4   *Per Capita Operating Expenditures for Parks and Recreation in Fifteen Selected Cities**

City	Expenditures 1960	Expenditures 1965	Budget 1968	Estimate 1973
New York	$4.22	$ 6.48	$ 6.19	$10.81
Chicago	7.57	8.97	11.72	14.45
Los Angeles	4.78	5.67	4.77	. . .
Baltimore	5.31	8.67	12.32	16.64
San Antonio	1.72	2.56	2.83	. . .
Saint Louis	4.82	5.57	5.85	6.90
Pittsburgh	5.71	7.73	9.13	. . .
Atlanta	3.67	4.76	9.11	. . .
Minneapolis	7.14	6.17	9.09	. . .
Nashville	5.09	4.50	4.52	7.81
Oakland	8.59	9.87	13.21	15.56
Tampa	2.30	5.82	7.33	. . .
Dayton	5.70	7.15	8.90	11.12
Peoria	8.63	10.63	14.69	. . .
Portland	4.44	9.12	8.76	9.21

SOURCE: *Recreation in the Nation's Cities: Problems and Approaches* (Washington, D.C.: Department of Urban Studies, National League of Cities, December, 1968), p. 14.

   * Derived by dividing financial data obtained from recreation personnel by actual or estimated population figures.

This extremely varied pattern of support raises questions about the fundamental role of recreation and park departments in our cities. Obviously, in many municipalities it is regarded as an important area of social service that must be supported generously. In others under financial pressure, budgetary support has been inadequate. The basic question is whether municipal administrators regard this area of service chiefly as a form of diversion or as a social necessity. The significant social contributions of organized recreation services are described in later chapters, and guides are presented for effective urban planning of recreation and park programs and facilities today.

4

Recreation in Other Settings:
Voluntary, Private, and Commercial

The previous two chapters have described recreation programs provided by government. A major portion of public leisure opportunity is provided by other types of agencies throughout the United States. These may be placed in three categories:

1. *Voluntary Agencies.* These are nongovernmental, nonprofit agencies and organizations which have been established to meet important social needs in American communities. They include both denominational and nondenominational agencies and are generally open to the public at large. They operate through contributions, fees, charges, and membership dues, although they may also receive support from public funds.

2. *Private Agencies.* These are generally established as nonprofit organizations and frequently are limited to a rather select clientele. One type of private recreation agency is the boating, golf, or tennis club which operates its own facilities and to which members are admitted through a careful process of screening and selection. Such programs are usually self-sustaining, governed by elected officers; they rely on their own income-generating powers rather than tax funds or contributions.

3. *Commercial Recreation Agencies.* The third major source for nongovernmental recreational opportunity is found in business-sponsored recreation programs. These include all sorts of commercial establishments which provide opportunity for leisure participation, such as privately owned and operated bowling alleys, swimming pools, golf driving ranges, movies, theaters, ice rinks, race tracks, sports stadiums, night clubs, and bars.

This chapter provides a detailed analysis of these three types of agencies. Recreational opportunity must be seen as a huge interlocking system. Often a single form of participation may cut across several types of sponsorship. For example, the boating enthusiast may readily become involved with four types of sponsors: (1) commercial: he purchases his boat and needed equipment from commercial manufacturers or dealers; (2) voluntary: he is a member of the Power Squadron, which gives courses to prospective boat-owners in navigation or seamanship; (3) private: he belongs to a private boating club and uses its marina facilities or other services; and (4) government: he makes extensive use of publicly owned lakes, reservoirs, and waterways.

It is generally government's responsibility to provide a basic floor of recreational facilities and services, while other types of agencies meet other more specialized or advanced needs. Within the broad sphere of social welfare, government and voluntary agencies often work side by side and cooperate intensively in meeting the needs of youth, families, disadvantaged population groups, the physically or emotionally handicapped, and the aging. Generally, private and commercial agencies are concerned not with meeting such social needs but rather with providing services and opportunities desired by their members or clientele.

VOLUNTARY AGENCIES IN THE LEISURE FIELD

Community organizations and agencies which are regarded as "voluntary" usually have the following characteristics:

1. They represent the voluntary wishes of community residents, in that they usually have been originated by community efforts to meet significant social needs through organized cooperation of citizen groups. Thus, they are voluntary in terms of *origin*.

2. They are governed by boards of directors or trustees which are usually composed of public-spirited citizens who accept such responsibilities as a form of social obligation. Thus, in terms of *membership* and *administrative* control, they are voluntary.

3. The traditional pattern of voluntary agencies has been to rely on public giving—either in the form of direct contributions to the agency's fund-raising efforts, or as part of a total "community chest" effort. Usually this is supplemented by a system of membership fees and charges; within recent years, many voluntary organizations have also undertaken special projects for which they receive governmental support.

4. In terms of *leadership*, voluntary agencies are staffed by professionals (often the administrative director has been professionally trained in social work, recreation, or education) at the top levels. At other personnel levels, leadership tends to be carried on by nonprofessionals, part-time or seasonal personnel, and volunteers.

Compared with government recreation agencies, voluntary organizations: (1) are generally less influenced by considerations of politics and freer to determine their own program objectives and emphases, (2) are more flexible and experimental, (3) are more specialized in program content, meeting specific needs for certain constituencies, rather than across-the-board services, (4) tend to be less facilities- or resource-oriented; and (5) since they are dependent on the success of fund-raising efforts, are somewhat less stable financially than government agencies.

Voluntary agencies tend to regard recreation as part of their total spectrum of service. It is generally seen as a way of achieving improved social welfare, character-building, reduced social pathology, enriched educational experience, and similar objectives.

Types of Voluntary Agencies

The following types of voluntary agencies may be identified:

Youth-Serving Organizations. These consist chiefly of nationally structured organizations which function directly through local branches, centers, or regional chapters. They have broad goals related to social development and character-building and operate extensive programs of recreational activity.

Religious Social Agencies. The major religious denominations sponsor membership organizations which may cut across various age groupings but which tend to focus most directly upon children, youth, and young adults. In many ways, they are similar to youth-serving organizations, although they may have special goals related to religious purpose.

Settlement Houses and Community Centers. These are community agencies which usually provide disadvantaged neighborhoods with a spectrum of social services, among which leisure activities are extremely important. Customarily, they are not part of national organizations but operate on an independent basis.

Antipoverty Organizations. A relatively recent phenomenon, such organizations serve disadvantaged populations, with special emphasis on minority-group clientele. Both their administrative direction and their staffing come more directly from the neighborhood groups being served than has been the case among traditional social agencies. They rely heavily on government antipoverty funding and special grants from foundations and business organizations, for support.

Special-Interest Organizations. These tend to be nationally structured organizations that promote special recreational activities. They rely on membership fees, gifts, and sometimes financial support by business organizations that share their interests.

Agencies Serving Special Populations. These are a number of large national organizations concerned with meeting the needs of various categories of the ill and disabled. Usually they operate through local chapters organized on a statewide or citywide basis and tend to focus heavily upon providing services for children and youth.

Professional Organizations Serving the Park and Recreation Field. These are membership groups which upgrade and expand professional practices in the park and recreation field. They have as members leaders, supervisors, and administrators in recreational agencies throughout the nation, including those who teach in recreation and park curriculums in colleges and universities.

Within each of these categories, the following section describes general characteristics and presents a number of specific examples.

Youth-Serving Organizations

Recreation has an important place in the programs of most voluntary youth-serving organizations, such as the Boy Scouts or Girl Scouts of America, the Campfire Girls, or the Boys Club of America. There are hundreds of such organizations, many of them junior affiliates of adult bodies, others denominational in origin, and still others independent and operated on a purely local level. They are sponsored by such varied bodies as civic and fraternal organizations, labor unions, veterans organizations and clubs, rural and farm organizations, and culturally oriented councils. Their stated goals may or may not include statements related to the constructive use of leisure; in most cases, however, they are heavily involved with the provision of recreational services.

The Boy Scouts of America. This national youth-serving body was founded in the United States in 1910; it is a powerful and widespread organization. Within the United States alone it has approximately 4.6 million boy members within 152,000 separate units; it also has branches in about 69 other countries and is part of a worldwide scouting movement which involves over 105 other countries. Since there are today over 1.6 million adults involved in Boy Scouting as leaders, the movement today comprises 6.2 million members. Since its inception, over 35 million boys have been members of the Boy Scouts of America.

It has as its primary purpose the development of desirable traits of character and good citizenship. These goals are achieved on three levels of membership: Cub Scouts for boys between eight and ten, Boy Scouts for those between eleven and thirteen, and Explorer Scouts for those between fourteen and seventeen. The total program places a strong emphasis on mental and physical fitness, vocational and social development, and the enrichment of youth hobbies and prevocational interests. It relies heavily on outdoor adventure and scouting skills and on community service activities.

The Boy Scout Advancement Program consists of a system of achievement tests in specified skills areas through which boys move up through membership ranks. There are today 112 merit-badge awards, which include special projects and achievement tests in such familiar areas as bird study, aviation, basketry, music, soil and water conservation, personal fitness, and canoeing and such newer subjects as American business, computers, engineering, landscape architecture, and theater. Over 1.75 million merit badges were awarded in 1967.

Approximately 50 percent of local Scout units are sponsored by religious bodies (although this does not mean that their membership is restricted to particular denominations); about 28 percent are sponsored by civic organizations, like the Lions, American Legion, or industrial groups; and about 22 percent are housed in schools or sponsored by Parent-Teacher Associations. In addition to over 3,600 paid professional Scout executives and regional staff members, the bulk of actual Scout leadership is provided by parents and other interested volunteer adults.

The Boy Scouts have been widely regarded as a middle-class organization in American society, and have not been active among lower-class children, particularly in inner-city, minority-group neighborhoods. There has, however, been a shift in emphasis over the past several years. Typically, in the city of Chicago, over 115 Scout units in low-income areas were established, with over 3,400 boy members. Similar programs have been developed in public housing projects in Dallas, San Francisco, Los Angeles, and other cities. Such programs have achieved, according to public housing authorities, major declines in vandalism and problems of maintenance and have brought about improved tenant-management relations. According to a Commissioner of the Federal Public Housing Administration, for boys in public housing projects,

Scouting can mean an introduction to physical fitness and team play; a channeling of energies; and a wholesome letting off of steam in recreation, in work, and in developing skills and participating in sports. Indeed, the Scouting program can effect considerable reductions in maintenance costs due to vandalism. Together, the Boy Scouts and local housing authorities can offer bold new custom-tailored youth opportunities to boys who are hard to reach. Through youth and adult activities, Scouting can make significant contributions to the almost half-million low-income families now living in public housing projects.[1]

In May, 1968, the Boy Scouts of America announced the beginning of a nationwide campaign of expansion in city slums and impoverished rural areas to increase total Scout membership to 6.5 million boys. The program, known as "Boypower '76," has already begun experimental programs in city slums, using storefronts and other experimental settings to attract greater numbers of Negro and Spanish-speaking boys. In addition, the Scouts have

[1] Marie C. McGuire, quoted in "Scouting for Boys," by Ray W. Sweazey, *Journal of Housing*, January 31, 1963.

established new services in institutions for juvenile delinquents and other special programs serving the physically handicapped and mentally retarded.

Boys' Clubs of America. Another national youth-serving organization is the Boys' Clubs of America. Founded in 1906 and chartered by Congress in 1956, this organization includes over 800 separate building centers, the majority in slum areas of major cities. In 1968 it served over 835,000 boys with programs consisting heavily of recreation in the form of sports and games, arts and crafts, and social activities—but also including services in remedial education, work training, job placement, and guidance.

The Boys' Clubs program is staffed by over 5,800 professional workers and 29,000 volunteers. In 1968, its total operating budget amounted to $28.9 million, and the replacement value of its buildings was estimated at $178 million dollars. Approximately fifty new Boys' Club centers were begun in 1967, and the American people contributed $24 million to facilities development of the organization during this year. Unlike the Boy Scouts, which relies heavily on the use of other agencies' facilities, the Boys' Clubs of America seeks to have its member organizations in local communities build their own centers.

Different Boys' Clubs provide many examples of unique services. Guidance and recreation programs for boys confined in the county jail are provided through the Syracuse Boys' Club. The Atlanta Boys' Club operates a "junior deputies" program designed to familiarize boys with the procedures and methods police employ to prevent crime. The Chicago Boys' Club provides basic education and prevocational training and job orientation programs in the clerical, automotive, and food-service occupations for hard-core out-of-school older boys. In Dayton, the Boys' Club operates a group therapy program for thirteen- to fifteen-year-old boys with educational and social-adjustment problems. Other centers have comprehensive programs in creative activities, such as drama and creative writing.

While voluntary citizen support has been the lifeline of the Boys' Club movement, it has increasingly received government aid. Approximately half of all Boys' Clubs now participate to some extent in such funded projects. Many operate Neighborhood Youth Corps and Community Action programs. Several have received grants for new building construction under the Neighborhood Facilities Act, and a number of clubs have been cooperating with neighborhood schools in tutorial and cultural enrichment projects funded under the Elementary and Secondary Education Act.

Girl Scouts of America. The leading voluntary organization serving girls in the United States is the Girl Scouts of America, a national movement for girls between the ages of seven and seventeen. It provides a sequential program of activities centered around the arts, the home, and the out-of-doors, with a primary focus on character and citizenship development, community service, international friendship, health, and safety. Its overall purpose is to inspire girls with "the highest ideals of character, conduct, patriotism and service, that they may become happy and resourceful citizens."

In 1968, total membership of girls and adult leaders in the Girl Scout movement climbed to 3.8 million, with over 158,000 separate troops throughout the United States. Today, one out of every seven girls in its age range is a Girl Scout. They are served with a variety of leisure interests and projects appropriate for each of four age levels: Brownie Girl Scouts (ages seven and eight), Junior Girl Scouts (ages nine to eleven), Cadette Girl Scouts (ages twelve to fourteen), and Senior Girl Scouts (ages fifteen to seventeen). This organization also is reaching out to disadvantaged girls in both urban and rural areas; today it conducts special programs with the poor, the handicapped, the emotionally disturbed, the mentally retarded, and similar groups.

Camp Fire Girls, Inc. This organization, which involves well over half a million girls, is primarily concerned with character-building through a program of outdoor-oriented recreation, community service, and educational activities. It makes use of varied interests, including sports and games, the creative arts, the home, and outdoor activity to develop the personality and character of its young members, ranging from the age of seven through high school. For some time, it has operated a Metropolitan Critical Areas project, reaching out into "long-neglected" areas and seeking to involve girls "whose problems of identity crisis, neglect, low educational levels, delinquency, fatherless families, and poverty are deep-seated."

The Camp Fire Girls have carried out demonstration projects in such cities as Boston, Detroit, and Washington, D.C., with funding by the Children's Bureau in the Department of Health, Education and Welfare. They have also intensified services in ten other cities across the country, with financial assistance from the Office of Juvenile Delinquency and Youth Development of the Welfare Administration. Thus, as in other formerly middle-class-oriented programs, a strong effort is being made to integrate recreation and social programs with special projects serving the disadvantaged.

The Police Athletic League. In over 100 communities throughout the nation, Police Athletic Leagues are sponsored by law enforcement agencies. Typically, they provide extensive recreation programming, indoor centers, and summer playstreets, with a heavy emphasis on sports and games, creative arts, drum-and-bugle corps, and remedial education. Many Police Athletic Leagues also maintain placement and counseling services which provide job training, and assist students who have dropped out of school. Such programs operate chiefly in poverty areas. They rely primarily on voluntary contributions for funding support, although they may receive technical assistance and some cooperation in the form of officers on special assignment, from municipal police departments.

4-H Clubs. Founded as self-improvement groups of rural young people around the turn of the century, 4-H clubs receive funding from various levels of government and also are assisted by county agricultural agents and land-grant college extension services. Much of their adult leadership, however, consists of volunteer adults in rural communities and so they may be regarded primarily as voluntary agencies. The primary purpose of the 4-H Club organization is to promote better living in primarily agricultural and rural areas. In the United States, well over two million boys and girls are involved in its programs, which include agricultural education, projects and competitions, home arts projects, conservation and other community service assignments, and a heavy program of recreational activities, including trips and hikes, camping, social programs, and cultural activities.

Religious Social Agencies

Among the most active voluntary organizations meeting leisure needs in America today are agencies affiliated with major religious denominations. While many local, social, and recreational programs are sponsored by individual churches or synagogues, this chapter focuses on three major examples of national organizations: The Young Men's and Young Women's Christian Association, the Catholic Youth Organization, and the Young Men's and Young Women's Hebrew Association. Each of these represents a nationwide network of facilities and programs with religious content and purpose but also with highly diversified recreation, education, and youth service activities.

Young Men's and Young Women's Christian Association. These are voluntary organizations affiliated broadly with Protestantism rather than any single denomination. They are devoted to the promotion of religious ideals of living, and view themselves as worldwide fellowships "dedicated to the enrichment of life through the development of Christian character and a Christian society." Typically, programs are heavily geared to serving young people through clubs, social events, sports and fitness, and educational and service activities. The specific relationship of the Y.M.C.A. program with recreation was defined in a study carried out by a national committee of the Y in 1946:

At their best Y.M.C.A.'s now engage in recreational activities not only for the purpose of wholesomely occupying the leisure time of young people and of affording the immediate development of knowledge and skill that results from such activities, but for the more comprehensive purpose of developing Christian personality and preparing for citizenship in a Christian society.[2]

The Y has assumed a major responsibility for meeting public recreation needs in many American communities. Frequently, in smaller cities

---

[2] Harry D. Edgren, "Public and Voluntary Agencies of Recreation in Our Society," *American Recreation Journal*, May–June, 1963, p. 11.

and towns, it provides the best facilities for indoor sports and games, physical fitness, social and cultural programs, as well as the most effective organization and leadership. The range of Y.M.C.A. involvement is indicated by the following statistics, reported in 1969:

Number of members	5,778,000
Number of Y.M.C.A.'s	1,718
Professional staff	4,000
Volunteers	545,900
Income	$234.3 million
Capital assets	$848.8 million
Endowments	$124 million
Campers	598,000
Youth clubs	46,000
Educational classes	17,000
Service contacts	$268.5 million

It should be made clear that neither the Y.M. nor the Y.W.C.A. restricts its membership either on the basis of sex or sectarian affiliation. One out of four members of the Young Men's Christian Association is a woman or a girl. During the 1960's, a study showed that the religious affiliation of Y members was 75.2 percent Protestant, 18.9 percent Roman Catholic, and 3.3 percent Jewish.

The Young Women's Christian Association has a major concern with world fellowship, public affairs, community service, education, and vocational development. It places a very heavy emphasis on health education and social programs; essentially, these are geared to meeting recreational needs and interests of girls and young women. As an example, in a large eastern Y.W.C.A. in a suburban city, the health education schedule includes dozens of classes each week for all ages from young children through adulthood in varied forms of dance, aquatic activity, and exercise.

Other activities at this Y include driving classes, activities for handicapped individuals, marching and cheerleaders' classes, a little theater program, a coffee house program, a dance hostess program for armed-forces social activities, various club programs, a West Point dance program, a high school age dance, road rallies, field trips and tours, a singles canteen for young adults, holiday dances, and a teen-age "Drop-In lounge."

The Y.W.C.A. places a heavy emphasis on promoting world fellowship and interracial and interreligious understanding. Both the Y.M. and Y.W.C.A. have in the past sponsored essentially racially segregated centers and programs. In many cities, until the 1960's, there were more or less formal restrictions against Negroes joining "white" Y's. In some cases, camping programs intended to serve the total Y membership have also been disproportionately white in membership. Within the past decade, however, both the Y.M. and the Y.W.C.A. have striven to serve a multiracial population more effectively and, in a period of rapidly shifting racial patterns, to meet the needs of urban minority groups and disadvantaged populations.

Catholic Youth Organization. The leading Catholic agency concerned with providing spiritual, social, and recreational services for young people in the United States is the Catholic Youth Organization. In New York City, as an example, the C.Y.O. offers the following recreational facilities and programs: 6 community centers, 4 settlement houses, 4 summer camps, an extensive Sea Cadet Corp, 17 antidelinquency recreation projects, 195 Teen-Age Leadership Clubs, leadership training courses, recreation programs for retarded children, swimming classes for handicapped children, nearly 600 Boy and Girl Scout Troops, 45 summer day camps, 36 young adult clubs, a Physical Fitness Council, and a Young People's Symphony and Music Program. Many of these are sponsored directly by the Catholic Youth Organization through its own centers, administered and financed by diocesan headquarters. Others are carried out within specific parishes under the direction of parish priests.

Within the Catholic Youth Organization, which serves in New York City alone over 278,000 teen-agers and young adults, there are both general social and specifically religious objectives. Recreational and social programs are seen as offering desirable outlets for youth in order to build constructive personal values. In the 1967 Annual Report of the New York Catholic Youth Organization, the following statement is made:

The most vulnerable period in the lives of our young people are the leisure-time hours when they are on their own, away from the positive influences of family, school and church. The values and standards of these significant institutions can then be challenged by the growing impulse for self-assertion and the natural instincts of pleasure-seeking and self-indulgence. This sensitive situation encompasses nearly half the lifetime of the pre-teen and teen-ager and it is the mission of the Catholic Youth Organization to "move in" on these idle hours as an extension of the family, church and school with recreation, spiritual, apostolic, social and cultural programming that will give the youngster attractive alternatives to the appealing excitement of the "offbeat" activities that are the root of delinquency.[3]

This general purpose is expressed in the same report by the statement, "Since 1936, the New York C.Y.O. has been in the thick of the struggle to prevent and overcome juvenile delinquency." However, the Catholic Youth Organization, like other religious organizations that work with youth, also sees its goals as directly related to spiritual content. Through participation in the program, Catholic youth are exposed to spiritual values and involved in retreats, religious education, and other functions which strengthen and enrich their faith. The social program also serves as a means of attract-

[3] "Youth . . . Apostles to Youth," *Annual Report of Catholic Youth Organization, New York City,* 1967, p. 3.

ing and involving young people in center activities based on religious affiliation, thus helping the parish priest to maintain a meaningful contact with the young people in his parish. One spokesman for the Catholic Youth Organization points out that religious leaders must be able to enter the lives of young people and that they cannot do this if religion and religious leaders are seen as narrow-minded and repressive. Therefore, he suggests, it is necessary to keep the religious program within the Catholic Youth Organization simple, free from "a lot of do's and don'ts"; ultimately, it must reflect and generate "Christian joy" rather than "straitlaced, pointed-nose Puritanism."[4]

This is a revealing statement about the contemporary religious approach to leisure and recreation. Rather than attempting to repress "sinful" forms of play, many religious agencies instead seek to promote joyous and affirmative programs of participation. They see leisure and the creative recreational involvement of young people, as having great potential for their total growth—both social and spiritual. It illustrates also a breadth of approach to the idea of ministry; increasingly, ministers of all faiths have been moving into unusual settings to bring their religious message to those who need them.

"Exceptional ministries" today include the following: an Omaha minister with a trailer chapel who works among occupants of mobile homes; a "taxicab priest" in Montreal who celebrates special masses for cab drivers and keeps in touch with them by two-way radio; a San Francisco minister who walks a nocturnal beat of hospital emergency wards, hotel lobbies, and bus stations; and a New York City minister who counsels his parishioners in the nightclubs of the city where they perform. Today, there are ministers who work exclusively in high-rise apartments or who have taken jobs in factories in order to meet and work more effectively with industrial employees. A comment recently made about the work of the Jewish rabbi is that a few decades ago he was expected to be a preacher and a teacher, whereas today he is also a counselor, administrator, and youth program director and is deeply involved in social action programs. This breadth of concern is well illustrated in the work of the Young Men's and Young Women's Hebrew Association.

Young Men's and Young Women's Hebrew Association. Like the Y.M. and Y.W.C.A., the Jewish Ys do not regard themselves primarily as recreation agencies but rather as community agencies devoted to social service, with a strong religious component. Specifically, the Y.M. and Y.W.H.A. defines its community role in the following way:

1. To meet the leisure-time social, cultural and recreational needs of its membership, embracing both sexes and all age groups.

[4] Albert Nimeth, address to Eighth National Catholic Youth Organization Convention, in *American Journal of Catholic Youth Work*, 1966, pp. 68-69.

2. To stimulate individual growth and personality development by encouraging interest and capacity for group and community participation.
3. To teach leadership responsibility and democratic process through group participation.
4. To provide certain limited guidance services, including individual counseling, in preparation for referral to specialized services when indicated.
5. To encourage citizenship education and responsibility among its members and, as a social welfare agency, to participate in community-wide programs of social betterment.[5]

The Y.M. and Y.W.H.A. identifies as its major professional discipline the field of social group work, although it also draws upon qualified staff members from nursery school education, health and physical education, adult education, and the arts. A typical Y.M. and Y.W.H.A. in the New York metropolitan areas serves about 3,500 members, ranging from children of nursery school age to older adults, and including special services to physically, mentally, and emotionally handicapped youth. Its services include a nursery school, an after-school play and recreation program and summer camping program for children, social, athletic, cultural, and prevocational activities for teen-age youth and young adults, parent education and other cultural programs for adults, and a day center for aging persons.

As an example, a large new Y.M. and Y.W.H.A. being built to serve the Jewish community in suburban Wantagh, Long Island, New York, involves construction of a $2.5-million "cultural, recreational and informal education center." Included are such facilities as separate lounges for various age groups, a large gymnasium and health club, an exercise room, a large auditorium and club rooms, an Olympic-size swimming pool, ceramic and woodworking shops, an art studio, drama workshops, an outdoor play area, and a fully equipped nursery. Like other religious agencies, the Y.M. and Y.W.H.A. provides special programs for young people and adults designed to further their religious orientation and sense of affiliation to Judaism. However, it also accepts non-Jews as program participants and thus provides an important component of public recreational opportunity.

Among the religious organizations which have set out deliberately to involve substantial numbers of disadvantaged and minority group populations not of their own denomination, Jewish community centers and Y.M. and Y.W.H.A.'s are presently extremely active. A recent study in 59 cities throughout the United States, carried out by the National Jewish Welfare Board, indicated that a high proportion, 64 of the 73 centers surveyed, were serving such populations. Their programs included operating Headstart centers, child care programs, tutoring and remedial reading clinics, training volunteers for participation in antipoverty programs, and similar activities.

[5] Irving Brodsky, "The New Role of the Community Center," in *The Social Welfare Forum* (New York: Columbia University Press, 1964), p. 201.

The report, issued in 1968, also indicated that in 31 centers the boards had established public affairs committees concerned with social legislation and that in 38 centers programs of membership education on urban crisis problems (mainly in the form of forum discussions for adults) had been undertaken. Despite some resistance by a minority of members or trustees, no center had changed its policy or procedures as a consequence of such objections.[6]

Settlement Houses and Community Centers

Another type of voluntary agency which provides extensive recreational services is the settlement house or community center. Such institutions (see Chapter 8) were founded in this country during the last decades of the nineteenth century and the first few decades of the twentieth century. Generally, they were established by pioneer social workers in the slums of large cities in the East and Midwest to help newly-arrived immigrant families in their adaptation to the United States. They have varied goals of education, counseling, health services, cultural enrichment, and recreation and are usually regarded as social work agencies, with their administrative personnel drawn from that field.

The Bronx River Neighborhood House, in New York City, is an example of a settlement house that has expanded rapidly over the past decades to meet pressing urban needs in a rapidly changing community. It began in Bronx River Houses, a low-income project serving 1,246 families. It has since expanded to several other operations within a large neighborhood known as Soundview-Bruckner. This neighborhood is a study in contrasts, including rundown tenements and a low-income public housing project, along with middle-income private housing in some areas. Within its borders are many stable and responsible families, as well as others that are involved in such chronic problems as drug addiction, prostitution, alcoholism, unemployment, and crime.

Soundview-Bruckner is the size of a small city, covering four square miles, and with a population that is approaching 125,000. Through urban renewal, many schools, parks, shopping plazas, amusement and recreational facilities and community centers have been constructed. The Bronx River Neighborhood Center sees its role as "helping the people who live in the neighborhood build a community capable of meeting their needs." Its budget has increased rapidly over the past several years, and it now operates three centers (one of which, a $650,000 structure, was built by the New York City Housing Authority with funds from the New York State Division of Housing and Community Renewal), plus special programs in three public schools, two churches, and the community rooms of three

[6] Irving Brodsky, *The Jewish Community Center and the Urban Crisis: A Report to the National Jewish Welfare Board,* 1968, pp. 1-8.

middle-income projects. Its activities include a variety of social and recreational services which are offered to serve all age groups and which stress character-development, the creative use of leisure, and special goals related to vocational development, remedial education, and leadership training. It operates playgrounds, nursery programs, social clubs, classes, teams, lounges, councils, work projects, study groups, day camps, and special services for mentally retarded children and the orthopedically handicapped.

Major segments of the Bronx River Neighborhood House operations are supported by foundations and by Federal, state, and city government funds—including Project Head Start, State Youth Commission grants, JOIN (Job Opportunities in Neighborhoods), and funding from the city's Social Service Department.

There are approximately 250 such settlement houses today, operating chiefly in disadvantaged areas of major cities, offering social, educational, and leisure services.

Other Organizations Serving the Disadvantaged

Closely linked in purpose to the work of settlement houses, but with a somewhat more restricted focus and without as strong an emphasis on social work leadership, are a number of voluntary agencies which concentrate on meeting the needs of the poor—particularly children and youth—in urban slums. Two leading examples of traditional agencies in this field are cited:

The Fresh Air Fund. This agency was founded in 1877, with the intention of giving deprived children of the tenements a unique vacation opportunity in healthy country settings over a twelve-state area along the eastern seaboard. In the early years, these were chiefly the children of immigrant families; today they come chiefly from nonwhite populations living in blighted urban neighborhoods. Through the years, almost one million children have been served, many of them from broken and fatherless homes and all selected on the basis of need alone by social agencies. The Fresh Air Fund, which is supported by voluntary contributions, operates its own network of seven camps on a 3,000-acre tract known as the Sharpe Reservation. It serves thousands of city children each summer with country living, natural science activities, and remedial education. Many other children are placed in private homes over a twelve-state eastern seaboard area ranging from Maine to Virginia through a "Friendly Town" program.

The Children's Aid Society. Another leading example of voluntary organizations which have been developed to serve disadvantaged children and youth is the Children's Aid Society. This was founded in 1853 as a nonsectarian agency. Initially its purpose was to focus "on the care of the orphaned and destitute children who roamed the streets of nineteenth-century New York, by operating lodging houses and industrial schools and placing children in homes in the West." Today it offers a variety of vital services which encompass every aspect in the lives of children, including child care, foster home placement, free hot lunches in schools, a visiting nurse and a school nurse service, an adoption service, a dental clinic, and a free day nursery. The Children's Aid Society provides a comprehensive group work, health, education, and recreation program in seven large centers in deprived areas of New York City. In addition, it conducts summer camps which provide three-week vacations for needy city children, including a special camp for handicapped boys and girls. Approximately 100,000 children are involved in a varied program of recreation and informal education each year, considerably more than receive its other types of services.

Since the inception of the Federal antipoverty program, the strictly voluntary approach has shifted sharply to a combined government–business–voluntary agency approach. Many "crash" summer recreation programs that have been instituted have received major support from business organizations for play-street programs, special entertainment, Junior Olympics programs (intercity competition in basketball, bowling, and track and field for eleven- to fifteen-year-olds), subsidized trip programs, teen-age film-making, repertory theater, night-lighting programs, and similar activities.

Other Antipoverty Organizations

It was part of the philosophy of the antipoverty program of the 1960's that one important ingredient of helping black and Spanish-speaking slum residents overcome poverty was to give them power to plan and run social action programs. In large cities all over the nation, major antipoverty agencies controlled largely by the poor and their representatives came into being. Their functions ranged from housing and legal assistance, political action, upgraded welfare services, remedial education, and vocational training to recreation, day-camping, and cultural programs.

Similarly, in a number of large cities, as part of the antipoverty effort, youth gangs in Negro, Puerto Rican, or Mexican-American slums have been supported by the government to carry out experimental programs. Typically, a fighting street gang in North Philadelphia known as "Twelfth and Oxford" has turned from fighting to working; it has become a corporation and makes profitable movies and carries on home rehabilitation projects. It has had a budget of $1.3 million, receiving funds from sources related to the Urban Coalition (an alliance of business, church, civil rights, labor, civic, and educational leaders working to advance city programs). Similar gangs that have been converted to socially constructive goals and programs have been the "Thugs United" of New Orleans, the "Sons of Watts, Inc.," of Los Angeles, and the "Real Great Society, Inc.," in New York City, a self-help group started by reformed leaders of Puerto Rican fighting gangs.

In a number of cases, such groups, which reach thousands of youths in the largest cities, have also been funded by the Office of Economic Opportunity. The latter organization is primarily concerned with economic advancement of ghetto youth; however, it also has supported courses in such areas as acting, dance, arts and crafts, karate, filmmaking and photography, and Afro-American and Puerto Rican history. Often, indigenous leaders in urban ghettos are discontented with the recreation and social programs which have been operated for them in the past by the Establishment; they have developed new kinds of activities and programs geared to meet their needs as they see them.

In a number of cities where major riots have occurred over the past several summers, special programs have been developed (combining the efforts of voluntary and government agencies and with financial assistance from business organizations and unions) to provide special summer programs to forestall and prevent fresh outbursts. In the Watts section of Los Angeles, scene of the first serious urban riots, the anniversary of the 1965 conflagration has been marked in succeeding summers by huge summer festivals, featuring parades, sports activities, jazz concerts, plays, panel discussions, and museum exhibits of Afro-American, West Indian, and modern art.

In the summer of 1967, the anniversary of the riot was marked by a second week-long festival and by a major camping program for thousands of Watts children, who went on a two-week vacation to Camp Roberts, a National Guard base, hundreds of miles away. Thus, within many community-based antipoverty organizations, recreation has been recognized as an important program function. When the Watts summer camping program was repeated in 1968, with an enriched program serving 3,000 children and young teen-agers, and with older community youth hired as staff, the director of the Watts Labor Community Action Committee commented on the necessity for this type of program in the following words:

It's impossible for kids to stay on the streets for 12 weeks during the summer with no recreation or recreational facilities and remain out of trouble. Many of those here already have prison records.[7]

Special-Interest Organizations

Another major type of voluntary agency promotes activities and public support for a particular type of recreation. Such organizations are usually developed on a national basis with full-time professional staff members who carry out promotional efforts through the mass media, pressing for favorable legislation and public action.

[7] Nancy J. Adler, "One Thousand Youths from Watts Encounter the Pastoral Life," New York *Times*, July 14, 1968, p. 55.

Special-interest organizations are often found in athletics, where they are concerned with the promotion of a given sport. Their memberships are composed of players, officials, coaches, and other groups; often they have committees responsible for playing rules, eligibility standards, and conducting national tournaments. Often such sports bodies are supported financially by businessmen who have a stake in the activity's success—such as manufacturers of bowling, billiards, or boating equipment. Organizations of this type may also be found in the cultural area—in the arts, music, dance, and theater. Often, too, they may represent participants in such hobbies as bridge, chess, rock-collecting, or antique-collecting.

Several examples of special-interest organizations with a special concern for conservation and outdoor recreation follow, as illustrations of the work of voluntary agencies in this field.

Sierra Club. Founded in 1892 and headed during its first two decades of life by John Muir, the famous naturalist, the Sierra Club has fought to achieve a growing awareness for Americans "of what we have lost and can lose during 200 years of continuing exploitation of our resources for commodity purposes and failure to realize their value for scenic, scientific and aesthetic purposes."[8] In recent years, the Sierra Club has become best known for its battles to protect major natural resources threatened by commercial exploitation, such as reservoir-development projects threatening the upper Colorado River and the Grand Canyon or the continuing legislative struggle to establish the Redwoods National Park. The Sierra Club is not, however, solely a conservation-promoting organization. It also is the nation's largest skiing and hiking club, operating a major network of ski lodges and "river runners." Since 1959, it has been a major publisher of books on conservation and natural resources in the United States. Its membership over a recent fifteen-year period has grown from 7,000 to about 60,000 members, and it expects to grow to 200,000 members in the years ahead.

Appalachian Mountain Club. A similar organization, founded on a regional basis in the East, has been the Appalachian Mountain Club, which has promoted such sports as skiing, snowshoeing, mountain climbing, and canoeing since its inception in 1876. Its original purpose was to "explore the mountains of New England and adjacent regions . . . for scientific and artistic purposes, and . . . to cultivate an interest in geographical studies." Through the years, it has explored and mapped many of the wildest and most scenic areas in Massachusetts, New Hampshire, and Maine.

While practical conservation has been and still is a prime concern of the Appalachian Mountain Club, it has also acquired various camp properties, published guides and maps, and maintained hundreds of miles of

[8] Lawrence E. Davies, "Sierra Club Maps Expansion," New York *Times,* December 9, 1967, p. 52.

trails and a network of huts and shelters throughout the White Mountains for outdoor recreation use by its 10,000 members. It promotes programs of instruction and leadership training in such activities as snowshoeing, skiing, smooth and white-water canoeing, and rock-climbing. It has chapters in a number of eastern cities and towns, as well as a number of college clubs which maintain their own trails and huts and carry out special trips and projects.

American Youth Hostels. A nonprofit organization founded for charitable and educational purposes, the American Youth Hostels gained much of its impetus from the European hostel movement which became extremely popular during the early part of the twentieth century. Its purpose is to "help all, especially young people, gain a greater understanding of the world and its people, through outdoor activities, educational and recreational travel and related programs; to develop fit, self-reliant, well-informed citizens." The American Youth Hostels maintains centers that provide simple overnight accommodations in scenic, historical, and cultural areas. Those who visit these centers are expected to travel under their own steam; cycling is used as a primary mode of travel, although bus, train, or ship transportation may often be used to get to the beginning point of a trip.

The American Hostel movement is an affiliate of the International Youth Hostel Federation Association. In 1965, more than eighteen million hostelers stayed overnight in 4,100 hostels in thirty-seven countries. In addition to travel and recreation for their own members, American Youth Hostel Councils help Scouts, Ys, schools, churches, settlement houses, city recreation departments, and organizations serving handicapped or disadvantaged youths initiate their own hosteling programs.

Throughout the year local Councils also carry on varied adventure trips and excursions for young people, and give leadership training in skiing, ski-touring, hiking, camping, cycling, snowshoeing, sailing, and canoeing. In a number of cities in Michigan, California, and New Jersey, municipal park and recreation departments have made hosteling programs available to the youth and families of their communities.

Voluntary Organizations Promoting Boating. Boating and related activities have been assisted in different ways by a variety of voluntary organizations. As an example, the Boy and Girl Scouts, Camp Fire Girls, and many other youth agencies have sponsored programs in swimming, life-saving, and safe boating. The American Red Cross Safety Service promotes and teaches life-saving, water safety, and first aid. Through its National Aquatic Schools, the Red Cross certifies teachers of swimming, life-saving, first aid, and small-craft handling. Basic courses in rowing, canoeing, and sailing are also offered to community groups by many Red Cross chapters; this organization also issues a number of publications promoting safe boating.

Other organizations which contribute to the development of safe boating in the United States include: (1) the U.S. Coast Guard Auxiliary, an organization of volunteer boatmen who work closely with the U.S. Coast Guard in providing education in seamanship, safety, and small-boat handling and conduct courtesy examinations of pleasure craft; (2) the U.S. Power Squadron, a volunteer organization whose members offer courses in small-boat handling, piloting, and navigation and which cooperates in the enforcement of boating laws (usually working through community adult education and recreation departments); and (3) the Outboard Boating Club of America, which provides similar services for this type of craft.

Other special-interest organizations are concerned with promoting open space and park programs in urban settings. One such example, in New York City, has been the Council for Parks and Playgrounds. Founded in 1962, this council is a nonprofit, tax-exempt organization that is

dedicated to promoting the widespread adoption of imaginative, safe and practical playground design, the preservation and expansion of park land and the formulation of novel, fulfilling and substantial recreation programs.[9]

Supported by over forty affiliated community groups concerned with local park and recreation needs, the Council (operating solely through funds contributed by its membership) (1) testifies at city budget hearings, (2) sponsors tours around city playgrounds and parks, (3) sponsors vest-pocket parks, mobile recreation units, and sports clinics, (4) promotes green-belt development and opposes encroachment on existing open space and park land, (5) carries out studies of park maintenance and presses for improved maintenance, (6) examines facilities in other cities in order to make innovative recommendations, and (7) promotes public awareness of outdoor recreation needs and fights for a higher priority to facilities acquisition and development programs.

In some cities, public recreation and park programs are also supported by community councils or councils of social agencies. These organizations generally represent major civic groups and voluntary and public agencies that provide services in the areas of aging, youth needs, children's day camps, health, education, and welfare, and antipoverty programs. Some, like the Youth Services and Planning Council in Los Angeles, focus especially on children and youth in the community. This council is particularly concerned with developing guides for youth services and evaluating existing services effectively. Through contracts with the Board of Education and City Council in Los Angeles, the Youth Services and Planning Council has carried out a number of major studies related to the more effective planning of recreation and other social services for youth. Councils of this type

9 *Annual Report of the Council for Parks and Playgrounds*, New York, 1968.

also serve to coordinate recreation, education, and group-work services among various agencies in the urban setting.

On the national scene, the task of coordinating the work of special-interest organizations in the park, conservation, and recreation field is carried out by the Natural Resources Council of America. This body combines thirty nonprofit associations and societies, all of which are active in outdoor recreation and conservation, including the World Wildlife Fund, Association, the American Fisheries Society, and the North American Wild-the American Conservation Association, the National Recreation and Park life Foundation. Total individual memberships in these organizations add up to more than two million public-spirited citizens. While they may have varying special concerns, all of them have an involvement with outdoor recreation. The Natural Resources Council, since its members have diverse and sometimes conflicting points of view, does not promote specific policy or engage in lobbying. Instead, its focus is on achieving mutual understanding and bringing about more effective public education within the broad field of conservation and outdoor recreation.

Voluntary Organizations Serving the Ill and Disabled

Another important category of voluntary organization in American communities today is concerned with meeting the needs of individuals with special limitations, such as the mentally retarded, the emotionally ill, and the physically handicapped or disabled.

While many public park and recreation departments have begun to establish special services to meet the leisure needs of such groups, the primary responsibility for initiating community action in this broad area has been assumed by voluntary agencies. Organizations like the American Cerebral Palsy Association or the National Association for Retarded Children have pressed vigorously to provide special services for the disabled. In many cases, local chapters of these voluntary organizations have encouraged municipal park and recreation agencies to expand their programs to include groups suffering from disability. They have urged the adoption of facilities standards which would prevent disabled persons from being excluded from participation because of physical barriers. Such voluntary organizations have established after-care centers, such as social clubs or half-way houses to provide counseling, vocational, and social programs for discharged mental patients. Organizations serving the mentally retarded have established sheltered workshops and social groups for retarded teen-agers and young adults in community life. In various other types of rehabilitation centers, recreation is today being provided to meet important needs of the disabled.

Typically, there has been a rapid expansion of Golden Age Clubs and social centers for aging persons during the 1960's; by the end of the decade,

1,200 such programs had been established throughout the country, chiefly by churches, local service organizations and other voluntary agencies.[10] A fuller description of recreational programs serving the ill and disabled is provided in Chapter 17; it is clear that voluntary agencies have provided a major portion of the impetus in this field.

PRIVATE AGENCIES PROVIDING RECREATION PROGRAMS

A major portion of recreational opportunity today is provided by private membership organizations. Within the broad field of sport and outdoor recreation, there are many organizations which provide facilities and organized services related to hunting or fishing, skiing, tennis, golf, and boating. Such clubs frequently exist as independent incorporated bodies, owning their own facilities, with policy set by elected officers or boards and with the actual work of maintenance, instruction, or supervision carried on by paid employees. Usually, membership policies are established which screen out those who might not be compatible with others in the club. Such private recreation and social organizations are often able to provide more extensive and varied services than public or voluntary agencies can. A golf club, for example, is usually less crowded and more attractively designed and carefully maintained than public courses; it is also more expensive. In the early 1960's, there were 3,300 country clubs in the United States—as an example of private recreation organizations. They had 1.7 million members who paid $250 million annual dues and consumed $500 million in food and beverages each year. Although recent statistics are not available, undoubtedly this figure has climbed sharply during the past several years.

In addition, many new forms of restricted leisure programs have come into being based on real estate ownership. Many real estate developers today have recognized that one of the key selling points in home-development projects is the provision of attractive recreational facilities. In many cities and suburban areas, apartment house or garden apartment developers have accompanied their projects with elaborate recreation facilities and programs (see Chapter 14). This is also true in many retirement communities, where recreational programs and club activities of all types are provided—usually with direction from a residents' council and a professional staff.

Another example of private recreational programs is the rapid growth of apartments designed for young men and women who are single and of a marriageable age. Often such buildings have lounges and social rooms, swimming pools, and saunas; they may also have actual programs of activ-

[10] Nancy N. Anderson, *Senior Centers: Information from a National Survey*, Report of Institute for Interdisciplinary Studies, American Rehabilitation Foundation, Minneapolis, June, 1969.

ities and events. What is important to recognize is that only those who can afford the cost of private recreation opportunities (in terms of rentals or membership fees) can avail themselves of such programs. In large measure, such individuals become less dependent on publicly sponsored recreation facilities and services. And since their needs are met through private programs, they are less likely to see the need for, or to strongly support, public programs.

COMMERCIAL RECREATION PROGRAMS

By far the largest amount of recreational participation in the United States today is offered by commercial enterprises. Such opportunities may be classified in various ways:

1. *Facilities and Areas for Self-Directed Activity:* Golf courses, swimming pools, ski centers, ice rinks, bars and taverns, bowling alleys, billiard parlors, riding stables, fish preserves, driving ranges, camp grounds, and boat marinas. In each of these, the individual is more or less active in providing his own recreation.

2. *Facilities of Enterprises Providing Entertainment:* Here the consumer is entertained in a generally passive way; this category includes theaters, indoor and outdoor movies, concert halls, nightclubs with floor shows, commercial sports stadiums, circuses, fairs, amusement parks, race tracks, carnivals, and similar enterprises.

3. *Commercial Enterprises Providing Instructional Services.* This includes special schools, studios, or health centers that give instruction in music, dancing, the arts, physical fitness (including gymnastics, trampoline centers, judo classes, and other forms of self-defense), riding schools, and similar enterprises.

4. *Commercial Enterprises Manufacturing Recreation Equipment.* A major portion of what people do for personal recreation in their homes and neighborhoods does not require special facilities or instructional services but does involve the purchase of special equipment or materials. Thus, musical equipment (phonograph records and players, tape recorders, instruments, and sheet music), toys, games, gardening equipment, books, magazines, radio and television sets, special clothing for play, barbecue cooking equipment, and a host of other products all represent a form of commercial recreation involvement.

As indicated earlier, all of these forms of opportunities, facilities, equipment, and services make possible a vast bulk of leisure participation by people of all ages. Chetkow comments:

It would appear that every aspect of recreation activities is being, or has already been, commercialized. In many instances (bowling, outdoor camping, tourism), commercial operators have capitalized on the original leadership of nonprofit recreation agencies. . . . If commercial recreation continues to program creatively, it may well remain a major provider of recreation services for years to come.[11]

A final category of recreation sponsorship involves the role of industry. In a sense, programs of recreational and social participation which are provided by major industrial firms for their employees fit none of the previous categories. They are obviously nongovernmental. They are not voluntary in the sense that they are organized by or in connection with profit-making organizations to promote the total efficiency of the business enterprise. Yet, they are not commercial, in that the recreation operation itself is not intended to make a profit. Perhaps they are closest to private recreation programs provided for specific memberships on a nonprofit basis.

INDUSTRIAL RECREATION SPONSORSHIP

Employee recreation began during the nineteenth century but expanded rapidly in the United States only after World War II. It was estimated by the *Wall Street Journal* in 1953 that expenditures by business and industry for employee recreation amounted to $800 million annually. By 1963, statistics compiled by the Philadelphia District Federal Reserve Bank estimated that company contributions to employee recreation programs were in excess of a billion dollars a year; two years later the sum was estimated at $1.5 billion. The leading organization in this field, the National Industrial Recreation Association, today serves 840 major companies which provide extensive recreation programs for their employees. In 1967, this organization (a nationwide nonprofit association organized by industry to assist in the development and coordination of employee recreation) estimated that there were 1,000 full-time industrial recreation directors and 500 park and recreation center managers employed by industries throughout the United States. Over all, N.I.R.A. estimates that there are 150 company-owned golf courses, 400 company-owned parks and camps, and 100 company recreation centers.

Three major purposes may be cited which justify making recreation an important aspect of industrial personnel programs:

1. *Improvement of Employer-Employee Relations.* At an earlier period in American industrial development, there was considerable friction between management and labor, often resulting in drawn-out and violent strikes. A major purpose of industrial recreation programs at this time was to create a favorable employer-employee relationship and to create a sense of loyalty among workers. Today, with relative peace in most industries, it is still an important purpose of employee recreation programs to establish

[11] B. Harold Chetkow, "Creative Programing in Commercial Recreation," *Parks and Recreation*, September, 1966, p. 698; see also John R. Thompson, "The Giant Nobody Knows," *Parks and Recreation*, March, 1968, p. 24.

harmonious relationships among personnel on all levels, within industries and business concerns. Specifically, it is believed to improve worker morale and foster good human relations among various levels of employees.

2. *Promoting Employee Efficiency.* It is generally believed that a constructive program of employee recreation improves worker performance. Personnel experts have found that when workers spend their free time at constructive recreational activities, absenteeism due to employees' emotional tension or illness, alcoholic overindulgence, or similar causes is reduced. Similarly, recreation helps combat workers' fatigue and boredom and thus reduces accident rates. American firms are not the only ones which take a major interest in providing recreational opportunities for their employees for such reasons. Many European firms do the same. As a single example, the Duhamel Textile Company at Harnes, in northern France, operates a handsome modern chalet near Grenoble, with an elaborate ski and winter-sports recreation center for employees who visit the chalet in groups of forty for four-week stays throughout the winter months. To make this program possible, employees voluntarily work an extra half-hour a day without pay through the full year. When they are at the ski center, they sew from 7 to 10 A.M., ski until 4 P.M., and then work for three hours more. There are many variations of this program, as well as extensive sports leagues and cultural activities sponsored by other European industries.

3. *Recruitment Appeal.* A closely linked purpose is that employee recreation programs assist firms seeking to recruit workers. In today's seller's market for skilled personnel, recreation is one of the lures held out to those considering employment. Particularly when an industry is a considerable distance from metropolitan centers and when adequate publicly sponsored park and recreation services are not available, it becomes virtually necessary for the industry itself to provide leisure opportunities.

There are a number of different administrative arrangements under which employee recreation is carried on. In some cases, the management provides facilities and leadership and maintains complete control of the operation. In other situations, they may provide only facilities, with an employee recreation association taking actual responsibility for administering the program. Frequently, profits from canteens and plant vending machines provide financial support for the program, along with moderate fees for participation.

A wide range of activities is provided in industrial recreation programs. The Teletype Company, a large concern in Skokie, Illinois, began in 1937 with 778 members in its recreation association; today there are approximately 5,800. The organization sponsors twenty clubs catering to varied interests and many sports leagues for both men and women. Such activities as basketball, bowling, softball, horseshoes, golf, tennis, and various hobby clubs are most popular, along with many tournaments and special events during the year. As many as 4,800 people attend club picnics or annual

Christmas parties at a single time. Varied trip programs, including European tours, are also part of the club's activities.

Other examples of current employee recreation may be found in governmental agencies. For example, the Brookhaven National Laboratory, a research center of the Atomic Energy Commission located in Brookhaven, New York, has about 3,500 employees, most of whom reside either directly on the property of the laboratory or in directly adjacent communities. The Brookhaven Laboratory maintains an extensive recreation program for all personnel. Facilities include a recreation building with a large gymnasium, a lecture hall, and a theater, lounges and social rooms, four softball fields, six tennis courts, a swimming pool, and many other areas for play. Organized activities include the following: archery, art exhibits, basketball league, bowling league, camera club, camping club, concerts, cooking courses, dances, fencing, fishing, folk-dancing and folk-singing groups, golf, judo, movies, picnics, rifle and pistol club, ski club, skin-diving, softball league, sports car club, theater group, touch football league, and volleyball league.

The program is administered by a recreation director hired by the personnel division of the laboratory. Assistance in carrying it out is provided by the Employee's Recreation Association. Membership is normally open to employees and their families, with some activities or special events open to outsiders by invitation.

This program is fairly typical of the recreation operation carried on within many large industrial plants. It also illustrates the fact that many government agencies are promoting extensive recreation programs for their employees. In 1957, agencies in Washington, D.C., formed a federation of recreation associations. This has since grown to over fifty, including such agencies as the Bureau of the Budget, Department of Labor, Department of Justice, and many similar groups, with a total membership of 120,000. The League of Federal Recreation Associations is a nonprofit organization, incorporated under the laws of the District of Columbia; it promotes various forms of cultural activities, sports, travel, welfare training, and publications for Federal employees. It has worked closely with the National Symphony Orchestra, the American Light Opera Company, and major sports organizations and concert bureaus to provide entertainment and cultural events for government employees at low cost. It organizes trip programs throughout the United States and abroad, sponsors sports leagues with hundreds of teams, and promotes other hobbies, social events, service activities, and courses.

Union-Sponsored Recreation Programs

In addition to industrial concerns, a number of leading labor unions sponsor extensive recreation programs and promote community recreation activities. Their interest has stemmed from four major factors:

1. Labor contracts over the past several decades have shortened the work week and provided extended vacations and improved retirement and pension benefits. Thus, unions have created huge bulks of leisure for their members. They recognize that it is essential that this time be used constructively and fruitfully; from a very realistic point of view, when workers are bored with their leisure, many tend to "moonlight" by taking second jobs, defeating the objective of creating more opportunities within each field of employment.

2. Labor unions recognize an important responsibility for the promotion of effective government programs in the broad field of social welfare. This includes stimulating and supporting local, statewide, and Federal efforts in recreation, community education, and conservation. A number of leading industrial unions have spearheaded political action in these areas.

3. Since the nineteenth century, labor unions have urged the promotion of leisure activities which help workers improve their education and intellectual development, enrich themselves culturally, and take on more effective citizenship roles. Programs related to adult recreation and education have been part of this effort.

4. Finally, just as in the case of industry-sponsored programs, unions have seen recreation activities as an ideal means of improving the loyalty and cohesiveness of their members. After World War II, many unions had a serious recruitment problem; the unionized percentage of the nonfarm labor force declined from a high of 35.1 percent in 1954 to 28.9 percent in 1964. Recreation has been seen as one of the important benefits that unions can bring to their members, and a means of promoting membership involvement; thus a number of the largest unions have been active in promoting recreation programs.

A leading example of such unions has been the United Automobile Workers. Recently, the UAW's president, Walter Reuther, announced the establishment of a new Department of Conservation and Resource Development; the name of the UAW Recreation Department was changed to the Department of Recreation and Leisure-Time Activities. A special eight-man Conservation and Recreation Committee was established by the UAW International Executive Board, and local unions are now playing a more active role in the following areas: (1) sponsoring and supporting local programs to solve air and water pollution, (2) supporting legislation in these areas, and in open-space development, (3) providing comprehensive education and leisure programs related to camping and conservation, family needs, and coordination with social service agencies, and (4) improving recreational services in deprived urban areas. The United Automobile workers recently initiated a new program in Detroit titled DART (Deprived Areas Recreation Team) to develop a network of vest-pocket parks by providing financial assistance and working with neighborhood organizations in inner-city areas. DART has also worked closely with the

Parks and Recreation Commission in Detroit to promote a citywide federation of neighborhood groups concerned with recreation and conservation.

Another active union in this field has been the International Ladies Garment Workers Union. The I.L.G.W.U. operates a $10-million vacation camp, Camp Unity, in Pennsylvania, for its members. The camp has seventy-eight buildings (including a million-dollar theater, a large administration building and dining room seating 1,100 guests, a health club, tennis courts, and a beach on a sparkling mile-long lake) plus a full activity program including such cultural activities as adult education and discussion groups, forums and classical music events. The I.L.G.W.U. has traditionally had a strong concern with promoting social-action programs. At the union's national convention in 1968, for example, its president, Jacob Potofsky, announced that it would donate $350,000 to the new Urban Coalition to help improve recreation facilities in urban slums. He stated:

In past years, one cause of the aggravated tensions in the cities during summer months has been a terrible lack of recreational facilities. Just a few dollars wisely spent could have saved uncounted costs in damage and destruction from people frustrated in their real grievances. . . . We must provide the children and young unemployed adults with facilities for recreation, education and entertainment—all the things that will keep them occupied and off the streets during the summer months.[12]

It is apparent, then, that a substantial portion of the leisure needs of many American citizens are met by programs provided by industrial firms and labor organizations. In addition, the role played by business and labor in promoting effective social action and open-space programs has helped to develop a groundswell of popular support for legislative sponsorship of such programs.

GOALS AND PROFESSIONALISM

This chapter and the preceding two have described in detail the four major categories of agencies that provide recreational facilities and programs in the United States today: public, voluntary, private, and commercial.

Both public and voluntary agencies exist primarily to meet the needs of the public at large. In the case of recreation departments sponsored by government on any level, programs operate under policies shaped by boards or advisory councils that have as a primary concern the public welfare. Although voluntary agencies may have more specialized purposes and are somewhat more independent with respect to policy, they too have a strong sense of values and social purpose.

[12] "Clothing Workers to Donate $350,000 for Slum Recreation," New York *Times*, May 26, 1968, p. 24.

In contrast, private and commercial recreation agencies do not have such altruistic purposes. Private organizations exist to meet the recreational and social wishes of their members, while commercial concerns are basically out to make a profit for their stockholders. Such a statement does not imply condemnation of either type of agency. Many of them provide wholesome and enjoyable entertainment or the opportunities for healthy and desirable sports, cultural activities, travel, or other leisure activities. In some cases, manufacturers and commercial providers of recreational services cooperate fully with public and voluntary recreation officials, aiding or subsidizing desirable community services; a number have also become affiliated with the National Recreation and Park Association.

However, public and voluntary agencies are generally regarded as being part of the recreation movement, in a formal sense, while private and commercial organizations are not. This is evidenced not only by the objectives they seek but also by their attitude toward the use of trained personnel. Because public and voluntary recreation practitioners are part of a social movement, they generally are expected to have special education that will equip them to operate as professionals; they are also usually affiliated with a field of professional practice and with its professional organizations.

This suggests that an extremely important element of organized recreation service today has to do with the training, background, and qualifications of those who staff public and voluntary recreation and park agencies. The following chapter examines this topic in detail, outlining the past development of professionalism in recreation and its current status, problems, and trends.

5

Professionalism in Recreation and Parks

The previous chapters have outlined the growth of recreation programs throughout the United States. Accompanying this expansion, the career field of professional leadership in recreation and park agencies has also grown rapidly. In 1965, Sylvia Porter, the financial columnist, stated:

As we move toward the peak recreation season of the year, the soaring profits-and-paycheck importance of "fun" in the United States emerges with brilliant clarity. . . . Today's surge in travel, sports, vacation, etc., has become a major creator of jobs—going far beyond the familiar categories of camp counselors, lifeguard, park ranger and the like.

Recreation, in sum, is becoming a big, booming, professional business—dazzling even the most optimistic projections of a few years ago—and it'll become bigger, boomier and more professional year after year.[1]

In the same year the U.S. Department of Labor issued a special *Occupational Outlook Quarterly* which dealt with recreation as a growing field of employment. The chief of the Labor Department's Occupational Outlook Service pointed out that there had been a more than 500 percent increase in spending on recreation since 1940, in contrast with the 45 percent population growth in the United States during the period. He documented employment in several leisure-connected fields: (1) radio and television broadcasting and manufacturing (200,000 persons); (2) travel resorts, including hotels, tourist courts, and motels (500,000 persons); and (3) manufacturing of toys, games, and sporting goods (90,000 persons).

[1] Sylvia Porter, "The Business of Fun," New York *Post*, May 14, 1965, p. 42.

Over all the *Quarterly* pointed out that the provision of leisure services involved employment of professionally trained workers in sixty different occupations.[2] However, not all those employed in the delivery of entertainment or leisure services should be regarded as recreation professionals. It is important that a distinction be made between two categories of individuals:

1. *The Broad Field of Leisure Services.* There is a broad field of involvement that includes manufacturing, travel, amusements, and entertainment, the operation of resorts, nightclubs and restaurants, and similar attractions. While those who are employed in these fields owe their careers to the public's desire for recreation (whether they are airplane pilots, motel managers, television repairmen, golf professionals, or marine biologists), they may hardly be regarded as recreation professionals.

2. *Specific Employment in Recreation Roles.* More narrowly, one might identify those public and voluntary agencies whose direct function is to provide nonprofit recreational services and opportunities and who employ individuals in leadership, supervisory, and administrative roles. Such persons are generally regarded as recreation professionals—assuming that they have appropriate educational qualifications and are employed at a professional level of service.

How many such individuals are there in the United States? In 1960, the first national survey of the social welfare field indicated that 116,000 persons were employed as social welfare workers, of whom 10,450 were identified as recreation leaders in government and voluntary agencies.[3] In 1965, Department of Labor studies indicated that the figure had grown rapidly. McCollum reported:

About 35,000 recreation workers were employed full time in 1965, the majority working for local governments and voluntary agencies. Most of the remainder were employed by religious organizations and by the Federal government in the National Parks, the Armed Forces, correctional institutions, and the Veterans Administration. Some recreational workers were employed by industry and a few by colleges and universities in teaching positions. . . . Shortages existed in all parts of the country for trained recreation workers, the need being particularly great in local governments, hospitals, and youth-serving organizations. Opportunities for recreation workers are expected to grow rapidly at least through the mid 1970's.[4]

A fuller analysis of employment in public, voluntary, and commercial recreation agencies was carried out by the National Recreation and Park Association, under a grant from the Administration on Aging of the U.S.

[2] Ego Ambre, "Recreation in Review," *Occupational Outlook Quarterly*, May, 1965, pp. 24-26.
[3] W. C. Sutherland, "Social Welfare Manpower Study," *Recreation*, October, 1961, p. 411.
[4] William J. McCollum, "Employment Outlook for Recreation Workers," in *Occupational Outlook Quarterly*, May, 1965, pp. 18-20.

Department of Health, Education and Welfare.[5] This 1968 report was based upon a stratified random sample of known public, county, and special districts with park and recreation programs, as well as reports from a variety of governmental, voluntary, and professional organizations. Over all, it found that there were approximately 1.4 million full-time and part-time workers in recreation; converted to full-time equivalents, the total was 949,431 persons.

These totals were broken down as follows. Employment in the public sector (over one-half of these persons were employed by local government) totaled 303,841 workers. There were 190,000 workers in the private non-profit sector and 455,590 in the commercial field. Specific totals were given for major Federal agencies in outdoor recreation, for branches of the armed forces, for state hospital recreation personnel, for Scouts, Y's, settlement-house workers, and many fields of commercial employment. This report should be viewed with reservations for three reasons: (1) many of the figures cited represent estimates, rather than actual head counts; in some cases they are projections of earlier totals, based on past rates of growth; (2) a number of the agencies cited, particularly in the voluntary agency field, do not regard themselves primarily as *recreation* agencies; and (3) the report includes *all* employees, including administrative, supervisory, research, maintenance, engineering, clerical, enforcement officials, and various other types of workers. For these reasons the 1968 Manpower Study should be regarded as an umbrella-like estimate of employment in the broad recreation field, rather than a precise tabulation.

The *1966 Recreation and Park Yearbook* reported that there were in the mid-1960's approximately 65,000 full-time year-round and 178,000 seasonal and part-time recreation and park workers in American city and county agencies, a total of 243,000 paid workers.[6] If one adds Federal, state, and voluntary agency personnel and allows for growth during the late 1960's, it would seem reasonable to assume that between 150,000 and 200,000 individuals are employed today in full-time, year-round nonprofit public and private agencies, with a primary concern for the provision of recreation facilities and services.

It is the purpose of this chapter to examine this field as an area of professional service and to determine its strengths and weaknesses as well as its present and future trends.

Characteristics of a Profession

Exactly what is a profession? Paul Douglass suggests that it is a body of career practitioners who by specialized education and skills assume the

[5] Donald E. Hawkins (project director), *Supply/Demand Study, Professional and Pre-Professional Recreation and Park Occupations* (Washington, D.C.: National Recreation and Park Association, March, 1968).

[6] *Recreation and Park Yearbook, 1966* (Washington, D.C.: National Recreation and Park Association, 1967), p. 56.

responsibility and power needed to (1) certify the adequate preparation of personnel and (2) assure ethical performance in the course of duty within a field of service that is regarded as a public trust.[7] These and a number of related aspects of professionalism are analyzed in the following pages in terms of the most recent developments in park and recreation practice.

Public Recognition of the Field. The rapid expansion of the field of recreation and park service provides evidence that there is public awareness of the need for organized recreation service and readiness to support programs manned by professionals in this field. There is also evidence, however, that the public is not yet fully aware of recreation as a distinct area of professional service. The problem, as Goodale sees it, is one of image:

Ask any high school senior to locate and identify a doctor. He might reply: "You'll find him in his office or the hospital, probably wearing a white jacket and carrying a black bag." An architect? "At his office drawing plans or at the site inspecting and supervising construction." A recreator? "A what?"

Most young people, by the time they start sorting through career possibilities, have met and been in contact with many recreation professionals, with perhaps one of two results—they don't identify those they've met as recreation professionals, or they don't project or envision the profession beyond the camp, pool, or playground with which they are familiar.[8]

In part, this lack of public understanding of the field is based on the way in which it came into being. As later chapters will make clear, when the playground movement came into being, it was heavily based on programs for young children operated by public school systems on an after-school or summer vacation basis. Many physical educators assumed responsibility for these early playground programs; usually they were required to take courses in game leadership and playground supervision as part of their training in physical education methods. Many state departments of education at this time established certification requirements for physical educators which included courses in the theory and skills and recreation leadership.

When the number of positions for full-time, year-round recreation administrators increased, those who filled these positions also tended to be drawn from the field of physical education. Many college departments of health, physical education, and recreation were established, and municipal school systems and state departments of education hired directors or supervisors of health, physical education, and recreation. Thus, from the beginning, recreation has been closely attached to physical education as a career field.

[7] Paul Douglass, "The Profession of Recreation on the Threshold of the Aesthetic Age," address at National Recreation Congress, Minneapolis, October, 1965.
[8] Thomas L. Goodale, "The Manpower Muddle," *Parks and Recreation,* February, 1969, p. 29.

A second field which has been closely linked to recreation is social work. Many pioneers in the settlement houses and youth-serving organizations of the late 1800's and early 1900's assumed that their concern with meeting the individual and group needs of participants included a major emphasis on organized recreational activity. At the outset, no sharp distinction was made between recreation workers and social workers. As late as the 1920's and 1930's, the development of group work theory and method brought together social workers, recreation workers, and educators in a mutually shared effort. Brodsky comments, "It was an unprecedented working collaboration. . . . It was also short-lived, lasting only until academic and professional loyalties began to harden and the separate fields began to move off along their own lines of emphasis."[9]

After World War II, a sharp distinction was drawn between the two fields. Social workers developed a body of theory based heavily on Freudian psychology and its offshoots and a major concern with individuals and groups who required special assistance—particularly the poor, the handicapped, and those with problems of psychosocial adjustment. By contrast, recreation leaders assumed the function of providing large-scale, communitywide programs for the public at large. They were less concerned with group process, the interaction of participants, or meeting pressing social needs in disadvantaged communities. Even today, however, there is a continuing linkage between the two fields. Many social work agencies carry on extensive programs of recreational activity; indeed, they tend to rely on recreation in many cases to attract participants who may then be involved in other kinds of services. Similarly, some recreation departments employ social workers to carry out special programs with groups that pose particularly difficult problems.

A third area of professional service which has been traditionally linked to recreation is park administration. During the early decades of municipal, state, and Federal park development, most park executives received their training in fields related to the management or design of physical resources —i.e., civil engineering, landscape architecture, forestry, or conservation. At the outset, they had comparatively little direct concern with recreation functions. However, the need to provide recreation facilities and programs requiring supervision and leadership became recognized by the bulk of park agencies, particularly on the municipal and county levels. Recreation was established as a division of special service within many park boards and commissions. In other cases, separate recreation and park departments operated side by side in larger cities, with the park department operating the facilities and the recreation department conducting the program.

Gradually, the most common form of municipal agency in this field became the merged park and recreation department with both areas of re-

[9] Irving Brodsky, "Problems and Perspectives in Group Work and Recreation Services," *American Recreation Journal*, April, 1962.

sponsibility under a single administrative head. As later sections will show, this trend has done much to unify the recreation and park field and to lend it status and identity in the public eye.

However, the concept of a single career field concerned with the provision of organized recreational services to the public is not yet clearly understood or accepted. In part, it is because recreation programs, when carried on by some public agencies, tend to be masked under other titles and descriptions. In many hospitals, recreation has been labeled as occupational therapy or as part of physical rehabilitation. In school programs it is often described as "informal" or "community" education or youth services. The major thrust of the Federal and state open-space programs of the 1960's was often attached to such titles as natural beauty or conservation rather than outdoor recreation. Thus, recreation has been part of many other programs but not clearly recognized in its own right as an integral form of service.

A closely related problem is that recreation professionals themselves have assumed such a wide variety of roles that no single clear image stands out. Sessoms comments that "we would like to be all things to all people: entertainers, promoters, counselors, psychiatrist aides, and social analysts." He writes:

I am afraid the public sees us either as ex-athletes, or gregarious, fun-and-game leaders wearing short pants, knee socks, and an Alpine hat, calling for all to join in.[10]

Fortunately, this narrow view of the profession is rapidly changing. With the increasing number of park and recreation agencies on all levels of government and with the growth of college and university curriculums specializing in this field, the public is gaining fuller awareness of it as a profession. What remains is for the field itself to clarify its role, so that a single clear image emerges.

Who is the recreation professional today, and what role does he play? In a major community agency (such as a public park and recreation department or school-operated program), the recreation professional is likely to be regarded as an individual holding a college degree in recreation or a related field, employed as an administrator or high-level supervisor. Depending on the size and scope of his department, he needs competence in such areas as the planning, design, construction, and maintenance of facilities, the recruitment, hiring, training, and evaluating of personnel, the supervision and administration of program services, program evaluation, budgetary procedures and reporting, the process of working effectively with

[10] H. Douglas Sessoms, "A Critical Look at the Recreation Movement," in *Recreation for the Ill and Handicapped* (Washington, D.C.: National Association of Recreation Therapists, July, 1965), pp. 11, 14.

municipal councils or boards and civic groups, and, finally, effective public relations and departmental promotion.

In other kinds of settings, the recreation professional may be an administrator of a major program related to rehabilitative service, multiservice programming for aging persons, adult education and recreation, or extensive cultural activities. He may also find himself involved, not as a direct practitioner but as a consultant, for a private organization or state agency, as a research specialist, as a planner, or in similar capacities. Thus, the task of recreation professionals has become more complex and demanding—and more worthy of recognition and status. Today, those who enter this field must have specialized training, if they are to operate effectively.

Professional Preparation in Recreation and Park Service

Although specialized training in recreation and park administration was available as early as the 1920's, through a one-year graduate training institute sponsored by the National Recreation Association, it was not until the late 1930's that colleges and universities began to develop curriculums in this field of professional service. After World War II, a number of colleges and universities initiated undergraduate and graduate recreation majors—usually as part of departments of health and physical education. By 1950, there were approximately fifty colleges that offered recreation majors. Through the decade and a half that followed, this figure remained relatively stable. In the mid-1960's, however, following the strong stimulus given to the merged park and recreation movement by Federal and space programs of resource development and the steady expansion of municipal recreation and park programs, a strong spurt in recreation and park enrollments was noted. In 1966, seventy-seven colleges reported 1,246 graduates; Sessoms wrote:

Enrollments in recreation and park administration are up. At every degree level there was significant increase in the number of students pursuing the recreation degree. The number of students identified as recreation majors was 4,274. Of these, 3,512 are pursuing the bachelor's degree. In 1963, the average undergraduate enrollment per major program was thirty-seven; this year there were forty-eight majors per institution.[11]

This expansion of professional preparation in recreation and parks continued on an abrupt upswing. In 1967, the Commission on Professional Preparation of the Recreation Division of the American Association for Health, Physical Education and Recreation identified 103 colleges and universities with an undergraduate curriculum in recreation and/or park

[11] H. Douglas Sessoms, "Recreation Enrollment Growth Reported," *Parks and Recreation*, October, 1966, pp. 867-69.

administration.[12] The most recent survey of colleges and universities in the recreation and park field was carried out as part of the National Recreation and Park Association 1968 manpower study, cited earlier. This report indicated that there were 183 colleges and universities offering recreation and park major programs; of these, 45 were two-year colleges, representing an important new trend. The report stated that 76 other colleges and universities indicated their intention to start a recreation curriculum by 1970, with 86 additional institutions reporting that they would start such a program by 1980.

Thus, there has been a dramatic and sudden growth in professional preparation in recreation and parks. There is, however, a continued need to clarify the objectives of professional preparation in recreation and parks, and to improve curricular content, organization, and staffing.

A number of conferences related to the establishment of standards and curriculum guides in recreation education were held during the 1940's and 1950's. One such conference was sponsored in 1962 by the American Association for Health, Physical Education and Recreation.[13] It provided guides for the development of both undergraduate and graduate recreation curriculums. For example, on the baccalaureate level, it suggested that 50 percent of required courses should be in *general education* (the humanities, language arts, physical and social sciences); 17 percent in courses related to *recreation education* (in such areas as group process, business procedures, human growth and development); and 33 percent in *professional recreation* courses (concepts of leisure, history of the recreation movement, place of recreation in the community, role of the leader, development of leadership skill, organization and administration of park and recreation programs and facilities, ability to train, supervise, and utilize both volunteers and professionals, and ability to work with community groups and to interpret the recreation department's objectives and role to others). On the graduate level, five areas were stressed as major concerns: philosophy and principles of recreation, administration of recreation, research and evaluation, personnel management, and public relations.

A second major project intended to upgrade higher education in recreation and parks has been the National Recreation Education Accreditation Project.[14] This effort was undertaken by the Federation of National Professional Organizations for Recreation in 1963 with a threefold purpose: (1) to develop a basic statement for presentation to the National Com-

---

[12] Jackson M. Anderson, *Annual Survey of Undergraduate and Graduate Curriculums in Recreation and Park Administration* (Washington, D.C.: American Association for Health, Physical Education and Recreation, October, 1967).

[13] *Professional Preparation in Health Education, Physical Education and Recreation Education* (Washington, D.C.: Conference Report, American Association for Health, Physical Education and Recreation, 1962), pp. 86-102.

[14] *Standards and Evaluative Criteria, National Recreation Education Accreditation Project*, Federation of National Professional Organizations for Recreation, March, 1965.

mission on Accrediting which would support recreation as a significant field of public service and as a profession, to justify having institutions preparing practitioners in this field accredited, to protect the public from substandard practice; (2) to develop standards and evaluative criteria for recreation education at both undergraduate and graduate levels; and (3) to raise funds to finance the completion of the standards and carry out the actual process of accreditation.

In 1965, the Recreation Education Accreditation Committee presented its first recommendations. On the undergraduate level, it urged that colleges prepare administrators for one of three settings: (1) general recreation program administration, (2) administration in joint recreation and park systems, or (3) administration with major responsibility for physical resource development and operation. On the graduate level, the Committee recommended that there be six possible options for specialization, including (1) recreation program supervision and administration in public or voluntary agencies, (2) recreation and park administration in municipal, county, and state agencies, (3) recreation resources administration, usually for a county, state, or Federal agency, with emphasis on physical sciences, ecology, and planning competence, (4) camping administration, (5) college union administration, and (6) therapeutic recreation administration. The Committee suggested that the purpose of doctoral programs was to develop top-level administrators, university educators, research and planning specialists, and consultants.

Under each of the recommended standards, the National Recreation Education Accreditation Committee proposed general guides for approved practices, as well as specific criteria through which college departments might be judged. The Committee's work has done much to stimulate colleges and universities to upgrade their practices in recreation education. Certain problems, however, continue to exist with respect to professional education.

A major problem is the danger of course repetition on three levels of professional study: undergraduate, master's, and doctoral. It is necessary to clarify the differences among these three levels of education. Undergraduate programs should provide a broad base of general education and the core of essential knowledge related to recreation as organized community service. Master's degree study should provide more advanced work in administration, an opportunity for specialization in one of the optional areas of service, and a research sequence which establishes a preliminary competence in this area. The doctoral level should focus heavily upon specialization in an advanced area of study and on research, planning, or consultation training.

The Growth of Community College Programs. A significant recent trend in professional education in recreation and parks has been the emergence of community colleges offering associate degrees in recreation. This development reflects two factors: (1) the rapid expansion of two-year colleges on the American educational scene and (2) the need to prepare individuals for direct leadership and program services (recognizing that most graduates of four-year programs are now moving directly into administrative roles). Verhoven comments:

Almost overnight, the junior college movement has skyrocketed to take its place as an established institution designed to meet the educational, social and vocational needs of the individual in today's complex technological society. Although the junior college was only established at the turn of the century, more than 800 two-year institutions are today meeting the needs of over one million students. Recent statistics of the American Association of Junior Colleges showed that "more than one student in every four beginning his program of higher education in the United States enrolled in a junior college."[15]

The term "junior college" was first used to describe two-year college programs. At the outset, it referred to privately operated institutions, often for young people of well-to-do families who were not sufficiently motivated academically to attend four-year colleges. Community colleges represent a later development, in which colleges were developed (often under public auspices) to provide transfer programs from which a person might transfer to a four-year college, or to provide terminal occupational training programs in specific areas of personnel shortages. Because of the shortage of leadership personnel in the recreation and park field, many community colleges are now preparing their graduates to move into technicians' roles.

Some professionals fear that the awarding of subprofessional degrees may lead to a downgrading of practice in parks and recreation. Verhoven points out, however, that in other areas there is an important role for subprofessionals; for example, doctors have medical technologists and nurses are assisted by practical nurses. In recreation and parks, the fully trained and qualified professional holding an administrative or top supervisory role may thus be assisted by a community-college-trained technician, who can assume direct program leadership roles in various activity areas.

Community college curriculums usually offer two program choices: terminal and transfer. Terminal implies that the individual will not continue with further study after completing his two-year course of study. Transfer prepares him to move to a four-year college to complete his baccalaureate degree. If professional standards for hiring are maintained, individuals taking the terminal program in recreation are unable to move into positions of higher pay and responsibility based on Civil Service codes or departmental hiring regulations. Therefore, those individuals who demonstrate in the community college that they have real academic potential and are highly motivated should be encouraged to take the transfer program.

[15] Peter J. Verhoven, "There Is Nothing Junior About the Junior College," *Parks and Recreation*, October, 1967, pp. 43-44.

It is necessary for community colleges to design their recreation curriculums with extreme care, to staff them with well-qualified faculty members, and to maintain full articulation with four-year colleges that may accept their graduates. Both general education and recreation courses must be acceptable to the four-year college that is to accept the community college graduate. Bartholomew pointed out that in a study of twelve selected two-year colleges, there was a great diversity of offerings; in general, the recreation curricula were minimal and lacked real direction or focus.[16]

Recognizing the need to strengthen community college recreation curriculums the National Recreation and Park Association carried out a study of community colleges in 1968, with funding by the U.S. Office of Education's Division of Manpower Development and Training. It supported the continuing need for more "equitable and realistic matching of job responsibilities with qualifications." The report urged that the founding of new post-secondary curriculums should be based on realistic knowledge of the employment market for graduates of the new community college programs; it also developed guidelines for staffing, student advisement, and placement.

As in other fields of professional practice, much stimulus and leadership has come from professional organizations in parks and recreation. Today, a single unified organization has emerged to meet the needs of this field, the National Recreation and Park Association.

The National Recreation and Park Association

In all professional fields in the United States, it is essential that practitioners be affiliated with strong, unified professional organizations. Professional organizations regulate and set standards for professional training, promote legislation for the advancement of the field, develop programs of public information, and press for higher standards of training, accreditation, and certification.

Because of the varied nature of professional service within the broad field of recreation and parks, as well as the strong role played by citizen's groups and lay organizations, a number of different organizations were founded to serve the recreation and park field. Five of these (the National Recreation Association, American Institute of Park Executives, National Conference on State Parks, American Association of Zoological Parks and Aquariums, and American Recreation Society) merged into a single body in 1965, under the leadership of Laurance S. Rockefeller as president. Within a year or two, other groups, such as the National Association of Recreation Therapists and specialized groups of professionals like the

[16] Warren M. Bartholomew, "Recreation Education in Selected Junior or Community Colleges," *Parks and Recreation*, January, 1967, pp. 25-26; see also Peter J. Verhoven, "Associate Professional Recreation Programs," *Parks and Recreation*, April, 1969, pp. 28-30.

Armed Forces Section of the American Recreation Society, fully merged their interests with the newly formed organization. This national body, the National Recreation and Park Association, is an independent, nonprofit organization intended to promote the development of the park and recreation movement and the conservation of natural and human resources:

As a national, non-profit, educational, public-service organization, NRPA's goals are to help preserve the balance between nature and man to allow him to live harmoniously with his surroundings both in the city and in the countryside; to help communities, states, and the federal government provide opportunities for recreation and for the enjoyment of the natural environment for our growing population, and to help all Americans develop a productive outlook and philosophy for the use of leisure time.[17]

The N.R.P.A. works closely, as a service organization, with public and private agencies, to foster the development and administration of resources, facilities, programs, and personnel. It helps communities conduct self-studies of recreation and park resources and needs, assists them in devising and applying standards for facilities, programs, administration, and budget, provides advice and technical aid in open-space programming, promotes citizen education on leisure problems and issues, gathers and disseminates current information on recreation trends and planning techniques, promotes recruitment of qualified leaders for careers in recreation and parks, sponsors annual national and district conferences, acts as a clearinghouse of information for national and local leisure-related agencies, and serves as an adviser to the growing number of Federal agencies involved in recreation and parks.

Members of the National Recreation and Park Association may be lay individuals interested in recreation, parks, zoos, and conservation, municipal agency board members, hospital, armed forces and industrial recreation program personnel, college and university educators, and practitioners in public and voluntary agencies. By the end of its second year of existence, 1967, the National Recreation and Park Association had 8,000 members in its Professional Division and 6,150 members in its Lay Division, with both categories increasing rapidly, as branch societies accelerated membership campaigns.

Structure. The National Recreation and Park Association is directed by a sixty-three-member Board of Trustees which meets several times each year to guide its major policies. The major thrust of activity is carried out through N.R.P.A.'s Professional Division, including several branches related to specialized areas of professional involvement (American Park and Recreation Society, the National Conference on State Parks, the American Association of Zoological Parks and Aquariums, the National Therapeutic Recreation Society, and the Society of Park and Recreation Educators).

[17] "The New National Recreation and Parks Association," *Parks and Recreation,* August, 1966, p. 621.

Functions. Among the specific activities carried out in a recent year by the National Recreation and Park Association were the following:

Conferences and Institutes. It held an annual Congress for Recreation and Parks, attended by 4,000 laymen and professionals, sponsored three Federal Assistance Institutes to help local and state park and recreation executives work with Federal agencies, and held eight district conferences and institutes, attended by 5,000 delegates, and a variety of other institutes and management training schools in special areas of service.

Publications. It issued a monthly publication, *Parks and Recreation*, with 25,000 subscribers, and newsletters serving specialty areas in twelve categories, operated a major book center with an extensive sale of publications, published the *Recreation and Park Yearbook* and a number of specialized management aids and other manuals related to park practices, and playground operation.

Field Services. Through district representatives, it provided consultation and planning assistance to over 800 communities, voluntary agencies, state and Federal agencies, military installations, hospitals and institutions, and colleges and universities.

Research. It carried out several studies on recreation manpower supply and demand, community college curriculum development, salary trends in municipal parks and recreation, and training of practitioners with financial support from major Federal agencies.

In addition, N.R.P.A.'s staff carried out an extensive Correspondence and Consultation service with over 5,000 requests for information and assistance from every state in the union and a number of foreign countries. Its officers and staff made extensive presentations before Congressional Committees and worked with civic groups and other national organizations to promote special programs. As a single example, it carried out an extensive program of sports instruction, reaching over 200,000 persons in 111 communities, through a $150,000 grant from the Lifetime Sports Foundation.

Under the direction of Dr. Sal J. Prezioso, the National Recreation and Park Association provides leadership for the total recreation and park movement. Its major problem is to maintain a single unified identity, without permitting its primary concern for outdoor recreation and open-space programs to overshadow such other important concerns as the work of voluntary agencies, school-oriented programs, the needs of special populations, and religious, armed forces, and industrial recreation programs.

Other Professional Associations

A number of other organizations continue to carry out programs supporting the recreation profession. A leading organization is the American Association for Health, Physical Education and Recreation, which embraces over 50,000 professionals with a broad interest in this field. Founded in 1885, A.A.H.P.E.R.'s Recreation Division today serves several thousand individuals who are employed for the most part by school systems and colleges and who have a specialized concern with school-sponsored recreation programs, education for leisure, the promotion of school camping and outdoor education, and recreation services for the physically handicapped and mentally retarded.

Other organizations which make an important contribution to this field include the American Camping Association, which acts as a voice for the organized camping field in the United States; the Association of College Unions–International, concerned particularly with social programs for college students; the National Association of Social Workers, Group Work Section; the National Industrial Recreation Association; the Society of State Directors of Health, Physical Education and Recreation; and the Athletic Institute. It would be a mistake to assume that the relationship among these bodies is entirely harmonious. Typically, the American Camping Association, the National Industrial Recreation Association, and the National Association of Social Workers, while they continue to regard themselves as linked to the recreation movement, have not affiliated themselves with the National Recreation and Park Association. A.A.P.H.E.R., in particular, continues to insist on its right to represent the recreation field with respect to certification and accreditation, despite N.R.P.A.'s being obviously the more representative organization. Similarly, the American Occupational Therapy Association continues to claim a responsibility for recreation service in treatment centers, although most occupational therapists today do not receive specialized training in recreation.

The Recruitment of Recreation and Park Professionals

One of the key problems over the past two decades in the field of recreation and parks has been the need to recruit larger numbers of competent individuals into the field. This is a problem faced by many other areas of public service, all of which compete strongly to attract students of high quality. Twardzik points out that recreation as a career still suffers from lack of public understanding; he agrees with Sessoms that the recreation professional is often seen as a playground leader rather than as a municipal executive with considerable responsibilities and importance. Therefore, he urges that a much more up-to-date and accurate image of the recreation and park field be promoted through films, brochures, and pamphlets, career days in high schools, youth development programs, internship programs for youth, and closer contact with guidance officers.

If greater numbers of capable young people are to be drawn into this field, Twardzik suggests that it must become more competitive in seeking them out and in insuring that they are hired on professional levels following graduation. Beyond this, it will be essential to convince these youngsters that recreation is still a young profession, too young to have become rigidly stratified in fixed concepts and practices and that, as a young profession, recreation continues to need the new ideas that young minds can bring to it.[18]

In another analysis of the recruitment problem, Saltzman urges that more effective use be made of the thousands of volunteers and part-time employees in the recreation field. Since large numbers of young people of high school and college age work in a seasonal or part-time basis in recreation and parks, it should be possible to guide the most qualified of these into professional study in college and university programs. He suggests also that recreation departments should institute more career plans and "work-while-you-train" programs which provide partial leave and tuition assistance for young people who wish to complete their higher education while on the job.[19]

Salary Trends in Recreation and Parks. Obviously a key factor in the ability of any professional field to attract high-quality applicants is the degree of financial reward it provides. Recreation and park salary trends have climbed steadily over the past several years and today compare very favorably with other public service fields. A study carried out by Cook and Hawkins for the American Park and Recreation Society in 1967, with the cooperation of the International City Managers' Association, reported the statistics given in Table 5-1.

TABLE 5-1   *Salaries of Recreation and Park Professionals*

Title	Pop. 10,000–24,999 West	South	100,000–249,000 West	South	500,000 and up West	South
Director of Parks and Recreation	9,133	6,750	15,333	10,875	24,500	16,167
Assistant Director of Parks and Recreation	7,500	5,375	11,500	8,500	23,500	9,750
Superintendent of Parks	6,900	5,333	11,750	8,285	18,000	8,750
Superintendent of Recreation	7,133	8,500	11,800	6,999	16,500	9,500
Director of Parks	6,000	5,667	12,250	9,500	18,500	
Director of Recreation	8,333	6,750	14,500	8,833	14,000	7,500
Division Head	7,125	5,200	11,250	7,250	13,500	12,500

SOURCE: Walter L. Cook and Donald E. Hawkins, *Salary Trends: A Survey, Analysis and Recommendations for Local Park and Recreation Administrative Personnel* (Washington, D.C.: American Park and Recreation Society, 1967), pp. 9–10.

[18] Louis F. Twardzik, "How We Fail in Recruitment," *Recreation*, November, 1964, p. 469.
[19] Donald Saltzman, "Recruitment Reappraised," *Parks and Recreation*, June, 1968, pp. 25-26.

The study illustrates a considerable variation in salaries, based on region and size of the community. Thus, the average salary of a director of parks and recreation is $6,750 in a small southern community and $24,500 in a large western community. What basis is there for comparing these figures, reported in 1967, with those in other professions? Probably the field with which recreation and park service is most frequently compared is that of teaching. According to the executive secretary of the National Education Association, the average salary in the elementary and secondary grades during 1967–68 was between $6,700 and $6,800 and was earned by a teacher who was thirty-nine years old and had been teaching for twelve years.

Compared with this standard, recreation professionals in 1967, according to the Cook and Hawkins study, were earning impressively superior salaries. Indeed, it seems clear that a more accurate analysis would be to compare recreation and parks administrators to school administrators, both in terms of degree of responsibility and salary range. Since school administrators normally work through the summer months and often through afternoons and into the evening, the two types of jobs are quite similar.

One may compare recreation with teaching in other ways, since they have frequently been professionally linked. Teaching tends to involve substantially the same subject matter and groups of children, in the same setting, month after month through the year. Administrative work in recreation involves a very different kind of challenge: working with participants, other staff personnel, civic groups, municipal boards, architects, builders, and professionals in other fields in a variety of settings. Thus, recreation and park administration demands initiative, imagination, and the display of community leadership. The very process of advancement demands mobility. Normally, while the teacher may remain in the same system and move up the salary scale year after year automatically, most recreation and park professionals move to larger communities and more responsible positions as they gain experience and competence.

In making comparisons, the American Park and Recreation Society study of salary trends found that recreation and park salaries in 1962 compared favorably with those of other municipal government positions requiring similar experience, education, and management skills. During the period between 1962 and 1966, salaries of recreation and park executives increased steadily, in amounts ranging between 9.9 percent and 18.0 percent. It seems clear that in terms of financial reward this field has improved its attraction for potential recruits and today compares favorably with other professions in a similar range of public service. For it to continue to improve in this respect, however, and for the field itself to grow in terms of effectiveness and degree of public understanding and support, it will have to become increasingly professionalized. This can only happen through developing higher standards for colleges and universities providing professional preparation and by improving procedures for screening qualified individuals at the point of entering the field, through two basic procedures: certification and registration.

Certification of Recreation and Park Professionals

Each of the recognized professions in our society has gone through a process of development in which its training gradually became more specialized and standardized, with the function ultimately assigned to colleges and universities. Customarily an individual qualifies today by studying in an approved college or university and then taking examinations that are given by state education departments—usually developed and administered with the assistance of professional organizations in each field. Through the years, the requirements have been raised in each profession. Typically, several decades ago, elementary and secondary school teachers were required only to have attended two-year normal colleges. Today, there is the universal expectation throughout the United States that a beginning teacher will have a four-year college degree with an approved program of studies established by state departments of education; graduate study in education is becoming increasingly necessary.

The situation in public departments of recreation and parks is generally less structured than this. Civil Service requirements and examinations tend to be poorly geared to the specific requirements of park and recreation agencies. There is a growing awareness that, in order to insure a high level of performance by qualified practitioners, some system of impartial certification or registration should be imposed.

The term "certification" refers to the process by which an applicant for entry within a profession is reviewed and, assuming that he meets specific qualifications, is approved. It may be based on such elements as education, experience, performance on written and oral tests, and personal recommendations. A number of states have now developed state certification procedures in recreation and parks. Two examples are New Jersey and Georgia.

New Jersey passed legislation in 1966 which established a Board of Recreation Examiners within the Department of Conservation and Economic Development. The main duty of this Board was to administer a plan of permissive certification and registration for recreation administrators (defined as any executive head or assistant to the executive head administering a major recreation program for the state, a county, municipality, or other public agency) and for recreation supervisors (defined as persons responsible for planning, organizing, or supervising parts of programs administered by a recreation administrator). The Board of Recreation Examiners, to be appointed by the Governor with the advice and consent of the New Jersey Senate, was charged with establishing and modifying qualifications for positions, holding examinations for the certification and registration of recreation supervisors, conducting research and studies relating to professional standards in recreation, and carrying out the total plan. Typically, the legislation established education and experience qualifications for administrators and supervisors and, through a grandfather clause, provided a waiver for those already employed in such positions throughout the state.

Similarly, the state of Georgia in 1968 passed legislation which implemented formal certification procedures for recreation and park professionals. It appears likely that such certification plans will be more and more widely adopted throughout the nation, particularly in states with strongly developed municipal recreation systems and effective state recreation and park societies.

In other states, notably Indiana, California, and New York, a system of registration by state professional societies has been instituted over the past several years to serve as a means of identifying qualified practitioners. In this case, it is not the requirement of the state certifying body that must be met but rather that of a professional organization in the field. Thus, the method has somewhat less force in application.

For a number of years, the Indiana Park and Recreation Association has operated a registration program through which qualified administrators might be identified. In 1966, the Indiana General Assembly granted the Indiana Outdoor Recreation Council the power to set standards, establish leadership criteria, and establish guidelines for local departments. Fifty-six items (including qualifications of administrators and other staff members) were set up through which local departments might be examined and accredited; departments would be evaluated every five years.

New York State has a voluntary registration plan, with standards established by the New York State Recreation and Park Society, on nine levels of responsibility. Classified by function and title (ranging from administrator of recreation and parks to recreation attendant) the personnel standards define for each level: the duties and distinguishing features of the position, the required knowledge and abilities for the positions, and the minimum education and experience required. This plan, initiated in 1957 and amended in 1968, seeks to clearly identify recreation and park leaders who meet minimum professional standards and thus certify properly qualified individuals who are employed as professional workers in New York State. The plan is administered by a Board of Examiners, with consultants from the New York State Division for Youth, the National Recreation and Park Association, the New York State Education Department, the New York State Department of Civil Service, and faculty representation from park and recreation curriculums in the state.

California has a similar registration plan, with a Board of Recreation

Personnel that establishes standards for administrators, supervisors and leaders and provides incentive pay in many communities for registered personnel. The problem with such plans is that they are more or less voluntary rather than compulsory. They depend on the cooperation of appropriate state and municipal agencies to respect and enforce their requirements.

Civil Service Procedures in Recreation and Parks

In the majority of states, Civil Service systems define protected positions for which educational and other qualifications are established and a system of examination and eligibility lists which will remove the element of political patronage from public employment.

A single example of how Civil Service operates in the recreation and parks field may be found in Suffolk County, New York. In this state, Civil Service was established as a hiring process under the 1941 Fite Law, with the form of administration left to local option. There are three alternatives: state administration, administration through a county personnel office, or county civil service commission. Several job titles, each with its own job description and requirements, have been established by the Suffolk County Civil Service Commission, including: Superintendent, Assistant Superintendent, Recreation Supervisor, Assistant Supervisor, Leader, Assistant Leader, Specialist, Instructor, and Town Park Supervisor. For each of these, specific requirements are established to become certified for appointment: (1) residence requirements within the county or the municipality itself; (2) examinations, usually constructed and graded by the State Civil Service Commission and administered by the county; (3) eligibility lists, which place individuals in a rank of eligibility; (4) certification, in which municipalities send a statement to the Civil Service Commission for the position they wish to fill, and the Commission determines the correct title and sends the certified list of eligible candidates, and selection of an appointee from one of the top three of eligible candidates.

The examinations given are classified into two types: "competitive," which applies to the majority of positions of a full-time professional nature, and "noncompetitive," in which a test is given but the individual need not compete with others for such positions as recreation specialist, part-time leaders, lifeguards, and swimming or skiing instructors. Because the bulk of positions tend to be in the latter category, Civil Service tests and eligibility lists are not fully utilized, and political patronage continues to exist in much recreation and park hiring.

The trend toward state certification and registration plans and the use of improved Civil Service hiring and screening procedures offers the best hope of upgrading professionalism in recreation and park practice. There is a need to strengthen such procedures and make them mandatory, as well as to increase recruitment efforts in order to swell the flow of qualified individuals entering the field.

Clarifying the Role of the Professional

As described earlier, the field of recreation and park service has expanded tremendously in terms of the numbers of individuals employed and programs of professional preparation. Public acceptance has become more widespread and the overall picture appears to be a favorable one. It is necessary to recognize, however, that American society is in an era of emerging social tensions and crises—particularly within the urban setting. This means that all areas of public service must examine themselves seriously in order to clarify their own roles, functions, powers, and responsibilities. They must make their case before the public and leading governmental authorities in a substantial and convincing way. In so doing, they must establish identities that are worthy of respect and based on reality, rather than a façade.

David Gray has suggested that the function of recreation professionals in the present period of rapid social change is to help "make sense out of our cities" and to develop new approaches to living in the twentieth century—including having a more adequate national philosophy of leisure, in which we are no longer dependent on work for meaning in life. Essentially, he sees organized recreation service as a vital force in combatting ugliness and commercialism in our lives, and substituting new values and badly needed human processes.[20]

Sessoms has examined several major trends in the uses of leisure, with implications for professionals in this field. He comments that five major changes have taken place: (1) fuller technology and mobility have made possible more long weekends and more intensive use of outdoor recreation resources (studies show that an increased portion of leisure time is being spent by families about an hour and a half's drive from home); (2) vacation patterns now include much more distant travel for many families, both as a desirable family activity and as a status symbol for all groups; (3) although the work day has been cut considerably over the years, many people have tended to accept other civic, social, or work-connected responsibilities; as a result, regular participation in locally sponsored recreation groups has not increased; (4) in many communities, particularly smaller towns and suburban areas, there is a trend toward the development of privately organized recreation clubs and associations, which minimizes the need for the development of public facilities and services; and, finally, (5) commercial opportunities provide an increasingly large bulk of actual leisure participation, with the result that a growing percentage of people

[20] David Gray, "The Changing Role of the Recreation Professional," address at National Recreation Congress, Minneapolis, October, 1965.

have developed a passive, consumer orientation toward leisure, characterized by apathy and lack of imagination.

Within this context, Sessoms suggests that we have failed to conceptualize sufficiently the specialized functions of professional services in the field of recreation and parks. What is lacking, he concludes, is a clear-cut sense of social purpose and a logical rationale for program development. In Sessoms' view, the professional recreation and park person today fits into one of three rather distinct categories:

1. The *park-recreation manager's role*, including administration of various facilities and programs, with responsibility for such functions as facilities development and maintenance, budget planning, personnel operations, and community relationships.

2. The *social-therapeutic role*, in which recreation is seen as the medium for bringing about desired social, physical, or psychological change for those with special needs.

3. The *traditional playground–community center role*, which was the original basis for the recreation movement during the period prior to World War II. This role has been drastically altered by growing mobility, affluence, and the suburban revolution; it is no longer needed by newer, well-to-do communities, and it is failing to serve the inner-city disadvantaged community. Typically, a person who is in charge of a playground or small recreation center does not perform truly professional functions today; his responsibilities might well be carried on more effectively by subprofessional workers.[21]

Sidney Frissell agrees that the role of recreation professionals has been changing. Rather than identifying three distinct roles, however, he sees the picture as being one of a broad range or spectrum of possible functions:

the width and diversity of the spectrum of recreation interests of Americans must be recognized when one is considering . . . programs to educate recreation leaders and managers. At one end of the recreation spectrum are the "activity-oriented" programs. Here we find the urban recreation programs—playgrounds, organized sports, arts and crafts and day camps. In addition are such specialties as hospital recreation, commercial recreation, and organized group camp programs. At the opposite end of the recreation spectrum we find the "resource-oriented" programs—visits to parks, monuments, historic sites, seashores, wild rivers, and lakeshores, administered by national and state park agencies.[22]

With respect to professional preparation, Frissell questions whether it is possible to develop a single recreation curriculum capable of producing super-administrators who can be all things to all people. Instead, he suggests that there should be increasingly refined curriculums, equipping

[21] Sessoms, "A Critical Look . . . ," *op. cit.*, p. 3.
[22] Sidney Frissell, "Educating Recreation Professionals," *Parks and Recreation*, April, 1967, p. 30.

people to work at specific points along the spectrum of services but with certain core courses that will serve the needs of all professionals. Implicit in most such views is the conviction that recreation and park development must remove itself from the orbit of physical education. Another critic, Loren Taylor, agrees that for too long recreation specialists have been confused with physical education teachers; similarly, in some institutions they are confused with forestry specialists or with sociologists. He suggests that recreation must be established as an independent department, drawing upon broad interdisciplinary sources and opportunities within colleges and universities.[23]

The question of curricular independence in higher education for departments of recreation and park administration must also take into account what colleges and universities themselves perceive as appropriate subjects for higher education. Louis Twardzik points out that this challenge comes at a time when universities themselves, at a time of considerable student body growth and under pressure from student groups for "relevance," are evaluating their own roles. Historically, the professions have looked to the universities for advanced training in their specialties, but the training of personnel to meet community needs in areas of public service is a relatively new concern. Within the field of recreation and parks, there have been two kinds of orientations: parks management, with its base chiefly in agricultural colleges and with curriculums centered on courses in earth sciences, and recreation leadership and administration, housed usually in schools of education, with courses stressing the social sciences and educational methodology and practice.

Now that the two fields have merged, it is essential that college study in recreation and parks justify itself in terms of appropriate scholarly content and in the eyes of higher education authorities. Twardzik points out that it must have its own philosophy, literature, techniques, skilled scholars, and body of research—rather than remain heavily dependent on allied areas of professional practice for subject matter. In Twardzik's view, we can no longer justify the requirement of a baccalaureate to carry on maintenance responsibilities in a park or prepare for recreation leadership of games and sports. Indeed, the community college movement is now preparing personnel who can fill these roles. Professional education in recreation and parks must be based on principles which "reflect a high level of intellectual pursuit and academic achievement." The graduate in this field must "understand recreation as an indispensable ingredient in man's aspiration for a quality of life and then be able to defend it as a high priority objective of public service." Twardzik illustrates this important point by suggesting the analogy of the barbering profession in past centuries. At first barbers had a variety of functions; ultimately they split into two fields.

[23] Loren Taylor, "Let's Get the Elephant Out of the Volkswagen," *Parks and Recreation*, pp. 18-19, 34-37.

One group of barbers became surgeons and the other hairdressers. Twardzik comments, "the university refuses to train barbers."[24]

In addition to the need to upgrade the scholarly content and quality of professional preparation in recreation and parks, there is also a need to review the premise that all persons working on a full-time basis in this field must be professionals. It seems increasingly clear that higher-echelon personnel should have truly professional training but that technical jobs concerned with face-to-face leadership can be done by people who are nonprofessionals in this field but have leadership skills or personal qualities which would equip them to work effectively in program leadership.

What implications are suggested for higher education curriculums in recreation and parks? Some have suggested that this should be a professional and graduate degree program only, so that recreation and parks preparation parallels that in other professional fields. Graduates would be selected from a variety of liberal arts fields and would then receive specialized training in a two-year graduate curriculum, including professional orientation in a carefully supervised internship program. Another suggestion is that we need to extend our view of the recreation professional's task far beyond the direct provision or administration of leisure services. In increasing numbers, recreation-trained individuals are being hired as consultants, researchers, directors of antipoverty training programs, and administrators of multiservice agencies. These roles imply the need for competences and understanding that go far beyond traditional concepts of recreation leadership.

Recreation and park professionals, if they are to play a truly significant role in modern society, must possess a fundamental understanding of the behavioral and social sciences. They should also have the kind of perspective that comes from a full knowledge of the history of recreation and leisure. To comprehend the value of recreation as a form of human service, it is necessary to understand its total relationship to growth and development, civic life, economic processes in society intergroup attitudes, governmental structure, and a host of similar concerns.

The professional, if he is to speak effectively for his field, must be more than a capable practitioner or administrator. He must see and understand the relevance of his field in terms of the rapid changes in society today and the needs imposed by these changes. But, first, to understand the present, he must know the past. Therefore, the following several chapters provide a chronological review and analysis of the development of recreation and leisure in human society.

[24] Louis F. Twardzik, "The University's Commitment to the Parks and Recreation Profession," *Parks and Recreation*, March, 1968, pp. 21, 57.

TWO

The History of Recreation and Leisure

6

The Early History
of Recreation and Leisure

As one examines the role of recreation and leisure in modern society, it is helpful first to view it through the lens of historical perspective. Throughout history, one must ask: What has been the nature of man's play? How much leisure has he had? How was work regarded, in contrast to recreation? Did the educational system of each period make use of play activities? How did philosophers regard leisure and its uses? Did the state make provision for the entertainment or recreation of the various classes of society? This chapter seeks to answer such questions with respect to the play of primitive man, the pre-Christian era, the Dark and Middle Ages, the Renaissance, the Reformation, and finally the period immediately preceding the Industrial Revolution.

The Play of Primitive Man

From a chronological point of view, one might begin by examining the play patterns of prehistoric man during the Palaeolithic and Neolithic epochs. However, knowledge of the lives of these early humans is so limited that it is more profitable to examine the cultural patterns of primitive tribes today or in the fairly recent past.

Primitive man does not make the clear distinction between work and leisure that we tend to make in modern society. Industrial man sets aside periods of time each day for work and other periods for rest and relaxation. Primitive man has no such precise separation; instead, he tends to work only when it is required and available. He may engage in an extended period of steady labor and then pause for a lengthy period to enjoy the fruit of his toil. Work itself is often infused with rites and customs that lend it variety and pleasure. Craven comments:

To every member of the community falls his share of labor and of play, his opportunity for participation in the important rites and mysteries; the orientation of life is physiologically and socially toward long periods of leisurely work, interspersed with occasional periods of intensive effort.[1]

Work in primitive society is varied and creative rather than highly specialized and demanding a narrow aspect of the worker's skill, as in modern industry. It is infused with ritual which is regarded as essential to the success of the planting or harvest, or the building or hunting expedition. Such ritual may involve prayer, sacrifice, and dance or feasting; these experiences thus become part of the world of work. This tends to explain the function of primitive art, which developed as a by-product of necessity. In primitive tribes, tools, weapons, and other implements are manufactured chiefly because they are needed for self-defense or to carry on the work of the tribe. Usually, however, implements, pottery, and weaving are decorated or formed in stylized ways which include special forms of symbolic decoration to provide magic identity, meaning, or power. Ultimately, the functional purpose of the decoration may be forgotten, and both it and the actual form of the object are carried on chiefly as a matter of custom or because they are aesthetically pleasing. In more advanced societies, art then becomes a professional activity which is carried out for its own sake, apart from the actual utility of an object. But in primitive cultures, it generally remains closely attached to the purpose of what is decorated or designed. In such settings, it is important to recognize that the urge to create art is never a matter of pleasure alone but is closely linked to practical functions.

In primitive societies, play may have many sources. Popular juvenile or adult games are often vestiges of warfare—now practiced as a form of sport. Not infrequently play activities depict historical events, practices of transportation, or the use of household or farming implements. When a given activity is no longer useful in its original form (such as archery for hunting or warfare), it becomes enjoyed as a form of sport. Often, the origin is religious ritual. Throughout man's history, games have been carried on as part of religious festivals or celebrations. McIntosh writes:

The Tailteen Games in Ireland, wrestling among the Aztecs, the team game of Tlachtli played by Maya people in central America, and ju-jitsu practiced by the Samurai Warriors of Japan, all had religious significance. In Britain, too, the early history of some games of football suggests that fertility rites were involved.[2]

---

[1] Ida Craven, "Leisure, According to the Encyclopedia of the Social Sciences," in Eric Larrabee and Rolf Meyersohn, eds., *Mass Leisure* (Glencoe, Ill.: Free Press, 1958), p. 5.

[2] P. C. McIntosh, *Sport in Society* (London: C. A. Watts, 1963), p. 4.

In many primitive tribes there is a dualism, or division of the community into two halves. These halves are often marked by their own distinctive totems (a totem usually being a sacred bird or animal), which in turn dictate a complicated system of obligations, taboos, and customs between the two tribal halves. In primitive societies, there tends to be a constant sequence of contests and rivalry between the two halves and at the same time a process of constant help and mutual assistance. Together, the halves carry on a series of precisely designed and performed ceremonies. Often the games played as part of such ceremonies are symbolic of a continuing struggle between good and evil, or life and death.

The game known as *tlachtli*, which was widely practiced in Central America centuries ago, is an example of such a contest. It was played on courts situated in the vicinity of temples. The courts were about 200 feet long and 30 feet wide; a stone ring was fixed about halfway up the walls at either end. The game was played with a rubber ball, which the players struck with their knees or hips, the purpose being to drive it through one of the rings. Spence characterized its symbolic purpose in these words:

The game of *tlachtli* probably symbolized the motions of some heavenly body, the sun or the moon. The ball with which it was played was represented in the Mexican manuscripts either as half-light and half-dark in color, or sometimes in four hues. . . . This dualistic myth assumes the character of an everlasting game of ball in which the fortunes of the universe are tossed, now into light, now into shadow, by the contending powers.[3]

Sometimes games of this type were so seriously regarded that the captains of losing teams were sacrificed following the contest. Indeed, sports were frequently carried on as a modified form of warfare, as in the case of the lacrosse games carried on by North American Choctaw Indians. These contests often involved as many as a thousand young braves and lasted many hours; they caused frequent injuries and deaths. Not only were such contests used as a means of testing warriors in battle-like situations but also of keeping their fighting morale high. In a sense they were simulations of actual fighting.

The play life of children in primitive cultures includes many games, contests, and rituals which were clearly designed to prepare them for adult roles. George Catlin observed North American Indian tribes in the early 1800's in which the boys of the tribe were formed into two companies which were headed by experienced warriors. They were led through various maneuvers and ultimately into pitched battles, using arrows made of spears of grass and knives made of blunt wood:

If any one is struck with an arrow on any vital part of his body, he is obliged to fall, and his adversary rushes up to him, places his foot upon him, and snatching

[3] Lewis Spence, *Myth and Ritual in Dance, Game and Rhyme* (London: C. A. Watts, 1947), pp. 18-19.

from his belt his wooden knife, grasps hold of his victim's scalp-lock of grass, and . . . twitches it off. . . . This mode of training generally lasts an hour or more in the morning, and is performed on an empty stomach, affording them a rigid and wholesome exercise, whilst they are instructed in the important science of war. Some five or six miles of ground are run over during these evolutions, giving suppleness to their limbs and strength to their muscles, which last and benefit them through life.[4]

Boys were also tested in riding and learning to survive unarmed and unclothed in the wilderness. Girls, through their play, were taught the household crafts expected of mature women. Thus, the activities carried on by the young were intended to prepare them for adulthood.

Clearly, the playlike activities that are carried out in primitive cultures are not viewed as peripheral to the needs of the tribe. Instead, they are (1) religious ritual, often providing a means of supplicating the gods or asking for their favor at times of marriage, birth, death, planting, harvest, or war, (2) a form of education, to prepare children and youth for adult responsibilities, (3) a means of achieving tribal solidarity and morale, (4) a form of therapeutic or healing experience, (5) a means of communication, (6) aesthetic pleasure, in the sense that even after primitive customs and rituals lose their religious meaning, they continue to be performed as a form of entertainment, and (7) recreation—carried out for the purpose of providing relaxation, recovery, and replenishment of one's strength and vitality after toil.

As early human societies grew increasingly complex, they came to be marked by a specialization of function. A class of shamans, or priests, developed, not only providing spiritual leadership but also engaging in governmental and scholarly activities. Ultimately, ruling classes appeared, along with soldiers, craftsmen, peasants, and slaves. Particularly as fixed villages and cities came into being and large estates were tilled and harvested by lower-class workers, upper-class societies gained increased power, wealth, and leisure. In the landed aristocracy of the first civilizations that developed in the Middle East during the five millenia preceding the Christian era, we find for the first time in history a leisure class. Since it was in the Mediterranean region that Western civilization had its birthplace, it is here that we will examine the first examples of recreation and leisure.

Recreation and Leisure in Pre-Christian Civilizations

Ancient Egypt. The Egyptian culture was a rich and diversified one; it achieved an advanced knowledge of astronomy, geometry, architecture, and engineering and various processes of manufacture and construction.

---

[4] George Catlin (1841), quoted in Thomas Woody, *Life and Education in Early Societies* (New York: Macmillan, 1949), pp. 29-30.

The Egyptians developed a varied class structure, with a powerful nobility, priesthood, and military class and lesser classes of workers, artisans, peasants, and slaves. This civilization, which lasted from about 5000 B.C. well into the Roman era, was richly recorded in paintings, statuary, and hieroglyphic records.

Apparently the ancient Egyptians led a colorful and pleasant life; it is said of them that their energies were directed to the arts of living and the arts of dying. For them, the life-giving Nile served as a highway, a marketplace, and a playground for sport and recreation. They engaged in a wide variety of sports, as a part of both education and the general culture. These included wrestling, gymnastic exercises, lifting and swinging weights, and ball games. Bullfighting was a popular spectacle and, at least at its inception, was religiously motivated. Hunting and fishing were both popular pursuits and, for the nobility, an elaborate form of recreation and entertainment. The Egyptians were known to have used fishing rods as early as 2000 B.C. Huntsmen in Egypt comprised a distinct social class, who either hunted by themselves or attended the nobles at the hunt.

Music, drama, and dance were all forms of religious worship and also of social entertainment. The Egyptians had complex orchestras, including cymbals, tambourines, drums, pipes, and other stringed and percussive instruments. Groups of female performers were attached to temples, and in the royal houses there were troupes of entertainers who performed on both sacred and social occasions. Slaves were taught both dancing and music. In the later dynasties, they developed into a class of professional performers who provided entertainment for the nobility at private dinner parties or in public squares in large cities.

The diversions of peasants and field laborers were few and inexpensive. They assembled in the "house of beer," which was probably the equivalent of modern bars and apparently were much given to drunkenness. Over all, there was much emphasis on entertainment of all sorts, by acrobats, conjurors, gymnasts, dancers, and other troupes. Egyptian children played with toy dolls, boats, marbles, tops, and balls. Such games as chess, backgammon, and other table games apparently also had their origin during this period.

When Egypt came under the rule of Rome, it was much influenced by the Roman way of life. During this period, clubs and drinking associations were common. Sex for the first time became a marketable item; prostitutes (who had originally been vestal virgins performing religious rites in the temples) now provided a secular form of entertainment. Apparently prostitution was licensed by the state or municipality, with girls being required to pay taxes in order to work at their trade. In addition, many other forms of popular entertainment were widely found. There were both private entertainments and public festivals on the occasion of imperial and religious holidays. Most large towns had theaters and regular mass athletic contests, including popular horse-racing events; the Egyptians spent great amounts for professional entertainment.

Thus we see among the ancient Egyptians a wide variety of recreational pursuits—at first largely reserved for the nobility and ultimately becoming available to all classes. Even in this early period of recorded history, it is worth noting that many forms of play related to gambling, drinking, and vice were apparently countenanced and controlled by the state.

Ancient Assyria and Babylonia. The land between the two great rivers, the Tigris and the Euphrates, known as the "fertile crescent," was ruled by two powerful empires, Assyria in the north and Babylonia in the south. These kingdoms were in power for a period of approximately twenty-six centuries, from about 2900 B.C. until the invasion by Alexander the Great, in 330 B.C. Based on clay tablets and cuneiform script, much information is known of both societies. In both Assyria and Babylonia, there were powerful centralized governments ruled by a strong nobility and military class, with slaves doing the needed productive labor.

Like the ancient Egyptians, the Assyrians and Babylonians had many popular recreation activities, such as boxing, wrestling, archery, and a variety of table games. Music and dancing were found both in religious practice and as social entertainment. Like the Egyptians, the Assyrians drank beer and palm wine; there were many wealthy tavern-keepers who catered to the public. Drinking at first was part of a religious act and then ultimately became a simple pleasure, a commercial enterprise, and finally a means through which the common people might find group companionship.

Contenau writes, "We may sum up the leisure occupations of a king of Assyria as the harem, listening to music, dancing, sedentary games, and the giving of banquets for his nobles." He was also devoted to hunting, however; what had been his duty as protector of the tribe now became "a recreation, not free of the spice of danger, despite the precautions with which he was surrounded."[5] The nobles of Assyria went lion-hunting in chariots and on foot, using spears. The chase was a daily occupation of the Assyrian nobility, recorded for history in numerous reliefs, sculptures, and inscriptions. Ceram writes that as early as the ninth century B.C.:

The Assyrians had animal parks, "paradises," as they called them, precursors of our zoological gardens. Within their large confines were kept freely roaming lions and herds of gazelles. They arranged battues—that is, hunts, in which the animals were driven by beaters and hunted with nets.[6]

[5] Georges Contenau, *Everyday Life in Babylon and Assyria* (London: Edward Arnold, 1954), pp. 132-33.
[6] C. W. Ceram, *Gods, Graves and Scholars,* quoted in Charles E. Doell and Charles B. Fitzgerald, *A Brief History of Parks and Recreation in the United States* (Chicago: The Athletic Institute, 1954), p. 7.

These early parks were primarily spectacular settings for royal hunting parties but were secondarily the places where feasts, assemblies, and royal gatherings were held. On the estates of other monarchs during the ninth and tenth centuries B.C. were vineyards, fishponds, and the famed hanging gardens of Babylon, featuring remarkable displays of vegetation and floral paintings. Contenau writes:

beside cultivating gardens for purely utilitarian purposes, the kings of Assyria enjoyed creating botanical gardens, containing collections of non-indigenous species—notably the plants and trees of the Amanus mountains. In much the same way, the Egyptian kings instructed their expeditions to collect and bring back the rarest species.[7]

In other lands throughout the Middle East and in the Orient, there were similar parks, hunting preserves, and botanical displays. Doell and Fitzgerald describe a park established in the twelfth century B.C. in the city of Polonnaruwa in Ceylon which featured displays of fountains, with pipes and machinery, which

made the place appear as though clouds were incessantly pouring down drops of rain. There was a great array of different baths that delighted masters and men. We hear also of other parks and other baths, and even of gardens that the rich made for the recreation of the poor.[8]

Among the ancient Israelites, both music and dancing were carried on for ritual purposes and also as social activities and for celebrations. A distinction was made by the early Hebrews between dances of a sacred or holy character and those which resembled pagan ceremonies. As an example, they condemned dancing around the Golden Calf as a form of idolatry which reflected the influence of the Egyptian religion (which worshipped the bull Apis as a major deity). The distinction between moral and immoral forms of play and ceremony which was made by the early Jews (first of the great monotheistic religions) was to be made even more sharply by the early Christians in the centuries that followed.

Thus the idea was established that recreation was related to morality. Some forms of play which had their origin in religious practice were ultimately condemned as immoral or pagan. The concept that through leisure and its uses a society might be strengthened or weakened was to be more fully developed by the Greeks and Romans, who accepted the state's responsibility for providing facilities for the physical, intellectual, or social use of leisure and for providing entertainment and amusement to the masses.

Ancient Greece. In the city-states of ancient Greece, and particularly in Athens during the so-called Golden Age of Pericles (from about 500

[7] Contenau, *op. cit.*, p. 109.
[8] Doell and Fitzgerald, *op. cit.*, p. 13.

to 400 B.C.), mankind reached a new peak of philosophical, cultural, and scientific development. The Athenians had a tremendous interest in all the arts, in learning, and in athletics. These were generally restricted to the well-born citizens of the state, who had full rights of voting and participation in affairs of state. Other citizens were craftsmen, farmers, and tradespeople who had limited rights and less prestige; the actual labor of the state was carried out by slaves and foreigners, who outnumbered citizens by as much as two or three to one.

The amenities of life were generally restricted to the most wealthy and powerful citizens. For them, there was the Athenian ideal of the balanced citizen—the man who was a combined soldier, athlete, artist, statesman, and philosopher. This ideal was furthered through education and the varied religious festivals, which occupied about seventy days of the year. All the arts of music, poetry, theater, gymnastics, and athletic competition were combined in the sacred games. At least five such festivals—the Olympic, Pythian, Istmian, Nemean and Panathenaic games—were celebrated each year. At these, running, horse and chariot racing, wrestling and boxing, and throwing the discus usually comprised the principal contests. They also had bardic, or musical events, in which contests on the harp and flute, poetry, and theatrical events were features. The very idea of sport and gymnastics was closely linked to art. Physical prowess was celebrated in sculpture and poetry, and strength and beauty were seen as gifts of the gods.

From earliest childhood, Athenian citizens engaged in varied athletic and cultural activities. Young children enjoyed toys, dolls, carts, skip ropes, kites, and seesaws. When boys reached the age of seven, they enrolled in schools in which gymnastics and music were primary elements. They were intensively instructed in running and leaping, wrestling, throwing the javelin and discus, dancing (taught as a form of military drill in the Pyrrhic dances), swimming, boxing, and ball games. Many of these activities were carried on throughout life.

The Athenian philosophers believed strongly in the unity of mind and body and in the strong relationship of all forms of human qualities and skills. They felt that play activity was essential to the healthy growth of children, both physical and social. Thus, in Book IV of *The Republic*, Plato had Socrates say:

our children from their earliest years must take part in all the more lawful forms of play, for if they are not surrounded with such an atmosphere they can never grow up to be well-conducted and virtuous citizens.[9]

He believed that education should be compulsory and that it should provide natural modes of amusement for children between the ages of

---

[9] Plato, *The Republic,* translated by Paul Shorey (Cambridge, Mass.: Loeb Classical Library, Harvard University Press, 1930, 1953), p. 335.

three and six. He suggested that classes should be held each day at village temples, with nurses seeing to it that children behaved in an orderly and proper manner. Plato wrote:

Education should begin with the right direction of children's sports. The plays of childhood have a great deal to do with the maintenance or non-maintenance of laws.[10]

Plato also decried the fact that law-givers tended to regard changes in children's games lightly:

they fail to reflect that those children who innovate in their games grow up into men different from their fathers; and being thus different themselves they seek a different mode of life, and having sought this, they come to desire other institutions and laws.[11]

Music and dance were also essential for the fullest development of youth. Plato urged that all children, boys and girls alike, be instructed in music and dance and that they be tested with frequent contests. These arts were to be consecrated to the gods, since the gods themselves were musicians and dancers. Both gymnastics and music were aimed at a total cultivation of the body and the emotions, as the foundation upon which to build a sound intellectual and physical life in the future. Athenian men continued to engage in sports, games, and the arts throughout their lifetimes. This was seen as essential to maintaining national security, by having citizens remain fit and active. Such exercises were seen not as a grim drill, however, but rather as creative and enjoyable experience. Pericles wrote:

We cultivate the mind without loss of manliness; whereas our adversaries from early youth are always undergoing laborious exercises which are to make them brave, we live at ease and yet are equally willing to face the perils which they face. We have our regular games to provide our weary spirits many relaxations from toil.[12]

In the philosophy of the ancient Athenians, the need for leisure and amusement were both clearly recognized, although they were regarded as distinctly different. Aristotle commented that it was necessary to work vigorously and to defend the state in order to secure leisure:

Therefore, a city must be temperate and brave and able to endure: for truly, as the proverb says, "There is no leisure for slaves," and those who cannot face danger like men are the slaves of any invader.

[10] Plato, *The Laws*, translated by R. G. Bury (Cambridge, Mass.: Leob Classical Library, Harvard University Press, 1926, 1961), p. 23.
[11] *Ibid.*, p. 37.
[12] Pericles, quoted in Allen V. Sapora and Elmer D. Mitchell, *The Theory of Play and Recreation* (New York: Ronald Press, 1961), p. 18.

He commented on the distinction between leisure and amusement:

Nature requires that we should be able, not only to work well, but to use leisure well; for, as I must repeat once again, the first principle of all action is leisure. Both are required, but leisure is better than occupation and its end; and therefore the question must be asked, what ought we to do when at leisure? . . . we should introduce amusements only at suitable times, and they should be our medicines, for the emotion which they create in the soul is a relaxation, and from the pleasure we obtain rest. But leisure of itself gives pleasure and happiness and enjoyment of life, which are experienced not by the busy man, but by those who have leisure.[13]

The Athenians regarded leisure as an opportunity for intellectual cultivation, including music, theater, poetry, and political and philosophical discussion. Gymnastics and sports were seen as being somewhat more purposeful, in the sense that they enhanced strength, fitness, and courage. They were regarded, however, as an obligation to the state and were carried out by all citizens.

The ancient Greeks developed the art of town planning to a high degree and customarily made extensive provision for small parks and gardens, open air theaters and gymnasiums, baths, exercise grounds, and stadiums where such activities might be carried on. In Plato's time, the gymnasium and the park were closely connected, in beautiful natural settings. Often they included indoor halls, exercise grounds, gardens, and buildings for musical performances. In its earlier periods, Athens had many public baths and some public parks. These gradually gave way to privately owned estates; under the reign of Alexander the Great, larger hunting parks were developed, as were private baths, gymnasiums, and academies for political and intellectual discussion.

A gradual transition took place in the ideals of the Greeks with respect to play. At first, it was taken for granted that all citizens would take part in sports and games. The Olympic games, as an illustration, were open to free-born Greeks only. It was believed that the active life was the best and that the amateur ideal strengthened the state and the individual citizen. Gradually, however, the religious and cultural functions of the Olympic games and other Panhellenic festivals were weakened by athletic specialization and commercialization.

Gradually, sports, along with other forms of performing activity, such as drama, singing, and dance, were performed only by highly skilled specialists before crowds of admiring spectators. Chariot races became more popular, and hippodromes were built for huge crowds to watch them. Interest in athletics as a popular pursuit for all citizens declined, and the strength of the state itself was weakened.

[13] Aristotle, *Education of Youth*, Book VIII, quoted in Robert Ulich, *History of Educational Thought* (New York: American Book, 1950), p. 17.

At its height, though, the Athenian ideal had developed a new concept of recreation and play as a means of preparing children for adulthood and for providing mankind with great creative impulses and enrichment. Play was seen as having the utilitarian purposes of maintaining physical fitness, courage, and readiness to defend the state and also in restoring the energies and health of citizens. It was in the period of the Periclean age that a philosophy of creative play emerged that gave birth to great forms of art, theater, poetry, and dance and that exalted a spiritual concept of democratic man that was not matched during the many centuries that followed.

Ancient Rome. Just as in the Greek city-states during the pre-Hellenic age, so the Roman republic during its early period of development was a vigorous and manly state. The Roman citizen, although he belonged to a privileged class, was constantly ready to defend his state and engage in its wars. He engaged willingly in the sports and gymnastics which kept his body hardened and his spirit courageous. Numerous games were carried on in connection with worship of various Roman gods. In time these developed into annual festivals. Such games were carefully supervised by the priesthood and supported by public funds, frequently at great cost. The most important of the Roman games were those which celebrated military triumphs; these were usually held in honor of the god Jupiter, the head of the Roman pantheon. Other leading festivals were held in honor of the goddess Ceres and the god Apollo.

Just as among the early Greeks, younger children had toy carts, houses, dolls, hobbyhorses, stilts, and tops and engaged in many sports and games. In youth, boys were taught various sports and exercises—running and jumping, sword and spear play, wrestling, swimming, and horseback riding. While intended to prepare for adulthood, they also were carried on in a spirit of friendly competition and play. Hunting and fishing were both popular, and there were many other forms of entertainment. The Romans, however, never had the same philosophical concepts supporting play that the Greeks had. They tended to support it chiefly for utilitarian rather than aesthetic or spiritual reasons.

In general, the Romans valued sport chiefly because of its practical benefits; the great medical authority Galen said, "The best gymnastics is that which not only exercises the body but delights the spirit." The Romans were much less interested than the Athenians in varied forms of cultural activities. They had many performing companies, chiefly of Greek and southern Italian slaves, but did not engage themselves actively in the theater. As for dance, after a brief period beginning at about 200 B.C., when it was fashionable for Roman patricians to dance, they began to disapprove of dance as a manly activity. Cicero wrote:

no man, one may almost say, ever dances when sober, unless perhaps he be a madman; nor in solitude, nor in a moderate and sober party; dancing is the last companion of prolonged feasting, of luxurious situation, and of many refinements.[14]

Even more than the Greeks, the Romans were systematic planners and builders. Their towns generally included provisions for baths, open-air theaters, amphitheaters, forums for public assemblies, stadiums, and sometimes parks and gardens. They developed buildings for gymnastic sports, modeled after the Greek palaestra, including wrestling rooms, rooms where the philosophers might have their conversations, and colonnades where in winter games might be carried on despite bad weather. Wealthier Romans often had private villas, many with large gardens and some with hunting preserves. Most of these were on the outskirts of town or in the countryside, but others were widely scattered through the city of Rome itself. The Romans also were the first to have floral greenhouses, using mica for windowpanes.

As the Roman empire grew more powerful, the sturdy agricultural democracy of the early years, in which all Romans were citizens and free men, shifted to an urban life with sharply divided classes. There were four social classes: the *senators*, who were the richest, owning most of the land and power; the *curiales*, who owned 25 acres or more of land and were office-holders or tax-collectors; the *plebs*, or free common people, who owned small properties or were tradesmen or artisans; and the *coloni*, who were lower-class tenants attached to the land. As the society grew more wealthy and corrupt, with immense fortunes being made by the conquest of vast provinces throughout Europe, the middle-class curiales tended to disappear. Some rose to join the ranks of the senators, but a greater number joined the plebs.

The society became marked by the wealth and profiteering of rulers and speculators. A huge urban population of plebs lived in semi-idleness, with most of the real work done by coloni and slaves brought to Rome by foreign conquests. Gradually, it became necessary for the Roman emperors and senate to amuse and entertain the *plebs*. They did so with doles of corn and bread and with public games—thus the slogan "bread and circuses." To maintain their political popularity with the indigent plebs, the rulers of Rome declared an increasing number of holidays as the occasion for popular entertainment.

As early as the reign of the Emperor Claudius, in the first century A.D., there were 159 public holidays during the year; of these, 93 were devoted to games at public expense. These included many new festivals in honor of national heroes, foreign victories, and other occasions. By A.D. 354 there were 200 public holidays, including 175 days of games. Even on working days, the labor which began at daybreak ended shortly after noon during much of the year.

[14] Cicero, quoted in Lincoln Kirstein, *Dance: A Short History of Classical Theatrical Dancing* (New York: G. P. Putnam, 1935), p. 7.

Plate 1. Even today primitive New Guinea tribes practice warfare regularly as a form of violent team sport. Here, rival tribes skirmish on a hillside, games of childhood are used to practice war-like skills, and warriors dance to celebrate a victory.

Plate 2. Combative pastimes in other primitive societies: Brazilian Kalapalo Indians wrestle many hours each day; ancient Mayan art depicts sport carried on as a religious ritual in temple courtyards; King Shamba of the Congo shown with the Mankala Board, a game popular in Africa and the Orient.

Plate 3. Ancient forms of recreation: the Egyptian Pharaoh Tutankhamen hunting lions; Ajax and Achilles, heroes of Greek mythology, playing an early form of checkers; Persian noblemen of the 16th Century enjoying a polo match.

Plate 4. During the Middle Ages and Renaissance, the court enjoyed jousting both as a form of amusement and training for warfare. One of the first vacation resorts in England was the King and Queen's Bath at Bath. European peasant recreation during this period, as portrayed by Breughel, was earthy and vigorous.

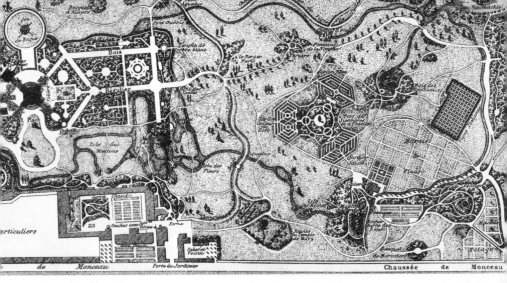

Plate 5. Popular recreation in 18th Century Paris included the use of handsome new parks and promenades, and such great public spectacles as this fireworks display on a bridge on the River Seine.

Plate 6. Nineteenth Century Americans enjoyed sport in many forms: a college boating regatta, ice skating on a frozen pond, and bowling.

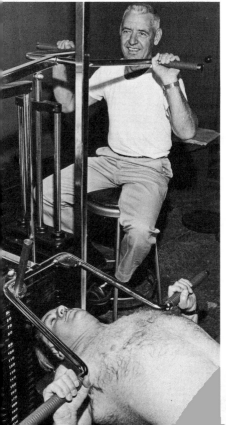

Plate 7. Municipal recreation today serves all ages in varied ways. Here, youngsters enjoy an informal game of baseball in Montclair, New Jersey, while preschoolers play "house" and older men work at physical conditioning in the Mountain View, California, recreation program.

Plate 8. The arts in recreation: a suburban Y.M. and Y.W.H.A. operetta company performs Gilbert and Sullivan; Canadian girls of Scottish ancestry demonstrate traditional folk dances; ceramics provides an absorbing challenge in this teenage "work camp."

As leisure increased and as the necessity to serve in the military or to engage in other forms of physical toil or effort declined for the Roman citizen, he began to do fewer and fewer things for himself. The normal practice was for him to be entertained or to engage in a daily routine of exercise, bathing, and eating. The Roman baths became popular social and athletic clubs. These were no longer exclusive; gradually huge public ·
baths were established throughout Rome. For the mass of the population in the city (about a million and a quarter during the second and third centuries A.D.), the physical facilities for recreation were elaborate and extensive. For example, the Baths of Trajan, huge in size, included hot rooms, cold rooms, and a swimming bath, two palaestrae for general exercise, and a running track. Other buildings in this establishment included a library, administrative offices, refreshment rooms, gymnasia, and courts for ball games. By the fourth century A.D., there were over 856 baths in Rome which could be used by over 60,000 people at the same time, either free of charge or for a nominal fee.

Roman citizens themselves were no longer as active in sports as they had once been. Increasingly, they sought to be amused and to entertain their guests with acrobats, musicians, dancers, and other artists. Athletes now performed as members of a specialized profession with unions, coaches, and training schools and with conditions of service accepted and approved by the emperor himself.

Gradually, the traditional sports of running, throwing, and jumping shifted into an emphasis on human combat—first boxing and wrestling and then displays of cruelty in which gladiators fought to the death for the entertainment of mass audiences. By the time of the Emperor Tiberius (A.D. 14–37) competitive sport in the Roman Empire had become completely commercialized and professionalized. To maintain political popularity and placate the bored masses, the emperors and the Senate provided great parades, circuses, and huge feasts. Fantastic sums were spent on sponsoring the games, often bankrupting both the public treasury and private fortunes. The Roman games featured circuses which included chariot races and other equestrian events. Contests were carried on to the death between gladiators in pairs or larger groups, using all sorts of weapons, on foot, on horseback, or in chariots. Even sea battles were fought in artificially constructed lakes in the Roman arenas. Imported wild beasts, such as tigers and elephants, were pitted against each other or against human antagonists.

The scale of these bloody entertainments was tremendous. The Circus Maximus was able to accommodate 385,000 spectators, and other amphitheaters held audiences that sometimes totaled half the adult populations of their cities. Often the taxes of entire provinces were expended on cruel spectacles. The Roman games were a visible, dramatic illustration of lust for power, as well as preoccupation with brutality and force.

Under the reigns of Caligula and Nero, the persecution of Christians became particularly unrelenting. Both animals and human beings were maimed and butchered in cruel and ingenious ways. Shows were often lewd and obscene, leading to a mass debauchery, corruption, and perversion of the human spirit. Over all, their vulgarity, cruelty, and lack of humanity reflected the spirit of the Roman people; the term "Roman holiday" came to mean a wild and corrupt celebration. Tacitus wrote that many Christians

were dressed in the skins of wild beasts, and exposed to be torn to pieces by dogs in the public games, that they were crucified, or condemned to be burnt; and at nightfall serve in place of lamps to light the darkness, Nero's own gardens being used for the purpose.[15]

During the seven centuries before the birth of Christ, the Roman empire had grown steadily. During the three or four centuries after his death, it declined and ultimately crumbled altogether under attack by pagan tribes from the north. Historians have concluded that a major reason for the downfall of Rome was that it was unable to deal with leisure; its citizens grew physically weak and spiritually corrupt. Although they were great engineers, soldiers, builders, and administrators, the Romans did not have the coherent philosophy of life that the ancient Athenians had. When faced by the challenge of excess wealth, luxury, and time, as a nation, they responded by yielding to corruption—and ultimately lost the simple virtues that had made them great as a nation.

An important consequence of the Roman experience was that the early Christian church became increasingly critical of the Roman way of life—particularly its entertainments, corruption, and hedonistic philosophy. During the later decades of the Roman Empire, Christians refused to admit any professional gladiator to baptism until he had pledged himself to abandon his profession. Preachers and writers of the Church frequently denounced the pagan games of the Romans, and a number of emperors, beginning in A.D. 365, after the Council of Nice, condemned the gladiatorial games.

The Dark and Middle Ages. Under attack by successive waves of northern European tribes, the Roman Empire finally collapsed. For a period of several centuries, Europe was overrun with warring tribes and shifting forces. The organized power of Rome, which had built roads, extended commerce, and provided civil order, was at an end. Gradually the Catholic Church emerged to provide a form of universal citizenship within Europe. Having suffered under the brutal persecutions of the Romans, the early Christians condemned all that their pagan oppressors had stood for—and particularly their hedonistic way of life. Indeed, the early church fathers believed in a fanatical asceticism which, particularly in the Byzantine, or

[15] *Ibid.*, p. 57.

eastern, Empire, was marked by the Anchorite movement—the idea of salvation through masochistic self-deprivation.

Even in western Europe, where the code of asceticism was not as strong, the Catholic fathers condemned Roman practices as displaying the essential depravity of human nature. In this setting, all forms of pleasure were seen as evil. H'Doubler points out that sharp distinctions were made between the "here" and the "hereafter," between good and evil, mind and body, spirituality and carnality:

the paramount consideration of all living was to save the soul. Consequently, the body was looked upon as a hindrance. To exalt the soul, the body was ignored, punished, and bruised. Anything that expressed the livelier feelings of instinctive human nature or in any way suggested former pagan ways and ideals of living, was banished.[16]

Many aspects of Roman life were forbidden during the Dark and Middle Ages, which covered a total period of almost a thousand years, between the accession of Theodosius in A.D. 408 and the beginning of the Renaissance. There was wholesale destruction of the stadia, the amphitheaters, and the baths that had characterized Roman society. Theatrical entertainment was forbidden. The Council of Elvira decided that the rite of baptism could not be extended to those connected with the stage or pantomime, and in A.D. 398, the Council of Carthage excommunicated those who attended the theater on holy days. While shows and games were reported to have been carried on for a period of time in the eastern Empire, the great spectacles and organized shows of imperial Rome were at an end.

They were replaced by a new morality, which had its roots in the monasteries that were founded in the fourth through sixth centuries in Egypt and the Near East and then spread to Europe. While Oriental and Greek monks lived primarily on the largess given to them by believers, those in western orders were convinced that salvation was obtained through faith and good works. The influential Benedictine order in particular insisted upon the dignity of labor. Their rule read, "Idleness is the great enemy of the soul. Therefore, monks should always be occupied either in manual labor or in sacred readings."[17]

Particularly in Ireland, France, the Low Countries, and Germany, monasteries were centers of learning and industry. With great zeal, monks cleared forests, reclaimed marshes, and cultivated barren plains. In many cases, monasteries formed the nucleus of what were to become cities. They

[16] Margaret H'Doubler, *Dance: A Creative Art Experience* (New York: F. S. Crofts, 1940), p. 13.
[17] James Westfall Thompson, *Economic and Social History of the Middle Ages* (New York: Frederick Ungar, 1928), p. 144.

were the symbol of stability in an age of turbulence and constant warfare. They helped to preserve Roman methods of agriculture, cattle-raising, and fruit growing and cultivated vast tracts of land throughout Europe. This was the beginning of what was later to be known as the Protestant work ethic—the idea that labor and toil were glorified and that play and idleness were evil.

It would be a mistake to assume that the Catholic Church completely wiped out all forms of play or even those ceremonies which in earlier pagan religions were the basis for community celebrations and festivities. In many instances, early Catholic priests based their religious practices on the rituals of earlier faiths, building their churches on existing shrines or temple sites, setting Christian holy days at the same time as earlier pagan festivals, and using such implements of pagan worship as bells, candles, incense, singing, and dancing. Douglas Kennedy writes that conversion to Christianity did not destroy the older forms of religious drama:

In fact, some of the old ritual was adopted by the early Church and embodied in its own practices. The yearly cycle of Miracle and Morality dramas, which played such an important part in the conversion to Christianity of the ignorant and illiterate peasantry in England, owed much of their appeal to the familiar pagan material which was widely included in their presentation.[18]

In addition, many forms of play were carried on in medieval society, which was marked by rigid class stratification. Below the nobility and clergy, there were the peasants, divided into such ranks as freemen, villeins, serfs, and slaves. Peasants did not live on the lands they cultivated but in crude huts huddled together in small villages ranging from as few as 50 to about 400 inhabitants.

Life in the Middle Ages, even for the nobility, was crude and harsh. Manors and castles were little more than stone fortresses, crowded, dark, and damp. Knightly responsibility consisted chiefly of fighting in the service of feudal rulers. In the intervals between wars, the favorite occupations were those of hunting and hawking. Hunting was considered the most noble pastime to which the nobility could devote themselves. They hunted bears, deer, boars, stags, lions, and leopards; many animals were imported from distant lands to lend variety to hunting.

As an example, the French emperor Charlemagne, who lived during the latter part of the ninth century, was a great hunting enthusiast. Although most of his career was spent in waging war, he

never missed an opportunity of hunting: so much so that it might be said that he rested himself by galloping through the forests. He was on these occasions not only followed by a large number of huntsmen and attendants of his household, but . . . by his wife and daughters . . . and surrounded by a numerous

[18] Douglas Kennedy, *England's Dances* (London: G. Bell, 1950), pp. 31-32.

and elegant court who vied with each other in displaying their skill and courage in attacking the fiercest animals.[19]

Hunting was considered a leading virtue of medieval heroes; kings and nobles, even saints, were mythologized for their skills in the chase. Among other values, it was seen as helping hunters escape the sin of idleness and thus be free from sin. (As a vigorous, tiring sport, it was believed to keep sensual temptation at bay.) It was also linked in a purposeful way to preparation for war. In a later period of history, the Italian Machiavelli pointed out that since the main concern of the Prince must be war, he must never cease thinking of it. In times of peace, thoughts of war should manifest themselves in the business of hunting:

he should be fond of hunting and thereby accustom his body to hardships, learning at the same time, the nature of topography, how mountains slope, how they are cut by valleys.[20]

The king himself designated certain royal forests for use by the nobility, and appointed officers to enforce rigorous game laws in every forest and district. Clergymen in particular were great hunting enthusiasts; bishops and abbots of the Middle Ages maintained numerous parks heavily stocked with game. Indeed, Chaucer upbraided the priests in "The Ploughman's Tale" because they thought more of hunting with their hounds and blowing the horn than of paying homage to God.

In addition to hunting, hawking was extremely popular during the feudal period. The richest nobles throughout Europe maintained extensive falconry establishments to hunt small game and other birds. A well-trained falcon was viewed as an object of great value, and hawking itself was considered a noble science. Typically, the office of Grand Falconer of France (established in 1250) was considered one of the highest in the kingdom. He was well-paid and influential and had over one hundred assistant falconers.

Other pastimes during the Middle Ages consisted of various types of games and gambling, music and dance, sports, and jousting. The games played in castles and medieval manors included early forms of chess, checkers, backgammon, and dice. At all times and in all countries during the Middle Ages, games of chance were extremely popular, although they were forbidden both by ecclesiastical and royal authority. "Dice shall not be made in the kingdom," said one law in 1256, and "those who are discovered using them, and frequenting taverns and bad places, will be looked upon as suspicious characters." Other table games were prohibited from time to

---

[19] Paul La Croix, *France in the Middle Ages: Customs, Classes, Conditions* (New York: Frederick Ungar, 1963), p. 179.
[20] Marcelle Thiébaux, "The Medieval Chase," *Speculum: A Journal of Medieval Studies*, 1967, p. 261.

time; the Council of Paris in 1212 condemned even chess. "We strictly forbid," said Louis IX, "any person to play at dice, tables, or chess."[21]

After the early period of the Middle Ages, life became somewhat more stabilized, and the chaos and anarchy of the eighth, ninth, and tenth centuries gradually began to yield to greater order and regularity. There was less violence, and travel with reasonable safety became more possible; commerce grew steadily during the eleventh century. It became customary for the nobility to fight on horseback; only common men fought on foot. Thus the term "chivalry" (from *cheval*, or horse) came into being. By the dawn of the twelfth century, the code of chivalry was developed. It came as an outgrowth of the profession of arms among feudal courtiers and involved a total ideal which glorified womanhood and the nobleman's fealty to his lord.

Tournaments and jousting became popular. At the outset, these were martial combats in which great numbers of knights engaged. They were violent and dangerous and were often condemned by the church. Gradually, they became more and more formalized, although they still represented war games of considerable military value. (The tournament was a contest between teams, and the joust was a trial of skill between two individual knights.) While there were different forms of attack, the basic object was to unhorse the opponent. An elaborate code of laws and regulations was drawn up for the preliminary arrangements and for the combat itself; no one below the rank of an esquire was permitted to engage in tournaments and jousting. McIntosh comments that the tournament, which in the thirteenth century was a serious form of military training for knights and their esquires, became a stylized and decorative pastime for the nobility of the fifteenth.[22]

Meanwhile, what of the life of the peasantry during the Middle Ages? Hulme suggests that life was not all work for the lower classes. There were village feasts and sports, practical joking, throwing weights, cockfighting, bull-baiting, and other robust exercises. "Ball games and wrestling, in which men of one village were pitted against men of another, sometimes resulted in bloodshed."[23] There was sometimes dancing on the green and, on holidays, miracle and morality plays. However, peasants usually went to bed at dark, reading was a rare accomplishment, and there was much drinking and crude brawling. For peasants, hunting was more a means of obtaining food than a sport. Although the lords usually tramped down and rode through the hedges and plowed fields of the peasantry, the lower classes were not even allowed to defend their lands against wild animals. If they were caught poaching, they were often maimed or hanged as punishment. The right of the peasant to engage in sport was viewed as different

---

[21] La Croix, *op. cit.*, p. 237.
[22] McIntosh, *op. cit.*, pp. 30-31.
[23] Edward M. Hulme, *The Middle Ages* (New York: Holt, 1938), p. 604.

from that of the nobility. Coulton comments that "some peasants played on holy days, and play in those days was mainly bound up with gambling, quite apart from the attendant temptation of shirking church service; therefore it is very rare to find a medieval moralist who makes any liberal allowance for sports and pastimes, among the lower classes."[24] Typically, certain games were classified as rich men's sports and poor men's sports; sometimes the distinction was made between urban and rural sports or aristocratic and plebeian pastimes.

Gradually during the Middle Ages, life became somewhat easier, and an increased number of pastimes, entertainments, and holidays came into being. Many sports in current practice today were found in rudimentary form during the Middle Ages. Typically, in England, a rough and ready form of football was played as a contest between the men of neighboring villages. Sir Thomas Elyot described the game as unfit for gentlemen: "foote-balle, wherein is nothing but beastlie furie and extreme violence, whereof proceedeth hurte, and consequently rancor and malice."[25]

Archery was extremely popular and was encouraged by English kings during the fourteenth and fifteenth centuries because of its military value. Every Englishman was commanded to have a bow of his own height, and butts were set up in every town; inhabitants were required to shoot on all feast days or be fined. Football was forbidden in some cities, including London, because it drew men away from the more useful sport of archery. Similarly, in France during the fourteenth century, Charles V wished to give a more serious and useful character to the games of the people; in a celebrated edict that forbade games of chance, he encouraged the establishment of companies of archers throughout his kingdom. Other forms of play were devised. In France, Rabelais collected a list of 220 games which were played during his era; these included variations of tennis, billiards, skittles, shuttlecock, and a French game, *la soule*, which was a type of mass ball game.

In addition, entertainment of various kinds became increasingly popular. While organized spectacles in stadia and arenas had died out with the fall of the Roman Empire, there continued to be village commons where people during the Middle Ages flocked to watch bear-baiting, bull-baiting, and even horse-baiting by dogs. Several places in London were set aside for such shows, and admission was charged. In effect, these were throwbacks to the cruel displays of the Roman era; in some cases in France, kings imported menageries of lions, bears, leopards, and other wild beasts and pitted them against each other in bloody public spectacles. Often the approach was more comic. At village feasts, wrestling matches between two men who were blindfolded, fighting a fat goose or pig with a stick, or at-

---

[24] G. G. Coulton, *The Medieval Village* (Cambridge: Cambridge University Press, 1925), p. 93.
[25] *Ibid.*, p. 95.

tempting to seize a greased pig were burlesques of more serious combats. Fitzstephen, in describing life in London in the twelfth century, wrote that each year on Shrove Tuesday, boys engaged in cockfighting in the morning and after dinner went into the fields to play ball. During the Easter holidays, water-jousting from boats on the Thames was organized and "upon the bridge, wharfs and houses by the river's side, stand great numbers to see and laugh there at."[26]

The people of the Middle Ages had an insatiable love of sightseeing; they would come great distances to witness amusing exhibitions or entertainments. There was no religious event, no parish fair, no municipal feast, and no parade or review of the troops that did not bring together great crowds of people. When the kings of France brought together their principal retainers once or twice a year, they distributed food and liquor among the common people and provided military displays, court ceremonies, and entertainment by jugglers, tumblers, and minstrels.

The nobility of the Middle Ages generally had a great amount of leisure. Peasants usually worked as long as twelve hours a day; during the later Middle Ages and the Renaissance, this was extended to fourteen to eighteen hours a day for craftsmen and other city workers. However, hours were shorter during the winter months, and holidays were plentiful. The Catholic Church had replaced the original Greek and Roman festival days with Christian holidays and had made the Sabbath the day of rest. As increasing numbers of saints' days were added, members of crafts guilds during the Middle Ages had as many as 170 days off (including Sundays, vacations, and special holidays) a year.

The Renaissance Period. Historians generally view the first half of the Middle Ages (roughly from A.D. 400 to 1000) as the Dark Ages and about the next 500 years as *le haut Moyen Age*, or high Middle Age. The Renaissance is said to have gotten under way in Italy about A.D. 1350, in France about 1450, and in England about 1500. It marked a transition between the medieval world and the modern age.

As the major European nations stabilized themselves during this period under more solidly established monarchies, power shifted from the rulers of the church to kings and their noblemen. There was an increase in urban manufacturing and trade and a growth of national states, along with a rising capitalist class. There were great new developments in terms of science and philosophy and a rebirth of interest in the arts and literature of ancient Greece and Rome.

In Italy and France particularly, the nobility became patrons of great painters, sculptors, musicians, dancers, and dramatists. These artists were no longer dominated by the ideals and values of the Catholic Church; instead they were free to serve secular goals. A great wave of music and literature swept through the courts of Europe, aided by the development

26 McIntosh, *op. cit.*, p. 32.

of printing. Dance and theater became more complex and elaborate, and increasingly lavish entertainments and spectacles were presented in the courts of Italy and France.

Life became marked by increasingly elaborate forms of amusement. Usually these were designated as appropriate for one social class or another. In England during the sixteenth century, tennis became popular among all classes, although Henry VIII tried to restrict it to noblemen and property owners. Cockfighting and archery were also enjoyed by all, although as firearms improved, archery became less popular. In England, football was seen chiefly as a lower-class sport. In contrast, McIntosh points out that one of the most popular pastimes of the Italian nobility during the fourteenth and fifteenth centuries was football, known as *calcio*. Regulations in Florence stipulated that only those of high social class might play, such as "honorable soldiers, gentlemen, lords and princes," and that "rapscallions, artificers, servants and low-born fellows" might not take part.

Similarly, Castiglione, a leading authority on the life of the Renaissance courtier, commended tennis and boating but criticized tumbling and rope-climbing as fit only for jugglers. The dance in particular was an important adjunct to court life in all of the palaces of the Renaissance. Queen Elizabeth of England was said to have selected her Lord Chancellor not because of his special knowledge in the law, but because he wore "green bows on his shoes and danced the Pavane to perfection." De Mille writes:

All courtiers took a lesson every day and their dances were exact and rigidly schooled. They were simple in steps, gracious and pretty and very intricate, involving fancy floor patterns, separation from one another, and changing and lacing of arms. The emphasis was always on deportment and manner.[27]

As the Renaissance continued, music, dance, theater, and opera all became professionalized. In courts throughout Europe, opera houses, theaters, and ballet companies were founded under royal sanction and subsidy. During the sixteenth and seventeenth centuries, the theater became particularly popular in England, where it was played in public squares and courtyards. Professional theaters were established such as the Drury Lane in London in the 1570's, and street theaters, such as Tabarin's, in Paris, in the early 1600's. Gradually, as more people entered the middle classes, the audience for such entertainments grew.

Meanwhile, a new philosophy came into being which gave much support to play—particularly as a form of education. Among the educators and writers who contributed to these newer concepts were Vittorino von Feltre, François Rabelais and Michel de Montaigne.

Von Feltre established a famous school in Mantua, Italy, in the early years of the fifteenth century, with a varied curriculum which gave much emphasis to games and play. He believed that games developed a grace and

[27] Agnes de Mille, *The Book of the Dance* (New York: Golden Books, 1963), p. 63.

agility of the body which affected the entire character and bearing of youth and that when play was enthusiastically indulged in, it kept "laziness and effeminacy" at bay. Noting that the most zealous scholars were also the most eager to play, Vittorino encouraged contests in archery and ball games and regular exercises in riding, fencing, running, and jumping.

Rabelais, who lived from 1490 to 1553, advanced a number of revolutionary theories on education and emphasized the need for physical exercises and games, singing, dancing, modeling and painting, nature study, and manual training. His account of the education of Gargantua makes considerable use of play as an exercise for mind and body. The French philosopher Montaigne, who lived during the sixteenth century, gave strong support to the concept of a unity of mind, body, and spirit, as opposed to the medieval ideal of a separation, or dualism, of mind and body. In his book *The Education of Children*, he wrote, "I would have his manner, behavior, and bearing cultivated at the same time with his mind. It is not the mind, it is not the body we are training; it is the man, and we must not divide him into two parts."[28]

These early educational philosophers thus rejected the ascetic view of the body as essentially evil and a source for temptation that required its being suppressed and punished. They saw the mind and body as unified parts of the total man and stressed that much learning took place through physical experience. During the Renaissance, the education of the nobility increasingly included such varied skills of a recreational nature as dance, music, riding, swordsmanship, and a variety of athletic and gamelike activities.

Locke, an Englishman who lived from 1632 to 1704, was also much concerned with play as a medium of learning. He recommended that children should make their own playthings and felt that important character training might be derived from games, provided that they were properly supervised and directed. "All the plays and diversions of children," he wrote, "should be directed toward good and useful habits."

Locke distinguished in his writing between the play of children and recreation for older youth. "Recreation," he said, "is not being idle . . . but easing the wearied part by change of business." At another point, he commented that a gentleman's serious employment should be "study: and when that demands relaxation and refreshment, it should be in some exercise of the body which unbends the body and confirms the strength and stamina."[29]

The French philosopher Rousseau (1712–1778) was one of the great theorists of experimental education in Europe. His revolutionary text *Émile* advocated full freedom of physical activity rather than constraint.

---

[28] Michel de Montaigne, *The Education of Children*, quoted in Ulich, *op. cit.*, p. 160.
[29] John Locke, quoted in McIntosh, *op. cit.*, p. 48.

Essentially, Rousseau suggested that man return to a state of nature marked by simplicity and freedom. He urged that children play freely in a variety of activities. Also, he contrived many learning experiences and problems of a mathematical and mechanical nature, many of which were based on play themes. Defending his method, Rousseau wrote:

You are troubled at seeing him spend his early years in doing nothing. What! Is it nothing to be happy? Is it nothing to skip, to play, to run about all day long? Never in his life will he be so busy as now.[30]

He commented that Émile's work and play were alike to him; his plays are his "occupations." Rousseau believed that play was an important element in character training; children should therefore be given activities which would satisfy their needs at each state of development. Sports and games had a therapeutic value in preventing idleness and antisocial activity. Rousseau was one of the first European educational theorists to propose that sport be used for political and nationalistic ends. He was asked to prepare a proposal on education for the reconstituted government of Poland and in 1773 published a report, *Considerations on the Government of Poland*. This document suggested that games were to make children's "hearts glow and create a deep love for the fatherland and its laws." Further,

The children should not be permitted to play separately according to their fancy, but encouraged to play all together in public; and the games should be conducted in such a way that there is always some common end to which all aspire to accustom them to common action and to stir up emulation . . . their games should always be played in public and shared by all. It is not merely a question of keeping them busy, or of cultivating a sound constitution and making them alert and graceful. The important thing is to get them accustomed from an early age to discipline, to equality and fraternity, to living under the eyes of their fellow citizens and seeking public approbation.[31]

Thus, there was increasing interest during the Renaissance in play, both as a form of popular entertainment for all classes and as a medium of education. It should not be assumed, however, that religious disapproval of play had died away completely. Within the Catholic Church, throughout the Middle Ages and Renaissance, there were constant edicts against various pastimes. However, the most severe attempts at repression came during the Protestant Reformation.

Influence of the Reformation.   The Protestant Reformation was a religious movement of the 1500's which resulted in the establishment of

---

[30] Jean Jacques Rousseau, quoted in Walter Wood, *Children's Play and Its Place in Education* (London: Kegan Paul, Trench, Trubner, 1913), p. 48.

[31] Jean Jacques Rousseau, quoted in McIntosh, *op. cit.*, p. 54.

Protestantism. It was led chiefly by Martin Luther, a German monk and scholar, although a number of other reformers, such as John Calvin in Switzerland and John Knox in Scotland, were also influential leaders. The Reformation was more than just a religious struggle but part of a broader stream which included economic, social, and political currents. In part it represented the influence of the growing middle classes, who allied themselves with the nobility to wrest power from the church. During the Middle Ages, the kingdoms of Europe had been marked by shifting boundaries and constant civil wars. As nationalism spread, rulers gained greater power, and challenged that of the church. After a series of savage civil wars, the Reformation resulted in increased power for the rising middle classes in Europe and for a number of monarchies. In some nations, Catholicism remained the state religion, in others it was displaced, and in still others it existed side by side with newer faiths. However, the new Protestant sects tended to be more solemn and austere than the Catholic authorities they had displaced.

For example, in Geneva, Calvin established an autocratic system of government in 1541, directed by a group of *Presbyters*, morally upright men who controlled the social and cultural life of the community to the smallest detail. There was ruthless suppression of heretics, and dissenters were burned at the stake. Miller and Robinson describe the unbending Puritanism that was established in Geneva:

"Purity of conduct" was insisted upon, which meant the forbidding of gambling, card playing, dancing, wearing of finery, singing of gay songs, feasting, drinking and the like. There were to be no more festivals, no more theaters, no more ribaldry, no more light and disrespectful poetry or display. Works of art and musical instruments were removed from the churches.[32]

In each of the countries where Protestantism took effect, there were similar strenuous attempts to curtail public amusements, sports, the arts, or the pleasurable use of leisure. In some cases, when rulers were overthrown and power assumed by new groups of antimonarchists, sports became an issue of politics as well as of religion. They were identified with the luxury-loving court, and the attempt to abolish them represented an attack on the monarchists by the new, hard-working middle class. Indeed, it was during the Reformation that the Protestant work ethic first came into being in Germany, England, Scandinavia, and elsewhere in Europe.

Throughout Europe there was a new aura of grim dedication to work and a determination to enforce old codes against play and idleness. This is illustrated in the following passage, describing school discipline exerted in Germany at the beginning of the eighteenth century. A schoolmaster, Franke, wrote:

[32] Norman P. Miller and Duane M. Robinson, *The Leisure Age* (Belmont, Calif.: Wadsworth, 1963), p. 66.

Play must be forbidden in any and all of its forms. The children shall be instructed in this matter in such ways as to show them, through the presentation of religious principles, the wastefulness and folly of all Play. They shall be led to see that play will distract their hearts and minds from God, the eternal good, and will work nothing but harm to their spiritual lives. Their true joy and hearty devotion should be given to their blessed and holy savior, and not to earthly things, for the reward of those who seek earthly things is tears and sorrow.[33]

The English Puritans carried out a constant battle to limit or condemn sports and various forms of entertainment and amusement during the sixteenth through eighteenth centuries, partly in an attempt to enforce religious observation of the Sabbath. Sunday football and tennis were banned during the reign of Richard II, but this was apparently intended to encourage archery practice rather than for religious reasons. Sunday fairs and markets were prohibited by Henry VI. Many Englishmen, however, having made an appearance at church, used to spend the rest of the day drinking in taverns, dancing, or enjoying other pastimes. "In the Sunday," wrote a moralist of Chaucer's period, "reigneth more lechery, gluttony . . . and other sins . . . than reigned all the week before."[34]

Under Henry VII, a document known as *The King's Book* stressed that Sunday should be spent in holy works and that those who spent it in "idleness, gluttony, riot or other vain or idle pastimes would be better occupied labouring in the field." This edict seemed to have little effect, however, and four years later, Thomas Cramer, Archbishop of Canterbury, complained that to sanctify the Sabbath was

not to pass over that day in lewd pastimes, in banqueting, in dicing and carding, in dancing and bear-baiting, in bowling and shooting, in laughing and whoring, and in such-like beastly and filthy pleasures of the flesh; nor yet in bargaining, buying and selling . . . but to apply own whole mind and body unto godly and spiritual exercises.[35]

Anglican preachers during the Elizabethan period bitterly attacked stage plays, church festive gatherings, dancing, gambling, bowling, tennis, and football and other such "devilish pastimes" as bear-baiting, cockfighting, hawking and hunting, holding fairs and markets, and reading "lascivious and wanton books." They were particularly antagonistic toward Sunday games and plays. The court, however, was tolerant of these, and people flocked to them despite the admonition of clerics. One preacher complained that a "fylthye play" might call to itself a thousand with one "blast of a trumpette," while "an hourse tolling of a Bell" would bring only a hundred to a sermon.

[33] See Harvey C. Lehman and Paul A. Witty, *The Psychology of Play Activities* (New York: A. S. Barnes, 1927), p. 1.
[34] See Peter Fryer, *Mrs. Grundy: Studies in English Prudery* (London: House and Maxwell, 1964), p. 90.
[35] *Ibid.*, p. 90.

James I, however, recognized that to prohibit such harmless amusements as dancing, archery, leaping, vaulting, and the erection of maypoles would give rise to public anger. In 1618, he issued a *Declaration on Lawful Sports*, in which he asked "When shall the common people have leave to exercise, if not upon the Sundayes and holy daies, seeing they must apply their labour and win their living in all working daies?" Rebuking some "Puritans and precise people" in Lancashire for unlawfully punishing those who engaged in "lawful recreation and honest exercises" on Sundays and other holy days after the afternoon sermon, James stressed the military value of sport and the danger of drinking and other vices if sport were denied to people. He concluded:

As for our good people's lawful recreation our pleasure likewise is, that after the end of divine service, our good people be not disturbed, letted or discouraged from any lawful recreation, such as dancing, either man or woman, archery for men, leaping, vaulting or any such harmless recreation.[36]

During the Civil War and the Commonwealth period in England, however, there were a series of ever-stricter laws to repress Sunday trade, travel without reasonable cause, and all forms of games, sports, and other pastimes. Existing maypoles were to be taken down, and no new ones put up. Those who could not pay the fines that were imposed were put in the stocks. Fryer comments that by the closing decades of the eighteenth century, people in England were forced to take their Sunday pleasures by stealth:

The hallmark of the English Sunday was hypocrisy. Many who would not walk in the fields for pleasure, where their wickedness would be seen and commented on, did not scruple to drink all day in private alehouses. If one were rich enough, one could be more open about Sunday recreation—go in for coach racing, perhaps, for very heavy wagers, or play cards in West End houses.[37]

The Development of Parks and Recreation Areas. During the Middle Ages, the need for defense required that cities be built in a compact way, surrounded by high walls that left little space for public gardens or sports or game areas. The invention of gunpowder and cannon, however, made the walled city difficult to defend; residents rapidly began to flow out of the central city and to develop satellite communities around it. In most cases, there was no definite planning of the area outside the existing walls.

As the Renaissance period got under way, however, European town planning became characterized to some degree by wide avenues, long approaches, vistas of handsome buildings, and similar monumental features. As the nobility began to acquire sizable estates and to develop elaborate

---

[36] McIntosh, *op. cit.*, p. 43.
[37] Fryer, *op. cit.*, p. 106.

gardens, some of these were opened to public use. This occurred first in Italy at the end of the thirteenth century. There were walks and public squares, often decorated with statuary. In some cases, religious brotherhoods built clubhouses, gardens, and shooting stands for archery practice; these were used by other townsmen for recreation and amusement. Increasingly, cities were equipped with large public squares and courts where gatherings and entertainments might take place.

In seventeenth-century France, other forms of space began to be provided for public use. Until this time, there was much reliance on the use of meadows for sport, on the outskirts of cities and towns. In crowded Paris, still constricted within its fifteenth-century walls, the banks and bridges of the Seine were used heavily by the public at play. Responding to public demands for more open space within the town in 1605, Henri IV had his planners design the Place Royale, an extensive plaza linked to a long promenade. In addition, two other types of areas were developed in seventeenth-century Paris—green lawns lying along the ramparts of the river, called "mails," which were useful for popular sports, chiefly croquet, and alleys of trees which were planted to create promenades, or "cours," where people might stroll during the evening hours.

During the period between 1500 and the latter part of the eighteenth century, throughout Europe the nobility began to develop extensive private grounds. These often included topiary work (trees and shrubbery clipped in fantastic shapes), aviaries, fishponds, summer houses, water displays, outdoor theaters, hunting grounds and menageries, and facilities for such games as tennis, bowling, archery, and racing. During this period, such famed gardens as the Tuileries and the Luxembourg in Paris and Versailles outside of Paris were established by the French royalty; similar gardens and private estates were found all over Europe.

Following the early Italian example, it became the custom to open these private parks and gardens to the public. At first it was done inconsistently or by caprice; some might be kept open for a time and then suddenly closed at the whim of the ruler or nobleman. In London, the great parks were the property of the Crown, and in the eighteenth century were completely given up to the use of the people, who came to expect this as a matter of right. When Queen Caroline had a fancy to shut up Kensington Gardens, she asked her adviser, Lord Walpole, what it might cost to do so; he gave the significant reply, "Only three crowns."

Three major types of large parks came into existence during the late Renaissance. The first were royal hunting preserves or parks, some of which have become famous public parks today, such as the 4,000-acre Prater in Vienna or the Tiergarten in Berlin. Second were the ornate and formal garden parks designed according to the so-called French style of landscape architecture. Third were the so-called English garden parks, which strove to produce naturalistic landscape effects. This became the prevailing style in most European cities, except in cemetery parks, where the formalistic style remained popular. Weir comments that, while most of these magnificent park creations were designed and built for royalty, they became a rich heritage to later generations, since practically all became public property, open to the use of the people. It was the French Revolution that ended the period of park-building for privileged classes and established the need of the common people as the primary concern.

Apart from the development of parks and gardens, what other sorts of recreative provisions were made for the public at large? In England, there were beginning efforts at city planning during the eighteenth century, when it became apparent that cities were becoming more crowded, dirty, and unhealthy. Business and residential streets were paved, and street names posted. Since it was believed that overcrowding led to disease (in the seventeenth century London had suffered from recurrent attacks of the Plague), an effort was made to convert open squares into gardens and create more parks and open spaces and greenery. Deaths from contagious disease declined during each successive decade of the eighteenth century; this improvement was believed to have been due to greater cleanliness and ventilation within the city. Thus, support grew for more parks and greenery.

Great outdoor gardens were established to provide entertainment and relaxation. Vauxhall, a pleasure resort founded during the reign of Charles II, represented the zenith of the tea-garden movement. It was heavily treed and had walks and bowers, lighting displays, water mills, fireworks, artificial caves and grottoes, entertainment, and eating places. It was supported chiefly by the growing class of merchants and tradesmen; the poor were excluded by a small admission charge. Also, it was far enough removed from London proper to "exclude the rabble" and so had a degree of exclusiveness.

Other pleasure resorts open to the public during the eighteenth century were gardens and amphitheaters at Ranelagh and the Pantheon. These featured music, singing, tea, and coffee; it was considered that they helped to raise moral standards. Even the caustic critic Dr. Johnson declared, "I am a great friend to public amusements; for they keep people from vice."

During the early decades of the eighteenth century in London, another social institution came into being—the coffeehouse. These were at first places where businessmen might meet to carry on trade informally or where professional men might gather to discuss topics of mutual interest. Thus, one became a center for lawyers, another for political figures. Coffeehouses became increasingly popular as places for social diversion; Botsford quotes a visitor to London:

If you would know our manner of living, it is thus; we rise by nine, and those that frequent great men's levees find entertainment at them until eleven . . . about twelve the beau monde assembles in several chocolate and coffee houses . . . the parties have their different places, where, however, a stranger is always received . . . there are other little coffee houses much frequented in this neighborhood . . . one for officers, one for stock-jobbers and paymasters, another for "sharpers."[38]

Gradually, some coffeehouses limited their membership and became exclusive social, political, or literary clubs. Others simply became taverns or restaurants open to the public. Still others, to serve a more complex and systematically organized business life, became banks or insurance exchanges. As an example, Lloyd's of London, the famous insurance firm, developed from a coffeehouse where businessmen met to gamble on the safe transport of cargoes overseas.

Following the days of the Restoration in England, Hyde Park and St. James Park became fashionable centers for promenading by the upper classes during the early afternoon. Varied amusements were held in the parks—wrestling matches, races, military displays, fireworks, and illuminations on special occasions. Aristocrats, merchants, and tradesmen all rode, drove carriages, and strolled in them. Horse-racing, lotteries, and other forms of gambling became new vogues. Indeed, government-sponsored lotteries became a popular means of raising money to pay for such public institutions or buildings as hospitals, bridges, or museums. Among the lower classes, tastes varied according to whether one lived in the country or city. Countrymen continued to engage vigorously in such sports as football, cricket, wrestling, or "cudgel-playing." Many Londoners sought more exciting spectator events in increasing numbers; bear-baiting, bull-baiting, cockfighting, and professional sports, such as professional boxing, were increasingly popular. Typically, boxing became an enthusiasm of the well-to-do, in which servants of the nobility fought each other while their masters watched. By the middle of the 1700's, this had become one of the most popular amusements, and was carried on commercially. Thus, in many ways, despite Puritan disfavor following the Reformation, parks and recreation areas were provided in increasing amounts for the public, and a variety of amusements found popular support in England.

France provides another example of the growth of recreational · interests during this period. For the wealthy during the eighteenth century, Paris was a "city of pleasure carried to a high pitch." They had the opportunity for leisurely play all week long—paying and receiving visits, dining, and passing evenings at gaming, at the theater, ballet, or opera, or at clubs. The working classes and industrial population had only Sundays and fête days, or holidays, for their amusements. LaCroix, however, points out that these represented a third of the whole year; in addition to those holidays decreed by the state, the church had authorized or tolerated many other special celebrations. Many economists and men of affairs argued that the ecclesiastic authorities should be called upon to reduce the number. For example, Voltaire wrote in 1756:

[38] Jay B. Botsford, *English Society in the Eighteenth Century* (New York: Macmillan, 1924), p. 211.

Twenty fête days too many in the country condemn to inactivity and expose to dissipation twenty times a year ten millions of workingmen, each of whom would earn five pence a day, and this gives a total of 180 million livres . . . lost to the state in the course of a twelvemonth. This painful fact is beyond all doubt.[39]

For the first time, one finds a concern about excessive leisure—both because of its economic effects upon industry and also because of its leading to "dissipation" among the lower classes. Within the large cities in France, many commercial places of amusement sprang up. These included cabarets or taverns of various types—some providing chiefly food and drink, others called *guinguinettes*, which were smaller and featured dancing and drinking. Cafés (of which there were 600 in Paris alone during the reign of Louis XV) provided meeting places for the unoccupied to chat, read newspapers, play dominoes, chess, or checkers, or play billiards. There were many complaints about the growing use of such establishments. The Marquis de Mirabeau stated:

The lower order of working men frequent the *guinguinettes*, licensed places of dissipation, which, it is rumoured, the authorities tolerate because of the taxes levied on them. They all go home tipsy and are unfit for work the next day. Employers of labour will tell you that their men work half time on Saturday and on Monday sleep off the effects of their dissipation; they are not up to much on Tuesday, and if there should happen to be a saint's-day in the middle of the week they do not see anything of them the other four days.[40]

Taverns did not represent the sole leisure outlet of eighteenth-century Parisians. There were many other opportunities for play; LaCroix comments that the upper classes still took part actively in fencing and riding, tennis, dice, cards, and scandal, while the lower classes had "the monopoly of bowls, skittles, and archery." There were frequent excursions to the country, where many took part in dancing in outdoor pavilions and a few in bathing. When the Seine was frozen over, a great crowd would enjoy sliding on the ice. The chief amusement of the Parisians of all classes and ages was the promenade, which the wealthy indulged in every day and the lower classes on Sundays and holy days. For these, they visited the great parks—the Bois de Boulogne, the Jardin des Plantes, the Luxembourg and Tuileries Gardens, and others. As in London, there were public gardens, where for a small fee people could be admitted and where there were a variety of amusements, such as fireworks, light shows, and dancing.

There were many public festivals on occasions of royal marriages, coronations, or other times of public celebration, when free wine and food were provided for the public, and as many as one hundred illuminated

39 La Croix, *op. cit.*, p. 346.
40 *Ibid.*, p. 346.

boats would go up and down the Seine, each with a band of music. Dancing continued through the year, with the lower classes taking part in commercial dance halls and rotundas and the upper classes giving private balls for invited guests during the winter only. The theater enjoyed a great vogue in eighteenth-century Paris; by 1719, there were the Opéra, the Comédie-Francaise, the Comédie Italienne, and the Opéra Comique. In each of these, the royal actors paid no rent for their theaters, and many of the production expenses were paid by the Crown. Lower-class people were admitted inexpensively to the pit, while the upper class sat in more expensive boxes and loges. By the 1770's, all the chief cities in the French provinces had theaters comparable to those in Paris, and there were many strolling companies that visited smaller towns.

Thus, we see in France and England (presented here as only one segment of the total European development during this period) widespread participation in varied forms of recreation by all classes. During this period, authorities in both nations exerted pressures to control varied forms of public amusement which they regarded as immoral. Linked to this was the economic concern, expressed especially in France, that unlimited play and amusement (particularly drinking in taverns) was a threat to economic productivity and that the number of holidays had to be reduced for this reason. As a final trend, there was the development of both public and private places of amusement and the emergence of varied forms of commercialized recreation which appealed to masses of people on all social levels.

This then was the status of recreation and leisure on the eve of the Industrial Revolution. The work ethic was not yet fully established, and leisure was still comparatively widespread. Dramatic changes were soon to take place, both in the nations of Europe and in the new society that was developing on the other side of the Atlantic.

7

Recreation and Leisure
in Colonial America

What was the history of recreation and leisure in the early American colonies? Tradition tells us that it was marked by stern Puritan repression of play. This was true chiefly in Calvinist New England; in the middle Atlantic and southern colonies, restrictions tended to be relaxed within a few decades after settlement.

It should be recognized that those who settled the shores of North America brought with them the pastimes and pleasures of their homelands as well as their attitudes of repression. There was a steady traffic back and forth to the British Isles of colonists, representatives of the Crown, fur-traders, and other commercial travelers, as well as newspapers, books, and other materials that imparted elements of culture. Yet there was also a long and dangerous ocean journey that cut the colonists off from too-easy communications or flight from the colonies.

The first need of the new colonists was to survive. They had to plant crops, cut down forests and clear away trees, build shelters, and defend themselves against Indians. Over one-half of the colonists who arrived on the *Mayflower* did not survive the first winter near Plymouth. In such a setting, work was of the essence; it was necessary for survival. There was little time, money, or energy to support amusements or public entertainment. Also, without a royalty that had the wealth, leisure, and taste to patronize the arts, there was little opportunity for music, theater, or dance to flourish. But most important of all, at the outset, was the religious attitude.

The Puritan settlers of New England came to the New World to establish a society that would be based on a Calvinistic interpretation of the Bible. There were strict ordinances against gambling, drama, certain forms of music, and dancing—particularly mixed dancing (between men and women). Dancing in taverns and maypole dancing were especially condemned; Governor Endicott of the Massachusetts Bay Colony cut down the maypole at Merry Mount, grimly warning the revelers against this "pagan" practice. The theater was completely prohibited in several colonies. Connecticut judged as "common rogues" and served fifteen lashes on the bare backs of those found guilty of practicing "common plays, interludes, or other crafty science."[1] A number of New England colonies banned dice, cards, quoits, bowls, ninepins, and similar pastimes in "house, yard or garden." There was especially strong enforcement of the Sabbath laws; Sunday work, travel, or recreation, even "unnecessary and unseasonable walking in the streets and fields," was prohibited.

Idleness in particular was detested and work enforced. At Jamestown, Virginia, Sir Thomas Dale ruled that any tradesman who failed to work daily at his trade should be "condemned to the Galley" for three years. The Virginia Assembly decreed in 1619 that any person found idle should be bound over to compulsory work. It prohibited gambling, regulated drinking, and penalized excessively rich attire. Gradually, however, these stern restrictions declined in the southern colonies. There, the upper classes had both wealth and leisure because of their larger estates and plantations, on which the labor was done by indentured servants and slaves. Many of them had ties with the landed gentry in England, and they shared their tastes for aristocratic amusements. Dulles writes:

Once the colony was firmly established and the need for incessant work began to lessen, Virginians were more generally permitted to make the most of whatever opportunities for recreation their expanding life presented.[2]

Plantation life became marked by lavish entertainment and hospitality in the southern colonies. Holidays, weddings, family reunions, and even funerals were marked by lavish feasting, dancing parties, and music. Hunting and fishing were especially popular, as was gambling. Card games of all types, lotteries, roulette tables, and dice were common. Carson writes:

Gaming was not considered an evil in itself; it became a vice only when "inordinate" pursuit of the amusement led one to neglect his business or lose more money than he could afford. Professional gamesters were condemned for cheating if caught red-handed, but controlled "deceit" was only a mark of the skillful player. In Virginia, as in England, gaming was a gentleman's privilege, forbidden

---

[1] Foster Rhea Dulles, *A History of Recreation: America Learns to Play* (New York: Appleton-Century-Crofts, 2nd ed., 1965), p. 6.
[2] *Ibid.*, p. 5.

by law to those who were supposed to be working: apprentices, artificers, fishermen, husbandmen, laborers, mariners, servants of all kinds.[3]

Such "unlawful games" as bear-baiting, bull-baiting, bowling, cards, cock-fighting, quoits, dice, football, ninepins, and tennis were usually forbidden to working men, servants, apprentices, and students. Yet it is clear that even they enjoyed these forbidden activities frequently. By the close of the eighteenth century, a French visitor, the Marquis de Chastellux observed:

The indolence and dissipation of the middling and lower classes of white inhabitants of Virginia, are such as to give pain to every reflecting mind. Horse racing, cock fighting, and boxing matches are standing amusements, for which they neglect all business.[4]

Horse racing became particularly popular, at first in the South and then throughout the middle Atlantic colonies. The theater too began in Virginia, where the first theater was erected in Williamsburg in 1716. By 1750, professional companies had begun to tour the colonies from New York to Savannah. The theater became a constant diversion among the upper classes in the middle and southern colonies. A host of other pastimes, including pleasure boating, shooting matches, golf, tennis, cricket, and concert-going became increasingly widespread.

In the northern colonies, Puritan magistrates attempted to maintain curbs on amusements long after the practical reasons for such prohibitions had disappeared. Early records show many cases of young people being fined, confined to the stocks, or publicly whipped for such "violations" as walking in the streets and fields, gambling, bowling, dancing, or carrying on other forms of "lascivious" behavior. Yet the Puritans permitted bundling, which was a fairly open invitation to premarital sexual activity. Despite the supposedly stricter religious principles in New England, there is evidence that

among New Englanders of all social classes in the early part of the eighteenth century . . . fornication if followed by marriage, no matter how long delayed, was considered a venial sin, if sin at all.[5]

Similarly, taverns were widely established throughout New England by the early part of the eighteenth century, providing places where gentlemen might "enjoy their bowl and bottle with satisfaction" and engage in bil-

---

[3] Jane Carson, Colonial Virginians at Play (Charlottesville: University Press of Virginia, 1965), p. 53.
[4] Dulles, op. cit., p. 35.
[5] James Truslow Adams, Provincial Society, 1690–1763 (New York: Macmillan, 1927), p. 159.

liards, cards, skittles, shuffleboard, and bowling. Drinking in particular was widespread throughout the colonies. Andrews writes:

the colonists were heavy drinkers and . . . consumed liquors of every variety in enormous quantities on all important occasions—baptisms, weddings, funerals, barn raisings, church raisings, house raisings, ship launchings, ordinations . . . at meetings of commissions and committees, and in taverns, clubs, and private houses. In New England a new officer was expected on training day to "wet his commission bountifully." Among the New England farmers beer, cider, cider brandy, and rum were the ordinary beverages. . . . Rum was distilled in all the leading New England towns, notably at Boston and Newport.[6]

Gradually, the restrictions against varied forms of play relaxed in New England, as elsewhere. Hunting and shooting contests gained popularity; dancing and horse racing became acceptable, and such diversions as sleighing, swimming, cricket, and town-ball were widely found. Typically in New England, however, many forms of play became attached to work. Thus, country fairs were the occasion for merrymaking. Social gatherings, with attendant drinking, singing, gaming, and dancing, were held in conjunction with communal work, such as house raisings, sheep shearing, log rolling, or corn-husking bees. Play thus could be seen as justified as a reward for work, and even as the means of restoring oneself for further work. Many social pastimes were linked to other civic occasions, such as elections or training days for local militia. Dulles comments that on training days in Boston, over a thousand men would gather on the Boston Common to drill, practice marksmanship, and then celebrate in livelier fashion at nearby taverns.

By mid-eighteenth century, the stern necessity of working hard for survival had lessened, and the religious antagonism that had existed toward varied forms of amusement was diminished. The Sunday laws continued in force in many settlements, however, and there still was a lingering undercurrent of disapproval of play. The young John Adams, who was destined to become the President of the United States, wrote in his diary during the mid-1700's:

Let no trifling diversion, or amusement . . . : no girl, no gun, no cards, no flutes, no violins, no dress, no tobacco, no laziness, decoy you from your books.[7]

Some religious sections maintained their stern opposition to all forms of play. For example, the Methodist Episcopal Church in the late eighteenth century showed graphically its distrust of idleness and the temptations of play, in its following statement of policy:

[6] Charles McL. Andrews, *Colonial Folkways* (New Haven, Conn.: Yale University Press, 1919), p. 104.
[7] John Adams, quoted in Dulles, *op. cit.*, p. 44.

We prohibit *play* in the strongest terms. . . . The students shall rise at five o'clock . . . summer and winter. . . . Their recreation shall be gardening, walking, riding, and bathing, without doors, and the carpenter's, joiner's, cabinet-maker's or turner's business within doors. . . . The students shall be indulged with nothing which the world calls play. Let this rule be observed with the strictest nicety; for those who play when they are young, will play when they are old.[8]

At a time of national emergency, with the Revolutionary War approaching, the Continental Congress set out to curtail the amusements of the colonial aristocracy. One of the Articles of the "Association" of 1774 called upon the colonies to prohibit every "Species of Extravagance and Dissipation, especially all Horse Racing, and all Kinds of Gaming, Cock Fighting, Exhibitions of Shows, Plays, and other expensive Diversions and Entertainment."

Why this drastic ban? Dulles speculates that it might have been an expression of discontent with an extravagant way of life of the rich planters of the South by frugal, hard-working New England delegates.[9] Because of it, many kinds of entertainment, including theater, music, dance, and horse racing, were prohibited during the period of the Revolution. After it, however, such activities were restored to legitimacy, and the social life, sports, games, and tavern pastimes of city and country people both north and south became more widespread than ever before. Only in rural areas and on the extending frontier was life still isolated and lonely. Even there, community gatherings, camp meetings, fights, circuses, traveling lecturers, and shows provided temporary entertainment and social interchange.

With the passing of the eighteenth century and the beginning of the nineteenth, an increasing number of Americans began to live in cities and towns. For the first time, land was not unbounded, and the simple rural sports that were taken for granted, such as hunting and fishing, began to be threatened. It was necessary to think about conserving the land; little provision had been made for parks and open spaces during the colonial period, although there were a few such examples.

Parks and Conservation in the Colonial Era

Compared with the nations of Europe during the same era, there was little concern for developing city parks in the early American colonies. With land so plentiful and little need for recreational areas in the isolated settlements that had sprung up along the eastern seaboard, there seemed to be little need for such planning. Even in the earliest colonies, however, particularly in New England, "commons" or "greens" were established in a number of towns and villages. They were used chiefly for pasturing cattle

---

[8] *The Doctrines and Discipline of the Methodist Episcopal Church in America* (Philadelphia: Parry Hall, 1792), p. 68.
[9] Dulles, *op. cit.*, p. 66.

and sheep, as well as for drill fields and market days and fairs. Similar open places were established in towns settled by the Spanish in the South and Southwest, in the form of plazas and large squares located in the center of towns or before principal churches.

Olmsted and Kimball comment,

In America, as abroad, the municipal park was a late development. In the New England colonies the traditionally largely utilitarian type of public ground known in the old country appeared again spontaneously in the new. Boston set aside a common as early as 1634, and in 1640 protected it from future diminution. In 1728 its improvement began in recognition of its long use as a recreation ground.[10]

All through Massachusetts, Connecticut, Vermont, and New Hampshire, there are still examples of beautiful village greens which were established during this early period.

Gradually, in the design of new cities throughout the colonies, attention was paid to the need for preserving or establishing parks and other open spaces. Among the first cities in which such plans were made were Philadelphia, Pennsylvania, Savannah, Georgia, and Washington, D.C.

In Philadelphia, there was a conscious effort to provide public parks in a plan drafted for the city in 1682 by William Penn's Surveyor-General. The following description is extracted from the plan:

The city, as the model shows, consists of a large-front street on each river, and a High-Street near the middle, from river to river, of one hundred feet broad, and a Broad-street, in the middle of the city from side to side, of the like breadth. In the center of the city, is a square of ten acres; at each angle to build houses for public affairs. There is also in each quarter of the city a square of eight acres, to be for the like used.[11]

In the plans developed by General James Oglethorpe for Savannah, the principal city of the colony of Georgia, in 1733, even more extensive provision was made for public open space and greenery. Oglethorpe had many large forest trees spared when the site of the town was cleared, and his land-grant scheme permitted each freeholder, besides his own plot of land within the town, to have five acres outside, which would serve him as a garden and orchard. Oglethorpe envisioned a populous city that would have a large square for markets and other public purposes in every quarter, with wide and regular streets crossing each other at right angles and shaded by rows of tall trees.

[10] Frederick L. Olmsted and Theodora Kimball, quoted in Charles E. Doell and Charles B. Fitzgerald, *A Brief History of Parks and Recreation in the United States* (Chicago: The Athletic Institute, 1954), p. 24.
[11] Thomas Holme, quoted in Doell and Fitzgerald, *ibid.*, p. 24.

The Public Gardens covered ten acres of rolling land near the river; in addition to it and to the Common, there were twenty-four other small squares and open spaces in Savannah, a remarkably generous allocation of parks for the colonial era in America. Wright points out that 150 years later, when many cities were conspicuously lacking in public grounds, Savannah had 33 acres in twenty-three public places, besides a 10-acre park and a 20-acre parade ground.[12]

When the plan was drawn up in 1791 for the new Federal city that was to become Washington, its creator, Major L'Enfant, envisioned a city with a number of majestic parks and pleasure gardens. His plan, developed with the guidance of Jefferson and Washington, included fifteen squares (each to be developed by one of the fifteen states then in existence), boulevards, a "grand cascade," a President's Park, and similar features. However, many elements of the plan were not carried out until a century later and some not at all.

The majority of colonial towns made very limited provision for parks and open recreation spaces. Typically, the Dutch colony of New Amsterdam (later to become New York) had houses built close together, facing extremely narrow streets. Only two open spaces were provided in the old part of the town, a small Bowling Green at the southern end and an open field, which later became City Hall Park, in the northern end of the settlement. It was to be almost two hundred years before Central Park would be established as a majestic open space in the heart of the city.

Early Conservation Efforts

Almost from the earliest days of settlement, there was concern for conservation of forests, open land, and, in time, wildlife. As early as 1626, in the Plymouth Colony, the cutting of trees without official consent was banned by law. The Massachusetts Bay Colony established a Great Ponds Act in 1641, which set aside 2,000 bodies of water, each over 10 acres in size, for such public uses as "fishing and fowling." This became supported as a recreational usage by the courts. In Pennsylvania, in 1681, there were laws that for every five acres of forest land that were cleared, one was to be left untouched. Other laws against unlawfully setting woods on fire or cutting certain types of trees were passed well before the Revolution.

As early as the late seventeenth century, Massachusetts and Connecticut defined hunting seasons and established rules for hunting certain types of game. Although at the outset hunting was primarily a matter of obtaining food, it rapidly became a sport in the colonies. Andrews writes:

The woods and waters offered endless opportunity in summer for fishing and in winter for such time-honored pursuits as hunting, fowling, trapping, and fishing

[12] *Ibid.*, p. 25.

through the ice. John Rowe of Boston was a famous and untiring fisherman; thousands of other enthusiasts played the part of colonial Isaak Waltons; and there was a fishing club on the Schuylkill as early as 1732.[13]

What appeared to be an inexhaustible supply of wildlife began to disappear with the advance of settlements and the destruction of the forests. Wildfowl in particular were ruthlessly hunted, particularly in New England, and "so unlicensed had the destruction of the heath hen become in New York that in 1708 the province determined to protect its game by providing for a closed season."[14] So, well before the American Revolution, we see the first establishments of parks and urban open spaces, as well as an initial concern for the conservation of forests and wildlife. Not until the latter part of the nineteenth century, however, were these to become well established in American society.

[13] Andrews, *op. cit.*, p. 113.
[14] *Ibid.*, p. 114.

8

The Nineteenth Century
in Europe and America

The nineteenth century in both Europe and America was a time of tremendous social change. Its most important single influence was the Industrial Revolution, a period of rapid development of production processes and industrial expansion, which began during the second half of the eighteenth century and continued throughout most of the nineteenth.

During the Industrial Revolution, industry was taken out of the home and the small workshop. Handwork carried on by individual craftsmen was replaced by large-scale machine operations. There were marked changes in production methods as a consequence of the invention of such devices as the spinning jenny, the water frame, the weaving machine, and the steam engine—all of which were invented during the 1760's. Increasingly, coal became used as a fuel; there was more widespread use of brick instead of wood for building and greater use of metals. Science and capital were combined to solve the problems of production, and businessmen invested in the development of new mills and factories where mechanical power was available.

Following the 1770's, there was a rapid expansion of new machines and processes of manufacture as well as new modes of transportation and communication. The invention of the locomotive, the steamboat, and the telegraph—all during the early 1800's—gave rise to greater world trade, exploration, and colonization. Networks of canals, rapidly expanded railroad lines, the completion of the transatlantic cable, and the scientific study of navigation made possible a vast expansion of industry and created a totally new way of life.

How did the Industrial Revolution influence the patterns of work, leisure, and recreational participation of various social classes during the nineteenth century? It had four major effects: it created a new urban society; it established a new, industrial way of life; it gave birth to a strengthened work ethic, which pervaded all social values and beliefs; and, finally, it encouraged more widespread recreational participation.

Urbanization

Throughout the nations of the western world, there was a steady shift of the population from rural areas to urban centers. Generally, factory wages were higher than those paid in domestic industry or agriculture, and so great numbers of country people came into the cities and new factory towns to work. Millions of peasant families left Europe in successive waves of immigration because of crop failures, being forced off their land, religious or social discrimination, and political unrest. The American population increased at a rapid rate. When Andrew Jackson became President in 1829, about 12.5 million people lived in the United States. In 1850 the total reached 23 million, and a decade later there were 31 million. In the large cities, the proportion of foreign-born was striking. In New York City in 1850, 45 percent of the population was foreign-born, with Ireland and Germany the source of most immigrant families. In Philadelphia, about one in every four residents was from Europe.

In 1850, about 85 percent of the population was still rural, living in places of less than 2,500 population. However, as more and more people moved into factory towns and large cities situated along the eastern seaboard or around the Great Lakes, the United States became increasingly an urban civilization. Both rural and foreign immigrants moved into the congested tenement areas of growing cities, living in quarters that were inadequate for decent family life (often a whole family lived crowded in a single room), under unsanitary and unsafe conditions. Counts described the new urban slums as marked by congestion, squalor, and disease; people were oppressed by starvation wages and recurrent unemployment, by monotonous and prolonged labor, including the use of women and young children in mines, mills, and factories and piecework tasks at home.[1]

The Reduction of Leisure

The trend in manual occupations in Europe during the period from the late Middle Ages to 1800 was toward longer working hours. In both France and England, the average working day climbed from 12 hours with a two-hour rest in about 1700 to a 14- to 18–hour day in 1800. By 1850,

---

[1] George Counts, *Social Foundations of Education,* Report of the Commission on the Social Studies, 1934, p. 12.

the average work week in French cities was about 70 hours. In addition, the number of holidays provided during the year, which during the Middle Ages had been as high as 115 (adding 52 Sundays to this meant that there were 167 days off a year), was sharply reduced.

The peak of working hours appears to have been reached during the first half of the nineteenth century. Gradually, pressure by trade unions and pioneering industrial legislation improved the situation. In England, for example, Factory Acts during the first four decades of the nineteenth century removed the youngest children from factories and limited the working hours of others. By law, the hours of labor were limited to ten in 1847; a nine-hour day was won by contract for most workers between 1869 and 1873. By 1919, the eight-hour day had been formally adopted in nearly all European countries.

The average industrial and agricultural work week in the United States for the period between 1850 and 1960 is illustrated in Table 8-1,

TABLE 8-1   *Changing Work Week, 1850–1960, in United States*

Year	All Industries	Agriculture	Non-Agricultural Industries
1850	69.7	72.0	65.7
1860	67.8	71.0	63.3
1870	65.3	70.0	60.0
1880	63.8	69.0	58.8
1890	61.7	68.0	57.1
1900	60.1	67.0	55.9
1910	54.9	65.0	50.3
1920	49.4	60.0	45.5
1930	45.7	55.0	43.2
1940	43.8	54.6	41.1
1950	39.9	47.2	38.8
1960	38.5	44.0	38.0

SOURCE: Sebastian de Grazia, *Of Time, Work and Leisure* (New York: Doubleday-Anchor, Twentieth Century Fund, 1962), p. 419.

which shows the steady decline of work hours (although it does not indicate other elements related to leisure, such as the number of holidays, the number of vacations, or the length of retirement).

The Development of the Protestant Work Ethic

Preceding chapters described the religious attitudes toward work which began during the early Middle Ages and during the Reformation in Europe. The Puritan ideal, which glorified work and demeaned leisure and play, became even stronger as a consequence of the Industrial Revolution. In part, it was seen as the way to religious salvation; in the United States, loyalty and dedication to work were also seen as the hallmarks of American life and the way to build a powerful nation.

As industrialization became more widespread, there was a renewed emphasis on the importance of "honest toil" and a strong antagonism expressed against play. The church fell in with the attitude of the merchant-manufacturing class that idleness led to drinking and vice and that consequently long hours of labor should be maintained for the sake of the wage-earner's moral welfare. Religious leaders supported the twelve- or fourteen-hour factory work day, as part of the "wholesome discipline of factory life."

Dubin comments that work ultimately becomes a cornerstone of society and a basis for man's self-justification. "Indeed, the capitalist system itself is asserted to rest upon the moral and religious justification that the Reformation gave to work."[2] Americans became more consciously dedicated to the Protestant work ethic than Europeans had ever been;[3] their single-minded dedication to work was noted by many foreign visitors. One British visitor commented about the grim, business-minded American way of life:

A Boston boy is a picture of prematurity. It can almost be said that every man is born middle-aged in every city in the Union. The principal business seems to be to grow old as fast as possible. The interval between their leaving school and commencing their business careers offers no occupation to give either gracefulness or strength to body or mind. Athletic games and the bolder field sports being unknown . . . all that is left is chewing, smoking and drinking.[4]

Henry Adams, the noted American historian, agreed with this picture, commenting that Boston offered "few healthy resources for boys or men. . . . Sports as a pursuit was unknown." As a youth he felt great guilt about occasional lapses into play, such as fishing.[5] Like all boys, he was constantly reminded that the most important thing in life was industry and intellectual development. But, throughout the Western world, life was a sober business. The great Scottish philosopher and historian, Thomas Carlyle, expressed the spirit of his times in such quotations as: "All work, even cotton-spinning, is noble; work is alone noble . . . a life of ease is not for any man, nor for any god," and "Even in the meanest sorts of labor, the whole soul of a man is composed into a kind of real harmony the instant he sets himself to work."[6] John Ruskin, the English social critic, wrote,

[2] Robert Dubin, "Industrial Workers' Worlds: A Study of the Central Life Interests of Industrial Workers," in Erwin O. Smigel, ed., *Work and Leisure: A Contemporary Social Problem* (New Haven, Conn.: College and University Press, 1963), p. 54.

[3] Henry Steele Commager, "On the Evils of a Foreign Education," *Saturday Review*, February 18, 1967, p. 83.

[4] Guy Lewis, "The Muscular Christianity Movement," *Journal of Health, Physical Education and Recreation*, May, 1966, p. 28.

[5] *Ibid.*, p. 28.

[6] Thomas Carlyle, *Past and Present* (Boston: Charles C. Little, 1843), Books II and III.

"Life without industry is guilt" and "When men are rightly occupied, their amusement grows out of their work."[7]

Thus, work came to be viewed as more than a necessity; indeed it became a source of social and moral values. It was therefore the proper concern of the church and subject to ethical precepts. This concern was marked by a renewed attack upon many forms of play. The church condemned many commercial amusements as "the door to all the sins of iniquity," and as late as 1844, Henry Ward Beecher, a leading minister of his time, savagely attacked the stage, the concert hall, and the circus, charging that anyone who pandered to the public taste for commercial entertainment was a moral assassin.

Despite these attitudes, many forms of play became increasingly popular throughout the country. City workers now had free time and money to spend on various forms of recreation. In addition, a new middle class was emerging—a class that began to seek out varied forms of entertainment.

Growth of Popular Participation in Recreation

Dulles writes that the first half of the nineteenth century, despite the period of religious repressions, was actually marked by the gradual expansion of popular amusements which have since played an increasingly important role in our national life:

The first half of the nineteenth century witnessed the growth of the theater as entertainment reaching out to all classes of people. It saw the beginnings of variety, minstrel shows, and the circus; the establishment of amusement parks, public dance-halls, concert saloons and beer-gardens; a revival of horse-racing and the rise of other popular sports. By the Civil War the nation was in the midst of these far-reaching changes in the recreational scene.[8]

The theater, which had been banned during the American Revolution, gradually gained favor in cities along the eastern seaboard and in a number of principal southern cities. Large theaters were built, holding as many as 4,000 persons. Frequently the theater was attacked by newspapers and religious leaders but none the less it persisted. Performances were usually given by touring players who traveled throughout the country, playing with local stock companies.

Gradually, stage performances moved in one of two directions: the legitimate stage, concerned with serious drama and directed to an audience that tended to be somewhat more upper-class and intellectual, and popular entertainment (which ultimately became burlesque and vaudeville), which

---

[7] John Ruskin, *Lectures in Art: The Relationship of Arts to Morals* (New York: Wiley, 1870), and "Sesame and Lilies," in *The Works of John Ruskin* (New York: Alden, 1885).
[8] Dulles, *op. cit.*, pp. 98-99.

presented variety shows to a more plebeian audience. By the 1830's some thirty traveling shows were regularly touring the country, presenting menageries and bands of acrobats and jugglers. Ultimately they added riding and tumbling acts and developed into circuses. Another popular form of stage entertainment, especially during the 1840's and 1850's (although they continued after the Civil War) were minstrel shows. These presentations, combining music, singing, dancing, and "blackface" comedy routines in which plantation Negroes were caricatured by white performers in burnt-cork makeup, did much to spread a caricature of Negro life that lingered in American folklore.

Sports

A number of forms of sport had their first strong impetus during the early nineteenth century. Before this, Americans had enjoyed watching amateur wrestling matches, foot races, shooting events, and horse races during colonial days or along the frontier. However, now sports events were professionally promoted. Crowds as large as 40,000 and 50,000 from all ranks of society attended highly publicized horse races, boating regattas, and five- and ten-mile races of professional runners during the 1820's. The first sports promoters were owners of resorts or of commercial transportation facilities (such as stage-coach lines, ferries, and, later, railroads). These new sports impresarios made money from transportation fares and by putting up spectators; in time, they erected grandstands for viewing and charged admissions.

Horse racing flourished; by mid-century, both running and trotting races were being held before crowds as large as 100,000. Boating and sailing regattas usually involved contestants from wealthy yacht clubs, men of the highest social class. Foot racing was a highly professional sport, with match races for large purses and heavy gambling on the outcome. Prize fighting also gained popularity as a professional sport. At first it was a brutal, bare-knuckled sport, often prohibited by legal authorities. By the time of the Civil War, gloves were used and rules established, and boxing exhibitions were becoming accepted.

Thus, by the time of the Civil War, there was widespread interest in a variety of sports. Baseball was enjoyed as a casual diversion in the towns of New England through the early decades of the nineteenth century (in the form of "rounders" or "town-ball"), and amateur teams which were usually organized by occupation (merchants and clerks, or shipwrights and mechanics) were playing on the commons of large eastern cities by the mid-1850's. However, the whole apparatus of sports in colleges and secondary schools, community sports clubs and societies, and parks and public playing fields was not yet developed.

Following the Civil War, there was a tremendous boom in public participation in team and individual sports. In an analysis of the pastimes of Union and Confederate soldiers during the Civil War, Crockett pointed out that men on both sides of the great struggle engaged in a wide variety of recreational pursuits. Soldiers in both armies took part actively in combative sports (boxing and wrestling), cock-fighting, fencing matches, boating and fishing, horseback riding, team sports, and a variety of other pursuits like tenpins, gymnastics, card-playing, table games (checkers, chess, dominoes), quoits, and similar activities.

For several reasons, the Civil War was a stimulus to recreational involvement. One was the spreading of interests; men from different sections of the land learned each others' games and sports and took them home with them. Compared with life at home, there was much more free time, and so men got in the habit of engaging in various activities. There was no Puritanical influence to prevent certain forms of play, and while some soldiers may have objected to card-playing on religious grounds, other activities all seemed acceptable in the rough-and-ready atmosphere of army camp life.

The Muscular Christianity Movement. Gradually, a number of leading mid-century preachers began to argue that physical prowess and sanctity were thoroughly compatible. Henry Ward Beecher drew a line between "harmful" amusements and those which contributed to well-being, saying, "Don't be tempted to give up a wholesome air-bath, a good walk, or a skate or ride every day [as] it will pay you back . . . by freshness, elasticity, and clearness of mind."[9] For the first time, Americans took a hard look at themselves and were not pleased with what they saw. Oliver Wendell Holmes argued that widespread participation in sports would create a physically fit citizenry:

I am satisfied that such a set of black-coated, stiff-jointed, soft-muscled, paste-complexioned youth as we can boast in our Atlantic cities never before sprang from the loins of Anglo-Saxon lineage. . . . We have a few good boatmen, no good horsemen that I hear of, nothing remarkable, I believe, in cricketing, and as for any great athletic feat performed by a gentleman in these latitudes, society would drop a man who ran around the common in five minutes.[10]

There suddenly developed a great interest in outdoor and athletic activities. Skating became a vogue in the 1850's, and rowing and boating grew popular, especially for the upper social classes. The Muscular Christianity movement—called this in part because of the support given to it by leading church figures and in part because sports and physical activity were seen as building morality and good character—had its greatest influence in schools and colleges, which began to initiate programs of physical educa-

[9] Lewis, *op. cit.*, p. 28.
[10] *Ibid.*, p. 28.

tion and athletic competition, and in the Young Men's Christian Association, which based its program heavily on active physical recreation and health education.

In Europe, since the late eighteenth century, sports were seen as an important means of achieving physical fitness and national morale. J. F. Jahn envisioned a national sporting movement which would regenerate the German people after their crushing defeats in the Napoleonic Wars. In his *Deutsches Volkstum* (German Way of Life) Jahn wrote:

Only when all men of military age have become capable, through physical education, of bearing arms, have become ready for combat through weapon training, prompt to strike through new kinds of war games and constant alertness, and battle keen through love of the Fatherland—only then can a people be called militarily prepared.[11]

In the early decades of the nineteenth century, Jahn's *turnen* (system of gymnastics) spread rapidly through Germany, with strong military and political support. It was not really play but a form of rigorous drill, involving exercises on horizontal and parallel bars, rope and ladder climbing, and pole vaulting. It represented, however, a socially approved form of organized physical activity and as such was an innovation that spread rapidly among other northern European nations. Emphasis on games and sports in the schools was not to develop until later.

In England, the development of recreational sports was heavily influenced by the factor of social class. The British aristocracy engaged heavily in such traditional rural sports as hunting, shooting, and angling. Only the land-owning aristocracy was permitted by the Game Laws to hunt on horseback; it was forbidden to buy or sell game, and the Game Laws, as late as 1816, threatened heavy penalties for poachers. Other aristocratic sports were golf and tennis. The lower ranks of society had a number of popular sports, including athletic competitions of various types carried on at country fairs, including a "mob" form of football, after work was done.

Team sports gradually gained approval in the fashionable English public (actually private, or preparatory) schools. At the outset, there was much hostility to them because of their origins. McIntosh writes:

Headmasters were hostile to sport. Dr. Keats at Eton tried to prevent cricket against Harrow; the headmaster at Westminster tried to prevent rowing races with Eton, and Dr. Butler, headmaster of Shrewsbury, thought that football was "only fit for butcher boys."[12]

However, students organized their own interscholastic sports competitions. Gradually Rugby football spread, then cricket and organized boating

[11] J. F. Jahn, quoted in P. C. McIntosh, *Sport in Society* (London: C. A. Watts, 1963), p. 57.
[12] *Ibid.*, p. 65.

matches. In time, leading headmasters began to believe that sport improved discipline and contributed to "valuable social qualities and manly virtues." The headmaster of one school, who had referred to the "idle boys, I mean the boys who play cricket," was succeeded by one who said, "Give me a boy who is a cricketer. I can make something of him." A number of leading clerical figures gave support to sports; one clergyman, Charles Kingsley, summed up this view in 1874:

that games conduce, not merely to physical but to moral health; that in the playing fields boys acquire virtues which no books can give them; not merely daring and endurance, but, better still, temper, self restraint, fairness, honour, unenvious approbation of another's success, and all that "give and take" of life which stand a man in such good stead when he goes forth into the world, and without which, indeed, his success is always maimed and partial.[13]

Thus, in both Europe and America, active participation in sports, games, and outdoor recreation at last became respectable and grew to new heights of popularity.

School and College Sports Programs. In Europe, early programs of physical education were chiefly based on formal approaches to gymnastics and drill-like activities. However, games and sports gradually became valued for their intrinsic appeal to youth. In Germany a Central Committee for Popular and Juvenile Games was formed, and by the 1870's and 1880's, games and sports were made an integral part of the school curriculum, first in the _Gymnasium_ (higher school) and then in the middle and lower grades. An "order" issued by the Prussian Minister of Public Worship and Instruction, in October, 1882, urged that

The School must foster play as an expression of youthful life salutary for body and mind, for heart and soul alike, along with increase in physical strength and skills and the ethical effects which attend it, and this must be done not merely now and then, but as a matter of course and in a systematic way.[14]

In America, the colleges initiated the first competitive sports programs. In colonial New England, youthful students had engaged in many pastimes: some were tolerated by college authorities and others prohibited. The first college clubs had been founded as early as 1717, and social clubs were in full swing by the 1780's and 1790's. By the early nineteenth century, most American colleges had more or less officially recognized clubs and social activities. The founding of Greek-letter social fraternities in the 1840's and the building of college gymnasiums in the 1860's added to the

    [13] Charles Kingsley, _Health and Education_, 1874, quoted in _ibid._, p. 77.
    [14] Lebert H. Weir, _Europe at Play: A Study of Recreation and Leisure Time Activity_ (New York: A. S. Barnes, 1937), p. 85.

social life and physical recreation of students. Intercollegiate participation in competitive athletics, particularly rowing, baseball, track, and football, came into being.

The first known intercollegiate football contest was between Princeton and Rutgers in 1869; the game rapidly became more complex, with new rules for running, kicking, and passing, for the size of teams, and for specific positions. Interest spread rapidly, first among Ivy League colleges in the East and then throughout the nation. By the late 1880's, college games were attracting as many as 40,000 spectators. But it was baseball that drew the greatest public interest. The National Association of Baseball Players was formed in 1858; two years later, with a membership of fifty clubs, it began to play games in an organized way, charging admission and drawing huge crowds of spectators. The National Baseball League got underway during the 1870's, and the modern professional game, with its system of major and minor leagues, was in motion. Along with this, baseball thrived as an amateur sport for millions of persons in other settings: colleges, high schools, Y.M.C.A.'s, and community life.

Many other sports became popular during the second half of the nineteenth century in the United States. Track and field events were widely promoted by amateur athletic clubs. Gymnastic instruction and games were sponsored by the German *turnvereins*, the Czech *sokols*, and the Y.M.C.A., which had established some 260 large gymnasiums in cities around the country by the 1880's and was a leader in sports activities. Other popular pastimes included croquet, archery, lawn tennis, and roller-skating, which became so popular that huge skating rinks were built that could accommodate thousands of skaters and spectators. Bicycling was introduced in the 1870's, and within a few years hundreds of thousands of people were participating in it. During the closing decades of the nineteenth century, there was a growing vogue for outdoor activities. Americans began to enjoy hiking and mountain climbing, fishing and hunting, camping in national forests and state parks, and nature photography.

Gradually, Puritan restraints were lessened, and while work was still valued as a moral virtue, recreation became more respectable. Church leaders of the 1880's and 1890's realized that religion could no longer impose arbitrary prohibitions. Instead, they chose to offer attractive equivalents to the forms of play which they viewed as undesirable. Thus, in many churches during the closing decades of the nineteenth century, provision was made for libraries, gymnasiums, and assembly rooms. Often they offered games and sports, social activities, concerts, and other forms of "sanctified amusement and recreation."

The twelve-hour work-day had now changed to the ten-hour day, and in some occupations and industries, the half-Saturday and two-week summer vacations were being provided. Dulles comments:

Visitors from abroad in the 1890's were as much struck by the way Americans were now seeking out opportunities for play as those who had come to this country in the 1840's had been impressed by our apparent lack of interest in amusements.[15]

Particularly in larger cities, whole new forms of commercial recreation sprang into being or expanded rapidly. The theater in its various forms—melodramas, variety shows and vaudeville, burlesque, and the circus—was more popular than ever. Dime museums, dance halls, shooting galleries, bowling alleys, billiard parlors, beer gardens, and saloons provided a new world of entertainment for pay. Added to these, many cities had red-light districts, where saloons and houses of prostitution flourished. Drinking, gambling, and commercial vice gradually became serious social problems, particularly when protected by a tacit alliance between criminal figures and big-city political machines. More and more, cities became viewed as centers of corruption.

Amusement parks sprang up on the outskirts of cities and towns. Often they were established by new rapid transit companies, which offered reduced rides for excursions to them in gaily decorated trolley cars. They featured such varied attractions as parachute jumps, open-air theaters, band concerts, professional bicycle races, sideshow entertainment with barkers, freak shows, games of chance, and shooting galleries. Roller-coasters, fun houses, and midget-car tracks sprang up. Dancing was now accepted for all levels of society; the upper classes had dancing schools and annual balls, while the lower and middle classes attended dance halls, beer gardens, and dances sponsored by fraternal or business organizations. Sports were more popular than ever: horse racing, professional rowing matches, prize fighting, professional baseball, and a host of college sports attracted huge crowds.

For the first time, a concern about the uses of leisure began to arise—not so much in terms of the sinfulness of play but rather a broader question about the potential of leisure in modern society.

Intellectual and political leaders began to raise searching questions. The English author, Lord Lytton, commented, "The social civilization of a people is always and infallibly indicated by the intellectual character of its amusements." In 1876, Horace Greeley, a leading journalist, commented that although there were teachers for every art, science, and "elegy," there were no "professors of play." He asked, "Who will teach us incessant workers how to achieve leisure and enjoy it?" And, in 1880, President James Garfield declared in a speech at Lake Chautauqua, "We may divide the whole struggle of the human race into two chapters, first, the fight to get leisure; and then the second fight of civilization—what shall we do with our leisure when we get it."

---

[15] Dulles, *op. cit.*, p. 203.

This new concern was an inevitable consequence of the Industrial Revolution. Americans now lived in greater numbers in large cities, where the traditional social activities of the past and the opportunity for casual, wholesome play were no longer available. They had increasing amounts of free time and, more and more, were able to afford to pay for recreation. It was increasingly apparent that there was a need for organized recreation services that would provide wholesome and enriching leisure experiences for all classes.

Beginning of the Recreation Movement

The term "recreation movement" describes those forms of leisure activity which are provided in an organized way by agencies of society, either governmental or voluntary, which are intended to achieve desirable social outcomes. Four major streams of development which had their roots in the nineteenth century may be identified: (1) the adult education movement, (2) the development of a network of national, state, and municipal parks, (3) the establishment of national voluntary organizations and of settlement houses, and (4) the playground movement in cities and towns.

The Adult Education Movement. During the first two or three decades of the nineteenth century, there was considerable civic concern for improved intellectual cultivation and continuing education for adults throughout the United States. It took the form of the so-called Lyceum movement, which consisted of a national organization with over 900 local chapters. Its program consisted chiefly of lectures, readings, and other educational presentations. Lyceum programs reflected the view that all citizens should be able to take part knowledgeably in affairs of government. For many decades, speeches and lectures were an important part of the leisure life of American communities.

Such organizations as Chautauqua, which sponsored a leading summer camp program in upstate New York for adults and their families, with varied cultural activities, sports, lectures, and other educational features and which also sponsored a lecture circuit, promoted the movement on a widespread scale. While the nominal purpose of Chautauqua was education, it actually provided substantial entertainment and amusement to its audiences. In an era in which there was a paucity of adult cultural opportunity, it filled an important need. Even today, lecture series—often provided or sponsored by colleges or universities, civic groups, or women's clubs—are extremely popular leisure activities in many cities and towns.

The Development of National and State Parks. During the nineteenth century, parks in the United States developed on three levels—national, state, and municipal.

Concern about preserving the natural heritage of the United States

in an era of increasing industrialization and despoilment of natural resources began during the first decades of the nineteenth century. The first
major action of this type was taken in 1864, when an act of Congress set
aside the first extensive area of wild land primarily for public recreational
use, consisting of the Yosemite Valley and the Mariposa Grove of Big
Trees in California, later to become a National Park. The first designated
National Park was Yellowstone, which was founded in 1872. Through the
years that followed, other major wild lands were added to the national
park system and to the national forests and increasingly became devoted
to recreational uses.

Gradually, there was an increasing awareness of the value of nature
and the need to preserve wild areas and wildlife, both for scientific reasons
and as part of the national heritage which should not be lost. As early as
1867, Michigan and Wisconsin established fact-finding committees to explore the problem of forest conservation, to be followed shortly by Maine
and other eastern states. Within two decades, a number of states had established forestry commissions. Between 1864 and 1900, the first state
parks were established, as well as a number of state forest preserves and
historic parks. All such developments did not automatically lend themselves to recreational uses. Brockman comments:

> the current interest in recreation as a resource of national forest lands was not
> typical of the initial years of the forest-conservation movement in the United
> States. Early foresters could not envisage the great public interest in the recrea-
> tional values of the national forests typical of the present day; at that time few
> people did. . . . Consequently, although a few forestry leaders began calling
> attention to growing public interest in and use of national forest for outdoor
> recreation about 1910, official U.S. Forest Service recognition of recreation as
> a valid part of national forest management did not develop for more than a
> decade.[16]

America lagged behind the European nations in the development of
municipal parks. In part, this was because we did not have a nobility that
possessed large cultivated estates, hunting grounds, and elaborate gardens
which might be turned over to the public, as was the case in Europe. The
first major park to be developed in an American city was Central Park in
New York City. It was particularly significant because its design and the
philosophy on which it was based strongly influenced other large cities
during the latter half of the nineteenth century.

There had long been a need for open space in New York City. During the first three decades of the nineteenth century, plans were made for
several open squares to total about 450 acres but were not carried out
fully. By the early 1850's, the entire amount of public open space in all of

---

[16] C. Frank Brockman, *Recreational Use of Wild Lands* (New York: McGraw-Hill,
1959), pp. 69-70.

Manhattan totaled only 117 acres. A letter printed in a New York newspaper which was addressed to the mayor and the city council illustrates public concern:

it is a very general complaint that there is not in this great city, nor in its environs, any one proper spot, where its numerous inhabitants can enjoy, with convenience, that exercise that is necessary for health and amusement.[17]

Pressure mounted among the citizens of the city for a major park that might meet the pressing needs for a large area that would provide relief from stone and concrete. The poet William Cullen Bryant lamented that no preparation had been made while the city was being laid out for a range of parks and public gardens that would provide refreshment and recreation for its citizens. In 1844, he wrote:

Commerce is devouring inch by inch the coast of the island, and if we would rescue any part of it for health and recreation it must be done now. All large cities have their extensive public grounds and gardens, Madrid and Mexico [City] their Alamedas, London its Regent's Park, Paris its Champs Elysees, and Vienna its Prater.[18]

When the public will could no longer be denied, legislation was passed in 1856 to establish the park, and construction was begun in 1857, with a total of 843 acres. Central Park, as designed by the leading landscape architects, Frederick Law Olmsted and Calvert Vaux, was completely man-made: "every foot of the park's surface, every tree and bush, as well as every arch, roadway and walk, has been fixed where it is with a purpose." The dominant purpose was to provide, within the densely populated heart of an immense metropolis, "refreshment of the mind and nerves" for city dwellers through the provision of greenery and scenic vistas. The park was designed to be heavily wooded and to have the appearance of rural scenery wherever possible. Although there were passages for traffic, these were screened from the view of most park users, and carriage ways were deliberately made twisting to avoid long straightways for trotting matches. Recreational pursuits that might be undertaken in the park included walking, pleasure driving, ice skating in the winter, and boating.

Before the park was built, some had been concerned about the behavior of those who would use it. The New York *Herald* declared in 1858 that it would be nothing but "a great bear-garden for the lower denizens of the city." Olmsted established strict rules for its use, however, saying, "A large part of the people of New York are ignorant of a park. . . . They will need to be trained to the proper use of it, to be restrained in the

[17] Charles E. Doell and Charles B. Fitzgerald, *A Brief History of Parks and Recreation in the United States* (Chicago: The Athletic Institute, 1954), p. 25.

[18] Henry Hope Reed and Sophia Duckworth, *Central Park: A History and a Guide* (New York: Clarkson N. Potter, 1967), p. 3.

abuse of it." As its executive head, he hired a special police force to enforce an extensive code of regulations, including restrictions against walking on the grass, turning domestic animals loose in the park, or damaging the landscape or wildlife in any way. Throughout its history, Central Park has been the scene of constant battle between those who sought to keep it a quiet, secluded, untouched scenic area and those who wished to develop it more fully for active recreational uses.[19]

In the decades that followed, other large city parks were developed— in Boston, Franklin Park, with 527 acres in 1883, in Philadelphia, Fairmount Park, with 2,816 acres in 1867, and numbers of others. Olmsted designed several of these himself; others were directly influenced by his policy and example.

The Establishment of Voluntary Organizations. During the nineteenth century, a number of voluntary organizations were established which played an important role in providing organized recreation services. On a national level, one such body was the Young Men's Christian Association, which was founded as a youth-serving organization in Boston in 1851. At first, the Y stressed a fellowship of youth and adults for religious worship. It gradually enlarged its program, however, to include recreational gymnastics, sports, and other group recreational activities. The first Young Women's Christian Association was founded fifteen years later in Boston; among its varied program features were religious activities, job training and placement, and recreational and cultural programs.

Another type of voluntary agency which provided significant recreational services was the settlement house. These were neighborhood centers which were established in the slum sections of large cities in the East and Midwest; among the first were University Settlement, which was founded in New York City in 1886, the Neighborhood Guild in New York in 1887, and Hull House, founded in Chicago in 1889. Their founders sought to help poor people—particularly immigrants—adjust to American life by providing services concerned with education, religious activities, family life, and community improvement. Many of the early settlement house workers saw recreation as a major concern and fought for the provision of adequate leisure opportunities. Typically, one of the best-known pioneer social workers, Jane Addams, urged that recreation be provided as a safety valve for slum conditions, saying

It is as if our cities had not yet developed a sense of responsibility in regard to the life of the streets, and continually forget that recreation is stronger than vice and that recreation alone can stifle the lust for vice.[20]

Other leaders, in cooperation with such outspoken social reformers as Jacob Riis, Walter Vrooman, and Louise deKoven Bowen, created a pub-

[19] *Ibid.*, pp. 40-51.
[20] Jane Addams, *The Playground*, March, 1910, p. 24.

lic awareness of the need for improved recreational opportunities in the cities. They welded public-spirited citizens, clergymen, educators, and newspaper editorialists into a force that ultimately compelled action from civic officials and brought about the playground movement.

The Playground Movement. To understand the origins of the playground movement in the United States, it is necessary to know what living conditions were like for poor people during the latter decades of the nineteenth century. The wave of urbanization which had begun earlier in the century was now at its peak. In 1850, there were only 85 urban communities in the United States with populations of over 8,000. There were almost seven times as many by 1900. The urban population more than doubled, from 14 to 30 million, between 1880 and 1900 alone. By the century's end, there were 28 cities with over 100,000 residents, chiefly because of the great masses of migration during the latter decades of the nineteenth century. A leading example was New York City, where the island of Manhattan had been a port of entry to America for millions of immigrants. Nearly five out of every six of the 1.5 million residents of New York in 1891 lived in tenements; social reformers of the period described these buildings as crowded, with dark hallways and filthy cellars and with inadequate cooking and bathroom facilities. In the neighborhoods populated by poor immigrants, there was a tremendous amount of crime, gambling, gang violence, and prostitution.

Within such districts, there were few safe places in which children might play. The first such facility—and the one which is generally regarded as a landmark in the development of the recreation movement in the United States—was the Boston Sand Garden, established in 1885. In Boston, a group of public-spirited citizens had a pile of sand placed in the yard of the Parmenter Street Chapel, in a working-class district. Young children came to play in the sand with wooden shovels. At first, supervision was provided on a voluntary basis, but that was not sufficient. By 1887, ten such centers were opened, and paid matrons were employed to supervise them. Two years later, the city of Boston began to contribute funds to support them. So it was that citizens, on a voluntary basis, began to provide play opportunities for young children.

In New York City, two model playgrounds were established in poor areas of the city in 1889 and 1891 by the newly formed New York Society for Parks and Playgrounds, with support from private subscriptions. Gradually, public interest was aroused to create improved play facilities for children in the city. Walter Vrooman, founder of the New York Society for Parks and Playgrounds, brought to the attention of the public that, in 1890, there were in New York City 350,000 children without a single public playground they could call their own. While the city now had almost 6,000 acres of parkland, none of it was set aside for children. Vrooman pointed out that the existing parklands tended to be at a great distance from the poorer sections of the city. He charged that those who walked were at a disadvantage compared with those who drove carriages and that the poor were sacrificed for the rich and children for grown men, who were permitted to engage in organized sports in the parks.

Some reformers vehemently demanded parks and playgrounds as an escape from crowded, filthy tenement houses. One leading physician wrote, "Foul air prompts to vice and oxygen to virtue, as surely as the sunlight paints the flowers of our gardens." Speaking of slum children, he said,

The varied opportunities of a park would educate him and his family in the enjoyment of open-air pleasures. Deprived of these, he and his are educated into the ways of disease and vice by the character of their surroundings.[21]

Other civic leaders pointed out that children whose parents worked lacked supervision and were permitted to grow up subject to varied temptations. Vrooman wrote that such children

are driven from their crowded homes in the morning . . . are chased from the streets by the police when they attempt to play, and beaten with the broom handle of the Janitor's wife when found in the hallway, or on the stairs. No wonder they learn to chew and smoke tobacco before they can read, and take a fiendish delight in breaking windows, in petty thievery, and in gambling their pennies.[22]

Gradually, reformers, social workers, educators, civic leaders, businessmen, church leaders, and newspapermen joined together to support demands for playgrounds. One businessman told Vrooman how his company had twice replaced all of the windows in its buildings up to the fifth floor, only to have them broken again by neighborhood youth. He ended by saying, "We must give them a playground or throw them in the river." Similarly, Jacob Riis concluded as a result of investigations elsewhere that where small playgrounds were developed, juvenile delinquency and vandalism declined. Gradually, the pressure mounted. A new organization, the Outdoor Recreation League, was established and finally opened a model playground, known as Seward Park in June, 1893. This park was jointly paid for by the League and by the city. They raised substantial sums to pay for maintenance and leadership, and also for costs that might accrue to the city through accident damage suits, which had been a major fear of the city fathers.

In the years that followed, New York City moved rapidly to develop a network of playgrounds that would be paid for and administered completely by the city. All schools constructed after this time were required

[21] Thomas E. Will, "Public Parks and Playgrounds: A Symposium," *The Arena*, July, 1894, pp. 276-77.
[22] Walter Vrooman, "Playgrounds for Children," *The Arena*, July, 1894, p. 286.

to have open-air playgrounds which would be operated in connection with school programs. In July, 1897, the first recreation piers were opened and became an immediate success; by 1902 there were seven such piers jutting out into the rivers surrounding Manhattan Island, providing new places to play and bathe. The movement simultaneously spread in other major cities. By 1900, some fourteen cities had made provision for supervised play facilities, and the playground movement was under a full head of steam. Among the leading cities were Boston, Providence, Philadelphia, Pittsburgh, Baltimore, Chicago, Milwaukee, Cleveland, Denver, and Minneapolis. In each case, private initiative and financial support were prominent factors in getting the first playgrounds under way, and in bringing pressure upon city governments to accept responsibility for providing play areas.

At the same time, municipal parks became increasingly well established throughout the country. In addition to the urban parks mentioned earlier, the first metropolitan park system was established in Boston (1892) and the first county park system in Essex County, New Jersey (1895). In the West, San Francisco and Sacramento in California and Salt Lake City, Utah, were among the first to incorporate large open spaces in town planning before 1900. The New England Association of Park Superintendents, predecessor of the American Institute of Park Executives, was established in 1898, to bring together park superintendents and promote their professional concerns.

Thus, in the last decade of the nineteenth century, the playground and park movement got fully under way. Before long, it was to become known as the recreation movement and was to concern itself not only with the needs of children but those of all ages. Before this was to happen, however, a fuller rationale for the need for public recreation was to be developed. This was provided by a number of major pioneers of the public recreation movement—men like Clark Hetherington, Joseph Lee, Henry Curtis, and Luther Halsey Gulick—as well as by the theories of psychologists and educators regarding the values of play in human growth and development. Both in Europe and America, major contributions were made to a growing body of play theory, which supported it as an important psychological and educational concern. These views and theories are presented in Chapter 11.

9

The Recreation and Parks Movement
During the Twentieth Century

This chapter is chiefly concerned with the development of municipal recreation and parks agencies, facilities, and services in the United States during the period between 1900 and 1950, and with the major trends and social influences which affected the recreation and parks movement.

The Growth of Public Recreation and Parks Agencies

It is difficult to document the growth of public recreation and park departments in the early decades of the century, because no unified effort was made to record this process. Certain statistics are available, however, relating to the number of cities operating playground programs, expenditures, number of leaders, or facilities.

Number of Cities. In 1900, only 12 cities were reported to be providing for recreation through public funds. In 1906, the number was reported as 41. In 1915, there were reported to be 83 cities which employed paid recreation leaders. In 1920, 465 cities reported public recreation departments; in 1930, there were 980; and in 1946, there were 1,530.

Expenditures on Recreation. In 1917, $6.6 million was reported to be spent by municipalities on public recreation. This figure rose to $7.2 million in 1920, $38.5 million in 1930, and $51.7 million in 1946.

Growth of Leadership. In 1915, municipal public recreation agencies reported 1,157 full-time, year-round paid leaders and 6,009 part-time or seasonal paid employees, for a total of 7,166. In 1930, there were 2,660 full-time, year-round leaders and 24,949 paid employees overall. By 1946, the number rose to 5,147 and 41,159, respectively.

186

During the ten years between 1910 and 1920 the concept of city governments assuming responsibility for recreation programs and services became widely accepted. During the 1920's, there was a considerable expansion of local facilities for recreation. By 1927, 32 states had expressly provided by law for the use of school buildings as community centers. By 1930, one-half of the states had passed enabling legislation permitting local units of government to operate recreation departments. In the ten years between 1925 and 1935, the number of municipal recreation buildings quadrupled.

Park departments also expanded rapidly in the United States at this time. During the period from 1892 to 1902, the number of cities possessing parks grew from 100 to 800. By 1926 the figure had reached 1,680. Butler comments that during the 1920's, "Playgrounds, golf courses, swimming pools, bathing beaches, picnic areas, and game fields were constructed in unprecedented numbers. Municipal park acreage, especially during the latter half of the decade, expanded more than in any other period of equal length."[1] New ways of adding parks were being discovered by municipalities. Many of them acquired parks outside their city limits, while others required that new real estate subdivision plans include the dedication of space for recreation. Some cities obtained substantial amounts of park property through gifts.

The pattern began to develop of having a network of small, intensively used playgrounds throughout cities, particularly where lower-class or working families lived. Usually these were operated by recreation departments or school boards. Larger parks tended to be located in outlying areas of the cities. In such cities as Boston, Minneapolis, and Chicago, forest preserves and outlying park systems were developed. By 1928, there were 86 county and regional park systems around major cities throughout the country, and by midcentury the number grew to about 400.

Among the major cities to initiate park systems at an early stage, Chicago was outstanding. Chicago was one of the first cities to develop a large-scale network of neighborhood recreation parks. In 1903, a $5-million bond issue was voted to acquire and develop small recreation parks (ranging in size between 7 and 300 acres) in crowded neighborhoods in the southern part of the city. Ten of these parks, combining excellent facilities for outdoor play with field houses that included gymnasiums, clubrooms, shower and locker rooms, and branches of the public library, were opened, in 1905. They set a new standard for American cities in park and playground development, particularly because the first playground convention sponsored by the Playground Association of America was held in Chicago in 1907. President Theodore Roosevelt called the creation of the South Park playgrounds and centers "the most notable civic achievement of any

[1] George D. Butler, *Introduction to Community Recreation* (New York: McGraw-Hill, 1967), p. 89.

American city." The South Park facilities were intended to serve all ages, year-round, with varied programs and opportunities; many included bandstands and outdoor swimming pools and were carried on under trained leaders who served under a general director of field houses and playgrounds.

Luther Gulick commented:

Chicago, within a brief two-year period, set aside over $10 million for small parks and playgrounds, and since that time millions have been spent in developing, administering and enlarging the system. . . . All this is paid for by the city, not by private philanthropy. . . . The places have become recreation centers in the most promising sense. It is said that aldermen in Chicago lose all popularity with their constituents unless they secure playgrounds in their wards.[2]

Chicago continued to expand, developing several other separate park boards and a large number of other smaller districts which were consolidated into the Chicago Park District in 1934; at that time, the city possessed 137 parks with 85 field houses designed for varied recreational uses.

The Development of the Recreation Movement

An early historian of the recreation movement, Clarence Rainwater, described seven stages through which the recreation movement passed, between the 1880's and the 1920's:

1. The sand garden (1885–95)
2. The model playground (1895–1900)
3. The small park (1900–1905)
4. The recreation center (1905–12)
5. The civic art and welfare center (1912–15)
6. Neighborhood organization (1915–18)
7. Community welfare (1918–20's)[3]

Although these stages were not mutually exclusive, they represented periods in which an important innovation was made or a particular rationale or development gained public interest. Rainwater also suggested that there were nine important transitions in the playground movement during this early period: (1) from provision for small children to services for all age groups, (2) from facilities operated during the summer only to those maintained throughout the year, (3) from outdoor equipment and activities only to both outdoor and indoor programs, (4) from an emphasis on serving congested urban districts only to both urban and rural communities, (5) from philanthropic support (as in the early model playgrounds) to public support and control, (6) from free play and casually organized events to directed play with leadership and carefully scheduled

[2] Luther H. Gulick, *A Philosophy of Play* (New York: Scribner, 1920), p. 7.

[3] See Martin H. Neumeyer and Esther Neumeyer, *Leisure and Recreation* (New York: Ronald Press, 1958), p. 68.

programs, (7) from a simple to a complex range of activities, including manual, physical, aesthetic, social, and civic projects, (8) from the provision of facilities to the definition of standards for the use of leisure time, and (9) from the satisfaction of individual interests to meeting group and community needs.[4]

During the 1930's, the so-called play movement became thought of as the "recreation movement." It began to embrace many other agencies and forms of service. It developed a close working relationship with public school systems and added to its focus on urban communities a concern for suburban and rural settings. It moved from being a form of community service which was largely under quasi-public control (receiving subsidies from public funds) to widespread acceptance as a government function, with substantial support from tax funds. Whereas originally playgrounds were the major type of facility, recreation centers and other types of facilities, particularly for adult use, were developed. Leadership shifted from volunteer or part-time to full-time, paid leaders and administrators, who came to regard themselves as specialists within a unique field of public service.

Social Factors Influencing the Recreation Movement

During the first several decades of the twentieth century several major social factors played an important role in influencing the shape of the recreation movement in the United States:

1. *Modern Science and Technology.* Major developments in industrial technology and production tended to make life increasingly easy for working people. Hours of leisure were expanded, and retirement became available for large numbers of working people. Medical science also made it possible for people to live longer and to spend their retirement years in leisure.

2. *Continued Urbanization.* As increasing numbers of people moved from rural to urban settings, and as life patterns adjusted to the needs of an industrial economy, still greater need was created for publicly sponsored recreation facilities, programs, and leadership.

3. *Changing Nature of Work.* As work became increasingly specialized and mechanical, in assembly-line factories, work ceased to have personal meaning for many employees. There was widespread agreement that recreation and leisure might provide a means of meeting these needs satisfactorily in industrial society.

4. *New Concepts of Recreation.* The religious objections toward play that had persisted throughout the nineteenth century in some sections of the country, tended to decline still further. Many churches accepted increasing responsibility for their congregation's leisure and recreation. How-

[4] *Ibid.*, p. 73.

ever, there was a serious concern about the negative influence of many forms of commercial amusement.

5. *Growth of Transportation.* Technology and increased affluence made it increasingly possible for people to travel widely in their leisure. The development of public transit lines and then the growing popularity of family automobiles and the development of highways meant that Americans could travel on vacations or visit night clubs, summer resorts, baseball stadiums, motion picture houses, and other forms of entertainment which became popular during the 1920's. Driving became a hobby for many, and the freedom that the car offered meant that the car became a setting for play both respectable and illicit.

6. *Role of the Schools.* Especially during the 1920's and 1930's, America's public schools provided many forms of community education. They became sponsors for youth and adult recreation or cooperated with other agencies that were direct sponsors, by providing buildings and other needed physical facilities. In addition, schools accepted the responsibility for "educating for leisure," thus strengthening the linkage between education and recreation.

7. *Expansion of Commercial Recreation Opportunity.* For the first time, recreation became a major industry in its own right. There was a wave of popular enthusiasm for all sorts of entertainment and recreational fads and amusements. During the 1920's, the growth of the radio industry and motion pictures, the rapid development of bowling alleys, commercial swimming pools, sports leagues and stadiums, gardening hobbies, and the commercial packaging and sale of games, hobby kits, and sports equipment and supplies were part of the total expansion of play as an important element in the nation's economy.

8. *Need for Conservation.* Public-spirited Americans began to support legislation and government programs designed to protect our national heritage by maintaining open spaces, protecting wild lands and wildlife, and providing green belts in and around densely populated urban areas.

A number of these social factors—particularly the concern with the need for recreation as a social service in urban slums, and the effects of commercial amusements—are discussed in this chapter. Others, particularly those related to the growth of leisure and the role of recreation in the economy, are analyzed in later chapters.

The Rationale for Organized Recreation Programs

The justification for expanded municipal recreation programs, which was formulated during the first three decades of the twentieth century, was largely that it was necessary to enrich life and to prevent social pathology. There was also much concern about the influence of commercial amusements and about "spectatoritis"—the negative or passive use of leisure. President Herbert Hoover, in addressing a White House Conference on Child Health and Protection held in Washington in 1930, summed up this rationale:

In the last half century we have herded 50 million more human beings into towns and cities where the whole setting is new to the race. . . . Perhaps the widest range of difficulties with which we are dealing is the betterment of children grows out of this crowding into cities. Problems of sanitation and public health loom in every direction. Delinquency increases with congestion. Overcrowding produces disease and contagion. The child's natural play space is taken from him. His mind is stunted by the lack of imaginative surroundings and lack of contact with the fields, streams, trees and birds. Home life becomes more difficult. Cheerless homes produce morbid minds. . . . Architectural wizardry and artistic skills are transforming cities into wonderlands of beauty, but we must also preserve in them for our children the yet more beautiful art of living.[5]

In large measure, the support for public recreation was based on the fear that leisure would be used unwisely. There was an increasing conviction among industrial leaders and civic officials that the growth of leisure for the working classes represented a dangerous trend. When periodic waves of unemployment occurred during the first three decades of the century, concerns were expressed about what idle men would do with their time. Similarly, when the 8-hour work-day laws first came under discussion in 1916 and 1917, temperance societies prepared for increased drunkenness and social reformers throughout the Western world held international conferences on the worker's spare time and ways of using it constructively.

The major concern, however, was about children and youth in the large cities and their need for healthy and safe places to play. Indeed, much "juvenile delinquency" arose from children being arrested for playing on city streets. Gulick wrote:

Playing baseball on the streets of New York is forbidden by a city ordinance. Yet every day during the spring a large proportion of the boys brought before the judge of Children's Court are there for the crime of playing ball. The black-robed judge questions them from behind a high desk; a big policeman stands near to give testimony. The boys are in the position of lawbreakers, yet most of them are decent, respectable boys, frequently very young and much frightened.[6]

The lack of suitable play opportunities as a cause of juvenile crime was noted by many authorities during this period. One English writer commented that, when left to the resources of the street, boys inevitably got into trouble, to be "birched in a police court" and to stand a "lively chance of becoming a criminal."

[5] Herbert Hoover, quoted in James E. Rogers, *The Child and Play*, Report on 1930 White House Conference on Child Health and Protection, 1932, p. 27.
[6] Gulick, *op. cit.*, p. 3.

We remember hearing the headmaster of a large Council school, in a very poor district in London, address the boys on the eve of the holidays; the burden of his long speech was simply: "Try and keep out of the hands of the police." He knew from bitter experience, in the long days there were to follow, when, for many of them, there would be no home, no school, no playground, and no games, whither the occupations of the streets were likely to lead his more daring spirits.[7]

The belief that the best solution to juvenile delinquency was to provide play facilities for city children was widely shared by educators and law enforcement authorities. Many positive statements supported this view. A Philadelphia Judge, William H. Staake, commented:

The public playground is the greatest deterrent of juvenile delinquency and lawlessness among children. It stands for body and character building, and produces better children, homes, morals and citizens. On the score of public economy alone, the playground is a necessity.[8]

Judge Ben B. Lindsey, one of the originators of the juvenile court system in America, stated that "our plea for public playgrounds is a plea for justice to the boy." Some number of authorities during this period reported on reduced rates of juvenile delinquency in slum areas where playgrounds had been established. A Philadelphia District Attorney described a 50 percent decrease in a slum neighborhood rate of juvenile delinquency, after a playground program was instituted. A probation officer of the Juvenile Court in Milwaukee described a "very noticeable dropping off of boys coming before the court" and a disappearance of "dangerous gangs," concluding that playgrounds and social centers were "saviors" for American youth. A Juvenile and Domestic Relations Court Judge in Richmond, Virginia, stated that, on the basis of his fifteen years' experience as probation officer and judge, supervised recreation was the best preventive of delinquency yet devised.

Typically, the Judge of the Juvenile Department in the Orange County Court in Anaheim, California, noted that after

the opening of supervised playgrounds in the public park in the summer of 1924, juvenile delinquency decreased. During the first six months of 1925, it was 70 percent less than for the same period in 1924.[9]

In part it was believed that street life exposed children to antisocial temptations and criminal examples, in part that the playground stressed desirable social values and constructive activities and put children in closer touch with adult authorities on a friendly and trusting basis.

[7] Walter Wood, *Children's Play and Its Place in Education* (London: Kegan Paul, Trench, Trubner, 1913), p. 181.
[8] *Ibid.*, p. 197.
[9] Rogers, *op. cit.*, p. 36.

One school administrator in a New England town which was heavily populated by poorer families that had recently emigrated from Europe, described his district:

many homes are merely sleeping places for the healthy, active children. The small yards, the congested and unattractive tenements, and the alluring attractions of the theaters and streets cause the children, especially the boys, at an early age to spend the greater part of their waking hours in play or work or mere idling away from home . . . cigarette smoking, the theater-going habit, petty stealing from fruit stands and stores, lawlessness and truancy, are some of the outward manifestations of the street-developed character.[10]

When this principal developed an extensive outdoor playground program for boys, he found a marked reduction in theft, vandalism, and delinquency; he was able to relax his discipline and make much less use of corporal punishment.

The outdoor gymnasium and supervised play made the boys happier in their school life. It raised the tone of the school by bringing about a better disposition toward teachers and toward school work. It brought the principal in closer touch with the children and, while increasing his knowledge of them, strengthened his influence over them.[11]

Although later studies were to question the validity of the delinquency-prevention function of recreation, there was little doubt during this period about it. A closely related factor was the matter of safety. Not only was play in city streets regarded as undesirable because children were arrested for it or were exposed to criminal temptation, but because they were literally in danger of their lives because of speeding traffic. One survey carried out by a major insurance company in 1930 revealed that in a single year there were 65,811 accidents to children playing in city streets, of which 2,310 were fatal. Most of these accidents occurred near the child's home; it was concluded that while better safety education and greater care by both children and motorists would be helpful, the better solution was adequate play spaces and play leadership.

For a time, there was some disagreement about the need for paid leadership in playground and playstreet programs. As an example, when the Playground Association of America was organized, President Theodore Roosevelt expressed the view:

It is a splendid thing to provide in congested districts of American cities spaces where children may play, but let them play freely. Do not interfere with their play. Leave them alone.[12]

[10] George E. Johnson, *Education by Play and Games* (New York: Ginn, 1907), p. 47.
[11] *Ibid.*, p. 51.
[12] Theodore Roosevelt, quoted in Gulick, *op. cit.*, p. 232.

The view that children were innately good and that the unsupervised play situation was most desirable was disputed by many others. Gulick pointed out that in a number of cities, including Toledo, it was necessary to close down playgrounds because, without leadership, apparatus had been destroyed and children mistreated by each other. He concluded:

Real freedom is impossible without protection. An unsupervised playground is nominally free; in reality it is controlled by the strongest and most vicious element in the crowd. It is a dangerous place for girls and small children; it can be converted from a direct source of evil to a source of benefit by having someone put in authority.[13]

Commercial Amusements

In city after city around the country, there was also considerable concern about the growth of commercial amusements. During the several decades prior to and immediately after the turn of the twentieth century, commercial recreation had become a lucrative business enterprise, involving considerable investment of capital, occupying much valuable property in the heart of cities, and receiving huge sums from the earnings of all classes of citizens. There was widespread concern about the moral impact of these new offerings.

Counts pointed out that prior to the rise of industrial civilization recreation had been almost completely a function of the family and the neighborhood. As cities grew, however, neighborhoods changed and families lost their self-sufficiency

business enterprise . . . was quick to grasp the opportunity for material gain presented by the breakdown . . . almost every form of recreation has a commercial aspect. . . . Commercial enterprise has provided for the American people a bewildering variety of cheap forms of amusement; dance halls, houses of prostitution, speakeasies, pool and billiard rooms, vaudeville performances, burlesque shows, amusements parks, and many others. In fact business has overlooked few opportunities for making profit out of the leisure time resulting from the growth of technology and the craving for excitement generated by the monotony of industrial occupations. And as the appetites of the population became jaded, thrill is added to thrill and sensation to sensation. That the consequent program of recreation was unsuited to the deeper cultural and spiritual needs of the people became clearly apparent.[14]

In such major cities as Milwaukee, Detroit, Chicago, Kansas City, and San Francisco, extensive recreation surveys were carried out, scrutinizing

---

[13] *Ibid.*, p. 232.
[14] George Counts, *Social Foundations of Education*, Report of the Commission on the Social Studies, 1934, p. 300.

the nature of commercial amusements, the extent and kind of their patronage, and their character. Typically, it was found that Coney Island alone had registered over 5 million paid admissions in a single season and that the five amusement parks in Kansas City, Missouri (at the time, a city of 248,000 residents), had a total attendance of almost 2 million people during the summer of 1911. In city after city, the figures were tallied. A survey of Detroit, for example, showed that it had 297 pool-rooms, 16 billiard rooms, 36 bowling alleys, and 5 shooting galleries. It was found typically that the majority of these catered to boys and young men and that many of them served liquor, involved gambling, and were in effect hangouts for criminals.

There was much concern about movies and stage performances. Edwards commented on the musical comedies and the burlesque of his period, saying that they

ordinarily have as little morals of any sort as the law allows, and frequently less. It is here that immorality in dramatic amusements has its chief stronghold. They do an incalculable damage to public morality, for their basic appeal is directly to the sensual passions. They frequently reek with suggestive songs and dances, vulgar jokes, with vile double meanings, and spectacular effects which have no other appeal than to sensuality.[15]

A study of vice in Philadelphia found that places of entertainment were closely linked to the underworld:

Many public dance halls, moving picture shows, and other amusement centers are breeding-places of vice—the rendezvous of men who entrap girls and of girls who solicit men. . . . The proprietors of these places are known to abet these vicious practices and, in many cases, to derive large revenue from them.[16]

It was found that in a high percentage of privately operated dance halls in Milwaukee, Chicago, and New York City, saloons were attached and were freely patronized by young girls. Dancing seemed to be only a secondary consideration. Pick-ups occurred regularly, often of young girls many of whom had come to cities from farms and small towns with a presumed degree of innocence; white slavers plied their trade with little interference. Dance halls were often attached to disreputable lodging houses. While there were laws regarding the conduct of dance halls, these were not enforced. Edwards cites the Chicago Vice Report, which established the link between commercial amusement and the vice problem:

In nearly every hall visited, investigators have seen professional and semi-professional prostitutes. Practically no effort is made by the managers to observe laws

---

[15] Richard H. Edwards, *Popular Amusements* (New York: Studies in American Social Conditions, Association Press, 1915), p. 45.
[16] *Ibid.*, p. 18.

regarding the sale of liquors. Nor is the provision of the ordinance relating to the presence of disreputable persons observed.[17]

It was not claimed that commercial amusements were the cause of vice. It was widely observed, however, that criminal behavior flourished in many such establishments and settings. The Crime Commission of the State of New York reported in the late 1920's that

the low-grade pool-room is the chief hang-out of the crook, and more burglaries among boys between the ages of sixteen and twenty-one are concocted there than in any other single place.

There was a widely shared conviction on the part of reformers, social workers, educators, and religious leaders that commercial recreation was pitched at the lowest possible level and represented a degradation rather than an enhancement of the human spirit. Edwards described amusement parks in these terms:

The crowd is barked and badgered, deceived and enticed into buying thrills of fleeting pleasure on shoot-the-shoots, topsy-turvy novelties, fake sideshows, sensational joy rides, carousels, ferris-wheels, merry-go-rounds, acrobatic shows, chariot races, daredevil rides, scenic panoramas, and the like. Some of them are harmless, some of them thoroughly vicious; many of them out-and-out fakes; all of them frankly sensational in appeal, and all calculated to separate the people from their money with the least possible return.[18]

The same studies that examined commercial amusements also surveyed the socially approved forms of recreation. They found that in many large cities, the schools were closed in the evenings and throughout the summer, that libraries closed at night and on weekends, that churches closed for the summer, and that publicly provided forms of recreation were at a minimum. Jane Addams concluded that the city had "turned over the provision for public recreation to the most evil-minded and the most unscrupulous members of the community."[19]

Gradually, pressure mounted for more effective controls of places of public amusement. In city after city, permits were required for operating dance halls, pool parlors, bowling alleys, and places for sale of liquor. The admission of minors, the prevention of gambling, the enforcement of closing hours, and the regulations concerning proper ventilation and sanitation were all more rigidly specified and enforced, although many cities continued to maintain red-light, or tenderloin, districts. Ultimately, with stronger

[17] *Ibid.*, p. 76.
[18] *Ibid.*, p. 106.
[19] Jane Addams, *The Spirit of Youth and the City Streets*, quoted in Edwards, *op. cit.*, p. 18.

and better enforced codes, the concern about commercial amusement and its contribution to the delinquency of minors declined.

A new fear emerged, however—that Americans were moving away from traditional, active ways of using their leisure to pursuits in which they were passive spectators. Edwards commented that instead of the "wholesome love of play," Americans now had a love of being "played upon." It had become wholly out of date to make one's "own fun." He wrote:

The professional entertainer holds sway in every field from which he is not rigidly excluded, every field in which the rights of the amateur are not vigorously asserted. . . . A social disease has been spreading broadcast among us. . . . The disease of *spectatoritis* is abroad in the land.[20]

Many shared Edwards' view of the "fan," whom he described as a "flabby creature symbolic of a multitude, a parasite upon the play of others, the least athletic of all men, never playing himself at anything, a spectacle hunter, not a sportsman." There was fear that with growing professionalism, America was moving toward a jaded sensationalism that would ultimately lead to the "Roman amphitheater and the Spanish bullfight."

In the effort to enrich leisure as a creative source of personal and social enrichment, several forces played a key part. One was the development of settlement houses and community centers, another the establishment of voluntary organizations which provided leisure services, a third the establishment of the Playground Association of America, and a fourth the acceptance by American education of the responsibility for educating for leisure and providing organized recreation services.

Settlement Houses and Community Centers

As indicated earlier, settlement houses and community centers had been established in such cities as Chicago and New York during the 1880's and 1890's. From the very beginning the directors of such agencies were vitally interested in play and recreation. Jane Addams, one of the pioneers in this field, was deeply concerned with the need to provide varied forms of play in urban slums. She was one of the original founders of the Playground Association of America and spoke widely on the theme of "recreation and social morality." It was her view that education, recreation, and social work were closely related functions. She was responsible for opening the first independent playground in Chicago, in a vacant lot adjoining Hull House, equipping it with swings, seesaws, slides, and sand bins. She also valued creative activities highly: the first building at Hull House contained

[20] Edwards, *op. cit.*, p. 134.

an art gallery; art, music, dance, and drama were all part of the total program.

The settlement house movement expanded rapidly in cities and towns during the first decades of the twentieth century. Well into the 1930's, these centers continued to regard the provision of recreation services as one of their important responsibilities; only after that did they more sharply define their social service and group work function and, in some cases, minimize their recreation responsibilities.

Growth of Voluntary Organizations

A closely related phenomenon was the widespread expansion of youth-serving organizations which provided extensive recreation programs. Many of these agencies were established as nationally organized movements; others were founded as local, autonomous organizations. All became active in recreation from the outset. The National Association of Boys' Clubs was founded in 1906, the Boy Scouts and the Camp Fire Girls in 1910, and the Girl Scouts in 1912. Major civic clubs and community service groups such as the Rotary Club, the Kiwanis, and the Lions Club were also founded during the period between 1910 and 1917.

By the end of the 1920's, these organizations had become widely established in American life and were serving substantial numbers of young people. Typically, by 1926, the Boy Scouts had 625,000 young members and 189,000 men serving as leaders and officials; one boy in every seven of the proper age group in the United States was a Scout. In the same year, the Girl Scouts had 167,000 members, and the Camp Fire Girls had a similar enrollment. The Y.M.C.A. had 961,000 men and boy members, and the Y.W.C.A. had about 600,000 members. In terms of the content of their programs, they were doing much to supplement the work of public agencies in the leisure field. Yet it was apparent that a strong national voice would be needed to pull these various groups together and to provide leadership to the growing recreation field.

Playground Association of America. In the early 1900's, as the playground movement gained momentum in larger cities, several leading municipal directors felt the need to call a national conference to effectively promote the entire field. Under the leadership of Luther Halsey Gulick, representatives of park, recreation, and school boards throughout the country met in Washington, D.C., in April, 1906. There was a unanimous conviction that a national organization was needed to promote community leisure services throughout the United States. On April 12, the Constitution was drawn up, and Gulick was selected as the first president of the Playground Association of America. The organization had President Roosevelt's statement of "earnest and hearty sympathy."

From the outset, the Playground Association was intended to provide places where children might play and to develop informational and promotional services that might assist those of all ages in using leisure time constructively. It was the founders' intent to establish a national playground museum and library and an information department which might assist cities and towns throughout the country in program development. As the organization got under way, with assistance from the Russell Sage Foundation, a monthly magazine, *The Playground,* was begun. Field workers were sent out from city to city, meeting with public officials and citizens' groups and helping in the development of playgrounds and recreation programs.

One of the functions of the Playground Association was to promote professional training. In this connection it developed *The Normal Course in Play,* consisting of three courses on play leadership which were designed to train normal school students and grade teachers to conduct play programs and recess periods, to help those entering professional work in playground leadership, and to give advanced training to professional directors. In keeping with its broadening emphasis, the organization changed its name in 1911 to the Playground and Recreation Association of America and in 1926 to the National Recreation Association.

The Role of the Schools

The concern about the negative uses of leisure was shared by school authorities. As indicated earlier, in a number of large cities, school boards had begun to operate after-school and vacation-play programs as early as the 1890's. In New York, all schools constructed after 1890 were required to have open-air playgrounds. In the same city, newly organized indoor programs became popular, and in 1903 the Public School Athletic League was organized to extend sports participation to all boys. Other cities, such as Rochester, New York (1907), Milwaukee, Wisconsin (1911), and Los Angeles, California (1914), initiated playground programs at an early stage. Los Angeles had twenty playgrounds in operation under school auspices in 1914 and thirty by 1921. Other leading communities to pioneer in school recreation sponsorship were St. Louis, Missouri, Columbus, Ohio, and Des Moines, Iowa.

These pioneering efforts were strongly supported by the National Education Association, which recommended the use of public school buildings for community recreation and social programs. The report of the fiftieth annual meeting of the N.E.A. in 1912 included a number of major presentations concerned with the school's role in leisure programming. One statement reveals the position of many leading educators of this era:

much of the millions of dollars invested in our school systems is wasted owing to the fact that, outside of school, children form wrong habits due to unwholesome play conditions, and develop traits of character which make much of their school training useless. Because of the size of the task before an adequate recreation system, because of the need of a recreation system to save from loss the enormous investments in schools and other municipal services, because of the call to avoid duplication and waste in the face of this unmet need, many communities are trying to find out and to plan systematically for their recreational needs.[21]

School authorities began to plan school facilities that would be useful for recreational purposes, providing space for gardening, assembly rooms, swimming pools, gymnasiums, and music and art rooms. The statement that education for "the worthy use of leisure" was one of the major objectives of modern education was made in the famous bulletin, "Cardinal Principles of Secondary Education," issued by the Commission on the Reorganization of Secondary School Education of the National Education Association:

Aside from the immediate discharge of these specific duties (home membership, vocation, and citizenship), every individual should have a margin of time for the cultivation of personal and social interests. This leisure, if worthily used, will recreate his powers and enlarge and enrich life, thereby making him better able to meet his responsibilities. The unworthy use of leisure impairs health, disrupts home life, lessens vocational efficiency and destroys civic-mindedness. The tendency in industrial life, aided by legislation, is to decrease the working hours of large groups of people. While shortened hours tend to lessen the harmful reactions that arise from prolonged strain, they increase, if possible, the importance of preparation for leisure. In view of these considerations, education for the worthy use of leisure is of increasing importance as an objective.[22]

The Cardinal Principles suggested that schools had a direct responsibility to guide and direct the use of leisure by youth. "The school should, therefore, see that adequate recreation is provided both within the school and by proper agencies in the community."[23] In a succeeding series of policy statements, educational authorities reaffirmed this responsibility of the schools during the decades that followed. In many school systems, extensive recreation programs serving children, youth, and adults were established by school boards. In others, schools have cooperated in the provision of school buildings and other facilities for use by other community recreation agencies.

Through the middle decades of the century, however, the school's role in the direct sponsorship of community recreation programs has

    [21] Journal of Proceedings and Addresses of the Fiftieth Annual Meeting of the National Education Association, July, 1912, pp. 233-34.
    [22] "Cardinal Principles of Secondary Education," Report of the Commission on the Reorganization of Secondary Education of the National Education Association (Washington, D.C.: Dept. of the Interior, Bureau of Education Bulletin No. 35, 1918), p. 10.
    [23] Ibid., p. 15.

tended to decline. In part, this was due to a failure on the part of many school administrators to accept fully the recommendations of the National Education Association. More important, it was a consequence of *other* types of community agencies arising to meet leisure needs as a primary concern.

World War I

As part of the nation's rapid mobilization during World War I, it was recognized that communities adjacent to army and naval stations and training camps needed more adequate programs of recreation as well as controls upon commercial amusements. The Council of National Defense and the War Department Commission on Training Camp Activities asked the Playground and Recreation Association to play a role in the creation of a national organization to provide special wartime community recreation programs. The Association quickly established the War Camp Community Service. This agency mobilized the recreation resources of 604 communities near military camps, providing wholesome recreation activities under leadership both for servicemen and civilians. A force of 2,700 full-time workers was employed, and 60,000 additional part-time or volunteer leaders were also utilized in varied sports and in social, cultural, and entertainment programs.

At the end of the war, servicemen who had become accustomed to these recreational opportunities desired similar programs for their own communities. Butler writes:

The people who saw during the war what community singing, pageants, athletic meets, and neighborhood parties could mean in community life insisted that means be devised for continuing them. Influential citizen groups and committees had come to realize the value of volunteer recreation service and the satisfaction obtained from it. Social, civic, and religious agencies had acquired common interest in community recreation and a sense of responsibility for providing it.[24]

A new agency, Community Service, Inc., was established in 1919 to take the place of the War Camp Community Service, for the purpose of developing an expanded peacetime community recreation effort. Many community memorial buildings in honor of the war dead were established by voluntary efforts; community centers, particularly for youth, were set in motion. Gradually, municipal recreation departments took over the responsibility for such programs. The net effect of the war was to promote the realization that recreation met universal needs—for those of all ages rather than just for children, and for all neighborhoods, rather than only congested and underprivileged areas.

[24] Butler, *op. cit.*, p. 88.

Growth of Public Recreation During the 1920's

The decade following World War I was marked by increased leisure, affluence, and public involvement in recreational activities of all types. Among the factors that contributed to recreation and park development throughout the United States at this time were the establishment of the National Park Service in 1916, which gave Federal emphasis to promoting outdoor recreation, the establishment of the National Conference on State Parks in 1922, the Izaak Walton League in 1922, and the American Association of Zoological Parks and Aquariums in 1924. Gradually, park administrators began to change their concepts of park development and design to make fuller provision for active recreation. This trend was promoted by a National Conference on Outdoor Recreation, called by President Calvin Coolidge and held in Washington, in May, 1924. This conference, attended by 309 delegates representing 128 national organizations, made a number of important recommendations for the development of publicly supported recreation programs in communities throughout the United States.

The conference recommended that a manual on parks be developed as a joint effort of the American Institute of Park Executives and the National Recreation Association. In response, a two-volume work, *Manual on Parks*, was written by L. H. Weir; it became widely used by park and recreation administrators and was an example of the merging relationship between the two groups. In 1926, the National Recreation School for graduate training in recreation was established by the National Recreation Association. It continued until 1935, graduating a total of 300 students, many of whom became leading practitioners in cities throughout the country.

A second major conference which helped to focus attention on recreation and leisure needs was the White House Conference on Child Health and Protection called by President Herbert Hoover in Washington, in November, 1930. Committees and speakers at this conference, including the Secretary of the Interior, Ray Lyman Wilbur, and Dr. William Heard Kilpatrick, an outstanding educational philosopher, stressed the importance of play in the lives of children. Shortages of play facilities and programs and the need for more widespread vacation opportunities were stressed.

Summing up, by the end of the 1920's, a solid base had been provided for organized park and recreation services. Both public and voluntary agencies were now widely established, although many municipalities still lacked organized programs and leadership and many park boards still resisted playing an active recreation role. The Federal government had become involved in the provision of outdoor recreation sites and armed forces recreation. There was now the awareness that recreation was needed for all ages and all social classes and that it involved far more than sports and games but included also many forms of cultural and social activities as well. In addition to public recreation departments, there were now numerous private organizations, such as golf and athletic clubs, fraternal orders, sports associations, nature study societies, choral groups, and hunting and fishing groups. In 1928 May and Petgen wrote:

> Underlying the whole recreation movement, commercial and noncommercial, is the enormous productivity of American industry which has reduced the average work day and yielded a wage that allows the working man increased spending money for the good things of life. In other words the industrial revolution has democratized recreation in the United States. Working people own not only homes but cars, radios, pianos and victrolas, and have a surplus of leisure and energy with which to enjoy these facilities. . . .
>
> The trend in the United States is to public control and direction of recreation. . . . The organized recreation movement has taken up good activities formerly enjoyed only by the rich and made them available to the general public through tax-supported recreation systems.[25]

The Depression of the 1930's

The great Depression of the 1930's was a sustained economic slump which resulted in mass unemployment and involuntary idleness for American workingmen. By the end of 1932, an estimated 15 million people, nearly one-third of the labor force, were unemployed. Even by 1940, just before the beginning of World War II, nearly half that number were still unemployed or on public work or relief projects.

Municipal recreation departments found themselves in a difficult position. Although attendance in park and recreation programs mounted considerably, tax revenues declined (by 1933, aggregate appropriations from the usual tax sources were only 54 percent of what they had been in 1930), and it became necessary to cut budgets sharply. In order to meet the increased demand for recreation by unemployed adults or young people who could not find work and had little money to spend on commercial amusements, recreation administrators attempted to reduce capital development, close down the least-used facilities, and rely heavily on the use of volunteers.

The Federal government soon instituted a number of emergency work programs related to recreation. At one time, about 49,000 persons were employed by the Recreation Division of the Works Progress Administration, and as late as 1940, 60,000 out-of-school youth between the ages of eighteen and twenty-four were employed in National Youth Administra-

[25] Herbert L. May and Dorothy Petgen, *Leisure and Its Uses* (New York: A. S. Barnes, 1928), p. 258.

tion projects involving leisure services. The Works Progress Administration provided leadership for a wide variety of recreational activities in local communities, including direct operation of 15,000 community centers, and assistance given to 8,000 more. Supervision was given to parks, playgrounds, athletic fields, beaches, and swimming pools. Community social events were organized, and classes formed in dance, crafts, drama, music, and social studies. In 1939, over 5 million people, not counting spectators, were estimated to be taking part in the programs of the WPA's Recreational Division each week, including at least 1.25 million youths between the ages of sixteen and twenty-four. Many of the employees of this program later found permanent employment in local recreation agencies.

In addition, the Federal Art Project operated many community art centers with a total attendance of 2.5 million in a single year. The Federal Music Project, which sponsored thousands of musical performances, had over a hundred Federal symphony and concert orchestras and over 160,000 in its classes. The Federal Theater Project, which had some 100 companies operating in twenty states, gave a monthly average of 2,800 performances. All these served millions of people with cultural activities and succeeded in bringing live performances and exhibits to millions of Americans who had previously not been exposed to the creative arts in a direct way. Altogether, the Federal arts program gave employment to over 30,000 writers, artists, musicians, dancers, actors, and directors.

Both the National Youth Administration and the Civilian Conservation Corps carried out numerous work projects involving the construction of recreational facilities. During the five years from 1932 to 1937, the Federal government is estimated to have spent about $1.5 billion dollars in developing and improving camps, buildings, picnic grounds, trails, swimming pools, parks, and playgrounds. Many large community center buildings, stadiums, and athletic complexes were constructed in urban areas. The Civilian Conservation Corps helped in the establishment of state park systems in numerous states that had no organized park programs before 1933. In 1939, there were some 300 camps operated by the CCC, and a vast quantity of work was done in national and state forests, much of it with recreational value. Many of the buildings that National Youth Administration workers constructed had recreational uses; this included, by 1940, over 9,000 schools, libraries, museums, art galleries, and other educational buildings.

In the large cities of the nation, cellar clubs emerged. These were youth-organized social and recreational programs, which sprang up spontaneously, often based on ethnic and racial ties. The cellar clubs made use of vacant stores, cellars, or building lofts, where young people were able to find meeting places free of adult supervision and interference. Often, they gained occupancy of premises simply by painting, cleaning, and maintaining them; they furnished them with second-hand furniture and operated them as clubrooms. The memberships of cellar clubs ranged between 20 and 100 boys and young men, usually ranging in age from about sixteen or seventeen to well past twenty-five. In New York City alone, there were 6,000 such clubs by 1940, and other cities had them as well. Obviously, they offered much potential for constructive youth work, as well as dangers related to gambling, sexual misbehavior, or other antisocial activity.

The Federal government was much concerned with this phenomenon. In large cities, federations of clubs were formed which established rules for behavior and operation. Settlement houses worked with club members, and the Youth Service Division of the WPA assigned many youth leaders to reach unaffiliated cellar clubs and to assist them in their programs and methods of financing and in their relationships with the police and the neighborhoods. It sought to end much of the petty racketeering and other forms of delinquency carried on by club members and attempted to help them achieve the status of youth agencies. Youth leaders employed by the WPA in this program were the forerunners of the street-club workers who emerged in large cities during the 1940's and 1950's to work with street gangs.

The effect of the Depression—while it was devastating in other ways —was positive in terms of recreation. Instead of simply channeling off billions of dollars in direct relief, according to the European dole system, people were put to work meaningfully. The lives of millions of people in thousands of communities was enriched. Recreation training was given to hundreds of thousands of leaders. Great numbers of indoor facilities were built and outdoor recreation areas constructed and improved. Recreation and park development, in the view of one analyst, was set ahead at least a decade by the services provided by the Civilian Conservation Corps alone.[26]

Another important effect of the Depression was to stimulate the concern of the American people about the crucial problems of leisure and recreation opportunity. The American Association for the Study of Group Work studied the problem and published an important report, *Leisure, a National Issue*, in 1939. Written by Eduard Lindeman, a leading social work administrator who had played a key role in government during the Depression, this document held that the "leisure of the American people constitutes a central and crucial problem of social policy." Lindeman pointed out that the view that leisure was only for the elite classes of society was now outmoded; it was now available to all social classes. In a democratic society, he concluded, it was essential that it be seriously considered and provided for. Lindeman pointed out that the relation of leisure to social policy was clearly evident in those totalitarian European

---

[26] C. Gilbert Wrenn and D. L. Harley, *Time on Their Hands: A Report on Leisure, Recreation and Young People* (Washington, D.C.: American Council on Education, 1941), p. 221.

states which during the 1920's and 1930's had embraced leisure as an integral part of their programs:

In Germany, the latest and most extreme of these new autocracies, leisure is organized primarily for the purpose of propaganda, of sustaining an attitude of loyalty toward the state, and of keeping the time of the people . . . fully occupied . . . in mass activities. Recreation in totalitarian nations is merely another form of subservience to the state, a planned form of action which follows the usual pattern of regimentation.[27]

Lindeman urged that in the American democracy, it was necessary to make recreation meet the true needs of the people. He urges that it be considered in terms of its relationship to work and that leisure not be thought of as the antithesis of labor but rather its complement. Pointing out that American workers were gaining a vast "national reservoir" of leisure which would be estimated at 390 billion hours per year, he suggested that the "new leisure" should be characterized by free choice and a minimum of restraint. He urged, however, that if the new increments of leisure were not to become "idleness, waste, or opportunity for sheer mischief," it was essential that an environment be furnished in which free choices would be expressed in positive ways. Lindeman urged that a national plan for leisure be developed and that the varied Federal programs in recreation be expanded and more effectively coordinated by a central bureau. He pointed out also that there was a growing need for professional trained recreation leaders if the quality of leisure was to be enhanced:

I have no doubt that a distinct profession of recreation leadership is now coming into being. Indeed it is my expectation that this newer occupation will enlist recruits at an accelerated rate of speed and that within the next quarter-century there will be a demand for at least one hundred thousand trained recreation professionals. Some of these will be concerned with problems of administration and planning; others will work in research; others will be engaged in developing newer forms of facilities; some will be supervisors, recreation teachers and trained specialists.[28]

Before Lindeman's urgent recommendations for formulating national policy in leisure could be acted upon, however, the nation underwent a second major crisis—even more sustained and dangerous to its existence than the Depression. This was World War II.

The Effects of World War II

This great conflagration, in which the United States became actively involved in December, 1941, compelled the immediate mobilization of

---

[27] Eduard C. Lindeman, *Leisure: A National Issue* (New York: American Association for the Study of Group Work, 1939), p. 11.
[28] *Ibid.*, p. 47.

every aspect of national life: education, manpower, industry, and a variety of social services and programs. Necessarily, many adjustments needed to be made in community life and new programs set in motion to serve the armed forces and those working in defense plants.

The Special Services Division of the U.S. Army provided recreation facilities and programs on military bases throughout the world, making use of approximately 12,000 officers, several times that many enlisted men, and large numbers of volunteers. About 1,500 officers were involved in the Welfare and Recreation Section of the Bureau of Naval Personnel, and expanded programs were offered by the Recreation Service of the Marine Corps. These departments were assisted by the United Service Organizations, formed in 1941, consisting of the joint military effort of six agencies, the Jewish Welfare Board, the Salvation Army, Catholic Community Services, Y.M.C.A., Y.W.C.A., and the National Travelers Aid. The United Service Organizations functioned in the continental United States and outside of camps, in clubs, hostels, and lounges throughout the western hemisphere. Through U.S.O. Camp Shows, Inc., it provided professional entertainment for troops overseas and in many Veterans' Administration Hospitals.

The American National Red Cross established approximately 750 clubs in theaters of operations throughout the world, along with about 250 mobile entertainment units, manned by over 4,000 leaders. Its military hospitals overseas and in the United States involved over 1,500 recreation workers as well.

In American communities, many programs had to be curtailed during World War II because of manpower shortage and travel restrictions. However, recreation and park departments instituted special new programs to assist the war effort, including victory gardens, learn-to-swim programs, salvage drives, and many teen-canteen programs to counteract the increase of juvenile delinquency throughout the nation. Youth-serving agencies, such as the Boy and Girl Scouts and the Camp Fire Girls, collected scrap metal and paper, made equipment and supplies for military recreation centers, and sold war bonds. The National Recreation Association established a new field to assist communities near military bases and training camps, helping them organize special programs for members of the armed forces.

Recognizing that wartime conditions made recreation especially important in newly established or expanded defense industrial centers, many municipal recreation directors extended their facilities and services to local war plants and changed their schedules to serve war-industry workers around the clock. Because of the rapid increase of industrial recreation programs, the National Industrial Recreation Association was formed in 1941 to assist in such efforts. Also, the Federal Security Agency's Office of Community War Services established a new Recreation Division to assist programs on the community level. This division's consultants helped to set up 300 new community programs throughout the country; it assisted the construction and operation of child-care centers and recreation buildings, many of which continued after the war as regular tax-supported community recreation departments.

By the war's end, great numbers of servicemen and servicewomen had taken part in extensive and varied recreation programs and services and thus had come to a new appreciation of this field of organized service. Many individuals had been trained and had gained experience in recreation programs and were ready to move back into civilian life as professionals in this field. Just as after World War I, many communities established parks, civic centers, pools, and other recreation facilities as memorials to their war dead or were now impelled to establish new public recreation and park agencies.

Trends During the 1950's and 1960's

Following World War II, there was a marked increase in the number of municipal park and recreation departments and indeed in all forms of participation in recreation throughout the nation. Certain trends affecting organized recreation service were noted during the post-World War II period. These included the following:

1. *National Concern with Physical Fitness.* Particularly during the 1950's, there was a marked emphasis on the need to develop and maintain the physical fitness of youth and adults. Comparative studies showing that American youth were less fit than the youth of other nations led schools to strengthen their programs of physical education. Many public recreation departments expanded programs involving fitness classes, conditioning, jogging, and sports for all ages. The President's Council on Physical Fitness and such organizations as the Lifetime Sports Foundation, the American Association for Health, Physical Education, and Recreation, and the American Athletic Union were particularly active in this area.

2. *Programs for the Disabled.* A second area of increased emphasis was the provision of special services for the physically and mentally disabled. Various agencies of government which were concerned with rehabilitation—particularly vocational rehabilitation—were strengthened to meet the needs of disabled citizens, especially large numbers of returning veterans, who sought to be reintegrated into community life. During the years of the Kennedy administration, the Federal government greatly expanded its aid to special education. In recreation, this took the form of new services to aid retarded children, youth, and adults. Beginning in the middle 1960's, there was greatly increased emphasis on developing social

and recreational programs for aging persons in both institutional and community settings.

3. *Outdoor Recreation and Park Development.* The major emphasis of both Federal and state governments was in the area of expanding open-space and beautification programs. The report of the Outdoor Recreation Resources Review Commission in 1962 and the establishment of the Bureau of Outdoor Recreation and the Land and Water Conservation Fund program led to increased Federal support for conservation and open-space development. State planning and accelerated municipal land acquisition programs were key elements during this period.

4. *Increased Government Assistance.* On various levels, the Federal government provided fuller assistance to community and state agencies and to colleges and universities in the park and recreation fields. Assistance was given by a number of agencies in the Department of Health, Education and Welfare and in the Department of Housing and Urban Development, both in facilities, in planning and development, and in support of consultation and research.

5. *Involvement in the Arts.* Following World War II, the nation embarked on a marked expansion of cultural centers, performing organizations, museums, and art centers. Chiefly, the growth in participation has been on an amateur or recreational basis. This "cultural explosion" has been encouraged by the assistance of the Federal government, through the Arts and Humanities Act of 1965, and by the establishment of various state art councils. The bulk of it represents genuine interest on the part of Americans in cultural activities, coming as a consequence of greater affluence and leisure and of increasingly higher levels of education.

6. *Other Trends in Participation.* Other major developments in terms of public interest and involvement have included (1) the growth of outdoor recreation, including family camping, (2) all forms of travel, including exploration of national and state parks and forests and a considerable growth of foreign vacation travel, (3) a continued growth in spectator activities (not so much in terms of direct attendance as in terms of vast numbers of people spending great bulks of time, on all age levels, in watching television, and (4) considerable interest in do-it-yourself activities, such as gardening, home-repair, craft, and minor construction activities.

Following World War II, the close cooperation between recreation, education, and social work which had characterized the earlier period of development tended to decline. Although recreation continued to be linked with physical education in many university departments, its orientation now moved sharply in the direction of parks management. As described in Chapter 5, the result was a new merger of park and recreation interests. A primary interest came to be placed on facilities development and maintenance—with lessened concern given to the provision of organized group services.

The major new challenge to recreation came as a consequence of the growing urban crisis that arose in the mid-1960's. This stemmed from the increased awareness of the needs of disadvantaged citizens, particularly members of minority groups, that had come about during the antipoverty programs developed under the Johnson administration. It also felt the sharp impact of growing black militancy and the wave of urban riots in black ghettos. Coupled with efforts on the part of the Federal government to improve services to the disadvantaged and to assist in major new programs of urban renewal, many cities developed improved services for inner-city areas. By the decade's end, it was still clear that the challenge of providing services to the poor had not been solved and would continue to represent a major difficulty for public authorities.

A new kind of challenge emerged also with the youth rebellion of the 1960's. Young people were challenging the establishment. They had developed new kinds of recreation for themselves, in many cases completely discarding traditional moral values as outmoded shibboleths. They were "doing their own thing," taking drugs in ever-growing numbers, and affirming new, permissive attitudes with respect to sexual behavior. The society was marked by a new "electronic" environment, in which drugs, light, and sound had invaded the arts and were used to "blow one's mind." The roles of work, conformity, patriotism, family stability, and respect for elders all were seriously challenged. As young people sought new kinds of sensation and personal relationships, many of the traditional forms of recreation seemed no longer as relevant as they had been in the past. With the pressure of increasingly severe social crises in the cities, austerity budgets, and shifting responsibilities of governments, it became more and more necessary for those responsible for recreation services to develop new and innovative approaches to program planning and to financial support. In doing so, it became obvious that the rationale for service—in effect, the philosophy upon which recreation programs were to be developed—had to be revised to meet the needs of a new technological age.

10

Recreation on the International Scene

This chapter examines the recent development and current status of recreation in a number of leading European and Oriental nations, as well as major aspects of international recreational service. Throughout Europe, recreation has not developed as a field of professional service as fully as in the United States. In several respects, however, European nations have promoted forms of recreational involvement which surpass those found in the United States. Typically, they have achieved a higher level of sports participation for the masses of people and have promoted the arts and folk culture far more vigorously than in the United States.

In contrast to the American system, the general pattern in European nations has been to view leisure as a national or Federal responsibility. It has been used as a means of promoting ideology, and serving important national goals. This was most evident during the period prior to World War II, when, in such nations as Italy, Germany, and Russia, one found a widespread organization of recreation

as a medium of indoctrination of the children, young people and adults with definite social-economic-political ideas, aims and purposes. In Germany it is the idea of totalitarian state; in Italy the corporative state; in Russia the communistic state.[1]

In the democratic states of Europe during this period, such as England and France, recreation tended to be approached through national minis-

[1] Lebert H.Weir, *Europe at Play: A Study of Recreation and Leisure Time Activity* (New York: A. S. Barnes, 1937), p. 12.

tries of labor, which assisted programs serving working people and their families, or through departments of education. The bulk of actual sponsorship of programs was carried on not through governmental agencies but rather through voluntary organizations interested in promoting sports, the arts, outdoor activities, folklore, and similar concerns. Weir wrote in the 1930's:

In European countries labor unions, churches, political groups or parties . . . recognized in leisure or recreation a powerful instrument for the promotion of their particular social, economic, religious, political theories, aims and purposes.[2]

In general, there was a greater concern with the leisure needs of adults than those of children. Owing to the close-knit family life in most European nations, the view was widely accepted that the place for children, outside of school, was the home (except for those totalitarian nations which established powerful youth organizations for purposes of indoctrination). Most playgrounds were under the control of schools, which used them for highly organized formal physical activities rather than casual play.

In most European nations, park planning was well-developed early in the twentieth century. Many cities had, by the early 1930's, extensive provisions for parks and other outdoor recreation spaces. Typically, both the state and the large cities owned extensive acreage, including many national, state, and municipal forests—all open to the public for recreation. Major sports and gymnastic organizations, with strong government support, developed networks of sports arenas, play fields, and stadiums. In addition, during this early period, riverfronts, beaches, and lake shores throughout the European nations were widely used for park and recreation purposes.

The following section examines the development of recreation and park programs in a number of major European and eastern nations.

Great Britain

As indicated earlier, parks and various forms of public entertainment had been well-established in England by the end of the eighteenth century. There was little concern with the needs of the working classes, however, until the growth of leisure for the building trades, clerks, and manual workers resulted in the Saturday half-holiday and a widespread interest in developing sports clubs and district sports leagues. Churches acted as sponsors for many football and cricket clubs during the 1870's; many of these later became independent professional teams. Church authorities regarded sport as the least of the evils that beset the urban population and felt that it might deter workers from vice and alcoholism during the newly acquired weekly half-holiday.

[2] *Ibid.*, p. 11.

Gradually, a broader concern about the use of leisure spread in Great Britain. Prime Minister Benjamin Disraeli said in an 1872 speech to the Conservatives of Manchester, "Increased means and increased leisure are the two civilizers of man." During the decade beginning in 1880, a system of loans granted by the national government through the Ministry of Health to local authorities helped them establish playing fields. The Bath and Washhouse Act assisted local authorities in building swimming pools. Play centers in settlement houses and working boy's clubs were established in the 1880's; soon there was a Federation of Working Boy's Clubs in London with over one hundred clubs and thousands of young members.

In 1925, the National Playing Fields Association was formed to promote the development of facilities for sports and outdoor recreation throughout Great Britain, a function that until this time had been carried out by local associations. The N.P.F.A. provided financial assistance for thousands of local playfield projects and developed an "Open Space Standard," consisting of a recommended minimum of five acres of public open space for every 1,000 persons, of which four acres should be set aside for team games. Other organizations and societies were developed in this period to promote public recreation opportunities, such as local "public garden" associations, footpaths, preservation societies, drama leagues, and music and folklore societies.

Local education authorities were empowered, by the Education Act of 1918, to provide camps, physical training centers, playing fields, and other "facilities for social and physical training." In 1935, government and education authorities concerned with physical education established a Central Council of Recreative Physical Training; two years later, Parliament passed a Physical Training and Recreation bill giving financial support to local school and community sports programs. During World War II the British government established a National Fitness Council which promoted programs of physical activity. In 1944 the Central Council of Recreative Physical Training was changed to the Central Council of Physical Recreation, with a primary concern with providing pleasurable leisure activities rather than training as such.

Since this time, the Central Council of Physical Recreation has been among the leading organizations to promote sports and various other types of active leisure pursuits in Great Britain. It directly sponsors many activities and also assists other organizations involved in physical recreation, including local authorities, sports bodies, outdoor activity associations, youth organizations, and industrial firms. It offers training courses in a wide range of sports, as well as mountaineering, sailing, and dance. Over two hundred national organizations are represented on the Council, including the major organizations in sport, outdoor recreation, education, health, youth, and social services. For a number of years, the C.C.P.R. operated three National Recreation Centers for leadership training and sports participation. These included Bisham Abbey on the Thames, a major sports center just six miles from London, which provides facilities for tennis, golf, sailing, canoeing, and similar sports; Lilleshall Hall in Shropshire, based on an old historic estate and offering extensive grounds for cricket, football, hockey, and lacrosse, as well as larger sports halls for indoor play; and Plas y Brenin ("The King's House"), situated in the Snowdonia National Park in North Wales, providing training and practice in every form of mountaineering, snow-rock-ice climbing, and orienteering.

In 1964, a magnificent new national recreation center, the Crystal Palace, was opened in metropolitan London. A multisports complex with a stadium and sports hall enabling several hundred persons to take part in a wide variety of activities simultaneously, the Crystal Palace cost 3 million pounds to build. Since then, three other centers have been established, a new sailing center at Cowes in the Isle of Wight and two others in Scotland, Inverclyde and Glenmore Lodge, operated by the Scottish Council of Physical Recreation.

The Central Council of Physical Recreation is regarded as a voluntary organization, although about half of its income comes from grants made by the British Ministry of Education; the other half is derived from donations and fees.

During the 1950's there was much concern in Great Britain about the role of sport in society. The Wolfenden Committee on Sport was established in October, 1957, to examine the total development of games, sports, and outdoor activities in the United Kingdom. The Wolfenden Report, issued in 1960, contained many valuable recommendations directed to the government, local authorities, industrial firms, sports bodies, voluntary youth organizations, and others. It took the view that sport was self-justified, although it also pointed out that it had strong links to the development of favorable character traits, social behavior, health, and aesthetic experience. Its major statement with respect to juvenile delinquency was

> The causes of criminal behavior are complex, and we are not suggesting that it would disappear if there were more tennis courts or running tracks; nor are we concerned to press for wider provision of opportunities for playing games just on the ground that it would reduce the incidence of those various forms of anti-social activities which are lumped together as "juvenile delinquency." At the same time, it is a reasonable assumption that if more young people had opportunities for playing games fewer of them would develop criminal habits. . .
>
> But our major thesis is that there is a positive "play" element in the life of young people, which can be neglected only to the disadvantage of both individual and society. Man in short, needs play. In the form of a game, a sport or an outdoor activity of some kind it is desirable in itself, for its own sake, as a valuable element in a full and rounded life.[3]

[3] P. C. McIntosh, *Sport in Society* (London: C. A. Watts, 1963), p. 114.

In 1965, the government established a Sports Council, which operates in four areas: "sports development and coaching," "facilities planning," "research and statistics," and "international," with the assistance of regional sports councils throughout the nation. Through its recommendations, the National Department of Education and Science provides substantial funds throughout England, Scotland, and Wales for coaching projects and capital expenditure on facilities. In addition, financial assistance is given by the Ministry of Housing and Local Government to local authorities to help develop parks and play facilities.

In 1959, the Recreation Grounds Act gave local authorities the power to acquire land for recreation, under loans sanctioned by the Minister of Housing and Local Government. With the passage of the Countryside Bill in 1968, it seems clear that national expenditure for parks and outdoor recreation will be much greater than in the past. In a 1968 publication of the Sports Council, *Planning for Sport*, the following statement was made:

It is the local authorities that have become most involved in the changing pattern of demand for physical recreation. The pressure on land, the expense of new capital facilities such as sports halls and swimming pools, a growing awareness of overlap in the provision of neighboring authorities or of two or more departments within the same authority, and the expectation of further demands, have all contributed to the need for local authorities to consider overall policies for recreational provision. It seems clear that . . . most large recreational facilities will in future be provided by local authorities.[4]

In Great Britain, youth services are promoted by the National Association of Youth Clubs, a national body with which thirty-six local associations of youth clubs in England and youth clubs of the Scottish, Welsh, and Northern Ireland Associations of Youth Clubs are affiliated. Its purpose is to help young people through leisure time activities "to develop their physical, mental and spiritual capacities that they may grow to full maturity as individuals and members of society." Each varied organization retains its own purpose and independence but subscribes to the overall goals of the Association. Approximately 3,300 affiliated clubs and groups (of all religious denominations, including voluntary and government sponsored groups), with 282,000 young members, mostly between fourteen and twenty-one, are affiliated with the National Association of Youth Clubs. The organization provides training for leaders, consultation, conferences, and courses for those in group work or youth work.

The National Association of Youth Clubs and its member groups receive assistance from the Ministry of Education's Youth Service Development Council and from many local educational authorities. Its work

[4] *Planning for Sport*, Report to the Sports Council of Great Britain (London: Central Council of Physical Recreation, October, 1968), p. 15.

is based on the Education Act of 1944, which required that all local education authorities provide adequate facilities for "continuing education" and also "leisure-time occupation, in such organized cultural training and recreative activities as are suited to their requirement." The Report of the Albermarle Committee in 1960 made a number of major recommendations to improve youth services by establishing a Youth Service Development Council, assisting building programs, providing an increased force of full-time leadership, and giving grants to national voluntary youth organizations, including for the first time denominational programs, as well as support to "problem youth."

Professional leaders of youth clubs are trained in several colleges which offer one- and two-year special courses; some training is also provided by the National Council of Y.M.C.A.'s. Special training in youth work is now offered through the Department of Education at the University College at Swansea and the University of Wales, with a one-year post-graduate diploma in youth leadership and organization as an aspect of education. Youth club programs include

hobbies and construction projects; self-improvement activities, social activities, trip programming, sporting activities, including skiing, sailing, surfing and canoeing, and gliding; camping; birdwatching; boat racing; service projects in community programs; fund-raising, providing services to the handicapped and to hospitals; artistic and cultural activities.[5]

In recent years, the directors of the N.A.Y.C. have raised serious questions about the place and value of youth clubs and their relevance in contemporary society. Many young people have challenged the traditional approaches of these organizations; they ask whether they are

significantly meeting the needs and wants of the contemporary generation of young people; and whether new forms of youth provision and opportunity are needed which allow more self-determination to the young, and get away from the structure, developed over the last decades, of an adult leader who is the proprietor of a group for which he provides programmes and facilities.[6]

Questions have been raised about programs serving young adults with respect to social behavior, moral standards, and such issues as whether liquor should be served through licensed bars in youth clubs. Realistically, it has been pointed out that "the majority of young adults will never join an organization which offers less than they can get outside." The rationale of the Youth Service program has been phrased in the following way, in response to those who have challenged the concept of voluntary youth

[5] *Annual Report, National Association of Youth Clubs of Great Britain, 1967–1968*, pp. 8-11.
[6] *Ibid.*, p. 6.

organizations, urging that youth work become a state-operated service carried on by central and local authorities:

In a free and open society such as ours, a wholly state organized youth venture tends to be anathema because people remember and are still disturbed by the fascist youth organizations which emerged in the 1930's. Every government report, every official committee which has made a study of youth work in Britain has suggested that the most effective pattern is a non-state, non-totalitarian one. . . . A state youth organization or a wholly state operated youth service with dangers of political manipulation is unlikely in this country. The demand is for variety, freedom of form in organization and development, a mixture of organizations and a real partnership between the state . . . and voluntary movements.[7]

Recreation in the Soviet Union

The Soviet Union is the leading example today of a major nation (actually a federation of autonomous Soviet Social Republics, regions, and national districts) with extensive centralized economic planning and social management, including a major concern with leisure and recreation. Every aspect of Soviet life is regarded as part of a collective scheme to build national morale, improve health, and increase national productivity.

The concept of leisure within the Soviet Union has been closely linked to the promotion of "socialist discipline" and the development of communal solidarity and morality. Economic expansion in the Russian system has required stringent controls over all aspects of life, including the use of leisure time. Whetten comments:

leisure activities are vitally important in a controlled society. Unless leisure time is carefully regulated, the "sense of sacrifice" which the worker is taught on the job could desert him in the hours he is away from it. Furthermore, the nature of leisure activities will, to some extent, determine the amount of capital available to the state for reinvestment and the type of products these investments will produce. Realization of the state's ultimate goal thus depends, at least in part, on its success in controlling leisure time.[8]

In the early decades, the Soviet concept of leisure carried a negative connotation of lazy, selfish indulgence. The Soviet citizen was expected to use it to "rest and gather strength for new labors and successes." Such use of leisure by workers became a social responsibility as well as a constitutional right. Provision of leisure programs for working men and women was aimed at increasing industrial productivity, with personal happiness a secondary concern. Thus, the Russians developed an elaborate system of

[7] Harold Haywood, *A Role for Voluntary Youth Work* (London: National Association of Youth Clubs, June, 1968), p. 2.

[8] Lawrence Whetten, "Leisure in the Soviet Union," *Recreation*, February, 1961, p. 91.

rest homes and vacation resorts for workers in coastal regions like Alupka, Yalta, or Socki, with the emphasis on providing nourishing diets, casual bathing, sunning, entertainment, and rest.

The Soviet Union provides recreational opportunities for all age levels. Beginning in the 1920's, it established a system of day-care centers for infants, kindergartens, open-air and other schools, and summer camps, which provided varied play involvements for children throughout the year. An extensive youth movement is under state guidance, including all ages from seven to twenty-five. In all divisions, games and athletics are an important part of the program. On each level there is indoctrination in the ideas of the Soviet state, with constant campaigns, drives, and parades and with a paramilitary approach to organization and membership. The Pioneers operate thousands of camps for children and youth; there are graduated admission fees which permit all children and youth to enter. Over all, there are over 3,200 Pioneer Youth Palaces, or centers, which enjoy spacious quarters in the former palaces of Czarist royalty or in more recently built modern structures.

For adults, there is an extensive provision of clubs and organizations which are built in many cases around individual membership or through neighborhood organizations or housing developments. Whetten writes:

Every effort is made to fill leisure time during the working year with as many culturally and educationally rewarding activities as possible. Local groups, such as hobby clubs, apartment-house councils, civil-defense units, the factory . . . study group, and the Komsomol or party cell, are organized and supported by the government. Activities of these groups center around . . . local palaces of culture, which are often the most impressive buildings in sight. Though the individual is not forced to join specific organizations, social pressure is strong enough to bring conformists to heel.[9]

In Russian cities, apartments, frequently occupied by several family groups, are often so crowded that families must depend on publicly provided resources, such as parks and outdoor recreation facilities.

Park Planning and Development. In a detailed study of the Soviet Union during the early 1930's, Weir reported that social planning included extensive provision of parks, playgrounds, sports fields, stadiums, swimming centers, winter-sports facilities, housing playgrounds, and indoor centers in cities as well as many camps and recreation establishments in the country. In addition, the Commissariat of Health established and enforced minimum requirements for playgrounds for younger children.

Russian planners also developed a type of general park, to be controlled by special municipal authorities. Called parks of "culture and rest," these facilities offer all sorts of recreation and educational facilities for

9 *Ibid.*, p. 92.

adults and children. Weir described the famous Moscow Park of Culture and Rest, which was opened in 1929 and comprised 731 acres, as being a "cross between an American amusement park and a large landscape park," including Ferris wheels, parachute towers, and similar equipment, as well as areas for games and sports, gymnastic apparatus, outdoor and indoor dancing places, exhibition halls, reading rooms, lecture halls, concert and theater facilities, children's playgrounds, and numerous places for reading and quiet enjoyment of nature. During its first six years, the park was visited by 47 million persons, and hundreds of thousands of organized events were held, including many literary and theatrical programs.

Cultural Activity. The Soviet Union is characterized by a tremendous amount of state-sponsored activity in the arts, including legitimate theater, opera, ballet, concerts, and circuses. Bowers comments that in the large cities, such as Leningrad and Moscow, there are far more houses of cultural entertainment per capita than in other cities of the world. The Bolshoi Ballet in Moscow has a large annual grant from the state running into millions of rubles. It invariably plays to packed houses and employs nearly three thousand people, including artists, stagehands, scene builders, administrative personnel, and musicians.[10]

But the primary focus of the Soviet government, within the area of leisure and recreation, is in the field of sport.

Sport in the Soviet Union. Among the Russians, physical education and sport are viewed as essential means of developing national strength, unity, and prestige. Physical education is a required subject for all students, and marks in it are considered as important as any other school subject. Physical culture and sports programs are provided for all ages; carefully planned achievement tests promote standards of national stamina and hardiness. When the working day is over, thousands of industrial and office workers, students, engineers, collective farmers, and sports lovers crowd the nation's courts, gymnasiums, stadiums, and water-sports areas. There are hundreds of sports events, presentations, and holidays in each Republic throughout the year, and events such as the National Games, World Festival of Youth and Students, and Soviet Sportakadiada, to promote Olympic participation. McLendon writes:

from early years through adulthood, millions compete . . . for badges signifying athletic achievement. All participants are provided with facilities, trainers, coaches, and—more important—opportunities for organized competition and awards for recognition. . . . Public works related to the development of parks, rivers, lakes, stadiums, arenas, and swimming pools are extensive, more and more modern . . . for all individual, team and recreational classifications.[11]

[10] Faubion Bowers, *Broadway, U.S.S.R.: Ballet, Theater and Entertainment in Russia Today* (New York: Thomas Nelson, 1959), p. 13.
[11] John B. McLendon, Jr., "The Soviet Union's Program of Physical Culture and Sports," *Journal of Health, Physical Education and Recreation*, April, 1962, pp. 28-29.

This program is supported by thousands of juvenile sports clubs, over one hundred special sports schools for youth (where training includes fitness, sports practice, and political indoctrination), and vast numbers of organizations. Morton writes that in 1961, there were approximately 186,-000 *Kollektivy* (sports groups), with a membership of 30 million, organized in factories, offices, and collective state farms, as well as in schools, labor reserve units, the armed forces, and the security police. Competitions are scheduled in over forty-six different sports, with the best teams from district, province, republic, and Federal levels competing for championships on each level. Facilities for mass participation in the Soviet Union include approximately 25,000 soccer fields, 200,000 basketball and volleyball courts, 7,000 gyms, and 2,200 ski centers, with major programs of such other activities as ice skating, hockey matches, hiking, and similar events.[12]

The spontaneous organization of sports groups without Party permission (through the U.S.S.R. Union of Sports Societies and Organizations) is forbidden, and all sports societies and groups are formed according to prescribed statutes.

Sport is also seen as an important means of impressing Soviet superiority on the rest of the world and inflating the U.S.S.R.'s prestige. Morton points out that Communist Party slogans since the 1930's have demanded of Soviet athletes that they beat bourgeois sport records:

It was a Central Committee resolution of December 1948 . . . which launched the Soviet sport offensive of the 1950's . . . after many years of preparation, Soviet sports machine challenged the world's top athletes. . . .

By systematically organizing sport exchanges with nations from all over the world the U.S.S.R. has won valuable beachheads of influence which have been exploited to create a positive image of the Soviet Union . . . as Soviet technicians are welcome in various parts of the world, so are Soviet coaches.[13]

During the 1950's and early 1960's, Soviet athletes emerged as leaders of the international sports scene, having outdistanced the world's leading competitors in the 1956 and 1960 Olympic games and in other international sports meets. Strong feelings of national pride and satisfaction were aroused, and team victories were identified with state triumphs over the capitalist nations of the world. When, during the 1968 Mexico City Olympics, the Russian performers had a sharp setback, it caused a national furor. *Trud*, the State union newspaper, blamed coaches and athletes for a "blunted sense of responsibility" and for the "easy life" that had sapped their stamina. New and harsher state controls were established to promote sports organizations and lead to renewed success, with Communist Party Chief Leonid Brezhnev saying crisply, "International standards for our sports must be improved." A number of Soviet athletes were dropped from

---

[12] Henry W. Morton, *Soviet Sport* (New York: Collier Books, 1963), p. 19.
[13] *Ibid.*, pp.17-18.

national teams for breaking training and for failing both in their moral standards and in "hard work and self-sacrifice in the fight for high sporting achievement."

Increasingly, as the Russian people gain a measure of affluence, the leaders of the Soviet society are concerned about the invasion of Western decadence, in the form of "easy living" or "immoral" entertainment. Constant drives are carried on against "shirkers" in industry and against the invasion of jazz music, rock-and-roll dancing, foreign films and publications, and modern art—all of which the Soviets see as an attempt to corrupt and undermine the morality of their youth.

Yet leisure and possessions are growing in the Soviet Union, and the "soft life" is seen as a severe threat to the national strength. Leisure has been expanded through a new five-day week and by the addition of many holidays throughout the year. New resorts and entertainment centers are being established, and vacations are more widely available. In 1969 a long article in *Pravda* pointed out the dangers in the "generation gap" and the decline of adult and state-imposed influence on youth, who are supported by well-to-do parents and have lost the disciplined work ideal of their parents. An editor of *Pravda* wrote in 1969:

We have nothing against your supermarkets and all your material facilities for leisure time, but they have to be combined with high standards of culture, which your middle classes do not have. Material facilities are dead without the supreme blessing of culture.[14]

A leading sociologist, G. S. Petrosian, warned that free time must not lead to idleness: "It is the time devoted to study, the raising of [occupational] qualifications, self-education and self-development." *Pravda* expressed the national view clearly in these terms:

To care about the cultural recreation of the people is above all to ensure the conditions making it possible for the working people to spend their free time in such a way as to raise their general cultural and professional level to improve [themselves] physically and aesthetically.[15]

Despite the vast apparatus of youth and worker's organizations, of parks, playgrounds, and sports facilities, of cultural and athletic programs, the Soviet people are now seeking more "bourgeois" forms of play. Alcoholism, long a problem in Russia, has continued to plague the Soviet state. Idling, the pursuit of "diversionist" arts, even the increase of television, which has now become much more widely available to the Russian people and which threatens their ideal of a vigorous and meaningful leisure life—

[14] "Modern Living: Discovering the Weekend in Russia," *Time*, May 9, 1969, p. 73.

[15] *Ibid.*, p. 73.

all these are problems which they are attempting to solve by new and stronger laws forbidding gambling, drinking, and other forms of "Western decadence." They see these as ways of "softening" the Soviet people; pictures of nude women in Western publications which have entered the country are described by Communist officials as containing an "extremely well-concealed ideological burden" designed to turn the thoughts of the people toward the "sweet life" when they should be concerned with strengthening Communism instead.[16]

Recreation and Leisure in Germany

During the twentieth century, the provision of recreation facilities and programs in Germany fell into three distinct periods: up to and including the 1920's, the era of Nazi domination, and the post-World War II period.

Germany had been one of the first countries to develop a strong gymnastics and physical education movement and had established many parks and outdoor activity areas during the nineteenth century. As a consequence of the kindergarten movement, many playgrounds were built in large cities, often directed by educational authorities. The Central Committee for Popular and Juvenile Games carried on national programs which promoted sports and games and published many books and pamphlets during the period before and after World War I. It organized and conducted a series of national congresses on games and sports, provided courses for the training of leaders and coaches, and organized tournaments, excursions, winter-sports events, and syllabi for all levels of participation, from young children through college and adult-age programs.

During the years immediately before and after World War I, general standards of city planning were developed with respect to parks and open spaces. These provided minimum requirements as to equipment and areas for children's play and general recommendations for gymnasiums, large indoor swimming and bathing centers, tennis halls, and other indoor sports facilities. German parks and open-space planning during the 1920's and early 1930's created an extraordinary amount of green space in the form of parks and forests radiating fanlike from the central, densely populated parts of cities or in green belts encircling cities. Smaller green spaces in the form of small parks and gardens were widely provided in older, more congested neighborhoods. Many large municipalities established botanical and zoological gardens and sponsored cultural facilities and programs, such as theaters, operas, museums, and libraries.

Sports activities were based on a flourishing workers' sports movement, with thousands of adolescents participating in games and with strong voluntary organizations providing organized instruction, leagues, and facil-

[16] "Soviet Finds Photos of Nudes Ill-Concealed Ideological Ruse," New York *Times*, April 7, 1969, p. 5.

ities. Although substantial assistance was given by the Ministers of Welfare or Education of the various German states, in the form of subsidies for the construction of sports facilities, the actual expenses of organizing and carrying on activities were carried on by independent organizations. There were many patriotic and military groups, both on the left and the right, which, during the 1920's, made sport a major part of their program.

Following Germany's defeat in World War I, military training was forbidden, and much of the increased sports activity was undoubtedly used as a substitute for it. Frequently, drill fields were converted into athletic fields; certainly the goals of maintaining physical fitness and high morale were important to the various German athletic societies. It was estimated in the middle 1920's that some 5 million adults from the age of fifteen up were connected with sports organizations. The vogue was for mass participation rather than spectatorship, as in the United States during this period.

The Nazi Era in Germany. After the National Socialist Party came to power in Germany, it took over direct control of all physical education, organized sports, and recreation activities. Just as in the Soviet Union, the government established a network of youth and adult organizations and used them intensively as a form of propaganda and social control. The Hitler Youth Organization systematically organized the out-of-school activities for both boys and girls from six to eighteen, including sports and games, camping, hiking, first aid and hygiene, and other cultural pursuits, under leaders who were fully indoctrinated in the Nazi social and political party line. They prompted National Socialist ideals and strove to develop patriotic idealism and physical vigor and strength. Typically, they stressed the need for Puritan simplicity in recreation and for the promotion of the German folk heritage.

Physical education was seen as having a fourfold purpose: (1) training in citizenship responsibility, by demanding obedience, coordination, needed social values, and behavior; (2) the systematic development of youth's innate instinct for movement, games, and competitive struggle, to the practice of physical accomplishment and the "militant engagement of self"; (3) development of a sense of "race worth," with healthy views about physical beauty and efficiency, rooted in *Volkstum* (folk tradition and unity); and (4) the development of courage, self-discipline, and the encouragement of leadership potential and training in personal will and character.

The program of the *Bund Deutscher Mädel*, the organization serving girls and young women, included gymnastics, handicrafts, folklore, foreign affairs discussions, games and music, and health service. Many forms of entertainment or the arts which were popular in the other Western nations became forbidden under Nazi ideology because they were thought to be degenerate. Even such activities as hosteling, camping, and hiking, which had become popular before the Nazis came into power, were approached in a new light. Baldur von Schirach, the leader of the *Hitler Jugend* (Hitler Youth Organization), stated:

> Everywhere now new youth hostels of the National Socialist type have come into being. . . . If German youth today takes hikes, it does not do so with a false and gushing sentimentality intoxicated with Nature, but even here it subordinates its action to a political purpose. German youth roams the countryside in order to know its fatherland and, above all, comrades in other parts of the Reich. . . .
>
> The deeper meaning underlying the idea of hostels is to get the youth of large cities away from the morally corrosive dangers of its environment and to show that there is a form of recreation which is more satisfying than movies and beer joints and which costs less money. Through the youth hostel movement, even the poorest children of our people are given a chance to know the homeland for which they may be called upon to stake their lives.[17]

Thus, in every way, the Nazis made use of recreational programs to promote the goals of the Third Reich. Following the catastrophic defeat of the Nazi Regime in World War II, Germany abandoned this approach to leisure.

German Recreation after World War II.   Immediately after the war, under Allied occupation, funds were allocated for the rebuilding of recreational facilities and for the operation of new youth centers. Many bombed-out sections of cities were turned into parks, green belts, sports facilities, and stadiums. Sports again became extremely popular; they are organized by voluntary sports clubs, of which there are about 35,000 in West Germany today, with a total membership of about 7.4 million. Of this number, about two million are below the age of eighteen; about 41 percent of all male youths are active members of sports clubs. Each different sport has an autonomous Federal sport association attached to it. In addition there are numerous state and regional sport associations and unions.

The work of these groups is promoted by the *Deutscher Sportbeirat* (German Sports Advisory Council), which also assists efforts to create broad programs of community recreation in cooperation with churches, trade unions, and employer associations. Many cultural, social, and non-sport recreational activities are promoted by the *Bundesjugendring* (Federal Youth Ring), a centralized union of youth organizations, which coordinates varied recreation and social programs for young people.

As in many other European countries, considerable support is given by local governments to the performing arts, such as theater, opera, and musical organizations. Substantial subsidies are given by state governments and municipalities to West Germany's 135 theaters and operas. In the cities, educational authorities sponsor playgrounds and community centers.

[17] George L. Mosse, *Nazi Culture* (New York: Grosset and Dunlap, 1966), p. 296.

Thus, we see in Germany a pattern of recreation sponsorship which has shifted from authoritarian control to a program heavily sponsored by voluntary organizations and educational authorities, free from political or social indoctrination.

Recreation in Other European Countries

Among other nations of Europe, there have been varying patterns of provision for recreation needs. In France, for example, the national government has had little concern with the provision of recreation facilities or leadership. Some interpret this as due to the French "temperament," which is seen as highly individualistic and resistant to attempts by authority to organize the lives of people.

Therefore, the three major forms of recreation sponsorship in France have all been voluntary in origin. Industrial firms and unions have provided fairly extensive programs; these include playing fields, equipment, meeting halls and recreation rooms, sports teams and leagues, cultural programs of art, music, and theater, and motion pictures. A second form of sponsorship is the church. Many youth and sports programs are operated by both Catholic and Protestant denominations. These provide buildings or "patronages," which offer extensive programs of drama, sports, social, and educational activity. Although church-sponsored recreation is a major source of leisure opportunity, it generally does not involve a religious focus and thus is regarded as a communitywide service. In France, a third source of cultural, social, and sports activity has been various political movements, which operate youth clubs and adult clubs.

Since World War II, the national government has begun to take more aggressive steps to provide recreational opportunities and programs. The High Commissariat for Youth and Sports, a division of the French Ministry of Education which was established in 1958, is responsible for all matters having to do with physical education, sports, outdoor activities, "popular" education (meaning the whole gamut of government-sponsored extracurricular activities which enable young people to develop their cultural, artistic, and health potential in leisure), and summer camps.

In 1964, a special French commission, the Commission on Leisure for All, surveyed the growing problem of leisure in French society, particularly for industrial workers. The Commission recommended that 2,000 new open-air recreation parks be built in the Paris area and that others be built over 6 percent of France's total national territory, to be fully equipped with facilities for tennis, golf, swimming, and track.

Other European countries tend to fall into a middle ground of involvement. The other nations behind the Iron Curtain provide substantial support to sports and youth and adult organizations, although not to the same degree as the Soviet Union. The Scandinavian countries promote sports and physical fitness to a high degree and also tend to offer highly developed networks of social programs, including extensive social services for aging and disabled persons. They have pioneered in the development of so-called folk schools, which have revived interest in many traditional forms of play, including folk dance and song. Denmark, Norway, and Sweden all have extensively developed park and playground programs under municipal sponsorship. In the Low Countries, Belgium has been active in promoting recreation, through a system of *Loisirs des Ouvriers* (Workers' Leisure) Committees. Many Belgian organizations, particularly the Roman Catholic Church and major industrial firms, promote strong recreation programs. Publicly supported *Maisons des Loisirs* (Leisure Institutes) are sponsored in many cities and towns; these provide various forms of social, cultural, and educational enrichment, as well as family activities.

In the comparatively new state of Israel, the bulk of public recreation is provided by the Sports and Physical Education Authority in the Ministry of Education and Culture. Since the establishment of the Zionist movement, Jewish nationalists have stressed the need for a "muscular Jewry" to enable a people who have traditionally been intellectuals, professionals, and craftsmen to survive in the harsh Palestinian desert. The *Maccabi* Sport Organization, the *Hapoel* Association, and similar athletic groups have strongly promoted international Jewish sports participation and competition. Emphasis in Israel is strongly on maintaining the physical vigor and involvement of all the people—thus, mass sports and popular community activities rather than spectator sports are heavily stressed. *Hapoel*, for example, encourages water sports, cross-country races, marches, folk dancing, and sports and games at places of employment. In a number of cases, these have involved so-called "Popular Sports Events," in which thousands of persons of all ages and both sexes take part; such events are often attached to patriotic or historic themes or celebrations. Combative sports, such as judo, wrestling, fencing, boxing, mountain climbing, sharpshooting, and scuba diving, are also stressed, as part of the need for developing physical vigor and high morale for national survival. Generally in Israel other recreational and club activities tend to be centered around the school, although municipal authorities also provide some parks and youth programs.

Summing up, the pattern of recreation development in European countries differs from American practice in several respects. First, the major thrust in most countries is through sports associations which promote various forms of physical activity for the public at large. These are operated through district and regional voluntary associations which tend to receive substantial government assistance—usually from a national department of education and youth services. In other areas of leisure activity, such as cultural arts, substantial grants are given to private groups by national and municipal governments.

Most after-school activities for young children are sponsored by local educational authorities, which in turn are assisted by national educational ministries, which train leaders, send consultants and advisers, and provide other aid. In general, while many European countries have highly developed parks, playgrounds, zoos, and sports facilities, they have not developed a single unified recreation movement, as has been the case within the United States. Recreation, when provided to special groups, such as the handicapped or aged, tends to be viewed as a form of social service or rehabilitation.

Recreation Development in Eastern Nations

Recreation and Leisure in Japan. Nixon and Vendien point out that recreation in Asia has traditionally come through the home, religion, private clubs, and great national festivals. The concept of organized recreation with trained leaders and government responsibility is meeting serious obstacles of vast needs, little money, and lack of government interest.[18] In Japan, however, the reverse is true. There, since the 1920's, there has been a major interest in Western sports, such as baseball, hockey, basketball, boxing, track and field, tennis, and swimming. As early as 1925, major sports stadiums were built; both the colleges and the Y.M.C.A. have been influential in promoting such activities.

Prior to World War II, Japan displayed considerable interest in the organized recreation movement. It founded a National Recreation Association based on the American model after the 1932 Olympic Games. Following World War II, the Association has functioned actively in developing public recreation and park programs, promoting leadership training, and issuing recreation publications. Japan itself has changed markedly since World War II in evolving from a nationalistic and autocratic way of life to a democratic society. Its powerful and expanding economy has created a higher standard of living for the Japanese people than anywhere else in the Orient, along with greatly increased leisure hours.

A Sports Promotion Law was enacted in 1961 to assist preparation for the approaching 1964 Tokyo Olympics. This Act established guiding principles for sports development and gave both local and national government agencies broad responsibility for developing programs, facilities, and leaders. Participation in various sports is widespread and is usually climaxed by local, regional, and national competitions, festivals, and sports events. National athletic meets are held each year in various localities throughout the country, and delegates from each section compete for the Emperor's and Empress's Cups in thirty-five different activities on a seasonal basis. The Japan Amateur Sport Association and the National Ministry of Education assist in the organization of these competitions.

[18] Thomas Rivers, quoted in C. Lynn Vendien and John E. Nixon, *The World Today in Health, Physical Education and Recreation* (Englewood Cliffs, N.J.: Prentice-Hall, 1968), p. 77.

Beyond such organized sports events, there is a tremendous amount of commercially sponsored recreation in Japan, much of it modeled on programs in the United States. The development of superexpress trains has encouraged millions of Japanese families to travel for fun; they enjoy camping in summer and skiing in winter. Boating, fishing, and other outdoor pursuits are extremely popular. There are many privately operated recreation centers, including huge ski complexes (some of which now use plastic slopes flowing with water for year-round skiing), several-tiered driving ranges, and other facilities described in *Life* Magazine:

> In Japan, golf courses, beaches and ski slopes are packed beyond belief, . . . newly affluent, they have leisure their fathers never knew and a restless vigor that demands outlet . . . Whatever the sport, the Japanese attack it with a fearsome determination to be *dai-ichi*—the very best. They play as hard as they work, and they like to see others do the same. . . .
>
> Skating rinks have to stay open almost all night to handle the crowds. Skiers have to get to the railroad station six hours before train time to be sure of a place—and once in the mountains, wait again for hours for a turn on the lifts. High school baseball teams pull 60,000 to their championship games. More than 250,000 climbed Mt. Fuji this year, leaving tons of debris on the sacred slopes. But the most ambitious project is privately owned Yomiuriland, a $20 million complex spread over 1,000 acres on the outskirts of Tokyo.
>
> Yomiuriland, though inspired by Disneyland, emphasizes sports instead of amusements. Besides its Olympic-size snowless ski jump, it has easier slopes for beginners, a 120-foot parachute jump, two golf courses, . . . a clubhouse with a Buckminster Fuller geodesic dome, a chain of stocked fish ponds—and its own monorail to carry visitors from sport to sport.[19]

With all these modern innovations, the Japanese people still carry on many of their traditional leisure pursuits, linked to folk art, dance, theater, ceremony, and ritual along with such combative activities as *Sumo, Kendo,* and *Judo.*

As they continue to strengthen their public recreation programs and services, the Japanese have established not only a National Recreation Association but also a number of other professional organizations in the broad field of health, physical education, and recreation. There is as yet no single institution for the training of professional recreation leaders, although many are trained in short courses and institutes provided by government and voluntary organizations, the Y.M.C.A. and the Y.W.C.A., and the Ministry of Education.

A considerable amount of organized recreation opportunity in Japan is provided by industrial firms, which tend to be highly paternalistic. For example, Japan's leading businessman, Konosuke Matsuchita, whose industrial empire manufactures a wide range of appliances used throughout

[19] "Frantic Lunge into Sport," *Life,* September 11, 1964, pp. 34-35.

the world, provides a broad welfare plan for his employees. Both at their plants and in special resorts and recreation centers, his workers take part in many sports, cultural, and social activities. The Matsuchita firms even sponsor employee weddings, giving newlyweds free honeymoons in company-owned inns; they also operate extensive dormitories and houses at which thousands of workers live, many with attached recreational opportunities.

Recreation in Other Eastern Nations. In a number of other Oriental countries, less industrialized than Japan and characterized by extreme problems of overpopulation and poverty, recreation and leisure are not so fully developed. In India and Pakistan, for example, although beginning steps have been taken by the national governments toward establishing physical education and recreation facilities and programs, the bulk of service is still provided by private or voluntary organizations, such as the Y.M.C.A. or Scouts. The mass of people still live in small agricultural communities, where there are frequent festivals and village fairs, where popular pursuits such as dancing, music, folk dramas, and traditional games are practiced.

With increasing industrialization and urbanization, these forms of play tend to decline or to be inadequate for the urban masses. Large cities like Bombay and Calcutta are therefore developing stadiums and other facilities for mass sports and cultural pursuits. Beginning in 1950, a number of recreation centers were established in Indian cities under national subsidy; it is the plan of the Indian government ultimately to provide sport and recreation centers in towns and villages throughout the country. These will include libraries and cultural programs to maintain interest in traditional Indian customs and folkways. Balkan-ji-Bara, the All-India Children's Organization, has been active for many years in promoting playground programs and other leisure opportunities for children and youth. In addition, an Indian Recreation Association was recently formed, with assistance from the national government, to promote recreational development and train leadership, particularly for industrial and urban populations. A number of industries in India, particularly large textile mills, have organized varied social-service programs, including child and maternity welfare centers, reading rooms, parks, gymnasiums, sports fields, and theaters.

In Australia and New Zealand, relatively industrialized and technologically advanced nations with small populations and a high standard of living, recreation has begun to make rapid strides as a form of public service. In Australia, recreation is closely attached to sports and physical education programs. In the schools, physical education is coordinated through a National Director of Training in a highly centralized federal system of education. School programs include varied gymnastics, games, and sports. Community sports are provided by independent sports clubs and municipal authorities. In Australia, there has been considerable concern about physical fitness; in 1939 the Federal government helped to form a National Coordination Council for Physical Fitness and later appointed National Fitness Organizers who established state councils to promote fitness. This program has included leader training, the encouragement of camping and youth hostels, general sports programs for the public at large, and national grants to assist both facilities development and programs. Schools today provide many recreational activities for children and youth; varied programs of dramatic, cultural, and social activities are also conducted by churches, community centers, settlements, and similar agencies. Special recreation programs are also provided for aging persons and for hospital patients. Recently, park development has accelerated; beginning steps are being taken to create administrative posts for professionals in this field and also to provide specialized training for them.

New Zealand, with a much smaller population and an outstanding natural environment, has thus far made fewer advances in local parks and recreation services. Youth organizations are assisted by Youth Activities Officers based in the Department of Internal Affairs, and the Physical Education Branch of the National Education Ministry provides Adventure Camps for school children. New Zealand has nine outstanding national parks which serve both her own people and visiting tourists with outdoor recreational opportunity.

In most other Oriental nations, programs tend to be poorly developed. In Communist China, however, the pattern is very much like that of Soviet Russia, with all forms of recreational activity—particularly sports—being used to promote national propaganda and social control. Within all the arts and media of communication, rigid censorship is exerted. In the field of sports, this vast land of over 700 million people has made striking progress since it launched a sports build-up two decades ago. A Swedish writer comments:

> The restless giant behind the Bamboo Curtain is flexing its muscles in a dramatic sports renaissance . . . to challenge the United States and the Soviet Union for worldwide athletic supremacy.
>
> The government has subsidized the entire project, spending billions of dollars for schools, facilities, stadiums, training and equipment. And China has become sports-minded, with 65 million athletes, huge crowds jamming the big new arenas for athletic events (admission free) and a widespread eagerness for physical fitness.[20]

Both in the development of huge new stadiums and arenas, and in the promotion of such sports as track and field, swimming, weightlifting, soccer, speed skating, and table tennis, Communist China promises to become a leading competitive nation. Like Russia, it has a utilitarian view of sport as a means of attaining international prestige and compelling recognition.

[20] Wolf Lyberg, "Communist China Bidding for Athletic Supremacy," New York Times, January 16, 1966, n.p.

Similarly, Communist China's entire approach to leisure is that all forms of recreation must contribute to national goals and be under the direct control of national authorities.

The International Recreation Association

There is a strong contrast between the programs of the industrialized nations of Europe and the poorer nations of the Orient, South America, and Africa. In such countries, the promotion of recreation as a national program and a form of international cooperation has been the direct concern of the International Recreation Association.

Efforts to build cooperative international relationships through the sharing of recreational interests came as early as 1932, when the first International Recreation Congress was held in Los Angeles, in connection with the National Recreation Congress of the United States and the 1932 Olympic Games. During World War II, owing to the considerable international exchange of games and sports and travel by military personnel, a fresh impetus was given to the idea. At the 1952 National Recreation Congress in Boston, the Japanese delegation requested that the National Recreation Association provide assistance in the development of the recreation movement in that country. This led to increased interest in the idea of forming an international body to promote exchange in leisure philosophies and services among the countries of the world.

In 1956, an international recreation exchange project sponsored by the United States Department of State enabled leaders from nineteen countries to spend four months studying recreation developments in the United States. In the same year, at the National Recreation Congress in Philadelphia, the International Recreation Association was founded. Thomas E. Rivers, since 1923 the Secretary of the National Recreation Congress and a highly experienced worker in the field of international exchange, was appointed Director General of the new organization. Lord Luke of Pavenham, president of the National Playing Fields Association of England, was elected chairman of the Board of Directors, with six vice-presidents representing India, Germany, the Philippines, Egypt, Japan, and Latin America.

The I.R.A.'s essential purpose has been to provide a central clearing house for the exchange of information and experiences among recreation officials throughout the world, to assist countries in establishing central recreation service agencies, programs, facilities, and leadership training, and, in effect, to promote a world recreation movement designed to enrich the human spirit through the wholesome use of leisure. It has worked closely with the United Nations and its affiliated agencies, has provided services to over ninety nations, and has organized exchange programs and published useful pamphlets on international recreation development. In 1964 it sponsored (in cooperation with the National Recreation Association of Japan) a World Recreation Congress in Osaka and Kyoto which was attended by five hundred delegates from thirty-two countries.

The work of the I.R.A. has been widely acclaimed. President Eisenhower commended its efforts by stating,

Mutual interest in recreation and sports forms a natural bond of understanding among individuals as well as among countries. In stimulating activities of this kind, the Association is contributing toward better international relations.[21]

And, in recognition of its work with the United Nations, U Thant, Secretary-General of that body, commented, "You are helping to create a climate where peace can flourish."[22] Unfortunately, however, substantial financial support has been difficult to obtain for the International Recreation Association, which is primarily dependent on voluntary contributions. Its projects have therefore necessarily been limited.

Special Programs for the Disabled

Another aspect of international recreation service which has expanded considerably since World War II has been the provision of special competitive events and other activities for disabled men and women. The Stoke Mandeville Games, founded in England in 1948, set the pattern for such competitions, including such activities as archery, basketball, swimming, weight lifting, and similar events. Following the Rome and Tokyo Olympics, special "Paralympics" were held, with several hundred disabled participants from over twenty countries. A number of international organizations, such as the League of Red Cross Societies, the International Society for Rehabilitation of the Disabled, and the World Rehabilitation Fund, have assisted the development of recreation programs for the ill, aging, and disabled. Increasingly, therapeutic recreation service is becoming a worldwide movement, with a considerable amount of international exchange helping to stimulate new developments around the globe.

Recreation Contributions of the Peace Corps

A final example of international recreation service has been the work of the U.S. Peace Corps, which has provided substantial assistance to underdeveloped nations in the areas of physical education and community recreation. Obviously, the major problem in such countries is to develop educational, agricultural, and industrial processes that will make it possible for them to feed their swarming populations and maintain a more acceptable standard of living. Since this is so, some question whether it is appropriate to provide assistance in recreation when the major problem is that of survival. Community development authorities point out, however, that

---

[21] Dwight Eisenhower, quoted in Vendien and Nixon, *op. cit.*, p. 74.
[22] *Ibid.*, p. 76.

the problem of unused time is an extremely serious one for underdeveloped nations. One authority has pointed out that among the "billion people who live in conditions of the most extreme poverty, there is a latent resource of not less than 75 billion man-days of unemployed manpower per year."[23] Another author cites the example of Indian tribes in Peru, where the "mass of the rural population only work for 60 to 80 days out of the entire year and spend the rest of the time doing practically nothing."[24]

In such settings, recreation serves a useful function in that it provides a constructive and morale-building experience to replace uses of free time which might otherwise be demoralizing and negative. Recreational activities have certain specific functions in underdeveloped nations, where, as Suhm points out,

poverty, illiteracy and a rigid social system inhibit the development of more complex means of expression and mass communication. In effect, they provide a safety valve for repressed emotions, effectively link the present with the past, and help reduce the tedium and drabness that go with chronic poverty in a rather rigidly defined social system.[25]

Leet comments that recreation can also contribute to the survival of family and community life by holding the interest of young people who might otherwise drift away to cities. There, all too often, they create a problem of chronic mass urban unemployment and become a menace to society. Another specific value of recreation in underdeveloped nations is that it provides a medium through which people may learn to work together to develop communal unity and improve their own lives. The development of play areas and building of playground equipment have been among the most successful initial projects of rural community groups. Peace Corps officials have found that recreation, particularly sports, helped Peace Corps workers make contact with people and integrate themselves in community life.

Thus, recreation and physical education have represented important project areas for the Peace Corps. Typically, the Ivory Coast asked the Peace Corps for ten recreation instructors to help develop local, regional, and national sports teams and to introduce the concept of teamwork to participants from its many tribes and regions. Peace Corps workers in this specialization have also been used to teach environmental sanitation, public health, and nutrition, organize scouting and youth activities programs, begin boys' clubs and build clubhouses, operate libraries, build recreation facilities, organize local women's clubs, provide services for the mentally ill, help organize museums, work with orphan children, develop summer

---

[23] Glen Leet, paper presented at World Recreation Congress, Kyoto, Japan, *International Recreation Association Bulletin*, December, 1964, p. 1.

[24] Lawrence L. Suhm, "Southern Peru Regional Development Project," unpublished training manual, University of Wisconsin, 1962.

[25] *Ibid*.

camp programs, carry on life-saving and water-safety programs, develop local crafts programs with economic potential, and provide recreation and educational classes for the blind.

Summing up the Peace Corps' experience in this area, one official commented:

> The efforts of recreation workers in the Peace Corps to help the people of developing nations appreciate the value of physical conditioning, teamwork, self-reliance and self-discipline have evoked a warm response from the host countries. Requests for volunteers with recreation skills have more than doubled this year. Recreation activities have great potential value in helping to widen horizons and build a healthier foundation for the improved standards of living which volunteers with other technical skills are trying to promote.[26]

Of the 12,000 volunteers at work in over fifty nations in 1968, more than half were reported to be devoting at least a portion of their time to sports and recreational activities. Sports in particular were found to be a built-in catalyst for social change. A number of underdeveloped nations welcomed Peace Corps assistance in coaching their Olympic teams because they felt that this would help them achieve a feeling of national unity. Peace Corps workers who were coaches were also particularly effective because they were regarded as least vulnerable to charges of neocolonialism and cultural imperialism. As one Volunteer in Ecuador put it, "Nothing communicates like sports—it's an international language."

On a more modest basis, the People-to-People Sports Program, initiated as a result of a White House Conference convened by President Eisenhower in 1956, has made it possible for American citizens to use worldwide interest in sports as a means of broadening understanding between our nation and other peoples of the world. Working with over one hundred sports organizations, this committee has sponsored scores of foreign teams visiting the United States and has helped to send hundreds of American teams abroad, for amateur competition in such sports as boxing, baseball, soccer, table tennis, gymnastics, basketball, and tennis. The Committee also raises funds to buy sports equipment for youth in underdeveloped countries. "It is not the billions in foreign aid that impress the Africans here," wrote a missionary from Basutoland, "but gestures of true friendship. A soccer kit talks a language that is well understood here, you can be sure."

In effect, this sums up the true meaning of sports and other forms of recreation on the world scene. Their purpose should be to help people live full and happy lives and to develop themselves creatively, physically, and socially. This has been the fundamental purpose of the International Recreation Association, and of other efforts at international exchange through recreation.

[26] Ruth Schumm, "Broad Horizons," *Recreation*, October, 1963, p. 356.

THREE

Concepts of Recreation
and Leisure

11

Early Theories of Play and Recreation

As the recreation movement sought public acceptance and support, it required a convincing rationale. During the nineteenth century, a number of theories of play were evolved which gradually became incorporated into a social philosophy of recreation in the twentieth century. Many of our present-day beliefs regarding the necessity for programs of organized recreation service are based upon these early theories of play and recreation.

During the eighteenth and early nineteenth centuries, two leading educational philosophers, Heinrich Pestalozzi and Friedrich Froebel, incorporated play as an essential element in educational practice. Pestalozzi (1746–1827), a Swiss, believed that play contributed to the total performance of students and, particularly through competitive involvement, led to the integration of body and mind. In his experimental school at Yverdun, such activities as games, skating, mountain climbing, jumping, and wrestling were engaged in regularly each day. Froebel, a German (1782–1852), believed that play represented not merely a means of distraction but was rather the most important phase in the spontaneous growth of the child, allowing him to exercise harmoniously all his physical, emotional, and intellectual qualities.

During the nineteenth century, a number of other investigators sought to develop theories of play which would explain its fundamental purpose and meaning. None of the theories which were evolved can today withstand a rigorous scientific examination; none the less, they were important in that for the first time, scholars were devoting serious attention to the nature of the play experience.

Early Theories of Play

There were essentially six widely recognized and discussed theories of play that gained prominence in Europe and America during the nineteenth and early twentieth century.

Surplus-Energy Theory. The English philosopher, Herbert Spencer, in his mid-nineteenth-century work, *Principles of Psychology*, advanced the view that play was primarily motivated by the need to burn up excess energy. His writing was influenced by the writing of Friedrich von Schiller, a German who had speculated on the nature of play almost a century before. Schiller's original statement on play was found in his work, *On the Aesthetic Education of Mankind*. He wrote:

When the lion is not tormented by hunger, and when no wild beast challenges him to fight, his unemployed energy creates an object for himself; full of ardor, he fills the reechoing desert with his horrible roars and his exuberant force rejoices in itself, showing itself without any object. The insect flits about rejoicing in the sunlight, and it is certainly not the cry of want that makes itself heard in the melodious song of the bird; there is undeniably freedom in these movements . . . the animal *works* when a privation is the motor of its activity, and it *plays* when the plenitude of force is this motor, when an exuberant life is excited to action.[1]

Schiller considered play to be essentially an aimless expenditure of exuberant energy, which serves as its own cause for action. Spencer extended this theory, adding two components: the elements of imitation and a physiological explanation for play. Using an "animal analogy," he pointed out that

play . . . is very commonly simulation of the types of activities which an organ carries on when it is being forced to exercise processes conducive to life. . . . so with the kitten running after a cotton-ball, making it roll and catching it, crouching as though in ambush and then leaping on it, we see that the whole sport is a dramatization of the pursuit of prey . . . an ideal satisfaction for the destructive instincts in the absence of real satisfaction for them.[2]

Spencer saw play among children as representing the dramatization of adult activities; the sports of boys, such as chasing, wrestling, and taking each other prisoner, involved "predatory instincts." Even the games of skill practiced by adults were seen as involving the same motivation—satisfaction in getting the better of an antagonist. He wrote:

[1] Friedrich von Schiller, *Essays, Aesthetical and Philosophical* (London: George Bell, 1875), p. 113.
[2] Herbert Spencer, quoted in Harvey C. Lehman and Paul A. Witty, *The Psychology of Play Activities* (New York: A. S. Barnes, 1927), p. 13.

This love of conquest, so dominant in all creatures because it is so correlative of success in the struggle for existence, gets satisfaction from a victory at chess in the absence of ruder victories.[3]

Spencer also attempted to develop a scientific explanation for play, based on an inner need of the organism to use bodily organs which are "over-rested and under-worked." He felt that in the lower animals, the occasion for play arose less frequently, since energies were more constantly expended in survival activities, whereas among the higher animals time and strength are not wholly absorbed in providing for immediate needs. Spencer developed a physiological theory that the nerve centers of the body, "disintegrated by action," must perpetually reintegrate themselves. Activity is necessary; if it is not provided by work, it must be expended in play.

Recreation Theory. Another early theory of play, which was regarded as the converse of the Schiller-Spencer theory, was suggested by Moritz Lazarus, professor of philosophy at Berlin University. It was his view that rather than serving to *burn up* excess energy, play provides a way of *conserving* or restoring it. In other words, when one is moderately exhausted, play recharges one's energy for renewed work.

Lazarus distinguished between physical and mental, or nervous, energy, pointing out that when the brain is "tired" (provided that it is not over-tired), a change of activity, particularly in the form of physical exercise, will restore one's nervous energy. As an illustration, the desk worker playing tennis after a hard day's work at the same time discharges surplus physical energy and restores his mental energy. The major emphasis in this theory was directed at adults, who were seen as requiring recreation in order to be restored for further work. Lazarus felt that children were most inclined to play when they have an excess of physical and mental energy; thus they have less need for it as a recreative function.

Instinct-Practice Theory. A more elaborate theoretical explanation of play, sometimes called the "practice-of-skills" or "instinct-practice" theory, was put forward by Karl Groos, a professor of philosophy at Basel, who wrote two major texts, a work on the play of animals in 1896 and another on the play of man in 1899. The Groos theory was heavily based on the Darwinian theory of natural selection. Groos conjectured that play helped animals in the struggle for survival, by practicing and perfecting the skills they would need in adult life; the more adaptable and intelligent a species is, the more it needs a period of protected infancy and childhood for such learnings to take place. Thus, among men, there is a lengthy early period during which children engage in a variety of activities to perfect skills before they are seriously needed. Play assumes the role of a single generalized instinct (the impulse to practice instinctive forms of behavior).

In his book on *The Play of Man,* Groos categorized play under four

[3] *Ibid.,* p. 14.

major headings: (1) fighting play, including contests, hunting play, and mental and physical rivalry; (2) love play, courtship activities, and love play expressed through art; (3) imitative or dramatic play; and (4) social play. He developed an extended theory involving physiological, psychological, aesthetic, sociological, and pedagogical elements to explain his total view. Using examples drawn from primitive tribes in Africa, he pointed out that children in these cultures have few toys as such, but their play consists instead of imitating adults in their daily activities, such as hunting, fishing, building, and trapping. On the other hand, children in civilized societies still retain in their play many games and songs which reflect old rites and customs but are not presently useful, thus showing the strength of "instinct."

Groos also saw value of play as an approach to instruction, in which "instruction may take the form of playful activity, or, on the other hand, play may be converted into systematic teaching." He warned that it was necessary to distinguish between play and study or other forms of work, yet he also believed that work might include a play impulse:

even the most serious work may include a certain playfulness, especially when enjoyment of being a cause and of conquest are prominent. . . . Since play thus approaches work when pleasure in the activity as such, as well as its practical aim, becomes a motive power . . . so may work become like play when its real aim is superseded by enjoyment of the activity itself. And it can hardly be doubted that this is the highest and noblest form of work.[4]

The major impact of Groos's theory of play was that it attempted to assign a serious biological purpose to activities which under the Schiller-Spencer view were regarded as aimless. The concept that play represented an important technique through which the young of various cultures are educated to carry out the tasks and functions of adulthood was probably his greatest contribution.

The Catharsis Theory. Another theory which was widely discussed during this early period is the catharsis theory of play. Briefly stated, this suggests that play activity—particularly competitive, active play—serves as a safety valve for the expression of bottled-up emotions. As far back as the ancient Greeks, Aristotle saw the drama as a means of purging oneself of hostile or aggressive emotions; by vicarious sharing in the staged experience, the on-looker purified himself of harmful feelings. Groos adapted this theory by suggesting that fighting activities and competitive play helped children become free from "hurtful emotions." This theory was expanded by a number of other early twentieth-century writers.

Carr, an American psychologist, expressed this view:

Catharsis . . . implies the idea of purging or draining of that energy which has *anti-social possibilities*. . . . The value of football, boxing, and other physi-

---

[4] Karl Groos, *The Play of Man* (New York: Appleton-Century, 1901), p. 400.

cal contests in relieving the pugnacious tendencies of boys is readily apparent as examples. Without the numberless well-organized set forms of play possessed by society which give a harmless outlet to the mischievous and unapplied energy of the young the task of the teacher and parent would be appalling.[5]

Others, particularly G. T. W. Patrick, challenged Groos's "naive" view of the emotions as internal forces which could do damage if they could not escape. He saw the cathartic effect of play as being primarily due to a restoring of disturbed balance in the psychophysical organism. Pointing out that under the influence of strong emotions such as fear or anger, a whole series of internal changes take place in the organism, preparing the muscular system for the strenuous responses demanded by the threatening situation (such as increased blood sugar and increased adrenalin), Patrick comments that in the past, "such preparations were usually followed by great muscular effort, flight or combat." In modern society, however, Patrick suggests, although such emotions often occur among men, with the body preparing itself for violent action, the physical means of discharging the tension or hostility usually are lacking. It is the specific cathartic effect of play—especially active sport—to use up such energies and help the body restore itself to a balanced state once again.

The catharsis theory, as modified by Patrick, was widely accepted by early recreation and social welfare professionals. Coupled with the surplus energy theory, it suggested that there was a vital necessity for play activity for children and youth—to burn up excess energy which might otherwise result in destructive acts and to channel aggressive, hostile emotions and drives of both youth and adults into socially acceptable forms of play.

The Recapitulation Theory. One of the most widely discussed theories of play at the turn of the twentieth century was the so-called recapitulation theory advanced by Stanley Hall, a prominent American professor of psychology and pedagogy, college president, and author, who was regarded as one of the fathers of child psychology. Hall's dual interest in evolutionary theory and in education led him to study children, observing their behavior with scientific rigor. Millar writes:

For the first time a serious scientist concerned himself with such questions as the kinds of dolls children prefer or how soon they are given names. His "Recapitulation Theory" of play rests on the notion that children are a link in the evolutionary chain from animal to man and pass through all the stages from protozoan to human in their lives as embryos.[6]

It had been observed that a number of the developmental stages which the human foetus passes through are similar to the evolutionary process of the historical development of mankind. This led to the belief that the development of the individual (ontogeny) repeats that of the race (phylog-

[5] Harvey A. Carr, "The Survival Values of Play," quoted in Lehman and Witty, *op. cit.,* p. 19.

[6] Susanna Millar, *The Psychology of Play* (Baltimore: Penguin Books, 1968), p. 17.

eny). Hall suggested that the child relives the history of the human race, just as the embryo relives that of its prehuman ancestors. He wrote:

The past holds the keys to all play activities. None survives unless based on pretty purely hereditary momentum. The view of Groos that play is practice for future adult activities is very partial, superficial and perverse.[7]

Hall's theory provided a convenient means of describing the detailed content of children's play. Thus,

children's delight in playing with water could be connected with their fishy ancestors' joys in the sea; their insistence on climbing trees and swinging from branches showed vestiges of the life of their monkey-like forebears.[8]

Through play, children were seen as re-enacting the lives of their caveman ancestors, engaging in activities like fishing, canoeing, hunting, or camping, which were vital to the species eons ago. Play was seen as "the purest expression of heredity, . . . not doing things to be useful later on, but . . . rehearsing racial history." Hall developed a detailed "culture-epoch" analogy, which showed how the child traverses in his play the successive periods of human history. It showed children going through several stages of evolution of man's past, such as the *animal* stage, the *savage* stage, the *nomad* stage, the stages of *agricultural* and *patriarchal* societies, and, finally, the *tribal* stage of historical development. To each of these, typical forms of children's play found at each stage of life development, were attached. Thus, Hall's primary view of play was that it was an instinctive process of rehearsing the past rather than practice for the future.

The Relaxation Theory. The recreation theory, which was briefly described earlier, was extended by the American psychologist G. T. W. Patrick. He took the position that it was essential for man's healthy functioning in modern society that he find active outlets in play. He based this on what he described as the demand of the "higher cerebral centers for relaxation." According to Patrick, the stress and strain of modern life meant that man was under excessive tension, resulting in an increase of nervous disorders and mental illness. He commented that, while there was less fear of communicable diseases, the death rate due to other causes had grown:

there is a marked decline in the power of American workers to withstand the strain of modern life. They wear out sooner than they did a few years ago. The chances of death after reaching the prime of life have increased because of . . . the breaking-down of the heart, arteries, kidneys, and of the nervous and digestive system.[9]

[7] G. Stanley Hall, *Youth* (New York: Appleton-Century, 1920).

[8] Millar, *op. cit.*, pp. 17-18.

[9] George T. W. Patrick, *The Psychology of Relaxation* (Boston: Houghton Mifflin, 1916), p. 13.

This trend, he speculated, was due to the nature of industrial life, involving considerable mental stress, tension, and nervous fatigue. Patrick also believed that modern man was forced to constantly repress the impulse to revert to primitive kinds of behavior as natural releases for emotion. As a consequence of this inhibition, he saw a growing, imperative demand for rest and relaxation through artificial means, such as narcotic drugs, tobacco, and alcohol.

It was Patrick's view that mankind needs healthy forms of physical and emotional release to compensate for these added strains and tensions and for his inability to use traditional activities as outlets for emotions. He pointed out that "mankind has come up through a history of warfare. It has been man against man, group against group, tribe against tribe, nation against nation, from the beginning." Concluding that man is at home on the battlefield and that his "soul is full of latent memories of strife and conflict," Patrick concluded that sports provided the most appropriate release for this now-denied outlet:

The football field is a mimic representation of this age-old field of battle. Here again is found the face-to-face opposition of two hostile forces, the rude physical shock of the heavy opposing teams, the scrimmage-like, melee character of the collisions, the tackling, dodging and kicking, and the lively chases for goals as for cover. . . . Football is more fun than baseball and attracts larger crowds, because it is more dramatic, more like a fight. It awakes in us deep-seated slumbering instincts.[10]

Finally, Patrick concluded that in "modern cities, supervised play as became necessary for the social order." Typically, he commented on the use of play in preventing youthful antisocial behavior:

boys *must* play. Take away the opportunity for legitimate play, and the play instinct, the instinct of rivalry . . . will manifest itself in anti-social ways. Hence the juvenile court and the reform school. "Better playgrounds, without schools," says one writer, "than schools without playgrounds."[11]

Patrick was one of the first writers to distinguish between the play of children and that of adults. He saw the play of children not as a form of relaxation but as a significant element in social growth and as a release for instinctive drives. The play of adults, in contrast, was chiefly valuable as a form of relaxation, to compensate from the stress of modern life. Patrick also developed an influential definition of play in modern life:

The term "play" may be applied to all those human activities which are free and spontaneous and which are pursued for their own sake alone. The interest

[10] *Ibid.*, p. 62.
[11] *Ibid.*, p. 7.

in them is self-developing and they are not continued under any internal or external compulsion.[12]

He sharply distinguished play from work, which has an extrinsic goal or purpose, necessarily involving mental effort and tension. This sharp dichotomy between work and play was accepted by writers within the developing recreation movement. In effect, they then gave support to the need for play, by suggesting that only through it, could man avoid the harmful effects of excessive work-caused fatigue and restore himself for further work. Of all the theories presented during this early period, those formulated by Patrick were the most useful for sponsors of organized recreation services in modern society.

During the early 1900's, a number of leading psychologists and authorities on child development carried out additional investigations of play behavior, and wrote favorably regarding its contribution to healthy growth and development and the educative process.

L. Estelle Appleton (1910) wrote that play for children and youth is closely related to the developmental exercise of maturing functions and skills. When a particular function has developed fully, the play impulse that is related to it subsides. Thus, play is dependent on the structure of the body, and the basic drive for play activity is the organism's need to grow and develop, and to improve skills and functions.[13]

Carl Seashore (1916), a leading psychologist, stressed the importance of play in the social development of the child, particularly his sense of kinship with a group. He suggested that child play reproduces on its level the struggles and achievements of adult life:

The child gradually approaches the stern adult realities, taught and trained, hardened and softened, warmed and cooled, roused and rationalized, through these very engagements in play, which without break or loss of their original character gradually blend into the duties, responsibilities, opportunities and achievements of adult life. Play is essentially social . . . one of its aims and rewards should be a sense of fellowship. . . . Play is the making of a social man.[14]

Another psychologist, William McDougall (1918), supported the function of play as a socializing influence. He suggested that play "molded" the individual, preparing him for social life, for roles related to both leading and following, and for cooperative group involvement.[15] Similarly, John B. Watson (1924), a leading behavioral psychologist, saw play as essential in human development. He wrote:

[12] *Ibid.*, p. 47.
[13] L. Estelle Appleton, *A Comparative Study of the Play Activities of Adult Savages and Civilized Children* (Chicago: University of Chicago Press, 1910), p. 77.
[14] Carl Seashore, *Psychology in Daily Life* (New York: Appleton, 1916), p. 8.
[15] William McDougall, *Social Psychology* (Boston: John W. Luce, 1918), p. 352.

In short, play is the principal instrument of growth. It is safe to conclude that, without play, there would be no normal adult cognitive life; without play, no healthful development of affective life; without play, no full development of the power of the will.[16]

Gradually, a climate developed in American education which viewed play as an essential element in education. It was supported as an important means of learning, more pleasurable and less fatiguing than work. It was pointed out that in play the child's attention was undivided and spontaneous and thus provided a natural means of learning. Educators also supported the view that experience was essential to healthy personal adjustment. Curiously, no writer in this period seemed to regard play as potentially dangerous or self-destructive; it was always described as desirable and constructive, and the play instinct was considered to be automatically beneficial.

As a consequence of this positive acceptance of the values of play, increased support was given to the expansion of organized playground and public recreation programs in American communities.

The Philosophy of Organized Recreation Service

During the first three decades of the twentieth century, several individuals emerged as highly influential spokesmen for the recreation movement. Their writings and theories were influential in developing public support and helping to create a philosophical base for organized recreation service.

Joseph Lee. Perhaps the most influential of the pioneers of the recreation movement, Joseph Lee was a lawyer and a philanthropist who came from a wealthy New England family. Born in 1862, he took part in a survey of play opportunities conducted by the Family Welfare Society of Boston as early as 1882. He was shocked to see boys arrested for playing in the streets and organized a playground for them in an open lot, which he helped to supervise. In 1898, Lee helped to create a model playground on Columbus Avenue in Boston, which included a play area for small children, a boys' section, a sport field, and individual gardens.

Gradually, Joseph Lee's influence expanded; he was in great demand as a speaker and writer on playgrounds and served as vice-president for public recreation of the American Civic Association. He was president of the Playground Association of America from 1910 to his death in 1937 and was also president and leading lecturer of the National Recreation School, a one-year course for carefully selected college graduates. Lee helped to

---

[16] John B. Watson, *Psychology from the Standpoint of a Behaviorist* (Philadelphia: J. B. Lippincott, 1924), pp. 439-40.

form and operate the War Camp Community Service and in many other ways contributed to the developing playground and recreation movement.

Lee had an idealistic and purposeful view of play. In his book, *Play in Education*, he expressed this philosophy in detail, outlining a set of major play instincts which he believed all children shared and which governed the specific nature of play activities. These were creation, rhythm, hunting, fighting, nature, curiosity, and team play. These were seen as the basis for most play activity. He did not believe, however, that instinct alone was enough; play required intelligent leadership:

Teaching is thus a necessary part of play because the play instincts themselves call for it. But teaching enhances play for another reason also—namely, because play, like all other pursuits, is itself a social as well as a physical inheritance, handed down partly by tradition, not wholly evolved by each generation for itself. Children do not inherit baseball any more than they inherit the Lord's Prayer. . . . They inherit tag in rudimentary form, just as puppies do, but they do not inherit cross tag, hill dill, or prisoner's base. The play instincts are a constant factor in every generation, but their satisfaction is partly a matter of discovery.[17]

Lee did not make a sharp distinction between work and play. He saw them as closely related expressions of the impulse to achieve, to explore, to excell, to master. He wrote:

True work is the highest form of play; but it is always the play element in work that is the most important. The play motive is the deepest and most serious. It is deeper than the hungers; the artist starves himself for art; the student renounces love and fortune to vindicate his vision of the truth; the artisan postpones reward to workmanship. The master of any calling cares for his work first; the pay is secondary.[18]

Exactly what was play? Lee suggested that it was the non-utilitarian motivation that impelled man into pursuits in which the desire to achieve was the primary one. He stressed that play was not carried on in pursuit of pleasure. Indeed, in a somewhat Puritanical fashion, he condemned the pursuit of pleasure:

Pleasure results from play, and may in the sophisticated become a conscious motive, but it is not the play motive. It is extraneous, a by-product; it does not in any way account for the play attitude or the direction of the play instincts. In play the motive of the act is the doing of it. . . . The pursuit of pleasure is an egotistical, self-conscious, almost a morbid, state of mind, notoriously self-defeating. Play implies the opposite, contrasted attitude, that of self-forgetfulness, subordination. The man who goes out to have a good time is usually dis-

[17] Joseph Lee, *Play in Education* (New York: Macmillan, 1915, 1929), p. 38.
[18] *Ibid.*, p. 52.

appointed. The one who goes out to play the game, and does play it for all it is worth, is never wholly so.[19]

Lee stressed that play might involve pain, sacrifice, and fatigue and that, for these reasons, it helped to "drill" the child to the service of ideals and a dedicated way of life. In addition to his views of play, Lee strongly promoted certain other concepts. One was the important role played by the neighborhood unit in community life; he saw this as a survival from the "ancestral heritage" of village life and urged that many forms of community activity, such as sports, festivals, and the arts, should be carried out on a neighborhood basis. Lee saw play as an important factor in combatting social pathology, not in the specific sense of its preventing or reducing juvenile delinquency, but because of its positive contributions to physical fitness, opportunity for group involvements, sense of joy, and appreciation of beauty. He wrote:

The battle with the slum is not primarily a battle against the obvious evils of drink, overcrowding, immorality, and bad sanitary arrangements. These are the evidences that the slum exists. The thing itself is not a positive but a negative phenomenon. The slum is what is left when from an aggregate of people living together you subtract the local personality. . . . Every social environment that is not a neighborhood is essentially a slum.[20]

His moralistic view of play was also illustrated in his reference to recreation as a means of combatting "excessive youth preoccupation with sex." This purpose, he believed, was a primary force behind the old "Muscular Christianity" movement, much of the work of the Y.M.C.A., and many youth, social-center, and school extension programs. Lee constantly fought for recognition of the need to use leisure constructively in modern society. He wrote:

The problem of civilization is the problem of leisure. For those to whom leisure is denied, to whom loss of expression in industry is not made up in art of play, civilization is of doubtful benefit.[21]

Because of his organizational leadership and personal inspiration, Lee was widely regarded as the father of the American playground movement.

Luther Halsey Gulick. Another leading pioneer in the early playground movement was Luther Halsey Gulick. A medical doctor by training, he developed a special interest in physical education and recreation. Born in Hawaii of missionary parents, he also had a strong religious orientation. Beginning in 1887, Dr. Gulick headed the first summer school of "special training for Gymnasium Instructors" at the School for Christian Workers

[19] *Ibid.*, p. 255.
[20] *Ibid.*, p. 385.
[21] *Ibid.*, p. 476.

(now Springfield College) in Massachusetts. He was supervisor of all physical education programs in the Y.M.C.A.'s in Canada and the United States and became director of physical education in the New York City school system. He was the first president of the Camp Fire Girls, was active in Y.M.C.A. war work, and was instrumental in the establishment of the Playground Association of America in 1906. It was his view that the work of the Association should not be restricted to the promotion of play-grounds; instead, he saw a need to develop municipal recreation commissions which would not encroach upon the functions of park or school departments but would broadly be concerned with the uses of leisure in community life and the promotion of varied recreation and social programs.

Gulick lectured extensively on the significance of play and recreation and taught a course in the psychology of play as early as 1899. He strongly promoted constructive recreation programs for girls and women, and it was primarily as a result of his efforts that the Camp Fire Girls of America was established in 1914.

Like Lee, Gulick was profoundly concerned with the nature of play, recreation, and work. He drew a distinction between play and recreation, seeing play chiefly as an attitude or motivation for involvement, while recreation was seen in terms of its relaxing and energy-restorative functions. He defined play as "doing that which we want to do, without reference primarily to any ulterior end, but simply for the joy of the process."

The term play is used popularly in many different senses. It is frequently contrasted with work and held to cover a series of activities which are highly enjoyable, but without utility or seriousness. Or it is confounded with recreation, and its usefulness is found solely as a means of relaxation for future work. As a result of this view, the plays of childhood are excused on the ground that children are not yet able to do the serious tasks of the world, and may therefore be allowed to enjoy themselves without much loss.[22]

But, he went on to say, play is not less serious than work. Being carried on chiefly as an "expression of the self, as the result of desire," play is essentially at the heart of a rich and free life, with the problem of recreation being only one of its phases. He went on to point out the nature of the difference between play and recreation:

The boy who is playing football with intensity needs recreation as much as does the inventor who is working intensely at his invention. Play can be more exhausting than work, because one can play much harder than one can work. No one would dream of pushing a boy in school as hard as he pushes himself in a football game. If there is any difference of intensity between play and work, the difference is in favor of play. Play is the result of desire; for that reason it is often carried on with more vigor than work.[23]

[22] Luther H. Gulick, *A Philosophy of Play* (New York: Scribner, 1920), p. 126.
[23] *Ibid.*, p. 125.

Gulick characterized recreation as being different in character, consisting for adults of a reversion to the "simpler fundamental activities" acquired during childhood. For the adult, it meant relaxation, in sharp contrast to the child's outpouring of energy in play. Commenting that adults may also engage in play that is as exhausting as the intense play of children, he suggested that this was inappropriate for the adult who worked strenuously in his business. Thus he accepted the view that recreation was primarily valuable as rest or relaxation for adults, since it restored them for further work—as opposed to play, which might be more dynamic, demanding, and creative and cover a wide range of involvements.

Gulick also pressed forcefully for recognition of the important place of recreation and leisure in contemporary life. It was his belief that the great bulk of modern crime, as well as antisocial or "degenerative" behavior throughout all history, has resulted from "wrong play and recreation." He took the position that restrictive efforts were not sufficient; instead, positive and constructive forms of social activity needed to be provided. Gulick pressed for recognition of the "recreation problem" as a nationwide concern, pointing out that huge sums of money were being spent each year on commerically sponsored activities. His moralistic viewpoint is illustrated in the following passage:

> The importance of having some leisure is no greater than that of the proper use of this time. An investigation in England showed that the result of shortening the day of anthracite coal-miners from eight to six hours resulted in a lessened output per hour. During their leisure time the men dissipated so much that they were less competent in working hours. The important fact to be noticed is not mainly the lessened productive activity, but the reason for it, which led to the degeneration of the workers. It is a commonly observed fact that Monday is a bad day in many if not most industries, and it is bad because of the unwise use made of the leisure time on Sunday.
>
> The recreation problem ranks in importance with the labor and education problems. Character is made predominantly during leisure hours.[24]

Other Contributions to Play and Recreation Theory

During the same period in which Lee and Gulick were exerting their influence on recreation professionals and public officials, other writers began to press for an increased concern with play within the school systems of the nation. The idea of using play as a meaningful kind of educational experience was strongly promoted by a number of philosophers and educators.

John Dewey, the leading American philosopher of the early twentieth century, was immensely influential in the development of modern educational practices. His view of meaningful education was that it was most

[24] *Ibid.*, p. 119.

effective when it was based on activity that challenged all one's faculties: physical, creative, and intellectual. One learned by doing. Dewey felt that the most important kind of learning activity was that which involved freedom of choice, deliberate and self-planned (rather than random or dictated) involvement, and activity which involved mental initiative and intellectual self-reliance. He saw physical activities as not solely physical but also intellectual in quality, both in the learning and the doing. He placed much reliance on the use of such tools as pencils, brushes, implements, and physical materials and substances, as means of achieving mastery of oneself and the environment.

Throughout all this, Dewey strongly supported spontaneous and creative learning processes that might best be achieved through playlike experiences. He distinguished between *work* (a creative and highly motivated activity), *labor* (an economic term meaning that form of work which is paid for, and in which the direct result accomplished, is valuable for the worker only as a means of exchange for something else), *toil* (unusually arduous or fatiguing work), or *drudgery* (activities which are quite disagreeable and usually performed only under strong compulsion). He saw *work* and *play* as being closely related, highly motivated, and creative activities:

Play and work cannot . . . be distinguished from one another according to the presence or absence of direct interest in what one is doing. A child engaged in making something with tools, say, a boat, may be just as immediately interested in what he is doing as if he were sailing the boat. He is not doing what he does for the mere sake of an external result—the boat—nor for the mere sake of sailing it later . . . his interest is free. He has a play-motive; his activity is essentially artistic in principle. What differentiates it from more spontaneous play is an *intellectual* quality.[25]

Dewey held that through play, children should be introduced to the idea and the experience of more formal work when they are ready for it; also that they should move gradually from projects which yield immediate satisfaction to those with deferred satisfactions, and from those which require little planning to those which require careful planning and intellectual analysis. Within the wide range of artistic, manual, and exploratory activities in the elementary grades, he felt that both play and work approaches were essential. He made his support of play completely clear in the following passage:

The idea that the need [for play] can be suppressed, is absolutely fallacious, and the Puritanic tradition which disallows the need has entailed an enormous crop of evils. If education does not afford opportunity for wholesome recreation

[25] John Dewey, "Interest and Effort in Education," in Joseph Ratner, *Intelligence in the Modern World* (New York: Modern Library, Random House, 1939), p. 611.

and training, capacity for seeking and finding it, the suppressed instincts find all sorts of illicit outlets, sometimes overt, sometimes confined to indulgence of imagination. Education has no more serious responsibility than making adequate provision for enjoyment of recreative leisure; not only for the fact of immediate health but still more, if possible, for the fact of its lasting effect upon habits of mind.[26]

As early as 1896, in Dewey's Laboratory School in Chicago, a normal day's activity consisted of conversation, construction projects, stories, songs, games, trips, dramatic play, and other kinds of creative handiwork and activities. In many experimental schools which were established as the "progressive education" movement gathered momentum, there was a similar reliance on playlike activities. In one of the leading progressive schools, the emphasis was on providing the children with

as rich a variety of first-hand experiences as possible—trips to parks, stores, zoos, the harbor, etc.,—and then to provide them with play materials—blocks, clay, paints, boxes, toys, and the like—through which they might imaginatively portray what they had experienced. The usual ingredients of an elementary education were there; reading, writing, arithmetic, history, geography, the arts and physical education were present; but the teaching situations themselves remained unstructured and unpatterned.[27]

A leading example of such programs was founded at the Berkeley campus of the University of California in 1913, under the direction of Clark Hetherington, a pioneer physical educator. Known as the Demonstration Play School, this center was a

combined play center and school, in which the child and his activities, rather than the subjects studied, were the major concern of the leaders. The outdoor center was designed through leadership "to fuse the joyousness and dynamic power of play and the social purpose of education."[28]

Hetherington's unique experiment attracted widespread interest among educators, influencing many school systems which developed after-school play programs; it also encouraged others in establishing physical education as a compulsory school subject. Probably at no time in American history was play regarded as a more significant concern in education than during the 1920's and 1930's, as a consequence of Dewey's philosophical writings and the total effort of progressive educators and experimental programs such as Hetherington's.

[26] John Dewey, *Democracy and Education* (New York: Macmillan, 1921), p. 241.
[27] Lawrence A. Cremin, *The Transformation of the School* (New York: Knopf, 1961), p. 205.
[28] George D. Butler, *Pioneers in Public Recreation* (Minneapolis: Burgess, 1965), p. 21.

During this period too, there was an increased concern about the changing nature of work. Many psychologists and educators pointed out that it was becoming increasingly specialized (as a consequence of the "machine age"), mechanized, and monotonous. They wrote of the need to make it more interesting and a greater source of satisfaction to the worker's ego, in order to avoid the danger of "collapse" from overwork. Two psychologists who explored the nature of work and play, Lehman and Witty, commented:

> With the rapid specialization of industry and business, the opportunities for expression of the personality and gratification of the ego at one's work are becoming more rare. The exceptions are to be found mostly in those fields that are devoted to experimentation and development, or that offer free play to the individual's initiative. . . .
>
> Those who have chosen their occupation in accord with their abilities and interests afford evidence of the increased joy in living that comes from finding one's work.[29]

Seashore pressed the point by writing, "those of us who get the most out of life are they whose work would be their preferred play, quite apart from its pursuit as a means of livelihood."[30]

Throughout the first three decades of the twentieth century, then, a number of writers, philosophers, educators, and psychologists developed a body of theory that gave strong support to the need for play in education and as a form of community service. Their writings were an extension of the early theories of play developed by Spencer, Groos, Hall, and Patrick, and they provided the basis for an immensely expanded public interest in recreation and the development of the organized recreation movement throughout the United States.

[29] Harvey C. Lehman and Paul A. Witty, *The Psychology of Play Activities* (New York: A. S. Barnes, 1927), p. 234.

[30] Carl Seashore, *Introduction to Psychology* (New York: Macmillan, 1923), p. 280.

12

Recreation, Play, and Leisure:
A Conceptual Analysis

The statement is frequently made that one of the most crucial challenges of the present day is the need to come to grips with the "new leisure." Exactly what *is* leisure? From a conceptual point of view, the term has at least four widely found meanings: (1) the "classical" view of leisure as exemplified by the writings of de Grazia and Pieper, (2) the view of leisure as a function of social class, presented originally by Veblen, (3) the concept of leisure as a form of activity, and (4) the concept of leisure as free time.

The word *leisure* is related to the early Greek word *scole*, which leads to the English *school* or *scholar* and implies a close connection between leisure and education. In addition to having the meaning of leisure directly, *scole* also referred to places where scholarly discussions were held. One such place was a grove next to the temple of Apollo Lykos, which became known as the *lyceum*. From this came the French *lycée*, meaning school. The English word *leisure* seems to have been more directly related to the Latin *licere*, meaning "to be permitted" or "to be free." It referred to the fact that the upper classes were not required to engage in work as such and thus were free to engage in intellectual, cultural, and artistic forms of activity. From *licere* came the French *loisir*, and such English words as *license*, meaning originally to be permitted to refrain from giving service, or immunity from public obligation, or *liberty*. These words are all related; they suggest freedom of will, lack of compulsion, and free choice.

The Classical View of Leisure

Aristotle regarded leisure as "a state of being in which activity is performed for its own sake." It was sharply contrasted with work, or purposeful action. Instead, it involved such pursuits as art, political debate, philosophical discussion, or learning in general. Historically, the ancient Athenians saw work as ignoble; to them it was boring and monotonous. Leisure was seen as the highest value of life and work as the lowest. Within modern philosophies of leisure which are descended from the classical Athenian view, leisure is still seen as occurring only in time that is not devoted to work. It is, however, far more than simply a temporary release from work intended to restore one's energies for more work. According to Pieper,

leisure does not exist for the sake of work—however much strength it may give a man to work; the point of leisure is not to be a restorative, a pick-me-up, whether mental or physical. . . . Leisure, like contemplation, is of a higher order than the active life. . . . [it involves] the capacity to soar in active celebration, to overstep the boundaries of the workaday world and reach out to superhuman, life-giving existential forces that refresh and renew us before we turn back to our daily work.[1]

De Grazia stresses the view that free time is not necessarily leisure; anybody can have free time, but not everybody can have leisure. "It is an ideal, a state of being, a condition of man, which few desire and fewer achieve."[2] Both authors agree that leisure involves a spiritual and mental attitude, an attitude of nonaction, inward calm, silence, contemplation, serenity, and openness.

How useful is this classical view of leisure today? It has two drawbacks. First, it is linked to the idea of an aristocratic class structure, based on the availability of slave labor. When Aristotle wrote in his *Treatise on Politics,* "it is of course generally understood that in a well-ordered state, the citizens should have leisure and not have to provide for their daily needs," he meant that leisure was given to a comparatively few patricians and made possible by the strenuous labors of many.

In modern society, leisure cannot be a privilege reserved for the few; it is widely available to all. It must exist side by side with work which is respected in our society and should have a meaningful relationship to work. Millions of people in Western society have leisure today and must learn not to feel guilty about it and to use it fruitfully rather than abuse it. Fur-

---

[1]Josef Pieper, *Leisure, the Basis of Culture* (New York: Mentor-Omega Books, New American Library, 1952, 1963), p. 43.

[2] Sebastian de Grazia, *Of Time, Work and Leisure* (New York: Doubleday-Anchor, Twentieth Century Fund, 1962), p. 5.

ther, the classical view of leisure imposes extremely narrow restraints. De Grazia specifically rejects the modern concept of recreation as an inappropriate use of leisure. Recreation, he says, is necessarily purposeful and intended to restore one for further work; therefore, it cannot be considered part of leisure. He suggests also that the tendency of modern Americans to fill their free time with chores, hobbies, trivial pursuits, and varied forms of community obligation and responsibility means that they have no real leisure.

This view of leisure essentially sees it as a privilege reserved for the well-bred few, rather than as an opportunity for all, without class distinctions. Great masses of people are interested in activity and involvement—in hobbies, the arts, sports, and active play. To suggest that none of these can be a legitimate use of leisure is to give the concept such narrow limits that it becomes meaningless for us today.

Leisure as a Symbol of Social Class

The view of leisure as closely related to social class structure stemmed from the writings of Thorstein Veblen, a leading American sociologist of the nineteenth century. Veblen showed how, through the various periods of history, ruling classes emerged which identified themselves most sharply through the possession of leisure. Veblen's major work, *The Theory of the Leisure Class*, pointed out that in Europe, during the feudal and Renaissance periods and finally the industrial age, the possession and visible use of leisure became the hallmark of the upper class. Abstention from labor became the evidence of wealth and social standing.

Veblen attacked the "idle rich"; he saw leisure as a total way of life for the privileged class, regarding them as exploiters who lived on the toil of others. He coined the phrase "conspicuous consumption" to describe their way of life throughout history:

The . . . gentleman of leisure . . . consumes freely and of the best, in food, drink, narcotics, shelter, services, ornaments, apparel, weapons and accoutrements, amulets, and idols or divinities. . . . He must cultivate his tastes . . . he becomes a connoisseur . . . and the demands made upon the gentleman in this direction therefore tend to change his life of leisure into a more or less arduous application to the business of . . . conspicuous leisure and conspicuous consumption.[3]

To maintain his status, Veblen said, the feudal nobleman and ultimately the self-made millionaire had to give valuable presents, expensive feasts, and entertainments. Veblen satirically attacked those who engaged in aristocratic sports, seeing these only as a badge to impress society or as a

[3] Thorstein Veblen, *The Theory of the Leisure Class* (New York: Viking Press, 1899, 1918), p. 73.

means of satisfying predatory and warlike urges. Chiefly as a consequence of Veblen's writing, the concept of the leisure class came into being. Obviously, his rigid dichotomy of social classes no longer holds true. Today, working classes tend to have far *more* leisure than industrial managers, business executives, or professionals. Veblen's contempt for leisure as the sole possession of the "idle rich" no longer applies, both for this reason and because the present generation of our most wealthy and influential families tend to become involved in business or public life. With the exception of a small group of jet setters, the class he criticized no longer exists.

Leisure as a Form of Activity

A third concept of leisure is that it is nonwork *activity* in which people engage during their free time. A leading French sociologist, Joffre Dumazedier, defines leisure in these terms:

Leisure is activity—apart from the obligations of work, family and society—to which the individual turns at will, for either relaxation, diversion, or broadening his knowledge and his spontaneous social participation, the free exercise of his creative capacity.[4]

Dumazedier goes on to suggest that leisure must be regarded also as liberation and pleasure and that it provides man with three essential functions: relaxation, entertainment, and personal development. Similarly, an American sociologist, Bennett Berger, points out that leisure has chiefly been investigated as a form of behavior. He points out that the sociology of leisure today is "little more than a reporting of survey data on what selected samples of individuals do with the time in which they are not working, and the correlation of these data with conventional demographic variables."[5] He writes:

leisure refers to those activities whose normative content renders them most important to us, those things that we want to do for their own sake or those things that we feel ethically (as distinguished from expediently) constrained to do.[6]

This point of view stresses that leisure is voluntary activity carried on in free time, in sharp contrast with work, which is required, is utilitarian, and is rewarded in economic terms.

[4] Joffre Dumazedier, *Toward a Society of Leisure* (New York: Free Press, 1962, 1967), pp. 16-17.
[5] Bennett Berger, "The Sociology of Leisure: Some Suggestions," in Erwin O. Smigel, ed., *Work and Leisure: A Contemporary Social Problem* (New Haven, Conn.: College and University Press, 1963), p. 28.
[6] *Ibid.*, p. 29.

Leisure as Unobligated Time

The most common approach to leisure, and the one used in this text, is to regard it as a form of non-obligated, or discretionary, time. In a number of sociological references, this concept of leisure is clearly stated. The *Dictionary of Sociology* offers the following definition:

Leisure is the free time after the practical necessities of life have been attended to. . . . Conceptions of leisure vary from the arithmetic one of time devoted to work, sleep, and other necessities, subtracted from 24 hours—which gives the surplus time—to the general notion of leisure as the time which one uses as he pleases.[7]

This concept of leisure sees it as time which is free from work or from such work-related responsibilities as travel, study, or social involvements based on work. It is also regarded as time not devoted to essential life-maintenance activities, such as sleep, eating, or personal care. Its most important characteristic, therefore, is that it lacks a sense of obligation or compulsion.

Certain activities which we carry on in nonwork hours have a *degree* of compulsion about them. For example, some uses of free time which are not clearly work nor paid for as work may contribute to work success. A person may read books or articles related to work, attend evening classes that contribute to his work competence, invite guests to his home because of work associations, or join a country club because it is of value in establishing business contacts. Thus, there is a shadow area in which what appears to be leisure time slips over into work time. Within community life, those tasks which have a degree of obligation about them, like serving on a school board or serving as a member of a town council, although unpaid, may also be viewed as part of a person's responsibility. In terms of time, energy, or degree of commitment, it would be difficult to distinguish them from work. Another shadow area lies in those uses of time which are normally part of maintenance. Usually, such activities as eating, sleeping, or shopping are regarded as obligated tasks, necessary for maintenance and therefore not part of leisure. However, eating frequently becomes a leisurely and pleasurable form of experience, as in the case of a group of friends going out to a fine restaurant for a gourmet meal or a country picnic. Such activities as gardening or do-it-yourself projects in the home may also involve creative interests, cheerfully engaged in beyond the necessity of maintenance.

Dumazedier comments that if leisure is governed in part by commer-

[7] See Martin H. Neumeyer and Esther Neumeyer, *Leisure and Recreation* (New York: Ronald Press, 1958), p. 19.

cial, utilitarian, or ideological concerns or purposes, it is no longer wholly leisure. He suggests that activities in which obligation or utilitarian purpose appear to a degree be regarded as "semi-leisure." This occurs when the world of work and of primary obligations partially overlaps with the world of leisure; semi-leisure is where they coincide.[8]

Even the notion of "voluntarism" or free will in choosing to take part in an activity is somewhat questionable. While one appears to make the ultimate choice in taking part in an activity, one is also dominated by community values and expectations and the knowledge that certain uses of leisure might prove advantageous, indirectly or in the long run. Very few actions are completely disinterested or free of compulsion; often as one continues to engage in an activity, one begins to perceive it as a source of social approval or other sorts of rewards that give it extrinsic purpose. One must also challenge the strict view of leisure as time that lacks *any* obligation or compulsion. If one chooses to raise dogs as a hobby or to play an instrument in an orchestra, one begins to assume a system of routines, schedules, and obligations to oneself and to others. De Grazia suggests that none of these "semi-leisure" activities should be regarded as true leisure. He points out that the eight hours left over each day after work and sleep are devoted to such activities as

shopping, grooming, chores, transportation, voting, making love, helping children with homework, reading the newspaper, getting the roof repaired, trying to locate the doctor, going to church, visiting relatives, and so on. Do all these activities rightly belong to free time?[9]

A somewhat more generous view of leisure than this would suggest that many of the activities cited here—such as going to church, making love, reading the newspaper, or visiting relatives—might all be construed as fitting within a definition of both free time and leisure. The most important element within such a definition would appear to be a substantial degree of non-obligation and a sense of freedom and personal choice on the part of the participant.

Another element which comes into the definition of free time as leisure is the question of values. Some authorities suggest that only those uses of free time regarded as "desirable" or "self-enriching" should be considered leisure. This definition assumes, however, that it is possible to identify what *is* desirable, i.e., that there is some universally acceptable set of values which can be used in this determination. This raises a serious philosophical question. How does one determine what is good? Is it in terms of what the individual regards as desirable for himself? Many individuals, operating on a free-choice basis, engage in activities which society

[8] Joffre Dumazedier in *International Encyclopedia of the Social Sciences*, Vol. 9 (New York: Free Press, 1968), p. 250.
[9] De Grazia, *op. cit.*, p. 59.

as a whole regards as harmful or antisocial, such as the use of illegal narcotics, criminal gambling activity, drinking to excess, or premarital or adulterous sexual activity. It is probable that many who engage in such activities would vigorously defend their right to carry them on and would argue that—in their view—they are self-enriching or self-fulfilling. Clearly, the task of determining which activities *are* desirable becomes extremely difficult if one relies only on the judgments of participants.

Similarly, the decision becomes difficult if one uses as criteria the judgments of society. There is widespread ambiguity as to what is legally or morally acceptable with respect to uses of leisure. This varies according to region and locality; it varies also according to religious affiliation. In some states, "wet" and "dry" counties exist side by side; a person may drink hard liquor at a bar in one community, must bring his bottle in a brown paper bag to a restaurant in another, and may not drink at all in a third. One may bet on horse races at a pari-mutuel window with complete legality (indeed many states rely heavily on income from such ventures) but may not drive half a mile away and make the same bet through a bookmaker. In the realm of sexual activity, both attitudes and actual behavior vary widely, with the professed codes of society being so freely disregarded that it becomes almost impossible to say what is right or wrong or what is self-enriching or degenerative, except in the eyes of a particular group of individuals or religious denomination.

All this demonstrates that it is extremely difficult to classify leisure solely as those uses of free time which are positive and desirable. A more realistic approach would be to suggest that leisure represents all free time and that it provides the potential for freedom of choice. Within leisure one may engage in a wide range of activities—including those which are negative, passive, and destructive or those which are positive, active, self-enhancing, and constructive for the community as a whole.

A final question is whether work must exist for leisure to exist. Traditionally, this view has been accepted both from a semantic and a moral point of view. Since leisure was seen as time free from work, how could one conceive of leisure without work? Dumazedier has said, "Leisure in the modern sense pre-supposes work." From a moral point of view, according to the Protestant ethic, which valued work highly and deprecated idleness, both leisure and recreative activity could be justified only if they helped to restore one for work. Leisure in this context has been viewed as a reward; if one did not work, one was not entitled to have it and by definition did not have it.

If the premise is accepted that those who do not work do not have leisure, one may logically ask, "Who does not work?" The answer would include several classes of people such as some very rich people, people in prisons, young children, retired persons, unemployed people, and the ill and handicapped. Obviously, leisure should not be a problem for very rich people; they have both the free time and the resources to do what they wish with it. Whether one regards this time as leisure does not really matter. Older persons, although they no longer work, once did, and so the leisure they now have comes as a complement to their earlier work. They therefore deserve leisure in retirement, as a reward for the efforts of their earlier life. Similarly, young children use their free time heavily in play as preparation for adulthood and work. In the context of a lifetime, as opposed to the narrow view of a day or week which must include both work and leisure, the child has a balanced life.

But what about the very poor person who does not work—or the ill or handicapped person who has no possibility of working? The position that they have no leisure and therefore that society need not be concerned about what they do with their free time becomes sheer nonsense. It is still free time, and it may be used productively, to provide pleasure and constructive self-enrichment, or negatively, passively, or self-destructively. The former position ultimately becomes destructive for the unemployed individual himself and for the society as a whole, as later chapters, showing the linkage between recreational deprivation and urban unrest and violence, make explicit. The ultimate absurdity of insisting that without work there is no leisure is illustrated by the point that housewives do not work in a formal, paid sense. By this definition, they would then not be entitled to leisure. Unfortunately, this might be very near to the truth; many women work longer and harder than men and have comparatively little free time.

A Conceptual Framework for Recreation

Historically, the term "recreation" stems from the Latin word *recreatio*, meaning that which refreshes or restores. In its traditional sense, recreation has been as a period of light and restful activity, voluntarily chosen, which restores one for heavy, obligatory activity, or work.[10] Even in the modern era, this point of view is often expressed. De Grazia writes:

Recreation is activity that rests men from work, often by giving them a change (distraction, diversion), and restores (re-creates) them for work. When adults play—as they do, of course, with persons, things and symbols—they play for recreation. Like the Romans, our own conception of leisure is mainly recreative.[11]

This concept of recreation lacks acceptability today for two reasons. First, as most work in modern society becomes less demanding, many people become more fully engaged, both physically and mentally, in their

[10] Max Kaplan, *Leisure in America: A Social Inquiry* (New York: Wiley, 1960), p. 19.
[11] De Grazia, *op. cit.*, p. 233.

recreation, than in their work. Thus, the notion that recreation should be light and relaxing is far too limiting. Second, the idea that recreation is primarily intended to restore one for work has no meaning for such groups as aging persons who have *no* work but who certainly need recreation to make their life meaningful. Recreation must be perceived as valuable in its own right, not simply because it makes it possible for one to engage in more work.

Most modern definitions of recreation have fitted into one of three categories: (1) it has been seen as an activity carried on under certain conditions or with certain motivations; (2) it has been viewed as a process or state of being—something that happens within the person while engaging in certain kinds of activity with a given set of expectations; and (3) it has been perceived as a social institution, a body of knowledge, or a professional field.

The bulk of definitions, particularly those advanced by authors within the field of recreation, have regarded recreation as a form of activity or experience. Thus, the Neumeyers wrote of recreation as

any activity pursued during leisure, either individual or collective, that is free and pleasureful, having its own immediate appeal, not impelled by a delayed reward beyond itself or by any immediate necessity.[12]

A second definition, offered by Hutchinson, offers the element of social acceptability:

Recreation is a worthwhile, socially accepted leisure experience that provides immediate and inherent satisfaction to the individual who voluntarily participates in an activity.[13]

Other definitions offered over the past three decades have included the following elements:

1. Recreation is widely regarded as activity (including physical, mental, social, or emotional involvement) as contrasted to sheer idleness or complete rest.
2. Recreation may include an extremely wide range of activities, such as sports, games, crafts, performing arts, arts, music, dramatics, travel, hobbies, and social activities. They may be engaged in briefly, or in a sustained way, for single episodes, or throughout one's lifetime.
3. The choice of activity or involvement is completely voluntary rather than because of outside pressures, compulsory, or obligated.

[12] Neumeyer and Neumeyer, *op. cit.*, p. 22.
[13] John Hutchinson, *Principles of Recreation* (New York: Ronald Press, 1951), p. 2.

4. Recreation is prompted by internal motivation and the desire for achieving personal satisfaction, rather than "ulterior purpose" or other extrinsic goals or rewards.

5. Recreation is heavily dependent on a state of mind or attitude; it is not so much *what* one does as much as the reason for doing it, and the way the individual *feels* about the activity, that makes it recreational.

6. Recreation has potential desirable outcomes; although the primary motivation for participation is personal enjoyment, it may result in intellectual, physical, and social growth. This is not to say that recreation is automatically desirable; it may consist of activities which are dangerous, undesirable, or degenerating to the personality. However, when engaged in as part of a program of community recreation service, it is assumed that recreation is designed to provide constructive activity.[14]

One might briefly challenge a number of these beliefs. First, although recreation *is* widely regarded as activity, rather than complete idleness or rest, it may range from the most physically challenging pursuits to others which are much milder in their demands. With respect to recreation's being voluntarily chosen, it should be recognized that free choice does not always operate fully in such matters. One's opportunity to select recreational activities is often limited by the lack of available choices. In treatment centers patients may be strongly urged to take part in certain activities. If they are forced to take part in these experiences against their will, surely it would not be regarded as recreation. If, however, they came to enjoy it and to take part willingly, it might then rapidly become recreation.

The view that recreation must provide immediate pleasure also raises certain questions. Why need the satisfactions be immediate? Many worthwhile pastimes take a lengthy period of time to master before they yield the fullest degree of satisfaction. Many complex activities may cause frustration and even mental anguish—as in the case of the golf addict who is desperately unhappy because of poor putting or driving. In such cases it is not so much that the participant receives immediate pleasure as it is that he is absorbed and challenged by the activity; his pleasure should grow as his sense of achievement increases.

What of the view that recreation must be carried on by individuals for its own sake and without extrinsic goals or purposes? It is important to recognize that human beings *are* commonly goal-oriented, purposeful creatures. When they engage in recreational activity, they frequently do so for reasons that go beyond personal enjoyment or satisfaction, such as the need to make friends, to keep fit, to obtain physical release, to become

[14] Harold Meyer and Charles Brightbill, *Community Recreation: A Guide to Its Organization* (Englewood Cliffs, N.J.: Prentice-Hall, 1964), pp. 32-34; see also Reynold Carlson, Theodore Deppe, and Janet MacLean, *Recreation in American Life* (Belmont, Calif.: Wadsworth, 1963), pp. 7-8.

involved in competition, or to gain prestige. There are many purposes for recreational involvement which transcend the search for diversion alone.

Indeed, within a society that is still dominated by Puritan overtones, the view that many recreation educators and professionals have insisted upon—that recreation is *not* purposeful—has been extremely damaging in terms of obtaining community support. All publicly financed programs *must* have significant goals and objectives, or they do not deserve and obtain support. It therefore becomes necessary to make an important distinction. Recreation, as such, does not imply social acceptability or a set of socially oriented goals or values. When, however, it is provided as a form of community-based service, supported by taxes or voluntary contributions, it *must* be attuned to prevalent social value systems and *must* be aimed at achieving desirable social outcomes, as seen by dominant groups and agencies in community life.

It is important to recognize that recreation as a personal experience may range from the most trivial or temporary kinds of involvement to those which involve sustained dedication and persistence. Sometimes activities such as art, music, or theater are regarded as cultural pursuits, rather than recreation as such. It must be understood that when individuals take part in community theater activity or join a regional symphony orchestra or ballet company, they do so as a form of personal recreation. Only a narrow bias that sees recreation as describing only children's summertime play or casual social or sports activity would exclude such cultural activities from the total range of recreational experience. Similarly, many forms of service activities, in which individuals serve on community boards or contribute their services voluntarily to hospitals or other civic enterprises, must also be regarded as part of the broad spectrum of recreational participation.

Finally, when one considers recreation as a total community institution, it is important to recognize that today it provides the basis for employment for large numbers of people. One often hears such phrases as the "recreation industry," or "leisure economy." In this sense, recreation becomes more than a concept, a form of activity, or a state of being. Instead, it refers to all the social institutions which have been formed to meet the leisure needs of people. It includes activities and organizations which are sponsored by government on various levels, schools, churches, industries, voluntary agencies, and the business world—all of which provide varied recreational opportunities.

The Meaning of Play

A final term which must be considered is "play." The words "recreation" and "play" have often been used synonymously, yet they should be distinguished from each other in certain ways. Etymologically, the word play comes from the Anglo-Saxon word *plega*, meaning a game or sport, sometimes also a skirmish, fight, or battle. This is related to the Latin *plaga*, meaning a blow, stroke, or thrust; it is illustrated in the idea of striking or stroking an instrument or playing a game by striking a ball.

In addition to the theories of play described earlier, a number of other authors have written on the meaning of play. John Dewey wrote of play as "activities not consciously performed for the sake of any result beyond themselves." Gulick described play as "what we do because we want to do it." Patrick indicated that it consisted of

those human activities which are free and spontaneous and which are pursued for their own sake alone. Interest in them is self-sustaining, and they are not continued under any internal or external compulsion.

Mitchell saw it as "Play is self-expression for its own sake."[15]

Each of these definitions seem closely linked to traditional definitions of recreation. Those who have attempted to distinguish between the two have suggested that play is generally carried on by children, while recreation is an adult's concern. Thus, Kaplan writes that the term play is currently used in one of two senses:

(a) a light, informal, make-believe action, such as the play of children; (b) a more formal, stylized, intense and even serious presentation of some aspect of life on a "stage."[16]

De Grazia shares this view, saying:

Play is what children do, frolic and sport. . . . Adults play too, though their games are less muscular and more intricate. Play has a special relation to leisure. Men may play games in recreation; indeed except for men who work, play is a form of recreation . . . when adults play, as they do, of course, they play for recreation.[17]

Slavson writes, "Play is the means whereby the child, in fantasy, comes to know reality."[18] Others write of play as "not serious" or "not real." It involves playing a game or being involved in something that does not count. The author has written elsewhere:

Often, to play or to be playful, suggests . . . that one is not serious in purpose; one is amusing oneself and possibly teasing others, although, of course, the games-player may be in deadly earnest. Play is frequently referred to as being part of the world of children, and thus somewhat casual, unstructured

---

[15] Allen V. Sapora and Elmer D. Mitchell, *The Theory of Play and Recreation* (New York: Ronald Press, 1961), pp.114-15.
[16] Kaplan, *op. cit.*, p. 20.
[17] De Grazia, *op. cit.*, p. 233.
[18] S. R. Slavson, quoted in Carlson, Deppe, and MacLean, *op. cit.*, p. 5.

and exploratory, although not purposeless. On the other hand, recreation is usually viewed as being more deliberately planned and purposeful, more sustained and repetitive, and as more of an adult activity.[19]

Play normally suggests a lively, light, or humorous attitude; Miller and Robinson write of play as "activities engaged in purposely with free, happy, natural attitudes, full of fun and expression."[20] It is often marked by the element of combativeness or competition and involves a process of challenge and testing. It must work itself out, either with a product being created, an audience being amused, a feat accomplished, or an opponent being overcome. While carried out with a general spirit of inventiveness and freedom, it is also frequently controlled by strict rules or ritualized forms of behavior.

Both play and recreation may be examined in their relationship to work. While, by definition, recreation cannot exist within work, play (both in terms of the spirit of participation and the manner in which one approaches a task) certainly is part of work for many individuals. They play at their work, they experiment with it, they despair at failure and exult at success, they devise strategies, they map campaigns, they assume roles and exert cunning; ultimately, work is perceived and enjoyed as a game or drama. On the other hand, play is only one aspect of recreation; that is to say, there are forms of recreation which are not playlike. Reading for pleasure is not really a form of play. When one goes to the symphony or opera, it is recreational but not really play. The tourist may enjoy exploring new environments but is not really playing during most of his journey.

The distinction between play and recreation mentioned earlier—that play is carried on by children, chiefly for developmental purposes, while recreation is primarily an adult activity—should also be examined. This is an arbitrary view, based on the old notion that recreation's purpose is primarily restorative. Even if one were to accept it, it is clear that many children do work very hard in school and therefore are in need of rest and relaxation which may be provided by recreation as well as vigorous and demanding forms of play. Similarly, adults require a range of leisure experiences, and both play and recreation should help to contribute to their growth and health throughout life. Thus the view of play as a developmental function or learning process applicable only to children is not meaningful. Clearly, adults may engage in both play and recreation, as may children.

The public has accepted "recreation" in recent decades as the term most applicable to the broad field of leisure services and experiences, including such institutional forms as community agencies, professional organizations, and occupational involvement. It would seem undesirable to attempt to re-

[19] Richard Kraus, *Recreation and the Schools* (New York: Macmillan, 1964), p. 3.
[20] Norman P. Miller and Duane M. Robinson, *The Leisure Age* (Belmont, Calif.: Wadsworth, 1963), p. 8.

verse this trend, although the word "play" will undoubtedly continue to be used by many who are concerned with the activities of young children or with philosophical or psychological aspects of leisure involvement. In summation, the three terms, "leisure," "recreation," and "play" are defined in the following passage.

Definitions of Leisure, Recreation, and Play

1. *Leisure* is that portion of an individual's time which is not devoted to work or work-connected responsibilities or to other forms of maintenance activity and which therefore may be regarded as discretionary or unobligated time.

2. *Recreation* consists of activities or experiences carried on within leisure, usually chosen voluntarily by the participant, either because of the satisfaction or pleasure he gains from them or because he perceives certain personal or social values to be derived from them. Like leisure, recreation does not have work connotations. When it is carried on as part of organized community or voluntary agency programs, it is designed to meet constructive and socially acceptable goals of the individual participant, the group, and society at large.

3. *Play* customarily is also regarded as an activity carried on within leisure for purposes of pleasure and self-expression. It tends to be active and to be carried on in a spirit of competition, exploration, or make-believe. Customarily, play is regarded as a child's activity, although an adult may also engage in play and under some circumstances may find play in his work.

Recent Theories of Play and Recreation

In Chapter 9, a number of early theories of play and recreation were discussed. During the past several decades, a number of other theories have analyzed the nature and significance of play activity and defined its role in society.

The "Self-Expression" Theory. Two leading educators, Elmer Mitchell and Bernard Mason, attempted to develop a more convincing philosophical basis for the development of organized recreation programs than had been provided by earlier authorities. In *The Theory of Play*, they saw play primarily as a result of the drive for self-expression; man was perceived as an active, dynamic crature with a need to find outlets for his energies, to use his abilities, and to express his personality. The specific forms of play that he engages in were believed to be influenced by such factors as his physical fitness level, his physiological and anatomical structure, his physical environment, and his social setting. Mason and Mitchell particularly stressed the importance of achieving a sense of accomplishment through play.

In addition to the elements just described, the "self-expression" theory also suggested that certain universal wishes of men were influential in shaping leisure attitudes and habits. These included: (1) the wish for new experience, (2) the wish for participation in a group enterprise, (3) the wish for security, (4) the wish for response and recognition from others, and (5) the wish for the aesthetic. Mason and Mitchell's theory avoided the pitfalls of earlier explanations of play by providing a rationale for the various forms it took among different individuals and also by explaining its appearance among persons of all ages. Their explanation of play incorporated many of the psychological theories which had begun to gain influence in the early part of the century. It was therefore widely influential among recreation professionals and educators.[21]

Other major theories of play were developed in the mid-twentieth century by two European writers, Johan Huizinga and Roger Caillois.

The Play Element in Culture. Huizinga, in his provocative work, *Homo Ludens*,[22] takes the position that play pervades all of life. He assigns play certain characteristics: It is a voluntary activity, marked by freedom and never imposed by physical necessity or moral duty. It stands outside the realm of satisfying physiological needs and appetites. It is separate from ordinary life, both in terms of its location and its duration, being "played out" within special limited time periods, in such places as the arena, the card table, the stage, or the tennis court. Play is controlled by special sets of rules and demands absolute order. It is also marked by uncertainty and tension. Finally, it is not concerned with good or evil, although it has its own ethical value, in that its rules must be obeyed.

In Huizinga's view, play reveals itself chiefly in two kinds of activities —contests *for* something or representations *of* something. He regards it as an important civilizing function in human society, citing as an example ancient Greece, where the entire society was permeated with play forms. He traces historically the way in which many social institutions began originally as ritualized forms of play activity. For example, in the evolution of legal processes and the administration of justice, the play element was initially dominant. Law consisted of a pure contest between competing individuals or groups. It was not a matter of being in the right or wrong; instead, trials were carried out through the use of oracles, contests of chance which determined one's fate, trials of strength or resistance to torture, or simply verbal contests which determined the winner. Even in modern society, many legal rituals and processes are reminiscent of these early beginnings.

Although we tend to regard play as not serious, it may obviously be

---

[21] The original source of this theory was W. P. Bowen and Elmer D. Mitchell, *The Theory of Organized Play* (New York: A. S. Barnes, 1923). Now see Sapora and Mitchell, *op. cit.*, pp. 90-103.

[22] Johan Huizinga, *Homo Ludens: A Study of the Play Element in Culture* (Boston: Beacon Press, 1944, 1960).

carried on for stakes that are as important as life and death. Indeed, Huizinga states that war developed historically as a kind of game. All the elements of competing national teams, stratagems and deception, elaborate codes for prisoners, hostages, noncombatants, permissible weapons, and honorable behavior—all these support the idea of war as a game on a giant scale. In primitive cultures, even today, warfare is practiced as a game and carried on within strict limitations rather than in a serious attempt to wipe out and actually conquer the other team. Many sports have descended from forms of warfare or are directly related to them: hunting, horsemanship, archery, fencing, and shooting are today recreational activities which were originally essential to warfare and which are still practiced as games.

In other cultural and social institutions today, one may observe the play element at work. The stock market, or "investment game," is an obvious form of gambling—and recognized by many stock counselors as such. Beyond this, the conduct of much actual business, including the development of new technology, advertising strategy, personnel "raids," alliances with other firms, moving into new territories by establishing franchises in competition with existing firms, and even the pervasive practice of company spying, suggests that business is often approached as an exciting game. Competitions for the best salesman, testimonial dinners, referring to the sales group as "our team," and the common practice in both Europe and America of hiring athletes as employees to take part in sports contests with competing companies are evidences of this motivation.

Huizinga explores the role of play in the development of poetry, art, and philosophy in ancient and primitive societies. He concludes that within contemporary civilization, play is slowly declining. In sports, for example, games have been "raised to such a pitch of technical organization and scientific thoroughness that the real play spirit is threatened with extinction."[23] It has become too serious a business. Similarly, he suggests that in many other areas of life, such as warfare, contemporary politics, or international law, the old play rules are no longer respected and that culture therefore suffers.

Huizinga's major contribution was that he was the first respected scholar to give serious attention to play as an intrinsic element of such fundamental social institutions as war, law, religion, and politics. Another author who has made an important recent contribution to the theory of play is the French sociologist, Roger Caillois.

Man, Play, and Games. Caillois has developed a systematic analysis of play forms, through which the characteristic games of a culture may be better understood and classified. Like Huizinga, he regards play as free activity, separated from ordinary life; however, he goes further than Huizinga in analyzing varied forms of play and identifying their functions in various cultural contexts.

[23] *Ibid.*, p. 199.

Caillois establishes four major types of play and game activity: *agon, alea, mimicry,* and *ilinx.*

Agon refers to activities which are competitive and in which the equality of participants' chances is artificially created. Winners are determined through such qualities as speed, endurance, strength, memory, skill, or ingenuity. Agonistic games may be played by individuals or teams; they presuppose sustained attention, training and discipline, perseverance, limits, and rules.

Alea includes those games over whose outcomes the contestant has no control; winning is the result of fate rather than the skill of the player. Games of dice, roulette, baccarat, or lotteries are examples of *alea.* Caillois writes:

The player is entirely passive; he does not deploy his resources, skill, muscles, or intelligence. All he needs do is wait, in hope and trembling, the cast of the die. In contrast to *agon, alea* negates work, patience, experience and qualifications. Professionalization, application and training are eliminated . . . it supposes on the player's part an attitude exactly opposite to that reflected in Agon.[24]

Mimicry is based on the acceptance of illusions or imaginary universes; it includes a class of games in which the common element is that the subject makes believe or makes others believe that he is someone other than himself. For children, he writes,

the aim is to imitate adults. . . . This explains the success of the toy weapons and miniatures which copy the tools, engines, arms and machines used by adults. The little girl plays her mother's role as cook, laundress and ironer. The boy makes believe he is a soldier, musketeer, policeman, pirate, cowboy, Martian, etc.[25]

On the adult level, mimicry is found in theatrical presentations or games involving simulation and role-playing. Caillois sees a strong relationship between agon and mimicry in contests such as boxing or wrestling, football, tennis, or polo games which are

intrinsic spectacles, with costumes, solemn overtures, appropriate liturgy and regulated procedures. . . . In a word, these are dramas whose vicissitudes keep the public breathless, and lead to denouements which exalt some and depress others. The nature of these spectacles remains that of an *agon,* but their outward aspect is that of an exhibition.[26]

The element of mimicry is reinforced when spectators identify strongly with competitors, and, as in boxing, "rock with the punches," strike out

[24] Roger Caillois, *Man, Play and Games* (London: Thames and Hudson, 1961), p. 17.
[25] *Ibid.,* p. 21.
[26] *Ibid.,* p. 22.

themselves, or assume the pose of a jockey as they urge on the horse they had bet on. Under such conditions, Caillois says, a competitive mimicry is born in the onlooker, which doubles the agon of the competitive event.

Ilinx consists of those play activities which are based on the pursuit of vertigo, or dizziness. These are many activities which momentarily weaken the participant's stability of perception, deliberately bringing on a kind of "spasm, seizure or shock." Historically, ilinx was found in primitive religious dances or other rituals which induced trancelike states necessary for worship. Today, it may be seen in children's games that lead to dizziness by whirling rapidly or the use of swings or seesaws; among adults, it may be achieved by certain kinds of dances, amusement park rides such as the whip or loop-the-loop, or the use of alcohol and drugs which destroy the user's equilibrium and self-control.

In Caillois' view the entire universe of play is based on these categories; to some degree they may overlap when activities include elements of more than one type. He also suggests two extremes of style which characterize play and games. The first of these, which he calls *paidia*, exemplifies exuberance, freedom, uncontrolled and spontaneous gaiety; the second, *ludus*, is characterized by rules and conventions and represents calculated and contrived activity.

Like Huizinga, Caillois provides a rich historical perspective to play activity, showing how many play artifacts and activities, such as masks, kites, tops, balls, songs, games, and dances, are cultural residues of past "magical" beliefs and rites which have lost their original potency and now are played as a matter of tradition and custom. He suggests also that the drives underlying primitive behavior still strongly influence modern man and that playthings and games must be regarded as meeting fundamental built-in needs of modern man.

Other Cultural Analyses of Play. A number of other investigators have examined the social role of play in primitive societies. One anthropologist, Felix Keesing, describes recreation as a behavioral zone which is an "open" system, marked by "fictional" premises, novelty, risk-taking, both utilitarian and nonpurposeful motivations, and relative freedom from demanding goal orientations and society sanctions. He suggests that within primitive societies, it may be observed to have the following important functions: (1) pleasurable, or hedonistic, effects; (2) relaxing, or energy-restorative, functions; (3) "integrative" effects, which develop stability and cohesion among both individuals and groups in the society; (4) therapeutic or sublimative functions, which channel off conflicts, aggressions, and hostilities; (5) creative opportunities for innovation and self-expression; (6) communicative functions which assist learning and habit formation among both children and adults; and (7) symbolic values, in terms of expressing cultural values and beliefs.[27]

[27] Felix M. Keesing, "Recreative Behavior and Culture Change," *Papers of the Fifth Congress of Anthropological and Ethnological Sciences*, 1956, pp. 130-31.

Keesing suggests that such characteristics are also shared by recreation's close cultural relatives, art and religion, two behavioral zones which in his view have frames of reference different from those of everyday "reality" situations.

He observes that recreative aspects of behavior are remarkably open to innovation and cross-cultural transfer; they provide important opportunities for the analysis of social and cultural change and development. Ultimately, traditional recreation activities are most likely to persist when they have a continuing functional relation to social structure, child-training, religion, or other behaviors pervaded by important social values. In some cases, the same activity may readily be adapted to new uses and needs while retained in another form for traditional purposes. As an example, the ceremonies of American Indians are frequently used for tourist exhibitions in one form and in another quite different form as part of traditional religious practice.

Similar documentation of the role of playlike activities in primitive societies is provided by the anthropologist Bronislaw Malinowski. He describes the use of varied rites and rituals in the communal lives of primitive tribes as being a unique blending of both practical and mystical beliefs and customs, intended to deal with the forces of nature which cannot be otherwise combatted or controlled. Such rituals are kept strictly apart from work:

Every magical ceremony has its distinctive name, its appropriate time, and its place in the scheme of work, and it stands out of the ordinary course of activities completely. . . . Work is always tabooed on such occasions, sometimes only while the ceremony lasts, sometimes for a day or two.[28]

All aspects of life (including the planting and harvesting of crops, initiation ceremonies, or even the preparation and eating of food) are surrounded by magical ceremonies and prayers, many of which are uniquely playlike. As an example, Malinowski writes:

food has also a conspicuous role in ceremonies of a distinctly religious character. First-fruit offerings of a ritual nature, harvest ceremonies, big seasonal feasts in which crops are accumulated, displayed, and, in one way or another, sacralized, play an important role among agricultural people. Hunters . . . or fishers, celebrate a big catch or the opening of the season of their pursuit by feasts and ceremonies at which food is ritually handled, the animals propitiated or worshipped.[29]

Ceremonies at birth, rites of initiation, mortuary attentions to the dead, and acts of mourning and commemoration are all collectively celebrated, involving the gathering together of all members of the tribe, often involving feasts carried on in a mood of happiness and harmony, with re-

[28] Bronislaw Malinowski, *Magic, Science and Religion* (New York: Doubleday-Anchor Books, 1955), p. 29.
[29] *Ibid.*, p. 42.

laxation of rules and taboos. In modern society, weddings, confirmation ceremonies, and even funerals may similarly provide occasions for get-togethers, social entertainment, drinking, and amusement—just as in primitive cultures. Malinowski points out too that there are many collective play acts in areas of life which are not dominated by religion. He writes:

Collective work in the gardens, as I have seen it in Melanesia, when men became carried away with emulation and zest for work, singing rhythmic songs, uttering shouts of joy and slogans of competitive challenge, is full of this "collective effervescence." But it . . . assumes no divine grandeur or godlike appearance. A battle, a sailing regatta, one of the big tribal gatherings for trading purposes, a . . . corroboree, a village brawl, are all from the social as well as from the psychological point of view, essentially examples of crowd effervescence.[30]

Thus, Huizinga, Caillois, Keesing, and Malinowski all see play and recreation as having an important role in cultural practice. They also suggest that humans at all levels of societal development have a strong urge to engage in group activities which strengthen identification with the society as a whole and provide an emotional affirmation of common cause. Humans take part in assemblies, wear uniforms, have feasts and testimonial dinners, march and sing, enjoy spectacles and displays—not as light or trivial forms of amusement but because they share fundamental needs for such group involvements.

This concept is widely illustrated in the modern world. In the Olympics, for example, we see a vast display of nations competing in varied sports and linked cultural activities, in order to affirm their own strength and prestige. In college or professional sports, the contests themselves are accompanied by the fervent rooting of fans in great numbers, along with colorful displays by bands, cheerleaders, drill teams, and drum majorettes. Sports thus demonstrate both a kind of communal identification and affirmation of group loyalty and what appears to be a universal need for panoply and display, color and excitement.

A final aspect of play and recreation as cultural elements has been suggested by such investigators as Robert Ardrey and Konrad Lorenz, who have concluded that man is dominated by fundamental inherited urges toward aggressive behavior toward others and by the need to symbolically and physically defend his territory against intruders.[31] These concepts suggest an important need to make public provision for controlled forms of violent and aggressive behavior, in order to provide comparatively harmless

[30] *Ibid.*, p. 58.
[31] See Robert Ardrey, *African Genesis* (New York: Dell, 1961, 1967); Konrad Lorenz, *On Aggression* (New York: Harcourt, Brace and World, 1963, 1966); and Desmond Morris, *Primate Ethology* (New York: Doubleday-Anchor Books, 1967, 1969). These, with other books by the same authors, comprise what some have described as an ethological theory of play.

outlets for what might otherwise be dangerous and antisocial individual and group behavior. While this line of investigation does not constitute a theory of play and recreation (instead it represents a general theory of human culture and behavior), it does have important implications for those concerned with leisure services. Therefore, it will be more fully discussed in Chapter 17.

13

Psychological Aspects of Play

During the first several decades of the twentieth century, a number of psychologists wrote extensively on the role of play and recreation in human growth and development. Their concern was directed to three broad areas: (1) the contribution of play experience to total personality formation, (2) its function in the learning process, and (3) its place in the expanding body of psychoanalytical theory, which sought to explain emotional adjustment and human behavior.

During the early decades of the century, despite the growing interest in play on the part of many educators, it continued to be regarded by some authorities as an experience of dubious worth. For example, the 1914–15 edition of *Infant Care,* the official publication of the U.S. Children's Bureau, represented the "infant as a creature of strong and dangerous impulses":

Playing with the baby was regarded as dangerous; it produced unwholesome pleasure and ruined a baby's nerves: "The rule that parents should not play with the baby may seem hard, but it is no doubt a safe one. . . . The dangerousness of play is related to that of the ever-present sensual pleasures which must constantly be guarded against."[1]

Gradually, however, in the decades that followed, the same publication came to regard play as natural and desirable, and it recommended

[1] Quoted in Eda J. LeShan, "The 'Perfect' Child," *New York Times Magazine,* August 27, 1967, p. 63.

that mothers play with their children. By the 1940's, Ruth Strang, a leading child-guidance authority, was to write, "The play life of a child is an index of his social maturity, and reveals his personality more clearly than any other activity."[2] Similarly, two noted child psychologists, Gesell and Ilg, stated, "Deeply absorbing play seems to be essential for full mental growth."[3]

The Role of Play in Personality Development

Play came to be regarded as an important experience, through which children developed emotionally, psychologically, and socially and formed patterns of behavior that would serve them in good stead throughout life. The psychologist Lawrence K. Frank wrote:

Play, as we are beginning to understand, is the way the child learns what no one can teach him. It is the way he explores and orients himself to the actual world of space and time, of things, animals, structures, and people. Through play he learns to live in our symbolic world of meaning and values, of progressive striving for deferred goals, at the same time exploring and experimenting and learning in his own individual way. Through play the child practices and rehearses endlessly the complicated and subtle patterns of human living and communication which he must master if he is to become a participating adult in our social life.[4]

Psychologists examined the role of play at each stage of life, beginning with infancy and moving through the preschool period, middle and late childhood, and adolescence. They identified the first form of play in infancy as "sense-pleasure" play, in which the baby discovers and relishes the experiences of movement and exploring his own body and such environmental stimuli as sounds, flavors, or tactile sensations. During later infancy, children begin to explore "skill-play," exercising their capacities for action. Early in the toddler period, young children take part in "dramatic play," re-enacting scenes from everyday life, using toy dolls and animals, and acting out functional relationships and roles. Erik Erikson describes this total process of development in the following terms:

The child's play begins with, and centers in, his own body. It begins before we notice it as play, and it consists first in the exploration by repetition of sensual perceptions, of kinesthetic sensations, and of vocalizations. . . . Next, the

[2] Ruth Strang, *An Introduction to Child Study* (New York: Macmillan, 1951), p. 495.

[3] Arnold Gesell and Frances Ilg, *The Child from Five to Ten* (New York: Harper, 1946), p. 360.

[4] Lawrence K. Frank, in Ruth E. Hartley and Robert M. Goldenson, *The Complete Book of Children's Play* (New York: Thomas Y. Crowell, 1963), p. 43.

child plays with . . . available persons and things . . . with the small world of manageable toys.[5]

The content of individual play often proves to be the young child's way of reliving difficult experiences and achieving a sense of control over them. Often his play becomes a projection of his uncertainties and fears. He learns that he is capable of dealing effectively with the outside world. Many play experiences provide an opportunity for what Bettelheim calls "self-regulation." He points out that many children's activities have important psychological significance, as in games of "not flinching . . . holding one's breath . . . not crying out . . . conquering a sense of revulsion, and so on."[6]

Often the child's purpose is to test dangers or dispel fears of the unknown, in what may appear to him to be a chaotic and dangerous world. Bettelheim suggests that as simple a game as peek-a-boo symbolically means to the child that even if he is temporarily out of her sight, his mother will not abandon him but will look for him and find him. Thus, he gains confidence and need not always be under her careful protection. Similarly, in activities centering around the use of swings, slides, and merry-go-rounds or being swung around or tossed in the air and then caught by a parent, the child deliberately seeks giddiness and danger—in order to be sure that the feat can be mastered and the danger will pass. Other forms of children's play which involve fear and risk—such as hide-and-seek in dark hiding places—symbolize the child's testing out the security of home, to which he can safely return.

Thus, play provides a medium through which children can develop inner strengths and processes of self-control. This growing independence is revealed in the changing nature of social relationships in children's play. As children move from the toddler age to about five or six, they shift from solitary activities to parallel, side-by-side play, and finally to integrated, cooperative play projects. Dramatic play during the first two or three years is episodic and incomplete. By the time they enter kindergarten, children act out more elaborate roles and themes in cooperation with others.

The environment of play gradually expands from the crib to the playpen to the entire room, and ultimately to the backyard, the playground, or the street. The child explores the air, the water, the ground; he climbs, he kicks, he runs, he wades and swims. Through all this, he practices language and manipulatory skills; he finds out about gravity, velocity, the weight and strength of objects and tools, and the way others respond to his behavior. All this is essential for his fullest possible self-realization. Many cases of mental retardation in our society today are aggravated by environ-

[5] Erik Erikson, in Morris L. Haimowitz and Natalie R. Haimowitz, *Human Development: Selected Readings* (New York: Thomas Y. Crowell, 1960), p. 303.

[6] Bruno Bettelheim, "What Children Learn from Play," *Parents' Magazine*, July, 1964, pp. 4, 9-10, 102.

mental deprivation; children lack sufficient varied stimuli in the form of language, ideas, objects, magazines, books, toys, play materials, and other elements needed for healthy growth. By the time he has reached puberty, the child should have achieved, through play, a variety of interests, skills and social competences which help him enter this difficult and challenging period of development.

The Role of Play in Adolescent Development. Psychologists who have done extensive research with teen-agers in areas related to play and recreation have been primarily concerned with the social and emotional growth of teen-agers. Such studies have generally been school-connected and have focused on extracurricular participation. Since extracurricular activities are voluntarily chosen within leisure, to obtain pleasure or other forms of personal satisfaction, and since they include such activities as sports, music, dance, hobbies, and social activities, they may be viewed essentially as play or recreation. In several ways such activities have been documented as being of particular value for adolescents in American schools.

It has been found that the adolescent's self-image is closely related to participation in extracurricular activities. A study of over 5,000 high school students of varying social, religious, and national backgrounds revealed that those with a high degree of self-esteem tended to take part actively in sports teams, musical organizations, publications, outdoor recreation, and social activities. Those with a low degree of self-esteem were much less involved. Such activities fill certain specific functions in the development of teen-agers. Jersild stresses their special value in providing meaningful social contact. Despite the popular notion that adolescents are constantly "ganging," he has found that for many, adolescence is a time of intense loneliness:

Adolescents live in solitary isolation when they cannot share their concerns with others and when the only close companions they can find are those who dwell within their own imagination . . . there are many conditions in adolescence and adult life that wall people off. . . . Loneliness occurs not only in those who physically are alone. It can occur in its most acute form when a person is in the midst of a crowd, joining in the banter and enforced sociability. Some adolescents feel their loneliness most vividly when they are at a party or dance.[7]

Obviously, extracurricular or other recreational experiences for youth can offer an opportunity for real involvement with others, and provide a sense of acceptance and security within the group, that will contribute to psychological well-being. Jersild found that the most popular teen-agers were those who had the spontaneity and willingness to enter into games and other activities; liveliness, cheerfulness, gaiety, and the ability to suggest or initiate group projects and social events were found to be important elements in being accepted by one's peers. A number of investigators have

[7] Arthur Jersild, *The Psychology of the Adolescent* (New York: Macmillan, 1963), p. 253.

also found that athletic prowess was closely related both to the individual's self-concept and the way he was regarded by others. Jersild has commented that this extended beyond the factor of being physically skilled; it included also the element of lifestyle. Whether or not a boy enters into sports is influenced

by his willingness to rub elbows with others, his ability to enter easily and freely into social contacts, his aggressiveness, his willingness to face the possibility of being roughed up a bit. . . .

There is perhaps no single department of the high school that offers greater opportunity than the physical education department for studying the individual student, his style of life, his potentialities for being spontaneous and free, his hesitancies and lack of self-confidence, his need to vanquish, or his need at all costs to avoid defeat or to avoid a contest in which he might look awkward.[8]

In other ways, participation in cocurricular activities has been seen by psychologists as having important implications for the adjustment of teenagers. They offer healthy outlets for the direct release of tensions or aggressions, as opposed to vicarious release through television, movies, or reading matter or such antisocial acts as vandalism, aggressive behavior against other youths, or harmful sexual promiscuity. Competition provides a particularly important element in extracurricular activities. Jersild comments that when children and adolescents try out their growing powers in spontaneous competition with each other, it leads to realistic self-discovery and self-appraisal and offers meaningful preparation for living in the adult world. Recognizing that competition may also be self-defeating, as in the case where a person suffers from low esteem and can prove his worth only by endlessly defeating others, there is a need to gain a sense of perspective about winning and losing.

Another important value of recreation in teen-age life is that it leads to the development of interests, some of which have important carryover values for later life. Particularly during the 1920's and 1930's, extracurricular activities were seen as having important utilitarian values in that they opened a pathway to occupational involvement by helping the individual understand his own interests and capabilities and begin to make intelligent choices for the future. This function was stressed during the Depression, when avocational interests and aptitudes were used as a means of providing vocational guidance. Many counselors working with unemployed young people found it necessary to provide them with guidance in the constructive use of leisure. In addition, since many lacked obvious vocational skills and experience, counselors examined hobby and other recreational interests in order to gather diagnostic information about potential aptitudes. One investigator carried out an extensive study of such hobbies as

[8] *Ibid.*, pp. 106-107.

model engineering, music, photography, and stamp collecting and concluded that there was considerable value in relating avocational and vocational interests.[9]

Since the 1940's, within the field of career development, a number of psychologists have advanced a theory of self-concept formation which places considerable stress on what they call the "exploratory" drive. Their view is that both animals and human beings are motivated to seek as well as to avoid or reduce stimulation. Jordaan writes:

A good deal is known about the ways in which hunger, thirst, sex, pain and the fear of punishment motivate the behavior of animals; much less is known about the behavior of animals when these drives are not present and about the other sources of motivation which might influence and direct their behavior. Some investigators . . . have postulated the existence of an exploratory drive and concluded that animals and humans are motivated to seek, as well as to avoid or reduce stimulation . . . with motives . . . which can be described by such names as manipulation, exploration, curiosity, and play.[10]

It is suggested that certain kinds of situations are believed to lead to stimulation of the individual—including both circumstances in which there are few stimuli (thus leading to boredom) and others which provoke risk-taking, self-inflicted stress, and a deliberate search for thrills and excitement. In either case, exploratory behavior is likely to result. Jordaan suggests that such exploratory activity may involve a wide variety of pursuits, such as music, writing, acting, art, or homemaking activities, along with student activities similar to certain occupations or other group recreational activities. Any such form of exploratory experience—which involves a sequence of experimenting, searching, trying out, testing, and getting one's bearings—is likely to produce changes in the individual's knowledge, attitudes, behavior, and perception. Avocational experiences are seen as extremely valuable in building positive self-concepts and helping individuals make sound vocational choices. Here, then, one finds continuing theoretical support for the value of extracurricular and out-of-school activities which enhance personal growth.

The Role of Play in the Learning Process

Earlier chapters in this text have described the use of play as a medium of education in many elementary schools during the early decades of the twentieth century. A number of psychologists who investigated child behavior during this period concluded that play was essential to contributing

---

[9] Donald E. Super, *Avocational Interest Patterns: A Study in the Psychology of Avocations* (Stanford: Stanford University Press, 1940).

[10] Jean Jordaan, in Donald E. Super, Reuben Starishevsky, and Norman Matlin, *Career Development: Self-Concept Theory* (Princeton, N.J.: College Entrance Examination Board, 1963), p. 42.

to the child's initiative, resourcefulness, and originality. Lehman and Witty wrote during the 1920's that "as educative forces, it is apparent that these play activities are vital, and indispensable tools to modern education "and that they should be used as "basic elements in curriculum construction and project planning."[11] Educational experiences, it was believed, should be presented so that the child would pursue them voluntarily as a form of play, giving them a time, place, and order of their own and engaging in them freely, with fullest absorption and without the need for punishments or rewards. There was comparatively little systematic analysis of the use of the play method in education at this time; what was done tended to be supported by enthusiastic sloganeering rather than by objective evaluation.

One leading experimenter at this time who made considerable use of playlike methods was Maria Montessori. She was an Italian educator whose innovations with preschool education in the slums of Rome early in the twentieth century produced remarkable effects. Since her work was based on psychological principles not in agreement with those generally in vogue in the United States, her work was largely ignored by American educators. Over the past decade or two, however, there has been a striking growth of Montessori schools on the preschool and primary grade levels throughout the United States.

The Montessori method was based on intensive observation of young children and on investigating and perfecting techniques for involving them in learning processes using so-called didactic materials (a variety of objects, tools, rods, blocks, boxes with bells in them, different-colored tablets, and child-sized furniture). Her method was to help children move from preliminary physical experimentation with these materials to a sense of abstraction about their use. Throughout, children were helped to gain a sense of order, control, and organization. While Montessori did not regard what she was doing with children as "play" (she avoided the use of this word entirely, instead referring to it as "work"), the activities themselves and the way in which they were carried on were extremely playlike. Montessori wrote, "It is *necessary* that the spontaneous development of the child be accorded *perfect liberty*."[12] The child was not to be told what and how he was to learn; instead, he worked at his own pace and rhythm, in a spontaneous process of exploration, skill development, and cognitive growth.

The progressive education approach which characterized the first several decades of the century died out in the 1950's under sharp attack by critics who sought increased rigor and academic emphasis in American education. This was particularly evident in two fields of education which

[11] Harvey C. Lehman and Paul A. Witty, *The Psychology of Play Activities* (New York: A. S. Barnes, 1927), p. 230.
[12] Maria Montessori, *Spontaneous Activity in Education* (New York: Schocken Books, 1965), p. 71.

had had a close connection with recreation: adult education and outdoor education. Adult education had traditionally included many activities not of a formal or academic nature, including sports, games, social activities, the arts, hobbies, and self-improvement courses. Beginning in the early 1950's, professional organizations in this field, as well as a number of state education departments, sought to distinguish sharply between adult education and recreation. In a number of cases they withdrew special subsidies from classes which were primarily social or recreational in nature because they lacked "educational" value. Similarly, in school camping and outdoor education programs, which had been widely established throughout the United States during the 1940's and 1950's, the earlier emphasis on recreational activities and education for leisure was cut sharply. Instead, the primary focus was given to science education and other academic subject fields which could be closely related to the outdoor setting.

But the sharpest retreat of educators who were promoting the value of play as learning experience came in the area of early childhood education. Here, as indicated earlier, most nursery schools and kindergarten classes had developed approaches based heavily on a rather free exploration of blocks, paints, tools, toys, cutting and pasting, singing, storytelling, rhythmic dancing, and varied forms of outdoor play. However, the appropriateness of such emphasis has recently been challenged. During the 1960's, special crash instruction programs at the preschool age level, designed to help children from disadvantaged backgrounds, developed entirely new priorities. The conviction has been expressed that these children cannot afford to have the kind of play-oriented, casual social experience that middle- or upper-class children are given. Instead, because of the deficiencies in their home backgrounds, it is held that they need more intellectual stimulation and more emphasis on cognitive development, as well as early intensive work in reading and arithmetic. As an example, in an experimental Head Start program at the University of Illinois, Bereiter and Engelmann have broken away completely from the play-oriented nursery school approach. Instead,

their brisk, two-hour schedule allows virtually no time for free play. Instead of having a central, motherly teacher for the whole class, the children are split into small groups that move from subject to subject, each with a different instructor. Instead of spending most of their time on nonverbal activities which hardly change from semester to semester, the children and teacher talk, shout, chant in full sentences—following a very specific plan.[13]

To a degree, this approach might be regarded as playlike, in that it seeks to capture and fully involve each child. One of the leading preschool experimenters suggests that the child must be "hooked" on learning, and

[13] Maya Pines, "Slum Children Must Make Up for Lost Time," *New York Times Magazine*, October 15, 1967, p. 70.

indeed that "a good match [of challenge to ability] produces so much in-trinsic motivation and pleasure, that learning becomes a sport, as engross-ing to children as baseball.[14]

The idea that slum children must make up for lost time by becoming involved in highly structured and academically oriented preschool classes rather than in play-oriented kinds of programs has been strongly criticized by a number of leading contemporary educators. They suggest that these new experimental methods are drill-like, repetitious, and unstimulating, similar to the educational methodology which is still widely used in under-developed and totalitarian countries and not geared to the development of well-educated citizens who will be able to meet the challenge of contem-porary society. Lois Murphy, Director of Developmental Research at the Menninger Foundation, comments that early education must nourish such cognitive functions as curiosity, reflectiveness, and problem-solving and that this can best be done in the following ways:

Learning to be active, to make things for oneself, to clarify observations, to de-velop concepts of space, size and weight, are contributions of block-construc-tion and work with plastic materials, such as clay or paints. . . . Cooking dem-onstrates measurements and effects of heat. Growth is observed in a garden. Information is extended by calendars, thermometers, heaters. Play telephones stimulate communication.[15]

In terms of resolving such disagreements, little empirical evidence has been gathered about the specific value of play as learning experience. In-stead, the major investigations that have been carried out have had to do with cognitive development and have seen play experience as an element in this process.

Probably the leading psychologist over the past several decades in the field of child development has been Jean Piaget, professor at the University of Geneva and director of the *Institut Rousseau*. Piaget suggests that there are two processes which are basic to all development—*assimilation* and *ac-commodation*. Assimilation is the process of taking in, as in the case of receiving information in the form of visual or auditory stimuli. Accom-modation is the process of adjusting to external circumstances and stimuli. Within Piaget's theory, play is specially related to the process of assimila-tion, mentally digesting new and different situations and experiences. Any-thing important that has happened is reproduced in play; it is a means of assimilating and consolidating the child's emotional experiences.[16]

Piaget carried out a careful stage-by-stage analysis of the various periods of child development, showing how the child moves from a sensory-motor

---

[14] J. McVicar Hunt, quoted in Pines, *ibid.*, p. 74.

[51] Louis Barclay Murphy, "Letter to the Editor," *New York Times Magazine*, No-vember 12, 1967, p. 42.

[16] See Susanna Millar, *The Psychology of Play* (Baltimore: Penguin Books, 1968), p. 55.

period through a period of individual symbolic, or make-believe, play to a later period of formal games with rules and collective discipline. He regarded play primarily as repetition of an activity already mastered rather than an attempt to investigate or explore it further and develop a capability for dealing with it more effectively, which would be part of accommodation. Some psychologists have criticized Piaget's analysis of play as being severely limited, concerned with play only as a "transient, infantile stage in the emergence of thought," lacking an originating or innovating role in the development of new concepts. In part, this is because Piaget regarded play and imitation as distinctly separate phenomena; while play was related to assimilation, imitation was part of the process of accommodation. In contrast, most systematic observers of children's behavior have regarded imitative activity as a basic element in play.

Another leading authority on cognitive development has been Jerome Bruner, a professor of psychology at Harvard University. Bruner's analysis of cognitive development in children suggests that it has three broad stages. In the first, which he calls the "pre-operational" stage, the child's mental task consists chiefly of establishing relationships between experiences and outcomes and of learning how to understand and represent the external world through symbols established by simple generalizations. The second stage, that of "concrete operations," involves the child's learning to gather data about the environment and to understand and be able to predict its operations within his own mind, rather than through trial and error. In the third stage, that of "formal operations," the child's ability becomes based on more hypothetical propositions and understandings of relationships, rather than immediate experiences and observation.[17]

Bruner describes the use of play materials, toys, and similar objects to help the child learn basic principles or scientific relationships through direct experience. He stresses the need to establish the child's sense of autonomy, as well as intense involvement, if the fullest degree of learning is to occur. Bruner urges that children be freed from the immediate controls of environmental rewards and punishments, the need to gain parental or teacher approval, or the avoidance of failure. Learning should be approached as a task of discovery of ideas rather than "learning about" something.

Other experts on cognitive development today stress the need for children to become more sensitive to the world around them, to be actively involved, and to work with raw sources rather than predigested materials. Mastery, not just the acquisition of knowledge, is the basic goal. Within such a framework, the role of out-of-class hobbies and other recreational pursuits obviously is important in providing opportunities for gaining new understandings and information. As Hunt puts it,

[17] Jerome S. Bruner, *On Knowing: Essays for the Left Hand* (Cambridge, Mass.: Harvard University Press, 1962), pp. 34-36.

the greater the variety of situations to which the child must accommodate his behavioral structures, the more differentiated they become, the more rapid is his rate of intellectual development and the greater is his range of interests in the novel and the new.[18]

Games and Games Theory

As indicated earlier, one of the areas relating play to the learning process which behavioral scientists have explored during the past several decades has to do with the function of games in society. A number of anthropologists and psychologists have examined the relationship of games to child-rearing in primitive societies; it has been found that games are indicative of the life styles and fundamental values of the tribes in which they are found. For example, games of physical skill tend to predominate in societies which stress achievement and success as important life goals. Strategic games which simulate war and combat are found chiefly in tribes with complicated social and political structures. Games of chance are found to reflect tribal religious practices and beliefs. In one study, carried out by Roberts and Sutton-Smith, game-playing was demonstrated to be a direct training ground for skills and behaviors that would be expected of children in later life.[19] In another series of studies, Sutton-Smith and Gump explored the role of children's games in more advanced cultures. They concluded that games provided children with "action-based social relationships," giving them the opportunity to assume a variety of roles and status positions and providing gratification and psychological release.[20]

There has been a marked increase in the use of specially devised games in education, as a means of teaching fundamental concepts, providing information, and encouraging strategic behavior. James Coleman, a leading authority on adolescent development, has written on the value of playing games as learning experience:

Recently, educators have begun devising games for high school and pre-high school students that simulate complex activities in a society. One of the ways that simulation and games were first combined was in war games. Many of the oldest parlor games (chess and checkers, for example) were developed as war simulations long ago, and today armies use war games to develop logistic and strategic skills.

From war games developed the idea of management games, a simulation

18 Barbara Biber, in Eli M. Bower and William G. Hollister, *Behavioral Science Frontiers in Education* (New York: Wiley, 1967), p. 126.

19 Brian Sutton-Smith and J. M. Roberts, "Child-Training and Game Involvement," *Ethnology*, 1962, pp. 1, 166-85; see also Brian Sutton-Smith, "The Role of Play in Cognitive Development," *Young Children* (Journal of the National Association for the Education of Young Children), September, 1967, p. 361.

20 Brian Sutton-Smith and Paul Gump, "Games and Status Experience," *Recreation*, April, 1955, p. 172.

of management decision-making which is used in many business schools and firms to train future executives by putting them in situations they will confront in their jobs.[21]

Coleman and his associates at Johns Hopkins have developed a number of games which simulate aspects of society—a *Life Career Game*, a *Family Game*, a *Representative Democracy Game*, a *Community Response Game* (in which a community responds to some kind of disaster), and a *Consumer Game* (in which the players are consumers and department store credit managers). Games developed in other settings have been used to help children learn simple scientific, mathematical, and language concepts and particularly to help lower-class children gain confidence in language as a mode of communication. One firm provides game kits and visual aids involving playlike approaches for teaching number relationships and mathematical symbols, puzzle boxes, equation games. Other games deal with civics, government, history and political science, banking, international trade, geometry, and physics.

What are the particular merits of games play as a learning process? Coleman suggests that games constitute an approach to learning that starts with a fundamentally different premise from traditional methodology:

The first premise is that persons do not learn by being taught; they learn by experiencing the consequences of their actions. Games which simulate some aspects of reality are one way a young person can begin to see such consequences before he faces the real actions and the real consequences as an adult. A second premise underlying the development of these games is that schools find it difficult to teach about the complexity that characterizes modern society, with the result that the students have had little or no experience to prepare them for facing a multitude of decisions and problems in adult life.[22]

Teaching through the use of games helps the student become aware that each of his actions has direct consequences and that he has the power to affect his own future. This is particularly important in a complex society, in which students perceive the world of business and vocational opportunity as distant and difficult to understand. Particularly for students who are not prepared for abstract intellectual learning, it becomes possible to approach learning through direct experience. Typically, a number of workers in underdeveloped countries have designed teaching games to help villagers learn to deal cooperatively with problems related to the construction of roads, schools, and hospitals and agricultural projects.

Obviously, the use of games for instruction does not represent play in the traditional sense of the word. The teaching game is a carefully designed and administered instructional device, a programmed learning ex-

[21] James S. Coleman, "Learning Through Games," *National Education Association Journal*, January, 1967, p. 69.
[22] *Ibid.*, p. 70.

perience. It depends for its success, however, on key elements involved in all play—absorption of the individual in the activity, a sense of involvement, the arousal of competitive instincts, and finally a sense of playfulness, and creative problem-solving.

The Role of Play in Psychoanalytical Theory

A final important aspect of play with respect to psychological analysis has been its interpretation by psychoanalytical writers and practitioners. The dominant influence in the development of psychoanalytical theory was that of Sigmund Freud, whose contribution during the early twentieth century was immense. Many of Freud's fundamental concepts of personality development and his exposition of psychological mechanisms have profound implications for the understanding of play.

Freud's basic formulation was that the child brings into the world a somewhat unorganized and chaotic mentality, called the *id*, which is dominated by powerful drives for self-preservation, the alleviation of hunger, and the expression of sexual love—all linked to the continuation of the species. As the child grows older, Freud suggested that a portion of the *id* becomes transformed into the *ego*, which attempts to govern the *id* when it behaves in lawless or antisocial ways. When sharp conflicts arise between the two (typically, the *ego* refuses to let the sexual impulses of the *id* express themselves freely), neurosis occurs. A third element, the *super-ego*, represents a modified part of the *ego*. It personifies all the prohibitions and strict rules of conduct which were imposed on the child by authority figures and may be perceived as a powerful conscience and sense of duty.

In the continuing attempt on the part of each human being to resolve the conflicts between the drives of his *id* and the controls exerted on them by his *ego* and *super-ego*, a number of psychological mechanisms are employed. Freud described these as "sublimation," "regression," "compensation," "repression," and "identification"; each may be directly related to human motivations for participating in play and recreation.

Sublimation is the process through which sexual energies and aggressions are rechanneled into socially desirable activities. Typically, artistic activities are regarded as a form of sublimation for those who are not able to express the primary drive of sexual expression and must divert it into other more culturally acceptable directions. In *regression* the individual returns to behavior characteristic of his childhood, a time which he found to be easier and more pleasurable. Play frequently provides an opportunity to engage in activities fixated at an early stage of development. *Compensation* occurs when an individual who has certain limitations—possibly of a physical nature—and consequent inability to be successful within one sphere of activity pours his energies into another form of activity and achieves success in that. Recreation provides many opportunities to find compensatory outlets. *Repression* consists of the individual's refusing to face the cause of his tension and anxiety; recreation may offer a means of reducing tension which repression has kept from being faced and relieved on a more fundamental level. A final mechanism, *identification*, may involve one's engaging in an activity because one identifies subconsciously with a person whom one loves or admires greatly. Thus a child may express this impulse by engaging in pursuits his parents had enjoyed.

While one may argue that the use of such mechanisms is basically unhealthy and that the desirable course of action is to recognize and solve the neurotic conflicts that cause the basic problem, none the less, through such mechanisms as compensation or sublimation, individuals are often able to reduce tension from conflicts that cannot easily be resolved.

A number of Freud's other theories had important relevance for play and recreation. He advanced the "pleasure principle," which suggested that man's basic desire is that of instinct gratification. Many of the substitute activities which occur because of lack of sexual gratification are thought to arise under the domination of this urge. In his later writings, Freud asserted that man was dominated by a "repetition compulsion," which forces individuals to re-enact earlier experiences without regard to their pleasant or unpleasant nature; this may also be regarded as a force prompting much play behavior.

Freud also hypothesized that the life and death instincts were primary motivating factors in human behavior. Some of his followers have concluded that high-risk activities, such as sky-diving, car-racing, mountain-climbing, or other extremely dangerous sports, represent the influence of the death wish. Freud saw hidden meaning in play involving wit and humor. Although many jokes or play expressions appear to be meaningless or nonsensical, he felt that they invariably contained double meanings and were used to mask or disguise the real impulses and thoughts of the individual. Thus, what is too openly hostile, sexual, or painful to be openly expressed is often stated as a joke. Humor may thus be a veiled form of attack on oneself or others and, when analyzed, may provide an important source of understanding.

Freud's general view of play was that it served as a means of denying and repressing reality; many of the interpretations of play and recreation that are based on his theories are essentially negative. It must be recognized, however, that Freud spent most of his career working with severely neurotic patients, and it was on the basis of his experience with this population that he developed his total theory of personality. It is not surprising that play and recreation from this vantage-point seem replete with negative or self-destructive elements. It is important to stress that play may serve in a number of highly positive ways—as an ego-rewarding activity, a means of obtaining security within group situations, a form of reality-testing, and an outlet for varied emotional drives and creative impulses.

In more recent decades, a number of other writers have examined play and recreation from a psychoanalytical orientation. S. R. Slavson, a leading social work authority, has written extensively on recreation and play.[23] He regards play as an important means of providing balance, satisfying major needs and drives, and compensating for personal inadequacies. Typically, he sees social recreation as meeting major needs for outlets related to the sex drive and dangerous sports as unconsciously satisfying the death wish. He also views recreation as an acceptable means of regressing to more spontaneous and less inhibited behavior. Play, to Slavson, provides escape from the pressures of reality; he stresses its importance in satisfying the need of many individuals for personal contact and meaningful association with others.

Another leading psychoanalytical theorist who has been concerned with play and recreation, particularly in the lives of children, has been Erik Erikson. His view of play is that it is

a function of the ego, an attempt to bring into synchronization the bodily and the social processes of which one is a part . . . the emphasis [being placed] on the ego's need to master the various areas of life.

In Erikson's view, play provides a way of testing fate and causality and a means of breaking away from the confinement of space and time, from sharply defined social reality, and from the compulsions of conscience. In working with disturbed children, Erikson has supported the use of play therapy as a form of creative expression and as a means of gaining security. He comments that "to play it out" is the most natural self-healing measure childhood affords.[24]

Another leading psychiatrist, Karl Menninger, has pioneered in the use of play and recreation in the treatment of the mentally ill and views a well-rounded play life as essential in maintaining a healthy emotional balance. Play, in Menninger's view, provides the opportunity for many miniature victories which compensate for the injuries inflicted by the daily wear and tear of life. Under his direction, a study carried out at the Menninger sanitarium compared the hobby interests in the earlier lives of a number of seriously ill patients with those developed by a group of comparatively well-adjusted ones. It was found that the well-adjusted were found to have pursued nearly twice as many hobbies as the maladjusted. Menninger comments that in his work with psychiatric patients, he has consistently found them deficient in the capacity to play and unable to develop balanced recreational interests and skills.[25]

[23] See S. R. Slavson, *Creative Group Education* (New York: Association Press, 1945), and *Recreation and the Total Personality* (New York: Association Press, 1948).
[24] Erik Erikson, *Childhood and Society* (New York: Norton, 1950), p. 184.
[25] Karl Menninger, *Love Against Hate* (New York: Harcourt, Brace and World, 1942), p. 185.

The concern that has been widely developed in the United States about the value of play for emotional well-being has been strongly supported by a number of leading psychotherapists. Menninger has put it in these terms:

If it were economically possible, beginning tomorrow, to relieve every man in the United States of half his present work requirements (or rather, his work opportunities) without decrease of income, the nation would be in peril. It would be absolutely impossible for the great majority of these people to utilize the suddenly acquired leisure in any psychologically satisfactory way, i.e., in play. *Some* of the energy thus released would undoubtedly be taken up with play, but most of it would be expressed in direct aggressiveness or in some form of self-destructiveness. People would begin fighting, drinking, and killing themselves and one another.[26]

This chapter has reviewed the role of play and recreation with respect to the total development of personality, their place in cognitive development and the learning process, and as part of a total psychoanalytical approach to personal adjustment and mental health. The following chapter analyzes recreation from an entirely different viewpoint—that of the sociologist.

[26] *Ibid.*, p. 184.

14

The Sociology of Leisure

One of the most familiar guides in the professional literature in recreation service has been the dictum that all community residents should be provided with *equal* opportunity for participation in recreation. A number of investigations have disclosed, however, that Americans differ very widely in their recreational interests, depending on their social class affiliations. The term "class" generally refers to the horizontal stratification of a population by means of such factors as family background, occupation, income, community status, group identification (race, religion, or nationality), and education. A leading sociologist, Lloyd Warner, has written:

By class is meant two or more orders of people who are believed to be, and are, accordingly ranked by the members of the community, in socially superior and inferior positions. A class system also provides that children are born into the same status as their parents. A class society distributes rights and privileges, duties and obligations, unequally among its inferior and superior grades. A system of classes, unlike a system of castes, provides by its own values for movement up and down the social ladder . . . in technical terms, social mobility.[1]

In a number of studies carried on over the past several decades, recreation and leisure participation have been analyzed in their relationship to social class, occupational status, occupational prestige, and related variables.

---

[1] W. Lloyd Warner and Paul S. Lunt, *The Social Life of A Modern Community* (New Haven, Conn.: Yale University Press, 1941), p. 82.

Studies of Leisure Participation

A Pioneer Study of Suburban Leisure Patterns. One of the first studies of leisure was carried out by Lundberg, Komarovsky, and McInerney in 1934.[2] It involved an analysis of 2,460 individuals in Westchester County, New York, grouped under the following headings: labor, white collar, professional and executive, housewives, unemployed, high school students, and college students. It was found that each of the groups spent different proportions of its daily time in leisure activities; for example, housewives were reported as having the most leisure (9.2 hours per day) and laborers the least (5.7 per day).

Lundberg and his associates reported that 90 percent or more of the leisure of all classes except students was divided among seven activities: eating, visiting with friends, reading, public entertainment, sports, listening to the radio, and motoring. It was found that each group examined had characteristically different patterns of behavior. For example, housewives tended to spend the bulk of their free time on sociability, while men who had substantial amounts of leisure tended to spend it on visiting, reading, public entertainment, sports, and radio. Within each area of participation there were marked qualitative differences. Thus, all classes spent considerable time in reading, but there were great differences in what they read. Lundberg summed up this point:

Perhaps our most important practical conclusion from the data . . . is that the difference of greatest significance in the leisure of the various groups lies not in the total amounts nor in the distributions of that leisure between different activities . . . [but] in the qualitative variations between the activities which we have been compelled to classify under the same captions.[3]

While this study provided only tentative generalizations about the varying uses of leisure of different groups in the population, it was unique in that it was the first major attempt to study the relationship of leisure and its uses to sociological variables.

Social Class and Leisure Behavior. R. Clyde White carried out a systematic analysis of the relationship between social-class differences and the uses of leisure.[4] White investigated several census tracts in Cuyahoga County, Ohio, using a sampling of families that was representative of income, education, racial composition, occupation, and age distributions

[2] George Lundberg, Mirra Komarovsky, and Mary Alice McInerney, "The Amounts and Uses of Leisure," in Eric Larrabee and Rolf Meyersohn, eds., *Mass Leisure* (Glencoe, Ill.: Free Press, 1958), pp. 193-98.

[3] *Ibid.*, p. 195.

[4] R. Clyde White, "Social Class Differences in the Uses of Leisure," in Larrabee and Meyersohn, *op. cit.*, pp. 198-205.

within the county's population. They were assigned to four major social classes: upper-middle, lower-middle, upper-lower, and lower-lower. White identified nine major categories of leisure use and grouped them under headings related to settings for leisure activity. These were: (1) parks, playgrounds, or other public recreation facilities; (2) group-work agencies financed by Community Chest; (3) church; (4) museums; (5) libraries; (6) home; (7) commercial amusements; and (9) other. He found that the home was the most frequently used setting for leisure involvement, with commercial amusements a close second. There was much less involvement in community-provided facilities, such as parks and playgrounds, and Community Chest agencies. In general, the study found that the lower social classes made greater use of such facilities than the upper classes.

Other distinctions were made between lower- and upper-class uses of such leisure facilities as radios, phonographs, or television, movies, theaters, or taverns. These distinctions grew sharper with age:

It is clear that the tendency to choose leisure activities on the grounds of membership in a particular social class begins in adolescence and becomes more pronounced in maturity. . . . As people get older and settle into the ways of the class to which they belong, they choose leisure activities which are congenial to their class. The growing divergence between the uses of leisure by the middle class and lower class is clear. Class differences are reflected by young people but are not fixed until maturity.[5]

Junior high school age youth of the upper lower class had more leisure than those of the upper middle class, devoting almost twice as much time to radio, television, movies, and sports as did their upper-middle-class counterparts. In contrast, upper-middle-class youth had more remunerative work and home duties. Certain sex differences were also found; boys tended to be more involved in entertainment and sports, and girls had more remunerative work and home duties. This investigation used a more sophisticated sampling method and statistical analysis than the Lundberg study and gave a more positive affirmation of the correlation between social class and leisure choices.

Leisure and Prestige Levels. A third major study of leisure patterns was reported in 1956, by Alfred C. Clarke.[6] Viewing leisure activity as an aspect of social stratification, he focused on the role of leisure as part of the life-styles of urban adult males. Identifying five levels along a continuum of occupational prestige, he selected five groups (each consisting of at least 100 respondents drawn from each prestige level). With them, he explored two basic questions: (1) whether participation in specific activities was significantly linked to occupational prestige levels and (2) if such

5 *Ibid.*, p. 204.
6 Alfred C. Clarke, "Leisure and Occupational Prestige," in Larrabee and Meyersohn, *op cit.*, pp. 205-14.

relationships were found, what kinds of preferences were displayed on each level.

Using a list of 27 activities, he found that men on the highest prestige level were most frequently involved in such activities as attending theaters, concerts, special lectures, or motion pictures, visiting museums or art galleries, playing bridge, reading for pleasure, studying, or community service work. Men on the lowest prestige level were the most frequent participants in such activities as watching television, going to the zoo or to baseball games, spending time in taverns, fishing, playing with their children, driving their cars for pleasure, playing poker, and going to drive-in movies.

Clarke found considerably less involvement in spectator-type and commercial activities than he had expected. The respondents who spent most of their leisure hours as spectators (41.3 percent) were on the middle occupational prestige level; on the highest and lowest levels, only about 25 percent of activities reported were of the spectator type. Involvement in such commercial activities as movies, night clubs, or dance halls was reported by only 3.8 percent on the highest prestige level, compared with 10.1 percent on the lowest. Other major differences were noted (Table 14-1) in the response to such questions as what respondents would do with an additional two hours of free time each day.

TABLE 14-1

Use of Added Free Time	I*	II	III	IV	V
Relax, rest, loaf, sleep	24.7	31.1	26.7	32.9	39.7
Read, study	27.9	18.7	14.8	11.2	12.8
Work at job	19.8	13.8	14.0	8.3	9.1
Work around house	8.5	7.9	12.3	18.4	15.7
Watch television	0.0	1.9	2.5	5.6	6.9

SOURCE: Alfred C. Clarke, in Erie Larrabee and Rolf Meyersohn, eds., *Mass Leisure* (Glencoe, Ill.: Free Press, 1958), p. 212.
* Class I is the highest prestige level; Class V the lowest.

Clarke concluded that while differences in leisure behavior were clearly related to prestige levels, certain new patterns of behavior seemed to be emerging. He speculated that some of the class-connected expectations with respect to the use of leisure might be dying out and called for new and more rigorous research which would take into account such elements as economic, religious, and political affiliations.

Occupation and Leisure Behavior. The emphasis on occupation rather than social status was also the basis of a study by Joel E. Gerstl, which explored the influence on leisure behavior of different occupations of approximately the same prestige level.[7] He selected three upper-middle-class

[7] Joel E. Gerstl, "Leisure, Taste and Occupational Milieu," in Edwin O. Smigel, ed., *Work and Leisure: A Contemporary Social Problem* (New Haven, Conn.: College and University Press, 1963), pp. 146-67.

occupations for his analysis: the independent professional practitioner (dentist), the organization man in the corporate business world (advertising man), and the salaried intellectual (college professor). He examined a sampling of 75 men in these three fields, all of about the same age, in an attempt to explore the links between occupational milieu and non-occupational behavior within leisure.

Distinct differences were found in the amount of leisure time each group had and also in the way business involvement seemed to influence leisure behavior. Professors generally had longer work weeks (averaging 56 to 60 hours), with much work being done at home, while advertising men averaged 45 hours a week, with some of this being done at home, and dentists averaged 40 hours of work a week, rarely doing any of it at home. In terms of sports activity as related to occupation, the subjects reported the involvement shown in Table 14-2.

TABLE 14-2 *Participation in Selected Sports, by Occupation*

Activity	Admen	Dentists	Professors
Golf	32	27	0
Hunting	7	18	1
Fishing	17	28	5
Bowling	8	4	0
Swimming	29	13	10
Boating-sailing	8	2	2
Hiking-walking	13	1	10
Skiing	10	0	3
Tennis	9	6	6
Other activities	18	19	10
Total score	151	118	47

SOURCE: Joel E. Gerstl, in Erwin O. Smigel, ed., *Work and Leisure*. (New Haven, Conn.: College and University Press, 1963), p. 151.

In terms of activities that might be regarded as cultural, such as theater or concert attendance, the professors rated the highest. In each case, specific characteristics of the individual profession were seen as relevant to recreational choices. The dentist's high level of interest in hunting and fishing suggests his need for change from a physically confining, delicate, and tense job. The advertising man's high involvement in golf, swimming, boating, and tennis may well be linked to the need to do business on the green or in the clubhouse. Gerstl concluded that the contrasts between occupations which were within a similar social stratum

indicate that the crucial explanatory factor is that of the occupational milieu— consisting of the setting of the work situation, the nature of the work performed, and the norms derived from occupational reference groups.[8]

[8] *Ibid.*, pp. 161-62.

One might speculate that it is not so much the influence of the occupation upon the leisure pattern of the individual as that the individual has a set of personality traits which in effect propel him both into the choice of a profession and also into the selection of leisure patterns and recreational interests. In any case, Gerstl's study suggested that the factor of life style, as related to specific occupations, was clearly instrumental in affecting leisure behavior, as opposed to the earlier view that social class represented the major influence.

The Decline of Social Class as a Determinant

In recent years, a number of sociologists have suggested that the traditional concept of social class is no longer useful in predicting leisure interests and needs. Max Kaplan suggests that the label of "class" in the social sciences is becoming increasingly dubious. Inexpensive travel, the mass media, and common affluence have brought varied forms of leisure within the psychological and economic reach of almost everyone. He concludes that in no area of American life more than leisure has the idea of social class become an outmoded concept.[9] Instead of class, one's life-style, which presumably is uninfluenced by the traditional yardsticks of income, family background, education, or occupation, is the key factor in determining leisure interests.

Similarly, the sociologist, Nels Anderson, comments that today class lines are less strictly drawn:

all classes attend the same ball games, the same prize fights, the same night clubs, even the same opera. All listen to the radio and view the same television programs. All attend dances or go to the horse races. The difference is in money outlay; how much is spent for the fishing outfit, the automobile, the television set, the seat at the opera or the table at the night club.[10]

To some degree these views may be justified. Certainly there has been a blurring of social class stratification in American society which is reflected in leisure behavior. Although, however, larger numbers of people now have both leisure and a degree of affluence, it would be sheer nonsense to suggest that basically the pastimes of all levels of society are the same and that it is only a matter of where we sit at the opera. There continue to be two important distinctions related to class—one being cultural taste and the second a matter of opportunity.

While it is true that all classes watch television, Clarke's study made it very clear that those in occupations on the lowest prestige level watched far more television than those in the upper level, who were also far more

9 Max Kaplan, *Leisure in America: A Social Inquiry* (New York: Wiley, 1960), p. 92.
    10 Nels Anderson, *Work and Leisure* (New York: Free Press, 1961), p. 34.

selective in their choice of programs. It is also clear that the so-called cultural explosion that followed World War II has not reached and involved all social classes equally. In a comprehensive study of the economics of the performing arts, carried out during the 1960's, Baumol and Bowan found that the audience for the professional performing arts is drawn from an extremely narrow segment of the American population and is remarkably alike in makeup from city to city and from art form to art form. It consists, they write,

of persons who are extraordinarily well educated, whose incomes are very high, who are predominantly in the professions, and who are in their late youth or early middle age. Even if there has been a significant rise in the size of audiences in recent years, it has certainly not yet encompassed the general public. If the sociological base of the audience has in fact expanded, it must surely have been incredibly narrow before the boom got under way.[11]

This report suggests that the view that all tastes have now become homogenized is poorly founded.

Another key factor which influences patterns of leisure involvement is economic. As earlier chapters have indicated, the vast expansion in recreational participation today is heavily dependent on financial capability.

Recreation and the Wealthy

Probably the best way to illustrate the disparity that exists between those who have comfortable incomes and those who live at or below the poverty line is to examine the way in which recreational opportunity becomes available based on one's residence. Increasingly, recreational units or facilities are being included as part of real-estate developments or large apartment buildings. Recreation has become an essential part of the packaging through which housing is offered to the well-to-do. As an example, a major apartment house developer in New York City recently advertised:

PREVIEW TODAY: EXCITING NEW RESIDENCE . . .

"The Happy Life!"

Your fourth dimension in apartment living. A totally new approach to total living, the Wellington '66 premieres all new design and appointments plus a galaxy of *happy-life* innovations: heated indoor swimming pool, saunas, squash courts, health spa, gymnasium, clubrooms, discoteen, arts and crafts, nursery school . . . even a new public school on the premises. . . .

Add these happy-life rewards of total living: on-site shopping, theatre, playgrounds, tennis courts, outdoor adult and kiddy pools, ice-skating rinks, restaurants, cocktail lounges, snack bars.[12]

---

[11] William J. Baumol and William G. Bowen, *Performing Arts: The Economic Dilemma* (New York: The Twentieth Century Fund, 1966), p. 46.
[12] Real estate advertisement, New York *Times*, April 11, 1965, p. R-9.

Home developments today may be based on particular recreational interests. Typically, the New York *Times* reports almost 125 residential developments which were planned with a golf course as the focal point of community life. About 400,000 persons were living in such communities in 1967, and the number was expected to rise to one million by the early 1970's.[13] In other cases, developments of single-family homes include extensive and varied recreational facilities. Inevitably, these are restricted to the wealthy. As an example, the Village of Oak Brook is a privately developed 30-square-mile enclave just west of Chicago where building sites, during the late 1960's, cost between $13,600 and $35,000 and where finished houses were priced between $50,000 and $250,000. Oak Brook includes three residential subdivisions built around an 800-acre sports center, an 1,800-acre forest preserve, an industrial park, a hotel, an office plaza, and a shopping center. The facilities include

a polo club and 12 polo fields, soccer fields, a private air strip that is the home of a glider soaring club, a golf course, a riding academy and riding trails with stables for 300 horses, skeet shooting, upland game-hunting areas and a fox-hunting preserve. . . . Inside the village limits also are another private golf club, a public course and a lake for canoeing, sailing and skating.[14]

Even in cities today, we are seeing increasing numbers of so-called urban country clubs, which offer swimming, clubhouses, basketball, paddleball, restaurants, saunas, lounge areas, and similar facilities to middle-class families.

There are many other examples of how the rich can meet their recreation needs in diversified and varied ways. There are a number of community flying clubs, in which members join together to provide share-the-cost weekends or longer trips throughout the United States and occasionally to Europe and South America. In many cases, such clubs operate their own planes and provide varied excursions throughout the year. Among the very rich, when ski resorts become overcrowded, the solution is to buy your own mountain and develop your own ski center, with members of private associations building their own homes and maintaining exclusive and tightly closed social groups. The sport of polo, while growing steadily in popularity, continues to involve a small, select group. Polo is a rich man's sport; the cost of equipment, transportation, ponies, and insurance for tournament players may run as high as $40,000 a year. Squash raquets is another example of a sport which is enjoyed chiefly by successful businessmen and professionals, many of whom learned it in college. Exclusive private childrens' dancing classes are found in all large cities today. They are highly

---

[13] Franklin Whitehouse, "Thousands Drive Home to Fairway," New York *Times*, October 22, 1967, p. R-1.
[14] William Robbins, "Houses in a Suburb of Chicago Offering Originality at a Price," New York *Times*, January 9, 1966, p. R-1.

class-oriented, with admission by invitation only. Waiting lists are long, with some parents putting their children's names on them at birth. These private dancing classes are the first stage of a process of social inbreeding and exclusive social participation that will continue through life.

The degree to which economic ability determines the use of leisure is best illustrated by a study carried out by the Outdoor Recreation Resources Review Commission. Based on an extensive sampling of the overall population over the age of twelve, the results shown in Table 14-3 were found. Generally, those with higher family incomes participate in all activities much more fully than those with less income. The difference is more marked in activities such as boating, camping, and horseback riding, which require mobility, equipment, or expense, than in the case of walking for pleasure or fishing, which may be carried on at almost no expense. Even here, however, it is likely that the *nature* of participation will be quite different. The rich man is likely to do his fishing for trout in the Rockies or salmon in Canada or for big-game fish from a cabin cruiser in the Caribbean, while the poor man may use a handline in a local pond or from the banks of a semi-polluted local stream.

TABLE 14-3 *Percentage of Population Taking Part in Specific Activities, Based on Income Levels*

Family Income	Boating	Camping	Horseback Riding	Walking for Pleasure	Fishing
Under 1,500	4	3	2	19	24
1,500–2,999	0	4	3	28	21
3,000–4,499	19	6	4	32	28
4,500–5,999	24	8	6	36	32
6,000–7,999	28	10	7	37	32
8,000–9,999	33	13	7	37	31
10,000–14,999	41	18	11	37	39
15,000 and up	36	10	13	46	27

SOURCE: *Outdoor Recreation for America: Report to the President and to Congress of the Outdoor Recreation Resources Review Commission,* Vol. 1 (Washington, D.C.: U.S. Government Printing Office, 1962), pp. 37–38.

Similarly, education affects participation sharply. In a study of a broad sampling of adults, the O.R.R.R.C. Report found that those with a college education engaged in such outdoor recreation activities as playing games, swimming, or sightseeing far more frequently than those with less education. With respect to occupation, it was found that farm workers, laborers, service workers, and proprietors engaged in outdoor recreation the least, while professionals, technical, clerical, and white-collar workers engaged the most.

Over all, there continue to be marked differences among the American people, in terms of leisure participation, based on certain social factors, which, taken as a whole, unmistakably constitute social class affiliation. The well-educated, affluent, suburban professional or executive individual engages in a greater variety of activities, far more frequently, than his less well-educated, poorer, urban-dwelling counterpart. Anderson's conclusion that poor people attend the same ball games, prize fights, night clubs, opera, or horse races as the rich but simply have cheaper seats is difficult to accept.

No sociological study has focused specifically on the use of leisure by poor people. A number of studies which have cut across class lines have, however, touched on this concern. During the Depression of the 1930's, the Welfare Council of New York City carried out a major investigation of three aspects of the life of young people: employment, education, and leisure.[15] Covering a wide range of socioeconomic classes and the major religious, ethnic, and national groups in the city, the report pointed out that, while there was abundant diversion in the city for those who could pay their way, for the great mass of young people recreation had to come primarily through public provision if it was to come at all. As it examined the leisure activities of city youth under four major headings (athletics, cultural activities, arts and crafts, and social activities and pastimes), the study concluded that there was an extremely low rate of participation in cultural activities involving museums, art galleries, or concerts or even in other more general forms of organized recreation activity. This was particularly true of young people on the lower end of the socioeconomic scale, who appeared to make extremely limited and passive use of their leisure time.

In a landmark study of the impact of social class on adolescent life, *Elmtown's Youth*, August Hollingshead devoted two chapters to participation by teen-agers in both organized and unstructured leisure activities. He showed in considerable detail how social class affiliation was closely connected to membership in clubs and youth organizations, extracurricular school activities, attending various social functions in the town, and such tabooed pleasures as drinking, gambling, smoking, and sexual activity. Lower-class youth tended to be excluded from many organizations, were financially unable to take part in many forms of commercial opportunity, and sought out the less-approved forms of pleasure-seeking. For them, it was the search for pleasure, Hollingshead noted, that led to delinquency charges. He wrote:

The nightly search for excitement by speeding, shooting firearms along the river roads, drinking, picking up girls, gambling, with now and again a fight, brings many of these young people face-to-face with the law. Pleasure-bent

15 Nettie P. McGill and Ellen N. Matthews, *The Youth of New York City* (New York: Macmillan, 1940).

youths violate the mores, if not the law, almost every night, but they are not overly interested in the consequences of their acts. . . . In almost every one of these cases [delinquency convictions] the delinquent behavior is a concomitant of clique activity or sex play.[16]

In a more recent study, Herbert Gans analyzed a lower-class Italian-American population in Boston. Much of his report is concerned with the out-of-school, nonwork activity of teen-agers. Describing these lower-class urban youth, Gans comments that the West End adolescent tends to be alive only with his friends, where the style of life is one of "action-seeking"; in other settings he is likely to be lethargic and sullen, seeking to avoid contact with adults. Adolescent peer-group life alternates between killing time and episodic searching for action.

"Action" generates a state of quasi-hypnotic excitement which enables the individual to feel that he is in control, both of his own drives and of the environment. Also, it allows him to forget that he is living in a routine-seeking world, where "they," that is, the routine-seeking adults, make and enforce most of the rules. As previously noted, this state may be achieved through a card game, an athletic contest, a fight, a sexual adventure, or through an attack on the adult world (in the form of petty mischief, minor thefts, vandalism, etc.)[17]

Gans takes the position that much of the action-seeking behavior of lower-class youth is similar to that of middle-class youth. However, the lower-class teen-agers and young adults that Gans observed tended to meet on street corners, in tenement hallways, or in and around the small soda shops that dotted the neighborhood. Those who came under the influence of the church, the school, and the settlement house appeared to accept this as symbolic of a "routine-seeking" and upward-mobile way of life. Those who resisted this kind of affiliation were apparently content to remain, in Whyte's phrase, "street-corner boys." Thus, even in this relatively homogeneous population, the nature of each individual's leisure involvement was symbolic of his class aspiration.

Recreation and Race

Another important area of sociological investigation with respect to leisure has to do with racial identification. As far back as the 1920's, Lehman and Witty examined children in elementary and junior and senior high schools and came to the conclusion that Negro children tended to participate much more actively in social forms of play than white children.

---

[16] August B. Hollingshead, *Elmtown's Youth: The Impact of Social Class for Adolescents* (New York: Wiley, 1949, 1961), p. 410.

[17] Herbert J. Gans, *The Urban Villagers: Group and Class in the Life of Italian-Americans* (New York: Free Press, 1962), p. 65.

They questioned whether this "excessive sociability" was desirable if it meant that other areas of development were being neglected. They speculated about the psychological meaning of play by Negro children, suggesting that it might serve as a form of compensation:

Although Negro children are relatively unsuccessful in academic endeavor, they play school more frequently than do white children. It appears likely that Negro children engage in playing school more frequently than white children because this activity symbolizes knowledge, power and prestige which they are unable to achieve in the world of actuality.[18]

In the New York City Welfare Council study of youth cited earlier, a contrast was drawn between the leisure participation of Negroes and whites. It was found that the recreational participation of Negro youth in the city tended to be extremely limited, particularly in sports and certain forms of cultural activities, when compared with whites. The study pointed out that some of the differences in participation could be:

accounted for by segregation and by the social prejudice when it prevents the Negro from relying on amusements and recreations supplied primarily by and for the white race. This situation, on the other hand, probably accounts also for ways in which his use of leisure is superior to that of the white youth. In some very important respects, notably in social activities, both Negro men and Negro women seem to enjoy a richer, fuller leisure than white men and women.[19]

The Swedish sociologist, Gunnar Myrdal, in his landmark study of the Negro in American Life, *The American Dilemma*,[20] commented at length about the inadequate provision of recreation programs and services for blacks in American communities and about patterns of segregation which were enforced by law in the southern and border states, and by social custom in the north. Documenting the inadequacy of facilities and play programs under leadership in city after city, Myrdal reported that Negroes everywhere expressed to him their concern about the "great damage" done to black youth by the lack of recreational facilities and programs (see page 388). As a consequence, Myrdal found that it had become necessary for the urban Negro of the 1930's and early 1940's to find much of his recreation in his own social and athletic clubs, churches, and lodges—on a racially segregated basis, of course.

Another striking analysis of the leisure of Negroes in America was provided by E. Franklin Frazier, in *Black Bourgeosie*. This work described

18 Harvey C. Lehman and Paul A. Witty, *The Psychology of Play Activities* (New York: A. S. Barnes, 1927), p. 161.
19 McGill and Matthews, *op. cit.*, p. 262.
20 Gunnar Myrdal, *The American Dilemma* (New York: Harper and Row, 1944, 1962), pp. 346-47, 1274-75.

middle-class Negro society in America as involved in an intense struggle for status, in which the social activities of business and professional people represented both a means of differentiating middle-class Negroes from the mass of poorer blacks and also of compensating for their exclusion from white society. Frazier saw the emphasis on play among many blacks as a way of avoiding reality:

The exclusion of middle-class Negroes from participation in the general life of the American community has affected their entire outlook on life. It has meant that whites did not take Negroes seriously; that whites did not regard the activities of Negroes as of any real consequence in American life. It has tended to encourage a spirit of irresponsibility or an attitude of "play" or make-believe among them. Consequently, Negroes have "played" at conducting their schools, at running their businesses, and at practicing their professions.[21]

Frazier believed that since prejudice against the Negro made it so difficult for him to succeed in any area of life, he fictionalized his efforts; playing became the one activity which he could take seriously. Frazier indicted Negro "society" for its excessive preoccupation with sports, gambling, and the numbers racket and for its self-deceiving attempts to exaggerate its own social status. Long before the "black is beautiful" movement of the late 1960's, Frazier charged that many American Negroes were ashamed of their racial origins, saw blackness as a source of self-contempt, and regarded Africans and African culture condescendingly. For many, "play" represented an escape from frustration:

the majority of the black bourgeoisie who seek an escape from their frustrations . . . have found it in magic or chance, and in sex and alcohol. Excessive drinking and sex seem to provide a means for narcotizing the middle-class Negro against a frustrating existence. A "social" function is hardly ever considered a success unless a goodly number of the participants "pass out." But gambling, especially poker, which has become an obsession among many middle-class Negroes, offers the chief escape into delusion. Among the black bourgeoisie it is not simply a device for winning money. It appears to be a magical device for enhancing their self-esteem through overcoming fate.[22]

Frazier concluded that American middle-class Negroes, despite their relative degree of success, were still beset by feelings of insecurity, frustration, and guilt; as a consequence, the "free and easy" life they appeared to lead was a mask for an unhappy existence. The prophetic nature of his writing is illustrated by the emphasis given recently to the development of black cultural programs among Negro organizations in the United States. In an effort to overcome the sense of inferiority that many American

[21] E. Franklin Frazier, *Black Bourgeoisie* (New York: Collier Books, 1957, 1962), p. 169.
[22] *Ibid.*, p. 190.

Negroes have attached to their blackness, organizations throughout the country have stressed the need for programs of Afro-American music, dance, and culture and for "black studies" in schools and colleges.

A number of recent studies have examined differences between blacks and whites with respect to leisure activities. A study of consumer expenditures carried out by the Wharton School of Finance in the early 1950's showed marked differences between Negro and white families with respect to spending on such items as admissions, radio, television, and musical instruments.[23] The 1962 Report of the Outdoor Recreation Resources Review Commission indicated that Negroes engaged in outdoor recreation activities far less frequently than whites.[24]

In 1967, Kraus studied participation in public recreation programs in selected urban and suburban communities, in the New York metropolitan area. He found that the involvements of Negro and white residents varied markedly in such activities as sports, cultural programs and activities for specific age groups.[25] Another study, reported by Short and Strodtbeck in 1965, examined the leisure behavior of several hundred Negro and white youthful gang members in Chicago.[26] This report found distinctly different patterns of involvement on the basis of race. Negro gang members tended to be more frequently involved in antisocial activities related to physical violence or sexual activity. On the other hand, white gang members were reported to be more frequently involved in homosexual behavior, the use of alcohol and hard narcotics, gambling, auto theft, and other kinds of delinquent acts. This study is particularly interesting because it includes both antisocial behaviors which are part of the leisure activity of lower-class gang youth and many socially acceptable activities, such as baby-sitting, track and field, work, Ping Pong, baseball, football, and bowling.

These studies suggest that while the concept of social class may no longer be as applicable to the study of leisure interests and needs as in the past, certain social factors continue to influence patterns of participation. Economics, education, residence, and cultural background play an important role in determining tastes and interests and the kinds of program services that are needed.

Changing Work Attitudes in American Society

A final area of sociological investigation has to do with changing work attitudes and the implications of these changes for the provision of leisure services. Traditionally, work has been seen as a central life interest of

---

[23] Kaplan, *op. cit.*, pp. 95-97.
[24] *Outdoor Recreation for America, op. cit.*, p. 28.
[25] Richard Kraus, *Public Recreation and the Negro* (New York: Center for Urban Education, 1968), pp. 36-53.
[26] James F. Short, Jr., and Fred L. Strodtbeck, *Group Process and Gang Delinquency* (Chicago: University of Chicago Press, 1965), pp. 36-53.

people and as the cornerstone around which one's life is built. Dubin writes:

it is a commonplace to note that work has long been considered a central life interest for adults in most societies, and certainly in the Western world. Indeed, the capitalist system itself is asserted to rest on the moral and religious justification that the Reformation gave to work.[27]

Santayana suggested that there have been three basic motivations for work: want (economic need), ambition (the drive for power, or to get ahead), and the love of occupation (intrinsic satisfaction in one's craftsmanship).[28] Dumazedier points out that work is a unique type of human experience, since "it puts man in rapport with materials, with tools and also with other men. Through work he acquires social status."[29] Clearly, work in the industrialized Western world has provided not only financial reward but also a sense of self-respect. In Soviet society, the worker has actually been made a national hero in the interest of promoting production. Berger writes:

The muscled worker raising his sledge-hammer above the rubble, the Stakhanovite overproducing his quota, the stocky, fresh-complexioned girl on the tractor, are proper topics for heroic treatment and glorious characterization. The collectivized Horatio Alger morality of the Soviet rhetoric confers heroic status on those types of individuals and roles that actually represent the collective purposes of the state.[30]

There has been a growing awareness, however, that this tradition of work being at the moral and religious core of life is no longer widely accepted. Much work today is of a highly specialized assembly-line nature; the individual is merely a cog in a machine and has little opportunity to use individual judgment or initiative. Instead of being responsible for turning out an entire product, as in the case of the old-time craftsman, the modern industrial worker rarely has a sense of total creation or individual responsibility for performance.

Anderson comments on "declining worker interest in the job," writing that "it is generally recognized that most workers who sell their time seem to have little interest in the job or in the enterprise."[31] Dubin supports this view, pointing out that an investigation of industrial workers revealed that the majority did not regard their job and work situations as central life

[27] Robert Dubin, "Industrial Workers' Worlds," in Larrabee and Meyersohn, op. cit., p. 215.
[28] See Anderson, op. cit., p. 26.
[29] Ibid., p. 26.
[30] Bennett Berger, "The Sociology of Leisure: Some Suggestions," in Smigel, op. cit., p. 32.
[31] Anderson, op. cit., p. xiii.

interests and found their preferred associations and major areas of interest outside of employment. Dubin concludes:

The factory and factory work as sources of personal satisfaction, pride, satisfying human associations, perhaps even of pleasure in expressing what Veblen called the "instinct of workmanship" seem clearly subordinated in the American scene.[32]

The trend away from work as a source of emotional and social satisfactions does not mean that it is no longer important for the worker. Obviously, he needs it for sustenance. Anderson writes:

The worker sells his time and skill, a business transaction; the transaction complete, at quitting time he puts work out of mind. He is no longer the slave of a routine job, but has worked out a sensible relationship with it. He is not bored with his job; he has come to terms with it. . . . He will give an honest day's work.[33]

For many workers the job continues to fill what would otherwise be a void in life. Reisman comments that it is not so much the work itself as simply having a job. It is the job and the "punctuations of life" that it provides that is an essential component of regular employment.[34] In a society where most men work, the job furnishes a metronome-like capacity to help regulate the individual's routine of waking and sleeping, time on and time off, life on and life off the job. Berger poses the issue raised by changed attitudes toward work:

As work loses its power to command the moral identifications and loyalties of men, as men look away from work to find moral experience, society loses an important source of normative integration. . . . In such a situation we may expect . . . the transfer of functions formerly performed by the institutions of work to the "leisure institutions," and this, it seems to me, is precisely the significance of the enormous increase in attention which the problem of leisure has received in recent years.[35]

Exactly how is this problem to be met? One alternative might be to restructure the nature of work so it would be less routine and more challenging. Reisman comments, however, that industrial engineers are not really interested in people and basically would rather replace them in order to make the job more automatic, simple, and predictable than change the nature of the job to suit the needs of people.[36]

[32] Dubin, *op. cit.*, p. 220.
[33] Anderson, *op. cit.*, p. xiii.
[34] David Reisman, "Leisure and Work in Post-Industrial Society," in Larrabee and Meyersohn, *op. cit.*, p. 370.
[35] Berger, *op. cit.*, p. 35.
[36] Reisman, *op. cit.*, p. 372.

This final aspect of the sociology of leisure suggests that it is becoming increasingly necessary for the American people to confront the problem of increased leisure, first, because of the changed nature of work and the necessity to provide new challenges and moral values in nonwork and, second, simply because work continues to decline over the life span of each new generation.

This chapter has explored the implications of leisure, particularly with reference to social class, economic status, and subcultural affiliation. The following chapters deal with the precise nature of leisure and its uses in America today and with the personal and social values to be derived from recreation.

Plate 9. Outstanding facilities for community recreation: the Seattle World's Fair left that city this huge auditorium for cultural events and a fine sports arena; Hackney Marsh, an extensive London playfield constructed with World War II bomb rubble.

Plate 10. Outdoor recreation—particularly camping and boating—have become tremendously popular. Here, the two are combined on a TVA lake. Closer to home, residents of Levittown, N.Y., have built a network of night-lighted swimming pools supported by their own dues, rather than public taxes.

Plate 11. In contrast, summer play opportunities in urban slums are sharply limited. Here, children wade in a curbside puddle, while adults play cards on the sidewalk. In another poor neighborhood, children have painted their own game areas on the pavement.

Plate 12. Efforts are being made to upgrade recreation for the disadvantaged. Here, portable play equipment is set up on a slum street, and city youngsters visit a state park. Mrs. Lyndon Johnson dedicates a Washington playground with equipment contributed by the Mexican government, and recreation and park authorities confer to improve urban park facilities.

From Chase Ltd., Washington.

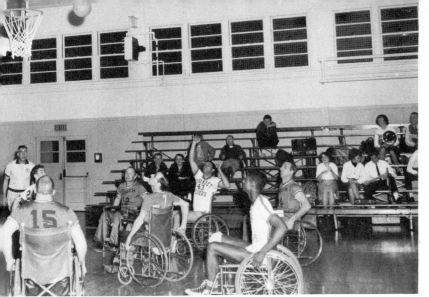

Plate 13. New programs and facilities are provided for the ill and disabled. A nature trail for the blind has been designed by the National Park Service. Mentally retarded and neurologically impaired children are entertained. "Wheelchair basketball" pits paraplegic veterans against a team of nonhandicapped servicemen.

Plate 14. Among the most popular park facilities throughout the world are zoological gardens. Otters and elk are on display at the Alpenzoo in Innsbruck, Austria, while polar bears enjoy a natural setting in the Milwaukee Zoo.

Plate 15. Man both destroys and protects nature. Millions of fish are shown killed by pesticides in a Texas lake, contrasting with the work of the Fish and Wildlife Service in propagating and protecting wildfowl.

Plate 16. Technology and overcrowding are vividly illustrated here. Japanese enthusiasts use a complex aquatic center, a ski slope with a plastic-brush slope, and a three-tiered golf driving range. Below, anglers struggle to keep lines untangled on the first day of the fishing season.

15

The Economics of Leisure:
Its Amounts and Uses

Over the past several decades, there have been two opposing viewpoints with respect to the meaning of leisure in modern society. One group of social critics have seen the expansion of free time as providing the potential for a great new era of individual and community cultural development. This viewpoint was expressed by W. Whitney Griswold, then President of Yale University:

Now we stand on the threshold of an age that will bring leisure to all of us, more leisure than all the aristocracies of history, all the patrons of art, all the captains of industry and kings of enterprise ever had at their disposal. . . . What shall we do with this great opportunity? In the answers that we give to this question the fate of our American civilization will unfold.[1]

On the other hand, there has been apprehension that leisure represented a great danger to the American society. Historically, it was expected that the laboring classes would misuse their free time in riotous dissipation. During the first half of the nineteenth century, "the fourteen-hour day" and the "wholesome discipline of factory life" were defended by preachers and employer alike as a deterrent to drunken leisure among urban workers, a view not entirely rejected by organized labor itself.[2] In more recent times, there has been the fear that people would grow slothful and passive in their

[1] A. Whitney Griswold, *Life*, December 28, 1959.
[2] Harold L. Wilensky, "The Impact of Economic Growth on Free Time," in Erwin O. Smigel, ed., *Work and Leisure: A Contemporary Social Problem* (New Haven, Conn.: College and University Press, 1963), p. 130.

uses of free time and would seek the cheapest and most tawdry kinds of amusement. Boredom, alienation, and the use of drugs, alcohol, and sex as time killers have all been seen as dangers of increased leisure.

What are the actual statistics and dimensions of today's leisure? How is free time used in American society? This chapter seeks to answer these questions on the basis of recent research findings.

The Availability of Leisure Today

As earlier chapters have shown, the peak of free time in Europe was reached during the Middle Ages, when there were great numbers of church-decreed holidays in European countries, resulting in about 160 workless days per year. Dumazedier points out that there was much opposition on the part of both working people and employers to holidays imposed by the church to promote the carrying out of spiritual obligations. In one of La Fontaine's fables, the poor man decries such holidays, saying that "Monsieur le Curé is always burdening us with a sermon on some new saint" to promote religion.[3] Thus these holidays were viewed not so much as opportunities for leisure as simply "workless" or "unemployed" days.

As religious authority declined in Europe and the Industrial Revolution accelerated, the workday increased to as much as 13 to 14 hours a day, six days a week. The number of holidays was radically slashed. During the early decades of the nineteenth century, work was at its height and leisure at a minimum. Progressive legislation and labor contracts gradually reduced the length of the work week in Europe and the United States. Here, the sharpest reduction of average weekly hours occurred between 1900 and 1930, when they declined from 67 to 55 for farm workers and from 56 to 43 for those in industry. The passage of the Fair Labor Standards Act in 1938 set 40 hours a week as a desirable standard for most American industrial workers. During the 1940's and 1950's, many major industries and business adopted a 37.5- or 35-hour work-week as standard practice. In some recent labor contracts, even more striking reductions of the work week have been achieved. As an example, the International Brotherhood of Electrical Workers in New York City achieved a pioneering contract in 1962 which set the basic work week for electrical construction workers at 25 hours a week.

Recently, there has been comparatively little change in the average hours worked by full-time industrial workers. Through the 1960's, weekly hours on the job remained high because of the current level of prosperity with attractive premium payments for overtime. Typically, over 400,000 General Motors employees worked an average of 42.6 hours a week in the mid-1960's. Similarly, in 1966, the average factory work week was 41.6

---

[3] Joffre Dumazedier, *Toward a Society of Leisure* (New York: Free Press, 1962, 1967), p. 34.

hours, its highest point since World War II. Indeed, the work week is actually increasing for many workers, particularly professional, technical, and managerial employees. In part, this is the result of overtime work. Statistics compiled in the middle 1960's indicated that approximately 11 million factory and white-collar workers worked substantial amounts of overtime hours.

In addition, there is a substantial amount of moonlighting, or dual job-holding, in the United States. During the middle 1960's, this practice was carried on by an estimated 5.7 percent of the labor force, (about 3.9 million employees), mostly in factory work, the retail trades, business services, home and equipment services, and repair industries. In addition, 1.6 million employed individuals are reported to be self-employed in second jobs. Workers holding two or more jobs average about 53 working hours each week.

Thus, it would be false to suggest that the workweek is continuing to decline at as rapid a rate as it did during the early decades of the century. Instead, increased leisure is being provided as a consequence of rapidly expanding holidays and vacation periods and liberal retirement programs.

Holidays and Vacations

In their investigation of Middletown, U.S.A., the Lynds commented on the rarity of time off from work during the latter years of the nineteenth century:

"Vacations in 1890?" echoed one substantial citizen. "Why, the word wasn't in the dictionary!" "Executives of the 1890 period never took a vacation," said another man of a type common in Middletown thirty-five years ago, who used to announce proudly that they had "not missed a day's work in twenty years."[4]

By the 1920's, two-week summer vacations with pay had become increasingly common among middle-class families but were still quite rare for working people. In 1940, only about one-quarter of all union members, and a similar proportion of all employees, received annual vacations with pay; for most of these, the maximum vacation period was only one week. The average number of paid holidays was about two per year, although many workers received additional holidays without pay. Since World War II, paid holidays and vacations have greatly increased. The number of paid holidays now include six nationally recognized days (New Year's Day, Memorial Day, Independence Day, Labor Day, Thanksgiving, and Christmas) and frequently others that are regionally recognized. Henle writes:

[4] Robert S. Lynd and Helen M. Lynd, *Middletown* (New York: Harcourt, Brace, 1929), p. 261.

Estimates for the economy as a whole, for the period 1940–1960 show that there has been on the average, an increase of 155 hours of leisure time annually for the full-time employee, thus providing the equivalent of almost 4 weeks of leisure for a person on a standard 40-hour week . . . this increase in leisure has been almost equally divided between a drop in the average workweek and an increase in paid vacations and paid holidays . . . in the most recent period, however, it is clear that a far greater proportion of the advances in leisure time has come in the form of paid vacation and holidays.[5]

Generally, the four-week vacation for longer-service employees came into common practice during the mid-1960's. In the automobile industry, for example, it was granted as an automatic job benefit for employees with fifteen years of service. In a number of other industries, five-week vacations are automatic after twenty years of service. In the steel industry, collective bargaining has achieved thirteen-week vacations every five years for older-service employees. Similar benefits were provided for the aluminum and can industries in 1968.

In addition, a substantial number of added holidays are being provided through new industry-union contracts and legislative action, frequently designed to provide extended weekends. In a number of industries, the newest holiday is the Friday after Thanksgiving or the day before Christmas or New Year's; in other industries, each employee is given a holiday on his birthday, taken as part of a three-day weekend.

In 1968, Congress passed a bill designed to create four permanent three-day weekends, by shifting Washington's Birthday, Memorial Day, Veteran's Day, and Columbus Day to specified Mondays. While the bill was compulsory only for Federal employees, it is widely expected that many other governmental and industrial agencies will follow suit.

Another dramatic source of increased leisure has come about for older persons as a result of two factors—longer age spans and improved employee retirement programs and benefits. Typically, life expectancy for male children rose from 48 years for those born in 1900 to 66.6 for those born in 1960. In addition, industrial retirement benefits, pension plans, and Social Security programs have made earlier retirement feasible. A 1963 report to the office of Manpower, Automation and Training of the U.S. Department of Labor pointed out that there had been a dramatic change in the work-life patterns of older men. In 1940, only 70 out of 1,000 men who were 64 years of age left the labor force within a year. By 1953, the figure was 83, and by 1960, it had jumped to 234, a fourfold increase over the twenty-year span. Increasingly, major union contracts of municipal employees are now providing improved retirement benefits. Typically, in 1968 New York City signed a pact with 120,000 nonuniformed municipal employees (in-

[5] Peter Henle, "The Quiet Revolution in Leisure Time," in *Occupational Outlook Quarterly* (Washington, D.C.: U.S. Department of Labor, U.S. Government Printing Office, May, 1965), p. 6.

cluding hospital, welfare, and clerical workers) providing a 25-50 formula, under which workers with 25 years of service may retire at the age of 55 with a pension equivalent to 50 percent of their most recent salary. With life expectancy continuing to rise, substantial numbers of early retirees are now able to look forward to 15, 20, or 25 years of nonwork life.

It would be easy to conclude that leisure is indeed becoming a vast new resource, easily available to all. However, the availability of leisure is sharply differentiated by sex, social class, and occupation, among other factors.

For example, sociologists have concluded that women are at a disadvantage compared with men, with respect to work and leisure—working women because they are burdened with both paid and unpaid (home-centered) responsibilities and nonworking women because their home labors are generally underestimated or undervalued and because their existence is generally much more drab and limited than that of men. A fourteen-nation study of 25,000 men and women carried out in 1967 by the International Social Council, an agency of UNESCO, indicated, for example, that working mothers had an average of only 2.8 hours of free time per day, compared with 4.1 for working fathers.

Another serious discrepancy, in terms of availability of leisure, affects many in the upper socioeconomic brackets—particularly those employed as professionals, business executives, and managers and the self-employed. Traditionally, upper-class persons were regarded as members of the leisure class. Today it is apparent that members of this social stratum have actually less discretionary time than those in white-collar or blue-collar areas of employment. Professionals, executives, officials and other civil servants, and the self-employed have generally gained little and in some fields have actually lost in the amount of leisure available to them. Professionals generally work more total hours in their lifetimes than blue-collar workers; Wilensky writes that the daily or weekly averages of time put in on the job obscure important inequalities in the distribution of leisure:

With economic growth the upper strata have probably lost leisure. Professionals, executives, officials and proprietors have long workweeks, year-round employment. Their longer vacations and shorter worklives (delayed entry and often earlier retirement) do not offset this edge in working hours. Although life-time leisure decreases with increased status, the picture is one of bunched, predictable leisure for elites whose worklives are shorter; and intermittent, unpredictable, unstable leisure for the masses, whose worklives are longer.[6]

Wilensky concludes that, considering both those occupations which *necessitate* long hours (proprietors, some young skilled workers, and foremen) and those in which men *choose* to work hard (professors, lawyers),

[6] Wilensky, *op. cit.*, p. 113.

there appears to be a slowly increasing minority of the male urban labor force working 55 hours a week or more.

De Grazia points out that in addition to these factors, those who hold executive or professional positions tend also to be community leaders, accepting numerous civic and organizational responsibilities which consume their time. In addition, they spend large amounts of time in traveling to and from work, on business travel, or on business entertainment; these factors, too, reduce their over-all free time. In contrast, the work of those on the lower levels of employment tends to be rigidly organized by union contracts, personnel policies, and guaranteed holidays and retirement plans which thrust leisure upon them without permitting options for extending work hours or postponing the retirement age. Wilensky points out that more than half the labor force is moving toward such less free occupations.

In addition, there are substantial numbers of people who have gained leisure in involuntary ways. These people "condemned" to leisure include the chronically unemployed, the intermittently unemployed, and the involuntarily retired. For many persons, retirement becomes a forced matter because of educational or occupational obsolescence, compulsory age retirement, or age discrimination in hiring. Unemployment tends to be concentrated among low-status service workers and unskilled or semiskilled manual workers in construction, manufacturing, and trade. The unemployed or underemployed are disproportionately very young, elderly, nonwhite, and foreign-born. Typically, in a year in which the national rate of unemployment averaged only 4 percent, at least 15 percent of the working force experienced one or more periods of unemployment.

The Leisure "Explosion"—Divergent Views. Some social analysts have concluded that the widely acclaimed growth in leisure has been exaggerated. Wilensky comments that much of the modern gain in free time is illusory and that most leisure is forced leisure.[7] Pointing out the extent to which people use their free time today in moonlighting, work-connected responsibilities, community involvements, and home chores, De Grazia concludes that "The great and touted gains in free time since the 1850's . . . are largely myth."[8]

While it is true that many older persons who have retired from work have done so unwillingly or that many industrial workers would be willing to work longer hours, the fact is they cannot. They have free time; it is essentially unobligated and must be regarded as leisure. Similarly, De Grazia's arguments are based on the classical concept of leisure described earlier, which regards it as a way of life, rather than as free time. The fact that members of the business and intellectual elite tend to assume roles in their nonwork time as officers or board members of community agencies

[7] *Ibid.*, pp. 131-32.
[8] Sebastian de Grazia, *Of Time, Work and Leisure* (New York: Doubleday-Anchor, Twentieth Century Fund, 1962), p. 79.

does not necessarily mean that this is time withdrawn from leisure. Such individuals accept responsibilities of this kind voluntarily; many gain pleasure and satisfaction from making contributions to community welfare, from the exercise of power, and the involvement with others that are part of the task. It might be argued that such voluntarily undertaken service activities represent a higher and more purposeful form of leisure than watching a baseball game on television or dozing in a hammock—which would clearly be accepted by most authorities as typical uses of leisure.

One must conclude that available leisure in the United States has grown tremendously over the past century as a consequence of all the factors which have been cited here.

Patterns of Leisure Availability

Leisure is available today in widely varying amounts and degrees, according to such factors as one's age, social status, and occupation. Typically, it is most often found in the evenings and on weekends for working people or those attending school. Major blocs of leisure come during special holidays during the year, which may provide several consecutive days of nonwork time or during vacations which may extend to several weeks of free time. There is bunching, too, in the amount of leisure available within one's lifetime. Obviously, there is a great deal of free time for young children and retired persons and much less during the working years of life.

Southern California Analysis of Leisure. This study provides one of the most detailed analyses of leisure, with its social and economic implications and projections for the future, to have been carried out in any region of the United States.[9] Covering fifteen counties with a present population of 12.6 million and the expectation of 19 million residents by 1985, the report's conclusions were based on a large sampling of all ages and social classes, throughout the year. It determined that approximately 110 billion hours were available to all the residents of southern California during the course of a year. These hours were used in the following ways:[10]

Time-Use for All Groups	Percent
Sleeping, eating, and personal care	47
Leisure	25
Work and related travel	12
Housework and child care	9
School and study	5
Other unpaid productive activities	2

[9] *The Challenge of Leisure: A Southern California Case Study* (Claremont: Southern California Research Council, Pomona College, 1967).

[10] *Ibid.*, pp. 15-17.

Each of these categories, however, varies greatly according to the age, sex, or social role of individual residents. Thus, "school and study" would obviously be much higher than 5 percent for young people and much lower for aging persons. Employed southern Californians, according to the state's Department of Industrial Relations, were found to work about 40.5 hours each week for pay. If part-time employees were excluded from this group, however, it was found that the typical full-time employee works about 46 hours a week.

The study found that southern Californians spend at least three-quarters of their time engaging in activities which are either necessary for existence or productive of goods and services. For most adults, the total time taken by these activities (including sleep) amounts to about 18 to 20 hours a day. The remaining time was defined in the study as "leisure." It occupies between 25 to 50 hours per week for most adults and between 50 and 70 hours per week for the young and the old. Most fully employed adults enjoy less than 30 hours of leisure each week. This estimate is close to that of Dumazedier, who calculated that the average fully-employed French worker had 2.5 hours of leisure on weekdays and 8 hours on weekend days, amounting to approximately 28.5 hours of leisure per week.

The Southern California Research Council summarizes the way in which this free time appears:

Leisure is taken in bits and pieces. According to our time budget for Southern California, about one-third of all leisure hours is taken as daily leisure, in small pieces after school or work. About one-fourth is absorbed by family members in weekend leisure pursuits. Vacations and holidays are the settings for yet another one-sixth of the total. The remaining one-fourth is time spent "at leisure" by children too young for school, retired persons, the chronically unemployed and the institutional population.[11]

Obviously, many factors influence the nation's use of leisure in recreational activity. Two of the most important of these are population growth and affluence.

Population Growth in the United States

According to the "census clock" of the United States Department of Commerce, we reached a population total of 200 million on November 20, 1967. It took the nation about four centuries after European settlement to reach its first 100 million in 1915; the next 100 million was achieved within only 52 years.

Of the 1967 total of 200 million, about 102 million were female and about 98 million male. Over two-thirds of the population live in counties

11 *Ibid.*, p. 18.

classified as metropolitan; this proportion is rising. White-collar workers exceed blue-collar workers, 33 million to 27 million. Twelve percent of the population is classified as nonwhite; this percentage is steadily growing. Nineteen million people are over 65, although the total population of the United States is becoming younger on the average. Because of the surge in births after World War II, the median age declined from 30.2 years in 1950 to 27.8 in 1966, the lowest it had been since the late 1930's. At the same time, life expectancy for men climbed from 53.5 years in 1920 to over 66.5 in the late 1960's and for women, from 71 to about 73.5 during the same period.

Farm population was reported in 1967 to be less than 6 percent of the total population and falling. Since 1960, it had declined by more than 4 million persons owing to the productive capability of agricultural workers, who by 1967 were capable of feeding almost 40 persons through the productive efforts of a single farm worker (compared with a ratio of one to seven at the turn of the century).

During the 1950's and 1960's there had been a spectacular population shift from rural to urban areas. This migration resulted in massive numbers of southern Negroes entering cities in the Northeast, the Midwest, and the Far West. Since most black in-migrants tend to be concentrated in the age bracket of 18 to 29, this trend contributes to a higher birth rate in metropolitan areas, particularly in the inner city slums to which most southern Negroes have moved. The prediction is widely made that unless the trend is halted, America's large cities will become predominantly black, while their surrounding suburbs will be almost exclusively white by the end of the century.

All of these elements of population growth and change have important implications for the provision of leisure opportunities.

Affluence of the American Economy. Although rapid, the population growth of the United States during the 1960's was at a much lower rate than the one at which the nation acquired goods and services. In 1966, for example, the population grew only 1.15 percent, while the nation's economic growth rate was 5.8 percent.

In 1968, records were toppled month after month in key economic and business statistics; records were set for industrial production, personal income, employment, retail sales, and capital outlays. During this year, personal income soared $57 billion, to $686 billion, and total employment increased by almost 1.5 million persons, to 76.6 million. During the five-year period between 1963 and 1968, overall unemployment declined from 5.7 percent of the labor force to 3.4 percent, the number of persons existing below minimum poverty levels declined by about 12.5 million, the average income of Americans rose by $535, corporate profits rose by about 50 percent, and the net financial assets of American families increased by $460 billion—over 50 percent. *Time* Magazine commented:

In material terms at least, the panorama of American progress is tremendous.
. . . No other nation has ever remotely matched the U.S. in both human and
material resources. . . . In the past ten years, the growth of the American
economy has far outstripped the comprehension of most individuals; even economists are at a loss for an abstract theory to explain it. But beyond dispute is
the fact that never before has man transmuted energy and raw material into
wealth at such a fantastic rate. With 7 per cent of the global land mass and 6
percent of its population, the U.S. produces about one-third of the world's
goods and services. . . . In 1968, the U.S. gross national product was twice
that estimated for the Soviet Union, and the output of one American corporation, General Motors, was greater than the G.N.P.'s of all but 13 of the world's
nations.[12]

During this period the U.S. government committed itself to an ever-
larger social program with the establishment of Medicare, far-reaching civil
rights laws on housing and voting, job programs that trained 5 million
persons, over 1.5 million college students on Federal scholarships, Project
Head Start for preschool children, and a host of other programs. Beginning
from a modest expenditure of $75 million in 1940, the Federal government
increased its subsidy for scientific research to a peak of $16.7 billion in 1967.
In 1961 there were 45 federal social programs with expenditures totaling
some $9.9 billion; by 1969, there were 435, involving $25.6 billion.

Total Spending on Leisure and Recreation

How has national affluence affected spending for leisure and recreation? Obviously, there has been a tremendous upsurge in leisure spending,
although there is no single authoritative measure of its actual amount.
The Statistical Abstract of the United States, published by the Department
of the Census, reported in 1967 that personal consumption for recreation
for 1965 (the most recent year available) was $26 billion. If one were to
bring this figure up to a more recent year, 1968, by extrapolating at the
most recent rate of growth, it comes to $32 billion per year. Even this
impressive sum, however, represents a gross underestimation of actual
leisure spending.

The Statistical Abstract describes expenditure in a limited number of
categories, such as money for admissions to movies and spectator sports,
sporting equipment, books, magazines, gardening equipment, musical instruments, and television sets. It does not include money spent on domestic
vacation travel, entertainment, liquor, gambling, or similar categories of
involvement, although all these involve uses of leisure. As a consequence,
other estimates of leisure spending have been much higher than that of
the Census Department. Typically, in 1959, the Statistical Abstract reported that the total amount spent for recreation was $16 billion; however,

[12] "What Is Holding Us Back?" Time, January 24, 1969, p. 24.

Fortune Magazine carried out a major study based on industry sales figures in the same year and concluded that the correct sum was $41 billion. A fuller statement of leisure spending by consumers is shown below.

TABLE 15-1   *Annual Consumer Spending on Recreation*
in the United States in the Late 1960's
(*in billions of dollars*)

1. Books, maps, magazines, newspapers, and sheet music	$ 5.5
2. Nondurable toys and sport supplies	3.2
3. Wheel goods, durable toys, sports equipment, pleasure aircraft, and boats	3.4
4. Radio and television receivers, records, and musical instruments	7.4
5. Radio and television repair	1.2
6. Camping equipment and supplies	5.0
7. Swimming pools and accessories	1.0
8. Equipment and supplies for home "do-it-yourself" activities	12.0
9. Motion picture houses, gross receipts	1.9
10. Admissions to legitimate theaters and opera and to entertainment of non-profit institutions	0.6
11. Spectator sports admissions	0.4
12. Gross receipts, including dues and fees, of clubs and fraternal organizations (luncheon, athletic and social clubs, and school fraternities)	0.9
13. Commercial participant amusements, including billiard parlors, bowling alleys, dancing, riding, skating, shooting, and swimming places, amusement devices and parks	1.6
14. Other purchases and fees, including photography, dogs and other pets, collectors' and other hobbies expenses, camping fees	2.4
15. Pari-mutuel betting on thoroughbred and trotting horse racing	5.4
16. Domestic pleasure travel	32.0
17. Foreign pleasure travel	5.0
18. Home entertaining	7.0
19. Purchase of alcoholic beverages	14.5
20. Purchase of tobacco and smoking supplies	9.2
21. Hunting and fishing licenses, equipment, and related expenses	4.0
22. Lawn and garden supplies and equipment	2.0
Total	$125.9

SOURCE: Statistics reported chiefly in 1968 and 1969, but to some degree earlier in the 1960's by: (a) the Securities Research Division of Merrill Lynch, Pierce, Fenner and Smith, a stockbrokerage firm; (b) *Forbes* Magazine; (c) *U.S. News and World Report*; (d) the annual National Economic Review of the New York *Times*; (e) studies of leisure spending reported by *Life* and *Fortune* Magazines; (f) the Statistical Abstract of the United States; and (g) other trade association or industrial reports which have appeared in the press.

It might be pointed out that such items as "books, maps, magazines, newspapers" or "home do-it-yourself" are not solely recreational involvements, although they are listed in economic reports as forms of leisure spending. While this is so, it should also be pointed out that this compilation is a conservative one, which does not attempt to assess actual spending in such areas as gambling and which reports extremely low figures in such areas as pleasure-boating, photography, and cultural participation. In terms of gambling, for example, knowledgeable analysts have pointed out that only about one-sixth of the money bet on horse races is ventured at the track and that the rest is gambled illegally through private bookmakers. The total sum wagered on professional and amateur sports, or bet in casinos and gambling houses has been estimated at $50 billion per year.

A leading stockbrokerage firm, Merrill Lynch, Pierce, Fenner and Smith, describes the leisure market in 1968 as rapidly approaching the $150-billion mark and predicts that it will reach $250 billion by 1975. Based on a comprehensive analysis of all segments of leisure spending, this study states:

we believe that leisure will be the dynamic element in the domestic economy in the 1970's, and that it will even outperform the economy.[13]

Other authorities support this view. The editors of *Forbes* magazine, a leading business publication, calculated in January, 1969, that the combined leisure and education market in the United States involved a total annual expenditure of $200 billion. (In this context, the term "education" does not include actual school or college budgets but does include books, magazines, newspapers, records, television, and varied other teaching aids—all of which have both educational and recreational uses.) The editors of *Forbes* write:

While amusement and education may sound quite different, both, in fact, stem from the same socioeconomic trend: the nation's growing leisure and affluence.[14]

They point out that a number of major companies in the knowledge and information field (such as major book companies or broadcasting networks) have moved into the ownership of sports teams or stadiums or have diversified widely within the leisure and entertainment field. The burgeoning of this field is described in the following terms:

The interaction of leisure and the Puritan ethic (people feel guilty doing nothing, so they "structure" their leisure time) has created a big opportunity for business; not for nothing are shrewd companies rushing to create "leisure-time activities" divisions, moving across traditional boundaries, from electronics into publishing, from publishing into motion pictures, and so on. . . . If Americans want to structure their leisure time, why not sell them the things to structure it with: riding lawnmowers; tape-recorders; home education courses; books; records; sailboats and other articles yet to be invented.[15]

13 *Leisure: Investment Opportunities in a $150-Billion Market* (New York: Securities Research Division, Merrill Lynch, Pierce, Fenner and Smith, 1968), p.4.
14 "Leisure and Education," *Forbes*, January 1, 1969, p. 170.
15 *Ibid.*, p. 174.

The estimate of the Statistical Abstract of the United States that personal spending for recreation amounts to about 4.5 percent of consumer spending is in sharp contrast to the analysis of economists, business and investment firms, and social research agencies, who calculate the percentage at close to 12 percent, about one-eighth of after-tax income.

What kinds of activities do Americans engage in most frequently in their leisure? What is their broad range of involvement and interest?

PATTERNS OF LEISURE ACTIVITY IN THE UNITED STATES

A number of studies have attempted to assess the total nature of leisure participation in the United States. One such analysis was done in 1960 by the Stanford Research Institute, based on data obtained from the Outdoor Recreation Resources Review Commission, Michigan State University, and the National Recreation Association.[16] This report suggests that Americans tend to engage most frequently in easily accessible activities that do not require specialized equipment, elaborate organization, or supervision. Of the ten most frequently listed activities (rest, relaxation, watching television, visiting with friends and relatives, reading, studying, etc.), seven are normally carried on at home. With the possible exception of the sixth activity listed (clubs, organizations), none of the leading ten require the assistance of community recreation agencies.

However, this report must be regarded as incomplete. It includes only those activities which are normally viewed as constructive or socially desirable, with emphasis on outdoor recreation. There is no mention at all of playing cards, going to a racetrack, attending movies or the theater, or spending time in a bar or night club. Nor does it mention arts and crafts, dancing, or active musical participation.

Other reports by the Outdoor Recreation Resources Review Commission confirm that such activities as driving or walking for pleasure rank high above strenuous or dangerous activities such as water skiing, canoeing, or mountain climbing. The most popular activities, in terms of frequency of participation, tend to be the simplest and most readily available, such as driving and walking for pleasure, swimming, playing outdoor games or sports, or bicycling.

While it is not possible to examine in detail every form of recreational involvement found in the United States, a number of major categories are described in the following section. These include sports, both as participant and spectator activity; outdoor recreation, including boating, fishing, and hunting; leisure travel; commercial entertainment and cultural activities; and television-watching.

[16] See "Participation in Selected Leisure Activities, United States, 1960," in *The Challenge of Leisure, op. cit.*, p. 21.

Sports Participation in the United States

Without question, participation in sports represents a major leisure interest for the great mass of Americans. There are many reasons for their popularity. They offer participants a chance to test themselves, by striving physically in a world that offers few other such challenges. They provide means of sublimating aggression and hostility, and they offer both competition and cooperation on intense levels. Their outcome is uncertain, leading to the heights of triumph or the depths of defeat. They are suspenseful and dramatic. They are widely regarded as desirable from the point of view of physical fitness and character development. Finally, as part of an industrial society, sports have become big business. They are money-makers, sponsored by powerful commercial interests and promoted by mass-media advertising, public relations, television, magazines, and newspapers.

On every age level, sports competition is widespread. Children and youth may participate in a variety of leagues operated by youth organizations, schools, or recreation departments—casually, in intramural play, or as part of more intensive competition. National organizations provide stimulus, guidelines, and even annual competitions for the top teams. On younger age levels, the emphasis is on such team sports as baseball, basketball, and football. For adults, it shifts to a personal involvement in golf, tennis, bowling, winter sports, aquatics, and the like and spectator interest in professional sports competition. Unlike the pattern in Europe, where national federations and sport societies promote a vast amount of adult sports activity on an amateur basis and where there are comparatively few professional athletes, in the United States the emphasis is very strongly on professionalism.

What are the most popular participant sports? For a number of years, the Athletic Institute, a nonprofit organization concerned with the promotion of athletics, physical education, and recreation, conducted an annual survey, which provided estimates of national participation in major sports activities (Table 15-2).

It is clear, however, that while certain activities such as fishing or hunting may be measured fairly precisely (based on the number of licenses taken out during the course of a year), others, like cycling, shuffleboard, or volleyball, can be estimated only in very broad terms. In 1968, the Athletic Institute concluded that sufficient confidence could not be given to statistics provided by business organizations or sports associations; it therefore discontinued its annual survey and report of sports participation.

Another means of assessing the relative popularity of sports activities in the United States is through the yearbooks published by the National Recreation and Park Association, which offer detailed information about the kinds of sports facilities which are provided to the public and about

TABLE 15-2   *Estimated Number of Participants (millions)*

Activity	1946	1956	1961	1965	1966
Cycling	. . .	. . .	. . .	57	59
Boating	20	28	30	39.3	40.3
Volleyball	. . .	. . .	20	40	40
Bowling (ten-pin)	12.5	20.5	30	39	39
Camping	. . .	. . .	5.5	37	37
Fishing	13.1	25	30.3	35.4	36.2
Softball	4.7	6.6	14.5	22.5	25.8
Roller skating	. . .	. . .	15	25	25
Billiards	. . .	. . .	. . .	20	23
Shooting sports	. . .	. . .	18	20	20
Golf	4.3	5.1	6	8.7	9.1
Shuffleboard	. . .	. . .	5	10	10
Water skiing	. . .	. . .	6	8.7	9.1
Tennis	4.1	6.6	7.5	8.5	9.1
Horseshoes	. . .	. . .	. . .	9	9

SOURCE: Drawn from "Sports and Recreation Participation Survey," published by the Athletic Institute, Chicago, January 31, 1967, and from previous annual reports of the *Athletic Institute Sportscope*.

general trends in programs which reflect popular interest and support. Generally speaking, the most popular activities reported in the mid-1960's were, for adults softball, swimming, tennis, basketball, volleyball, and picnicking and for youth baseball, basketball, swimming, tennis, volleyball, and picnicking. There has been a dramatic rise in the number of baseball diamonds, bathing beaches, golf courses, softball diamonds, swimming pools, and tennis courts offered by local park and recreation departments. Among the activities whose popularity had more than doubled in the five-year period between 1960 and 1965 were such sports as bowling, regulation and touch football, golf, track and field, boating, horseback riding, synchronized swimming, water skiing, and skiing.[17]

Other reports on sports participation provide information not only on the number of participants in each activity but on the amounts they spend. A 1968 report indicated that there were 9 million golfers, 3.5 million tennis players, and 35 million fishermen, all of whom were spending freely for equipment, facilities, and memberships related to their sports interests. It went on:

The number of American skiers has soared from just 50,000 at the end of World War II to more than 4 million at present, and they spend hundreds of millions each year for equipment, travel to the slopes, food and shelter. Water skiing is an even newer sport, but it now has about 10 million devotees. . . .

[17] *Recreation and Park Yearbook, 1966* (Washington, D.C.: National Recreation and Park Association, 1967), p. 53.

The popularity of surfing is also a recent phenomenon, yet surfers bought $12 million worth of surfboards in 1967. Overall purchases of archery equipment, baseball goods, bicycles, fishing supplies, skates and tennis equipment each increase approximately 8 to 10 percent per year; it is estimated that purchases of golf equipment will rise by 13%, billiard and pool tables, 16%; equipment for winter sports . . . by 21% . . . the number of registered bowlers climbed from 2 million in 1951, to 7.9 million in 1966-67.[18]

Thus, sports make a major contribution to the national economy. A survey by the American Camping Association estimated that cash outlay for participation sports had increased 600 percent during a fifteen-year period in the 1950's and 1960's. Another phenomenon of the 1960's was greatly increased attendance at spectator sports events.

Spectator Sports

Horse Racing. The number of those attending thoroughbred and harness-racing tracks throughout the nation was 61.5 million in 1968; total betting rose to $5.4 billion in the following year. As an example of the financial importance of this type of spectator sport, state revenues from racing in 1968 were close to $400 million.

Automobile Racing. The second major area of spectator sport, automobile racing, attracted paid attendance by 40 million persons in 1968. As contrasted to those attending horse-racing events (who come primarily to bet at pari-mutuel windows), automobile racing fans come chiefly because of the spectator appeal of the sport itself. Because automobile racing must necessarily cover large areas, the crowd is spread out, and huge numbers may watch at a single time:

The Indianapolis 500 brings in perhaps 225,000 spectators. Daytona has gates of 100,000 and Riverside 80,000. Auto racing is even more popular abroad. One event alone, the Twenty-Four Hours of Le Mans, has had as many as 400,000 spectators.[19]

The huge crowds that attend auto racing events have been compared to those attending the ancient Roman Circus Maximus. Few other sports are as dangerous to participants and sometimes to the audience. While such huge events are strictly professional, much stock-car racing and hot-rod competition (drag racing) is either semiprofessional or amateur. Many clubs sponsor rallies for amateurs; these too attract numbers of spectators. Car racing is a unique blend of technical appeal, hero-worship, and the ever-present risk of sudden death.

Major Team Sports. The three leading team sports in the United

18 *Leisure: Investment Opportunities in a $150-Billion Market, op. cit.,* p. 7; see also "Recreation: A Record Boom," *U.S. News and World Report,* July 22, 1968, pp. 52-54.

19 "U.S. Auto Racing," New York *Times,* February 4, 1968, p. 15-S.

States are baseball, football, and basketball. The leading sport in terms of attendance is baseball, which has traditionally been recognized as the national pastime. It has experienced something of a decline in interest since World War II. Some attribute this to television; others suggest that because many baseball parks are located in the older areas of cities, spectators hesitate to travel into these neighborhoods in periods of urban violence. Still others complain that baseball is too slow, not action-oriented.

Interest in baseball has been falling off for years as people discover how exciting other sports and forms of leisure activity can be. Compared with the violence and sophistication of pro football, the frenetic pace of hockey and basketball, baseball seems elementary, antiquated and soporific. It still draws more fans in total than other pro team sports. But that is only because there are 1,620 big league baseball games each season (v. 182 pro football games).[20]

While baseball has climbed slightly from a major-league attendance low of 20.9 million in the early 1950's to 24.3 million in 1967 (a rise of 16 percent, due largely to league expansion and increased numbers of games), football attendance at professional games rose from 1.5 million in 1948 to 8.2 million in 1967—a climb of 438 percent. All forms of professional sport have expanded their leagues and numbers of teams, with a rapid shifting of franchises. Unlike their early years, when sports teams were regarded with great loyalty in their home cities, they have recently moved rapidly around the country, in search of municipal or county governments that would subsidize huge new stadiums or huge new audiences of unjaded fans. Even more important has been the need to get advantageous locations for television broadcasting contracts. The major networks, with tremendous advertising revenues based on sports programs, have competed hotly for the right to broadcast games. In the late 1960's, the Columbia Broadcasting System paid $41.6 million for a two-year contract with the National Football League, and the American Broadcasting Company paid $4.5 million to cover the Olympic Games in Mexico.

Thus, sports have become big business, and television has been the key factor in making them so. This trend has influenced the nature of college and even secondary school sports. While they are nominally amateur, many college teams can no longer be seriously regarded as a form of cocurricular or recreational activity. Instead, they are a kind of training ground, or minor league, for highly skilled performers, most of whom have been recruited into colleges because of their sports ability rather than their academic potential.

This system of highly competitive and publicized secondary school and college sport is uniquely American; it is found in no other nation in the world and is essentially an expression of the fact that our approach to sport is heavily spectator-oriented.

[20] "Baseball: Slump at the Turnstiles," *Time*, July 26, 1968, p. 47.

Outdoor Recreation Activities in the United States

Another major area of participation on the part of Americans is in outdoor recreation. In 1965, the Bureau of Outdoor Recreation of the Department of the Interior reported that the participation of individuals in outdoor recreation—including everything from hiking to surfing—had reached a total of 6.5 billion "occasions" (acts of participation by one person in a given activity) during the calendar year. The Bureau predicted that there would be 10 billion such sporting occasions in 1980 and 17 billion in the year 2000, based on a projection of current trends.

Boating as Recreation. Figures released at the close of 1967 by the National Association of Engine and Boat Manufacturers and the Boating Industry Association indicated that there were a total of 8.2 million boats in the nation's pleasure-craft armada, belonging to approximately 7 million Americans. The total fleet of pleasure craft was broken down approximately as follows: outboard boats, 4.8 million; inboards, including auxiliary-powered sailboats, 591,000; sailboats without power, 561,000; and rowboats, canoes, dinghies, etc., 2.3 million. In all, the total number of those who participate in recreational boating with some degree of frequency during the year was estimated to have climbed to 41.7 million persons.

Boating is particularly dependent on the provision of public marinas and launching ramps and on government development of huge reservoirs, lakes, and waterways. Many municipal recreation and park departments today provide facilities and services. Boating is closely related to camping as a major outdoor recreation interest. Of the over 40 million people who spend one or more days each year camping outdoors, studies report that well over 50 percent seek out lake or reservoir campsites. Typically, 47.5 percent of campers surveyed own outboard motors, and 41.5 percent have boats. The Bureau of Outdoor Recreation, in its predictions for the year 2000, foresees a 238 percent increase in camping activity and a 215 percent increase in boating.

Fishing and Hunting. It was reported in 1967 that the number of licensed fishermen and hunters in the United States had risen from 34.8 to 35.6 million. This included 21.3 million fishermen and 14.3 million hunters who bought licenses. Since many other sportsmen are not counted because they are exempt from having to have licenses (including children, elderly persons, servicemen, landowners on their own properties, and those who fish in the ocean), it would appear that a far greater number than 35.6 million actually engage in these sports.

Travel as a Form of Leisure Activity

Another major form of recreational activity for Americans involves vacation and weekend pleasure travel. The nature of the recent growth of leisure (more holidays and longer vacations) has given emphasis to this form of recreation. In 1968, the gross income of hotels, motels, and restaurants was estimated at $39.3 billion. While a proportion of this is attributed to business travel, the bulk of it stems from domestic pleasure travel. Typically, the motel industry has shifted its emphasis from providing places to stay while en route to a destination to developing places which have become places to stay in themselves. Major chains now emphasize recreation and entertainment facilities to encourage weekend vacations with package deals for couples and families. One motel chain executive comments:

Swimming pools, air conditioning and room T.V. are just points of departure now. Some of our motels offer golf, horseback riding, tennis, boating, fishing, even duck hunting and skeet shooting.[21]

Many motels situated near large cities now offer vacation gateways. Travel that makes use of such facilities may be part of a total vacation, a vacation in itself, or even part of a business trip. It becomes increasingly difficult to separate the elements of business and pleasure. Similarly, eating, usually thought of as a maintenance activity, often becomes a form of pleasure:

As a nation, we are now spending more than $20 billion a year for food away from home, quadruple the amount we spent in the late 1940's. . . . Eating out has rapidly developed into one of the biggest industries in the United States. . . . City families in the $15,000 and over after-tax income bracket actually spend one-third of their food dollars on eating out. . . . The travel-vacation-leisure time booms have spurred a dramatic growth in roadside restaurants, airline meals, restaurants in airline and bus terminals, in resorts and national parks.[22]

Foreign travel has also become a major form of recreational activity. By the mid-1960's, more than 16 million Americans each year were spending over $3 billion a year on travel outside our national borders. How much of this was for recreation? It was reported in 1968 that of every 100 travelers to Europe, 24 were on business, usually making a fairly short trip, 45 on vacation with an average stay of three or four weeks, and 34 persons with incomes, or visiting relatives or friends, who tend to make extended stays (a small number of these going to study or teach but much greater numbers clearly pleasure-bound). By the end of the decade, it was reported that American vacationers were spending $5 billion a year abroad. Some companies have been founded based solely on the idea of vacation travel.

[21] Frank Litsky, "Motels Aren't Just for Sleeping Anymore," New York *Times*, July 18, 1966, p. 38.
[22] Sylvia Porter, "Restaurant Boom," New York *Post*, January 7, 1966, p. 66.

For example, the Paris-based Club Méditerranée operates 47 vacation villages in thirteen countries (including Europe, North Africa, the Near East, Tahiti, the Caribbean, and the United States). Its 700,000 members, each of whom pays $10 annual dues, enjoy comparatively inexpensive, relaxed, and informal vacations on exotic islands, in ski resorts, and in a host of picturesque settings throughout the world.

Major Entertainment Complexes. Linked to travel as a form of recreation has been the expansion of "fun centers" throughout the United States. These become targets of travel for millions of families whose members, like the Soviet Premier Khrushchev, would not think of going to California without visiting Disneyland.

This major entertainment complex is the leading example of such business ventures. Built in 1955, at a cost of over $50 million, it covers 65 acres in Anaheim, California. Disneyland is a unique amalgam of the past and present, of fairyland fantasy and modern space science, including a massive, independently operated hotel complex. Accommodating as many as 60,000 persons at one time, by the mid-1960's, Disneyland had attracted over 45 million visitors, including many kings, queens, and heads of states. In recent years, many similar complexes have been built throughout the country.

Another example of widespread investment in recreational facilities has been a wave of stadium construction throughout the nation in the 1960's, often housing a variety of entertainment and business-exposition functions. A leading example is the Astrodome in Houston, Texas. This marvel of modern technology is a fully enclosed structure (the temperature is always 72 degrees, and events are never rained out) which cost $37 million to build and which attracts 4 million persons a year. Beautifully designed and decorated, the Astrodome is so huge that the eighteen-story Shamrock-Hilton Hotel could stand on second base and not touch its dome or walls. The stadium complex also includes a $26-million, 116-acre amusement park called Astroworld, a 12-acre Astrohall exhibition center, and a $16-million group of motor hotels. The major sports teams that play in the stadium itself are owned by the controlling corporation. In addition to professional and college baseball, football, and basketball, the Astrodome schedules boxing, motorcycle racing, polo, bloodless "bullfights," Gaelic football, religious revivals, and the circus.

Throughout the country, other cities have built huge new stadiums, often with cooperation of government and business groups. In Los Angeles, five major sports palaces have been built within the past twelve years, the latest being the Inglewood Forum, an elegant $16-million structure designed to accommodate audiences primarily for professional basketball and hockey. The new $150-million Madison Square Garden in New York City has been called the greatest sport and entertainment center in the world. Another trend in the building of entertainment centers today has been toward providing commercial recreation in suburban shopping centers. With the increased reluctance of the suburban dwellers to drive into cities for shopping, entertainment, or sometimes even cultural programs, huge new regional shopping complexes today offer motion-picture houses, restaurants, bowling alleys (which often provide child-care facilities for women players), and even legitimate theaters.

Cultural Activities in the United States

Another major area of leisure development in the United States has been rapidly growing public interest and involvement in the arts, including the performing arts (music, drama, and dance) and the plastic and graphic arts (such as painting, sculpture, and drawing). This cultural explosion has been evidenced by the building of cultural centers and museums, growth in spectator events and mass participation, and personal consumption related to all the arts.

As an example, there has been a remarkable growth in all forms of musical activity in the United States since World War II. During the period from 1939 to 1965, the number of American symphony orchestras more than doubled, from about 600 to 1,401 (more than one-half the world's 2,000 orchestras). In the mid-1960's, there were a total of 732 opera-producing companies in the United States, compared with only 77 companies in 1941. The sale of records, musical instruments, and other forms of musical expenditure increased by 857 percent during the same period, a rate markedly faster than that of the country's total economic growth during the same period. By the late 1960's, there were estimated to be over 37 million amateur musicians in the United States, and it was stated that more Americans attend symphony concerts than go to major- or minor-league baseball games.

Consumer spending on the arts increased by about 130 percent during the period from 1953 to 1960. By the mid-1960's, Americans were spending nearly $400 million a year at theaters, opera, and concert performances, buying over $1 billion worth of books and spending $200 million for painting, prints, and art materials, $300 million to operate art museums, and $600 million a year for musical instruments. It was predicted that the renaissance in culture would result in an annual expenditure of $7 billion by the early 1970's.

Hundreds of cities have planned or carried out major building programs for the performing and graphic arts, ranging from New York City's $142-million Lincoln Center for the Performing Arts, to the $30-million National Cultural Center for the Performing Arts in Washington, D.C. The establishment of the National Arts Council by Federal legislation in 1965 and subsequent funding of programs in the arts and humanities, as well as the efforts of many state art councils, have undoubtedly stimulated these developments.

There has been a rapid increase in community-sponsored recreation programs in the arts, as revealed by statistics in the 1961 and 1966 *Park and Recreation Yearbooks* (Table 15-3).

TABLE 15-3   *Percentage of Local Public Recreation Agencies Offering Arts Programs*

	1960		1965	
Activity	Youth	Adults	Youth	Adults
Painting	24.0	11.8	38.5	38.0
Sculpture	4.7	2.8	12.2	13.1
Ballet	10.5	1.8	21.0	5.2
Choral activities	9.2	8.0	22.8	22.8
Community theater	7.5	7.4	16.6	19.2
Modern dance	10.6	3.7	20.1	6.1
Orchestral concerts	6.3	6.2	15.7	14.9

SOURCE: *Recreation and Park Yearbook*, 1966 (Washington, D.C.: National Recreation and Park Association, 1967), p. 55.

The Growth of Television

Probably the most important influence on the present-day use of leisure has been television and the degree to which the home screen today has captured huge bulks of the leisure time of people of all ages. An extensive international study was carried out by UNESCO in 1965; it indicated that, depending on the native country's television availability, school-age children spent from 12 to 24 hours a week watching the home screen. In the United States, peak watching time was found to be between the ages of twelve and thirteen, when the average daily viewing time was found to be three hours. Schramm writes:

The cumulative statistics in the TV-oriented countries, such as the United States, are staggering. The total time spent in front of the television set during the typical span of the 13 years of school attendance ranges between 6,000 and 12,000 hours, with the latter figure about equal to the total number of hours the average child spends in school during that period.[23]

A 1968 study revealed that the average American home with preschool children has the television set turned on between 55 and 60 hours a week. Based on Nielsen Survey statistics, it concluded that the "average American adult will spend from 10 to 15 years of his life watching TV."[24]

[23] "T.V. Children," New York *Times*, February 28, 1965, p. E-7.
[24] *New York Times Magazine*, July 14, 1968, p. 26.

By 1968, 95 percent of the American homes had television sets; 25 percent had more than one set. In terms of the fears expressed as long ago as the 1920's that we were becoming a spectator-oriented nation in our use of leisure, this has extremely serious implications. The sports interest of many Americans seems to be increasingly diverted to watching on television. As an example of the tremendous audience captured by sports events on television, the Columbia Broadcasting System reported in January, 1968 that an audience of 70 million persons watched its broadcast of the world championship Super-Bowl football contest—a number greater than those who actually attended all professional sports events during the entire year.

The appeal of television is due in large measure to the ingenuity of its producers. Using small portable cameras that capture all sorts of sports events, such programs as the "Wide World of Sports" have telecast over 90 different sports events in 31 different countries. In 1965, when a team of mountain climbers scaled the Matterhorn to celebrate the hundredth anniversary of the first climbing of the mountain, they were met on top by an ABC camera team that had climbed up the day before to film the occasion. Television cameramen today film under water, place microphones in quarterback's helmets to pick up the sounds of the huddle and the game action, and use missile-tracking devices to keep cameras fixed on skydivers who are falling at 160 miles per hour. They use instant replays, slow-motion closeups, split screens, and other newly devised techniques to insure that the home watcher can see far more accurately and vividly than the fan who is actually on the scene ever can.

Television-watching has obviously displaced other forms of leisure activity to a marked degree. Attendance at movie theaters declined from about 3.4 billion admissions in 1948 (the year television networks got under way) to about 1.1 billion a year in the late 1960's. It is clear that many other forms of participation must have been cut into seriously by television-watching. Its appeal, of course, is that it is easily available (being right at home in an age of danger in the streets constitutes a major advantage) and requires no strain or effort on the part of the onlooker—only that he stay awake and suffer through numbers of commercials that punctuate the actual entertainment. In addition, it offers every level of taste and entertainment, from animated cartoons for little children to rock-and-roll shows for teen-agers, low-grade situation comedies, talk shows, action and soap-opera dramas, and old-movie replays.

Television, in a sense, epitomizes American attitudes toward leisure. Studies cited earlier indicate that the most popular activities are those which are simple, easily available, and inexpensive and require limited risks or inconvenience. What is negative about television, apart from its questionable level of taste and preoccupation with violence and sadism, is its essentially passive and lonely character. Instead of creatively expressing himself or being meaningfully involved with others, the television watcher becomes little more than a blotter that soaks up sight and sound. In millions of homes throughout the country, exactly the same pictures appear on the screen. This leveling of taste through the cumulative impact of the standardized media could be achieved only by modern technology. And it is technology that must ultimately be recognized as the most important modern influence on the use of leisure.

Technological Influences on Leisure

Not only has technology given us leisure, it is also shaping and changing our use of it. In addition to television, the most obvious example, technology has created whole new forms of recreation and undoubtedly has others on the drawing board.

Technology permits man to alter his environment and to create new environments for play. The growing ski industry is based on the ability of ski promoters to make artificial snow, extending the ski season and making it feasible to build expensive winter-sports complexes far to the south of regions that would normally be able to provide this sport. Artificial ice rinks, refrigerated toboggan chutes, and other devices such as the newly popular snowmobiles, which are being sold at the rate of 150,000 a year, are technological innovations that have created whole new approaches to winter sports.

Boating is an example of how technology has made what was once a highly exclusive sport available to large numbers of people for entirely new forms of aquatic play. Mass-produced power boats, many made of plastic, are used for recreation by millions, in combination with fishing, water-skiing, and such other technologically based pursuits as skin and scuba diving. New processes have made it possible to build giant dams and reservoirs and even to locate large lakes in desert areas with the use of plastic undercoatings which prevent drainage into the subsoil. Many marinas in northern climates are now equipped with automatic bubbling mechanisms which prevent freezing, so that boats may remain safely in the water throughout the year. The year-round heating of pools in cooler climates and the invention of artificial surf (Japanese technicians have developed machines that create four-foot breakers in large pools) are other examples of how technology can make swimming more comfortable and appealing throughout the year.

Leaving the earth and the water, even in the air one finds new forms of technologically based recreation. Flying has gained widespread popularity as recreation. The Aircraft Owners and Pilots' Association reports that of 600,000 airmen in the United States, about 250,000 are private pilots who fly about 120,000 private aircraft. Of these, a substantial number are used primarily for family or individual recreation or, when owned by industrial firms, for combined business and leisure functions. In addition to flying for recreation, many hobbyists have taken up skydiving, ballooning, and gliding—all based on new technological developments.

There are many other examples of how modern technology has created new forms of leisure activity. The automobile was the first invention to give Americans easy mobility in the search for recreation and was responsible for radically changing our patterns of family living and social participation. Today, Americans enjoy many forms of play which are based on the automobile; it seems likely that entirely new forms of mobility—perhaps individual flying platforms—will contribute to recreational opportunities in the near future.

At the same time that one appreciates the positive contributions that technology has made to our leisure lives, it is necessary to raise two serious questions about its effects.

First, mechanically based forms of play both extend and supplant man's capability and at the same time limit the extent of his personal participation and involvement. One might compare the slot-car racing fad of the 1960's (a highly technological amusement in which players sit at control boards in commercial centers, pressing a switch with one finger, while complicated little cars zoom around a table-top raceway) with the nature of the experience the participant might have while bicycling, running, or being involved in any other form of direct personal recreation. When applied to leisure, technology tends to reduce the level of involvement, individual expression, and group contact.

A second concern that stems from the growing influence of technology on leisure is that it inevitably results in more expensive activities. Most such recreational innovations are provided by business firms and have a price tag attached. While this is understandable in a society committed to the free enterprise system and the profit motive, it means that an increasing proportion of recreational experiences tend to require admissions fees and charges or the purchase of equipment. For those who cannot afford to pay their way, the use of leisure necessarily becomes limited. Thus, the entire question of recreational opportunity is closely linked to financial capability. This poses serious issues of public policy in recreation and parks which are discussed later in this text.

FOUR

Goals and Problems in Organized Recreation Service

16

Recreation and Human Values

This text now examines the contributions of recreational experience in meeting the needs of people as individuals and with respect to societal functions.

Behavioral scientists have recently characterized the major areas of human growth and development as fitting under three major headings: *cognitive* (meaning mental or intelligence development), *affective* (relating to emotional or feeling states), and *psychomotor* (referring to the broad area of motor learning and performance).[1] Because these terms are somewhat narrow in their applications, however, this text will instead use the more familiar headings of *physical, emotional, social,* and *mental* development, in examining the personal values of recreational experience. Obviously, these areas are all closely related; growth must be seen as a total process, involving every aspect of human functioning. In order to focus on each specific area of recreation's contribution, however, they are here treated separately.

Physical Growth and Development

Here we are concerned with the outcomes of those forms of recreational activity which demand physical output to a greater or lesser degree. This includes games and sports, outdoor recreation such as swimming and camping, dance, and even such activities as gardening or walking.

[1] Benjamin Bloom, Ed., *Taxonomy of Educational Objectives, Handbook I, Cognitive Domain* (New York: McKay, 1956); and David Krathwohl, *et al., Taxonomy of Educational Objectives, Handbook II, Affective Domain* (New York: McKay, 1964).

The values of such activities obviously differ according to the age level and developmental needs of the participant. For children and youth, the major need is to promote healthy structural development, organic growth, and the acquisition of physical skills. In addition, it is essential that children gain interests and habits of participation in varied physical activities which will carry over into later periods of life.

Even in today's mechanized society, there is a need for all individuals to be able to accept the stresses of life and to respond to physical demands and emergencies. Thus, it was a matter of serious national concern that physical fitness testing programs during the 1950's revealed that American youth were considerably less fit than those of the British Isles, Japan, and a number of other nations. Physical education programs were strengthened to remedy this situation, and more recent tests have revealed that American youth have improved significantly in their levels of physical performance. It is recognized, however, that the effects of crash training programs, while impressive, tend also to be temporary. Therefore, it is essential that programs of physical activity be continued beyond the school years. This can best be done through group programs of physical recreation and participation in such individual activities as walking, swimming, golf, tennis, skiing, and bicycling.

In adulthood, the need for regular physical exercise is directly related to maintaining health and minimizing physical degeneration. Hein and Ryan write:

In the last decade, a growing body of evidence derived from clinical observations and experimental studies points to definite values for exercise in (a) maintaining desirable weight, (b) preserving the health of the cardiovascular system, (c) aiding the individual to meet emergencies, and (d) prolonging life.[2]

Control of Obesity. Scientists are generally agreed today that the level of one's physical activity plays a major role in weight control. This is a serious problem, since there has been a steady growth of obesity among Americans. There is also evidence that per capita energy consumption has decreased by as much as 10 percent over the past fifty years because of the use of automobiles and other mechanical devices and the popularity of television and spectator sports. Hein and Ryan comment:

Comparison of the food intake and body weights of height-matched individuals grouped according to the amount of physical activity in their lives revealed that, in general, inactivity loomed more important in overweight than the amount of food consumed.[3]

[2] Fred V. Hein and Allan G. Ryan, "Contribution of Physical Activity to Human Well-Being," *Research Quarterly*, May, 1960, p. 264.
[3] *Ibid.*, p. 267.

Generally, physical inactivity has been discovered to precede rather than follow the onset of obesity. Dr. Jean Mayer, a leading authority on nutrition at Harvard University, has taken the stand that exercise is essential to the control of both obesity and circulatory illness and is particularly helpful to those of middle age and beyond in preserving youthful body contours and maintaining the general level of condition of the body.[4] A continuing practice of moderate exercise helps each individual maintain the capacity to meet emergency situations which pose sudden demands for heavy or prolonged physical activity and which may occur even under conditions of modern living.

Preserving Cardiovascular Fitness. Americans are known to have far more coronary attacks than the people of any other nation; heart and circulatory system diseases claim nearly a million lives in this country each year. The continuing rise in the percentage of such deaths is believed to be caused in part by more accurate diagnosis as well as the fact that more people are escaping such illnesses as pneumonia or tuberculosis and living to the age when degenerative vascular disease becomes more of a threat. Doctors have also noted, however, an alarming growth of mortality from cardiovascular illness among comparatively young men. Among the conditions leading to coronary disease are overweight, poor diet, emotional stress, cigarette smoking, and the lack of suitable exercise.

A healthy regimen of physical recreation helps to reduce overweight and emotional stress and thus contributes significantly to the individual's resistance to heart attack. Studies have shown that the occupations in which the highest incidence of coronary disease occur are those which involve the least physical exertion. In British medical studies, when bus drivers and conductors on London buses or postal clerks and postmen (situations in which one class of employee is physically active and the other inactive) were compared, it was found that there was a much higher rate of heart disease among the inactive workers.[5] Dr. Paul Dudley White, one of the nation's most distinguished heart specialists, has strongly urged regular exercise—whether walking, swimming, golf, tennis, or bicycling. Some practitioners have urged the use of fitness programs such as the Royal Canadian Air Force exercises. Other fitness specialists have urged jogging as an ideal form of exercise for the cardiovascular and respiratory systems, particularly in the age group beyond thiry-five, where regular exercise is frequently neglected. The particular value of jogging is that it has elements of recreation, with social overtones, especially when practiced in a group situation:

[4] Jean Mayer, "The Best Diet Is Exercise," *New York Times Magazine*, April 25, 1965, p. 34.

[5] Henry L. Taylor, "The Mortality and Morbidity of Coronary Heart Disease of Men in Sedentary and Physically Active Operations," in Seward C. Staley, Ed., *Exercise and Fitness* (Chicago: The Athletic Institute, 1960), pp. 20-39.

Although it does tone muscles, shrink girths and condition the heart and lungs, jogging's appeal seems more psychological than physiological. A recent study of 422 male joggers in Eugene [Oregon] found that the regimen left them feeling more "vital and alive."[6]

An increasing number of recreation departments have initiated conditioning programs for men and women. Sometimes these programs consist of varied sports, games, or aquatic activities; sometimes they are based on gymnastics or exercise sequences known as "slimnastics." They demonstrate an increasing awareness that exercise is essential to maintaining sound physical health in middle and later life and that the most sensible and attractive way in which to gain exercise is through an enjoyable, recreational experience.

Emotional Aspects of Recreational Participation

The emotional and psychological benefits of recreational participation have been heavily documented in the medical literature. Dr. William Menninger has written:

Mentally healthy people participate in some form of volitional activity to supplement their required daily work. . . . Their satisfaction from these activities meets deep-seated psychological demands, quite beyond the superficial rationalization of enjoyment. . . . There is considerable scientific evidence that the healthy personality is one who not only plays, but who takes his play seriously. Furthermore, there is also evidence that the inability and unwillingness to play reveals an insecure or disordered aspect of personality.[7]

Dr. Paul Haun, another respected psychiatrist, has written that the medical case for play is undisputed. In his view, it constitutes an essential aspect of healthy life, and provides a natural rhythmic alternative to work. This concept has been fully accepted in treatment programs for the mentally ill. Haun describes the use of recreation in the hospital environment, as a "potent normalizer" that helps to dispel the threat of isolation and social rejection for hospitalized patients. Recreation can provide the patient with familiar social roles through which constructive interaction with others can occur:

It offers a gratifyingly wide opportunity for instinctual discharge in socially acceptable channels. . . . Competently administered and skillfully presented, it encourages the timid, disarms the aggressive, motivates the lethargic, calms the restless, and diverts the melancholic. As a necessary part of a hospital en-

[6] "Guides for the Flabby," *Newsweek*, October 2, 1967, p. 90; and "Gerontology: Good News for Joggers," *Time*, February 7, 1969, p. 39.

[7] William C. Menninger, "Recreation and Mental Health," *Recreation*, November, 1948, p. 343.

vironment, genuinely attuned to the needs of the sick, it merits our serious attention.[8]

A leading heart research specialist, Dr. Joseph B. Wolffe, formerly president of the American College of Sports Medicine and Medical Director of the Valley Forge Medical Center and Heart Hospital, has reported on the specific value of recreational activities prescribed for patients suffering from acute thrombosis, congestive heart failure, and allied illnesses:

Recreation . . . is one of the best medicines when properly adapted for the individual's age and capacity for effort. Suitable group activity offers many psychological advantages. It affords the patient an opportunity to become interested in others, provides an outlet for aggressive drives, teaches cooperation and team play.[9]

In a clinical study of recreation in the hospital setting, Dr. Wolffe found that a special activity program resulted in lessening drug requirements for various types of patients from 35 to 50 percent and actually shortened hospital stay by approximately 15 percent. As an example, in neurocirculatory asthenia, a reduction of 35 percent in the need for sedatives and tranquilizers was noted. Wolffe concluded:

Recreation is more than physical medicine. It helps to make the patient . . . a part of a social milieu in the hospital. . . . The recreator's evaluation of actions and attitudes helps to fill an important gap in the physician's appraisal of a patient's physical and mental status. Opportunities for recreational activities in a hospital setting help to minimize introspection, lessen anxieties and neuroses irrespective of the patient's physical and mental conditions.[10]

Such statements from medical practitioners support the recognition of recreation as a potent force in maintaining or improving mental health. They are supported by findings of mental health specialists in educational settings. Dr. James Jan-Tausch of the New Jersey Department of Education found, in a study of suicides occurring among public school children in New Jersey during a three-year period (1960–63), that nonparticipation in school recreational and extracurricular activities was closely related to despondency, isolation and suicide attempts. He writes:

With very few exceptions, the suicides in this study were not members of a chorus, a team, a cast or a publication. The most significant factor related to

[8] Paul Haun, "The Place for Recreation in Mental Health," *Parks and Recreation*, November, 1966, p. 906.
[9] Joseph B. Wolffe, "Recreation as Prophylactic and Therapeutic Measure in Diseases of the Cardiovascular System," *Recreation in Treatment Centers* (American Recreation Society Hospital Section), September, 1965, p. 28.
[10] *Ibid.*, p. 30.

suicide among school children was the relationship between the child and the people with whom he socialized. In every case of suicide, the child was described as having no close friends, with whom he might share confidences or from whom he received psychological support. This investigator is of the opinion that participation in extra-curricular activities is a good deterrent of suicide.[11]

A related study was carried out by L. H. Richardson, a consulting psychologist at the City University of New York, who examined college students who were receiving psychological counseling. Comparing them with students who were not being counseled, Richardson found that the counseled group had engaged in significantly more passive leisure-time activities than had the noncounseled group; his implication was that active recreational participation was closely linked to maintaining emotional stability and well-being.[12]

Generally, then, it is accepted that recreation provides an extremely useful means of channeling the emotional and psychological development of children, youth, and adults. It helps to establish and reinforce positive and realistic self-concepts and offers pleasure and a sense of personal creative accomplishment. Finally, as indicated earlier, it provides a means of applying such psychological mechanisms as substitution, compensation, and sublimation, all of which can help individuals maintain healthy emotional balance.

Social Values of Recreation

As indicated earlier, most people today do not find their primary social contacts and important relationships in their work lives. Instead, such opportunities are found chiefly within family life and voluntary group associations during leisure hours. The primary value of recreation in this respect is that it provides an opportunity for people to overcome a sense of isolation by joining social groupings. These may include not only informal neighborhood associations or religious or professional groups but also the varied kinds of social groups in which people become involved on the basis of friendship, sociability, or common interests.

In our society, such groups are extremely important in that they provide individuals with a sense of belonging rather than isolation. Group participation offers a realistic training ground for both cooperation and competition. The youngster who is part of a group in an after-school center or a member of a teen-age social club is testing his social role and preparing for involvement in the adult world. He must learn to cooperate

11 James Jan-Tausch, *Suicide of Children, 1960–1963*, Report of New Jersey State Department of Education, Trenton, 1964, p. 3.
12 L. H. Richardson, "Relationship of the Use of Leisure Time in High School to Effectiveness in College," *School Activities*, May, 1962, pp. 262-64.

with others, to accept group rules, to impose self-discipline, and to subordinate his own wishes, when necessary, to the desires of the over-all group.

Sports in particular are seen as playing an important role in character development. This view is typified in a recent statement by Dr. Frederick Hovde, president of Purdue University:

College football breeds discipline and leadership. We are a peace loving people, but we defend what we have and believe in. Competitive team sports keep us strong and vigorous. . . . I find no convincing evidence that leadership can be taught. It is something that can only be learned by facing successfully its demand on the individuals' total capability.[13]

One of the most important elements of sport is thought to be the rigorous process of training in which an individual must dedicate himself to a total way of life. A leading college long-distance runner describes distance running as a character-building experience, in which the daily routine of workouts becomes more enjoyable and valuable than the weekly ordeal of competition:

The essence of the enterprise lies in the daily workout. It is the workout that regulates the runner's whole life—his eating habits, his social schedule and his academic future . . . the distance runner enjoys the daily routine of workouts more than the weekly ordeal of competition. The lust for victory is too often overemphasized as the motive to run.[14]

Similar views have been expressed of college rowing, a sport in which the competitor is subject to tremendous physical demands and in which he engages almost anonymously, part of a total team effort. College crew captains stress that rowing is sport for its own sake, with no "good deals, no glory, no money" to be gained. They comment:

An oarsman must have a burning desire to excel, the ability to push oneself to the limits of human endurance and still maintain poise and concentration . . . it's a discipline, a way of life. One's whole attitude changes under the value of crew. . . . The unity of the boat, the fanaticism and religious ardor of oarsmen all contribute to the crew's growth.[15]

The conviction that sports participation helps to build character is widely shared. It must be recognized, however, that often sport is misused and its values seriously distorted. Typically, high school and college sports directors today place great emphasis on winning rather than on other goals

[13] Frederick Lawson Hovde, quoted in *Miami Herald*, December 6, 1967, p. 3-F.
[14] "Happiness for a Distance Runner," *New York Times*, August 11, 1968, p. 6-S.
[15] William N. Wallace, "Why Row? College Captains Provide Answer," *New York Times*, April 26, 1964, p. S-7.

of participation and competition. A leading American historian, Henry Steele Commager, suggests that the more fundamental problem lies in the extent to which the purpose of school and college sport has been distorted. No longer, he says, do athletics contribute to the physical fitness of the young or to the development of sportsmanship:

On the contrary, the tremendous emphasis on winning the game has largely destroyed sportsmanship and has corrupted both players and spectators. It does not contribute to initiative, independence, alertness and other desirable qualities. Instead, by centering authority in paid coaches whose primary interest is winning games, it has gone far to destroy initiative and independence on the part of players. . . .

No impartial student of college and high-school athletics today can doubt that, on balance, these sports—far from making any contribution—actually do immense and irreparable harm. It is not only sports that are corrupted by the current malpractices; it is the whole educational enterprise.[16]

The claims that are made for sport as a means of character development depend entirely on the circumstances under which they are played. This is true not only in scholastic or collegiate competition but also in community recreation programs. The development of desirable character traits, such as the ability to play by the rules, evidence good sportsmanship, and win and lose gracefully, essentially represent middle-class values. Lower-class youth often find it difficult to accept such values. Short and Strodtbeck suggest that gang athletics tend to emphasize individual performance and to serve immediate rather than long-term goals. Adolescent gangs are often so completely committed to the idea of winning at all cost that

the rules of the game seemed to have a tenuous hold on their loyalties. It was not unusual for them when stern adult supervision was absent to avoid impending defeat in a sports contest by precipitating a fight.[17]

Often the gang itself is not cohesive enough to be able to withstand the effects of defeat; thus, sports failures can be highly demoralizing.

Thus, it would be wrong to assume that sports automatically yield desirable social adjustment and character development. There is some evidence to suggest that the social attitudes and group behavior of high school athletes may be destructive or antisocial. Hollingshead found that Elmtown's varsity high school athletes tended to be the most active drinkers in the high school and that it was impossible for the coach to discipline or control them. Similarly, Coleman, in *The Adolescent Society*,

---

[16] Henry Steele Commager, "Give the Game Back to the Students," *New York Times Magazine*, April 16, 1961, p. 27.

[17] James F. Short, Jr., and Fred L. Strodtbeck, *Group Process and Gang Delinquency* (Chicago: University of Chicago Press, 1965), pp. 161, 244-46.

concluded that athletic participation was detrimental to educational attainment by discouraging a stress on scholarship and diverting school resources and student energies away from the mission of academic excellence.

On the other hand, a number of investigators have found that sports participation provides social mobility for many disadvantaged young people. In effect, it has become a realistic way of realizing upward aspirations. Hodges comments that football "has functioned as a highly effective status elevator for thousands of boys from blue-collar ethnic backgrounds."[18]

Loy points out four important values of sports play with respect to upward mobility: (1) early participation may develop skills which permit direct entry into professional sports, (2) sports participation may promote educational achievement by providing scholarships and strengthening the student's motivation to remain in school, (3) it may lead to occupational sponsorship or assistance or to the kinds of contacts that lead to later business careers, and (4) it may lead to the development of attitudes and behavior patterns valued in the larger occupational world.[19]

Recent sociological studies of midwestern high school boys have demonstrated that on all social-class levels, athletes performed on a higher level academically than nonathletes and were working toward college entrance at a much greater rate. Almost five times as many nonathletes as athletes dropped out of high school.[20] Even when students with similar intelligence quotients were compared, athletes did better academic work than nonathletes. One might speculate that the discipline of sports led athletes to make better use of study time or that the sense of personal worth and the prestige gained from sports brought greater all-around confidence.

In general, participation in student activity programs seems to be closely related to the school's holding power and to provide constructive outlets for student's social and psychological needs.[21] Student organizations serve as a means through which students are able to define their social status, and those who participate in cocurricular activities tend to be more successful academically than nonparticipants. Indeed, it has been found that leading business and industrial executives were extremely active participants in cocurricular activities while at school or college.[22]

One might, however, ask whether it is participation itself that causes improved student performance—or whether it is not that students accu-

[18] Harold Hodges, *Social Stratification* (Cambridge, Mass.: Schendkamn, 1964), p. 167.

[19] John W. Loy, *The Study of Sport and Social Mobility*, paper presented at Sociology of Sport Symposium, University of Wisconsin, November, 1968, pp. 14-15.

[20] Walter E. Schafer and J. Michael Armer, "Athletes Are Not Inferior Students," *Trans-Action*, November, 1968, pp. 61-62.

[21] Percy V. Williams, "School Dropouts," *National Education Association Journal*, February, 1963, pp. 10-12.

[22] Robert M. Wald and Roy A. Doty, "The Top Executive—A First Hand Profile," *Harvard Business Review*, July–August, 1954, p. 48.

rately perceive sports and other cocurricular activities as avenues to success and status. William F. Whyte, in a study of slum youth, found two social groupings. One group, which he called the "corner boys," was content to hang around on street corners; this group had low occupational and prestige goals. The other group, which he called the "college boys," was much more ambitious and upward-mobile.

Whyte found that the "college boys" realized that certain kinds of affiliations and social behavior would help them in getting ahead. Perceiving the neighborhood settlement house as representative of middle-class, goal-oriented values, they tended to join and become active in its program. Thus, not the recreational activity itself but the social setting in which it is carried on as well as the values it stresses accounts for recreation's contribution to social growth and academic success.

Intellectual Growth Through Recreation

The previous section has pointed out that sports participation and cocurricular involvement in general are highly correlated with overall school success. In addition to motivational factors, it would appear that the element of physical activity itself promotes more effective mental performance. One writer states,

the youngster who gets plenty of exercise . . . is more likely to do better academic work and be freer from tension than his passive, non-athletic roommate. . . . Participation in sports relaxes and challenges the student and enables him to concentrate more intensely.[23]

A study of West Point cadets revealed that academic failure occurred much more frequently (43.4 percent) in a group that was classified as "inferior" on physical performance tests than among students whose physical performance was "superior" (18.8 percent). Another study conducted at Phillips Academy in Andover, Massachusetts, demonstrated this linkage even more conclusively. The physical education department introduced an experimental morning physical activity program; it was found at the end of a testing period that those in the morning gymnasium classes had twice the number of honors and half the number of failures of those who continued with the regular school program.[24]

In many ways, recreation contributes to the individual's intellectual growth. As Chapter 13 has indicated, it promotes creative learning and self-expression for young children and stimulates conceptual growth. Such hobbies as reading, art, music, drama, amateur radio, nature study, and similar interests all make an important contribution in this regard.

[23] Phyllis Lee Levin, "Putting Muscles into Marks," New York Times Magazine, November 28, 1965, p. 118.
[24] Ibid., pp. 118, 125.

Recreation can be particularly important for those who suffer from disability. Typically, a British study of physical activity programs with mentally retarded children showed that the effect of these programs was not only to improve the physical but also the mental performance of the subjects.[25] A three-year study of a remedial program for infants of under-privileged Negro families in Washington, D.C., conducted by the National Institute for Mental Health, found that, over a 21-month period, the subjects' average intelligence quotient climbed to 106, compared with 89 for a control group. While the program was described as "tutoring," its report indicated that

since the children were too young for any formal schooling, the tutoring, con-ducted by women college graduates, consisted of play activities designed to stimulate mental and verbal capacity.[26]

There is widespread acceptance of the value of recreational experience in antipoverty programs. This trend was pointed up in a 1968 conference dealing with the role of the arts in meeting the social and educational needs of the disadvantaged. At the meeting, sponsored by the Arts and Humanities Program of the U.S. Department of Health, Education and Welfare, the following statement was made:

Ironically . . . such projects in the arts which appear to offer the greatest promise for the education of poor children are being conducted—not within the formal school system—but in neighborhood centers, settlement houses, community action agencies, recreation centers, museums, churches, and in a variety of other settings outside the schools.[27]

It was agreed that such artistic and cultural programs helped dis-advantaged children to

Have a continuing experience of accomplishment and achievement and thus acquire the confidence necessary to develop a sense of worthiness.

Develop a greater refinement of taste and sensibility—the ability to dis-criminate the fine and true from the coarse and false.

Appreciate a wide range of sensory, intellectual, emotional and aesthetic experiences.

Acquire an understanding of the importance of work and discipline in order to achieve desired ends in life.

25 J. N. Oliver, "The Effect of Physical Conditioning Exercises and Activities on the Mental Characteristics of Educationally Sub-Normal Boys," *British Journal of Edu-cational Psychology*, 28:155-65, 1958.

26 John Leo, "I.Q.'s of Underprivileged Infants Raised Dramatically by Tutors," New York *Times*, December 26, 1968, p. 24.

27 Judith Murphy and Ronald Gross, *The Arts and the Poor, New Challenge for Educators* (Washington, D.C.: United States Department of Health, Education and Welfare, 1968), p. iii.

Increase the capacity to manage effectively verbal and symbolic non-art tasks, like the three R's. . . .

Improve in general mental and emotional health and provide . . . more adequate personality growth and role functioning.

Develop perceptual skills which might contribute to the more complex and subtle view of reality that culturally disadvantaged children often fail to develop.[28]

In this and many other ways, recreation can be perceived as contributing to the intellectual development of participants as well as to physical, emotional, and social development.

Recreation and the Needs of Major Age Groups

Any analysis of the personal values of recreational experience must necessarily examine the special needs of major age groupings in the light of rapidly changing patterns of family life in modern society.

Family Life Today. The changing nature of American family life has had profound implications for the upbringing of children. As increasing numbers of families have moved to suburban housing developments, much of the actual responsibility for raising children has shifted from the home to other settings. Urie Bronfenbrenner, a leading developmental psychologist, points out that while parents still have the moral and legal responsibility for raising children, they often lack the power or opportunity to do the job adequately. Parents tend to spend much less time with their children, and in many ways children and youth have moved away from adult influence. Years ago, families were both larger and more diversified, including more adults (grandparents, uncles, aunts, and cousins) who lived close by and with whom one had close ties. Bronfenbrenner suggests that families today usually include only one or two adults, and functioning suburban neighborhoods have withered to a small circle of friends, chiefly accessible by automobile or telephone:

Whereas the world in which the child lived before consisted of a diversity of people in a diversity of settings, now for millions of American children the neighborhood is nothing but row upon row of buildings inhabited by strangers.[29]

Many suburban housing developments today lack nearby stores, community services, institutions, and social structures; the way of life for many working adults in the neighborhood is to come home, have a drink, eat dinner, mow the lawn, watch television, and sleep. This is the sterile

[28] *Ibid.,* p. 9.

[29] Urie Bronfenbrenner, "The Split-level American Family," *Saturday Review,* October 7, 1967, p. 60.

world, Bronfenbrenner says, in which many of our children grow up. Children tend to be grouped with other children who are much like themselves, in terms of age, social class, and even levels of ability. Often it becomes hard for them to communicate with and understand their parents.

Coleman adds to this picture by pointing out that in modern society the natural processes of education in the family have been replaced by the formal structure of the school. Children no longer are helpful to families economically, and parents cannot help train them for a place in community life. Children are set apart in schools for ever-longer periods of time. High school students in particular are cut off from the rest of society and made to carry on their entire social lives with their own groups, in

separate subcultures [which] exist right under the very noses of adults—subcultures with languages all their own, with special symbols, and most importantly, with value systems that may differ from adults.

Teen-agers, in effect, become a distinct social system which offers

a united front to the overtures made by adult society . . . the adolescent is dumped into a society of his peers, a society whose habitats are the halls and classrooms of the school, the teen-age canteens, the corner drugstore, the automobile, and numerous other gathering places.[30]

What are the implications of this, with respect to leisure and recreation?

First, as later sections of this text make clear, many of the most serious problems of teen-agers are related to the forms of play they engage in. Beyond this, it is clear that the lack of meaningful contact between many parents and their children during leisure hours is a source of much difficulty. Bronfenbrenner points out that research on middle-class adolescents indicates that those children whose parents had been away from home for lengthy periods of time rated significantly lower on such traits as responsibility and leadership. Father absence was responsible for low motivation, the inability to work for deferred satisfactions, low self-esteem, susceptibility to group influence, and juvenile delinquency, especially among boys. It would seem then that close and continuing contact between parents and their children, such as might be found in family recreation activities, would be extremely important in the healthy personality development of children.

Many families, however, do not seem able to achieve this kind of relationship. Bronfenbrenner points out that American children depend on television to fill their leisure hours far more than the children of any other nation. He writes,

[30] James E. Coleman, *The Adolescent Society: The Social Life of the Teen-Ager and Its Impact on Education* (New York: Free Press, 1962), p. 4.

whereas American children used to spend much of their time with parents and other grownups, more and more waking hours are now lived in the world of peers and of the television screen.

Bronfenbrenner points out that television has been shown in controlled experiments to have a marked effect on the attitudes and actions of observers. Recognizing that television has become a major aspect of the leisure behavior of children and youth, he asks:

Is it any wonder that children, as they grow to adolescence, often turn out to be complete strangers to their dismayed parents? Why do an enormous number of young people from educated and middle-class families find it difficult or impossible to relate to anybody and therefore drop out?[31]

A leading educator, S. I. Hayakawa, president of San Francisco State College, has suggested that television is a "powerful sorcerer" which is largely responsible for much of the alienation, rebellion, and deviant behavior of today's youth. Hayakawa's view is that, in contrast to parents, relatives, and teachers, whom children may find censorious or dull, the child prefers the nonthreatening, nondemanding world of television. A youngster who watches television for several hours daily between the ages of three and eighteen will spend over 20,000 hours in passive contemplation of the screen; these hours are "stolen from the time needed to learn to relate to siblings, playmates, parents, grandparents, or strangers.[32]

Hayakawa describes television as a source of pleasant fantasy, a means of "turning on" and waiting for something beautiful or exciting to happen. Even in its commercials, which teach that there is an instant, simple solution to all problems, Hayakawa suggests, television fails to teach the lessons of real life—that study, patience, effort, and training are necessary before one may enjoy what the world has to offer. Certainly, the tremendous number of hours which children and youth spend in watching television suggest that there is a great need for fuller involvement in activities that might provide a fuller physical, social, emotional, and intellectual challenge.

Trends in Sexual Behavior of Youth. At the same time that we have permitted adolescents to become a distinct subculture in our society and have glamorized them by offering public adulation and spending power, we have also frustrated them by lengthening the required period of schooling before they can marry, hold a job, or play a meaningful adult role. Much of the rebellion of teen-agers is based on this development; they are challenging adult controls and seeking new forms of freedom and power— much of it in terms of a pleasure-oriented rationale that rejects traditional standards of behavior and value.

[31] Bronfenbrenner, *op. cit.*, p. 63.
[32] "Television: Kids Turning On," *Time*, September 13, 1968, p. 96.

There is considerable evidence that premarital sexual activity is becoming increasingly accepted by youth. One major study has found that the number of young Americans who still are virgins at the time they marry is rapidly declining and that American youth is "undergoing a revolution in its attitudes toward sex, life, and proper behavior."[33] While there are conflicting reports as to the incidence of pre- or extramarital sexual intercourse, one convincing evidence of the change in mores of youth comes from statistics about illegitimate births.

Despite the development of effective birth-control techniques, especially the "Pill," about one out of every 18 babies born in the United States today is born out of wedlock. Typically, in the quarter-century since 1940, the proportion of all births that were illegitimate increased from 3.8 to 7.7 per thousand per year, and the number of illegitimate births for each 1,000 unmarried women from fifteen to forty-four years of age (commonly regarded as the child-bearing years) rose from 7.1 to 23.5.[34] In March, 1968, the National Center for Health Statistics of the U.S. Public Health Service reported that the number of illegitimate births in the United States had more than tripled over the past twenty-five years, from 89,500 illegitimate births in 1940 to 291,200 in 1965. The stereotype that illegitimacy is chiefly a problem of the poor, and especially of nonwhites, is no longer valid; during the period from 1960 to 1965 the illegitimacy rate for nonwhite women declined 1 percent, while that of white women increased by 26 percent.[35] The problem affects youth particularly. Medical authorities in Connecticut, for example, have estimated that in a given year, one out of six of all teen-age girls in that state between the ages of thirteen and nineteen were illegitimately pregnant.[36]

In the face of new demands for sexual freedom, many college authorities have been forced to relax their regulations. In a number of large universities, rules which had formerly governed visiting by students in the dormitories of the opposite sex have been widely relaxed. In some, there are almost no restrictions today; the press frequently publicizes examples of unmarried college students of the opposite sex who are living together, both on and off campus. Entirely apart from the challenge this poses to traditional values, a number of very practical questions are raised. Beyond the problem of premarital pregnancy, research suggests that premarital intimacy may be closely linked with mental problems. A study carried out at the University of Wisconsin, reported in the *Journal of the American Medical Association*, revealed that a very high percentage of female students (86 percent) who had become psychiatric patients had engaged in

[33] New York *Times*, October 7, 1968, p. 49.

[34] Malcolm W. Browne, "Increase Is Found in Premarital Sex," New York *Times*, July 15, 1967, p. 27.

[35] Harold M. Schmeck, Jr., "Study Reports Illegitimate Births Have Tripled," New York *Times*, March 14, 1968, p. 20.

[36] New York *Times*, March 13, 1966, p. E-9.

premarital sexual intercourse, 72 percent of these with more than one person. The head psychiatrist concluded that "permissive sexual activity seems to be highly correlated with mental illness."[37]

While one might argue that powerful sexual drives are primarily responsible for such behavior, it might also be concluded that premarital sexual activity stems from important needs for human contact and meaningful relationships with others. It represents, in a sense, the other side of alienation or withdrawal. It may also be part of a philosophy of hedonism —a determined attempt to seek pleasure in many forms. To the degree that other kinds of social involvements and personal creative leisure experiences fail to provide such satisfactions, the area of sex is likely to have increased attraction for young people in schools and colleges.

The Use of Drugs. Another aspect of youth rebellion has been the explosion of drug experimentation and use, particularly by young people in high schools and colleges throughout the United States. This consists chiefly of involvement with such mood-changing or mind-expanding drugs as marijuana, hashish, the amphetamines and barbiturates, and LSD and other hallucinogenics rather than such hard narcotics as heroin or cocaine. While estimates vary greatly, there is evidence to suggest that a majority of the students in many schools and colleges are at least occasional users of marijuana.[38] There is sufficient knowledge of the link between this and other more dangerous forms of drugs, as well as the total linkage of the drug culture with a dropout mentality among today's youth, to suggest that this is a serious problem in American society.

What are the underlying causes of this recent revolution? One might point out that our total society has become tremendously dependent on drugs, both as medication and in the form of tranquilizers. For young people, they appear to have appeal both in terms of bringing about a sense of euphoria and because they provide an escape from reality. One college mental health authority suggests that "for people who are chronically unhappy, drugs bring some relief from a world without purpose." Corry writes:

Students themselves are not particularly articulate about why they take drugs. For kicks, they say, or because they are bored, or because drugs are easy to get or because drugs offer them deep personal insights. . . . They offer an illicit pleasure that is almost entirely without sanction in the adult world and they open an immense gap between parent and child.[39]

Often they are used because of curiosity or as a deliberate form of protest and rebellion against the Establishment. Hechinger suggests the

[37] Donald Janson, "Campus Sex Found Vexing Students," New York *Times*, May 20, 1967, pp. 1, 41.
[38] New York *Times*, March 11, 1969, p. 35.
[39] John Corry, "Drugs a Growing Campus Problem," New York *Times*, March 21, 1966, p. 27.

most fundamental cause of the problem, which was virtually nonexistent among middle-class youth before the 1960's, is the "chain reaction of a combination of permissive homes with the speed-up of youth's experiences in an affluent society." The early onrush of adolescence encourages youth to experiment with partying, dating, sex, smoking, drinking, and, before long, glue-sniffing and "pot." "As old thrills wear off, the search is on for new ones."[40]

Some authorities suggest that the use of drugs comes about because of youth's awareness of its own alienation and because of discontent with the world. Godfrey Hochbaum writes:

> For thousands of years, starting long before recorded history, man has found a variety of means to cope with the drudgeries, pressures, boredom and fears of everyday life . . . intoxicating beverages, tobacco, or similar substances, narcotics, and hallucinogens are only a few of these means that are themselves older than recorded history. . . . But in one form or another they have, with only few exceptions, always and everywhere been favored and widely used as a means to help people escape from or cope with the oppressive forces of reality. In fact, these means are in essence not very different from others to which all of us turn every day—going to a movie, reading a book, engaging in sports, or playing cards. All are means of escape, all help to relieve the constant daily stresses and strains on our minds and bodies.
>
> In short, smoking, drinking, or the use of various drugs can under certain conditions serve some constructive, useful, and satisfying purpose, just as the other mental and physical divertissements just mentioned.[41]

However, Hochbaum, who is acting director of the Social Analysis and Evaluation Program in Health Services and Mental Health Administration of the Department of Health, Education and Welfare, points out that the reason society disapproves of such dependencies and attempts to control their use is that the benefits and pleasures which they may yield are far outweighed by the health hazards which they create. For many young people, these health hazards are dismissed, and the use of drugs, particularly marijuana, is seen primarily as a means of achieving an accepting, friendly, social setting. Corry points out that on college campuses marijuana is often used in small groups, where it is associated with feelings of "conviviality and warmth."[42] Young people frequently make the argument that drugs are taken for reasons similar to those for drinking alcohol.

The use of alcohol is widely accepted throughout the United States with the exception of a few states that have local option. Two out of three

[40] Fred Hechinger, "Drugs: Threat on Campus," New York *Times,* April 10, 1966, p. E-7.

[41] Godfrey M. Hochbaum, "How Can We Teach Adolescents About Smoking, Drinking and Drug Abuse?" *Journal of Health, Physical Education and Recreation,* October, 1968, pp. 34-35.

[42] Corry, *op. cit.,* p. 27.

adult Americans who are twenty-one and over drink occasionally. One in eight persons drinks to excess, and one person in sixteen, about 6.8 million, drinks enough to be considered a problem drinker. Most people today are "learning to accept . . . drinking . . . as a social custom that is as ineradicable as it is harmless when practiced in moderation."[43]

Nor is alcohol our only mood-changing dependency. It has been estimated that one adult American in every four has taken a tranquilizer, sedative, or stimulant drug during the past year and that fully half of American adults have done so at one time. We continue to smoke cigarettes at a high rate despite the report of the Surgeon General of the United States which clearly linked cigarette smoking with cancer and other illnesses and despite other emphatic warnings from health authorities. For one year, the consumption of cigarettes fell from the 1963 level, when 509.6 billion cigarettes were sold. Since then the rate has continued to rise, reaching a total of 551 billion cigarettes in 1967; only recently has it begun to decline again.

Returning to marijuana, the widespread view that its users are necessarily alienated and socially withdrawn does not seem to be valid. A study of Michigan high school seniors showed that marijuana users tended to be more politically active and to have fuller social involvement than nonusers. The report stated:

Our data appeared to support the thesis that drug use by young people, particularly use of marijuana, represents a social form of recreation far removed in nature from the traditional problem of narcotics addiction or alcoholism.[44]

Some have pointed out that at the famous Woodstock Music Festival, a rock-and-roll concert in 1969 which attracted 300,000 young spectators to an upstate New York farm, the use of marijuana was widespread, and yet there was not a single example of violence in any form. In contrast, they suggest that 300,000 adolescents and young adults who were drunk, rather than "stoned," would have engaged in a mass three-day brawl. Despite such arguments, many mental health, legal, and educational authorities today agree that the use of drugs is an artificial means of achieving release or escape and often potentially harmful. For many drug users, it becomes self-defeating, encouraging a withdrawal from real life and from stable, meaningful relationships.

Why is this significant for those concerned with recreation and leisure in the lives of young people? It must be recognized that sex experimentation and drug use often stem from boredom, apathy, or the need to find meaningful relationships or relaxed sociability with others. Despite the

[43] "How America Drinks," *Time*, December 29, 1967, p. 15.
[44] "Marijuana Users Are Sociable, Michigan Student Survey Shows," *New York Times*, December 17, 1968, p. 20.

higher priority which is placed on academic and intellectual concerns today, it is a fact that the bulk of college students continue to value the non-academic side of college life. A study of almost 20,000 college freshmen and sophomores carried out in the mid-1960's by the Educational Testing Service indicated that of the varied values which college might hold for them, students were most concerned with "collegiate life," meaning cocurricular activities, athletics, and the social life of the institution. Fifty-one percent of those responding indicated that this was their most important value, while 27 percent indicated that preparation for a career or occupation was most important to them, and only 19 percent assigned greatest importance to academic goals.[45]

Thus, it is extremely important that young people of high school and college age be given opportunities for involvement in activities which are meaningful, which challenge them, and which offer the basis for creative expression and satisfying interpersonal relationships. It is essential that such opportunities be provided as imaginatively and fully as possible in our schools and colleges and in programs operated by community agencies.

The Leisure Needs of Adults. A primary need of many young adults is to find social groups which provide enjoyable activities in which they may make friends and carry on the process of selection and courtship that leads to marriage. Particularly in the cities, where so many young adults find employment after school or college, the environment tends to be anonymous and impersonal, with limited opportunity for social interaction. Apart from the work setting or being a member of clubs or church groups (which involve only a small proportion of young adults), there are comparatively few such opportunities. Thus, many commercial ventures have sprung up to help young adults find companionship and social involvement. Often they consist simply of "dating bars," where easy pickups and relaxed, alcoholic conversation are possible. Many apartment house builders have developed houses for "singles" only, where young unmarried people may mingle easily. Such activities as skiing, sailing, vacation travel, or stays at resorts provide leisure outlets for many young people in cities. Far too few public recreation departments or other voluntary agencies have recognized this need and made serious attempts to provide programs for young adults.

Gradually, most young adult Americans shift from single status to marriage during their twenties. As they begin to have children, their social involvement tends to center around the neighborhood in which they live and in programs sponsored by religious agencies, civic and neighborhood associations, or P.T.A.'s. Families begin to enjoy community-sponsored recreation opportunities, and the home itself is a center for parent-and-child activity. As their children move into organized community activities, par-

[45] "Student Goals: Why They Go to College," New York *Times*, November 8, 1964, p. 20.

ents begin to use their leisure as volunteer adult leaders for Scout groups, Little League coaches, or volunteer teachers in cooperative nursery schools.

In some communities, recreation departments provide mothers of school-age children with activity programs during the day. Social centers in many housing projects or settlements provide classes, exercise programs, and similar activities for mothers, at the same time providing day-care programs for younger children. Similarly, many community recreation departments and school adult education programs provide evening classes in skills, hobbies, current events, self-improvement, or cultural activities which attract substantial numbers of married adults.

Throughout this age span, recreation continues to serve the function of providing relaxation, helping the family strengthen its ties, gain new interests and social, cultural, and intellectual involvements—and, finally, to prepare for that period when the demands of raising a family lessen and leisure becomes more readily available.

This change tends to happen first for married women in the American society. Their lives are rather clearly structured through the age span of about twenty to the early forties. The task is to finish education, get married, establish a home, and raise a family. Once children have become fairly independent, however, many mothers find that the demands posed by the home and family are much less pressing.

At this point, many find it necessary to decide what they will do with the remainder of their lives. Some women return to school or college to complete their education or take an advanced degree. Still others return directly to work, in some cases with their husbands, where they may help operate family businesses or assist in office work. For many, the availability of increased leisure means that they are able to become involved in various community projects or causes. In many communities, women at this stage of life take on voluntary responsibilities in community nursery schools, teen-age canteens, libraries, mental health clinics, art museums, community theater programs, or choral groups. Often, they hold positions on church or school boards, work with the League of Women Voters, serve as volunteer nurses' aides, or participate in other activities dedicated to public welfare. Without the volunteer assistance of women who are able to devote substantial portions of their time to such efforts, many of the health, welfare, and educational programs in American communities would be seriously handicapped.

Many other women at this stage do not choose to become involved in volunteer programs and instead join recreational, cultural, or educational programs that are not degree-oriented but that serve to make their lives less lonesome, provide companionship, and help them develop their own personalities and talents. An example of the mushrooming interest in this field is found in Van Nuys, California, where a program called "Every Woman's Village" was established by housewives (mostly middle-class women whose husbands were professional men) in the early 1960's. They regarded themselves as typical of millions of women whose children attend school and whose gadgets do most of their housework but who are too intimidated by the competitiveness and the huge classes of the university to be able to return to formal educational institutions. Lacking the study skills or self-confidence needed to compete with young students and without a need for formal degrees, they sought a new kind of educational environment. One officer commented:

Everybody worries about factory workers displaced by automation, but no one seems to worry about women who are in the same dilemma. We do.[46]

Before long, Every Woman's Village had a student body of 800 women and a faculty of 55 paid and highly competent teachers. Offering no degrees, giving no grades, seeking no accreditation, and without intellectual pretense, it includes a blend of many recreational offerings with others that are clearly academic in nature. The curriculum of one hundred courses, aimed at "relaxed learning," runs a gamut from yoga, papier maché, and rug-making to courses in applied economics or automation and cybernetics. Many classes are in fairly typical "think courses," such as conversational French, or the "new math," while others are more esoteric, dealing with extrasensory perception and the use of hallucinatory drugs.

Every Woman's Village has met a growing need of many American women in the middle years. Delegations of women from other cities have come to observe it, with the intention of beginning similar programs elsewhere. It seems clear that it represents a trend that will continue to grow, whether in community-operated volunteer programs of this type or through non-credit university extension offerings.

For both men and women during the middle decades of life, leisure and recreation have the important function of providing a transition to the coming years of later maturity and aging. As earlier chapters have indicated, an increasing number of Americans cut their work ties sharply at retirement and are able to look forward to an extended period of comparatively healthy and independent living. While many professionals and self-employed businessmen have the option of continuing to work beyond the age of sixty-five, most persons who work in business organizations, Civil Service, or similar fields of empoyment must retire fully from formal occupation.

The sudden transition from an active work life confronts them with a great bulk of free time. For some older persons, this is not an insurmountable problem. They are able to live independently and to maintain family ties and social contacts that keep them happy and involved. Many

[46] Peter Bart, "Every Woman's Village: Challenge for the Bored Housewife," New York *Times*, December 3, 1965, p. 34.

who are financially well off move to "Leisure Villages" or other retirement communities, where with others like themselves they are provided with a wide variety of recreational opportunities.

It is apparent, however, that for the mass of retired persons, problems related to loneliness, boredom, and lack of meaningful personal and creative involvement pose serious difficulties. It is to meet this need that organized recreation services for aging persons in American communities must play an increasing role.

This chapter has dealt with the personal values of recreational experience in a number of areas: physical, social, emotional, and intellectual. It has examined a number of special problems and needs that relate to family living and to each of the major age levels. Chapter 17 analyzes recreation's contribution to community life, both in terms of meeting the personal needs which have been suggested here and with respect to its broader economic and social role.

17

Recreation and Social Functions

This chapter examines the role of organized recreation service in meeting important social needs, first with respect to the total community and second in terms of groups of people who have special disabilities or social problems.

Improving the Total Quality of Community Life

The general purpose of organized service is to improve the total quality of community life by helping to make it richer, fuller, more creative, and happier for all.

Providing Social Opportunity. Particularly for those who live in larger cities, varied recreational outlets are needed to provide opportunity for involvement with others. This problem was illustrated in a major mental health study carried out in the Midtown Manhattan district of New York City in the early 1960's, which found the city to be marked by hustle, frantic speed, life set to a highly competitive tempo, and a pervasive feeling of loneliness for many.

In a big city like New York, sickness, loneliness, trouble, a need for help, can be inches away from you . . . on the other side of the wall . . . and you may never know.[1]

---

[1] Leo Srole, in Leo Srole, Thomas S. Langner, Stanley T. Michael, and Thomas A. C. Rennie, *Mental Health in the Metropolis: The Midtown Manhattan Study* (New York: McGraw-Hill, 1962), p. 119.

The casual interpersonal relationships of the metropolis cause problems of isolation and unhappiness; often individuals find themselves in the state described as *anomie*, or alienation. The loneliness of the city, particularly for large numbers of unattached young adults, is illustrated by the rapid increase of computerized dating services, which match single adults in terms of their background, age, and interests. This indicates the need for more meaningful ways in which people can make contact with each other in the modern metropolis, in direct, open, and friendly forms of group involvement. While recreation cannot provide a total solution for the pathological loneliness and lack of communication that characterize much of modern urban life, there certainly is an important need for activities and groups in which people may find personal enrichment and social involvement.

Contributing to Mental Health. As suggested, recreational opportunity makes an important contribution to the maintenance of sound mental health. Some social scientists have pointed out that there has been no reliable empirical evidence of the value of recreation (particularly outdoor recreation) in reducing or preventing mental illness. Gans states the view that "leisure and recreation are, comparatively speaking, relatively unimportant causal factors in achieving . . . mental health."[2] He goes on, however, to describe "satisfying" leisure behavior as the kind of activity that provides the individual with physical and emotional relaxation, reduction of fatigue, restoration of energy lost elsewhere, and avoidance of activity with ill-effects. He concludes:

If satisfying leisure behavior as I have defined it is part of the good life, it would follow that it is a constituent part of mental health. Therefore, the recreation facilities which help to make leisure satisfying are necessary for the maintenance of mental health.[3]

In a major conference of psychiatrists, sociologists, ecologists, and city planners which examined the relationship between outdoor recreation and mental health, it was agreed that:

within the total environmental context, the social and physical environments associated with outdoor recreation have beneficial effects on the individual's physical and mental well-being. . . . Recreation appears as a contributor to mental health by offering a change from one's daily patterns and an opportunity to find self-identification and personal adjustment in ways that the daily patterns do not afford.[4]

[2] Herbert J. Gans, "Outdoor Recreation and Mental Health" in *Trends in American Living and Outdoor Recreation,* Vol. 22 of the Report of the Outdoor Recreation Resources Review Commission (Washington, D.C.: U.S. Government Printing Office, 1962), p. 236.

[3] *Ibid.,* p. 235.

[4] Melvin M. Webber, "Relations Between the Social-Physical Environment of Outdoor Recreation and Mental Health," in *Trends in American Living and Outdoor Recreation, op. cit.,* p. 244.

In response to the charge that valid evidence is lacking of this relationship, it must be pointed out that in *many* areas of community service, such evidence is lacking. Typically, in a number of major research and demonstration projects involving remedial education, individual psychotherapy, group therapy procedures, vocational training, and social welfare, it has not been possible to demonstrate clear-cut positive outcomes. Yet it is widely accepted that such programs have positive value.

Improving Intergroup Relationships. Another important function of recreation is to improve the relationships among people of different racial, religious, or class backgrounds by giving them an opportunity to work or play together in programs of mutual interest. Community recreation committees or neighborhood improvement associations may provide the medium through which people can express civic pride and community spirit. When the barriers of misunderstanding caused by lack of contact among people of different backgrounds are removed, intergroup relations may be markedly improved.

In addition, recreational programs may provide a medium for sharing customs, values, and folk traditions, thus helping to remove the stereotypes that account for intergroup hostility. In the early decades of this century, many social scientists characterized the American society as a "melting pot." It would appear that instead we seem to be achieving what has been called an American mosaic, in which citizens of different backgrounds maintain distinct subcultures (retaining national traits, customs, and values). Within such a mosaic, recreation can provide an ideal means for sharing folk culture and traditions and at the same time permit each group within the society to retain its own pride and self-identity.

It would be overoptimistic to say that we have fully achieved this goal. Indeed, the 1960's was a period in which Americans moved toward greater polarization in terms of racial identity and hostility between blacks and whites. Yet it is possible that such a period is necessary before there can be true harmony and social acceptance among different racial and ethnic groups. In this context, recreation programs in many large cities have been serving as the medium through which Negroes have begun to discover their own culture through programs of Afro-American music, dance, and theater and courses in black history.

In general, organized recreation programs have been perceived as a means of improving community morale and unity. When citizen groups work together to determine recreation needs and to press city councils and elected officials for improved park and recreation facilities and programs, they develop a sense of teamwork and commonly shared objectives. As the needs of various community groups are met, rewards of accomplishment are shared by those who have shared in the process, strengthening their sense of citizen participation.

Alternatives to Socially Harmful Activity. A key value of organized recreation service is that it provides healthy and constructive outlets for many drives and interests which might otherwise be expressed in socially harmful or personally destructive activities. Venereal disease, drug addiction, compulsive gambling, and the highway accident rate are only four examples of the outcomes of the search for pleasure and thrills that dominate many in our society. While the mere provision of other forms of socially desirable recreation will not insure that the majority of people will avoid harmful forms of play, yet it is essential that such alternatives be provided.

Summing up, then, it is the total purpose of recreation as a form of organized community service to provide happiness and pleasure, to enable those of all ages to enjoy their leisure in personally and socially constructive ways, to promote positive forms of social interaction in order to achieve community morale and a sense of unity, and to provide appealing alternatives to less desirable forms of activity.

Closely linked to this purpose is the function of recreation and park agencies in helping to make communities more attractive, pleasant, and livable in a physical sense.

Improving the Quality of the Urban Environment

Our cities suffer from a variety of ills that are closely related to overcrowding, including clogged transportation arteries, atmospheres that are poisoned by smog, and lakes and waterways that have become fetid cesspools of human and industrial waste. One authority writes:

It becomes increasingly obvious that the major challenge of our time is to make our cities livable. . . . Noise, congestion, polluted air, and traffic are the bane of urban, and, indeed, suburban existence. Green areas provide an antidote. As man cannot live by bread alone, so he needs to be surrounded by more than stone and concrete. . . .

Today, if people are to survive, their communities must provide relief from the tensions of life, and must provide it within easy reach. The national, state, and county parks fill a real need; it is a matter of record that millions of people enjoy their advantages. But there are also millions who no longer have the time or energy to seek these parks. For them, in spite of the rapid transit and freeways, whatever refreshment their spirits receive must come from the immediate surroundings where most of their lives are spent—the places they work, the places they live, and the roads between.[5]

It is no longer possible to permit our cities to become increasingly congested by cars, poisoned by smog, cut off from natural vistas, and scarred by the random dispersal of industrial debris, elevated highways, ugly and unreadable signs, auto junkyards, railroad yards, and decaying piers and by

---

[5] Margaret Winters, "Green Areas Provide an Antidote," New York *Times,* October 8, 1967, p. D-27.

the scattering of slum tenements in commercial and industrial districts. Instead, it is essential to protect and grace rivers with shaded walkways, boating, trees, and cafés; to take traffic off the street by creating pedestrian shopping plazas with sculpture, water displays, and sitting areas; to open up increased numbers of malls, playgrounds, and vest-pocket parks; and to provide opportunities for both active and passive uses of leisure for all ages.

The task is to create a total environment in which people can live most fully and happily. In this process, city planners, architects, engineers, and housing officials must all share responsibility. But it is the recreation and park professional who is chiefly concerned with the need for parks, play areas, and other outdoor sites that will contribute to the visual environment and provide useful settings for play. It is he who must make sure that in total environmental planning and design (including the rehabilitation of older cities as well as the design of newer ones), physical aspects relating to recreation and enjoyment of the environment are given strong priority.

The mere replacement of run-down and abandoned tenements and factories with high-rise apartment buildings and business complexes will not make cities more livable. Instead, they must be rebuilt so that they provide environments where people can live on a human scale, with opportunities for meaningful human contact and a sense of neighborhood. There are many ways in which natural beauty can be introduced into the urban environment. Green areas bordering parkways, small parks in the midst of business districts, municipal and commercial structures that are set into large open plazas, transforming lots into vest-pocket parks—all these help to make communities more livable.

The Economic Functions of Recreation

As described earlier, recreation has become a major source of business investment and income and thus an essential element in the total economy of the United States.

On the national level, while many forms of recreational involvement contribute to the economy, one of the most easily identifiable is the impact of the national park system travel on the national economy. In a study carried out for the Department of the Interior, it was reported that the approximately 150 million visitor days spent in travel to national parks in 1967 resulted in a total expenditure of $6.35 billion.[6] This in turn was responsible for $4.76 billion in personal income, $5.71 billion added to the Gross National Product, and $952 million in Federal taxes. The economic contribution of such recreation-based vacation travel is particularly impressive because it involves the use of national assets which are preserved

---

[6] Ernst W. Swanson, *Study of Impact of National Park System Travel on the National Economy* (Washington, D.C.: U.S. Department of Interior, 1968), p. 1.

for the future, unlike mining and oil uses, which deplete nonrenewable resources.

On a regional level, New England is a leading example of recreation's economic contribution. Only a short time ago, this was an economically declining area, with factories closing, jobs increasingly scarce, and more people leaving its six-state area than arriving. During the 1960's, New England went through a boom unprecedented in its history; a major source of its economic comeback was its expansion as an ideal winter-summer recreation region. The New England states, because of their attractive terrain, undeveloped rural areas and cool climate, had long been a popular area for summer vacations. The mid-1960's, however, brought a new winter-vacation boom:

Ski resorts are rising all over, especially in the northern tier. Building of the new lodges, motels and roads has had a major impact on the construction industry. . . .

Vermont has the fanciest of the new ski resorts. Some offer such lures as heated outdoor swimming pools, sauna baths, ice skating, closed gondolas to take people up ski slopes, rather than T-bar lifts or rope tows, and cocktail lounges, night clubs and theaters.[7]

Like other forms of recreation, skiing has a multiplier effect. State officials estimate that for every dollar spent on skiing directly winter visitors spend an additional $4 for food, lodging, liquor, entertainment, gasoline, and other goods and services.

On the statewide level, many states base their economies heavily upon tourism and vacation industries. Probably the outstanding example of a state which depends heavily on tourism is Hawaii. This recent member of the union has been swept over by a kind of tidal wave, or "kai mimiki," which has rushed "over the Pacific in jet planes, a lei-decked flood that is causing an upheaval in the 50th state's way of life, its economy, culture and landscape."[8] In 1968, it was reported that the number of tourists, nearly all from the mainland United States and a third from California, had actually exceeded the number of inhabitants: 1,005,790 versus the state's own population of 750,000. Tourist spending expanded from about $130 million per year in 1960 to about half a billion dollars in the late 1960's.

On the municipal level, many major cities depend heavily upon conventions and the tourist trade to support their economies. Their appeal is based on culture and entertainment in the form of great museums, symphonies, night clubs, theater, circus, and sports events. Many cities depend heavily on huge arenas and halls which house business, professional, and political conventions. In New York City, the Convention and Visitors Bu-

---

[7] "New England's Big Comeback," *U.S. News and World Report*, February 14, 1966, p. 74.

[8] "Hawaii: Too Much Prosperity?" *Newsweek*, April 8, 1968, p. 94.

reau announced in 1969 that during the previous year the city had a total of 16.5 million visitors, including almost 3 million convention delegates and 1 million foreigners—all of whom spent a total of $1.5 billion during their stay in New York. Tourism has been identified as the second largest industry in the city, producing 375,000 jobs, largely unskilled, in such employment areas as hotels and restaurants.

Recreation is also used as a means of upgrading economically disadvantaged rural areas throughout the United States. With assistance from government, many rural landowners have converted their properties into recreational resources—thus attracting increased numbers of visitors to their regions and adding generally to the local economy:

Participation by the farmer . . . varies considerably in kind and degree. He may rent cabins to hunters, fishermen, skiers, hikers, climbers, horseback riders, rock collectors, or families on vacation; he may offer facilities for those who camp in tents or live in trailers; he may cater to picknickers by supplying tables, stoves, wood, toilet facilities, electric light, and play areas. . . . He may sell by day or season the right to hunt. . . . He may beautify natural lakes or create artificial ones for fishing, boating, canoeing, swimming . . . to his artificial or natural lake development he may add a marina for the rental of boats and tackle and the sale of bait . . . or set up stands to [sell] his farm produce to visitors.[9]

Recreation has also been one of the ways in which Indian tribes have improved their economies. As an example, when the $110-million Kinzua dam and reservoir was planned for western Pennsylvania, the Bureau of Indian Affairs assisted the Seneca tribe, which was forced to give up much of its property, in developing a huge new tourist program, including shops, lodges, museums, an Indian village, a motel, a 100-boat marina, and an outdoor amphitheater and an indoor theater for Indian ceremonials and folklore festivals. It was estimated that this huge new development would draw several hundred thousand tourists each year.

Adequate provision for leisure is regarded as one of the hallmarks of healthy and sound communities. Typically, when regions or municipalities seek new business development or residential expansion, they stress their cultural, recreational, and educational resources. A former president of the National Association of Manufacturers has commented:

Nothing is more important to the physical and emotional health of the men and women of industry than proper recreation activities. So important is this considered that few modern companies would consider locating a new plant or facility in a community without first surveying its recreation possibilities. Management knows that, in seeking competent and gifted personnel, its ability to attract and hold the men and women it wants often is decided by the little theatre, the park system, or the Little League. The intelligent person indus-

[9] John A. Torney, Jr., "Farmer Brown—Recreation Specialist," *Journal of Health, Physical Education and Recreation*, September, 1964, pp. 20-22.

try desires as an employee is certain to insist upon living in a community worthy of his family.[10]

Generally, then, recreation is considered to be an important economic asset, in terms of helping to stabilize population, reduce turnover of employees in business, and attract new industries to American communities.

Recreation as a Health-Related Service

Recreation is vital for the health of residents in American communities, including both the over-all population and those who have physical, mental, or social disabilities. Luther Terry, formerly Surgeon General of the U.S. Public Health Service, confirms the value of recreation in this respect. He writes of health as

the measure of man's capacity for coping with or adapting effectively to the physical, emotional, intellectual, social and economic demands of his environment. This is clearly a dynamic life process involving a variety of stimulus-response relationships. . . . Meaningful activity is important to health throughout the life span. In order to mature—physically, intellectually, emotionally and socially—a child must be exposed to appropriate stimuli. And so too must the adult if he is to remain at his peak. Today, people are increasingly involved in leisure activity. . . . More and more people have time on their hands. Moreover, the injudicious use of leisure time is a characteristic feature of both maladjusted teen-agers and adults, and of retired, elderly persons. Too often, because of ignorance, indifference, or inertia we are faced with the time-consuming and difficult task of reestablishing a human capacity which need never have been lost. Recreation has an important—and an increasing—role in rehabilitation.[11]

All people need diversified recreational opportunity. Generally, those within a normal range of development are able to meet this need satisfactorily—provided that activities, programs, and leadership are available.

Those who suffer from disability, however, frequently find difficulty in meeting their recreative needs in constructive and varied ways, in part, because serious physical handicaps obviously limit the extent of participation. Much recreative deprivation of the disabled is, however, caused by the reluctance of society to permit them to engage in activity to the extent of their real potential. Sometimes communities or recreation agencies do not make the kinds of adaptations in the design of facilities needed for disabled persons to use them fully. Sometimes recreational and park agencies actively bar disabled persons from their programs because they feel that to

[10] Rudolf F. Bannow, "What Is Expected of Recreation by Management," *Recreation*, January, 1960, p. 15.
[11] Luther Terry, *Recreation in Treatment Centers* (American Recreation Society, Hospital Section), September, 1965, p. 3.

serve them would require specialized leadership to a degree they could not afford. Frequently it is feared that the presence of blind, retarded, or orthopedically handicapped participants would be distasteful to the public at large, who might then not enter facilities themselves. Sometimes parents or relatives shelter the disabled excessively. Finally, the lack of skill of the disabled person or his fear of rejection often limits his recreational participation. Whatever the reasons, many disabled persons are unable to make use of available community recreation resources.

A special function of recreation with respect to groups with disability lies in its use as a therapeutic or rehabilitative technique. Originally, such services were provided primarily in hospitals, and the field itself was known as "hospital recreation." More recently, the term "therapeutic recreation service" has become widely accepted, both by its own practitioners and by medical authorities. A publication of the National Center for Health Statistics of the Public Health Service defines it:

Therapeutic recreation is the specific use of recreational activity in the care, treatment and rehabilitation of ill, handicapped and aged persons with a directed program.[12]

In the past, this area of service has been described as "recreation therapy," similar to "occupational therapy." There is increasing agreement, however, that recreation is not usually applied as a specific therapy on a one-to-one basis under medical prescription with the specific purpose of curing illness. Instead, the emphasis is being placed on the role of recreation in facilitating healthy social interaction and creative experience and making life more enjoyable and rewarding—thus contributing to rehabilitation in the broadest sense. This function has been broadly described by E. Mansell Pattison in a passage dealing with adjunctive therapy in psychiatric institutions:

The thrust of milieu therapy is not to unlock specific psychodynamic conflicts, but rather to provide integrating, guiding, rehabilitating social experiences. This begins with those socializing activities that the most regressed patients can participate in, then on to social activities requiring more ego control and personal-relatedness, and finally to reality-oriented social functions that are part and parcel of every day living. Seen in this perspective, the adjunctive therapies are experiences in socialization and social interaction. The task of the adjunctive therapist is not that of individual therapist or extension thereof, but that of a social system specialist.[13]

[12] *Health Resources Statistics, 1968* (Washington, D.C.: U.S. Public Health Service, 1968), p. 185.
[13] E. Manswell Pattison, "The Relationship of the Adjunctive and Therapeutic Recreation Services to Community Mental Health Programs," *Therapeutic Recreation Journal* (Washington, D.C.: National Therapeutic Recreation Society, 1969), pp. 19-20.

This suggests that the primary purpose of recreation, when used with individuals who suffer from disability—hospitalized or not—is to promote social integration and rehabilitation, to make life more rewarding, to prevent further disability, and to help patients or clients make the fullest possible use of their existing resources.

This chapter now considers the specific functions of recreation with the mentally retarded, the mentally ill, the physically handicapped, and the rapidly growing aging population.

Recreation Service for the Mentally Retarded. Mentally retarded persons are children and adults who, as a result of inadequately developed intelligence, are significantly impaired in their ability to learn and to adapt to the demands of society. The U.S. Department of Labor has estimated that about 125,000 retarded children are born each year and that approximately 6 million Americans suffer from some degree of mental retardation. Some 30 million Americans, the families of the retarded, are closely affected by this problem.

A substantial number of mentally retarded individuals are believed to be the victims of environmental deprivation, in the sense that their initial disability has been seriously compounded by the lack of adequate stimulation, challenge, and instruction. Play, as a normal aspect of development, is often consciously lacking among retarded children. Stein writes:

mentally retarded boys and girls do not play spontaneously or innovate as normal children; they have to be taught to play whether the play be individual, parallel, or group. Many of the motor skills and abilities basic to play and recreation that most normal children learn from association and play with the gang on the block must be taught to the retarded.[14]

Several studies have explored the value of physical activity programs—including games and sports—for the mentally retarded. One study carried out in England by J. N. Oliver brought about marked improvement in athletic achievement, physical fitness, and strength (mentally retarded children are often poorly coordinated and obese) and also was responsible for an average increase of 25 percent in I.Q. of its subjects.[15] Similar efforts with educable mentally retarded boys demonstrated improved scores on the Wechsler Intelligence Scale for children after only 20 days' duration.

Social adjustment and group interaction are also extremely important to mentally retarded children, who frequently suffer from isolation from others. Skeels and Dye reported a striking change in mentally retarded children who were taken from an orphanage where they had received minimal attention and placed in an institution where they received much more attention from older patients and attendants. After a year and a half, these

---

[14] Julian U. Stein, "The Mentally Retarded Need Recreation," *Parks and Recreation*, July, 1966, p. 574.
[15] *Ibid.*, p. 575.

children showed an average increase in I.Q. of 27.5 points, while a similar group that remained in the orphanage dropped an average of 26.2 points.[16] Clearly, recreational experience can provide physical and social experiences which are crucial to the retarded child's reaching his full intellectual and social potential.

Comparatively little attention had been paid to the recreational and social needs of the retarded until the early 1960's. In 1962, the President's Panel on Mental Retardation urged that local communities, in cooperation with Federal and state agencies, expand community services for retarded children and youth. More and more communities have since initiated services in this field, many with stimulation or financial assistance from the Joseph P. Kennedy Foundation, the National Association for Retarded Children, and the American Association for Health, Physical Education and Recreation. In a number of states, new residential centers for the retarded are providing extensive facilities and programs.

The majority of mentally retarded children and youth are not institutionalized but live with their families. It has been estimated that in the average community, for each 1,000 school-age children, there will be approximately 1 totally dependent child, 4 trainable mentally retarded children, and 25 educable mentally retarded children; only the more severely retarded children are institutionalized. Ramm writes:

the retarded child living at home has little recreation opportunity. He may make friends with the children in his special class at school, but unlike the normal children who can play with their school chums in the neighborhood after school hours, retarded children are transported from their homes in different parts of town and have few friends in their own neighborhoods. A similar situation exists with mentally retarded adults who work in a centrally-located sheltered workshop, or who do not work at all. These people are victims of enforced leisure. They have a six-to-eight-hour time block each weekday and more on weekends or holidays during which little or no activity is available to them. Many just sit and watch television.[17]

A number of city and county recreation departments are now providing extensive recreation services for the mentally retarded. Their objective is not only to provide diversion but also to assist in the total development of the retarded. Avedon described the total purpose of socio-recreative programming for the retarded as including the following important elements: (1) providing recreation education and information which will develop the individual's capacity for meeting his own leisure needs;

[16] Harold M. Skeels and Harold B. Dye, "A Study of the Effects of Differential Stimulation on Mentally Retarded Children, *Proceedings and Addresses of the Sixty-Third Annual Session of the American Association on Mental Deficiency*, 44:114-136, 1939.

[17] Joan Ramm, "*Challenge: Recreation and Fitness for the Mentally Retarded,*" American Association for Health, Physical Education and Recreation, September, 1966, p. 1.

(2) using recreation to improve general health, minimize atypical appearance, and modify behavior to help retardates become more socially acceptable in community settings; (3) offering a variety of recreational and social experiences to help individuals learn and practice needed skills; (4) counseling retarded youth and adults about recreational resources in the community and arranging opportunities for involvement; (5) acting as a liaison between the community and the retarded individual and his family to assure acceptance of retarded persons in community programs and facilities; and (6) coordination of communitywide efforts to meet the vocational, educational, social, and recreational needs of the retarded.[18]

In terms of diagnosing the potential of retarded persons for living reasonably independent and satisfying lives in the community, Avedon and Arje suggest that the traditional ways of classifying the retarded child which were based largely on I.Q. scores are not as useful as categories which reflect the individual's level of social independence and ability to function in social groupings.[19] It is becoming increasingly clear that young adult retardates who have developed the necessary skills to hold down jobs in the community must also develop the ability to use leisure constructively if they are to operate successfully in job situations.

Recreation Service and the Mentally Ill. Approximately 9 million people today are described as being mentally ill; half of the hospital beds in American hospitals are occupied by mental patients. Traditionally, recreation has been an important area of service in many mental hospitals throughout the United States. In some, it has been approached primarily as a form of diversion, used to relieve boredom and improve patient morale. In others, it has been provided on the basis of medical prescription to help the patient in terms of resocialization and the development of leisure interests and skills.

Today, the provision of recreation services in programs serving the mentally ill has been radically altered by rapidly changing concepts and techniques of diagnosis and treatment. The modern concept of psychiatric care is based on the local community mental health center, which ties together such relevant psychiatric resources as out-patient clinics, in-patient services in general hospitals, day centers, night centers, halfway houses, and social clubs. Progressive mental health programs today place emphasis on early diagnosis of mental illness, out-patient treatment, and social rehabilitation rather than custodial hospital care.

New treatment methods—especially the use of tranquilizers—are responsible for these drastic changes and have brought with them a new concept of treatment:

---

[18] Elliott M. Avedon, "Recreation's Responsibility and the Rehabilitation Process," *Journal of Rehabilitation*, January–February, 1969, p. 29.
[19] Elliott M. Avedon and Frances B. Arje, *Socio-Recreative Programing for the Retarded* (New York: Teachers College Bureau of Publications, 1964), pp. 15-18.

a continuity of care from the point at which an illness is identified to the time when the former patient completely resumes his place in the community. The day is not far off when communities across the country will be prepared to offer a spectrum of services designed to support returned patients and also to prevent many persons from ever having to be hospitalized.[20]

As an example, one might cite the state of Illinois, where the total number of patients in mental hospitals is being steadily reduced. The emphasis is being placed on voluntary admission and commitment, with patients assuming major responsibility for their own management. The population of out-patient departments has increased tenfold, and psychiatric patients are being increasingly admitted to local general hospitals rather than to large, distant psychiatric hospitals.

Illinois has been divided into eight mental health zones, so that no citizen will be more than 90 minutes by automobile from a mental health center. A crucial aspect of such programs is the provision of recreation and social programs, such as social clubs for the mentally ill or halfway houses that help patients bridge the gap between the hospital and the community. Hong and Bauer describe one such halfway-house program:

The club provides opportunities for mental patients, discharged patients, and persons under psychiatric care to participate in social rehabilitation programs, recreation and other activities. Through this means they can make social contacts, reestablish social adequacy, reorient social status, regain lost skills, and restore lost self-confidence . . . to make the gradual readjustment back into the mainstream of community life. . . . Inpatients from selected state hospitals make trips to the club three days a week and participate in scheduled activities with club members, staff, and volunteers.[21]

Another important trend in the treatment of hospitalized mental patients is the development of "recreation counseling," which has the following objectives: (1) to assist patients to maintain and strengthen their existing affiliations with family, friends, church, lodges, and civic groups; (2) to help patients form new ties with individuals and groups; (3) to teach patients to make effective use of available community resources for recreation; and (4) to mobilize community resources for fostering mental health.

Studies have indicated that patients who receive recreation counseling tend to have a greater awareness of the importance of constructive use of leisure and recreation in maintaining physical and mental health and more clearly structured plans for the effective use of leisure after leaving the hospital than patients who have not had counseling. Avedon stresses that

[20] Paul Douglass, "Community-Based Volunteers in Illinois Mental Health Therapy," *Parks and Recreation*, April, 1967, p. 26.

[21] Jerry S. Hong and Ralston S. Bauer, "Have You a Halfway House Program?" *Parks and Recreation*, November, 1966, p. 914.

helping disabled persons meet their own needs for recreation must be a crucial goal of therapeutic service:

Personnel responsible for recreation service in the rehabilitation process must be primarily concerned with guidance and counseling rather than activity programming per se.[22]

Such an approach is necessarily dependent on the willingness and capability of community recreation departments to offer recreation programs which the disabled, including the mentally ill, may enter. Haun comments on the artificial barrier between recreation for the ill and handicapped and community programming for the so-called normal population. He writes:

I have been in turn outraged, depressed and bewildered by . . . the baseless anxiety of municipal, county and state program directors at the prospect of broadening their services to include, not just an arbitrarily chosen segment, but the entire residential population for which . . . they do have responsibility. . . . I have been equally unsettled at the hesitancies and fears expressed by line personnel in playground work, in camping, physical education, and parks at the prospect of developing programs for all comers.[23]

Haun suggests that there needs to be a much fuller concern on the part of recreation workers with serving the disabled as a vital part of their total spectrum of activities. Even today, comparatively few public recreation departments have developed cooperative relationships with mental health centers such as those described earlier. While the number of social clubs and halfway houses has been growing steadily, there are still few of them, and they tend to lack skilled personnel, particularly in the area of recreation programming and leadership.

Recreation Service and the Physically Handicapped. Another major segment of our population includes those with serious physical disability, such as amputees, paraplegics, and post-polio patients, the blind or partially sighted, and the deaf. Other conditions that may create a degree of disability include arthritis, which is estimated to affect about 11 million persons, cerebral palsy, about 600,000, multiple sclerosis, about 300,000, and muscular dystrophy, about 200,000. Of those who are orthopedically disabled, an estimated 250,000 persons in the United States are confined to wheelchairs, 200,000 wear leg braces, and 140,000 wear artificial limbs.

People with disabilities have the same need for a full range of recreational opportunity as the nondisabled. Many disabled persons, however, are today unable to use public recreation facilities freely. According to the Bureau of Outdoor Recreation,

[22] Avedon, *op. cit.*, p. 29.
[23] Paul Haun, "The Place for Recreation in Mental Health," *Parks and Recreation*, December, 1966, p. 974.

great numbers of disabled persons are not receiving the benefits of our nation's recreation resources. The severity of their disabilities, architectural barriers, nonacceptance by society, and slowness of the recreation profession to adjust its programs and facilities to their needs all have contributed to a serious lack of opportunity.[24]

Efforts have recently been made to provide full access to recreation facilities for persons with limited mobility and with wheelchairs, crutches, and braces. On the national level, the General Services Administration has ordered all new Federal construction contracts to permit easy access to the disabled, and the National Park Service and Forest Service are moving rapidly to make sure that the steps, curbs, doors, and other barriers of their hundreds of facilities are modified to permit entry to the handicapped.

A number of states are also taking action. Georgia, for example, is creating a state park designed solely for the disabled. This $1.3-million project, financed in part by a grant from the Department of the Interior, will be situated within Fort Yargo State Park and will include day and residential camping, nature walks, swimming, picknicking, fishing, and bicycling.

In an attempt to involve the physically and mentally disabled and to give them greater confidence and interest in outdoor recreation, separate facilities are provided. It is the expectation of the Georgia Park Department that as they become increasingly confident, they will no longer need the protection of separate facilities. Thus the special facility will have contributed to the goal of full integration of the disabled into society.

Many other state and public authorities have made similar efforts to make recreation and park facilities available to the disabled. Several states have improved access to rest rooms in service centers along their thruways and freeways. Such states as Oregon and New Jersey have developed ramps for wheelchair anglers along lakes and rivers. Major fairs like Montreal's popular Expo, in 1967 and 1968, and the San Antonio Hemis-Fair in 1968 were designed for total access by the disabled. The city of Fort Worth, Texas, has built a large new playground at its Child Study Center designed for safe and creative use by the blind, mentally retarded, cerebral-palsied, and other disabled groups. Other voluntary agencies place a heavy emphasis on trip and outing programs for disabled persons, including those with cerebral palsy, muscular dystrophy, polio, and other crippling disabilities. One such agency, the Federation of the Handicapped in New York City, sponsors weekly and monthly outings, usually by train or chartered bus, and has even taken groups abroad, including wheelchair travelers.

More and more, standards have been established which must be observed by municipalities that wish to qualify for state or Federal assistance in the development of park and recreation facilities. These standards seek

[24] *Outdoor Recreation Planning for the Handicapped* (Washington, D.C.: Bureau of Outdoor Recreation Technical Assistance Bulletin, 1967), p. 1.

to make all kinds of facilities accessible, safe, and convenient for the disabled.

Recreation Services and the Aging

The aging population clearly represents one of the most important areas of concern in the American society today and poses a major challenge for organized recreation service. During the mid-1960's, the population over sixty-five numbered about 18 million, representing over 9 percent of the total population.

Thanks to growing life expectancy (which lengthened by 17.6 years for men and 20.3 years for women between 1900 and 1950), the proportion of older persons in the United States has rapidly expanded. It had been estimated that the number of persons over sixty-five would total 25 million by 1970. Further in the future, it is expected that by the year 2000 the United States will contain approximately 310 million persons, of whom over 30 million will be over sixty-five, with about 20 million in the over-seventy-five age group that consumes the bulk of health, hospital, and nursing services. It is predicted that the average retirement age will be sixty years or less.

We tend to oversimplify the concept of retirement and aging and to assume that all older persons are very much alike. Far from this, they vary widely in terms of their economic, physical, and social status and their ability to accept the changes thrust upon them by the process of aging. Service to aging persons should therefore be viewed in relation to the following four major life periods, as formulated by Avedon.

Pre-Retirement. During the period between fifty and sixty-five, economic burdens related to child-rearing, education, and home furnishing and improvement generally lessen. For many individuals, with the lessening of other responsibilities, this period includes increased involvement in public and commercial recreation activities as well as participation in community affairs related to church, political activities, or volunteer service on hospitals, libraries, or school boards. It is during this period that thoughtful preparation should be made for retirement.

Post-Retirement. When work responsibilities are ended, many individuals develop problems related to the increase of free time, accompanied by a decrease in income. For many, the social contacts and sense of importance derived from work, which now are ended, pose the need to find new associations and commitments. Some older persons become involved in community programs for senior citizens. Others join retirement communities. While some persons in the period immediately after retirement may become hospitalized or institutionalized, the larger number continue to be fairly healthy and to maintain a degree of social independence.

Transitional Period. This generally describes the span between the mid-70s and mid-80s. In this period, many older persons experience a marked physical decline, become more socially isolated, and enter homes for the aged. Even though there is an inevitable loss of mobility and other physical capacities, however, major organic damage need not occur, and many older persons continue to function extremely well, emotionally and socially.

Later Years. The remaining years of life tend to be marked by increasing disability, often with serious physical or intellectual incapacity. Although some older persons in their late 80s or 90s continue to be active participants in community life, the majority become increasingly dependent and often enter treatment-oriented or custodial institutions.

Williams writes about aging persons in modern society:

We know that some, but not all, experience a decrease in close companionship, and an increase in personal loneliness. Some lose the fullness of living of previous years, and too often . . . respected places they formerly held in the family group, their circle of friends, and in society itself. . . . There is no accepted pattern for satisfying living in the later years, and no satisfactory plan for the transition from middle years to old age.[25]

John Gardner, formerly Secretary of Health, Education and Welfare, commented before a congressional committee on aging that although the American society had given some assistance to solve the problems of income, housing, and health that face many old people, it had done little to provide them with interest and purpose in life. He stated, "Our society is now designed to put most older people on the shelf . . . to deal them out of the game."[26]

The isolation of the aged in the second half of the twentieth century has been accentuated by major changes in family structure. Homes with three generations in them have vanished almost as completely as the horse and buggy. There are many communities in America in which almost no aged persons live, while there are many others in which only older persons live. About half the aged in the early 1960's (8.4 million persons) were married couples living together but for the most part away from other family members. Another 4.9 million persons were single and lived alone in their own homes; about 3 million lived with relatives. The rest were lodgers, living in residential hotels, Y's, institutions for aging persons, and S.R.O.'s (single-room-occupancy units).

Many older persons today tend to withdraw from meaningful contact and involvement with others. One group of sociologists has evolved a theory of disengagement to explain this phenomenon, viewing withdrawal from social interaction as a normal process of aging. The disengagement

[25] Arthur Williams, *Recreation in the Senior Years* (New York: Association Press, 1962), pp. 16-17.
[26] "Gardner Urges Retirement Aid," New York *Times,* June 8, 1967, p. 49.

theorists hold that gradual withdrawal from meaningful human contacts and involvement is a necessary and inevitable process which the aging choose for themselves and which others should accept. Generally, this theory has been rejected, and most authorities today believe that older people do not withdraw because they wish to but because it is forced upon them.

Many people tend to view the process of aging with fear and distaste and to see older persons in stereotyped and inaccurate ways. For example, it is widely believed that aging is accompanied by a sharp decline in sexual activity and interest. A number of studies, however, reveal that a significant number of individuals display an actual increase in sexual interest and activity as they pass through their 70s and 80s and that substantial numbers of aging persons are capable of carrying on heterosexual activity and are maintaining such relationships, both in and out of marriage.[27] Curiously, our Social Security laws, which penalize the widowed who remarry in terms of Social Security benefits, make it necessary for many retired older persons to live with others "in sin" to avoid having their retirement allotments cut.

The basic point is that old people retain human needs and appetites and if they are to be physically and emotionally healthy, must continue to have a full range of social and recreational opportunities which provide settings for friendship, social involvement, and creative activity.

When these are not provided, many older persons tend to decline abruptly, following retirement or serious personal losses. The suicide rate for persons sixty-five and older is higher than for any other age group. Loneliness often leads to alcoholic problems among older persons. A substantial proportion of older persons who are classified as mentally ill are alcoholic, and the death rate due to alcoholic disorders among older persons rose by 52 percent between 1950 and 1968. Among aging persons with special disabilities, social isolation is even more pronounced. A conference on the aged blind, sponsored in 1967 by the American Foundation for the Blind and the United States Administration on Aging, concluded that social isolation was the most serious problem confronting the older visually handicapped person.

Too often, the admission of aged persons to public or private nursing homes or to psychiatric hospitals (which have increasingly large geriatric units) comes about because they are unable to exist independently in the community rather than because they are actually mentally ill. The aged make up 27 percent of initial admissions and occupy a third of the beds in mental hospitals. Often when they are hospitalized, the long-standing disabilities of older persons are aggravated, and they move into a rapid decline. It is possible to arrest this pattern and to counteract the feelings of rejection and isolation, insecurity, and loss of self-esteem that affect many

[27] "Normal and Abnormal Sex Behavior in Aging," *Geriatric Focus* (published by Knoll Pharmaceutical Company, Orange, N.J.), July–August, 1968, p. 1.

older persons. Studies have demonstrated that purposeful mass activities in hospitals and nursing homes have been useful in remotivating sizable numbers of patients who are withdrawn and unresponsive.[28]

The most important challenge facing us today is to make the lives of aging persons in the community as rewarding and happy as possible, to prevent disability, withdrawal, and institutionalization. Senator Walter Mondale, Chairman of the Senate Subcommittee on Retirement of the Committee on Aging, has suggested that earlier retirement policies and medical advances have made it reasonable to assume that the average person will soon be spending twenty to twenty-five years in retirement. He suggests the need for mid-career clinics to help workers prepare for retirement by examining the goals of their working life, considering changes of direction, and developing added interests and involvements outside of work.

The Administration on Aging in the Department of Health, Education and Welfare has authorized substantial sums to assist states and communities in planning, demonstration projects, and the training of personnel to work with older persons. It has also provided several million dollars in grants to public and private agencies to finance research in problems related to aging. Much of this research has focused on the role of leisure in the lives of older persons. Friedman and Havighurst, who carried out a study of older persons at the University of Chicago, concluded that recreation could act as a useful routinization of life activity. They suggested that recreation provided a great potential for self-expression for many older persons and that "leisure time can be organized and scheduled so as to fill the day and make time pass happily. Play can be made to service this function as well as work."[29]

To meet the needs of older persons most effectively, recreation should not be isolated from other services but instead be meaningfully integrated with health, housing, legal, and economic assistance and other special services. When considered as part of a multiservice approach, recreation has the unique function of being attractive, interesting, and easy to enter; it may be regarded as a threshold, or entry, activity that brings older persons into centers for varied kinds of service and involvement. Both Federal and state agencies concerned with aging have recently lent strong support to the education of recreation professionals in the field of gerontological services. Increasingly, such individuals are taking responsibilities as administrators, researchers, and consultants in the field of services to the aging.

It is particularly important that recreation activities for older persons be suitable for their stage of life, in terms of dignity and maturity. Too often, the programs provided in senior centers are juvenile and childlike.

---

[28] "Geriatric Patients Improved by Purposeful, Mass Activity," *Geriatric Focus*, November 15, 1966, p. 3.

[29] Eugene A. Friedman and Robert J. Havighurst, *The Meaning of Work and Leisure* (Chicago: University of Chicago Press, 1954), p. 191.

Often, the most meaningful activity may be in the area of community service, through which retired people with special skills help others. Such programs, which are often part of a total range of recreational and social activity, provide retired persons with a deep sense of satisfaction and continuing worth.

Recreation and Juvenile Delinquency

As the historical review of the growth of recreation in the United States during the early twentieth century indicated, one of its primary functions was considered to be the prevention or reduction of juvenile delinquency. Since many young people were arrested simply for playing in city streets, the provision of supervised programs in playgrounds and community centers was obviously a useful means of reducing the juvenile "crime" rate. It was widely accepted that vigorous group activities—particularly sports and games—were helpful in burning up the excess energy of youth and keeping them off the streets and out of gambling halls or pool parlors where they might be exposed to criminal influences.

Based on such expectations, recreation was widely supported as an important form of community service for children and youth. In time, as sociologists began to examine the nature of delinquency and youth-gang behavior, questions were raised about the value of recreation as an anti-delinquency measure. More complex theories of juvenile delinquency were proposed; few of these attached major value to the lack of recreation as a cause of deviant behavior or to organized programs as a means of preventing or treating such behavior. None the less, most public and voluntary agencies that provide recreation services for youth continue to regard the reduction of delinquency as one of their primary objectives. How valid is their assumption?

First, it is necessary to define juvenile delinquency and to understand its causes. The concept of juvenile delinquency is extremely vague and ambiguous. Local jurisdictions vary widely in the definition of delinquent acts. These may range from leaving home, truancy, refusing to help parents with chores, smoking, turning on water hydrants, or hitching rides on buses to more serious criminal acts such as burglary, arson, armed robbery, or assault. Generally, juvenile delinquency is regarded as a form of deviant and antisocial behavior by youth, usually involving defiance toward authority and a threat to its security. Frequently, legal descriptions of delinquent behavior stress the idea of youth being "incorrigible" or "habitually" delinquent.

Exactly how serious a problem is juvenile delinquency? The Task Force Report of the President's Commission on Law Enforcement and Administration of Justice in 1967 described delinquency as the "single most pressing and threatening aspect of the crime problem in the United

States."[30] According to this study, one in every nine children will be referred to juvenile courts for an act of delinquency before his eighteenth birthday. Extremely high percentages of those arrested for certain criminal acts are under the age of eighteen. Specifically, 52 percent of all persons charged with burglary, 45 percent of all persons charged with larceny, and 61 percent of all persons charged with auto theft are juveniles.

However, much of the image of youth engaging in senseless and random violence is simply not justified. The 1967 President's Task Force Report indicates that while there is more juvenile delinquency today, it is chiefly in the area of property offenses:

The public image of a vicious, violent juvenile population producing a seemingly steady increase in violent crime is not substantiated by the evidence available. . . . Violence appears neither as a dominant preoccupation of city gangs nor as a dominant form of criminal activity . . . even among those toughest of gang members.[31]

Causes of Juvenile Delinquency. What are the fundamental causes of juvenile delinquency, and how do these relate to the value of recreation as a form of community service for youth? There are two basic schools of thought, one which sees it primarily as a psychological, or psychogenic, problem and the other which sees it from a sociological, or cultural, viewpoint.

The Psychological View. Here, delinquent behavior (referring not to occasional antisocial acts but to habitual patterns of antisocial and criminal activity) is regarded basically as an attribute of the child's personality. In psychiatric terms, it may mean that he has an inadequate *superego* or *ego* or that delinquency has become a symptom of, or method of coping with, fundamental problems of adjustment.

It is a paradox that even in high-delinquency neighborhoods, many children manage to survive and to build constructive lives for themselves while others fail to do so. Some investigators have found the family to be the key factor where such contrasts exist. Healy and Bronner maintained that where the tie between parents and children was strong, stable and integrated personalities would be built, with socially acceptable traits and behavior patterns that could withstand the temptation to crime and antisocial gang affiliation.[32] Other investigators have developed psychological classifications of juvenile offenders, which indicate that while some delinquents are "relatively integrated" and have a reasonably good chance to move ahead to independent and mature adulthood, other groups of delin-

---

[30] *Juvenile Delinquency and Youth Crime,* Task Force Report of the President's Commission on Law Enforcement and Administration of Justice (Washington, D.C.: U.S. Government Printing Office, 1967), p. 1.

[31] *Ibid.,* p. 150.

[32] William Healy and Augusta Bronner, *New Light on Delinquency and Its Treatment* (New Haven: Yale University Press, 1936, 1957).

quents have relatively weak ego controls, are highly insecure, and have strong tendencies toward aggressive and hostile behavior. A final category of delinquent youth includes "defective superego" cases, those who have refused to accept the values of the larger society, have no qualms of conscience over their behavior, do poorly in school, and generally are in difficulty with the police at an extremely early age.[33]

The psychological approach to the phenomenon of juvenile delinquency all too frequently assumes that behavior and personality are firmly fixed by early childhood experiences within the family, whereas the evidence is that later environmental factors play an important role. In addition, the delinquent act itself is taken as evidence that the youth committing it is mentally abnormal; thus, the teen-age girl who is an addict, an alcoholic, or a prostitute or the boy who runs away from home regularly or is highly aggressive and hostile is considered to be "sick." Socially deviant behavior itself is made the basis for diagnosing personality disturbance, whereas in fact such behavior may be typical for all members of a gang and not, in that sense, deviant.

The Sociological View. This position holds that juvenile delinquency today is more of a cultural than an individual problem and that its real roots are to be found in the society itself. It is supported by research which has clearly demonstrated that delinquency is closely linked to slum housing, poor schools, broken or unstable homes, the lack of desirable adult models, and the lack of opportunity. It rejects the notion that the juvenile delinquent is necessarily disturbed and disorganized and suggests instead that he is a member of a cultural group that deliberately rejects established social values, obtaining reinforcement from peers within an immediate subculture which is stronger and more real than the overall culture.

Talcott Parsons suggests that the problem is one of masculine identification. In his view, gang members strive to emphasize their own masculine self-image through delinquent behavior. Parsons suggests that particularly among middle-class youth, where females tend to dominate and the father's role may not be evident, or in Negro families lacking fathers, delinquency may represent a robust and destructive protest against femininity.[34] Block and Neiderhoff considered delinquent affiliation to be closely linked to the problem of adolescents growing up in society:

The adolescent period in all cultures, visualized as a phase of striving for the attainment of adult status, produces experiences which are much the same for all youths. . . . When a society does not make adequate preparation, formal or otherwise, for the induction of its adolescents to the adult status, equivalent

[33] For a fuller discussion of psychogenic theories of delinquency, see August Aichorn, *Wayward Youth* (New York: Viking Press, 1935); and Kate Friedlander, *The Psychoanalytic Approach to Juvenile Delinquency* (New York: International University Press, 1944).

[34] Talcott Parsons, *Essays in Sociological Theory* (Glencoe, Ill.: Free Press, 1954), pp. 304-306.

forms of behavior arise spontaneously among adolescents themselves, reinforced by their own group structure, which seemingly provide the same psychological content and function as the more formalized rituals found in other societies.[35]

Robert Merton explains socially deviant behavior in terms of the inability of lower socioeconomic class youth to reach the success goals of society by legitimate means:

when a system of cultural values extols . . . certain *common* success goals *for the population at large,* while the social structure rigorously restricts or closes access to . . . these goals for a *considerable part of the population* . . . deviant behavior then results on a large scale.[36]

Albert Cohen suggests that the behavior of delinquent gangs represents hostility toward middle-class values, such as ambition, self-reliance, the postponement of immediate satisfaction, courtesy, good manners, disapproval of physical violence, and respect for property. Delinquent acts typically display malice toward things that are virtuous; they exhibit hedonism, or thrill-seeking, on a short-term, impulsive basis.[37] Walter Miller identifies a number of typically shared values of lower-class youth which lend themselves to antisocial gang behavior. These include a respect for toughness, in the form of masculinity and physical prowess, for smartness, in terms of the ability to outwit others, a wish for autonomy—a desire to be one's own boss—a fascination with trouble as a way of life along with a craving for excitement, and a tendency to accept fate, rather than one's own actions, as the key influence in one's life.[38]

The idea that the baffled aspirations of lower-class youth account for much gang behavior was developed most fully by Cloward and Ohlin. They established a typology of gangs, which they saw as subcultural groupings, with different kinds of memberships, environments, and goals. These included the fighting gang, hostile and aggressive, with status derived from making war on the community and on other gangs, the criminal gang, involved in deviant behavior for financial gain through racketeering, theft, and the sale of illegal items, and the retreatist gang, which is involved with drugs, sex, and alcohol and withdraws from actual conflict, except for survival or as a means to an end.[39]

[35] Herbert Bloch and Arthur Niederhoffer, *The Gang: A Study in Adolescent Behavior* (New York: Philosophical Library, 1958), p. 17.

[36] R. K. Merton, *Social Theory and Social Structure* (Glencoe, Ill.: Free Press, 1957), p. 105.

[37] Albert K. Cohen, *Delinquent Boys: The Culture of the Gang* (Glencoe, Ill.: Free Press, 1955).

[38] Walter B. Miller, "Lower Class Culture as a Generating Milieu of Gang Delinquency," *Journal of Social Issues,* 14:5-19, 1958.

[39] Richard A. Cloward and Lloyd E. Ohlin, *Delinquency and Opportunity: A Theory of Delinquency Gangs* (New York: Free Press, 1960), pp. 20-30, 161-86.

The Role of Recreation. Each of these theories tends to ignore the role of recreation in the development of delinquent patterns of behavior. Yet a number of investigators have identified play as one of the ways in which delinquency becomes established as a way of life. Frank Tannenbaum, for example, locates the beginning of the alienation process of gang youth in the somewhat random play activities of youngsters:

In the very beginning, the definition of the situation by the young delinquent may be in the form of play, adventure, excitement, interest, mischief, fun. Breaking windows, annoying people . . . playing truant—all are forms of play, adventure, excitement. To the community, however, these activities may and often do take on the form of nuisance, evil, delinquency, with the demand for control . . . punishment, police court.[40]

An early investigator, C. R. Shaw, reports testimony from youthful gang members, showing that stealing stemmed from a search for excitement:

When we were shoplifting we always made a game of it. For example, we might gamble on who could steal the most caps in a day, or who could steal in the presence of a detective and then get away. This was the best part of the game. I would go into a store to steal a cap, by trying one on when the clerk was not watching, leaving the old cap. . . . I might do this all day . . . it was the fun I wanted, not the cap. I kept this up for months and then began to sell the things to a man on the West Side. It was at this time that I began to steal for gain.[41]

Cohen points out that much juvenile crime is carried on "for the hell of it," entirely apart from considerations of gain or profit:

There is no accounting for the effort expended and the danger run in stealing things which are often discarded, destroyed or casually given away. . . . Unquestionably, most delinquents are from the more . . . "underprivileged" classes, and . . . many things are stolen because they are intrinsically valued. However . . . stealing is not merely an alternative means to the acquisition of objects otherwise difficult of attainment. Can we then account for this stealing by describing it as another form of recreation, play or sports?[42]

Whyte's study of Boston lower-class youth quotes a leading gang member's description of fighting among gangs in his neighborhood: "There was a lot of mutual respect. . . . We didn't go out to kill them. We

[40] Frank Tannenbaum, *Crime and the Community* (New York: Columbia University Press, 1938), pp. 17-20.
[41] C. R. Shaw, *Juvenile Delinquency: A Group Tradition*, Bulletin of the State of Iowa, No. 23, 1933, p. 3.
[42] Cohen, *op. cit.*, p. 26.

didn't want to hurt anybody. It was just fun."[43] Such explanations of the playlike nature of much juvenile gang activity are disputed by a number of sociologists. Block and Neiderhoff conclude that juvenile crime today is almost invariably utilitarian and carried out for concrete gain. Short and Strodtbeck write:

Weapons and the intent of gang conflict are more lethal, and "kicks" more addicting. Theoretically, delinquency is seen as rooted less in community tradition and "fun," and more in frustration and protest or in the serious business of preparing for manhood as conceived by the gang members, including the "mysterious and powerful underworlds of organized crime."[44]

It should be recognized, however, that only a part of today's juvenile delinquency is committed by lower-class gang youth in urban slums. A considerable amount of crime is carried out by unaffiliated teen-agers, many of them middle- and upper-class, for whom there is no utilitarian purpose in crime—and surely no intention to join the adult underworld of organized crime. Recent reports of growing youth involvement in such activities as shoplifting, auto theft, and vandalism support this view.

Shoplifting has become a major area of concern in recent years. Between 1960 and 1966, its incidence rose 93 percent, according to the Federal Bureau of Investigation, whose director, J. Edgar Hoover, called it the "fastest-growing larceny violation in the nation." It is estimated today that there are 150,000 such thefts per week in department, food, variety, drug, and other stores. Professional security sources estimate that over 50 percent of all shoplifters today range in age from ten to nineteen. One authority comments:

In the case of the low-income teen-age thief, often the drive represents a craving for possessions that the parents can't afford or simply won't consider buying. . . . But for the youth from a better and even high-income background, the stimulus is curiosity, a desire for "kicks," an escape from boredom. . . . They want a thrill.[45]

The same motivation is responsible for much amateur auto theft, a crime which has been rapidly increasing in the United States. Of the 635,000 car thefts in 1967 (the total was expected to rise to almost one million by 1970), more than half were committed by teen-agers. Of the total arrests for auto theft, persons under eighteen accounted for nearly two-thirds, with the highest number being among fifteen-year-olds. The

[43] W. F. Whyte, *Street Corner Society: The Social Structure of an Italian Slum* (Chicago: University of Chicago Press, 1955), p. 6.
[44] James F. Short, Jr., and Fred L. Strodtbeck, *Group Process and Gang Delinquency* (Chicago: University of Chicago Press, 1965), p. 77.
[45] New York *Times*, December 1, 1968, p. F-1.

rate of car thefts is going up most rapidly in suburban areas; a preponderance of young offenders are middle-class and white. Why do they steal cars? While a few do it for profit—to sell or cannibalize—a recent F.B.I. survey found that 81 percent of teen-age auto thefts are for joy-riding or convenient transportation. Delegates to a Texas youth conference listed thrill-seeking, joy-riding, satisfying a dare, and gaining admission to a gang as the primary reasons for auto thefts by teen-agers.[46]

In many instances, car theft is linked to destructive impulses. In one eastern city, police picked up a gang of fourteen-to-sixteen-year-old boys who drove stolen cars to an isolated wooded area for "demolition derbies." Many other forms of juvenile delinquency involving gang rampages, wholesale destruction of homes, or other forms of vandalism illustrate this angry need to be destructive. Typically, the American Telephone and Telegraph Company must spend millions of dollars a year repairing and replacing its pay telephones, which are pulled, kicked, or picked apart by vandals and thieves. *Time* Magazine comments:

Teen-agers rip out wires or steal receivers and dials just for perverse fun or an adolescent sign of protest. Some psychologists see similarities between the wrecking of telephones and the destruction of school property or cars. Such acts are believed to be caused, in part, by what psychologists call "the feeling of anonymity" that stimulates teen-agers and others to destroy property.[47]

In addition to these forms of youthful crime, many other acts reveal a search for excitement on the part of teen-agers. Drag racing, youthful pranks involving desperate risks (like playing "chicken" and risking head-on collisions on highways or in tunnels), escapades on landing fields (in which teen-agers stand on the airstrip in front of landing planes until the last possible moment)—all are examples of such thrill-seeking stunts.

Here, then, is one aspect of recreation's role with respect to juvenile delinquency. Activities and youth programs which offer challenge and excitement might well make it less necessary for many youths to become involved in pointless lawbreaking and life-risking activities. A research study of athletics in several midwestern high schools has demonstrated that only 7 percent of the boys who had participated for at least one full year in an interscholastic sport were apprehended for delinquent behavior, compared with 17 percent of nonathletes.[48] This suggests that sports may provide a useful means of harnessing the energies and loyalties of young people by giving them the opportunity to identify with a cause, accept rules and discipline, and do battle against a common enemy. It may well be that the excitement, the physical risk, and the use of athletics as an exercise of skill,

[46] Donald Johnston, "Don't Help a Good Boy Go Bad," *New York Times Magazine*, October 1, 1968, pp. 107, 109.

[47] "Mother Bell's Migraine," *Time*, February 28, 1969, p. 92.

[48] Walter E. Schafer, *Interscholastic Athletes and Juvenile Delinquency*, research paper presented at Symposium on Sociology of Sport, Madison, Wis., November, 1968.

strength, and masculine competitiveness drain off many of the impulses that among nonathletic teen-agers are channeled into delinquent activity.

Few studies have attempted to assess in a valid way the effect of organized recreation services on delinquency-prone neighborhoods,[49] chiefly because of the difficulty in isolating recreation as a factor when numerous other influences, both good and bad, are also at work. It is possible, however, to give some illustrations of its observed influence.

The Effect of Recreation Programs. In New York City, in the late 1950's and early 1960's, youth-gang activity reached a new and virulent high. Throughout the area of East Harlem, the rate of juvenile delinquency over a ten-year period had consistently been twice as high as the city rate. The proportion of habitual narcotics users was from three to eight times that of the city as a whole; there were similarly high statistics of venereal disease among youth and of homicides, infant mortality, and other forms of social pathology. In this area, a major youth and adult center, the Wagner Center, was opened by the Board of Education in January, 1959, with a new wing built adjacent to the school to provide needed recreation facilities. The center included a large new swimming pool, gymnasium, game rooms, and special activity rooms; it was manned by a varied staff, including licensed school teachers, recreation leaders, correction officers, Youth Board workers, and other activity specialists. The program included a wide variety of sports and social activities (including boxing, judo, karate, and wrestling), along with vocational and educational courses in many occupational and remedial areas. It also incorporated such supportive services as guidance workers and psychological counselors, career planning experts, and others who leveled an attack on the school dropout problem.

The Wagner Youth and Adult Center developed an extensive membership of 3,500, of whom 1,800 were teen-agers. There was much initial hostility among the members of the eleven fighting gangs that came to the center, based largely on ethnic tensions among Italians, Negroes, and Puerto Ricans. Through careful work with gang leaders, rules governing behavior in the center were developed, and a council was established to enforce them.

Within a year, the New York *Times* reported that all eleven fighting gangs in East Harlem were disbanded and no new gangs had risen to take their place. Two hundred and fifty boys who had been gang members were now free of such affiliations. The number of youth in the area arrested for delinquent activity declined from 88.8 to 70 per 1,000 within a single year.[50] One might question whether it was recreation which contributed to the

[49] As an example, see Roscoe C. Brown, Jr., *A Boys' Club and Delinquency*, Monograph No. 2, New York University Center for Community and Field Services, 1956, which assessed the impact of a new boys' club program on delinquency rates in selected districts of Louisville, Kentucky.

[50] Sam Kaplan, "Eleven Gangs Disband in East Harlem," New York *Times*, August 8, 1960, p. 1.

decline of delinquent activity and to the dissolution of the gangs or whether it was the total program of the center that was responsible. Gans writes:

It is true that playground programs or community centers activities sometimes convert a delinquent into a pillar of the community. When this happens, however, I suspect that it is not due to the facility itself, but to the therapeutic talents of a leader who provides the delinquent with a surrogate father or brother; or to the existence of a group that offers him enough support to convince him that society is not always his enemy. This explains to me the success of the gang workers who have transformed fighting gangs into baseball teams. Although the surroundings in which this transformation often takes place may be recreational, this does not mean that recreation is a casual factor.[51]

This comment, typical of much negative writing by sociologists regarding recreation, needs to be examined. Of course, it is not the facility as such which reduces delinquent behavior; it is the use of the facility and the total experience it provides that is important. Recreational programs often attract youthful gang members who would not come to centers to take part in activities that they perceived as overtly out to change or improve them. As they participate, it becomes possible for understanding adults to assist them personally and in vocational or legal problems, to refer them to other agencies or services, to help them enlarge their life perspective and ultimately to become contributing and valuable members of society. If the community center or baseball field were not there, and if the recreation program did not exist in the first place, it is likely that the initial contact would never have been made.

It should be recognized that many recreation departments disclaim responsibility for working with problem youth and bar gangs from entering their programs. Usually this is because they find such youth disruptive and difficult to work with and because they discourage other participants from entering the program. On the other side of the coin, many hard-core teenagers are unwilling to enter public or voluntary agency programs because of the restraints they impose.

As a consequence, those agencies that seek to attract and involve delinquent or potentially delinquent youth must adopt special approaches. One of the most widely used techniques in recent years has been the roving-leader approach. Such workers are generally detached from organized programs and go out into the street, neighborhood hangouts, or other places where problem youth may be found. Typically, in Washington, D.C., where the Roving Leaders Program of the Recreation Department has been in operation since 1956, roving leaders work directly with several hundred gang youth, as well as others who are sporadically associated with

[51] Herbert J. Gans, "Outdoor Recreation and Mental Health," *op. cit.*, p. 236.

gangs. They receive special on-the-job training in group-work techniques, street-corner contact methods, community resources, and psychological counseling. Most of their time is spent in informal meetings with gangs or individual youths. They work closely with other community agencies to assist their clients in matters of discipline or academic standing. Although recreation is not their primary concern, they help to organize trips, sports events, and other recreational involvements for gang youth.

Another example of experimental approaches to working with problem youth in large cities was the Pre-Delinquent Gang Project carried out by the Henry Street Settlement in New York City. This settlement sought to work constructively with groups of younger boys, ranging in age from eight to thirteen, who were emulating their older brothers by defying adult authority and beginning to engage in violent and unlawful activity. Believing that it was an almost fruitless attempt with older gang youth, the directors of the settlement decided to work with younger gangs that might still be open to adult influence:

Our challenge was to find ways of winning these children back to friendlier ties with adults who could control and redirect them . . . before antisocial patterns became hard and fixed . . . and the adult community . . . lost interest and the chance for wholesome influence.[52]

The purpose of the program was to foster more socially acceptable behavior, to spur parental interest and involvement, and to help individual children free themselves of undesirable peer controls by asserting their own individuality. The groups were affiliated with the settlement house as clubs; the activities that were designed to meet their needs included athletics, crafts, trips, camping, dramatics, and other special projects appropriate for their age level. Parents were invited to the settlement whenever possible to observe or work with the children in special programs, parties, celebrations, picnics, and trips. As ties were developed between the project's leaders and the parents, the latter became better able to deal with such family problems as health, unemployment, school adjustment, housing problems, and parental alcoholism. The project's leaders referred individual children and family members to family casework, psychiatric, and other remedial services and coordinated their work closely with schools, courts, clinics, hospitals, public welfare, and other social agencies.

In the four youngest groups, behavior improved over a period of time until most of the members could be absorbed into the agency's regular program. On the basis of this experience, the directors of the Henry Street project concluded that antidelinquency efforts were most likely to succeed if they were able to reach problem youth at an early age (between eight

---

[52] Ruth S. Tefferteller, "Delinquency Prevention Through Revitalizing Parent-Child Relationships," paper presented at New Orleans Youth Problems Clinic, April, 1966, p. 3.

and twelve), before antisocial attitudes and behavior patterns were firmly fixed. A second implication of this project is that the provision of recreation services alone is not sufficient to meaningfully influence potentially delinquent youth in difficult neighborhoods. In this case, special attention was given to family involvement because disintegrated family structure and lack of parental influence and authority were seen as closely related to the problem behavior of the children in question.

A New Concept of Recreation's Role. A thoughtful statement of recreation's role in working with problem youth is presented by Bertram Beck, executive director of the Henry Street settlement. He suggests that the traditional view of recreation as nonpurposeful activity, sharply differentiated from work, is no longer meaningful for youth in urban slums, who are seeking to discover more adultlike roles for themselves. Simply "getting young people off the street" or "giving them something to do" is not sufficient to meet their needs.

Beck urges that work and play be combined to serve total developmental goals of youth and that recreational experiences be designed to help them systematically explore their environment and develop competences and attitudes useful in getting and keeping jobs. In part, the recreational system itself can provide jobs and training experiences for youth. He says, "employment of young people as recreation, group work or community aides can be the beginning of new career lines which will provide a fresh new cadre for the recreation system."

To provide such experience, the recreational system should be integrated . . . with . . . educational, cultural, and community welfare facilities. The roots of organized recreation in child's play have been destroyed. It must now strive to mix work, learning, and play to serve both social ends and the purpose of self development. Only then can it be an effective instrument in socializing the young and preventing delinquency.[53]

Many of the antipoverty programs which were financed by the Community Action Programs of the Federal Office of Economic Opportunity included such work-study-play approaches for teen-age youth.

A final aspect of the relationship between recreation and juvenile delinquency lies in the development of programs in custodial institutions for youth. Typically, in such institutions, recreation is provided as a means of keeping morale high, substituting constructive interests to supplant negative ones, and helping children develop favorable and constructive relationships with staff members.

Particularly in institutions which serve emotionally disturbed youth, recreation plays an important role in rehabilitation. Often it is found that disturbed youth who enter treatment centers are unable to play. Redl and Wineman write:

[53] Bertram M. Beck, "A Role for Recreation," in *Juvenile Delinquency and Youth Crime, op. cit.,* p. 404.

It is . . . important that the institution as a whole and every person in it are openly and explicitly accepting of children having "Fun." . . . By their very definition, our hyperaggressive and extremely destructive children are in need of a good deal of program activity which involves the happy discharge of surplus aggression, diversion of destructiveness into excited large-muscle activity.[54]

Such activities provide informal situations in which children can receive affection and trust from adults and begin to build ties of confidence and trust with them. They also provide situations in which children develop mechanisms for group control by its own members rather than always rely on the adult leader to stop them from misbehavior. Gradually, disturbed and delinquent youth learn to accept losing and failure with equanimity, to exert self-discipline, to have a sense of their own autonomy, and to place trust in others; all these are purposes of recreational programs in such remedial settings.

Recreation's Function with the Disadvantaged

An important function of organized recreation services in American communities is its special role with the economically and socially disadvantaged. Although America's economic development during the 1960's was unparalleled, a substantial number of Americans are still living in conditions of grinding poverty. While the top 5 percent of Americans earn 20 percent of the nation's income, the bottom 20 percent earn only 5 percent of its income.

The actual percentage of Americans who can be described as being below the poverty line—that is, below the income level considered minimal for an adequate standard of living—varies widely according to different government estimates. Economists in the Office of Economic Opportunity estimated that the number of American poor in 1968 included about 30 million people, based on a flexible "poverty line" of about $3,500 per family. Nearly half of the poor are twenty-one or younger, and a quarter are fifty-five or older; a third of all Americans over sixty-five, totaling 5.4 million, are regarded as below the poverty line. Living chiefly in cities, the poor suffer from poor municipal services, deteriorated housing, inferior schools, higher prices, and inadequate food. A high percentage of them are members of racial minority groups.

How effectively has organized recreation service met the needs of the non-white poor in American cities? For two reasons its role has been extremely limited until comparatively recently. First, the early emphasis on providing recreation as a social service in slum neighborhoods shifted to providing it chiefly as a middle- and upper-class amenity for those who

---

[54] Fritz Redl and David Wineman, *Controls from Within: Techniques for the Treatment of the Aggressive Child* (Glencoe, Ill.: Free Press, 1952), p. 54.

could afford to pay for expensive facilities and services. Second, recreation as an integral part of American life has been influenced by patterns of social segregation, both north and south. To fully understand the present situation, it is necessary to look at the past.

Within the southern and border states, the first several decades of the twentieth century were marked by systematic racial segregation in the use of public park and recreation facilities. Negroes were excluded from play-grounds, public parks, swimming pools, and organized sports that were pro-vided for white residents, and any form of social or recreational contact between blacks and whites was rigidly prohibited by state laws and mu-nicipal ordinances.[55] The recreation profession itself accepted this situation, and the National Recreation Association operated a special Bureau of Colored Work from 1919 until the early 1940's, which sought to expand recreation facilities and programs for Negroes—on a racially segregated basis. Both north and south, the public recreation facilities that were pro-vided for Negroes tended to be inferior to those in white neighborhoods.

The pattern of segregated park and recreation facilities began to break down after World War II and was particularly shaken by Supreme Court decisions which affirmed in 1963 that no municipally owned and operated facilities might be segregated (this included parks, playgrounds, libraries, museums, publicly owned stadiums, community centers, and similar facil-ities) and by the Civil Rights Act of 1964. Many southern and border com-munities have opened formerly segregated recreation facilities to Negro residents; in some cases, they have closed down certain recreation and park facilities rather than have them used by blacks and whites together or have transformed them into "privately owned" facilities, operated for all-white memberships.

Not until the 1960's did the recreation profession begin to take a special interest in meeting the leisure needs of the poor—especially the non-white poor—in urban slums. This came about as a consequence of the Federal antipoverty program, which provided special funding to serve the disadvantaged; it did not gain full impetus until urban rioting erupted throughout the nation in 1964 and 1965 and brought the needs of inner-city residents forcefully to the attention of the public.

Recognition that large numbers of unemployed Negro teen-agers and young adults roamed the streets—out of work, bored and frustrated, ready for violent action—led to a determination to use recreation to keep the summers "cool." In May, 1967,

The Senate voted $75 million additional in anti-poverty funds today to try to head off rioting in big cities this summer. President Johnson told a news con-ference that he had asked for the money on the basis of staff reports from San

[55] Gunnar Myrdal, *The American Dilemma* (New York: Harper and Row, 1944, reissued 1962), pp. 346-47, 1274-75.

Francisco, New York, Chicago, Baltimore, Washington and five other cities he did not name. He said the money would be used to provide new jobs, supervise recreation, light playgrounds, and provide swimming pools, and would be sent to areas that need it immediately.[56]

In city after city, recreation and park administrators began to develop expanded recreation programs in black and Spanish-speaking neighborhoods. Sports clinics and tournaments were initiated, along with busing programs, workshops in Afro-American arts, dance, and the theatre, and similar activities. Increasing numbers of Negroes were hired—many through Neighborhood Youth Corps programs. Since recreation and park facilities in Negro neighborhoods were often minimal, vacant lots, littered with garbage, were quickly transformed into vest-pocket parks, often with community participation and supervision. Portable pools and other mobile recreation units were rapidly built or purchased and trucked into disadvantaged neighborhoods. Busing programs transported large numbers of Negro children and youth to municipal, county, or even nearby state parks.

The need for improved recreation facilities and programs was documented by the report of the National Commission on Civil Disorders to President Johnson, in the spring of 1968. It showed that in city after city where serious riots had occurred in recent summers, one of the angry complaints of ghetto residents had been about the lack of adequate parks, swimming pools, recreation programs, and leadership. Grievances on this score were found in fifteen of the twenty American cities that had accounted for the most serious summer riots and were rated as high in intensity as ghetto concerns about inadequate education or ineffectiveness of the political structure. Indeed, the lack of adequate recreation and parks was more frequently cited as a grievance by Negro residents than the discriminatory administration of justice, inadequate welfare programs, or poor municipal services.[57]

It was pointed out that in several cities where rioting had occurred, initial flare-ups had come from the inability of Negroes to use certain recreation facilities (as in Chicago, where blacks could not enter public swimming pools in nearby white neighborhoods and were prevented from turning on water hydrants in their own streets during the hottest days of the summer).

In many of the crash summer programs, recreation became perceived as a way in which community groups could work together constructively for community improvement. In addition to added funds from the Federal government, assistance came from business firms, service clubs, and religious and fraternal groups. Typically, new partnerships were quickly

[56] "Senate Votes More for Poverty Funds," *New York Times*, May 21, 1967, p. 41.
[57] *Report of the National Advisory Commission on Civil Disorder* (New York: Bantam Books, 1968), pp. 7-8.

formed. In one eastern city where an outstanding summer recreation program was developed to meet inner-city needs, new outdoor basketball areas were developed at the last moment, using space donated by the Urban Renewal Agency, paved free by the construction union, lighted free by General Electric, and staffed by the Recreation and Parks Department on a seven-day, round-the-clock basis, with heavy participation and spectators.

The important role played by recreation in urban communities was stressed by a Federal official in the Department of Housing and Urban Development, who commented that political leaders in every city should realize

that the recreation or parks department is one of the most important communication links with the inner city, with the ghetto. . . .

Few other agencies have the opportunity to work inside ghetto neighborhoods on a day-by-day and people-to-people basis. Few other city programs offer opportunity for direct participation in all phases of program development and execution by the neighborhood people themselves. In better ways than the police, and schools, recreation programs can reach large numbers of people and bring city government face to face in friendship with individual families and people, bridging economic barriers, ethnic differences, age differences and neighborhood boundaries.[58]

Generally, city officials throughout the nation have felt that these special new programs have been successful in reducing tension and delinquency, "sublimating hostile, antisocial activities on the part of gang leaders . . . contacting gang members, reducing intergang friction."[59] There have been few careful efforts, however, to measure the actual outcomes of special recreation programs in ghetto neighborhoods. One attempt at assessment was made of a crash summer program sponsored in low-income projects by the New York City Housing Authority during the summer of 1967. This program involved extensive trips, athletic events, and social activities, with cooperative leadership by thousands of parents, Community Service Aides, and project managers. Involving 235,504 tenants, it was supported by a $575,000 grant from the city's Human Resources Administration.

Evaluations came from staff and participants on every level. It was unanimously agreed that this program's unique feature was the way it brought people together in constructive involvement. Neighbors became acquainted and worked together for the first time, and project residents turned out in huge numbers to cheer their teams on. Parents volunteered as bus-trip supervisors, as team managers and coaches, and in other roles. The final report of the program stated:

[58] Dwight F. Rettie, paper presented to Urban Affairs Seminar, 1968 Congress on Recreation and Parks, Seattle.

[59] *1967 Expanded Summer Program*, report of New York City Housing Authority, November, 1967, pp. 6, 18-22.

A major qualitative change in management-tenant relations occurred. Managers reported a vast improvement in tenant relations as communications with the broader tenant body improved. They found that working together with the tenants in a cooperative relationship tended to humanize management . . . and improve its image. An air of mutual confidence was established. . . . Project Managers reported a lessening of tenant complaints, of anti-social and disruptive behavior with fewer violations and less vandalism.[60]

One Community Service Aide commented that the program as a whole brought the residents of the housing projects together:

they played and worked with people they never knew or had spoken to since they lived here. The teen-agers were more courteous and respectful than I have known them to be before. They took initiative as leaders and were always ready to help with younger children.[61]

The image of the Housing Authority as a vast impersonal operation was transformed into more human terms. Tenant leadership was brought to the fore, and there was less disruption and antisocial behavior by teen-agers. While statistics cannot prove a cause-and-effect relationship between such programs and their social outcomes, the Housing Authority's Police Department reported a 16 percent reduction in vandalism, a 50 percent reduction in offenses, and a 21 percent reduction in misdemeanors during the summer this program was carried on, compared with a similar period in the previous year.

The support of recreation primarily as a means of preventing urban riots represents an unfortunately narrow view of this field. It should be recognized as a legitimate area of community service in its own right and not merely as a way to buy time and placate angry ghetto residents. Too often, special recreation programs that have been provided on an emergency summertime basis are phased out as soon as the summer months are over. Recreation in itself cannot possibly meet the varied needs and frustrations that cause urban riots. The only way to do this is to improve all areas of opportunity in the inner city—including education, housing, employment, health, and other important services. It is now clear, however, that recreation must serve as a vital component in any such battery of social services.

Recreation as an Outlet for Violence

Another important function of recreation in American communities is its potential for discharging violent and hostile drives in socially acceptable ways. Over the past several years, there has been an increasing concern

---

[60] *Ibid.,* p. 3.
[61] *Ibid.,* p. 3.

about American preoccupation with violence. Typically, this nation ranks extremely high among the industrial nations of the world, in terms of criminal violence. As an example, the U.S. homicide rate stands at about 11 per 100,000 in Georgia and Alabama, to 6.1 in New York and 0.5 in Vermont. By contrast, the homicide rate per 100,000 is 0.7 in England, 1.4 in Canada, 1.5 in France, and 1.5 in Japan. *Time* Magazine comments that, as a consequence of our past preoccupation with a folklore of violence, our bloody riots of past history (many carried out by whites against blacks), our bizarre multiple murders by demented drifters, and our recent assassinations of major national figures,

the rest of the world is ready to adjudge America as an excessively violent country in which brutal, irrational force can erupt any minute on a massive scale.[62]

The fact, however, is that violence and hostility are innate components of human nature—along with gentler, socially cooperative instincts. The writings of Freud, and more recently Ardrey and Lorenz, suggest that man has inherited such impulses from his biological past and that the problem is to control and use them constructively. Freud's theory was that man's instincts are heavily dominated by aggression, which often must be displaced on substitute targets. Bettelheim suggests that there are two ways to minimize the dangers of violence—to control it through education that provides understanding and mastery and to provide acceptable outlets for it. He asks:

What measures are we taking to help our children do a better job of mastering the disturbance of their communal life that comes from the instinct of aggression. . . . Children are supposed neither to hit, nor to swear at their playmates. They are supposed to refrain from destroying their toys or other property. . . . But what outlets for violence *do* we provide for them?[63]

The same point has been made by John Fischer, who suggests that crimes of violence and urban riots have been spreading rapidly all over the world—often as a form of protest by lower-class people who are bored with their work and frustrated by their vision of the future. Fischer writes:

rioting and hooliganism are on the rise in nearly every country, including England, Sweden, and Russia. Bloodshed in the big cities naturally gets most of the headlines, but it seems to be almost as widespread in predominantly rural areas—the Sudan, for example, India, the Congo, and Colombia, where *La Violencia* has taken hundreds of thousands of lives during the last two decades.[64]

[62] "Violence in America," *Time*, July 28, 1967.
[63] Bruno Bettelheim, "Violence: A Neglected Mode of Behavior," *Annals of the American Academy of Political and Social Science*, March, 1966, p. 51.
[64] John Fischer, "Substitutes for Violence," *Harper's Magazine*, January, 1966, p. 16.

Fischer points out that until comparatively recently in human history, it was necessary to be a fighter to survive. For the caveman, life was an incessant battle against the hostile Pleistocene environment, against other mammals for food, against humans for shelter, a water hole, or a hunting range. Through history, violence was necessary and socially approved:

Success in battle was the basic status symbol. The best fighters were feted in victory celebrations, heaped with honors and plunder . . . the weak and timid, on the other hand, were scorned . . . and in many societies cowardice was punished by death. For nearly all of human history, then, the aggressive impulse—so deeply embedded in our genes—had no trouble in finding an outlet. This outlet was not only socially acceptable; it was encouraged and rewarded by every resource at society's disposal.[65]

In modern society, however, we have banned socially approved outlets for pugnacity that were once found on the frontier or in rough-and-ready occupations. In a nation of city-dwellers, the traditional testing-ground of man against nature has disappeared. Life itself has become easier and safer, and war no longer provides an outlet for the primitive instinct for violence that it did in past centuries. Fischer points out that we have shown remarkable ingenuity in inventing fashionable surrogates for violence, including such strenuous and risky sports as skiing, skin-diving, surfing, mountain climbing, and sailing small boats in rough weather. These serve chiefly the well-to-do, however; they are too expensive and remote for the poor. Ultimately, he says, many of the poor turn to crimes of violence, largely because of the need to give vent to aggressive and violent impulses:

Gang fights, vandalism, robbery are, in an important sense, more "real" than any game. And for large groups of disadvantaged people, any form of antisocial violence is a way of striking back, in blind fury, at the community which has condemned them to disappointment and frustration.[66]

Those who have observed major ghetto riots in America's cities during the summers of the 1960's understand that they represent the expression of unbearable frustration and anger on the part of slum residents. Yet there has also been a curiously playlike aspect of these riots. To those who ask, "How can mass rioting, marked by killing, wholesale looting and destruction of sections of cities, be a form of play?" it should be pointed out that many forms of recreation involve extreme risk to participants. People often seem to seek pain and danger in their play. It has been estimated that 10 percent of the nation's skiers incur a serious injury each year. Certain professional sports in Europe and South America, particularly soccer, are marked not only by injuries but by bloody rioting by fans that frequently

[65] *Ibid.*, p. 19.
[66] *Ibid.*, p. 22.

results in widespread destruction and injuries. Automobile racing is almost suicidal in its statistics of sudden death; leading racer after racer is killed in crackups, year after year. Many contestants, both professional and amateur, are killed each year in such sports as boxing and football. Even for those who do not run such risks, sports often demand a marked degree of pain and consecration from competitors.

Thus, it is not altogether impossible to conceive of the recent riots in America's slums as a distorted and pathological form of play. It is clear that they stem in large measure from boredom and frustration. Harrington writes:

Harlem is distinctive because it lives so much of its life in the streets. The statistics on Negro unemployment may be abstract and distant. An afternoon block of milling, waiting men is not. The rooms of Harlem are, more often than not, small, dingy, and mean. Everyone wants to get out, to get away. Work is harder to get in Harlem than anywhere else in the city. So the bars are doing a good business in the early afternoon, and there are men on the streets, simply standing talking. One might walk into a sidewalk crap game . . . or (on occasion) there will be violence. Many of the fights of Harlem, or of any slum, are the consequence of mass enforced idleness.[67]

Riots themselves have a curious air of holiday about them. Again and again, eyewitness accounts have commented on this phenomenon. In 1967, a policeman commented bitterly about Puerto Rican rioters in New York City's East Harlem district: "they're like kids. They get a big kick out of the riots. It's like a carnival to them." And, in the same disturbance, a Puerto Rican antipoverty official commented, "It wasn't a gang effort but a series of unrelated incidents—kids in it for the fun of it." In Newark, New Jersey, during the tremendously destructive 1967 conflagration, Governor Hughes said after inspecting the district that he had found the "holiday atmosphere" among the looters most repelling. The Governor and the Mayor of Newark drove through the core of the riot area and "watched helplessly as men, women and children almost gaily raided wrecked stores." During the 1967 Puerto Rican riot, a passing nun remarked, "They were doing it out of sport, you know, not maliciously. They were laughing like: 'Isn't this great fun, getting something for free.' "[68]

Even the element of racial antagonism is often surprisingly low-keyed in urban rioting. During the 1968 Washington riot, after the assassination of Dr. Martin Luther King, Jr., Tom Wicker commented that most of the looters, far from appearing angry or mournful at the news from Memphis, appeared to be having a good time.

[67] Michael Harrington, *The Other America* (Baltimore: Penguin Books, 1962), p. 177.

[68] For a number of eyewitness accounts of riots in major cities, see New York *Times*, July 15, 1967, pp. 10, 11; July 26, 1967, pp. 18, 29; April 7, 1968, p. 62.

Negroes and whites mingled in apparent harmony on downtown sidewalks . . . members of both races watched as repeated waves of Negro youth ransacked a department store before burning it.[69]

In Detroit, the 1967 riot was marked by angry antiwhite feelings in the heart of the Negro ghetto. However, "elsewhere, especially in integrated neighborhoods, Negro looters smiled and waved at white policemen and newsmen." In one huge food and clothing center,

a Negro looter boosted a white looter through a window. Scores of other Negroes and whites looted and chatted side by side in the store . . . when a busload of police arrived at the scene, the white and Negro looters scampered away, shouting to each other to run fast.[70]

Obviously, no experience which involves arson, tear gas, shooting, sniping, mass looting, and destruction can be regarded as recreational in any true sense. Yet it is worth noting that the riots serve a need for excitement, release, abandon. They are real, as television is not. They fulfill the same needs for aggression and violence in the human makeup as war, battle against nature, and the highly competitive sports. The challenge to the organized recreation movement, then, is to see whether it can provide other kinds of experiences which will provide the same kinds of deep involvement and self-testing as riots but without their devastating social consequences.

Recreation and the Need for Ritual

A final important function of recreation in modern society is its role in meeting the needs of people for ritual. In past ages, there was a succession of year-round ceremonies related to religion and communal celebration. Some of these still survive in modern communities, in the form of festivities, fairs, and carnivals. Often, at the time of the return of a national hero or a successful national achievement, we celebrate by having great tickertape parades; major holidays, political events, and sports contests are also marked by celebrations and rituals. There is even in modern, industrialized man a need to take part in displays and rituals which are marked by music, parades, dancing, costumes, and ceremony. The love of color and excitement, and the need to merge with others in huge cheering throngs are historically ancient, yet found even today.

Typically, Independence Day provides an occasion for such rituals; it remains an example of what John Adams called for in July, 1776:

It ought to be commemorated as the day of deliverance, by solemn acts of devotion to God Almighty. It ought to be solemnized with pomp and parade,

[69] Tom Wicker, "Thousands Leave Washington as Bands of Negroes Loot Stores," *New York Times*, April 6, 1968, p. 23.
[70] "Federal Troops Sent into Detroit," *New York Times*, July 25, 1967, p. 19.

with shows, games and sports, guns, bells, bonfires and illuminations, from one end of this continent to the other, from this time forward, forever more.[71]

Even today, our Presidential inaugurations and major party nominating conventions are marked by lengthy speeches, presentations of the colors, anthems, invocations, benedictions, pledges of allegiance, inspirational readings, presentation of badges and honors, and seemingly endless demonstrations in honor of the nominees:

Balloons cascade from the ceiling. Sober men who earn their bread at the law, at the bank, at embalming, trot through the aisles in party hats, expressions of joy frozen rigidly on sweating faces, shouting and whooping like freshmen being hazed by the sophomores during hell week.[72]

The urge to take part in such displays seems to be universal. It is perhaps most vividly displayed in college sports events. These—particularly football—are marked by marching bands, drill teams, dancing choruses of elaborately costumed girls, banners, huge crowds with color-card displays, cannons booming, cheerleaders dressed in symbolic animal costumes, often huge parades before the event, bonfire pep rallies, and similar ceremonial aspects. Perhaps the purpose of such celebrations is to identify with a larger whole or (as in the case of Latin-American carnivals at the time of Lent) to break down distinctions of class and status and to abandon the year-round code of seriousness, hard work, social restraints, and formality. It has been commented that even a machine must have a little play if it is not to break down; the same axiom applies to people, both as individuals and as a society.

The function of recreation in this light is to provide occasions and opportunities that extend beyond the purely utilitarian, providing the opportunity for enrichment of life, for aesthetic involvement, for testing of oneself against others, and for personal joy, release, and reward. All such experiences, whether they relate to the need for ritual and celebration, artistic involvement, or education, are part of the first function cited, that of enriching the total quality of life. Although this chapter has focused primarily on the role of recreation in meeting the needs of groups with special problems, by far its largest area of service is concerned with meeting the needs of the public at large. The great majority of the American people, who do not require social welfare programs and who are economically and socially independent, are the ones who are primarily served by public recreation programs. Their needs and interests must be regarded as of primary importance, along with the special problem areas outlined in this chapter.

[71] From a letter from John Adams to his wife, speaking of July 2, 1776, the day the Continental Congress passed a resolution calling for the independence of the American Colonies.
[72] "That Time in the Nation . . . ," New York Times, August 8, 1968, p. 24.

A final point to be made is that recreation, even when it is aimed at serving the disabled or socially handicapped, can never be regarded as a cure-all for any major social problem. Carlson, Deppe, and MacLean have written perceptively:

Recreation is part of a whole. We would not wish to suggest otherwise. No claims are here made for recreation as the only answer for social illness, fullness of life, emotional balance, physical well-being, or an improved society. Recreation is not a panacea, it is not a substitute for work, economic security, or emotional stability.[73]

This implies that when recreation is directed at meeting significant human needs, it must always be seen as part of a total social context and must be provided along with other essential services and opportunities. To claim more for it than it can reasonably accomplish is to do it a disservice.

If wholesome leisure opportunities are to be provided to serve all ages and classes in society, recreation administrators must operate under sound policies and with a coherent philosophy of purpose. The following chapters examine a number of major issues and problems that face professionals in park and recreation service in America's communities today and provide guidelines that may be taken as the basis for such a philosophy.

[73] Reynold Carlson, Theodore Deppe, and Janet MacLean, *Recreation in America* (Belmont, Calif.: Wadsworth, 1963), p. 21.

18

Problems and Issues in Organized Recreation Service

The remarkable growth of organized recreation service throughout the United States has been documented in earlier chapters of this text. The expansion of recreation and park personnel, acreage, facilities, and expenditure, linked to growing national leisure and affluence, has led to a general impression that this field of public service is flourishing, with few obstacles or difficulties.

There are, however, a number of serious problems that relate directly to the recreation and park profession's role in society. How are this field's major priorities to be determined? What yardsticks should be used in decision making about facilities, programs, and population groups to be served? What solutions can be found for overcrowding in our cities and for the pollution of the environment throughout the country? What is the financial outlook for the support of public and voluntary services, and what are the implications of increased fees and charges? How can professionals in this field obtain fuller public recognition and support for program development in parks and recreation? These problems are discussed at length throughout this chapter.

The Social Role of Community Recreation Service

Probably the most important issue that must be faced today is the need to clarify the social role of community recreation service. At its inception, the recreation movement was reformist and socially purposeful. Its intent was to combat the pathology of the slum, to prevent or reduce juvenile delinquency, and to provide educational and cultural enrichment. Gradually, however, as it merged with the parks movement, it moved vigorously into the development of such facilities as boating marinas, ski centers, golf courses, and sports and cultural complexes serving middle-class or well-to-do residents. Programs designed to meet the needs of disadvantaged populations or those with special problems became more and more the concern of voluntary social agencies in the cities. David Gray describes this process of change:

The recreation movement was born with a social conscience. It grew up with the settlement house movement, the kindergarten movement and the youth movement that fostered the great youth agencies of the nation. Its earliest practitioners had a social welfare motivation in which the social ends of human development, curbing juvenile delinquency, informal education, cultural enrichment, health improvement and other objectives were central. Gradually the social welfare mission weakened and a philosophy which sees recreation an end in itself was adopted; this is the common view in public recreation agencies throughout the country.[1]

During this period of development, recreation practitioners developed a rationale for service which, while poetic and inspiring, had little relation to social reality. Typically, the *Credo* of the American Recreation Society during the 1940's and 1950's stressed "happiness, well-being and self-expression" as the goals of recreation; its purpose was expressed in the following passage:

because of the recreation movement, more men have a song in their hearts and sing it out, sense more of the drama of the world, see beauty more clearly in all about them, feel the poetry of the world, like to be among the trees, find joy in watching plants grow, have pride in their bodies, want to be more skillful in the use of their hands and all their powers, are happy to use their minds for just the fun of it, enjoy people more, find satisfaction in serving their neighborhoods and their cities.[2]

While professionals and recreation educators generally claimed that recreation was also a useful means of reducing delinquency, moral turbulence, or mental disorder, they developed few programs that actually sought to accomplish these ends. Although lip service was paid to the ideal of equality for all, residents in affluent neighborhoods were more successful in obtaining parks, centers, and well-staffed programs than the poor. Recreation was seen as an ideal means of promoting group harmony, yet, its practitioners made few efforts to bring about improved social relationships in racially mixed communities.

[1] David E. Gray, "The Case for Compensatory Recreation," *Parks and Recreation,* April, 1969, p. 23.
[2] *Credo for the Recreation Profession,* American Recreation Society, n.d., p. 1.

Today, parks and recreation administrators consult with planning authorities, develop land-use schemes and bond proposals, build buildings, buy and operate heavy machinery, work with engineers, architects, and builders, develop personnel codes, prepare budgets and annual reports, and carry out public relations. Comparatively few seem to be impressed by recreation's potential for influencing the lives of people. That their programs might somehow help reduce the growing alienation of youth, bring people together and alleviate racial antipathy, or resist the tide of technology that threatens to overwhelm individual creativity—such ideas appear irrelevant or impractical to many recreation and park administrators.

Particularly over the past decade, however, there has been increasing pressure upon recreation and park administrators to involve themselves in socially purposeful programs. Especially in metropolitan areas, they are developing more extensive services for the physically and mentally disabled and for aging persons. With the help of Federal antipoverty funding, many have improved programs for racial minority groups and the poor. Yet what is lacking is a clear sense of social purposefulness and a sharply defined social role. Gray urges recreation and park professionals to sharpen their objectives in terms of social welfare:

We have narrowly defined our services in the past. In the future will we be concerned about contributions to the education of our people, the welfare of the elderly, maintenance of domestic tranquility, the quality of American life, beauty and conservation of the urban environment, the design of our cities, improvement of community life, development of the young and cultural affairs? If we are not, which agencies in local government will be? These are much greater concerns than scheduling and staffing activities and managing recreation and park properties.

We should be attempting an enlarged contribution to the solution of enlarged urban problems. . . . We cannot divorce ourselves from the great social issues of our time. As we seek ways to make a contribution to the solution of social problems we will rediscover our social consciousness and begin to define our goals in terms of human welfare.

Our end then will not be activity; activity will be the means. Our end will be development of human potential in all its richness and variation. The poor, the potentially delinquent, the elderly and the disadvantaged are groups with the least resources and the highest need for community-supported recreation services. They will be the recipients of programs of compensatory recreation.[3]

If this role were more fully accepted, it would be necessary to abandon the idea that recreation is activity carried on for its own sake, without extrinsic goals or purposes. Recreation administrators would seek to identify the needs, interests, and recreational capabilities of many groups in society in order to serve them in highly differentiated ways. Those groups with the

[3] Gray, *op. cit.*, p. 48.

greatest level of need and the lowest capability for serving themselves independently would need to be given specially subsidized services and facilities—the "compensatory" approach that Gray speaks of.

To make such goals a reality, it will be necessary to link recreation in a team effort with other social services, such as antidelinquency and roving-leader programs, experimental storefront operations, multiservice housing-project centers, job training, remedial education and career-ladder programs, antinarcotics projects, programs to serve the disabled, and other community improvement ventures. All this implies a totally new concept of recreation as a form of social service. It does not mean that recreation would no longer be concerned with providing pleasure to participants. This would continue to be a primary function. Yet "fun" cannot be an end in itself; it must lead to constructive human outcomes, both for the individual and for his social group. Realistically, in many disadvantaged neighborhoods today, the operation of playgrounds, small parks, and centers has become so threatened by problems related to the threat of crime and violence, drug addiction, and lack of control that unless the administrator is able to deal constructively with these difficulties, his entire program is threatened.

A Changing Framework of Leisure Values

We have traditionally assumed that community recreation service must be socially desirable and constructive. This, however, poses certain problems. First, whose standard of social or moral desirability is to be used? Second, if community recreation departments exclude many of the activities that appeal most forcefully to large segments of the public, how will they be able to attract substantial numbers of participants?

The Basis of Moral Judgment. It is widely assumed that social desirability may be determined by a set of values which have been evolved by those who represent the Establishment (opinion-makers and responsible citizens—educators, ministers, civic officials, parents' groups, businessmen, and other professionals concerned with civic welfare). Yet there is growing disagreement in our society on such matters as well as increasing awareness of the gap between what we profess in terms of social and moral values and what we practice. The Kinsey report revealed that many of our most strongly accepted shibboleths regarding sexual behavior were secretly flouted by substantial proportions of the population. We have had a highly ambivalent attitude toward gambling. On the one hand, it is generally regarded as a social evil; on the other, it is widely licensed by state governments and even religious agencies, which use it as a means of obtaining revenue. It is difficult for many young people to accept adult strictures against marijuana or other illegal mood-changing drugs when they observe their parents regularly "turning on" with alcohol.

Our rejection of attempts to govern leisure behavior in particular is illustrated by America's response to national Prohibition during the 1920's. It became a national pastime to defy and circumvent the law; a huge illicit liquor industry was supported by the public and frequently operated hand in glove with elements of local government. Thus, in many ways Americans have demonstrated that while they will pay lip service to official preachments of what is desirable or morally worthwhile, in terms of private behavior they will operate quite differently. In recent years, resistance to traditional moral codes has become far more outspoken. In varied forms of entertainment—books, magazines, movies, television, and the stage— there has been a revolutionary relaxation of earlier prohibitions:

The old taboos are dead or dying. A new, more permissive society is taking shape. Its outlines are etched most prominently in the arts—in the increasing nudity and frankness of today's films, in the blunt, often obscene language becoming endemic in American novels and plays . . . in the undress of the avant-garde ballet, in erotic art and television talk shows, in freer fashions and franker advertising. And, behind this expanding permissiveness in the arts stands a society in transition, a society that has lost its consensus on such crucial issues as premarital sex and clerical celibacy, marriage, birth control and sex education, a society that cannot agree on standards of conduct, language and manners, on what can be seen and heard.[4]

Dr. Mary Calderone, who has fought for improved programs of sex education in American schools and colleges, comments that there is no longer time "for the usual stereotypes of thinking and old clichés . . . lessons in nineteenth-century morality are ineffective and hypocritical in an age of sexual freedom." Today sexual matters are openly dealt with everywhere; "erotic stimulation is all around us and pouring in on the young people from every available source."[5] Improved techniques of contraception and other medical advances have removed much of the effectiveness of the threat of unwanted pregnancy and venereal disease. None the less, for reasons that include ignorance, irresponsibility, and rebellious attitudes, statistics of teen-age pregnancy and venereal disease have been rising sharply in recent years. A 1969 Gallup Poll report indicates that the nation's young people are on the verge of a revolution in their attitudes toward sex.[6]

Such changing attitudes and behavior patterns may also be seen as the consequence of the declining role of parental authority, increase in the divorce rate, and the general rebellion of youth against adults. Similar changes are occurring throughout the civilized world. Even in the Soviet Union (which, despite its status as a "revolutionary" nation, has been far

---

[4] "Anything Goes: Taboos in the Twilight," *Time*, November 13, 1967, p. 74.

[5] "Debate Grows over Sex and the Single Student," New York *Times*, March 13, 1966, p. E-9.

[6] "Poll Finds Young Shifting on Sex," New York *Times*, June 22, 1967, p. 41.

more prudish than any Western nation), the urban divorce rate has climbed rapidly in recent years. In the city of Moscow, for example, the number of divorces per 100 has climbed from three in 1950 to thirty in 1967.

Accompanying and reinforcing such changes, there has been a striking decline in both the stability and the strength of many major religious institutions. In the Catholic Church, accepted practices such as the cloistered life for priests and nuns or the prohibition of birth-control practices have been seriously challenged by the younger clergy and many Catholic laymen. The number of young Catholics entering seminaries has dropped steadily in recent years, and Catholic schools have been undergoing a severe threat from declining enrollments and tightening financial support. There is evidence that other faiths are losing their influence over young people. Studies disclose that many young Jews are rejecting Jewish education as irrelevant and are demanding more meaningful religious practices. While church and synagogue membership in the United States has remained high (approximately 126.4 million, according to the 1969 Yearbook of the National Council of Churches), it has failed to keep pace with the population growth, and there is widespread agreement that formal organized religion is losing its influence in the United States.[7] This general trend is reflected throughout the Western world; even in those nations where extensive reforms have taken place, major religious bodies are facing serious problems of stability and public support.

All this is particularly relevant to policies concerning the use of leisure, since, as shown in earlier chapters, our strictures related to recreation in past societies have traditionally been based on religious beliefs and influence. With the power of institutionalized religion weakened, we must begin to search for new and convincingly rational bases for making moral judgments. This problem is of acute importance to the field of recreation, since many forms of leisure activity are on the borderline of traditional codes of appropriate moral behavior. Beck points out that participation in leisure-time activities is more volitional and less easily controlled than many other areas of human behavior. He writes:

The recreational system differs from other community systems because it abets and guides behavior that is natural and spontaneous to man. This is hardly true of the law enforcement system or the local welfare system. Recreation embraces all those actions that involve the pursuit of pleasure, and therefore aims to influence something that comes naturally to all people.

The definition of what kind of experience constitutes recreation is particular to the individual. One man's recreation is another man's work—or ennui.

---

[7] "Religions' Rolls Put at 126 Million," New York *Times*, February 16, 1969, p. 58; "70% in Survey See Religion on Wane," New York *Times*, June 1, 1969, p. 39; "Organized Religion Is Fading, Symposium Is Told," New York *Times*, March 25, 1969, p. 32.

Therefore, a recreational system that seeks to use recreational activity to deter crime cannot superimpose any particular concept of what is and what is not pleasurable. It can only rule out of its orbit activities which, while pleasurable, are also criminal.[8]

It should be recognized that a vast portion of organized crime in the United States is based on the satisfaction of leisure interests of Americans in sub rosa ways. The most obvious of these relate to illegal gambling interests, ownership of resorts and amusement areas, control of organized prostitution, bootlegging and sale of alcohol, operation of slot machines, bars that cater to homosexuals, and the distribution and sale of illegal narcotics. The scale of these involvements is tremendous; each year, for example, the Mafia exploits the human urge to gamble to the extent of handling $20 billion in illegal bets on racing and a variety of other major sports events, of which it keeps $7 billion in profits.[9]

The Role of Government Agencies. One might take the position that all these would be clearly inadmissible forms of activity as far as sponsorship by government agencies is concerned. Such a view would be supported by the traditional philosophy of organized recreation service. Yet government often treads a narrow and shaky line between what is morally acceptable and upright and what could, under other forms of sponsorship, be regarded as criminal.

For example, many state governments license parimutuel betting and lotteries. Such activities, if carried on privately, would be illegal. Although alcoholism is viewed as a major social problem, in a number of states the state government itself provides the only legal outlet for the sale of liquor through its own stores. Many municipal governments have tolerated and protected organized vice in red-light districts which have been regarded by governments as a social necessity in order to funnel off the sexual drives of men, prevent them from corrupting the innocent, keep venereal disease and sex crimes at a minimum, and, through special districting, keep other areas of the city "clean." In Nevada, for example, not only is gambling legal; prostitution is also tolerated in fifteen out of the state's seventeen counties. *Time* Magazine comments that in many communities

the brothel is practically an institution, like the corner drugstore and the county courthouse . . . grounds for civic pride. . . . One year, the town fathers of Wells noted that visitors seemed to be having trouble locating the red-light district, so they helpfully installed directional signs. . . . According to the Los Angeles *Times*, prostitution is one of the biggest industries in rural Nevada.[10]

8 Bertram M. Beck, "A Role for Recreation," in *Juvenile Delinquency and Youth Crime*, Task Force Report of the President's Commission on Law Enforcement and Administration of Justice (Washington, D.C.: U.S. Government Printing Office, 1967), p. 400.

9 "The Mob," *Life*, September 8, 1967, p. 91.

10 "Modern Living: Manners and Morals," *Time*, June 27, 1969, p. 54.

Such industries are regulated by local government; they submit to regular health inspections, and their books are audited by tax agents.

Even the Rest and Recuperation program of the U.S. armed forces in Vietnam, which flies servicemen on leave to cities of their choice throughout the Far East, recognizes that it is offering transportation to recreational experiences which are likely to include contact with organized vice. Official advice is given to soldiers on leave: "Do not purchase the company of a girl for more than 24 hours at a time; they seldom look as good in the morning."[11]

Thus government, by tacit agreement or cooperation, tends to condone gambling, vice, drinking, and similar uses of leisure. It seems to take the position that since people have a craving to engage in such activities, government agencies might as well control them in order to remove their worst evils and also to make money out of them. Generally, recreation agencies as such have been consistent to their traditional reformist philosophy. Some changes are beginning to occur, however; increasing numbers of park and recreation departments, for example, are operating clubs or other facilities which serve liquor as an accepted practice.

Some planners suggest that public recreation agencies should not seek to impose values on the public. Gans, for example, believes that it is inappropriate to use "leisure" as a means of achieving "nonleisure goals." He decries the tendency to provide recreational activities that are intended as "societal therapy" and urges that leisure behavior be viewed as completely nonutilitarian and spontaneous.[12]

If one carried this position to its logical extreme, public recreation agencies would simply seek to give people whatever they wished—regardless of its social or moral desirability. With a freer hand, they could attract large crowds of participants and earn substantial sums with which to finance other public services. After all, why permit the Mafia to have almost complete control of gambling, vice, and narcotics? Why not have the park and recreation department (which, after all, is concerned with meeting people's leisure needs) operate gambling halls with roulette, poker, and blackjack, with dollar machines for older folks and nickel-and-dime machines for the kiddies? And how about night clubs, saloons, strip joints, and even a few unobtrusive houses of prostitution? Carefully inspected and run with decorum, they might be called "health clubs." Or, if recreation agencies did not wish to run such operations directly, they might lease them to concessionaires or set up legal red-light districts and skim the cream off the profits through a heavy amusement tax. And how about race tracks and dog racing? Why not stage auto racing and "demolition derbies"?

[11] "Recreation: Five Day Bonanza," *Time*, December 22, 1967, p. 52.
[12] Herbert J. Gans, "Outdoor Recreation and Mental Health," in *People and Plans: Essays on Urban Problems and Solutions* (New York: Basic Books, 1968), pp. 115-18.

These suggestions might well be justified if recreation and park professionals were willing to accept the premise that their only basis for selecting program activities is what people will buy. It would mean that public agencies would be in full competition with commercial recreation; ultimately they would have little justification for existing except as a money-making operation that helped to finance other areas of municipal government. Obviously, this is not a tenable position for public agencies in the park and recreation field.

Instead, it must be their function to provide activities that are positive forces for personal enhancement and community growth, that respect the worth and integrity of each human being, that build physical, emotional, and social well-being, that stress active participation rather than spectatorship, and that draw people together rather than set them against each other. Yet how can such distinctions be made? What scale of values can be used to determine which activities are desirable and which are not?

Whose morality is to prevail? Should the recreation department reflect the values of the community in which it exists or those of the nation as a whole? And if so, from what segment of the nation—fundamentalist religious leaders, intellectuals and social scientists, artists, business executives —or others?

Ultimately it becomes necessary to recognize that recreation and park directors must, as a general rule, respect the views that are generally shared by the most responsible, influential, and active members of their communities. Through elected or appointed boards, advisory committees, or neighborhood councils, the recreation director tests out his own judgment as to appropriate goals and policies for his program. Except in areas of extreme disagreement, it should be possible for him to find consensus in issues related to morality, social purpose, good taste, or similar concerns.

A second source of values stems from the philosophy of service formulated by park and recreation leaders throughout the nation. Yet the park and recreational professional must also have a degree of independence in his thinking. He must be able to take positions that do not fall within the conventional system of values. Typically, in a number of cities throughout the country, many young people in the hippie or radical fringe of social protest have recently taken over public parks to establish their own programs and centers of activity. In some cases, they have been ousted by extreme force, with the use of National Guard troops, tear gas, and consequent loss of life. Such responses have in effect stemmed from a hard-line response by the Establishment to what it viewed as a threat to property and the existing value system. Yet could recreation and park executives come up with new and creative responses to dealing with such demands more constructively? In one city, the recreation department established a major community center to serve the hippie population. It perceived that, far from being menacing and dangerous, this bedraggled group actually consisted of middle-class young people who were runaways, estranged from their families, reduced to begging on the streets, demoralized, dependent on drugs, and often badly abused by other rougher and stronger elements in the slums. Such an approach was not consistent with the total community attitude toward this segment of the population, yet it was creative and constructive. Recreation and park professionals must be free to make such value judgments within their own sphere of professional service, even when they may be in opposition to accepted community beliefs.

Preserving and Improving the Physical Environment

Another major problem which faces recreation and park professionals today is the crucial need to preserve and protect our nation's land, water, and wildlife resources. It has become increasingly apparent that we have permitted great rivers and lakes to be polluted by industrial and human waste, forests to be ruthlessly razed by lumbering interests, and wildlife to be ravaged by uncontrolled hunting, chemical poisons, or thoughtless destruction of breeding and feeding grounds. Stewart Udall, formerly Secretary of Agriculture, has commented that our national goals have been oriented to the machine and to full production rather than to man and the full life:

The Gross National Product is our Holy Grail; the economists and statisticians its keepers. Statistics concerning auto output, steel production, heavy construction, housing starts, freight-car loadings, have become the indices of the American advance. We have no environmental index, no census statistics to measure whether the country is more or less livable from year to year. A tranquility index, a cleanliness index, a privacy index, might have told us something about the condition of man, but a fast-growing country bent on piling up material things has been indifferent to the "little things" that add joy to everyday living.[13]

Ultimately, as a consequence of this ruthless destruction of his environment (stemming from the twin specters of overpopulation and unbridled technology), man has himself become a threatened species. Greater and greater demands are placed upon our natural resource bank. Open space has been shrinking at an unprecedented rate. A million acres or more are lost each year to development for residential or commercial uses. In California alone, 375 acres a day (amounting to 140,000 a year) of agricultural land has been turned to urban uses. Of the original 127 million acres of wetlands and marshlands in the United States, crucial to many forms of wildlife, over 45 million have been destroyed by draining, filling, and dredging.

[13] Stewart Udall, quoted in *Man . . . An Endangered Species?* Conservation Yearbook No. 4 (Washington, D.C.: U.S. Department of the Interior, 1968), p. 3.

In terms of pollution, probably the most dramatic example of our unwillingness to protect the natural environment has been in the failure to construct adequate sewage and waste-treatment facilities by cities and states. Widespread industrial pollution has made dead, inert cesspools out of what were formerly sparkling lakes and rivers. We have built thousands of combined sewer systems which handle both sewage and storm water; these overflow during heavy precipitation, spilling raw sewage into streams and rivers. Many other communities are pouring huge amounts of raw, untreated sewage into rivers that were formerly pure-flowing streams, ideal for fishing and water sports. Information compiled by state and Federal biologists indicates that nearly 13,000 miles of streams and hundreds of natural lakes have been affected by surface mining activities.

The problem has been complicated by the widespread use of hard pesticides, such as DDT and Dieldrin. DDT is now everywhere in our environment and is believed to have the power to remain so for perhaps a century or more. Bryant writes:

Nothing we eat or drink is free from it. It is in oceanic fish, it is in birds and animals, it is in the milk a nursing mother gives her child.[14]

The total problem is summed up in an Interior Department Conservation Yearbook:

Degradation of environment is a gradual process; unfortunately, it has been accelerating rapidly. The stench and ugliness of pollution are apparent in too many waters which, only a few years ago, supported thriving populations of fish and wildfowl. Habitat for wild creatures is being engulfed by urban sprawl. The quality of our landscape is deteriorating, as the need for recreation grows.

All living things, including man, are meshed in an interdependent web of life. Even the most subtle change may have far-reaching effects. Every bite of the dragline alters this environment for better or for worse. Time and again biologists, ecologists, and other scientists have urged caution in connection with land and water resource development to insure that changes are for the better.[15]

Although a small group of determined conservationists has fought for years to prevent this steady deterioration of our national environment, it has only been over the past two decades that their efforts have begun to bear fruit. The recommendations of the Outdoor Recreation Resources Review Commission in 1962 helped to promote a wave of open-space development by the Federal government, states, and municipalities. All fifty states

[14] Nelson Bryant, "Wood, Field and Stream," New York *Times*, March 14, 1968, p. 57.
[15] *Man . . . An Endangered Species, op. cit.,* p. 42.

have now developed outdoor recreation plans. There is increased resistance to the dredging, filling, and polluting of our nation's estuaries. The Federal Water Pollution Control Administration has divided the nation into twenty major river basins and has promoted regional sewage treatment programs in them. The Water Quality Act of 1965, the Clean Water Restoration Act of 1966, the Solid Waste Disposal Act of 1965, the Highway Beautification Act of 1965, the Mining Reclamation Act of 1968—all have been instrumental in committing the nation to a program of conservation and protection of our natural resources.

Yet progress is unbearably slow, and in many cases there is strong resistance to more vigorous conservation efforts. With the growing shortage of open space in metropolitan areas, there is increasing pressure to use publicly owned land for schools, highways, water supply and sewerage systems, hospitals, urban renewal projects, and similar community ventures rather than for open space and parkland. Often proposals are made by well-intentioned people to peel off just a little piece of "useless" parkland for badly needed public projects. William Ballard, former Chairman of the New York City Planning Commission, comments:

The great threat to park lands is not that they will be preempted for unworthy purposes. It is rather that worthy causes pose a threat as they tempt us into sacrificing park land by way of an urgent need of the moment, a glamorous and timely project, or an attractive architectural design. These worthy causes are seldom in accord with the purposes for which parks are intended.[16]

In many other cases, powerful commercial interests have resisted the establishment of new Federal and state parks. Typically, the battle to develop Redwood National Park in California has been fought by spokesmen for the redwood lumber industry, who have claimed that the National Park Service's plan to preserve the giant redwoods along that state's Northern coast was "unnecessary, confiscatory, and economically depressing" and would threaten employment in the area. Such opposition has continued even after a study by the National Geographic Society, which revealed that 85 percent of the original redwood forests had been logged, that only 2.5 percent were protected in state parks, and that the remaining forests would disappear within thirty years. A similar battle has been waged between the giant oil companies that have been sinking offshore wells along the nation's West Coast and conservationists who have fought to prevent further damage to wildlife and the total environment by huge amounts of escaping oil.

Another example of continuing resistance to needed conservation efforts has been the struggle against those who have proposed a huge jetport

---

[16] William Ballard, in *The Green*, Newsletter of Park Association of New York, December, 1965, p. 2.

north of Florida's million-and-a-half-acre Everglades National Park. It is estimated that the jetport, involving a solid block of construction 38 square miles in size, would cut off the vital flow of water from the north, and by damaging the intricate ecological system of the Everglades, turn this magnificent natural region into a wasteland.

To increase the political effectiveness of those determined to protect and restore the natural environment, Henry Diamond, counsel for the Citizens' Advisory Committee on Recreation and Natural Beauty, has urged that five groups be assembled into a power base for political action for recreation and natural beauty. This coalition would consist of (1) the park and recreation movement (2) the conservation movement, a diverse and far-ranging group with varied interests and causes, (3) the new urbanologists—planners, urban renewal experts, sociologists, architects, and all those who seek to rebuild the cities and make them livable, (4) civic organizations which have an interest in the environment as an important social concern, and (5) the business community, which is often responsive to causes affecting community welfare.[17]

Even within this assembly of interests, there are marked conflicts. Many conservationists strongly resist the use of natural areas for recreation and fight to maintain parks as untouched areas of greenery. Often they have fought successfully to keep recreation structures and outdoor sports facilities out of major urban parks.

Their position is that recreation itself is often destructive to the natural environment—either in terms of temporary litter and disarray or, through continuous overuse, serious permanent damage. Many campgrounds and state and Federal parks suffer abuse to grass, exposed tree roots, eroded stream banks, and similar damage. Lake Powell, only five years after its construction in Glen Canyon in Arizona and Utah, has been noticeably afflicted by man-made pollution. Although huge in size (186 miles long, with a jagged shoreline of 1,800 miles), Lake Powell receives over 115,000 visitors a month in over 10,000 boats; the sheer accumulation of their sewage and garbage is beginning to ruin this giant lake.

Similarly, the use of great urban parks inevitably entails abuse. Recently, a free public concert in New York's Central Park attended by 135,000 people, left, in the words of Parks Commissioner August Heckscher, an "incredible sight." It took thirty garbagemen and machines three days to clean up the residue of broken glass, cigarette butts, cans, gum wrappers, chicken bones, wine bottles, blankets, and newspapers, while conservationists angrily protested against the historic park's desecration.

In part, the problem stems from irresponsibility in the use of recreation areas. When the Coho salmon boom began in Lake Michigan, 25,000 anglers a week jammed the lake; an official of the state's Department of

[17] Henry L. Diamond, "The Political Process," *Parks and Recreation,* April, 1968,

Natural Resources said that what he saw "was enough to turn my stomach."

It was like a prehistoric mob scene. Men waded waist-deep into the water and began clubbing, netting and spearing the silvery salmon. Some carted their catch away in tubs and they kept coming until 60 Michigan conservation officers directed by a helicopter moved in to make more than 100 arrests.[18]

Much of the problem stems from sheer overcrowding. When millions of people push out from the cities, the open space becomes a battleground where opposing factions clash for the use of space. The nation's most frequently visited national park—the Great Smokies in Tennessee—regularly has commuter-size traffic jams. There is insufficient space to accommodate the mass of campers and visitors during peak periods of demand (during the 1950's, visits to state parks increased by 123 percent, while their acreage increased by only 22 percent). As a consequence, the biological and physical ability of the land to support recreation use is severely strained, and hundreds of thousands of campers must be turned away from parks on busy weekends. One solution is to build additional access roads and camping and outdoor recreation areas. Yet there is strong resistance by many conservationists to such approaches. Typically, they have opposed proposals to build a second major highway through the Great Smoky Mountains along the North Carolina–Tennessee border, arguing that further development and use would destroy the wilderness quality of this unspoiled preserve. A similar battle raged in 1969, when plans to develop Mineral King, an area of majestic 12,000-foot peaks in California's Eastern Sierra Mountains, as a year-round vacation resort were announced by associates of the late Walt Disney. Angry conservationists claimed that this opening of part of Sequoia National Park to road traffic—for a $35-million yearround outdoor recreation complex expected ultimately to accommodate about 2.5 million visitors a year—would despoil the natural glories of the region.

Simply stated, the problem is one of balancing recreation, park, and conservation needs and values against other legitimate public concerns. A scale of national priorities needs to be set, based on an awareness that open space, once lost or destroyed, cannot be retrieved. Real progress has been made on a number of levels, including both the steady increase in open-space development on the state and municipal level and such actions as the recent banning of DDT by a number of states and the Federal government. Whenever possible, alliances of the sort suggested by Diamond will need to be forged. The action to ban DDT, for example, received the strong support of commercial fishermen in Michigan because it was revealed that this powerful pesticide threatened their livelihood as well as recreational opportunities in the region, Similarly, if it can be shown that

[18] "Recreation: Coho A Go-Go," *Newsweek*, October 7, 1968, p. 86.

loss of employment in such industries as logging due to the establishment of major national parks can be offset by increased employment in recreation-related occupations, stronger support may be given to conservation and recreation efforts.

In terms of conflicting conservation and recreation priorities, more effective implementation of the ORRRC Report's guidelines for the management of outdoor recreation resources will provide a basis for logical decision-making and development. If properly carried out, such plans will provide badly needed outdoor recreation space for much greater numbers of users, while keeping other areas as close as possible to the pristine wilderness.

Developing Needed Financial Support for Parks and Recreation

Although the amount of money spent annually on parks and recreation by government has grown steadily in recent decades, the need for additional budgetary support represents one of the field's most serious problems today. *Newsweek* Magazine commented in 1966:

Meeting recreation needs in goods and services, in fact, is now one of the nation's largest industries. . . . And yet, from Congress to county boards or supervisors, recreation is still puritanically regarded as a luxury. Despite all the oratory about natural beauty, physical fitness and mental health, when it comes to trimming the budget, most legislators put the shears first to parks.[19]

Because of inadequate Federal funding, the acquisition of already approved Federal parks and other outdoor recreation sites has been held back, while during the same period land prices have climbed steadily, making the ultimate cost of their acquisition and development far more expensive. This seems in surprising contradiction to the picture which has been painted of national affluence and growing expenditure on parks and recreation. It is true that during the 1960's, 2.4 million acres were added to the National Park System, compared with fewer than 30,000 acres during the 1950's. The states, too, have been involved in major open-space and conservation programs.

During the late 1960's, however, the mounting expenses of the Vietnam war and the nation's total military effort, the space program, and major social programs have imposed severe drains upon the Federal budget. Within the great cities of the nation, there are crucial problems caused by declining revenues, coupled with ever-growing demands for increased school, welfare, police, health, and housing services. As state budgets have swollen enormously, causing a cutback of state funds to municipalities, many large cities are facing severe financial crises. Compounding the fi-

---

19 "Race for Recreation Space," *Newsweek*, June 20, 1966, p. 99.

nancial problem of many municipalities has been the new militancy of civil service workers, with rapidly spiraling salary demands by policemen, firemen, teachers, and sanitation workers—and for the first time, strikes or job-action demonstrations by their unions to support their demands.

Owing to such factors, there have been severe limitations imposed on park and recreation spending by government, chiefly on the Federal and local levels. As an example, the National Park Service, the largest outdoor recreation program of the Federal government, has consistently suffered from inadequate financial support. During the five-year period from 1963 to 1968, visits to the National Parks increased by 48 percent and forty-two new areas were added to the National Park System, while permanent employment increased by only 13 percent. Based on budgetary and manpower restrictions under the Revenue and Expenditure Control Act of 1968, George B. Hartzog, Jr., Director of the Park Service, found it necessary to announce in 1968 that a number of severe cuts in the total program would have to be carried out. There was a nine-point program of reduced operations, including shorter visiting days and hours, off-season closing of campgrounds, imposition of new fees for visitors, postponement of traditional opening days, reduced visitor-center and information services, and the linking of small park areas so they could be administered together by single superintendents. There has been sharp Congressional criticism of such cuts; the Chairman of the House Subcommittee on National Parks stated:

For nearly a hundred years the Federal Government has been able to operate camping and picnic areas in national parks. Now, when the need and the demand for these facilities are greater than at any other time in our nation's history, we would close them and reduce services in the national parks.

The Federal Government, pursuant to congressional authorization, is spending $200 million each year for new national parks and seashores, and recreation areas. Why spend this money for more areas if we are unwilling and unable to continue operating the Government-owned facilities in our existing national parks. If private enterprise can operate these campgrounds profitably on a fee basis, why cannot the Federal Government do the same? . . .

It has been estimated that the annual tourist expenditures to private business generated by the National Parks amount to $6.5 billion. We are crippling one of the best revenue-producing agencies owned and operated by the Federal Government.[20]

While a number of the planned cuts have been restored, it is clear that unless the Federal government is able to reduce other areas of major expenditure and to assign fuller financial support to the acquisition of park areas and maintenance of facilities, this important area of public opportunity will continue to suffer.

Similarly, a number of major cities have found it necessary to reduce

[20] Roy A. Taylor, *Congressional Record*, January 16, 1969, p. H-386.

support of vital municipal services, including parks and recreation. New York, largest of the nation's urban centers, provides an example. Spending by the city's government tripled during the decade of the 1960's, outpacing the rise in state and local government costs throughout the country by one-third. The operational budget of the city rose from $1.99 billion in 1958–9 to $5.99 billion in 1968–9. Yet during this period the rising cost of welfare services compelled cuts in the proportion of support given to other services: public schools dropped from 26 percent of the budget to 21.9, police work from 9.5 percent to 8.3, and firefighting from 4.9 percent to 3.8 percent. In 1969, an "austerity budget" was presented that extended highest priority to basic protective services—police, fire, sanitation, and water supply—and then to the public schools, health services, and the City University. Sums granted to parks, recreation services, libraries, museums, cultural programs, and other special services to the poor were slashed by many millions of dollars.

This retrenchment in support meant a substantial reduction of workers in cultural institutions, with shorter seasons of operation and poorer levels of maintenance. As an example, the Board of Education was forced to cut its Office of Continuing Education (the bureau providing a major network of recreational and adult education services throughout the city) by approximately 40 percent, seriously affecting after-school and evening community centers, vacation day camps, swimming pools, and athletic programs. The Parks, Recreation and Cultural Affairs Administration announced that it would be necessary to reduce playground operations, close comfort stations, and eliminate preschool and day-camp programs and other recreational opportunities throughout the city.

The problem of maintaining adequate budgetary support is thus becoming increasingly difficult for park and recreation departments in many large cities. Within the realm of cultural activity, a number of large orchestras and other major musical organizations are suffering from deficits which threaten their very existence, primarily because of increased operating costs but also because much of the financial support formerly given to the arts by government, corporations, and private donors is now being given to antipoverty programs.[21]

What are the alternatives for support if it is not possible to raise the relative priority of such programs in the years ahead? Will it be necessary to reduce services sharply, to ration them, or to discontinue them? In more and more park and recreation departments, one solution has been to impose increasing fees and charges and to rely on these for the support of current operations and for the capital development of recreation areas and facilities.

---

[21] Howard Taubman, "Five Major Symphonies Share Woes," New York *Times*, May 20, 1969, p. 17; "American Orchestras: The Sound of Trouble," *Time*, June 13, 1969, p. 71.

Fees and Charges as Sources of Revenue

Traditionally, the major source of support for public recreation and park agencies has been general tax funds. To some degree, special taxes have been levied for the support of recreation programs, and bond issues have been widely used to finance capital development. Secondary sources have included grants-in-aid from Federal or state agencies (particularly for programs serving youth, the aging, or disabled persons) and gifts or donations of land, property, or money from private sources.

As indicated earlier, however, there has been increasing reliance on what are commonly called fees and charges to provide income for park and recreation agencies. Such charges fall into several categories:

1. *Entrance Fees:* Charges made to enter large parks, botanical gardens, zoos, or other developed recreational areas, such as fairgrounds, game preserves, or historical sites.

2. *Admission Fees:* Charges for entering buildings offering exhibits or performances, such as grandstands or museums.

3. *Rental Fees:* Charges for the exclusive use of property which is not consumed or destroyed and which is returned, such as boats, cabins, canoes, checking facilities, skis, archery equipment, or parking.

4. *User Fees:* Charges made for the use of facilities or participation in activities usually carried on simultaneously with others, such as artificial ice rinks, ski lifts, driving ranges, swimming pools, or golf courses.

5. *Sales Revenue:* Revenues obtained from the operation of stores, restaurants, or snack bars or from the sale of equipment and supplies.

6. *License and Permit Fees:* Charges for the right to carry out certain activities, such as hunting, fishing, or camping; vending or exhibition permits.

7. *Special Service Fees:* Charges for special or unusual services, such as entry fees for team competition, instruction in organized classes, summer camp enrollment, and workshops or clinics.[22]

The early recreation movement had few such charges, since its primary purpose was to provide basic facilities for general public use. Similarly, fees were not normally charged for the use of urban parks or state or Federal wilderness areas. As park and recreation facilities became increasingly complex and expensive, however, and with mounting pressure by the tax-paying public for budgetary economy in all municipal agencies, the imposition of fees and charges has become a widespread practice. Hines points out the economic background of this development:

During the ten-year period from 1952 to 1961, property tax revenues for all cities in the country increased 75 percent, while during the same period charges

[22] Thomas I. Hines, *Fees and Charges*, Management Aids Bulletin No. 59, National Recreation and Park Association, 1966, pp. 10-13.

for current services increased 134 percent. A greater portion of the financing of city government has shifted from the ad valorem tax to charges for current service.[23]

Therefore, the argument has been made that it is necessary to develop additional sources of revenue to support the acquisition and development of recreation facilities and areas and the cost of current services. Other arguments in favor of the increased use of fees and charges to support public park and recreation programs include the following.

A substantial portion of the public is able to pay reasonable fees for recreational opportunity and, particularly when it demands new, expensive, or specialized facilities, should be required to do so. It is argued that the payment of admission charges tends to increase appreciation and respect for park and recreation facilities and makes it easier to supervise and control patrons. In communities where substantial numbers of nonresidents may use park and recreation facilities, fees and charges may provide a means of requiring visitors who have not paid taxes to provide their share of upkeep and operational costs. The imposition of fees and charges is ultimately seen as a means of providing better and more varied park and recreation facilities and programs. The economic argument for them is summed up by McCormack:

> Meeting the demands of the public for parks and recreation has become so costly that existing tax moneys have become inadequate. The tax dollar has reached its stretching point. Taxes generally lag behind the kind of continuing upward economic spiral which this country is experiencing. The cost of land, the cost of equipment and materials, and in particular the costs of labor have skyrocketed out of sight. . . .
>
> There is a tremendous competition among . . . governmental functions. Parks and recreation often occupies the low position on the totem pole at appropriation time.
>
> The attitudes of the people today, the problems of balancing tax apportionments, and a severe shortage of money for parks and recreation are all factors trending toward the development of revenue-producing facilities and the charging of fees to fill the gap between supply and demand. Revenue facilities and fees and charges are the only remaining hope to many departments to enable them to provide quality programs and facilities.[24]

Gradually, public support has been given to the use of fees and charges in parks and recreation. The Outdoor Recreation Resources Review Commission recommended that fees should be charged for the exclusive use of facilities or programs which required the construction of spe-

---

[23] *Ibid.*, p. 6.
[24] John R. McCormack, "History, Principles and Objectives of Fees and Charges," report given at Revenue Sources Management Institute, 1967 Congress for Parks and Recreation, p. 4.

cialized and expensive facilities. It suggested that rates should be geared to recover a reasonable portion of the cost of administering, operating, and maintaining such facilities and, where feasible, recovering part or all of the capital costs of development.

Criticism of Fees and Charges Policies. There has been some continuing opposition to this trend. One objection is that it consists of double taxation, since people are taxed to construct and operate a public facility and then taxed again to be allowed to use it. Some argue that government should not operate as a proprietary, or profit-making, agency; many private campground owners believe that fee-charging state park and campground operations compete unfairly with their businesses.[25] Others point out that recreation has been accepted as an important governmental function and should not have to rely on fees and charges for support. They point out that if recreation and park development becomes increasingly dependent on such revenue sources, ultimately government will only initiate programs that are able to pay for themselves; other facilities or services that must depend upon general tax support will simply not be provided.

This leads to the major criticism of the growing use of fees and charges —that it tends to discourage recreational participation by economically disadvantaged groups. As more and more services—including entering zoos, beaches, camping areas, museums, and botanical gardens, the use of swimming pools, golf courses, tennis courts, and other outdoor recreation facilities, and registration in day-camp and adult-instruction programs—become based on the payment of fees, it may well be that in time the only free opportunity for poor people will consist of the limited use of neighborhood parks or playgrounds. There has been some evidence that the imposition of fees and charges has resulted in sharply reduced attendance in community recreation programs and in participation by organized groups.[26]

Despite such concerns, the use of fees and charges has become a widely accepted part of park and recreation operations on every level. Today, professionals are busy developing standards for operating methods and procedures and new kinds of revenue-producing facilities and services. In an increasing number of cities, income from fees and charges comprises a substantial portion (ranking as high as 30 or 40 percent) of annual departmental budgets. Many facilities and programs are today expected to support themselves entirely through revenues and even in some cases to support other less profitable services.

A single example of thriving fee-and-charge operations may be found in Oglebay Park, a thousand-acre municipal park in Wheeling, West Virginia. This pay-as-you-go operation received a tax subsidy in a recent year

[25] Curtis G. Fuller, "Cooperation Between Government and Private Campground Owners," in *Trends in Parks and Recreation,* National Conference on State Parks, July, 1969, pp. 27-32.
[26] "Notes for the Administrator: Fees Backfire," *Recreation,* June, 1962, p. 302.

of only $18,900 from the city of Wheeling and yet had an over-all operating cost of nearly one million dollars. The financially self-sustaining operation includes a huge lodge, family vacation cabins, a swimming pool, tennis courts, horseback riding, dancing, boating, fishing, a golf course and driving range, skiing, a museum, an outdoor theater, day and overnight camps, a park restaurant, and refreshment stands. No charges are attached to picnicking, a garden center, concerts, vesper services, an arboretum, hiking and nature trails, and a nature center. Gaylor writes:

Although Wheeling is a city of only 53,000 population, the recreational facilities at Oglebay Park attract visitors from practically every state, and the participation of these visitors enables the people of Wheeling to enjoy and finance park facilities and programs far beyond what a citizenry of 53,000 might rightfully expect.[27]

Obviously, the possibility of operating such varied and successful facilities without the need to compete for support with other, higher-priority community services is tremendously attractive to many recreation and park administrators. As indicated earlier, the major problem lies in large metropolitan centers, where such policies might result in a dual system with extensive networks of elaborate facilities and programs for the well-to-do but with the most meager and limited opportunities for the financially deprived. Even when charges are moderate, they tend to be too high for many families on public welfare, particularly when the cost of transportation (since most facilities tend to be at a distance from inner-city neighborhoods) is added to them.

What solutions are there for this problem? Mechanisms must be provided to permit the poor, the retired older person on a pension, and other groups in special need to participate as fully as possible. In some cases, facilities that normally have an admission charge may be opened for certain sessions during the week without charge. In others, facilities in poorer neighborhoods may operate without charge, while those in more affluent areas have fees. Arrangements may be made for sliding scales of fees for participation, or to have members of families in financial need admitted free, while others pay. It is extremely difficult to do this, of course, without determining extent of need, which tends to be an embarrassing or humiliating process.

While it seems clear the implementation of revenue-supported park and recreation operations will continue to grow, municipal administrators must bear in mind the urgent need to provide all persons in the community with a reasonable range of available leisure opportunities. At the same time, every effort must be made to educate the public to the need to support

[27] Earl E. Gaylor, "Active Recreational Use of Park Areas," *Journal of Health, Physical Education and Recreation*, January, 1963, pp. 40-41.

recreation and park development as a public function through tax monies rather than simply permit it to become a governmentally sponsored counterpart of commercial recreation operations. Otherwise, recreation may completely lose its justification as a form of publicly sponsored social service.

The Changing Role of Voluntary Agencies

Many voluntary agencies have traditionally provided varied leisure programs to the American public. Whereas public agencies have offered broad-scale programs, facilities, and leadership, voluntary agencies have met the need for social-service-oriented programs for special population groups, including the poor, the disabled, those on a particular age level, and those in specific religious denominations.

Today voluntary agencies are undergoing radical shifts in their function and structure. Those which have been accustomed to serving population of a particular social class or ethnic background are being confronted by the need to serve entirely new kinds of clientele. Major youth-serving agencies which have traditionally had white middle-class memberships, such as the Boy and Girl Scouts, are reaching out to minority populations and the poor.

To an increasing degree, voluntary agencies are being funded by government to operate special programs. Many settlement houses and community centers have undertaken remedial education and job-training programs with assistance from the Office of Economic Opportunity. Others provide programs for elderly people with funds from municipal welfare agencies or state departments for the aging. Still others operate Head Start programs or train and employ Neighborhood Youth Corps workers under Federal contracts. The traditional distinction between public agencies, which were supported entirely by the tax dollar, and voluntary agencies, which relied on their own financial resources, is rapidly blurring.

In effect, government has been able to carry out major new social projects only by assigning many important responsibilities to voluntary agencies. In so doing, it is acknowledging the special competence and experience of such agencies in these fields. In part, also, it is taking advantage of the administrative flexibility of voluntary agencies, which are much freer than governmental bodies in such areas as hiring, firing, and policy development. In the antipoverty field, well over half of the 900-odd newly created community action agencies supported by the Office of Economic Opportunity in the late 1960's were private, nonprofit organizations. In an analysis of this trend, Pifer writes:

The phenomenon of government by grant and contract . . . will almost certainly continue to grow despite the opposition of some members of Congress who believe it would be preferable for federal agencies to develop their own internal capacity to take on all the new tasks society is assigning to Washington rather than to hire others for this purpose.[28]

To solve many of the complex new problems in the field of municipal government requires the capacity to move swiftly, flexibly, and imaginatively into new areas of need—which voluntary agencies have demonstrated. On the face of it, it appears to be a fair exchange; voluntary agencies are providing vitally needed programs and services in exchange for financial support from government. Pifer points out, however, that government is essentially buying a commodity on a short-term basis and that this involves risks for the voluntary agencies that are involved:

This kind of support is in the long run harmful to the nongovernmental organization. It tends to produce mushroom growth and to place them in a position where they must continually seek further project support of the same nature to prevent the laying-off of staff and closing-down of programs. Thus, the paths of these organizations become characterized by frequent changes of direction induced by Washington's concerns of the day, rather than deliberate courses set by the organizations' own boards of trustees.[29]

The danger is that many voluntary organizations will become little more than appendages of government, with the interest and policy-making powers of their own trustees sharply limited and with diminished sources of support from business and foundation grants and private giving. Thus, their independence and freedom of action is threatened. The issue emerges: Is the nongovernmental organization of the future to become increasingly an auxiliary to the state or a strong, independent body that provides society with a type of capability that government itself cannot readily offer?

In the park and recreation field, based on developments of the past several years, it seems probable that the responsibility for providing special programming on a year-round basis for the disadvantaged and for disabled population will fall increasingly upon the shoulders of voluntary agencies. If this should happen, it will be necessary to increase efforts to coordinate such programs with the work of major public agencies in this field. Despite recent efforts to improve cooperative relationships, many public and voluntary agencies in our large cities still fail to work closely with each other. It is essential that coordination be improved, to avoid overlap and to insure the most effective and economic program service.

The Role of the Schools in Recreation and Leisure

As indicated in earlier chapters, the schools of the United States were among the first agencies to provide playground, after-school, and vacation

[28] Alan Pifer, *The Nongovernmental Organization at Bay* (New York: Carnegie Corporation Report, 1966), p. 6.

[29] *Ibid.*, p. 9.

programs for children and youth. By the mid-1920's approximately one-quarter of the public recreation programs throughout the country were operated by boards of education. Those in favor of the school's providing leisure services took the position that it had the needed personnel, facilities contact with children and youth, and status within the community to carry out this function effectively. The view was widely advanced that the goals of education and recreation were strongly complementary; therefore, the sponsorship of play programs was seen as a logical responsibility of public education.

Many recreation and park professionals, however, held that there was a basic conflict in philosophy between educators and recreation professionals and that educational administrators regarded the provision of recreation programs as a secondary concern. Further, they felt that school personnel and facilities were not suitable, in many respects, for recreation sponsorship. Finally, they charged that recreation, when provided by the schools, was limited in scope and quality.[30]

During the period between the 1920's and the 1940's, many state departments of education legalized the school recreation function in their codes and encouraged public education authorities—particularly health and physical education directors—to assume this responsibility. In this period, the community school idea became popular; the school served as a center for much community activity, including forums, vocational projects, cultural programs, and recreational activities.

Following World War II, however, several factors reduced the school's role as recreation sponsor. For one, the rapid population boom after the war coupled with the population shift to the suburbs meant that thousands of new schools had to be built, with ever-climbing school taxes. In many school districts, financial stringency sharply reduced such special services as school busing, library and guidance services, and recreation. A second factor in the decline of the school's role in recreation was the increasing professionalization of this field. As park and recreation authorities merged their departments in many communities and formed a single, united organization in the National Park and Recreation Association, it became apparent that recreation service needed to be regarded as a primary function of government rather than as a secondary function or offshoot of other services.

Finally, during the late 1950's and early 1960's, a critical examination of American education was prompted by a number of leading academicians. It resulted in the widespread conviction that the schools needed to be concerned much more deeply with academic functions and to relinquish other sorts of responsibilities. There was a sharply strengthened emphasis on science, mathematics, and similar academic subject areas along

---

[30] See Richard Kraus, *Recreation and the Schools* (New York: Macmillan, 1962), pp. 175-96.

with a general upgrading of standards and requirements in schools and colleges. These were accompanied by a sharp attack upon cocurricular programs and school activities which did not contribute to clearly educational goals.

Because of these trends, the percentage of public recreation programs sponsored by school authorities declined during the middle decades of the century. By 1960 only about 9 percent of the public recreation programs were sponsored by schools, and by 1965 the number declined to 4.5 percent. Although many boards of educations continued to provide excellent recreation programs serving all ages with diversified activities (particularly in California, where such school systems as those in Los Angeles, Pasadena, and Long Beach were enabled by state education laws to provide adequate funding for recreation), as a general trend, the schools became less involved in the direct provision of recreation programs.

Education for Leisure. The need to prepare young people for leisure was first identified as an important educational concern in the 1918 report, "Cardinal Principles of Secondary Education," which stressed that education for the "worthy use of leisure" was one of the seven major goals of American education. In successive statements of the Educational Policies Commission, the position was taken that the "unworthy" use of leisure impaired health, disrupted home life, lessened vocational efficiency, and destroyed civic-mindedness. American schools were urged to move vigorously to guide and direct the use of leisure in constructive recreation by children and youth.[31]

The concern of educational authorities with education for leisure, has, however, generally represented little more than lip service. One study of school administrators during the early 1960's found that few regarded education for leisure as a matter of important academic concern. In such fields as outdoor education and adult education, which had formerly promoted social adjustment and leisure skills, the emphasis shifted sharply toward strictly academic and intellectual goals.

A 1967 report revealed that a high proportion of today's schoolteachers accept the 1918 statement of the Cardinal Principles of Secondary Education as still valid; however, they felt that these goals were not being successfully achieved in modern schools. Specifically, they identified education for leisure as the area of concern in which the least was being accomplished today.[32] Assuming that leisure is still a valid objective of education, how is it to be achieved?

[31] *Policies for Education in American Democracy,* Report of the Educational Policies Commission of the National Education Association and the American Association of School Administrators (Washington, D.C.: National Education Association, 1946), pp. 65, 192, 203, 206.

[32] National Education Association Research Division, "A New Look at the Seven Cardinal Principles of Education," *National Education Association Journal,* January, 1967, pp. 53-54.

The schools should strive to teach skills and implant habits and attitudes to insure that individuals will use their leisure time in a full range of creative, active, and self-enriching pursuits. Such efforts can most easily be carried out in classes offering sports and games, music, dance, the theater, literature, and other subjects which have obvious carry-over potential for leisure. Some schools throughout the country provide experimental programs in such activities as skiing, skin and scuba diving, and even flying. Other schools are approaching problems of leisure—such as gambling, the use of alcohol, or drug experimentation—as part of instruction intended to create healthy and informed attitudes about these activities. Still others, although all too few, are approaching problems of leisure as a topic in economics, government, and other social studies courses. If students are to be provided with what might be called "leisure literacy," they should have not only recreational skills and habits but also an awareness of the implications of leisure in their lives and as a community and national concern. Such related problems as the need for conservation of our national resources should be taught far more seriously than they are in the present day.

Robert Maynard Hutchins, president of the Center for the Study of Democratic Institutions, urges that we begin to make a transition from a "working" to a "learning" society. He writes:

> The man who is truly educated, rather than narrowly trained, is ready for anything. He has developed his human powers and is able to use them and his understanding of the world to meet any new problem he has to face. He is prepared by his education to go on learning. Hence he is prepared for the human use of his free time. This is, in fact, the purpose of education in childhood and youth. . . . If work is our salvation, we are lost indeed, and we are on the way from full employment to full unemployment. But if we will only recognize it, the great opportunity that men have always yearned for is ours at last.
>
> Other nations have had affluence and leisure, or their ruling classes have had them. They have been destroyed, usually from within, and usually from causes associated with affluence and leisure.[33]

Hutchins' suggestions are supported by the report of a major research study carried out by the Carnegie Corporation, which concluded that America's schools were in many ways ineffectual and irrelevant to the real concerns of students. One of their most serious flaws, it stated, is that they have "separated mind from feeling and feeling from mind" and, by destroying a sense of spontaneity and joy, have failed to reach and involve students.[34] Clearly, education for leisure would have the twin values of

[33] Robert Maynard Hutchins, "Are We Educating Our Children for the Wrong Future?" *Saturday Review*, September 11, 1965, p. 83.
[34] "Schools Assailed in Carnegie Study," New York *Times*, January 26, 1969, p. 48.

helping to make the on-going school experience of the student more meaningful and enjoyable and of preparing him in concrete ways for his future life.

With respect to the school's role in community recreation sponsorship, while a smaller percentage of community recreation programs are now actually provided by boards of education, many of them continue to make extensive use of school properties. In 1965, for example, of 16,401 indoor recreation centers used by public recreation and park authorities, 14,294 (87 percent) were owned by school authorities. Since this administrative arrangement will undoubtedly continue, school buildings and outdoor areas should be carefully designed with such joint uses in mind. The reciprocal exchange of facilities among schools and other community agencies is the surest way of guaranteeing their full use at all hours and seasons and of providing the greatest range of educational and recreational opportunity for all citizens.

Within many cities and towns, as recreation and park departments continue to gear their programs toward the provision of outdoor recreation facilities and programs, it may well be that the school's role will be to provide special kinds of indoor, year-round instructional activities and small-group programs that are not being provided by other agencies. Indeed, in working with the socially and economically disadvantaged, the school is in the best position of all public agencies to link remedial education, vocational counseling, and similar services with attractive recreational programs that will attract and hold youth, broaden their horizons, and strengthen their self-concepts.

Professional Development in Recreation and Parks

As Chapter 5 indicated, there has been substantial growth in the numbers and status of recreation and park professionals. Nevertheless, there is a strong need to strengthen their public image, improve the process of professional development, and develop more effective research programs in recreation and parks.

A number of factors have clouded the public's understanding of the role and identity of practitioners in recreation and parks. Those in the field itself have contributed to the confusion by labeling every person working on any level and in any position related to recreation and parks as a professional in this field. Clearly, such a designation should not be attached to laborers and clerical and maintenance workers or to architects, lawyers, accountants, or biologists who happen to be employed within the broad field of recreation service. It should be extended only to those who have a primary concern for the planning, development, and maintenance of areas and facilities or for leadership, supervision, administration, consultation, research, or teaching directly related to the delivery of recreation services—and whose role requires specialized training in this field rather than some other area of professional competence.

Such individuals should be identified by job titles and Civil Service personnel codes, as well as by training and organizational affiliations, as recreation professionals. Others in the field should be clearly recognized as subprofessional, or support, personnel or as professionals in other disciplines who happen to be employed in leisure-related agencies. Such distinctions will help to clarify and strengthen the public's image of recreation professionals.

A second major problem is the need to strengthen the recruitment, selection, training, certification, and accreditation of those working on a professional level in this field. As an example, vigorous recruitment efforts must be made to identify talented young people and encourage them to gain early job experiences in this field as well as to enter college programs or professional training in recreation and parks rather than to have them make such decisions after preparation in other fields. Such efforts will require career days, sophisticated recruitment literature and films, and the combined efforts of colleges and universities, school guidance counselors, professional organizations, and local recreation agencies.

Simultaneously, as personnel benefits and job rewards are improved, it will be possible to apply higher standards of selection to those who seek admission to the field. Closely linked to this will be the process of upgrading recreation and park curriculums in colleges and universities. On every level—courses, admissions requirements, faculty, field-work requirements, facilities—these will have to be strengthened. Accreditation of qualified institutions will be necessary in order to eliminate substandard programs and permit this field to compete with other professions for highly qualified entrants and for foundation and government grants for research or other forms of support. In addition, certification and registration must become a reality throughout the nation as part of the process of upgrading professional selection.

A closely related problem is the need to fit the professional preparation of those entering the field to the demands of the jobs they will be holding. Some job-holders in recreation and parks today are overqualified for their positions in terms of academic background. Larger numbers are underqualified in the sense that they hold responsible positions without having had formal training in the field. One solution for this problem may be found in the growing number of community colleges providing associate degrees which prepare students for direct leadership or other technical roles in recreation and parks.

Some fear that if large numbers of community college graduates enter the field, the effort to upgrade academic requirements for professional recreation and park positions will be reversed. It is possible that individuals will be promoted to supervisory or administrative positions which, according to recommended job standards, should go only to those with four-year college training. Thus, hard-won minimum educational qualifications for professionals would be threatened; there is widespread agreement that these standards should not be abandoned.

A closely related problem is the need to hire greater numbers of minority-group individuals in recreation and park positions that will provide real opportunities for advancement. During the 1960's, many Negro and Spanish-speaking young people were employed in Federally funded antipoverty recreation programs in inner-city neighborhoods. Because of the temporary nature of such programs, if permanent employment in recreation for these individuals is to be found, it will have to be in established municipal agencies. To make this possible and to provide job mobility for young people from disadvantaged neighborhoods who enter recreation and park employment, a number of municipal agencies have initiated work-study programs which permit promising candidates to hold jobs while attending nearby community colleges with majors in this field. For those who are both ambitious and academically capable, such career-ladder programs may also continue while the individual is completing work for the baccalaureate degree in a four-year college.

Another problem is the need for more effective programs of research in recreation and park service. If the field is to solidly justify its claims for support, it will be necessary to document its values and tangible outcomes. While it is extremely difficult to measure the effects of any form of social service or social welfare, it is still important that such attempts be made. Sherwood writes:

Why isn't there greater demand from various segments of our society—public officials, the public itself, program administrators—for hard evaluations of action programs that attack one or more of the social ills of our social system? . . . More and better evaluation studies of social action programs are needed if our society is going to be able to make increasingly more rational allocations of resources to the solution of social problems.[35]

Improved programs of research within recreation and parks will have the dual effect of achieving a higher level of public understanding of recreation as a significant form of public service and of helping recreation administrators determine needs and user preferences more intelligently. Today, government, business, and all professional fields have come to rely increasingly on research as the basis for knowledgeable policy and action; recreation professionals must do the same.

As an example, the U.S. Forest Service has developed an extensive list of problems in its field which need to be carefully researched. These in-

[35] Clarence C. Sherwood, "Issues in Measuring Results of Action Programs," *The Research Letter*, October, 1967, p. 1.

clude the need to (1) obtain better understanding of visitor preferences and attitudes with respect to forest recreation opportunities, (2) develop better procedures for measuring current recreation uses in terms of numbers, duration, and type of activity, (3) determine the factors that influence recreation demand and reliable procedures for predicting trends and estimating future needs, (4) develop guidelines for recreation resource planning and allocation, (5) determine the compatibility of various types of recreation uses with each other and with other forest uses, (6) develop methods for improving visitors' understanding and appreciation of natural areas through visitor information services, (7) determine direct and indirect monetary costs and returns associated with recreation development and uses, and (8) determine nonmonetary individual and social values accruing from recreation development and use.[36]

Far more sophisticated ways of assessing benefits and costs, determining appropriate activities for different populations and agencies, and achieving a realistic order of priorities (particularly in urban settings) need to be developed. In addition, there is a crucial need not only to carry out research projects but also to insure that their findings are disseminated and used, in terms of having actual impact on real programs.

Over the past several years, considerable progress has been made in this area. The first national conference on recreation research was held in the fall of 1965, at Pennsylvania State University, cosponsored by the National Recreation and Park Association and the American Association for Health, Physical Education and Recreation.[37] The National Recreation and Park Association has carried out a number of major studies related to recreation manpower and curriculum development under contract with Federal agencies, chiefly in the Department of Health, Education and Welfare. It has also published the *Research Letter*, a monthly discussion of research developments and problems with respect to recreation and leisure, and the *Journal of Leisure Research*, a quarterly publication which reports and reviews major recent studies in this field. A comprehensive statement of research objectives and priorities in outdoor recreation was developed by a special conference convened in 1968 by the Bureau of Outdoor Recreation and the National Academy of Sciences.[38]

In order to promote more effective research in recreation and parks, it will be necessary for four types of agencies to collaborate more fully. These are *professional organizations*, which sponsor national studies, hold conferences and symposiums, and publish research findings, *colleges and universities*, which contribute to scholarship in this field, particularly

---

[36] See *The Research Letter*, April, 1966, p. 3.

[37] *Recreation Research*, Report of National Conference on Recreation Research (Washington, D.C.: American Association for Health, Physical Education, and Recreation, and National Recreation and Park Association, 1966).

[38] National Academy of Sciences, *A Program for Outdoor Recreation Research* (Washington, D.C.: Bureau of Outdoor Recreation, 1969).

through graduate theses, and provide trained faculty personnel to man sophisticated interdisciplinary studies, *state and Federal agencies*, which are able to fund significant research projects related to their areas of concern, and *recreation and park agencies*, which can carry on much direct research as well as provide settings and populations through which other agencies can conduct meaningful studies.

National Awareness of Recreation and Leisure

A final important problem which must be faced today is the need to develop fuller public concern about recreation, leisure, and problems of conservation and open-space development. It is essential that people become more fully aware of the role of recreation in their own lives and of leisure-related issues affecting the entire society in order to assure support for desirable public programs in this area.

Even today, many individuals have an extremely narrow view of the meaning of leisure; they are content to take part in a limited range of activities that do not begin to challenge their capabilities or contribute to the total quality of their life experience. The widespread reliance on television to "kill" great bulks of time is probably the best example of this. While certainly no individual or professional body should tell others what they must do with their time, it seems clear that we need to be able to make more intelligent and rewarding use of our growing leisure. The fact that so many strive for leisure and then do not know what to do with it— particularly after retirement from business—and that so many of our social pathologies stem from boredom and the search for "kicks" suggest that more attention should be given to understanding the relative roles of work and play in our lives.

Particularly with respect to the growing number of unemployed or underemployed persons which will be the probable outcome of increased mechanization and automation, it will be necessary for us to develop a national policy that comes to grips with the needs of a leisure-oriented society, that values rather than scorns free time, and that sees importance in human experiences other than work. Similarly, we will need a much clearer understanding of our relative priorities with respect to governmental support of conservation, spending to meet leisure needs, and the values of recreation and park service. Since its inception, the National Recreation and Park Association has played a vigorous role in interpreting the field to the public and in pressing for conservation, state and municipal recreation agency development, leadership training, and varied forms of legislation and Federal aid to recreation and parks. Such efforts will need to be redoubled if there is to be a fuller awareness and support of efforts to solve national problems related to leisure.

19

Urban Planning for Recreation and Parks

This chapter is concerned with what is probably the most serious logistical problem facing recreation and park authorities today—the need to plan effectively to meet leisure and open-space needs in America's cities. Nowhere in our society are there problems more acute than those found in our huge metropolitan centers:

"The serious problems of the cities are largely insoluble now and will be for the foreseeable future," insists one of the nation's most astute urbanists, Prof. Edward Banfield of Harvard. Few would go quite that far. But everyone agrees that the cities are at once the victims and the perpetrators of a larger crisis in America—a clutch of racial, economic, technological and generational frictions —that has strained the social fabric to a new and dangerous degree.[1]

Much of the problem has to do with the changed nature of the relationship between the central city and its outlying townships and satellite communities. Following World War II, with the country experiencing the greatest baby boom in its history, there was a mass migration from the central cities to the suburbs, chiefly of white middle-class families. At the same time, increasing numbers of poor people—many of them Negro and Spanish-speaking—moved from rural areas into rundown inner-city neighborhoods.

Many businesses leave the city, both to follow their customers to the suburbs and also because they find the cities difficult places in which to

[1] "The Cities: Waging a Battle for Survival," Newsweek, March 17, 1969, p. 41.

operate because of transportation tie-ups, increased crime, and growing taxes. Thus the municipal tax-base shrinks still further. Those suburbanites who use the city generally do not pay a fair share of its expenses for providing them places to work, highways, utilities, cultural facilities, and police protection. Increasingly, as the city requires ever more expensive health, welfare, education, and law-enforcement services, middle-class whites tend to move out in even greater numbers. Total welfare payments in cities climbed from less than $2 billion to almost $6 billion between 1960 and 1968; during the same period, violent crimes in cities of 250,000 or more approximately doubled.

Thus, the cities are left in a traumatic financial squeeze and, in a number of major instances, are approaching bankruptcy:

"We have a $1 billion economic blueprint," says Newark Mayor Hugh Addonizio, "but where are we going to get the $1 billion?" Fully half of Boston's taxable real estate is held by churches, schools, and other tax-exempt institutions—symptomatic of the financial squeeze strangling the cities. "It's just gotten beyond us," admits Frederick O'R. Hayes, budget director of New York City, where the million-plus welfare rolls hold more people than the entire population of Baltimore and will cost an incredible $1.7 billion next year.[2]

Part of the problem of the cities, in terms of being able to attack major social problems, is that they are handicapped by a great diffusion of authority. In many metropolitan areas, there is disarray bordering on actual chaos. The National Commission on Urban Problems reported that in 1967 U.S. metropolitan areas were served by 20,745 local governments. Greater Chicago has 1,113 different and often competing local authorities; in the Philadelphia area, there are 876 separate municipal governments. With the intrusion of Federal and state programs and the often overlapping influence of county and township governments surrounding independent unified governmental muncipalities, it becomes almost impossible to bring action to bear upon major social problems.

Within the total context of urban problems today, what special concerns relate to parks and recreation? First, there is the obvious need to preserve and acquire more park and recreation areas as part of renewal planning rather than permit the few remaining open areas to be swallowed up by urban sprawl or when slum areas are razed, have them replaced entirely by housing. A second important problem is the need to plan facilities and programs that effectively meet the differing needs of urban populations of varied economic and social backgrounds, as opposed to the shotgun approach that has characterized most agencies in the past.

Closely linked to both concerns is the need to develop more adequate budgetary support for capital development and operational support of parks

[2] *Ibid.*, p. 41.

and recreation. Park development has stagnated in some larger cities because of the increased priority given to other city concerns and because, as Higbee suggests, enthusiasm for public parks has been superseded by other interests. It is his view that public parks do not fit into the recreational pattern of privileged persons as they once did. Several decades ago, men of prominence in private and public affairs felt a social obligation to help make the city healthful and attractive. Today, many such persons satisfy their own leisure needs through private means. Gradually, recreation and parks come to be seen as peripheral to other important purposes. Higbee writes:

The city fathers are too distressed by the agonies of welfare services, harassed by traffic pressures, and embarrassed by inadequate public schools to dwell on the more pleasant aspects of existence which parks and playgrounds represent. These facilities seem to be regarded as frills rather than as the absolute necessities which they really are.[3]

Since this is so and since the once widely accepted view of recreation as an amenity, carried on for its own sake and without extrinsic purpose, is no longer important enough to justify substantial public support, it is necessary to conceive and plan for the delivery of recreation as a vital community service. It is necessary also to broaden the focus of urban planning for parks and recreation. Traditionally, most planning efforts have placed the major stress on the acquisition of land and the development of facilities. This has been particularly obvious in programs that have been developed with the assistance of the Federal government over the past several years. The Department of Housing and Urban Development has repeatedly urged cities to take swift action to save their rapidly vanishing open space. The Department of the Interior has been moving steadily toward the conviction that it must put its money where the people are by "working with the states and matching their money for central-city swimming pools, urban area hiking trails and bicycle pathways, vest-pocket parks and the like."

Such statements assume that the greatest need of inner-city people is for outdoor recreation, perceived chiefly in terms of more physical areas. There is considerable evidence, however, that the mere provision of play spaces—even if close at hand—does not guarantee satisfactory use. The failure of disadvantaged persons to take part in outdoor recreation programs may not only be because of their lack of funds and transportation; it may also be related to a different set of tastes and interests. This suggests the need in urban recreation planning to explore perceptively the needs and interests of all residents within the city and to analyze the city itself as a total living organism in order to determine what provision should be made for recreation, in terms both of facilities and programs.

[3] Edward Higbee, *The Squeeze* (New York: William Morrow, 1960), p. 235.

APPROACHES TO URBAN PLANNING FOR RECREATION AND PARKS

There are essentially three levels of planning with respect to park and recreation facilities and services. They consist of (1) total master planning that considers all aspects of municipal growth, including residential and industrial development, transportation, education, housing, health, and other major aspects of community life, (2) planning which focuses sharply on park and recreation development within the total context of a municipality's needs, often as a separate portion of a total master plan and (3) planning concerned with the development of a particular facility or the needs of a single neighborhood.

An example of the scope of total master-planning may be found in a statement of objectives of a major planning study carried out for the city of San Francisco:

1. Improvement of the city as a place for commerce and industry by making it more efficient, orderly, and satisfactory for the production, exchange, and distribution of goods and services, with adequate space for each type of economic activity and improved facilities for the loading and movement of goods.

2. Improvement of the city as a place for living, by aiding in making it more healthful, safe, pleasant, and satisfying, with housing representing good standards for all families and by providing adequate open spaces and appropriate community facilities.

3. Organization of the two principal functional parts of the city—the working areas and the community areas—so that each may be clearly distinguished from but complementary to the other, and so that the economic, social, and cultural development of the city may be furthered.

4. Protection, preservation, and enhancement of the economic, social, cultural, and aesthetic values that establish the desirable quality and unique character of the city.

5. Coordination of the varied pattern of land use with public and semipublic service facilities required for efficient function of the city, and for the convenience and well-being of its residents, workers, and visitors.

6. Coordination of the varied pattern of land use with circulation routes and facilities required for the efficient movement of people and goods within the city, and to and from the city.

7. Coordination of the growth and development of the city with the growth and development of adjoining cities and counties and of the San Francisco Bay Region.[4]

Planners receive training in a variety of disciplines; some are drawn from public administration, others from sociology, and still others from the fields of landscape architecture, law, engineering, economics, or social work.

[4] F. Stuart Chapin, *Urban Land Use Planning* (New York: Harper, 1957), p. 28.

In each case, the planner is likely to apply the standards and values of the field in which he received his professional training. For example, a number of planners who have a specialized background in economics tend to favor a systems approach, in which recreation is seen as part of a total ecosystem subject to the laws of supply and demand. Lowden Wingo, Jr., describes the economists' perspective on recreation planning:

Leisure activity can be viewed as a quasi-market system whose performance results from the interaction of demand and supply factors which are subject to analysis. When costs are measured in terms of both money and time, and when transportation costs are specified as variables, it becomes possible to construct a model of the space economy of recreation activity which should become an important analytical perspective for the recreation planner in the future.[5]

Wingo points out that recreation must be seen as an important dimension of the complex organization of an urban civilization. Leisure behavior must be analyzed as a form of economic behavior, dependent on costs and other influences on consumer decision making. He urges that the consumer must be able to cast his economic vote for the recreational services he prefers; it will then be possible to expand or contract recreation activities (viewed as economic goods, some produced by the private market and others by public agencies) in order to respond to the profitability signal.

This systems approach would seem to exclude the possibility of poor people receiving adequate recreation opportunity. Wingo suggests, however, that instead of offering them free but inferior services which they do not care for, we should create popular activities and services which they will want—and then provide "a set of policies for rational subsidization of groups which would be priced out of the market by access costs or by the pricing mechanisms."[6]

A number of other specialized approaches to planning may be cited. Planners trained in architecture or landscape architecture tend to be primarily concerned with the visual effects of the urban environment and the need to create an aura of open space, beauty, pleasing design, and lovely vistas. A closely related planning approach is conservationist-oriented; it gives primary emphasis to the need to retain and protect open spaces, green belts, natural areas, historic sites, and parks and to resist their use for any purpose, including recreation, that might alter the natural environment. Other planning efforts may be strongly dominated by political motivations: parks and recreation are viewed as positive and attractive governmental functions and constantly played up for political capital. Still others, particularly those related to urban renewal programs in large cities today, are

[5] Lowden Wingo, Jr., "Recreation and Urban Development: A Policy Perspective," *Annals of the American Academy for Political and Social Science*, 1964, p. 129.
[6] *Ibid.*, p. 138.

influenced by what might be called a social needs approach, which stresses planning that provides social opportunities and services through which disadvantaged people may solve their problems.

THE TRADITIONAL APPROACH TO URBAN PLANNING

This approach is essentially based on an imagined model of what the good community should be like. It assumes that each type of land use, such as light manufacturing or heavy industry, commercial development, cultural and educational facilities, residential development, transportation, and parks and recreation, may be seen in a logical kind of physical juxtaposition with others. This juxtaposition is generally based on a scale of desirability, which keeps the least attractive uses away from those at the upper end of the scale. Thus, heavy industry would normally be placed close to highways, rivers, or railroads for convenient transportation but away from residential areas (particularly high class). Certain types of diagrammatic approaches have been developed to show how these varying land uses, sometimes complementary, sometimes mutually antagonistic, may be distributed in a master plan. One such approach consists of a concentric-circle pattern, in which heavy industry is in the innermost sector of the city, surrounded by light industry, lower-class housing, shopping, and sectors of middle- and upper-class housing, interspersed by rings of green space to provide insulation from the less desirable parts of the city. Another approach makes use of sectors, or wedges, of land which strike into the heart of the city and which provide a logical means of zoning various uses for convenience and comfortable living.

This approach to planning has been based on two important elements: (1) the concept of self-contained, relatively homogeneous, and protected residential neighborhoods and communities and (2) the development of minimum standards for park and recreation open space and facilities which provide a basis for making recommendations with respect to land-use.

The Neighborhood Concept

The "neighborhood" is viewed as a section of a city or town in which people have grouped themselves with others of relatively similar background. It offers a social and physical environment in which the family may satisfy its basic needs for schools, shopping, churches, and centers for recreational or other social activities. Neighborhoods may occur in various sizes and shapes but are generally characterized in the planning literature as being about three-quarters of a mile to a mile square, including about 6,000 residents (about the population needed to support a single elementary school).

The Community Concept

The term "community" commonly refers to larger residential areas of a city (comparable in size to a high school district, just as a neighborhood is seen as comparable to an elementary school district). Communities are often composed of about three to five different neighborhoods, with populations ranging between 20,000 and 40,000 residents, extending for about two or three miles in diameter. The community is regarded as a natural grouping of neighborhoods within a city; while each has an identity of its own, the aggregate community is perceived as a recognized area of the city.

Recommended Recreation and Park Facilities

City planners have generally used the concepts of "neighborhood" and "community" as a basis of identifying and locating the kinds of recreation and park facilities needed in cities and towns:

1. *Neighborhood Play Lots.* The play lot is described as a small area set aside for the play of preschool children, chiefly in crowded neighborhoods where backyards are lacking or unsuitable for play. The play lot may be as small as 2,500 to 5,000 square feet. It is often placed in the center of a large housing project or may be part of a larger playground or neighborhood park.

2. *Neighborhood Playgrounds.* The neighborhood playground is seen as the chief outdoor play center of a neighborhood. It is primarily for children and youth between the ages of six and fifteen, with limited opportunities for older youth and adults. Neighborhood playgrounds commonly include the following: an area with play apparatus, a wading pool, a shaded quiet area with benches and a sandbox, areas for informal play, other areas for games, and, in many cases, a small building with storage space, lavatories, an office for the playground director, and sometimes an indoor room which can be used for activities. It is usually recommended that there should be a playground within a quarter-mile radius of each home in heavily crowded neighborhoods and within a half-mile of each home in less dense areas. It has been recommended that neighborhood playgrounds should range in size from about 4.5 to about 7.5 acres.

3. *Neighborhood Parks.* These are landscaped areas designed to provide attractive open space and opportunity for passive recreation. Their size may range from very small areas up to 30 or more acres; they may be located independently or in conjunction with neighborhood playgrounds, playfields, or elementary schools.

Suggested community facilities generally include the following:

1. *Community Playfields.* It is recommended that there be a community playfield within a half-mile to a mile of every home, depending on

the area's population density. Playfields offer varied activities, with emphasis on serving older youth and adults. They frequently include a children's playground, fields for popular team sports (softball, football, soccer), tennis courts, and multiple-use courts for basketball and such games as shuffleboard, roller-skating, handball, and badminton. It is generally recommended that playfields offer at least one acre of space for each 800 of the total population served; thus, a community of 16,000 would have a 20-acre playfield. Space standards suggest that playfields should range between about 12 and 30 acres and that they either be located close to junior or senior high schools which offer indoor recreation facilities or possess their own community center.

2. *Larger Community Parks.* These are good-sized parks which provide facilities for any of the following: family and group picnicking, day camping, horseback riding, boating, swimming, or fishing. They may also include golf courses, zoological gardens, athletic fields, ornamental gardens, athletic complexes, and winter-sports areas and may provide a setting for city wide community centers, museums, or libraries. Standards usually recommend that there be at least one large community park with a minimum of 100 acres for each 40,000 to 50,000 persons. It might serve as a regional center for several small cities and towns or as the main outdoor recreation resource for a medium-sized city.

Planning guides often generally include recommendations for "reservations" (large tracts of land, kept primarily in a natural state, which are usually owned by county, state, or Federal authorities) and for recreation centers which house auditoriums, gymnasiums, lockers and shower rooms, lounges and clubrooms, arts and crafts rooms, offices, kitchens and snack bars, and similar facilities. Other recommended facilities include golf courses, swimming pools, beaches, athletic complexes and stadiums, museums, zoological gardens, botanical gardens, nature trails, fairgrounds, winter-sports centers, and hunting and fishing centers.

Recommended Park and Recreation Space Standards

City planners have also developed guides for the minimum provision of park and outdoor recreation space, expressed usually in terms of the ratio of recreation acreage to the total population. The development of such standards has been briefly described:

Quite early in the century someone proposed that a municipality should provide ten acres of recreation space per thousand of the population. The actual origin of this standard is not known; however, the National Recreation Association accepted the ten acres per thousand figure and promoted it as a desirable standard. Because it was reasonable, and, no doubt, partly because of its simplicity, the figure was widely accepted in this country, and is still the most commonly accepted standard. It is generally applied only to recreation areas located within or immediately adjacent to the city, but not to outlying parks.[7]

Through the years, various professional or regional planning bodies have recommended variations of these standards. For example, the Committee on Park and Recreation Standards of the American Society of Planning Officials concluded in 1943 that the original standard was not practical for larger and more densely populated cities and that 10 acres per 2,000 of population should be set as a minimum in cities of over 500,000 and 10 acres per 3,000 in cities of over one million. On the other hand, the International City Managers Association has consistently supported the traditional standards:

Experience has demonstrated that, in general, any city seeking to furnish a well-balanced recreation program will need at least one acre of permanent, publicly owned open space for each 100 inhabitants. This ratio applies only to park and recreation areas within or immediately adjoining the city and not to properties at a distance from the city. In the future, cities will undoubtedly have higher requirements.[8]

In 1965, the National Recreation Association presented a revised formula of acreage standards (Table 19-1) geared to meet anticipated popula-

TABLE 19-1   *Space Standards Recommended by National Recreation Association, 1965*

Near-at-hand areas:	
Neighborhood recreation parks	2.5 acres per 1,000 population
District recreation parks	2.5 acres per 1,000 population
Within an hour's travel:	
Large urban parks	5 acres per 1,000 population
Large extra-urban parks	15 acres per 1,000 population
Total acreage provided by local governments per 1,000 of expected population	25 acres
Areas provided by state government	65 acres
Total recreation area provided by local and state governments per 1,000 ultimate population	90 acres

SOURCE: *Outdoor Recreation Space Standards* (Washington, D.C.: National Recreation and Park Association, 1965), p. 20.

tion needs which took into account both the property provided by local municipal authorities and that controlled by counties, park districts, metro-

---

[7] *Outdoor Recreation Space Standards* (Washington, D.C.: National Recreation and Park Association, 1965), p. 5.

[8] *Municipal Recreation Administration* (Chicago: International City Managers' Association, 1960), p. 66.

politan authorities, and state or Federal agencies of government. In addition, various authorities have proposed minimum requirements for recreation buildings, sports areas, or other special facilities. These include such guides as the following:[9]

Type of facility	Number of persons per facility
Archery range	1,500
Baseball diamond	6,000
Bridle trail	2,500
Boating facility	2,500
Handball court	1,500
Recreation pier	2,500
Golf course	3,000
Tennis court	2,000
Multiple-use room	4,000 or less
Gymnasium	10,000
Auditorium	20,000
Social room or playroom	10,000
Indoor game room	10,000
Indoor swimming pool	50,000

Authorities in the field of recreation and parks have stressed that such standards are not simply theoretical objectives but are realistic and attainable. Rodney comments that they are widely used

by planning commissions and other planning bodies in many cities of the United States, and they have been incorporated, practically without change, in many publications of agencies of our federal government.[10]

Traditionally, then, city planning for parks and recreation has been based on the concepts of "neighborhood" and "community," on the provision of specific types of facilities, and on the application of minimal space and facilities standards. In addition, a number of general guides have been developed by professional organizations and authors in this field.

Guides for Park and Recreation Planning

1. Recreation and park systems should be established in order to meet total community leisure needs and should provide equal recreational opportunity to all, as far as possible.
2. Planning should be based on a comprehensive and thorough evalua-

[9] Lynn S. Rodney, *Administration of Public Recreation* (New York: Ronald Press, 1964), p. 313; and Harold Meyer and Charles Brightbill, *Community Recreation: A Guide to Its Organization* (Englewood Cliffs, N.J.: Prentice-Hall, 1964), p. 404.
[10] Rodney, *op. cit.*, p. 311.

tion of existing public, private, and commercial facilities and services, including the public schools. It should strive for the fullest possible coordination of these agencies.

3. Planning should reflect the needs and wishes of all citizens and should involve them in data-gathering and decision-making processes.

4. Each recreation center or park should be centrally located within the area it is planned to serve and should provide safe and convenient access for all residents. In so far as possible, facilities should be equally distributed throughout the major areas of the city.

5. Design of each park or recreation facility should be carried out on an individual basis to insure that it be most adaptable to the needs of the specific population it is to serve; smaller and simpler facilities should be geared to serve nearby users, particularly with limited mobility, while larger, more complex facilities serve a wider range of interests and participants.

6. Beauty and functional efficiency are equally important goals of planning, with convenience and economy of maintenance important additional considerations.

7. It is essential to have a long range plan for site acquisition, with a total master plan that insures that properties will be acquired within the path of urban development while still available.

8. Every effort should be made to achieve space standards through acquisition in advance of anticipated needs, even if limited financial resources delay actual development of areas and facilities. Varied sources of funds should be used, including taxes, fees and charges, gifts, and bond issues.

9. Properties acquired should be held in perpetuity (protected by law against diversion to other than park and recreation uses).

10. Public school buildings and grounds should be designed for the fullest community use, through reciprocal agreements and operational coordination between school and park and recreation authorities.

11. Recreation properties should be developed to permit the fullest possible use by different groups at different times, on a yearround and round-the-clock basis.

12. It is the function of the park and recreation board to meet the needs of the city for wholesome recreation rather than to act primarily as a land acquisition or development agency; thus, planning should not be in physical terms alone but rather on a programmatic and administrative level.

While these guides for park and recreation planning are generally sound, it is necessary to examine critically the acreage and facilities-standards approach, which lies at the heart of much actual planning. Increasingly, experts are coming to recognize that these standards lack validity. The fact that they have been widely accepted by professional bodies and practitioners and that similar standards have been evolved in a number of foreign countries does not lend them authenticity. A number of the standards lack internal logic, particularly those which cite the need for specific types of facilities based on population totals. On what basis is it possible to say that there should be four recreation piers in a community for every game room or four bridle trails for every gymnasium?

The most serious criticism to be made of the space and facilities standards approach is that it is unrealistic, particularly in large cities today. A 1955 study of almost 200 cities revealed that only 27 percent achieved the standard of one acre per 100 population. In New York City, a 1967 study by the National Recreation and Park Association concluded that the city should have at least one 10-acre community park and one 8-acre athletic field for every 80,000 persons, as well as numerous other facilities. Apart from the projected cost of over a billion dollars, to achieve these standards in the crowded borough of Manhattan would mean that all buildings would have to be razed and the borough turned into one large park.

It is apparent that the application of a uniform set of standards to all cities does not take into account their differences with respect to population makeup, availability of open space, recreational needs and interests, financial capability, topography, and similar factors. Further, any planning approach which sees the American city as composed of neat, tidy, and relatively homogeneous neighborhoods and communities is simply not realistic. In larger cities, business and industrial uses, along with public service facilities, are widely intermingled with lower-class housing and shopping districts. In such cities, populations are often so mixed in terms of racial or religious background, age, and socioeconomic class that the assumption that each "neighborhood" needs a uniform set of playlots, playgrounds, and small parks has little validity.

The traditional approach is also meaningless in many of the newer suburbs, which often consist of large residential areas which lack central cores of services and in which municipal and township lines, school districts, police and fire districts, postal offices, and sewer, sanitation, and highway services all tend to be provided by different jurisdictions. This pattern is completely different from the view of the community as a relatively self-contained unit, with a core of central services and a constituency that takes responsibility for guiding the development of its own public services. It is clear that the nature of American communities has radically shifted, making traditional approaches to planning no longer valid.

Herbert Gans has commented that city planning has been ineffective because it has been based on nineteenth-century ideals of efficiency, order, and beauty couched within a small-town framework of white, Protestant, middle-class values.[11] It has assumed that the ideal city can be developed

[11] Herbert J. Gans, "City Planning in America: A Sociological Analysis," in *People and Plans: Essays on Urban Problems and Solutions* (New York: Basic Books, 1968), pp. 58-61.

by providing an ideal physical environment. Therefore, it has permitted architects and engineers to dominate the planning process and assigned little importance to the social, economic, and political processes that influence human behavior. Gans concludes that master planning seldom reflects the natural living areas of established social groups or deals effectively with political realities. Urban renewal programs which have wiped out huge residential neighborhoods in our cities and substituted high-rise, low-income public housing projects for them have, in his view, created more problems than they have solved.

Another authority, Jane Jacobs, takes the position that low-income projects segregate people by income, race, and often age and deprive them of the healthy and vital sense of neighborhood affiliation that should enrich community life.[12] She criticizes particularly the practice of continuing to build small parks and playgrounds on traditional models throughout our cities. When there are outbursts of gang violence or delinquency in large cities, she writes, one of the remedies usually called for is to have more parks and playgrounds. This ignores the reality that street gangs in large cities have tended to do their fighting predominantly in parks and playgrounds. (The worst gang outbreaks, feuds, and battles of the 1950's occurred in city parks, and some of the highest urban delinquency rates have been reported in the parklike belts around public housing projects.) Small parks and playgrounds have tended to become isolated and secluded, not part of the normal passageway of life, and often the most dangerous places in the city—feared and shunned particularly by smaller children.

Jacobs' observations have been corroborated by other planning authorities who have systematically examined the use being made of park and recreation facilities in American cities. They have found that to a great degree they are no longer used by middle- and upper-class families and in poorer neighborhoods have often become dangerous and unsavory hangouts for youth gangs and derelicts. Instead of the carefully organized and structured programs that were provided for children and youth in earlier decades, playgrounds in slum neighborhoods today offer chiefly casual play, with the use of slides, swings, and other equipment, informal sports played by older boys, smoking, "jiving," and generally just hanging around. Often small parks become lounging places for "winos" and drug "pushers" or hiding places for muggers. Indeed, the problem of maintaining safety in many recreation areas and facilities has become an ever-growing concern for recreation and park administrators, in large cities.

Jacobs proposes that playgrounds and small parks be made more meaningful and attractive through the fuller provision of more varied and attractive kinds of activities. They should be carefully located for easy access and have a constant flow of people passing through and around

[12] Jane Jacobs, *The Death and Life of Great American Cities* (New York: Random House, 1961).

them. "Demand goods" should be provided in the form of swimming, sports fields, fishing, boating, music, concerts, dancing, kite flying, model-boat sailing, artificial skating rinks, and other kinds of attractive features that will draw involvement of people of all ages, through the day and evening.

While a number of Jacobs' suggestions appear to be romantic throwbacks to an earlier era (such as her suggestion that streets remain narrow and winding or her resistance to bigness in shopping centers or housing), her appraisal of the present uses of playgrounds is solidly based. While such criticisms have been leveled chiefly at playgrounds in urban settings, their current use in small towns and suburbs has also been under challenge. Sessoms points out a number of changing patterns of American leisure which have important implications for park and recreation planners:

The changing trend in recreation patterns . . . stimulated tourism, day and week-end outings, and the use of water areas. Movie sales declined while admissions to golf courses, historic sites, and marinas soared. . . . Mass programs such as the playground, the most singularly popular program of the Thirties and Forties, lost their appeal. . . . Instead of enjoying their leisure at local parks and community centers, Americans were either on the move, seeking out some new recreation complex or remaining at home, relaxing on their patio or in their game room.[13]

While this description applies more directly to middle-class suburbanites than to the bulk of city dwellers, it accurately depicts some of the shifts of recreation interest that have taken place in recent years. It reinforces the conclusion that we need to develop entirely new approaches to the planning of parks and recreation services and facilities in cities, small towns, and suburbs.

What should be the basis for such changes? Some city planners have suggested that the criterion of social need be employed. The Community Council of Greater New York did a thorough analysis of recreation facilities, agencies, and leadership in the city's 74 officially-designated neighborhoods in the early 1960's. It placed them on a continuum, comparing each neighborhood's resources with those elsewhere in the city. It then analyzed the comparative need for service of each neighborhood, using three socioeconomic characteristics as criteria: (1) median family income, (2) juvenile delinquency rates, and (3) changing ethnic composition. The basis for this process was stated in the following passage:

There is no measure of absolute need for group work or recreation services, and adequacy of service cannot be measured either, since it is a percent of an unknown quantity. It is, however, reasonable to assume that certain socioeconomic conditions in neighborhoods are usually associated with need for

[13] H. Douglas Sessoms, "New Bases for Recreation Planning," *Journal of the American Institute of Planners*, February, 1964, p. 28.

community-subsidized services, and to measure these conditions. But knowing income level or delinquency rate in a neighborhood, for example, is not enough; it is also necessary to know something about existing programs, facilities and leadership, so that these can be taken into account. When the neighborhood index of socio-economic conditions is related to the neighborhood index of existing services, there is a basis for estimating comparative need in the neighborhood . . . on the basis of those "most" and "least" served, in relation to the average level of neighborhood services in the city as a whole.[14]

The Community Council study further justified the use of such criteria as juvenile delinquency rates (seen as a sensitive index of social disorganization and need) by stating:

Community-subsidized recreation is not assumed to be the cure for social disorganization, and, in fact, that is not its primary focus. The healthy neighborhood has a wide variety of services to meet various needs. Where special problems exist, however, group work and recreation services are presumed to have a role in the reduction of tension, by the provision of opportunities for people to obtain satisfactions through socially approved activities. The extent of social disorganization in any neighborhood, therefore, is assumed to be another indication of a particular need to strengthen community-subsidized group work and recreation services.[15]

It was found that 9 of the city's 74 neighborhoods contained over 53 percent of the total parkland and outdoor recreation acreage in the city. In contrast, 45 of the city's neighborhoods (particularly those in poorer and older areas) had only 10 percent of the park and recreation space. As a general pattern, it was found that the 16 neighborhoods with the highest degree of socioeconomic need and community disorganization rated well below the city average in terms of available public and voluntary agency group work and recreation services and resources.

A similar study was made in Los Angeles, following the Watts riot during the summer of 1966. Later, the Recreation and Youth Services Planning Council in Los Angeles developed a more sophisticated instrument for use in urban settings, which statistically related the degree of social need to the adequacy of provision for recreation and youth services.[16]

As interest in this new approach grew, the New York City Planning Commission carried out a more detailed study which identified areas of the city where social pathology and disorganization were highest and assigned them the highest level of priority for recreation and park development. This was done by dividing the city into three types of areas: *major action areas*, where problems of poverty, deteriorated housing, disease, and

[14] *Comparative Recreation Needs and Services in New York Neighborhoods* (New York: Research Department, Community Council of Greater New York, 1963), p. 3.

[15] *Ibid.*, p. 12.

[16] Edwin J. Staley and David Gray, *Study of Recreation Needs and Services, South Central Los Angeles* (Los Angeles: Recreation and Youth Services Planning Council, 1966).

crime are the worst and where facilities and programs are generally the poorest; *preventive renewal areas*, densely populated neighborhoods generally located in the path of outward migration from major action areas; and *sound areas*, in which social problems tend to be minimal and recreation opportunity relatively adequate. It then recommended budgetary allocations aimed at bringing major action areas up to the citywide average for facilities and programs by assigning them highest priority. Next highest priority was given to preventive renewal areas, and the lowest allocation of resources was recommended for sound areas. It was estimated that this approach, if followed over a projected sixteen-year period, would do much to eliminate the glaring disparity among the various areas of the city.[17]

Another respected urban planner, Charles Abrams, sees the problem as involving much more than simply building more parks, playgrounds, and community centers; instead it is a matter of providing a range of opportunities and situations which make the city a visually attractive, interesting, and exciting place to live in or to visit. He urges that we reverse our widely shared view of large cities as places to be dreaded and shunned. When Americans vacation in Europe, they visit the great cities of Paris, London, Amsterdam, and Rome—centers of culture, architecture, and entertainment. In America, we tend to avoid cities like the plague. Businessmen work in them but usually flee nightly to dormitory communities where their homes are located. When Americans take vacations they usually travel through the countryside rather than to the cities.

Somehow, the cities must be made more beautiful and attractive both for tourism and day-by-day living. Abrams points out that originally most American cities were blessed with good landscapes and waterscapes. During our great surge of industrial development, however, we have polluted and harnessed into industrial use our lakes, rivers, and streams, and we have blocked the landscape with factories, piers, railroad yards, and residential and industrial structures. Abrams stresses that larger city parks must become centers not only of natural beauty but of more active sports and other outdoor recreational activities that smaller areas cannot provide. Such activities as strategically placed chess centers and coffee-service areas, theater productions, concerts, dancing, and other planned evening recreational events would bring people into the parks and make them safer places to visit instead of luring grounds for muggers, delinquents, and sexual deviants. Abrams suggests also that we need much more relief from steel and concrete façades; we must vastly multiply the number of trees, parks, and green spaces. Trees are far more than "aesthetic props"; instead, they provide ventilation and shade and absorb noise and dust. Waterfronts, which too often are hidden behind highways, screened by housing projects and

[17] Steven Reichstein and Neiland Douglas, *Recreation Facilities in New York City: A Method of Assigning Budgetary Priorities* (New York: Department of City Planning, 1968).

industry, or lined by rotting wharves, railroad yards, or factories, should be opened up to the fullest. Abrams suggests that these have many potential uses for sightseeing, strolling, and casual recreation for tourists and residents, such as heliports and hydrofoil bases, marinas, seafood restaurants and fish markets, and other developments which encourage visitors. As in many European cities, we can build recreational facilities such as fishing piers, sunbathing areas, swimming barges, and boating centers along our rivers; as water pollution decreases, these will become increasingly attractive.

The streets of the city should be enhanced as places to stroll, sightsee, and bicycle. The character of such special ethnically oriented areas as Chinatown, Greenwich Village, Little Italy, or similar neighborhoods with outdoor markets, special celebrations and festivals, and other colorful customs should be protected. We need to encourage rather than discourage (through special taxes and overstringent regulations) such enterprises as the theater, dance halls, night clubs, supper clubs, art galleries, bookstores, sidewalk cafés, cabarets, and coffee houses. Fuller municipal support should be given to opera and dance companies, folklore groups, orchestras, and choral groups, as many European states and cities have done.

There is also a great need to provide leisure opportunities for specific groups in the population—places where young adults can meet each other socially under desirable circumstances, where mothers can bring their young children to play, where older people can find companionship and varied leisure opportunities. Abrams urges that we need many more neighborhood institutions—places where people can lose their anonymity and really get to know their neighbors. Public schools, churches, and universities can all play a role in providing such community centers. The city should be ideally equipped to do this: it has a wide pool of institutions, including universities, special schools, libraries, museums, and other organizations that are able to meet a much wider range of interests than suburban areas or small towns.[18]

All of these suggestions provide important new ideas for urban planning. They must, however, be fitted into a total approach toward solving the problems of the city. The following is a series of guides for municipal planning for parks and recreation, stated in terms of contemporary needs and foreseeable future trends.

Guides for Urban Recreation and Park Planning

1. *Planning as a Total Community Concern.* Recreation and park planning today must deal with the total structure of leisure opportunity, including facilities, programs, and services offered by public, voluntary,

---

[18] Charles Abrams, *The City Is the Frontier* (New York: Harper-Colophon Books, 1965, 1967), pp. 287-353.

private, and commercial agencies. It must see recreation and parks as part of the total spectrum of social, educational, health, environmental, and transportation services. As such, it must involve the participation of all agencies and groups in the community. It must also be concerned with the needs of citizens on every socioeconomic level, of both sexes, and of all ages and ethnic backgrounds and must involve them meaningfully in planning programs that will affect them.

2. *Planning for Operational Effectiveness.* Traditionally, park and recreation planning has placed a primary emphasis on the acquisition and development of physical resources, such as parks, playgrounds, beaches, and recreation centers. Today it is recognized that planning must also consider operational elements of providing recreational opportunity, including the administrative structure of recreation agencies, policies related to financial support, fees and charges, the costs of maintenance, and the provision of leadership. Particularly for people who lack mobility and easy access to recreation facilities that are at a distance from their homes, planning must deal with problems of transportation. In order to determine priorities for the development of new facilities or programs, the criterion of social need must be considered in the planning process.

In making recommendations for specific facilities, it is necessary to ask who will use them, at what times of the day, week, or year, what the costs of operation will be and how they will be met, and other similar concerns. Particularly when there are several agencies in the community that provide similar services, the planning process should make recommendations for their cooperation and coordination. This might include the interchange of facilities and staff throughout the year—thus cutting down on the cost of the over-all operation for the municipality by obtaining maximum usage. The fullest possible use of schools, museums, and libraries as centers for community activity should be promoted by effective planning.

3. *Determination of Program Emphases and Priorities.* As indicated earlier, uniform standards for recreation areas and facilities are no longer useful as the major basis for making resource-development decisions. While such standards will continue to be used by some planners and municipal officials (chiefly because they are simple to apply and have had broad professional support), they will be of greatest value when applied as general guidelines rather than as fixed and rigid standards. Particularly within large cities, other ways of determining priorities for development must be established.

One such approach has been suggested in this chapter: the needs-index approach, which assigns neighborhoods or districts in a city degrees of priority based on their social need and the extent to which they already have recreation areas, facilities, and programs in comparison with other neighborhoods in the city. Obviously, the success of this approach will be dependent on the willingness of civic officials and taxpayers to assign such a system of priorities to recreation and park development.

It will also be necessary to develop new kinds of classifications of recreation services and facilities in order to help identify program opportunities that will meet the varied needs of residents. Considerable progress has been made in terms of facility classification with respect to outdoor recreation. Clawson, for example, has outlined a system of facility classification ranging from *user-oriented* (areas most accessible to the public, involving considerable artificial development, such as pools and playgrounds), to intermediate facilities (those used primarily on day or weekend outings, with opportunities for such activities as boating, fishing and skiing) and *resource-based* areas (primitive and comparatively untouched, remote outdoor recreation places).[19] More meaningful classification of recreation programs and resources to cover the range of urban recreation opportunities will have to be developed in order to meet high-priority urban needs.

4. *Intergovernmental Planning an Essential.* With the exception of a few studies which have been carried out by regional authorities, most planning efforts are done within a municipality, township, or county. Meaningful urban planning today must, however, come to grips with the resources, capabilities, and problems of total metropolitan districts. Particularly in the suburban areas surrounding large cities today, the multiplicity of municipalities often leads to the duplication of some services, while others are completely lacking. A clear-cut assignment of responsibility for functions (such as the county providing major outdoor recreation resources and meeting specialized program needs for all residents, while local municipalities meet daily needs and provide close-to-home recreation opportunities in playgrounds and community centers) is essential to effective planning. A key problem in this respect is the willingness of outlying communities to cooperate with central cities in the solution of jointly shared problems. It has become increasingly clear that suburbs cannot thrive while the cities they surround are decaying. Planning must point the way to meaningful cooperative relationships between these two levels of government.

The Federal and state governments must also play a meaningful role in urban planning today. Since the enactment of the Bureau of Outdoor Recreation and the Land and Water Conservation Fund, state outdoor recreation plans (including detailed analyses of urban needs) have been developed throughout the nation. Increasingly, Federal and state agencies are being drawn into local planning for parks and recreation. The most obvious example is in Model Cities areas. Both the Federal and state governments are, however, also beginning to develop large independent facilities in or close to major urban centers. New York City is a leading example, with its new State Park District and with the Federal government planning to create a new Gateway National Recreation Area, both within

[19] Marion Clawson, *The Crisis in Outdoor Recreation* (Washington, D.C.: Resources for the Future, 1959).

the boundaries of the city itself. Particularly when many suburban communities refuse to let nonresidents use their outdoor recreation facilities (a policy dictated by economic considerations, problems of crowding, and feelings against outsiders for social-class and ethnic reasons), it becomes necessary for larger units of government, such as the state or Federal government, to provide such opportunities.

5. *Meaningful Community Representation in Planning Process.* Urban planning today must provide meaningful opportunities for representation and involvement by all members of the community. During the war on poverty of the mid-1960's (particularly in Community Action Programs which were generated and funded by the Office of Economic Opportunity), the principle of "maximum feasible participation" in the planning and administration of community-based programs was established. Through the development of "community corporations" and other organizations that represented disadvantaged people themselves, residents were given a fuller voice in making decisions that affected themselves or their neighborhoods. In the past, middle- and upper-class residents were usually able to make their wishes known with respect to recreation and park needs. Now, influence is demanded by all socioeconomic classes; poor people, particularly those who are black or Spanish-speaking, are demanding a larger share of actual policy-making and administrative roles in such programs.

What is a workable and constructive approach to meeting this challenge? Clearly, it cannot be to abandon decision-making and planning functions entirely to such groups. These are often technical processes which demand a high level of background and special knowledge if they are to be carried out efficiently. In addition, it is often difficult to tell which group does represent the community in a true sense. Often a number of conflicting groups claim to speak for the people in a given neighborhood, particularly when funds are to be dispensed or jobs to be shared. It is essential that the planning process be made responsive to the voice of community residents through a variety of mechanisms. This might involve using interest inventories, forming local study committees, having local people represented on planning and policy-making boards, hiring greater numbers of local people, and submitting proposals to community organizations for their approval. Community residents should be consulted not after decisions are made but throughout the planning process, including the design of facilities and program development. Only in this way can planning take into account the great variations existing among neighborhoods and communities with respect to recreational interests, needs, and capabilities.

6. *Sharper Focus on Disadvantaged Urban Areas.* Preceding sections of this text have made clear that for recreation and park service to be a viable area of contemporary urban life, it must address itself much more forcibly to significant social problems, particularly with respect to serving disadvantaged and minority-group populations.

Urban park and recreation administrators must become part of the total community effort attacking such vexing domestic problems as environmental blight, poverty, and racial confrontation. This does not mean that services to other elements in the community will be slighted. It is essential that the needs of the middle and upper classes be imaginatively and intelligently served, not only because they too have crucial needs for leisure opportunities which can best be met by public provision but also because recreation must meet communitywide needs if it is to receive community wide support.

In what specific ways can urban planning for parks and recreation serve disadvantaged areas more effectively than in the past? One approach should be the improvement of services in low-income housing projects, where large numbers of poor people live. Considerable Federal assistance has been given to the construction of community centers, playgrounds, and other recreation facilities in such housing developments. The problems of recreation directors in low-cost housing projects are many. They must work with senior citizens who are usually unemployed and living on small welfare payments or pensions, with large numbers of adults who may also be unemployed, with younger adults who have often married at an early age and are raising large families which limit their opportunity for leisure involvement, with a general cultural impoverishment, and often with rebellious and antisocial teen-agers. Gage comments:

the recreation director must recognize that his obligation also includes non-recreation needs. A recreation director in a housing project is more than a representative of an agency—he is a neighbor . . . the recreation center is a centralized meeting place with a built-in clientele.[20]

Recreation becomes a key means for counteracting the anonymity and lack of neighborliness within housing developments or on a larger scale in the total metropolis. Similarly, it is a means of establishing meaningful links between the people themselves and the authorities and social institutions that are intended to serve them.

7. *Linkage of Recreation with Other Community Services.* It is therefore essential that recreation and park planning be closely integrated with other areas of social service. This suggests that facilities must be designed to house a multiplicity of functions. Typically, community-center buildings should be able to serve a variety of age groups with relevant programs: nonworking mothers and preschool children during the day, children of working mothers in day-care centers, elementary school-age children after school, teen-agers and adults during the evenings, retired persons during the day. Centers should provide places where children may do home-

[20] Sandra M. Gage, "Recreation in a Housing Project," *Parks and Recreation*, April, 1968, p. 62.

work and receive tutoring or be part of cultural-enrichment programs. Job counseling, health and family counseling services, legal assistance, narcotics addiction programs, after-care programs for discharged mental patients, sheltered workshops for retarded youth and adults, and similar ventures are all part of the potential role of urban recreation centers. Centers may also provide a base for meetings of local organizations, antipoverty agencies, and other community groups.

In such multiservice situations, administrative control may be held by a recreation director if recreation is viewed as the primary function of the center and if he is qualified for such a responsibility. As an alternative, if recreation is viewed as only one of many services, the administrator may be an individual trained in the field of social work, education, health services, or another appropriate discipline.

8. *Design of Areas and Facilities.* The ability of recreation facilities to house such varied services is dependent on intelligent and flexible planning and design. Much of the past design of park and recreation facilities has been hidebound, based on standardized layouts appropriate only for narrow and stereotyped patterns of use. Entirely new approaches to the design of facilities are needed. A single example of innovative planning has been the recent expansion of mobile and portable recreation programs. Particularly in crash summertime programs, extensive use has been made of mobile stages and theater units, arts and crafts and science wagons, traveling libraries and museums, and portable pools and playstreets. Through such devices, immediate service has been provided to much wider areas than could possibly be done through the construction of permanent facilities.

The design of playgrounds is another example of innovation in facilities planning. In a number of cities, there has been what might be described as a playground revolution in recent years. Increasingly, designers are making use of new kinds of equipment for experimental and exploratory play by young children—free-form playhouses, animals, mounds, pyramids, tunnels, and climbing areas. They stress the use of walls and separators that become play equipment in themselves and make imaginative use of benches and low walls to create sitting areas that are like outdoor rooms on different levels. Even in comparatively small housing plazas, small amphitheaters are developed for varied entertainment and social activity. Playgrounds today have become much more visually and aesthetically pleasing; increasingly the effort is being made to design them for year-round use by all ages and family members and to offer possibilities for both solitude and sociability and for the full range of active, passive, and creative play.

Today some designers are creating playgrounds which, instead of being merely places where mothers may supervise young children in sandboxes or wading pools or where older children may use swings, slides, and seesaws, are becoming centers for total neighborhood activity. In them, both indoor and outdoor areas are provided where teen-agers may hold social events and sports activities, where senior citizens may read, have discussions and parties, play chess and checkers, and listen to music, where families may hold parties and picnics, and where entire neighborhoods may have social events and community festivities.

In the slum areas of many cities, where open space is usually limited, there are often small parcels of land in the form of vacant lots or back-yards. Often heaped with garbage and junk, they are rotting and dangerous eyesores. Such areas may be reclaimed through the joint efforts of local community groups, block associations, and religious or social organizations, frequently in cooperation with public authorities. Hoving writes:

Vest-pocket parks, carefully spotted in an over-all plan, can help correct . . . inequities. Easily accessible in the heart of congested neighborhoods, they can be as large as a block or as small as a lot. Equipped with facilities that meet the community's needs and desires, they can be places for kids to play or the elderly to relax. And as a spur toward the creation of active community groups . . . the small-parks program can help speed the broader social and economic reforms that the war on poverty is all about.[21]

Such parks had their beginning in Europe after World War II, when bombed-out building sites in such cities as London and Amsterdam were converted into small neighborhood parks. In the United States, Karl Linn, a professor of landscape architecture, originated a number of vest-pocket parks in Baltimore, Washington, D.C., and Philadelphia. He persuaded Philadelphia officials to make available municipally owned, tax-delinquent land to create what he called "neighborhood commons." There, both adults and teen-agers helped to build small parks, using materials salvaged from old building sites and other equipment donated by utilities companies. Particularly in slums, where apartments are small, dirty, hot, and crowded, there is a crucial need for such vest-pocket parks and playgrounds; they provide close-to-home out-of-doors living rooms.

Eve Asner, development coordinator of a Neighborhood Park Program in Philadelphia, describes the process of having slum residents serve as partners in the planning, construction, and maintenance of their own neighborhood parks. In Philadelphia, a "land bank" was established which made it possible for individuals or groups to lease, without cost, city-owned lots for open-space purposes judged to be in the public interest. A self-help program was established, with funds derived from foundations, Federal urban beautification grants, and the city itself, for over 120 projects, involving several hundred separate properties. These have been transformed into attractive gardens, tot lots, small parks, and sitting areas. Asner describes this program:

[21] Thomas P. F. Hoving, "Think Big About Small Parks," *New York Times Magazine*, April 10, 1966, p. 12.

We have set a pattern of self-help by requiring residents to *begin* the process by requesting their parks and by serving as partners in planning, construction, and maintenance. This is done to develop their initiative, resources and powers of decision-making. It is also done in self-defense. We know that residents feel a sense of proprietorship in something they ask for and help build. We also know they participate more if the facility is designed to meet valid needs which they pinpoint. The finished park produces a spirit of neighborhood solidarity and a close-at-hand focal point for getting together to plan community events, including additional neighborhood improvement.[22]

In addition to such efforts, we will need to become increasingly experimental in the use of space. Roof-top recreation areas and high-rise recreation centers in congested areas, waterfront installations and the development of facilities in the air-space over transportation lines, the use of air-supported structures for convertible yearround programs—these are but a few of the possibilities for innovative planning of urban recreation facilities. At all times, the design of facilities will need to be closely integrated with the operational needs of recreation programs. Such planning must also enable the physically disabled and other special population groups to have full and easy access to the city's leisure resources.

9. *Continued Emphasis on Open-Space Acquisition.* Linked to these operational concerns, urban planning must place a high and continuing priority on acquiring open space for recreation and park use. The acquisition of open space must, however, be done within a total framework of meeting the human, social, economic, and ecological needs of each region and community. Some properties should be preserved in their natural state—some because of their beauty and primitive quality, others because they are essential to wildlife. (Even within the boundaries of some modern cities, there are major flyways for wildfowl, breeding grounds, and similar areas that must be protected.) This intelligent assessment of the proper uses of land should be accompanied by resistance to the encroachment pressures that seek to take over parkland for other uses. Under some rare circumstances, it may be that other social needs (for schools, hospitals, or similar purposes) may justify the use of property originally acquired for park purposes. If this is to happen, planners must insure that other suitable properties are exchanged for those that are taken away. In the case of major parks which provide outstanding examples of landscape design and civic beauty, there can be no justification for any form of encroachment. It has been pointed out that if every proposal to put buildings and recreational or cultural facilities into Central Park had been accepted, the park would today be a hodgepodge of drill grounds, stadiums, airplane fields, underground parking lots, police garages, radio towers, armories, elevated railroad stations, housing projects, outdoor cafés, and dozens of roads, promenades, and cultural centers.

[22] Eve Asner, "Vest Pocket Parks," *Parks and Recreation,* May, 1968, p. 33.

10. *The Involvement of Park and Recreation Professionals in Planning.* Finally, if urban planning is to be most effective in this sphere, it must incorporate the professional judgment of park and recreation professionals. There is a crucial need to assign skilled planners to recreation departments and also to assign recreation professionals and administrators to work with urban planning departments. Too often, in municipal government, detailed plans for total urban renewal or even for the design of specific park and recreation areas and facilities are submitted to the recreation personnel only after their completion.

While our present problems appear to be overwhelming in many respects, they are trivial in comparison with the urgent social concerns that will be facing our nation in the future. Therefore, planners, as well as all those who are professionally involved in park and recreation administration, must consider the trends that we will encounter in the decades and centuries that lie ahead. A number of the most striking of these, as projected by social scientists, are described in the final chapter of this text.

20

The Challenge of the Future

As the United States moves into the 1970's, we face the need for long-range planning to meet the challenge of the future.

Among the social trends which have been predicted for the next several decades which will influence the demand for leisure services and the nature of organized recreation programs, are (1) population shifts, including changes in age, racial, and socioeconomic class composition and residential distribution, (2) general affluence and income level of the economy, (3) new forms of technological development affecting planetary and space exploration, medicine, communications, education, business, travel, and urban development, (4) changing human relationships and value systems, (5) revision of the industrial structure, and, finally, (6) changes in the availability of leisure.

A number of studies have attempted to predict the changes that we may expect during the early twenty-first century. The most thorough of these was carried out by a committee of leading scientists under the direction of a board founded by the American Academy of Arts and Sciences. Its findings, known as the Hudson Institute Report, *The Year 2000: A Framework for Speculation on the Next Thirty-Three Years*,[1] describe in considerable detail the areas of technological advancement and major social change which are seen as likely to occur during the last third of the

---

[1] Herman Kahn, Anthony Wiener, and staff members of the Hudson Institute, *The Year 2000: A Framework for Speculation on the Next 33 Years* (New York: Macmillan, 1967).

twentieth century. The report concludes that the United States is fast becoming a post-industrial society, which it defines as one in which the organization of theoretical knowledge and intellectual institutions become central in the social system. It establishes statistical baselines for the future, and sketches a number of alternative directions in which we may move as a nation. Over all, it suggests that the rate of change in every area of life will become increasingly accelerated as the result of research, innovation, and the diffusion of new ideas and processes.

Population Growth

Predictions for the worldwide growth of population suggest that the present number of about 3.5 billion people inhabiting the planet (more than double the number alive at the beginning of the century) will increase to 7 billion by the year 2000. It is presently growing at a rate of nearly 2 percent a year—double the rate of two decades ago. Since the percentage of young people under the age of fifteen is much higher in underdeveloped countries than in the industrialized nations of the world, it seems probable that the birth rates of poorer countries will continue to rise at a much higher rate than in the developed nations of Europe and the United States. Thus, feeding the world's steadily growing population will become an increasingly difficult task. In the United States itself, it is predicted that the population will reach the 300 million mark by the year 2000.

In the past we have seen a number of major population shifts, including a great wave of farm-to-city migration. Perhaps the most dramatic effect of this exodus has been the conversion of America's Negroes from a rural to an urban population (of the 22.3 million blacks estimated to be living in the United States in 1968, only a little more than a million, about 5 percent, were estimated to be living on farms). While some further migration is expected, the crest of this wave now appears to have passed. Population reports in the late 1960's indicated that the over-all farm population was stabilized at about 10 million, with only negligible numbers of rural people continuing to move to the cities.

Where will the 100 million new Americans expected by the end of the century be living? Some authorities have pointed out that the flow from rural to urban areas has in effect given us more potentially valuable open land today than at any time since the 1890's. Although about 75 percent of our population is now urbanized, less than 1 percent of our 2.27 billion acres of land falls within urban boundaries. Even if our population were to expand to one billion, its density over the total land mass of the United States would be less than that of present-day Switzerland. Scammon comments, "It is unlikely that—as some theorists assume—we are all going to be herded, strangling and suffocating, into some vast . . . ghetto."[2]

Instead, it seems clear that the big cities have in many cases reached their saturation points and begun to decline. It is expected that continuing development around metropolitan areas will result in vast belts of almost continuous residential, industrial, and other commercial building. The Hudson Institute suggests that there will be at least three such gargantuan megalopolises, which they have labeled Boswash, extending between Boston and Washington; Chipitts, concentrated around the Great Lakes, probably from Chicago to Pittsburgh; and Sansan, ultimately reaching from San Francisco to San Diego. It is predicted that the bulk of people in these areas will live in suburban districts which will include a mix of business and light industrial development as well as varying residential uses.

National Income Level

Forecasts of the nation's financial future are in general extremely favorable. By the year 2000, the Hudson Institute scientists forecast that 58 percent of U.S. families will reach the $25,000 income level and that about one family in twelve would have an income after Federal income taxes of at least $50,000 a year. The forecast is less optimistic, however, with respect to our ability to narrow the economic gap between the rich and poor that now exists. The present relationship, in which the poorest 20 percent of American families receive only about 5 percent of the nation's income, is not expected to be radically altered by the end of the century. Social scientists also predict that the gap between technologically advanced and less developed nations will continue to widen. This, coupled with the more rapid population growth of the latter countries, seems to lead inevitably to a polarization of the "have" and "have-not" nations of the world and to represent a serious threat to world peace.

The Effects of Technology

Technological innovations, which will affect such diverse areas of human activity as medicine, exploration, communications, housing, business, social relationships, and leisure, are expected to undergo marked changes by the year 2000. In contrast with the great era of mechanical invention of the Industrial Revolution, which was chiefly concerned with improving productivity in agriculture and manufacturing, the coming post-industrial period is expected to stress innovation of a software character, placing major emphasis on new techniques of management and marketing, the flow of products and materials, and the use of computer-based pro-

---

[2] Richard M. Scammon, "This Is What a Baby Can Look Forward To," *Life*, December 1, 1967, p. 29.

cedures for the mathematical simulation of businesses, organizations, and regional economies. Brooks writes:

The increasing power of symbol manipulating machines—computers—opens up a whole new field for innovation in the increasingly important service and knowledge-handling sectors of our economy.[3]

Economic researchers predict that computers will become objects of personal ownership, like wristwatches, and will be used in every form of activity. Education is expected to rely heavily upon computer-based games for more effectual instruction. The colleges of tomorrow will, according to predictions, rely on computerized control centers and closed-circuit TV operations in which students and teachers who are thousands of miles apart may engage in verbal interchange and with leading educators being recorded as a routine procedure, so that they may continue to be presented to future generations. It is anticipated that education will become a much more prevalent leisure activity, extending throughout the human life-span, with businessmen taking sabbatical leaves for study in universities as a matter of course.

The nature of employment is expected to change radically. Primary jobs, such as fishing, forestry, hunting, agriculture, and mining, and secondary jobs, which are concerned with processing the products of primary occupations, will become less important. Instead, it is expected that there will be a steady growth in such new fields as biomedicine, nuclear energetics, environmental studies, cybernetics, information systems, microelectronics, social technology, transport development, and oceanography. It is predicted that in the heavily automated factories of the future, work will be light and flexible, with unskilled and clerical jobs disappearing entirely and with men and women holding positions without distinctions as to sex. The computer is expected to transform many jobs and services; scientists predict that it will diagnose diseases for doctors, search for information for lawyers, monitor traffic flow, and assist social technology by indicating in advance the outcomes of alternative policy decisions.

Medical science is expected to move rapidly in the direction of new experimental procedures and devices for spare-parts surgery, transplanting hearts, lungs, stomachs, and other organs—possibly even the human brain. Life is expected to become longer, safer, and more physically enjoyable, and it is believed that through selective breeding and genetic change (brought about through prenatal selection, treatment, and implantation), many diseases and mutations will be eliminated. There are predictions that blind people will be able to direct themselves by radar and that the crippled will be able to walk on automatically controlled limbs that employ atomic power.

[3] Harvey M. Brooks, "Innovation: The Force Behind Man's March into the Future," *National Economic Review*, New York *Times*, January 8, 1968, p. 1.

Scientists also predict that man will be able to explore his environment in new and exciting ways. Following the space triumphs of the late 1960's, it is expected that the moon itself will be fully explored and ultimately colonized by man. Before long, there will be extensive exploration of other planets, with a continuing search for extraterrestrial life. The ocean will be fully explored by scientists, and new ways will be found to make it productive through submerged mining techniques to bring up vast deposits of oil, uranium, silver, and other minerals. There may ultimately be huge cities on the floor of the oceans, new ways of farming its living resources, and large-scale, inexpensive desalinization.

Personal travel in automobiles is expected to continue as a major form of personal transportation, but the responsibility for much driving will be taken away from humans by computerized guidance systems that feed routing, weather, and road conditions to drivers by means of television-computers. Guidance cables set into roads may instruct drivers with speed, braking, and other signals, and dual-mode cars may be developed which hook onto electric-rail roadways for highway travel. Similar predictions are being made that there will be supersonic and then hypersonic transports for round-the-world travel in less than an hour, with helicopters and versatile land-sea hovercrafts to facilitate access to central cities.

Changes in Human Behavior and Relationships

Scientists have also made a number of encouraging forecasts with respect to changes in human behavior and personality. Generally, it is predicted that man will have much greater control over all aspects of his physical, intellectual, and emotional growth. Brzezinski suggests that it will be necessary to place a much higher emphasis on human values to prevent man's personal existence from becoming increasingly depersonalized. He writes:

There is the real danger that human conduct will become less spontaneous and less mysterious; more predetermined and subject to deliberate programming. Man will increasingly possess the capacity to determine the sex of his children, to affect through drugs the extent of their intelligence and to modify and control their personalities. . . . The human body will be improved and its durability extended. Some estimate that during the next century the average life-span could reach approximately 120 years. The prolongation of life will alter our mores, our career patterns and our social relationships.[4]

It is expected that after 2000, people will become far less inhibited than they are today in openly expressing their impulses and feelings toward each other and acting out these feelings in public. Today's hippies and "flower children," some suggest, are actually the forerunners of a new way

[4] Zbigniew Brzezinski, "The Search for Meaning amid Change," National Economic Review, New York *Times*, January 6, 1969, p. 147.

of life; it may become accepted practice to artificially induce mood changes and openness. "We will have more, and more powerful drugs, capable of making men gay or sad, suicidal or ecstatic. How society will use and control these drugs is another matter."[5]

There is considerable concern about the changes that may occur in our societal value systems. It is speculated that increased general affluence may lead to a collapse of traditional bourgeois values. John Maynard Keynes, the distinguished British economist, pointed out several decades ago that man's economic struggle for existence has in the past been his most pressing problem. When this problem is finally solved and mankind becomes deprived of a major area of purpose and motivation, what will happen? Keynes speculated:

If one believes at all in the real values of life, the prospect at least opens up the possibility of benefit. Yet I think with dread of the readjustment of the habits and instincts of the ordinary man, bred into him for countless generations, which he may be asked to discard within a few decades . . . for the first time since his creation, man will be faced with his real, his permanent problem—how to use his freedom from pressing economic cares, how to occupy his leisure, which science and compound interest will have won for him, to live wisely and well.[6]

There are two possible alternatives. The Hudson Institute Report suggests that with increased freedom from necessity, man may become more generous, public-spirited, and humane, with a considerable reduction in personal aggressiveness. On the other hand, it is possible that many of the work- and responsibility-oriented attitudes which we have accepted in the past would decline as over-all living standards, with improved welfare services and public facilities and programs, diminish the need for personal initiative and conformity to societal goals. It is predicted that there may be

a great increase in selfishness, a great decline of interest in government and society as a whole, and a rise in the more childish forms of individualism. . . . Thus, paradoxically, the technological, highly productive society, by demanding less of the individual, may decrease his economic frustrations but increase his aggressions against the society. Certainly here would be fertile soil for what has come to be known as alienation.[7]

It is also predicted that accompanying such changes, the conscience-dominated character type and such virtues as diligence, punctuality, and the willingness to postpone or forego satisfactions may also tend to disappear. How realistic are these speculations? Is it likely that we will shift to

[5] Ithiel de Sola Pool, quoted in J. Robert Moskin, "Scientists Forecast the Year 2018," *Look* Magazine, May 28, 1968, p. 110.
[6] Kahn et al., *The Year 2000, op. cit.,* p. 198.
[7] *Ibid.,* p. 199.

a society in which the mass of people are no longer dominated by work ideals and preoccupations? It has already been shown, earlier in this text, that industrial mechanization has brought about a general decline of job-oriented social values among many workers. A key factor, if such a change is to be more pronounced, will be the extent to which automation is adopted in our economy.

The Effects of Automation

Automation represents more than just advanced mechanical processes. Instead, engineers define it as the transference of control functions from human beings to computers and servomechanisms. Automated devices are those which can essentially run themselves without human supervision or direction. They correct their own errors and respond to various kinds of informational imputs with preprogrammed responses. Automated machines work with a speed and accuracy that human beings cannot match.

Obviously, automation has had a tremendous influence on employment. In the coal-mining industry, for example, the number of production workers in the United States plummeted from 411,000 in 1947 to 123,000 in 1962; similar statistics apply to the broad field of agriculture. Yet there is some disagreement about the extent to which automation has proved a cause of major unemployment problems for the total economy. Some have taken the position that it eliminates a substantial number of jobs each year. A leading economic adviser, John L. Snyder, Jr., commented in 1964,

To my mind, there is no question that automation is already a major cause of unemployment in this country, or that automated machines will essentially take many more jobs from men than they have already.[8]

Snyder calculates that automation eliminates 3 million jobs a year not only through direct lay-offs but through the "silent" firing of workers who would have become employed had not their potential job been wiped out. The American Foundation on Automation and Employment has estimated that automation is eliminating 40,000 jobs a week, or more than 2 million a year. George Meany, president of the AFL-CIO, has estimated job losses attributable to automation to run as high as a possible 4 million each year.

On the other hand, some economists take the position that while automation eliminates some jobs, it creates many others and generally helps to build a sound and growing economy that is able to absorb those who enter the labor force each year. Gardner Ackley writes:

Technological change has been destroying jobs since the beginning of civilization—faster and faster since the Industrial Revolution—and yet the *total* number of jobs has, with occasional interruptions, risen continually. It is clearly

[8] Gardner Ackley, "Automation: Threat and Promise," *New York Times Magazine,* March 22, 1964, p. 16.

one-sided, therefore, to concentrate on the job-*destroying* effects of automation without considering the job-*creating* ability of our economy as a whole.[9]

Some have pointed out that the effects of automation have been much exaggerated in the popular press, partly because not as much automation has actually been put to work in production centers as is generally supposed and also because writers on it have failed to distinguish between what is scientifically possible and what makes economic sense. The most convincing argument against the job-destroying effect of automation is that during the two decades in which it was argued that new processes were eliminating at least 2 million jobs a year (which would amount to a total of 40 million unemployed if new jobs were not created), we have actually had an unemployment rate that has remained fairly consistently between about 3 to 5 million.

It seems clear, however, that the long-range effect of automation, if it is permitted to develop with a degree of freedom, will be powerful. First, it will inevitably change the character of employment. Increasingly, jobs will become more and more automatic and increasingly less physical and menial. Unskilled, semiskilled, and blue-collar workers will tend to disappear. A second effect will be the probable increase in unemployment, or in underemployment. What will happen to the millions of American families whose wage-earners may be displaced by the new technology and who will lack the skills or adaptability to find jobs in the new areas of employment that are expected to open up? What economic strategies can be brought to bear to insure that the section of society that is chronically underemployed, underpaid, or unemployed will have adequate financial support in the future?

As indicated earlier, there has been a meteoric growth in the municipal welfare rolls, even during a decade of unparalleled general prosperity. As an example, in 1957 the ratio of those on public welfare to those earning a paycheck in private industry in New York City was one to ten. By 1968, the ratio had changed to one in three. A number of proposals have been made to insure a minimum floor of economic support for all families, at the same time avoiding the destructive aspects of the present welfare system. One such proposal has been for a "negative income tax," which would involve a national payments system (viewed not as a dole but as a right insured by law) for all families below a stated income level. Closely linked to this is the proposal for a "guaranteed annual income," which would consist of a national system of income guarantees and supplements, available both to those who are unable to work because of age or disability and to those who are employed but underpaid. Hawkins describes this approach:

Under this plan the government would set a minimum income level that is necessary for a family. Each family with income less than this level would receive

[9] *Ibid.*, p. 16.

a subsidy from the government. Sliding scales would be established to provide for family size and to encourage family heads to seek work.[10]

Such a system would do much to eliminate the harsher forms of poverty and to bring a degree of income uniformity throughout the regions of the United States, where state and municipal welfare payments vary so widely that many poor people have migrated to areas where more generous programs are offered. A number of leading economists have endorsed the general principles of such an approach, as essential to banishing the indignities of the existing system and heightening inducements to take jobs. Estimates of the costs of a guaranteed annual income plan range from about $12 to $30 billion a year, however, and it seems improbable that it will be enacted to any significant degree in the immediate future.

Another approach to prevent automation from wiping out huge areas of employment is through labor-management agreements and personnel policies which shorten the work week, lengthen vacations, and provide for extended sabbaticals for older workers, earlier retirement, and periods of retraining. Such programs would spread out the available work among larger numbers of employees. Even with such policies, however, it seems likely that we are moving toward a situation in which substantial numbers of people will no longer be involved in work as it is presently conceived. Eric Hoffer, the longshoreman-philosopher, predicts that this will occur and explores its social implications:

What worries me is the prospect of a skilled and highly competent population living off the fat of the land without a sense of usefulness and worth. There is nothing more explosive than a skilled population condemned to inaction. Such a population is likely to become a hotbed of extremism and intolerance, and receptive to any proselytizing ideology, however absurd and vicious, which promises fast action. . . .

My feeling is that an energetic, skilled population deprived of its sense of usefulness would be an ideal setup for an American Hitler.[11]

Intellectuals tend to view this prospect with considerable alarm. Typically, the historian Arthur Schlesinger Jr., has written, "The most dangerous threat hanging over American society is the threat of leisure . . . and those who have the least preparation for it will have the most of it."[12] Nor are such concerns limited to the United States. The Council of Europe, an association of leading European social scientists, has predicted that the "age of leisure" would become a reality within one generation. They

[10] Donald E. Hawkins, "Pro and Con: The Guaranteed Income," *Parks and Recreation*, March, 1967, p. 45.
[11] Eric Hoffer, "Automation Is Here to Liberate Us," *New York Times Magazine*, October 24, 1965, p. 48.
[12] Arthur Schlesinger, Jr., quoted in Edward T. Chase, "Four Days Shalt Thou Labor," *New York Times Magazine*, September 20, 1964, p. 28.

view this both as a threat and as a promising possibility. One leading European economist described leisure as "one of the three great dangers facing our civilization," the other two being nuclear war and overpopulation. Another expert forecast that leisure would be turned over to "lifelong learning," which would help people exploit natural and cultural resources on an ever-increasing scale.[13]

The Predicted Growth of Leisure

How much free time is it predicted that we will have by 2000, and what forms will it take? The Hudson Institute Report predicts that by the year 2000 our employed labor force will consist of 122 million people, who will have an average working year of 1,100 hours (compared with a standard work year of about 1,900 hours today). The year would be broken down as follows:[14]

> 7.5-hour working day
> 4 working days per week
> 39 working weeks per year
> 10 legal holidays
> 3-day weekends
> 13 weeks of vacation per year

This projection would give the average working man 147 working days and 218 days off each year—considerably more free time than at present, although not remarkably different from the Middle Ages, when the laboring force had 170 holidays a year. While the majority of workers will have schedules of this type, it is also predicted that others will work for longer hours than normal, either for added income, for compulsive or altruistic reasons, or because their high-level skills are in special demand. Similarly, others will be employed only intermittently because of lack of motivation or because of cyclical unemployment due to business declines or geographical shifts in industry. Finally, it is estimated that about 20 percent of the population will be work "dropouts," deliberately dependent on the dole and not participating in the vocational life of the nation to a significant degree.

Another analysis (Table 20-1), drawn from projections made by the National Commission on Technology, Automation and Economic Progress, includes a number of alternative ways in which leisure may be used during the period immediately ahead.

It seems clear that no one of these alternatives is likely to prevail as the single preferred way of using the free time made available by more

---

[13] "Economists Foresee 'Age of Leisure,' " *Christian Science Monitor*, January 6, 1966, p. 27.
[14] Kahn *et al.*, *The Year 2000, op. cit.* p. 195.

TABLE 20-1   *Alternative Uses of Potential Nonworking Time*

Year	Length of Work Week (hours)	Vacation Time (weeks)	Labor Force Retraining (per cent)	Years of Extended Education	Retirement Age
1965	40	3	...	...	65
1970	34	10	13.8	5.1	57
1975	30	16	26.2	9.4	50
1980	25	21	37.2	13.8	44
1985	22	25	45.2	17.5	38

SOURCE: National Commission on Technology, Automation and Economic Progress, cited in *The Challenge of Leisure: A Southern California Case Study* (Claremont: Southern California Research Council, Pomona College, 1967), p. 11.

efficient production. There is evidence that the majority of workers will prefer to take the benefits of productivity in the form of higher real income, rather than through employee benefits and increased leisure. The Southern California Research Council reports that a survey of union officials and corporate managers indicates that, of the alternatives suggested, workers will prefer to use their free time in the form of sabbatical leaves, early retirement, and extended vacations and more holidays rather than across-the-board reductions in the work week.[15]

Whatever form the added free time takes, how will it be used? Two reports (the first issued by the Outdoor Recreation Resources Review Commission in 1962 and the second by the Bureau of Outdoor Recreation in 1967) offer projections for outdoor activities. The 1962 report suggests that participation in outdoor recreation would climb from the 1960 total of 4.4 billion separate activity occasions (participation by an individual in a single outdoor recreation activity during a day) to 6.9 billion occasions in 1976 and 12.4 billion occasions by 2000.[16] Only five years later, however, the Bureau of Outdoor Recreation's report, part of its research leading to the development of a Nationwide Outdoor Recreation Plan, estimated that by the year 2000 there would be 16.8 billion activity occasions, far more than originally anticipated.[17]

It is clear that the combination of increased population, affluence and leisure will lead to the need for greatly expanded facilities and organized recreation services.

15 National Commission on Technology, Automation and Economic Progress, cited in *The Challenge of Leisure: A Southern California Case Study* (Clarmont: Southern California Research Council, Pomona College, 1967), p. 12.

16 "Outdoor Recreation for America," *Report to the President and Congress by the Outdoor Recreation Resources Review Commission* (Washington, D.C.: U.S. Government Printing Office, 1962), p. 32.

17 Bureau of Outdoor Recreation, *Outdoor Recreation Trends* (Washington, D.C.: U.S. Government Printing Office, April, 1967).

Defining the Needs of the Future

Based on these projections, the following specific challenges face the United States with respect to recreation and leisure needs in the twenty-first century.

1. *The Need to Preserve and Expand the Nation's Outdoor Recreation and Park Resources.* As this text has indicated throughout, the need to reduce pollution and prevent constriction of open space and the natural environment must become a far greater concern of government on all levels. The problem of environmental protection extends far beyond merely setting aside land or waterfront areas; it involves such fundamental challenges as the need to halt offshore oil-drilling, which has done great damage to our natural environment and wildlife, or the use of immensely destructive chemicals which are poisoning the earth and the atmosphere in deadly and irretrievable ways.

According to Barry Commoner, director of the Center for the Biology of Natural Systems, and W. H. Ferry, vice president of the Center for the Study of Democratic Institutions, nothing less than a change in the political and social system of the nation is needed to save the country from destroying its natural environment. Through the uncontrolled use of inorganic fertilizers, high-compression automobile engines, and insecticides, we have been steadily poisoning our environment. Typically, the massive use of nitrogen fertilizers greatly increases crop yields for a few years but damages the soil by altering its physical character. In addition, it filters into rivers and destroys their self-purifying capability. Commoner has concluded:

Our present system of technology is not merely consuming this capital [of land, water and other resources] but threatening, probably within the next 50 years —to destroy it irreparably.[18]

The ultimate solution will require far more than simply providing better sewage treatment, fume traps on automobile exhausts, or scrubbers on smokestacks. Instead, it will demand fundamental redefinition of many of our agricultural, economic, and social policies. Similarly, our national and regional policies with respect to the process of urban development must be critically examined. If the prospect that lies ahead is really one of major sections of the country becoming dense megalopolises, then, as former Secretary of Agriculture Orville Freeman points out, our continued dumping of millions of Americans into great metropolitan areas is national suicide. He suggests that we must deliberately create new living spaces—far out in the countryside—for the 100 million additional people who will inhabit the United States by the year 2000.

[18] Robert H. Phelps, "Technology and Environment: Senators Hear Gloomy Appraisal," New York *Times*, April 28, 1969, p. 26.

2. *The Need for More Effective Urban Planning.* The approaches to city planning which were described in Chapter 19 deal chiefly with the ways in which our existing cities might be restructured and made more livable. We must, however, consider the problem of developing whole new cities which will have organic unity and logic as an alternative to the present policy of permitting unplanned and formless spreading out of our major metropolises.

A number of attempts to design new, experimental cities have been made in the past in both Europe and America. In Great Britain, during the early decades of the twentieth century, a number of so-called garden cities were established, such as Letchworth (1903) and Welwyn Garden City (1920). Following World War II, a New Towns Committee was established to promote the founding of new communities which would house expanding industry and population from congested areas, particularly London. In each of these, a wide range of clubs and societies, playfields and parks, youth centers, theaters, pools, cricket and hockey grounds, all-weather training areas, and sports halls have been established.

In the United States, a number of such experimental communities have been begun, under the sponsorship of private developers, with funds supplied primarily by major financial institutions such as banks and insurance companies.

One of the leading examples of such efforts has been Columbia, Maryland, sponsored by the Rouse Company of Baltimore. This city was begun in 1963 on 14,000 acres of farmland midway between Baltimore and Washington, D.C., and is scheduled ultimately to have 110,000 residents. Columbia's planners are noteworthy for having set aside 23.3 percent of the total area of the city-to-be for permanent open space, to be preserved largely in a natural state, for park and recreation purposes:

We invited the land to impose itself as a discipline on the form of the community. . . . Sprawl is ugly, oppressive, massively dull. . . . It squanders the resources of nature—forests, streams, hillsides—and produces vast armies of housing and graceless, tasteless clutter. In Columbia, the major stream valleys will be preserved, along with hundreds of acres of forests. These green acres will interlace the entire community, separating and collecting the nine villages and leading into the heart of downtown, which will have a 50-acre forest on one side and a lake on another.[19]

Of the 3,180 acres of open space in Columbia, 1,410 are being devoted to such specialized uses as golfing, hunting and game preserves, fishing and swimming on five manmade lakes, horseback riding, and tennis. The remaining 1,770 acres, woven throughout the entire fabric of the city, will

[19] David Colley, "Nature Disciplines a City," *Parks and Recreation*, May, 1968, p. 41.

be unrestricted open space and woodland. Each of the nine villages in Columbia is to be divided into a half-dozen neighborhoods. As an example of the extensive provision of recreation facilities, each of these neighborhoods, including about 800 families, will have two pools, many with wood superstructures with removable Plexiglas panels to permit longer swimming season. Over all, the Columbia planners have stressed the need for a wide variety of facilities for sports, outdoor recreation, and cultural pursuits, with convenient access from their homes for all residents. The final blueprint of Columbia, which was devised with the help of leading architects, engineers, and social scientists, incorporates the best aspects of late twentieth-century urban and suburban living and seeks to shut out the worst—such as choking traffic, air pollution, and parking problems. Its ability to attract residents and investment will undoubtedly be based heavily on its attractiveness and the quality of life promised by its open spaces and by park and recreation opportunities.

Another new town which makes important use of recreation and parks as essential planning elements, is Reston, Virginia. Situated on 6,819 acres of rolling countryside, Reston is scheduled to be completed by 1980 and to house about 75,000 people, who will live in high-rise apartments, one-family houses, and perhaps as many as 17,000 cluster houses which will provide the maximum possible outdoor space. Here, too, it is expected that ideal recreational environments will make life as enjoyable as possible, through careful planning, for residents. In all, it is expected that about 200 new communities like Columbia and Reston will be built across the country, many of them consisting of "leisure villages" built as retirement communities.

The most radical plans for new cities are today being developed by a leading scientist, Dr. Athelstan Spilhaus, with the support of the Federal Departments of Housing and Urban Development, Commerce, and Health, Education and Welfare. His approach has been to plan for an entirely new kind of experimental city that would be built at least 100 miles from any other urban center. Spilhaus urges that, unlike Columbia and Reston, which are dependent to a degree on nearby cities, cities should be developed that will be self-sufficient economically and that will provide new nuclei for urban development. Spaced at generous distances from each other, these cities, even when they have reached their optimum sizes, will have substantial open land around them.

Preliminary descriptions of Spilhaus' Experimental City suggests that it will be concerned from the outset with the provision of a total healthful and asthetically satisfying environment. It plans to make use of entirely new technologies, including pollutionless factories, noiseless and fumeless underground transportation systems, and methods for removing sewage and other waste materials in semiliquid form for processing and at least partial recovery of useful materials. Many of the essential services of the city—power, water, gas, communications lines, pneumatic tubes and parcel delivery, and express tunnels for police, ambulance, fire, and other emergency vehicles—will be underground. Buildings will be designed for a lifetime of perhaps twenty to thirty years, whereupon they would be disassembled and taken underground, with some portions stowed for future construction use, and the rest hauled off for salvage.

In Spilhaus' Experimental City, there would be no suburban sprawl. As in medieval walled towns, beyond the city limits one would enter directly into open country, with land set aside for recreation and farming. The boundaries of the city would be extremely compact and would permit any resident to reach open land by walking on the traffic-free ground level in 15 minutes or less. The whole field of culture and recreation is seen as a vital aspect of the city's development; however, it is viewed as an intercity concern:

> By the use of 400-mile-an-hour underground transit systems, which are presently in design, we could go from the center of one city to the center of its neighborhood in the same commuting time—15 minutes. Thus, mobility, not only within a city, but between cities, is a vital part of the concept of making dispersed, controlled-sized cities multiply the choices offered.
>
> Neighboring cities would then not compete, each for a baseball team, each for a symphony orchestra, each for an art gallery—but would complement each other.[20]

Thus, three levels of city planning are being carried out today, all of which have vital implications for recreation and park development in the future. First, there is the process of renewing and remodeling the existing cities and their surrounding suburbs in order to make them more livable and efficient. Second, there is the process of developing outlying fully planned communities like Columbia and Reston, which are close to existing metropolitan areas and partially dependent on them economically. Third, there is the more visionary prospect of developing entirely new population- and space-controlled cities at a considerable distance from existing cities and with the fullest possible use of modern and future technology, as in Spilhaus' Experimental City. In each case, recreation and park planning is heavily interwoven throughout the entire scheme.

3. *The Use of Technology in the Delivery of Leisure Services.*   Earlier chapters have described the influence of modern technology on our modern uses of leisure. Without question, continuing innovation in this field will provide us with more environmental-changing devices, greater mobility, and entirely new kinds of recreational activities. It seems likely that the computer will become increasingly important in sports and recreation. Typ-

20 "A City of Future, No Cars, Pure Air," New York *Times*, December 28, 1967, p. 20; see also "One Man's Vision of the City of Tomorrow," New York *Times*, January 9, 1969, p. 145.

ically, it is just beginning to be used in certain highly specialized ways. For example, transatlantic sailors today make use of the computer to calculate weather conditions and determine their course most safely and efficiently. Urban planning experts have begun to make use of computer techniques to examine the use patterns of park and recreation areas, determine priorities, estimate future demand, and determine the effects of new installations, fees and charges, assignment of manpower, or program innovations.

In their application of new technologies, recreation administrators will be able to learn much from professional educators. Experimentation in the field of education is creating revolutionary new devices with which more effective learning experiences on all age levels will be made possible. It has been predicted, for example, that grade schools of the future will be run by electronics engineers, with children working in "individual cubicles where they are taught to reach with the aid of TV screens and electronic light pens, headphones and speaker systems, multiple-choice buttons," and similar aids, all connected to programmed computers for mechanically-assisted instruction.[21]

If recreation is to become truly a part of the twenty-first century, it must share fully in the technological revolution rather than permit itself to be tied to concepts of a horse-and-buggy age. Yet it should be realized that technology does not promise unmixed blessings. It threatens to create a new class of passive, uninvolved human beings—people who have everything done for them and are simply spectators. If a computer can play bridge or chess better than a man possibly can—why should a man play such games at all? If, in an age of technologically determined recreation, everyone becomes exposed to a rubber-stamped model of entertainment through the mass media, we will be losing sight of one of the great values of recreation—that it permits each person to be involved in creative self-discovery and individualized activity.

The problem will be to maintain the elements of personal challenge and involvement and to promote meaningful human relationships within leisure rather than permit recreation to become an experience in which the player simply presses a switch or button, pulls a lever, guides a missile, or steers a vehicle. The seductive power of technology is best illustrated through television. This medium today actually far surpasses the naked eye; the television watcher is able to see two separate events going on simultaneously, can watch slow-motion, split-screen replays of the most exciting moments of ball games, can virtually be in the helmet of the football quarterback or dangling from a rope along with the mountain-climber who is scaling Mount Everest. The danger of all this is that it makes the event both unreal and removed and yet far more exciting in some ways than the real activity. Thus—and because it is too easy—it becomes likely

[21] Hillel Black, "Automation Still in Future," New York *Times*, January 12, 1968, p. 74.

to displace actual participation, which is frequently laborious, slow, inconvenient, and dangerous.

An allied risk is that technological devices are inevitably expensive. Unlike the simple, homemade recreation of the past, complex mechanical equipment such as ski tows or snow-blowing machines or any of the other technological devices that permit new kinds of recreation tend to demand fees for participation. Thus, the danger is that new forms of recreation may become restricted to the well-to-do and that the less affluent will be ignored as far as the provision of recreation opportunity is concerned. So, as recreation moves into the age of the future, its professional leaders must take full advantage of the potentialities offered by modern science and technology and at the same time, avoid their hazards and pitfalls.

4. *Establishing National Priorities for Recreation and Leisure.* As previous chapters have indicated, there is an urgent need to redefine and strengthen the role of recreation in modern society so that it becomes perceived not just as an amenity or frivolous diversion but as an important national concern. Some have commented that it is only the social scientist, the intellectual, or the recreation professional who is concerned about the problem of leisure—and that the average working man could not care less about it. It seems clear, however, that for great numbers of individuals —working men who are gaining increased bulks of free time and are turning to moonlighting because they are unable to use their free time enjoyably, retired men and women who lack interests and leisure opportunities, the physically and mentally disabled who are barred from recreational participation, the socially and economically disadvantaged, who turn to pathological forms of play for lack of other possibilities—for all these, leisure has indeed become an extremely serious problem.

It seems clear that if we are to retain our strength and morale as a nation, we must be certain that we do not permit increasing bulks of our time, at all ages, to be spent in negative, self-destructive, or empty ways. This is a clear challenge to the nation. There must be a total new awareness of the problem of leisure and a sense of national priority in this area. With fuller leadership by the Federal government and more extensive provision of facilities, services, and recreational opportunities by states and local governments, the task can be accomplished.

At the same time, it is crucial that we not permit the concept of recreation to be narrowly defined. Typically, some critics have suggested that recreation cannot possibly meet the needs for meaningful activity that future generations will share. Sylvia Porter, the financial writer, comments:

> Since extended leisure time is inevitable, what's the answer? It's not more golf, more gardening, more fishing, bowling or TV-watching. These pleasures can become tortures if there is little else.

The answer is a step-up in education of the American adult . . . to prepare all of us to reach a higher plateau of literacy in every sphere—economic, political, social, cultural. The voluntary return to classes of adults across the nation to learn new aptitudes and hobbies indicates how far we have moved from the popular image of night school. The campaigns launched by far-sighted unions, business and community leaders to spur adult education during vacation and off-hours telegraph what is on the way.[22]

What Porter describes as "adult education" includes many activities that are in reality adult recreation. Classes in the fine and graphic arts, in languages, music, dance, theater—and other areas that are explored not for vocational or other practical reasons but because people wish to develop themselves by expanding their interests, knowledge, and personality—represent clearly recreational uses of leisure. Some have taken the position that only the well-to-do and highly educated in our society are interested in such cultural involvements and that the rest are content to drink beer, bowl, or sit by the television set. The Community Action Programs which brought cultural programs into urban ghettos during the 1960's showed, however, that great numbers of economically disadvantaged and poorly educated young people in these slums had great potential interest in the arts and similar learning experiences. The real challenge of the future will be to develop not only better facilities and resources for outdoor recreation but, in alliance with other community agencies, to develop extensive learning and participating leisure experiences for all people. The total enrichment of life through the use of the arts, personal hobbies and pursuits, travel, civic activity, sports, and games must be made available for all persons as a matter of primary national concern.

5. *The Role of the Recreation and Park Professional.* Finally, what will be the role of the recreation and park professional in the period that lies ahead? It would almost appear that if he is to provide meaningful leadership, he will need to be a philosopher, a planner, a psychologist, a sociologist, an engineer, and an administrator. Clearly, no single profession can embody all these specialized areas of competence. Yet the recreation and park professional must be reasonably conversant within each of these spheres of knowledge and able to communicate effectively with specialists in each of them. But, more important, he must provide vigorous leadership to expand the prestige and influence of his own field of service on the national scene.

A leading recreation and park administrator, Joseph Curtis, has pointed out the need to bolster this field's degree of public awareness and acceptance. In order to achieve a concerted and unanimous professional focus, Curtis offers a set of suggestions which might well be termed a Magna Carta for recreation in the closing decades of the twentieth century. His proposals include the following.

He urges that we establish a billion-dollar trust or foundation to carry on continuous experimentation and research within the field of leisure

[22] Sylvia Porter, "Education for All," New York *Post*, December 12, 1963, p. 32.

services—this to be financed by major industries with a vital stake in recreation. Linked to this, Curtis suggests that we annually invest at least 1 percent of our Gross National Product in parks, open spaces, and recreation facilities, using income from recreational motor vehicle, boating, and aircraft use for such projects.

Curtis further urges that the Federal government establish a Department of Recreation and Leisure on the cabinet level and that within each of the fifty states this be supported by vigorous state societies and associations. He urges that to promote public concern we annually convene a summit conference of leaders in industry, education, medicine, transportation, social planning, recreation, and parks to develop plans for leisure development. To improve professional development, he suggests that a super-university be developed by the National Recreation and Park Association to give high-level training to community leaders in this field and that the N.R.P.A. promote career development and internship and national certification plans aggressively. Further, Curtis urges that a Recreation Youth Service Corps be established through which young people might work in recreation, enabling them to gain cash credits toward college by such early experience. The profession, he says, should be much more widely represented in the armed services and on college campuses and, finally, should be promoted by a massive public relations program carried on by the National Recreation and Park Association.[23]

While some may conclude that these proposals are too ambitious to be realistic, the fact is that steps of such magnitude will be necessary if our society is to come to grips with the onrushing reality of the leisure age of the twenty-first century. Without imaginative and sharply focused efforts to strengthen national support of recreation programs and to develop new concepts of leadership, this field cannot hope to cope with the challenges that will be posed by fantastically rapid social change. Marshall McLuhan comments that the present age of technology is reshaping and restructuring every aspect of our personal lives and all our patterns of social independence.

It is forcing us to reconsider and re-evaluate practically every thought, every action, and every institution formerly taken for granted. Everything is changing, you, your family, your neighborhood, your education, your job, your government, your relation to others. And they are changing dramatically. . . . Innumerable confusions and a profound feeling of despair inevitably emerge in periods of great technological and cultural transformation. Our age of anxiety is in great part the result of trying to do today's job with yesterday's tools . . . with yesterday's concepts.[24]

[23] Joseph Curtis, "The Cowardly Lion," *Parks and Recreation*, August, 1967, pp. 18, 42.

[24] Marshall McLuhan, quoted in Hugh C. Davis, "Recreation Planning in the Technological Age," *Parks and Recreation*, November, 1968, p. 22.

If we are to cope effectively with the changing physical and social environment of the future, and to provide leadership in an age of unbelievably rapid change, we must do so with entirely new concepts and approaches to providing leisure literacy and recreational opportunity to America's masses. This, then, is the challenge of the future.

Suggested Topics for Examination Questions, Student Papers, or Panel Reports

Part One

1. What major social factors have been responsible for the growth of the recreation movement in the United States during the past several decades? Identify and discuss these in detail.

2. What are the primary responsibilities and functions, with respect to recreation and parks, of government in the United States on federal, state, and local levels? Discuss the relationship among the different levels of government, with respect to overlapping functions and need for coordination.

3. Describe the major types of voluntary agencies which have a responsibility for recreation and social programs in the United States. How do they differ from governmental agencies in this field in terms of purpose, administrative control, personnel, and budgetary support?

4. Special emphasis has been given recently to improving recreation and park facilities and programs for disadvantaged population groups, particularly urban minorities. Describe what has been done in detail, and analyze the strengths and weaknesses of such programs.

5. Outline the development of park and recreation service as a professional field during the past three decades, including such points as public recognition, professional preparation, and standards for employment. Formulate several specific recommendations for upgrading professionalism in this field.

Part Two

6. Describe a number of major forms of play in primitive societies and pre-Christian civilizations. Contrast these early forms of play with the recreational pursuits of modern man.

7. Briefly trace the history of organized religion as it influenced man's recreative involvement in Europe and America, during the period from the Dark and Middle Ages to the Industrial Revolution. To what extent does organized religion today affect the legal status of, or public attitudes toward, recreation and leisure?

8. To what extent has recreational participation and opportunity been linked to social class structure in the United States, both in the past and present? Draw on historical and sociological data to support your statements.

9. Outline the major forces that led to the development of the playground movement in the United States, with emphasis on the role of schools, voluntary organizations, and municipal governments. What were the major justifications for providing play opportunities during this period?

10. Contrast the provision of recreation and park facilities and programs in three European countries described in this text, including the rationale for such programs, the role of the national government, and the relationship to the prevailing political philosophy of each country.

Part Three

11. Define *recreation, leisure* and *play*, in terms both of the discussion in the text, and your own understanding of their meaning.

12. Develop a systematic and carefully documented statement of the value of recreational experience in human growth and development. Then select a single age group (such as adolescence or old age) and analyze its special needs for recreation and how they may best be met.

13. Briefly summarize the four major concepts of leisure which are presented in this text. Which of these, in your judgment, is most relevant to understanding the place of organized recreation service in modern society? To what extent, and in what ways, is leisure growing, and what challenges does it pose for the health of our society?

14. Trace the past relationship between public school systems and recreational concerns in the United States. In so doing, discuss the task of educating for leisure as a responsibility of the schools, and the role of the schools in sponsoring or co-sponsoring community recreation programs.

15. Some authorities believe that recreation should be regarded primarily as a health-related field. What is the rationale for this belief? What should the role of recreation in institutional and community programs be with respect to the groups in the population that suffer from physical or mental disability?

Part Four

16. Although some authorities question its relevance, a major objective of community recreation has been to prevent or reduce juvenile delinquency. Discuss this statement in detail, citing both positive and negative arguments. Then indicate how you believe recreation can be most effective in anti-delinquency programs.

17. Programs of conservation, preservation of natural beauty, and pollution control have gained considerable support recently. What are the commonly-shared goals of these programs and recreation and park agencies? What are the points of possible conflict? Indicate how the two fields may work together cooperatively for their mutual benefit.

18. Many recreation and park agencies have come to rely increasingly on fees and charges as a means of financial support. What are the positive arguments supporting this trend? What are some of its negative implications? Develop a set of guides with respect to the use of fees and charges in recreation and park administration.

19. Describe and critically analyze traditional planning concepts as they affect the development of recreation and park facilities in American communities. How meaningful is the reliance on space and facilities standards that are commonly used in urban planning? What bases for determining community needs and developing recreation and park facilities can you suggest?

20. Basing your answer on the final chapter of this text, what do you see as the major problems and opportunities that will face recreation and park professionals during the remaining decades of this century? What constructive policies should this field adopt if it is to meet its responsibilities most effectively by the year 2000?

Bibliography

Textbooks on Recreation and Leisure

Nels Anderson, *Work and Leisure* (New York: Free Press, 1961).

Charles K. Brightbill, *Man and Leisure: A Philosophy of Recreation* (Englewood Cliffs, N.J.: Prentice-Hall, 1961).

C. Frank Brockman, *Recreational Use of Wild Lands* (New York: McGraw-Hill, 1959).

George D. Butler, *Introduction to Community Recreation* (New York: McGraw-Hill, 1967), and *Pioneers in Public Recreation* (Minneapolis: Burgess, 1965).

Roger Caillois, *Man, Play and Games* (London: Thames and Hudson, 1961).

Reynold Carlson, Theodore Deppe, and Janet MacLean, *Recreation in American Life* (Belmont, Calif.: Wadsworth, 1963).

Marion Clawson and Jack Knetsch, *Economics of Outdoor Recreation* (Baltimore: Johns Hopkins Press, 1966).

Sebastian de Grazia, *Of Time, Work and Leisure* (New York: Twentieth-Century Fund, 1962).

Charles E. Doell and Charles B. Fitzgerald, *A Brief History of Parks and Recreation in the United States* (Chicago: The Athletic Institute, 1954).

Paul Douglass, John Hutchinson, and Willard Sutherland, eds., *Recreation in the Age of Automation* (Philadelphia: Annals of the American Academy of Political and Social Science, 1957).

Foster R. Dulles, *A History of Recreation: America Learns to Play* (New York: Appleton-Century-Crofts, 1965).

Joffre Dumazedier, *Toward a Society of Leisure* (New York: Free Press, Collier-Macmillan, 1967).

Arnold W. Green, *Recreation, Leisure and Politics* (New York: McGraw-Hill, 1964).

Elinor Guggenheimer, *Planning for Parks and Recreation Needs in Urban Areas* (New York: Twayne Publishers, 1969).

Paul Haun, *Recreation: A Medical Viewpoint* (New York: Teachers College, Columbia University Bureau of Publications, 1965).

Johan Huizinga, *Homo Ludens: A Study of the Play Element in Culture* (Boston: Beacon Press, 1950).

John L. Hutchinson, *Principles of Recreation* (New York: Ronald Press, 1951).

Max Kaplan, *Leisure in America—A Social Inquiry* (New York: Wiley, 1960).

Richard Kraus, *Recreation and the Schools* (New York: Macmillan, 1964), and *Recreation Today* (New York: Appleton-Century-Crofts, 1966).

Alfred La Gasse and Walter Cook, *History of Parks and Recreation* (Washington: American Institute of Park Executives, 1965).

Eric Larrabee and Rolf Meyersohn, *Mass Leisure* (Glencoe, Ill.: Free Press, 1958).

Robert Lee, *Religion and Leisure in the United States* (Nashville: Abingdon, 1964).

Pauline Madow, *Recreation in America* (New York: H. W. Wilson, 1965).

Peter C. McIntosh, *Sport in Society* (London: C. A. Watts, 1963).

Harold D. Meyer, Charles K. Brightbill, and H. Douglas Sessoms, *Community Recreation, A Guide to Its Organization* (Englewood Cliffs, N.J.: Prentice-Hall, 1969).

Susanna Millar, *The Psychology of Play* (Baltimore: Penguin Books, 1968).

Norman Miller and Duane Robinson, *The Leisure Age* (Belmont, Calif.: Wadsworth, 1963).

Jay B. Nash, *Philosophy of Recreation and Leisure* (Dubuque, Iowa: Brown, 1960).

Martin Neumeyer and Esther Neumeyer, *Leisure and Recreation* (New York: Ronald, 1958).

Josef Pieper, *Leisure: The Basis of Culture* (New York: Mentor-Omega Books, 1952, 1963).

Bernard Rosenberg and D. M. White, *Mass Culture* (Glencoe, Ill.: Free Press, 1957).

Allen V. Sapora and Elmer Mitchell, *The Theory of Play and Recreation* (New York: Ronald, 1961).

Jay Shivers, *Principles and Practices of Recreational Service* (New York: Macmillan, 1967).

Samuel Slavson, *Recreation and the Total Personality* (New York: Association Press, 1946).

Erwin O. Smigel, ed., *Work and Leisure: A Contemporary Social Problem* (New Haven: College and University Press, 1963).

C. Lynn Vendien and John Nixon, *The World Today in Health, Physical Education and Recreation*, (Englewood Cliffs, N.J.: Prentice-Hall, 1968).

Other Reports and Publications

Ago Ambre, ed., *Occupational Outlook Quarterly, Recreation in Review* (Washington, D.C.: U.S. Bureau of Labor Statistics, May, 1965).

Nancy Anderson, *Senior Centers: Information from a National Survey* (Minneapolis: American Rehabilitation Foundation, June, 1969).

The Challenge of Leisure: A Southern California Case Study (Claremont, Calif.: Southern California Research Council, Pomona College, 1967).

Charles J. Cicchetti *et al, The Demand and Supply of Outdoor Recreation* (New Brunswick, N.J.: Bureau of Economic Research, Rutgers University, June, 1969).

Donald E. Hawkins, *Supply/Demand Study, Professional and Pre-Professional Recreation and Park Occupations* (Washington, D.C.: National Recreation and Park Association, March, 1968).

Journal of Leisure Research (Washington, D.C.: published quarterly by National Recreation and Park Association, beginning Winter, 1969).

Janet R. MacLean, ed., *Therapeutic Recreation in the Community* (Bloomington, Ind.: Conference Report, Indiana University, 1962).

"Outdoor Recreation for America," *Report to the President and Congress by the Outdoor Recreation Resources Review Commission* (Washington, D.C.: U. S. Government Printing Office, 1962), Vols. I and XXII.

Outdoor Recreation Research (Washington, D.C.: Bureau of Outdoor Recreation and Science Information Exchange of Smithsonian Institution, U. S. Government Printing Office, 1968–1970).

Martha J. Premo, ed., *Parks and Recreation in the Urban Crises* (Washington, D.C.: Report of National Forum on Urban Affairs, National Recreation and Park Association, 1969).

Recreation in the Nation's Cities: Problems and Approaches (Washington, D.C.: Department of Urban Studies of National League of Cities, for Bureau of Outdoor Recreation, December, 1968).

Recreation in Treatment Centers (Washington, D.C.: American Recreation Society, Hospital Recreation Section, 1962–1965).

Recreation Research (Washington, D.C.: Conference Report of American Association for Health, Physical Education and Recreation, and National Recreation and Park Association, 1966).

Therapeutic Recreation Journal (Washington, D.C.: published quarterly by National Therapeutic Recreation Society, 1967–1970).

Picture Credits

Plate 1. All pictures from Robert Gardner and Karl G. Heider, *Gardens of War* (Random House, New York), and used courtesy of Film Study Center, Harvard University. They also appear in the film *Dead Birds* available from Image Resources, Inc., New York. Photographs: battle scene, Karl G. Heider; boys playing "spear the hoop," Samuel Putnam; warriors dancing, Michael C. Rockefeller.

Plate 2. Kalapalo Indian wrestlers, Stan Wayman, *Life* Magazine © Time Inc. Maya, the Ball Player, c. 750 A.D., from Irene Nicholson, *Mexican and Central American Mythology* (Hamlyn, England). Photograph: Eugen Kusch. King Shamba, from Geoffrey Parrinder, *African Mythology* (Hamlyn, England), courtesy of the Trustees of the British Museum.

Plate 3. Wall painting, Tutankhamen Hunting Lions, c. 1357 B.C., Cairo Museum. Polo Game, School of Bokhara, Persia, c. 1522 A.D., Hewitt Fund Collection, Metropolitan Museum of Art. Achilles and Ajax, detail of vase by Exekias, c. 550 B.C., Vatican Museum, from Gisela M. A. Richter, *Greek Art: A Handbook* (Phaidon Press, London).

Plate 4. Jousting scene from 15th Century miniature in Bibliothèque Royale, Brussels. Frank Scherschel, *Life* Magazine © Time Inc. Peasant Dance, by Pieter Breughel, c. 1567, Kunsthistorische Museum, Vienna. King and Queen's Bath at Bath, by Thomas Johnson, 1672, courtesy of the Trustees of the British Museum.

Plate 5. Plan of the Parc de Monceau, executed in 1718 by Carmontelle for the Duc d'Orleans. Walk upon the ramparts of Paris, rendering, after St. Aubin. Fireworks on the Pont-Neuf, old print, Paris, 1745.

Plate 6. The Columbia College Regatta, from *Harper's Weekly*, June 1, 1878. Artist: W. P. Snyder. Skating In Central Park, from *Harper's Weekly*, Feb. 24, 1877. Artists: Schell and Hogan. A Ten-Strike, from *Harper's Weekly*, Aug. 28, 1869. Artist: C. G. Bush.

Plate 7. Kid's baseball, from *Montclair Times*, courtesy Recreation and Parks Department, Montclair, N.J. Photograph: Don McKee. Preschool program and physical fitness class, courtesy Mountain View Parks & Recreation Department, Mountain View, Calif., Merle Butler, Recreation Superintendent.

Plate 8. Mid-Westchester (Scarsdale, N.Y.) Y.M. and Y.W.H.A. Gilbert and Sullivan Company, courtesy of Victor Trasoff. Highland Fling dancing at Fergus, Ontario, courtesy of *Recreation* Magazine. Photograph: Ontario Dept. Travel & Publicity. Ceramics scene, Lincoln Farm Work Camp, Roscoe, N.Y.

Plate 9. Seattle Sports Arena and Civic Opera House, courtesy Seattle Visitors Bureau. Rugby playfield on Hackney Marsh, copyright Associated Newspapers Limited, London.

Plate 10. Water skiing on Guntersville Lake and camping on Land Between the Lakes, courtesy of Tennessee Valley Authority. Swimming pool, courtesy of *Parks and Recreation Magazine.* Photograph: Levittown Public Recreation Association, N.Y.

Plate 11. Children playing in gutter, courtesy of *Parks and Recreation Magazine.* Street marked with games, *New York Times.* Photograph: Jack Manning. Men playing cards, *New York Times.* Photograph: G. Gerald Frazer.

Plate 12. Playstreet scene, courtesy of *The News. New York's Picture Newspaper.* Children at pond, New York State bussing program at Bear Mountain, courtesy Katrina Thomas. Mrs. Johnson dedicating playground, White House Photograph by Abbie Rowe. National Recreation and Park Association conference on planning, photograph courtesy Chase, Ltd.

Plate 13. Wheelchair basketball at Quonset Naval Air Station, U. S. Navy photograph by Frazier. Nature trail for blind at National Arboretum, U. S. Dept. of Agriculture photograph by Rana. Party for handicapped children, from Aurora, Ill., Playground Department, courtesy of *Recreation* Magazine. Photograph: Spring Studio.

Plate 14. Otters and reindeer at Alpenzoo, Innsbruck, Austria, courtesy of Austrian Information Service, New York. Photographs: Richard Frischauf. Polar bears in Milwaukee County Zoo, courtesy Milwaukee County Park Commission. Photograph: Warner E. Bartram.

Plate 15. Dead fish at Lake Odessa, Texas, from Water Pollution Control Administration. Bird-banding, courtesy of Bureau of Sport Fisheries and Wildlife. Photography: Luther C. Goldman. Bird sanctuary, from Fish and Wildlife Service. Photograph: P. J. Van Huizen.

Plate 16. Japanese recreation. Larry Burrows, *Life* Magazine © Time Inc.

Index

Abrams, Charles, *cited*, 444–446
Addams, Jane, 182, 196–197
Administration on Aging, 11, 34–35, 374–375
Adolescence. *See* Youth
Adult education, 179, 281, 355, 470–471
Adults, leisure needs of, 353–356
Administration of recreation and park departments, 59–74, 400
Affluence, in American society, 7, 20–21, 315–316, 407, 456, 461
Aggression, 383, 386–387, 391–395
Aging persons, leisure needs of, 11, 34–35, 67–68, 71, 94–95, 208, 355–356, 372–376
Alcohol. *See* Drinking
Alienation of youth, 339–340
American Association for Health, Physical Education, and Recreation, 109–110, 115–116, 208, 367, 427
American Association of Zoological Parks and Aquariums, 113–114, 202
American Athletic Union, 208
American Camping Association, 116
American Institute of Park Executives, 113, 185, 202
American National Red Cross, 207
American Park and Recreation Society, 114, 117–118
American Recreation Society, 113–114, 399
American Youth Hostels, 92
Anderson, Nels, *cited*, 295, 304–305
Anthropological view of play, 270–272

Anti-poverty programs, 37–41, 77, 79–81, 86–90. *See also* Disadvantaged, recreation programs for
Appalachian Mountain Club, 91–92
Aquatics, 71, 294, 319–321, 324–325, 330
Ardrey, Robert, 272, 392
Aristotle, *cited*, 137–138, 254
Armed Forces recreation, 41–45, 405
Arts in recreation, 10–11, 67, 204, 327–328, 345–346, 471. *See also* Cultural expansion in United States; Performing arts
Assyria and Babylonia, in pre-Christian era, 134–135
Athens, during Periclean age, 135–139
Attendance in recreation and park programs, 4, 27–30, 66–73, 83, 323. *See also* Participation in recreation activities
Australia, 229–230
Automation, 13, 460–464
Automobile thefts, 381–382
Auto racing. *See* Racing
Avedon, Elliott M., *cited*, 367–369

Ballet. *See* Performing arts
Baltimore, 388–389
Bartholomew, Warren M., *cited*, 113
Baseball, 173, 177, 321, 323, 326
Baumol, William, *cited*, 296
Beck, Bertram M., *cited*, 403–404
Berger, Bennett, *cited*, 256, 304–305
Bettelheim, Bruno, *cited*, 276, 392
Blacks. *See* Negroes, and recreation

485

Boating, 25, 76, 93, 173–174, 294, 298, 321, 324, 330
Boston, 182, 185, 187, 245
Boston Sand Garden, 185
Bowen, William, *cited* 296
Bowling, 321–322, 327
Boys' Clubs of America, 80, 198
Boy Scouts of America, 78–80, 198, 207, 419
Brodsky, Irving, 86–87, 107
Bronfenbrenner, Urie, 346–348
Brown, Roscoe C., 383
Bureau of the Census, 27, 33
Bureau of Indian Affairs, 29–30
Bureau of Land Management, 26, 29
Bureau of Outdoor Recreation, 17, 26, 31–32, 46, 50, 209, 324, 370–371, 427, 447–448, 464
Bureau of Reclamation, 30
Butler, George, 201

Caillois, Roger, 267–270, 272
California, 47, 49–50, 120–121, 422
Calvinism, repression of play under, 152–154, 160–163
Camp Fire Girls, 81, 198, 207, 248
Camping. *See* Outdoor recreation
Cardinal Principles of Secondary Education, 15, 220–201, 422
Cardiovascular fitness, 336–338
Careers in recreation and parks. *See* Employment in recreation and parks; Professional development in recreation and parks
Carr, Harvey A., 240–241
Catharsis theory of play, 240–241
Catholicism. *See* Religious attitudes toward recreation
Catholic Youth Organization, 84–85
Central Council of Physical Recreation, 213–214
Central Park, 166, 180–182, 410, 452
Certification, in recreation and parks, 119–122
Character development, role of play in, 340–341
Chautauqua, 179
Chicago, 62, 185, 187–188, 194–195, 197, 388–389
Children's Aid Society, 88–89
Children's Bureau, 35, 81
Christianity, under Roman persecution, 142–143. *See also* Religious attitudes toward recreation; Religious social agencies

Cicero, 139–140
Circus Maximus, 141, 322
Civilian Conservation Corps, 204–205
Civil Service, 52, 121–122, 425
Civil War, 173–174
Clarke, Alfred C., *cited*, 292–293, 295
Clawson, Marion, *cited*, 20
Cloward, Richard A., *cited*, 379
Coast Guard, 29
Co-curricular activities in schools and colleges, 277–278, 339–340
Cohen, Albert, *cited*, 379–380
Coleman, James, *cited*, 284–285, 342–343, 347
Colonial America, recreation in, 160–167
Columbia, Maryland, 466–467
Commercial recreation, 6, 96–97, 103–104, 156–158, 172–173, 177–178, 194–197, 228, 326–328
Communism. *See* Soviet Union; Communist China
Communist China, 230–231
Community Action Programs, 37, 38–40, 386, 448. *See also* Office of Economic Opportunity
Community colleges, professional preparation in, 111–113, 425–426
Community councils, 93–94, 442–444
Conservation and open space programs, 9, 17, 49–50, 91–92, 165–167, 190, 407–412, 452, 465–466
Coolidge, Calvin, 202
Coordination of recreation and social agencies, 71–73
County recreation and park programs, 55–59
Crime. *See* Juvenile delinquency
Cultural expansion: in United States, 10–11, 209, 296, 327–328, 414; in the Soviet Union, 219; *See also* Performing arts
Curtis, Joseph E., 471–72

Dance. *See* Performing arts
Dark Ages. *See* Middle Ages
Definitions of recreation, leisure, play, 266
De Grazia, Sebastian, 254–255, 258, 264, 312–313
Delaware River Basin, 53–54
Department of the Air Force, 42–43
Department of the Army, 42
Department of the Navy, 43–44
Depression, influence on recreation in United States, 203–206

Detroit, 194–195, 395

Dewey, John, *cited*, 249–251

Disabled persons, recreation needs of, 11, 16–17, 67, 69, 208–209. *See also* Therapeutic recreation service

Disadvantaged, recreation programs for, 20–21, 37–41, 68, 73, 79–81, 83–90, 299–300, 387–391, 398–401, 418–419, 442–444, 448–452. *See also* Anti-poverty programs; Urban problems

Douglass, Paul, *cited*, 105

Drama. *See* Performing arts

Drinking, as leisure activity, 133–134, 152–154, 157–158, 162–163, 191, 195–196, 216, 351–352, 374, 379, 402

Drug use, 23–24, 350–355, 379

Dubin, Robert, *cited*, 171, 304–305

Dulles, Foster R., *cited*, 161–162, 172, 177–178

Economic basis of recreation and park planning, 19, 26–27, 52, 74, 414–419, 433, 456

Economic functions of recreation, 307–331, 361–364, 413. *See also* Recreation spending

Educational values of play, 149–151, 177, 246–252

Education for leisure, 7, 15, 199–201, 424

Edwards, Richard, 195–197

Egypt, history of play in, 132–134

Eisenhower, Dwight D., 234

Emotional values of recreation, 338–340

Employment in recreation and parks, 103–105. *See also* Professional development in recreation and parks

Enabling legislation, 46, 48

England, history of play in, 147, 153–154, 175–176, 211–217

Entertainment complexes, 326–328

Environment. *See* Conservation and open space programs; Urban planning

Erikson, Erik, 275–276, 288

Ethological view of play, 272–273

Europe, recreation and park programs in, 211–227

Every Woman's Village, 354–355

Exercise, value of, 335–338

Expenditures on leisure. *See* Recreation spending

Exploratory drive in play, 279

Extra-curricular activities. *See* Co-curricular activities in schools and colleges

Facilities for recreation, 64–74, 86, 96, 321, 324, 326, 330, 435–440, 450–452

Family life, 23–24, 346–348

Federal government, role in recreation, 3–4, 25–46, 203–206, 388–389, 400, 408–413, 447–449

Fees and charges in recreation and parks, 19, 67–68, 415–419. *See also* Economic basis of recreation and park planning

Fischer, John, *cited*, 392–393

Fish and Wildlife Service, 30–32

Fishing, 30–33, 49–50, 54, 321–322, 324

Flying, as recreation, 330–331

Football, 177, 320–323, 326, 329, 341, 396

Forest Service, 26, 28–29, 32, 180, 326–327, 371. *See also* Outdoor Recreation Resources Review Commission; Outdoor recreation

Four-H Clubs, 33

France, during modern era, 211, 225
  early history of play, 144–145, 147
  park development in, 155, 158

Fresh Air Fund, 88

Freud, Sigmund, 286–287, 392

Frissell, Sidney, *cited*, 123–124

Froebel, Friedrich, 237

Functions of municipal recreation and park agencies, 60–61

Galbraith, John Kenneth, *cited*, 20–21

Gambling as leisure activity, 145–146, 161–162, 195–196, 317–318, 404–405

Games theory, 284–286

Gans, Herbert, *cited*, 299, 384, 440–441

Georgia, park development in, 165, 371
  recreation and park certification in, 119–120

Germany, 175, 206, 211, 222–225

Gerstl, Joel E., study of leisure behavior, 293–295

Girl Scouts of America, 80–81, 198, 207, 419

Golf, 294, 320–321, 325

Goodale, Thomas, *cited*, 106

Graduate study in recreation and parks, 109–111, 124–125

Gray, David, 122, 399–400

Groos, Karl, 239–241

Guaranteed annual income, 461–462

Guides for recreation and park planning, 434–453

Gulick, Luther Halsey, 185, 188, 191, 194, 198, 247–249, 264

Halfway houses, 369
Hall, G. Stanley, 241–242
Haun, Paul, *cited*, 370, 388
Hawkins, Donald E., 105, 117–118, 461–462
Health, Education and Welfare, Federal Department of, 26, 34–36, 46, 81, 104–105, 209, 375, 427
Health-related functions of recreation, 364–377
Hebrews, ancient, 135
Henry Street Settlement House, 385–386
Hetherington, Clark, 185, 251
Hiking, 294, 298, 319
Hines, Thomas I., *cited*, 415–416
History of recreation and leisure, 129–234
    in Colonial America, 160–167
    in Dark and Middle Ages, 142–148
    in 19th Century, 168–185
    in pre-Christian era, 132–142
    in Renaissance and Reformation, 148–159
    in 20th Century, 186–210
Hjelte, George, *cited*, 63
Holidays, source of leisure, 140, 148, 157–158, 212, 309–310, 314
Hollingshead, August, *cited*, 299–300
Hoover, Herbert, 191, 202
Horse racing. *See* Racing
Hospitals, recreation programs in, 51, 338–339, 364–365. *See also* Therapeutic recreation service
Housing programs and recreation, 36–37, 64, 68, 390–391
Housing and Urban Development, Federal Department of, 34, 36–37, 209, 390, 431, 449. *See also* Real estate and recreation; Urban planning; Urban recreation problems
Hudson Institute Report, 454–456, 463
Huizinga, Johan, 267–268, 272
Hull House, 197–198, 182
Hunting, 133–134, 144–145, 294, 317, 321, 324
Hutchinson, John, 261
Idleness, during Depression, 203–206. *See also* Unemployment; Work, attitudes toward
    seen as evil, 161–164
Ill and disabled, organizations serving, 94–95. *See also* Therapeutic recreation service

Illinois, 49, 369
India, recreation in, 229
Indian tribes, 29–30, 131–132, 363
Indiana, recreation and park registration in, 120
Industrial recreation, 97–102, 228–229, 363–364
Industrial Revolution, effects of, 168–185, 308
Instinct-practice theory of play, 239–241
Intellectual growth through play, 344–346
International athletic competition, 220–221
International City Managers' Association, 437
International Ladies Garment Workers' Union, 101
International Recreation Association, 231–234
Israel, recreation in, 226
Italy, recreation in, 211

Jacobs, Jane, 441–442
Jahn, J. F., 175
Japan, recreation in, 227–229
Jersild, Arthur, 277–278
Job Corps, 37–38, 41
Jogging, as conditioner, 337–338
Johnson, Lyndon B., 37, 210, 388–389
Juvenile delinquency, 20–21, 80–81, 89–90, 183–184, 191–196, 204–205, 247, 299–300, 303, 347, 376–387, 441
    causes of, 377–383
    effects of recreation, 383–387, 443

Kansas City, Missouri, 66–67, 194
Kaplan, Max, 264, 295
Keesing, Felix, 270–272
Kennedy, John F., 11, 31
Kennedy Foundation, 11, 367
King County, Washington, 57
Kraus, Richard, 303, 421

Labor unions. *See* Union-sponsored recreation
Land and Water Conservation Fund, 17, 26, 31–32, 209, 447–448
League of Federal Recreation Associations, 99
Lee, Joseph, 185, 245–247
Lehman, Harvey C., 252, 300–301
Leisure. *See also* Education for leisure; Recreation spending
    availability today, 308–314
    class, 255–256

concepts of, 253–260
concern about, 13–14, 178, 191, 197, 203–206, 213, 217–218, 247, 249, 307–308, 462–463
defined, 266
historical development of, 148, 169–170
predicted growth of, 460–464
sociology of, 290–306
in Soviet Union, 221–222
uses of, 319–331
Life expectancy, 382
Lifetime Sports Foundation, 208
Lindeman, Eduard, 205–206
Little League, 65
Local governments. *See* Municipal recreation and parks programs
Locke, John, 150
Loneliness, 339–340, 356–358, 374
Long Beach, California, 70–71, 422
Lorenz, Konrad, 272–273, 392
Los Angeles, California, 62, 93–94, 199, 422, 443
Loy, John W., 343
Lundberg, George, and associates, study of suburban leisure, 291

McCormack, John R., *cited*, 416
McIntosh, Peter C., *cited*, 175
Malinowski, Bronislaw, *cited*, 271–272
Marijuana. *See* Drug use
Marine Corps recreation, 44–45
Massachusetts, recreation in, 165–167
Mechanization of industry, 168
Menninger, Karl, *cited*, 288–289
Menninger, William, *cited*, 388
Mental health, recreation's contribution to, 357–359, 364–377
Mental illness, 368–370, 374–375. *See also* Emotional values of recreation; Psychological aspects of play
Mental retardation. *See* Retarded children and adults
Middle Ages, recreation and parks during, 142–148
Military recreation. *See* Armed Forces recreation
Miller, Norman P., *cited*, 265
Milwaukee, 195, 199
Minneapolis, 185, 187
Mitchell, Elmer D., 264, 266–267
Mobility of American population, 9–10. *See also* Travel, as recreation
Model Cities programs, 37, 447
Montaigne, Michel de, 149–150
Montessori method, 280

Moonlighting, 309
Moral values in leisure, 258–259, 348–353, 401–407, 458–460
Motion pictures, 195, 317, 329
Mountain View, California, 65–66
Municipal recreation and park programs, 59–74. *See also* Anti-poverty programs; Urban planning for parks and recreation; Urban recreation programs
Muscular Christianity movement, 174–177, 247
Music. *See* Cultural expansion in United States; Performing arts
Myrdal, Gunnar, 301

Nassau County, New York, 58
National Association of Counties, 55–56
National Association of Recreation Therapists, 113
National Association of Youth Clubs (British), 215–217
National Commission on Civil Disorder, 389
National Conference on State Parks, 113–114, 202
National Education Association, 199–201, 422
National Industrial Recreation Association, 97, 116, 207
National League of Cities, 74
National Park Service, 25, 27–28, 30, 32, 53, 179–180, 202, 361, 371, 412–413
National Playing Fields Association (British), 213
National Recreation Accreditation Project, 110–111
National Recreation and Park Association, 51, 62, 104–105, 113–115, 421, 427–428, 440, 472
National Recreation Areas, 28, 54, 447
National Recreation Association, 109, 113, 199, 202, 207, 388, 436–437
National Therapeutic Recreation Society, 114
National Wilderness Preservation System, 28, 33
National Wildlife Refuge System, 31
Nazi era in Germany, 223–224
Negroes: and recreation, 20, 68, 73, 79, 83, 86–90, 173, 210, 300–303, 345–346, 359, 378, 383, 387–391, 429–431, 455; population trends of, 315
Neighborhood Youth Corps, 37–39, 419
Neumeyer, Martin H., and Esther, 257, 261

New England: during Colonial period, 160–167; economic benefits from recreation, 362
New Jersey, 48–50, 53, 119–120
New York City, 53, 84, 87–88, 93, 183–185, 199, 383, 385–386, 388, 414, 440, 442–444, 447–448
New York State, 49–51, 53, 120
New Zealand, recreation in, 229–230
Nixon, Richard M., 41
North Carolina, 47, 68–69

Office of Economic Opportunity, 37–41, 90, 386, 389, 419, 448
Oglebay Park, 417–418
Ohlin, Lloyd E., 379
Older Americans Act, 11
Olmsted, Frederick Law, 181–182
Olympic Games, 219–221, 227, 231
Omaha, Nebraska, 68
Open space. *See* Conservation and open space
Opera. *See* Performing arts
Oriental countries, recreation in, 227, 231
Outdoor education, 71
Outdoor recreation, 25–34, 48–54, 91–93, 177, 179–180, 209, 290, 321–322, 324, 330, 361–363, 435–440
Outdoor Recreation Resources Review Commission, 7, 31, 55, 209, 298, 303, 319, 408, 416–417, 464

Pakistan, recreation in, 229
Parks. *See also* Facilities for recreation
in Colonial America, 164–167
modern development, in America, 107–108, 187–188
in Great Britain, 213–215
in Soviet Union, 218–219
urban park councils, 93
in 19th Century, 179–188
in pre-Christian era, 134–135
in Renaissance and Reformation, 154–157
Parsons, Talcott, 378
Participation in recreation activities, 316–331
Pasadena, California, 422
Patrick, G. T. W., *cited*, 241–244, 264
Peace Corps, 232–234
Pennsylvania, 49, 53
Pennsylvania State University, 427
People-to-People Sports Program, 234
Performing arts, audience for, 296

during Depression, 204
history of, 133, 137, 139–140, 148–149, 158–159, 204
spending on, 317
trends in community recreation, 64–74, 327–328
Pestalozzi, Heinrich, 237
Philadelphia, 62–63, 71–73, 165, 182, 185, 195
Philosophy of organized recreation service, 245–252
Physical education, linked to recreation, 51–52, 106
Physical fitness, 208
Physical values of recreation, 335–338
Physically handicapped, 370–372. *See* Therapeutic recreation service
Piaget, Jean, 282–283
Pieper, Josef, *cited*, 254
Planning in recreation and parks, 18–19, 58. *See also* Urban planning
Plato, *cited*, 136–137
Play, defined, 266
in adolescent development, 272–279
in child development, 274–277
early theories of, 237–252
in learning theory, 279–286
modern concepts of, 263–273
in pre-Christian era, 136–139
in primitive societies, 130–132, 270–273
psychological mechanisms in, 286–288
Playground Association of America, 187–188, 193, 197–199, 245, 248
Playground and Recreation Association of America, 199, 201
Playground design, 435–436, 441, 450–452. *See also* Facilities for recreation
Playground movement, 183–184, 245
Police Athletic League, 5, 63, 81
Pollution. *See* Conservation and open space programs
Poor. *See* Disadvantaged, recreation programs for
Population growth in United States, 8–9, 169, 183, 314–315, 372, 407–412, 455–456
Portland, Oregon, 69–70
Prezioso, Sal J., 115
Primitive man, play patterns of, 129–132, 270–273
Private organizations and recreation, 5, 77, 95–96, 317
Problems in organized recreation service, 398–428

Professional development in recreation and parks, 11–12, 21–22, 26, 51–52, 73, 103–125, 186, 206
issues in professional development, 424–428
professional preparation in, 109–113
recruitment in, 116–119
role of professionals, 435
Prostitution, 133, 156, 194–196, 404–405
Protestant Reformation, 151–154
Protestant work ethic. *See* Work ethic
Psychological aspects of play, 274–289, 338–340, 357–358
Puerto-Ricans. *See* Spanish-speaking, recreation for
Puritan attitudes toward play, 12, 153–154, 157, 160–164

Rabelais, 147, 149–150
Race and recreation. *See* Negroes, and recreation; Spanish-speaking, recreation for
Racing, 162, 173, 317, 322, 394. *See also* Gambling as leisure activity
Rainwater, Clarence, *cited*, 188
Real estate, linked to recreation opportunity, 58, 95–96, 187, 296–297
Recapitulation theory of play, 241–242
Recreation, concepts of, 260–263
definition of, 266
federal role in, 3–4, 25–46
history of, 129–234
human values in, 335–356
movement in United States, 13–24, 179–210, 398–401, 454–473
in other nations, 211–234
role of local government, 55–74
social factors supporting, 6–13
social functions of, 367–397
state functions in, 4, 46–54
Recreation and Park Yearbook, 27, 47–48, 57, 60, 62, 105
Recreation counseling, 369–370
Recreation spending, 7, 19–20, 60, 64–74, 186, 303, 316–318, 320–331, 361–362
Recreation theory of play, 239
Registration of recreation and park professionals, 120–121
Rehabilitation Services Administration, 35–36
Relaxation theory of play, 242–244
Religious attitudes toward recreation, 84–85, 142–145, 151–154, 160–164, 170–172, 177, 189, 212
Religious social agencies, 77, 82–87
Renaissance, play during, 148–151
Research in recreation and parks, 426–428
Reston, Virginia, 467
Retarded children and adults, 11, 80–81, 88, 94, 208, 366–368
Retirement, 310–314, 355–356, 372–375
Riesman, David. *Cited*, 305
Riis, Jacob, 182, 184
Riots. *See* Urban riots
Rivers, Thomas E., 231–232
Rockefeller, Laurance S., 113
Rome, recreation in ancient, 139–142
Roosevelt, Theodore, 187, 193, 198
Rousseau, Jean Jacques, *cited*, 150–151
Roving leaders, 384–385
Rural recreation enterprises, 363. *See also* Outdoor recreation
needs, 32–33

Sabbath laws, 153–154
Safety, in city streets, 193
St. Louis, Missouri, 199
Salaries in recreation and parks, 117–119
Saltzman, Donald, *cited*, 117
San Francisco, 185, 194, 388, 432
Savannah, Georgia, 165–166
Scandinavian countries, recreation in, 225–226
Schiller, Friedrich von, 238–239
Schools, role in recreation, 62–63, 70–73, 93, 187, 190, 196, 199–200, 383–384, 414, 421–424
Seashore, Carl, *cited*, 244, 252
Seattle, Washington, 57
Self-expression theory of play, 266–267
Senior centers, 375–376. *See also* Aging persons, leisure needs of
Sessoms, H. Douglas, *cited*, 108–109, 122–123, 442
Settlement houses, 77, 87–88, 182–183, 197–198, 205, 385–386, 399
Sexual involvement. *See also* Prostitution
of youth, 133, 205, 247, 348–350, 379, 401–403
of older persons, 374
Short, James F., *cited*, 303, 342, 381
Sierra Club, 91
Single persons, recreation for, 95–96
Skiing, 294, 297, 321–322, 330, 362
Slavson, S. R., *cited*, 264, 288
Slums. *See* Urban recreation problems

Social class, linked to recreation participation, 145–149, 156–158, 161–162, 175, 205–206, 255–256, 290–300, 302–303, 311–313, 381, 393

Social functions of recreation, 340–344, 357–397, 398–401

Society of Park and Recreation Educators, 114

Socrates, *cited*, 136–137

Southern California Case Study, 313–314, 464

Soviet Union, recreation in, 211, 217–222

Space standards in recreation and park planning, 435–440

Spanish-speaking, recreation for, 79, 89–90, 394, 429–431

Special interest organizations, 77, 90–95

Spectatoritis, 196

Spencer, Herbert, *cited*, 238–239

Spilhaus, Athelstan, 467–468

Sport, character-building values of, 341–343, 382–383
in foreign nations, 213–230
in Middle Ages, 146–148
in modern era, 213–221
in pre-Christian era, 133–134, 136–141
primitive origins of, 130–132
in Renaissance, 149–151
school and college sport, 175–177, 199–200
in United States today, 321–324

State governments and recreation, 4, 46–54, 179–180, 447–448

Stein, Julian, *cited*, 366

Strodtbeck, Fred L., *cited*, 303, 342, 381

Suburban development, 8–9, 58–59, 346–347

Supply-Demand Manpower Study, 51, 104–105, 110

Surplus-energy theory of play, 238–239

Sutton-Smith, Brian, *cited*, 284

Swimming. *See* Aquatics

Taylor, Loren, *cited*, 124

Tennis, 320–322, 325

Technology, influence on recreation, 10, 189, 330–331, 456–457, 468–470

Television watching, 292, 295–296, 317, 323, 328–331, 347–348, 469–470

Tennessee Valley Authority, 25, 30

Theater in America, 172–173, 327–328. *See* Performing arts
in community programs, 69–70

Therapeutic recreation service, 51, 64, 67, 69, 232, 338–339, 364–377. *See also* Aging persons, leisure needs of; Disabled persons, recreation needs of; Hospitals, recreation programs in; Retarded children and adults

Tock's Island Reservoir, 53–54

Totalitarianism and recreation, 205–206

Tourism. *See* Travel

Tournaments, 146

Travel, as recreation, 9–10, 52–53, 190, 317, 324–327, 361–363, 458

Turnvereins, 175, 177

Twardzik, Louis, *cited*, 116–117, 124–125

Undergraduate preparation in recreation and parks, 109–111, 124–125

Unemployment, 203–206, 312, 388, 460–463

Union-sponsored recreation, 99–101, 212

United Automobile Workers, 101

United Nations, 231–232

United Service Organizations, 41–42, 207

United States Army Corps of Engineers, 29, 53–54

United States Department of Agriculture, 32–33

United States Department of Labor, 103–104

United States Office of Education, 34, 113

United States Public Health Service, 35, 364–365

Urban planning, 18–19, 22, 50–51, 213, 215, 218, 222, 224, 360–361, 429–453, 466–468

Urban recreation problems, 37–41, 58, 64–74, 79–81, 210, 301, 409

Urban riots, 16, 40–41, 210, 388–391, 393–395. *See also* Disadvantaged, recreation programs for

Urbanization, 8–9, 169, 189, 455–456

Vacations, 309–310, 314, 324–327

Values, changing, 23. *See also* Moral values in leisure

Veblen, Thorstein, 255–256, 305

Verhoven, Peter, 112

Veteran's Administration Hospitals, 26, 42, 45

Vietnam War, 44–45, 405

Violence in America, 391–392. *See also* Aggression; Urban riots

VISTA (Volunteers in Service to America), 37–38

Vocational values of recreation, 278–279

Voluntary organizations and recreation, 4–5, 75–102, 181–182, 198–199, 419–420

Vrooman, Walter, 182–184

War Camp Community Service, 201

Washington, D.C., 166, 384–385, 394

Watts riot, 90, 443

Welfare departments and recreation, 63, 81, 461

White, R. Clyde, study of leisure and social class, 291–292

White House Conference on Children and Youth, 35

Whyte, William F., *cited*, 300, 344, 381

Wildlife preservation. *See* Conservation and open space

Wilensky, Harold L., *cited*, 307, 311–312

Williams, Arthur, *cited*, 373

Witty, Paul A., 252, 300–301

Wolffe, Joseph B., *cited*, 339

Women, leisure problems of, 353–356

Work, attitudes toward, 13–14, 160–162, 303–306
  changing nature of, 189, 252, 457, 460–464
  during life span, 310–313
  ethic, 143–144, 151–153, 171–172, 259–260
  linked with play, 163, 246–248, 250, 265

Works Progress Administration, 203–205

Work week, 170–171, 177–178, 191, 308–310, 463–464

World War I, 201

World War II, 207–208, 388